Uncle John
was here

31

Uncle John's

ACTUAL
~and~
FACTUAL

Bathroom Reader

Bathroom Readers' Institute

Portable Press

San Diego, California

Portable Press / The Bathroom Readers' Institute
An imprint of Printers Row Publishing Group
10350 Barnes Canyon Road, Suite 100, San Diego, CA 92121
www.portablepress.com • e-mail: mail@portablepress.com

Copyright © 2018 Portable Press

All correspondence concerning the content of this book should be addressed to Portable Press / The Bathroom Readers' Institute, Editorial Department, at the above address.

Publisher: Peter Norton • Associate Publisher: Ana Parker
Publishing / Editorial Team: Vicki Jaeger, Lauren Taniguchi, April Farr, Kelly Larsen, Kathryn C. Dalby, Carrie Davis, Leah Baltazar • Editorial Team: JoAnn Padgett, Melinda Allman, Dan Mansfield
Production Team: Jonathan Lopes, Rusty von Dyl

Created and produced by Javna Brothers LLC

Interior design by Lidija Tomas
Cover design by Adam Devine
Endpaper design by Rusty von Dyl

Dedicated to our parents, Claire and Stephen Javna, who taught us to love facts

"I never apologize. I'm sorry, but that's just the way I am." —Homer Simpson

ISBN: 978-1-68412-493-0
Library of Congress Cataloging-in-Publication data available on request.

Printed in the United States of America

First Printing: September 2018
22 21 20 19 18   1 2 3 4 5

OUR "REGULAR" READERS RAVE!

I absolutely love your books. I learn more from them than I do from any other history book or book I've ever read. You keep printing them and I'll keep buying them.
—Bill M.

I enjoy all the humor, information, and trivia…and the fact that most of the articles are short enough to finish while visiting my "Reading Room."
—Dave G.

I love these books. The way they're written makes facts and trivia fun.
—Julia K.

I have enjoyed many issues of Uncle John's Bathroom Readers over the years (I'm 82) and always look forward to a new one. My son-in-law (also a nut who loves your books) gave me the new one a week ago and I dove into it as soon as I got to the bathroom! Thank you very much.
—Richard G.

Big fan here. I love everything you publish. You're my "fun encyclopedia." Never stop doing what you do.
—Terry D.

Your books bring my family a lot of pleasure.
—Lou B.

I own about 30 of your books. I read them partly for entertainment, but mostly to illustrate my sermons (I'm a preacher). Thanks for your help over the years.
—Jeff S.

I'm near the end of this book and I'm eagerly awaiting the next one.
—Jon L.

CONTENTS

Because the BRI understands your reading needs, we've
divided the contents by length as well as subject.

Short—a quick read

Medium—2 to 3 pages

Long—for those extended visits, when something
a little more involved is required

*Extended—for those leg-numbing experiences

ACTUAL & FACTUAL
Short
Nailed It!............................ 6

The Naked Tooth 92

What the Fact? 235

Fun Gun Facts..................... 336

The End 469

Hamburger Facts................... 481

Medium
Totally (You)Tubular................ 161

Save Ferris! 233

Long
It's About Lyme.................... 389

BATHROOM NEWS
Short
Bathroom Music 40

Medium
Uncle John's Stall of Fame 142

Farts in the News 185

Stall of Fame: "The Tinder Poo Date" . . 223

Uncle John's Stall of Fame 293

Extreme Recycling: Bathroom Edition. . 379

Stall of Fame: The "Shady Lady" 473

CREATURE FEATURES
Short
Weird Animal News.................. 5

Moos in the News.................. 247

Medium
Escape From Monkey Island.......... 89

Run, Gobi, Run!................... 153

Remember Me..................... 271

Animal Invaders 344

Historic Horses 412

CUSTOMS & SUPERSTITIONS
Short
The Sayings of Lao-Tzu 80

Happy Bermuda Day! 365

Medium
Today Is *What* Day?............... 111

The Gävle Goat 131

Golden Slumbers 441

GOVERN-MENTAL
Short
The "Andy Griffith" Show 49

Cat-Idates for Public Office 77

Medium
Filibuster? More Like Bladder Buster 37

Presidents Who Partook 169

Political Animals 183

Whatever Happened to Al Smith?..... 332

Presidential Also-Rans 415

HISTORY MAKERS
Short
The Fatal Glass of Beer 95

Medium
Are You Smart Enough to Work
   for Edison? 11
James the [Bleep!] 63
Queen for a Day 195
Anne Frank, Reconsidered 248
Fat Club 288
King Otto the Crazy 382

Long
A Baker to Remember 145
Dustbin of History: Chalmers Goodlin . . 227
History's Wonder Women 400

INTERNATIONAL AFFAIRS
Short
"Alo! Sollunga!" 218
Loonie Canadian Laws 353

Medium
A Whale of a Tale 47
Russia 1.0 139
Naming Canada 165
Weird Canada 283
Russia 2.0 358
Russian Spy Wars 425

Long
A Long, Strange Trip 267
A Long, Strange Trip, Part II 395

IT'S A WEIRD WEIRD WORLD
Short
"Don't Eat the Paper" 9
A Cure for Insomnia 253

Medium
Spite Houses 44
Fright White 115

A Week of Naked News 263
Ironic, Isn't It? 295
Odd-Time Radio 310
Beyond Spite Houses 334

Long
The Kid Who Stayed Up Really Late . . . 347

IT'S JUST BUSINESS
Short
We ♥ Our Workers 32
Fish and Pzza 88

Medium
Child Labor Lows 27
Last One Standing 61
Apollo Insurance Covers 65
Real Estate "Holdouts" 175
Branded 251
Largest American Business Layoffs 384

Long
Thinking Outside
   (and Inside) the Box 302

LANGUAGE & LINGO
Short
"I'm Serindipidating" 33
Maine Men 138
"It's a Situationship" 309
100 Words for Snow 339
Just Say No to Chicken Powder 424

Medium
Balance Your Rack 19
Talk Pidgin "Talk Story" 199
Wiseguys and Whales 239
Hen-Scartins with a Chance of Blenky . . 280
Found in Translation 438

GOOD SPORTS
Short
Sports One-Hit Wonders 84

Medium

Would You Buy Sneakers from
  This Man?. 21

Fighting the Good Fight. 126

Best Sports Owners. 197

Sports Lasts. 243

The International League. 340

Take Me Out to the Ba' Game 453

MISTAKES WERE MADE
Short

Terrible Typos 172

Typo-Rrific!. 285

Medium

Dude, Where's My Car? 13

Vexed by Texts 56

Lost in Space. 86

Oops!. 208

Here Comes Boaty McBoatface! 241

Sorry, Wrong Number. 354

Broadway Bombs. 393

MMM…FOOD
Short

Meat-Free 298

Vegetables, Schmegetables 299

Medium

Name That Soup. 75

Food for Thought 113

Your 1981 Grocery List. 167

Food Myths. 231

Dairy Queen: The "Butter-Cow Lady" . . 259

Name That Soup, Too 325

Food That's Art & Art That's Food 369

MOUTHING OFF
Short

Strange Celebrities 16

Thoughts from Thurber 29

"Just Be Yourself" 43

The Jeff Abides. 46

You're Fired! 72

Wise Women. 96

Celebrity Advice?. 152

The Mayor of Flavortown. 226

Celebrity Wisdom. 282

More Strange Celebrities 375

Medium

We Are Not a Fan. 106

ORIGINS
Short

You're My Inspiration 3

Card Game Phrase Origins. 180

Name the Place. 238

A Girl with Heart. 324

Medium

All That and a Bag of Chips. 100

A Store Is Born. 129

Classroom Origins. 158

Sweet History 203

The Paper Chase. 257

Taking It to the Streets. 286

A Store Is Born, Part 2 327

Go Ahead—Have Some More Chips. . . 404

POP SCIENCE
Short

Danger: Magnetars 317

Medium

Everyday Science 7

The Social Life of Trees 34

The Fungus Among Us. 117

Wanted: Planetary Protection Officer . . 173

Missed It by That Much 205

Good News 337

That's Very Cool. 372

Long

Planet 9 from Outer Space 420

The Hunt for "Planet X". 482

According to the Latest Research 490

POP-POURI

Short

Forget Paris 79

Uncle John's Page of Lists. 105

"Princess Takes a Ballet Class" 297

By the Numbers Quiz 444

Medium

Q&A: Ask the Experts 41

Life in 1948. 351

PUBLIC LIVES

Short

The Occupational Name Quiz 273

Medium

The "Barbra Streisand Effect". 58

The *Candid Camera* Hijacking 181

One Last Hit 192

Not My Best Work 433

It's About Lyme: Celebrity Edition. 445

Long

Twantrums. 319

The Matilda Effect 456

READING & WRITING

Short

Stop the Presses! 466

Medium

The Secret Lives of Authors. 98

The Final Issue 133

Writer's Block! 255

Long

The *Princess* Letters. 407

Thou Shalt Read! 427

STRANGE CRIME

Short

"What's Your Emergency?" 4

Strange Crime: Tattoo Edition 97

Medium

Parking Ticket News 25

Pirates of the Front Porch. 163

Dumb Crooks 342

Strange Crime: Selfie-Incrimination . . . 386

Strange Crime. 467

Long

The Force Is Not Very Strong With

This One. 313

SURVIVAL MODE

Short

Safe Spaces 10

What Would *You* Take?. 160

Medium

A Good Place to Get Bombed 291

Long

Danger Everywhere! 187

Surviving '17. 475

Sunk by the *Titanic* 495

TECH-NO

Short

"Keep Panicking" 217

Medium

The Last VHS Tape 17

Attack of the Drones 53

Robots in the News. 124

DNA Kit Discoveries 178

The First Viral Video?. 215

Pet Tech 265

THAT'S DEATH
Medium
They Died Onstage 81
Murder, He Wrote 108
Weird Deaths 150
Recipes to Die For 221
Too Much of a Good Thing 307

Long
William Henry Harrison,
 Reconsidered 274
How We Die 366

THE BIG SCREEN
Short
Bottles & Chokers 318
Actors Who Direct 436

Medium
For Your Eyes Only 70
Star Wars, Starring Jodie Foster 103
Not Coming to a Theater Near You 236
The Sound of Movies 277
You're a Winner *and* a Loser 363
Attention Earthlings! Warning! 417

THE MEDICAL FIELD
Short
"Total Loss of Tongue" 262

Medium
The Bumhole Resuscitator 51
Rescue Annie 73
Strange Tales of Sleepwalking 119
Your Mind Is a Sewer 201
Miracle Feet 212
Never Events 300

Long
A Letter to the Editor 447

THE SMALL SCREEN
Short
You've Been Eliminated 24
Television by the Numbers Quiz 254
Mmm…Everything 357

Medium
All in the Family 121
Big Screen 👍 Little Screen 👎 156
Watching the Detectives 210
Bunkerisms 330
The Censored 11 463
Life Imitates *The Simpsons* 479

TOYS & GAMES
Medium
The ABCs of RPS 30
The Minecraft Story 67
The Scrabble Scandal 135
Toy Origins 219
Getting in on the Action (Figures) 376
Video Game Lawsuits 470

WORDPLAY
Short
Gone Coastal 144
Groaners 191
Turn Left on Ugley 312
Horse Jokes 371
The Contronyms Quiz 378
The Art of the Pharm-Manteau 437

Medium
It's the Ant's Pants! 93
"Two Chickens to Paralyze" 245
Don't Call It That 361

ANSWERS 500

As a matter of fact…

GREETINGS, FELLOW TRIVIA HOUNDS!

We're happy to have you with us for our thirty-first annual edition:

Uncle John's ACTUAL *and* FACTUAL *Bathroom Reader*

A while ago, I was talking with some of the info-nerds here at the Bathroom Readers' Institute about the fact that facts are the building blocks of the *Bathroom Reader*—the atoms that bind this book series together. But there's another facet of the fact that I find fascinating: facts are fun! In fact, sharing a few facts here and there can make you sound like a know-it-all without actually having to know it all. (That's one of Uncle John's secrets.)

Quick story: I recently ran in to my old friend Sheila Burns, who asked me what I'm working on these days. "A new *Uncle John's Bathroom Reader*," I told her. "Really?!?" she exclaimed. "How long have you been writing these books?" "Thirty-one years," I replied. Then came the question I'm asked most often: "Is there even anything new to write about? Haven't you covered *everything?*"

Quite the opposite, Sheila. There's a whole universe of stuff out there to write about, and our dedicated writers are constantly mining it from books, magazines, newspapers, TV, radio, the Internet. We're like the Terminator: If there's an interesting fact out there, we *will not stop* until we find it, verify it, and share it with you. For example, I just learned that grasshopper meat has four times the calcium and twice the iron as beef. (You still won't get me to eat a bug.) It's fun facts like that one that earned our previous book, *Uncle John's Old Faithful Bathroom Reader*, a Gold Medal at the 2018 Independent Book Publishing Awards, thank you very much.

I slept through the awards ceremony, so let me thank my rag-tag team right here:

Gordon Javna	Pablo Goldstein	Trina Janssen
John Dollison	Megan Todd	Jack Mingo
Brian Boone	Brandon Hartley	Rachelle Sparks
Jay Newman	Lidija Tomas	Mighty John Marshall
Jahnna Beecham	Derek Fairbridge	Dave Blees
Kim Griswell	John Javna	Cuthbert J. Twillie
Thom Little	J. Carroll	Thomas Crapper

Year after year, these weirdos amaze me (and Shelia) with their uncanny ability to find not only great material, but fun, new ways to present it. Speaking of which, you've no doubt noticed that this edition has some stylish new page styles, and it's a bit more colorful. Yes, after 30 years, we decided to add blue. (It's the same color as Mrs. Uncle John's brown eyes.) Our goal was to spruce up the look while staying true to what we all love about the *Bathroom Reader*. And there's a whole lot to love in here:

- **History:** Women who were "Queen for a Day," why the U.S. never adopted the metric system, and a fateful glass of beer that changed the course of American history (hint: President Lincoln's bodyguard was drinking it during a play).

- **Blunders:** The dumb crook who stole some meatballs and was caught "red-faced," the news typo that reported Lance Armstrong "used rugs," and the biggest bombs in Broadway history.

- **Strangeness:** Cats that ran for public office, trees that use fungi to communicate, a teenager who stayed awake for 11 days, and the bizarre tale of Boaty McBoatface.

- **Good ol' facts:** How a filibuster works, the inside story of Lyme disease, casino lingo, the first viral video, the last VHS tape, and a page of facts about butts.

Yep, when it comes to finding stuff to write about, I'd say we're "good to go" for at least another 31 years. As a matter of fact, we've already begun mining facts and fun for *Bathroom Reader #32*.

Last but not least: Without you—our fans new and old (and Sheila, of course)—there'd be no way we could keep making these books. So thank you for keeping this dream alive.

As always…Go with the Flow!

—Uncle John and the BRI Staff

YOU'RE MY INSPIRATION

*It's always interesting to find out where the architects of pop
culture get their ideas. Some of these may surprise you.*

THE CREATURE FROM THE BLACK LAGOON: When it came time to design the titular
character for the 1954 horror classic, director Jack Arnold handed his art department
a photo of an Oscar statuette and told them, "If we put a gilled head on this, plus fins
and scales, that would look pretty much like the kind of creature we're trying to get."

EMPIRE: Fox's music industry drama, created by Lee Daniels and Danny Strong, is based
on Shakespeare…and Shakespearean drama. "The whole idea just flooded through my
head," recalled Strong. "I'd do it like *King Lear* or *The Lion in Winter*. Make the main
character like a dying king, and he's got three sons." That's the premise of *Empire*.

MICHIGAN WOLVERINES: At the turn of the 19th century, a bitter land dispute
between Ohio and Michigan led to both states' militias sending troops to the mouth
of Maumee River on Lake Michigan. Shots were fired, but there were no casualties on
the battlefield. When Congress awarded the land to Ohio in 1836, Michigan governor
Stevens T. Mason promised to "resist to the utmost every encroachment or invasion
upon the rights and soil of this territory." So stubborn were the Michiganders that the
Ohioans started calling them wolverines—"the ugliest, meanest, fiercest creatures from
the north." The University of Michigan adopted the nickname in the 1860s.

THE JOKER: Heath Ledger's sadistic turn as the Joker in *The Dark Knight* (2008) is
considered one of the best villain portrayals in film history. His inspirations for the role
are known to include punk rocker Sid Vicious, and Malcolm McDowell in *A Clockwork
Orange*. But in 2012, a viral video added another possible inspiration: gravelly voiced
singer Tom Waits. In 1979 Waits did an interview on Australia's *The Don Lane Show*, and
he looks and sounds exactly like Ledger's Joker (minus the makeup). It's likely that Ledger,
who was raised in Australia, saw a tape of the interview. According to *Slate*, "Even Waits'
hunched-over, lopsided posture brings to mind the Joker." (Google it and see for yourself.)

ERIC CARTMAN: In the late 1990s, *South Park* co-creators Matt Stone and Trey Parker
wanted one of the characters on their irreverent cartoon to be an eight-year-old
version of Archie Bunker, the cantankerous old conservative from the 1970s sitcom
All in the Family. But Archie had his soft side, and as *South Park* progressed over
the years, Cartman got nastier. He became less Archie Bunker and more, as Parker
describes, "the garbage in everyone's souls."

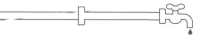

A journey begins with a single step…which requires 200 muscles working together.

"WHAT'S YOUR EMERGENCY?"

These are all real calls people made to their local emergency hotlines…that were not quite emergencies.

☎ A woman parked at a Florida Walgreens called 911 when her car wouldn't start…and she was locked inside. The dispatcher told her to pull up on the lock…and she was freed.

☎ **Another Florida woman called 911 three times in one day to complain that a McDonald's was out of Chicken McNuggets.**

☎ A married woman in Germany called the local police emergency number (110) because her husband wouldn't stop watching a dirty movie.

☎ **When she was dissatisfied with the number of shrimp in an order of shrimp fried rice at a local Chinese restaurant and was denied a refund, a Texas woman called 911 to summon police.**

☎ A woman called 911 to report that her cat was stuck in a tree. But she didn't want the fire department to come rescue the cat—her husband had climbed into the tree to retrieve it…and he got stuck, too.

☎ **A man called 911 when he spotted what he thought was a brush fire burning on top of a hill very early in the morning. Then he realized that what he was actually seeing was the sun rising.**

☎ When he couldn't figure out a math problem, a four-year-old boy called 911 for help. (The dispatcher helped him solve it.)

☎ **It's perfectly reasonable to call 911 if you think somebody's opening fire on you in your home. That's why one elderly woman called, only to realize that the exploding noises were eggs— she'd left them on the stove to boil, forgot about them, and they "popped."**

☎ A woman called 999 in England when two unauthorized intruders entered her home. Except that they were authorized: They were police officers who'd come to serve an arrest warrant on the woman.

☎ **One man in central Florida called 911 more than 16 times to demand the arrest of "TV news," but that it wasn't an emergency.**

☎ A woman in Deltona, Florida, was arrested for calling 911 four times in one day to complain that a salon had cut her nails too short.

☎ **A man called the cops on a convenience store clerk when they wouldn't sell him beer. The clerk refused to sell it to him unless he produced an ID proving he was 21, which he said he couldn't do because he wasn't 21. He told dispatchers that he'd purchased beer at the store in the past by bribing the store clerks… and he wanted police to come and force the clerk to both take his bribe and sell him beer. (The police did come…to arrest the caller.)**

Monkeys floss. They use feathers or blades of grass.

WEIRD ANIMAL NEWS

In this edition: sluggish snails, captivating camels, restrained reptiles, and an ornery owl.

The Ugly Side of Beauty. Camel beauty contests are a big deal in parts of the Middle East. Winners become national heroes; their owners make millions. So it shouldn't be surprising that some unscrupulous men go to great lengths to win. How? With Botox injections. In January 2018, a few days before the King Abdulaziz Camel Festival in Rumah, Saudi Arabia, a veterinarian was caught administering the muscle-paralyzing neurotoxin to 12 contestants. Why do they use Botox? As one of the breeders explained: "It makes the head more inflated so when the camel comes it's like, 'Oh, look at how big that head is. It has big lips, a big nose.'" There are strict rules against harming the animals, so the dozen camels and their handlers were disqualified.

Nobody Home. It was so cold in England in the winter of 2018 that the snails went into hibernation. That was bad news for patrons of the Dartmoor Union Inn, a pub in Devon, who had come there in February for the annual snail races. According to the pub's Facebook page, "Unfortunately, due to our snails being extra sleepy we have had to cancel the snail racing championships." (It must have been a slow news day because the story made international headlines.)

Owly Matrimony. It seems that the Harry Potter movies have given us some unrealistic expectations about owls' behavior. At a fancy wedding ceremony in Wiltshire, England, the bride secretly arranged for two handlers to emerge during the vows and release a large, white barn owl to deliver the rings to the altar. "The idea was it would be amazing and would swoop over the heads of the guests, and they'd all feel the air rushing from its wings," said Reverend Chris Bryan, "but it didn't quite work like that." Instead, Darcy (the owl) flew straight to the highest point in the 900-year-old church, landed on a rafter, and fell asleep for an hour. (Thinking ahead, the bride had brought two "back-up rings.")

Sticky Situation. There are so many lizards and snakes in Australia that if you want to catch a few, apparently you just throw a ball of tape on the ground and wait. In March 2018, animal-control officers in New South Wales responded to a call about a snake that was stuck to a ball of tape. They expected it to be some kind of heavy-duty tape, but, said a spokesperson, "Our rescuer was surprised to find that the tape was normal masking tape which had been crumpled up and discarded. Of even more surprise, the tape had caught not only a dwarf crown snake but also a little lizard." The snake and the lizard were carefully freed and sent on their way.

18th-century fashion fad: wearing fake moles made from velvet, silk, or mouse skin.

NAILED IT!

Fascinating facts about the things that grow out of your fingers and toes.

Fingernails and toenails are made of the fibrous structural protein keratin, which is also the major component of hair, hooves, horns, and the outer layer of human skin.

Technically, the cuticle—the piece of skin where the finger meets the nail—is called the *eponychium*, the skin around the edges of the nail is the *paronychium*, and the skin that connects the nail to the fingertip is the *hyponychium*.

The fastest growing nail is your middle finger.

Toenails are twice as thick as fingernails.

The cuticle creates a seal that keeps moisture and germs out of the body.

The top part of the nail—the part you polish—is called the nail plate.

On average, fingernails grow about 0.1 inch per month.

Contrary to popular myth, nails do not keep growing after we die. The skin retracts after death, making the nails look longer.

Scientific term for nail biting: *onychophagia*.

The nail bed, which is the tissue under the nail, is sometimes called the quick, and hurts when you cut it.

Nails grow faster in summer than in winter.

The white half-moon at the base of the nail is the *lunula*.

As we age, our nails tend to peel and crack more readily because they've lost their moisture.

Ridges on nails also come from aging.

Fingernails grow three to four times faster than toenails.

Women's nails grow faster during pregnancy.

White spots under nails, while harmless, are sometimes caused by trauma to the end of the fingertips.

Nails grow from the bottom out.

Are you right-handed or left-handed? The nails on your dominant hand grow faster.

Men's nails grow faster than women's.

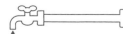

NASCAR drivers have to weigh 200 pounds. If they don't, weights are added to their cars.

EVERYDAY SCIENCE

Most people buy tea strainers to, well, strain tea. Not scientists. Apparently, they use everyday objects for purposes other than what the manufacturer intended. How do we know? Because scientists are now sharing their clever (and cringeworthy) uses for these items in online product reviews. We collected a few to show just how mad—and ingenious—the scientific method can be.

T-Sac Tea Filter Bags. "These bags are fantastic for soaking small fish in formaldehyde. We write on the bag itself, drop the fish in, and place it into formalin (or ethanol) to preserve for later analyses. This way we can easily label many individual fish in the same jar."

Reach Mint Waxed Floss. "Works great as noose to collect small lizards. Pretty durable but can snag on undergrowth. No comment from lizards on mint flavor."

Chinese Takeout Boxes. "Ideal for weighing and transporting mice. Likely to confuse non-scientists who think you are carrying your lunch through lab."

TashiBox 2 oz. Disposable Portion Cups with Lids. "Perfect-sized temporary containers for tiny poison frogs when you need to ID and process 100+ frogs in a morning. Some brands are more durable than others."

Colgate Extra Clean Toothbrush, Soft. "Great for cleaning pottery, stones, animal bones and even ancient teeth!"

> **DID YOU KNOW?**
>
> The ubiquitous Chinese takeout box was invented in the U.S. by Frederick Weeks Wilcox in 1894. Wilcox called it a "paper pail," because he based the design on the wooden oyster pails used by fishermen at the time. The image of a Chinese pagoda on the side wasn't added until 1970.

Sheaffer Skrip Ink Bottle, Blue/Black. "This is the ONLY ink that will stain *Arbuscular mycorrhiza*. I have tried several other brands and none stain or dissolve well in the acidified water. Great product."

MaxFactor Glossfinity Nail Polish. "Must-have in any tropical rainforest first aid kit! Apply topically over entrance to bot fly pupae until maggot dies, then extract. Colored polish helps track infestation over course of field season. Also festive."

Jif Creamy Peanut Butter. "Great for luring flying squirrels (and other rodents) into live traps. They love this stuff."

Estimate: The average American home has about $10 worth of pennies lying around.

MontoPack Bamboo Wooden Toothpicks. "Make perfect splints for injured songbird legs! Snip to size, wipe the leg with an alcohol swab, attach with superglue, and improve outcomes for that rare injury that occurs when bird banding or from a window strike."

Ziploc Brand Containers, Medium. "Great for transporting queen bumblebees from the field for captive breeding. Ziploc is better than no-name option that tend to split when air holes are poked. Downside is humidity buildup. Disinfect by throwing in the dishwasher."

Coleman Camp Oven. "Fits perfectly on a propane tank and brazier for drying monkey poop when you have no electricity. Get an oven thermometer to monitor internal temperature, and make sure everyone knows you're not baking brownies."

TePe Interdental Brushes. "Really excellent for getting the brains out of very small bird skulls."

Bead Organizer. "Bought this for storing small bags of ancient human teeth. Box makes it easy to keep the teeth separate and transport them."

Hard Plastic Champagne Glasses. "These are listed as party essentials & champagne glasses, but they're really for suspending fecal samples in tidy packages of cheesecloth held by bamboo skewers to grow up and isolate parasite larvae."

Knee-high Pantyhose. "Perfect for 'burrito-ing' (the technical term) bats in order to keep them still (and flightless) when weighing them. (Note: imagine the hose as the tortilla and the bat as the filling.)"

Hamster Exercise Ball. "A convenient chamber for isolating individual crayfish."

Self-Adhesive Reinforcement Labels, Round. "Reinforcement rings, perfect for making wells of just the right depth for mounting whole bee brains for microscopy."

* * *

TOOTHPICKS OF THE RICH & FAMOUS

Today's toothpicks are cheap, single-use items. But in medieval England, toothpicks were a status symbol. They came in fancy cases, were made of gold or silver, and were even set with jewels. In 1570 Queen Elizabeth was gifted a set of six golden toothpicks. One of her most prized possessions, they were kept on display for all to see.

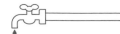

Action movie hero John Rambo was named after a variety of apple called the Rambo.

"DON'T EAT THE PAPER"

Sometimes fortune cookies contain a helpful bit of sage wisdom. Other times, they're ridiculous. These are those. (And they're all real.)

"About time I got out of that cookie."

"You will go on a date with a beautiful woman. She could do so much better."

"The fortune you seek is in another cookie."

"Stop procrastinating—starting tomorrow."

"You are not illiterate."

"If you think we're going to sum up your whole life on this little bit of paper, you're crazy."

"Some men dream of fortunes, others dream of cookies."

"It is a good day to have a good day."

"You love Chinese food."

"I am worth a fortune."

"You have rice in your teeth."

"This cookie contains 117 calories."

"You think it's a secret, but they know."

"What's the speed of dark?"

"Make love, not bugs."

"Help! I am being held prisoner in a Chinese bakery."

"Some fortune cookies contain no fortune."

"Today is probably a huge improvement over yesterday."

"You will receive a fortune. (Cookie)"

"It is easier to resist at the beginning than at the end."

"The greatest danger could be your stupidity."

"When in anger, sing the alphabet."

"Pick another fortune cookie."

"The rubber bands are heading in the right direction."

"Avoid taking unnecessary gambles. Lucky Numbers 12, 14, 17, 20, 28, 36"

"Ask your mom."

"I cannot help you, for I am just a cookie."

"Don't eat the paper."

"Ignore previous fortunes."

SAFE SPACES

*We all want to be in the safest place possible, especially
when we're in these harrowing situations.*

SAFEST PLACE TO SIT ON A PLANE. In 2015 *Time* magazine analyzed data from the
Federal Aviation Administration's Aircraft Accident Database and studied accidents in
which some passengers survived and others died. The findings: Passengers riding in the
middle seats in the back third of the plane had the highest rate of survival.

SAFEST PLACE TO SIT IN A CAR. The University of Buffalo studied data about car
accident fatalities, paying special attention to where deceased occupants had been
sitting at the time of impact. On average, the back seat is approximately 70 percent
safer than the front seat. The middle seat in the back is a full 25 percent safer than
window seats. Reason: If you're sitting in the middle, you're as far away from impact as
possible—if a car gets sideswiped, for example, the side of the car will absorb most of
that impact.

SAFEST COUNTRY TO BE IN WHEN NUCLEAR WAR BREAKS OUT. Switzerland is
well known for its staunch neutrality and refusal to engage in any large-scale conflicts.
That means if World War III between superpowers were to break out, those two allied
networks would blow each other up while Switzerland stayed out of it. Enhancing the
nation's safety, the Swiss have taken aggressive steps to prevent getting pulled into a
war or getting invaded. Hundreds of its bridges and roads are rigged with explosives, as
are the sides of mountains that sit on borders with neighboring countries.

SAFEST PLACE AGAINST ALL NATURAL DISASTERS. A geographical data service
called Sperling's Best Places considered what American cities were most likely to
endure hurricanes, tornadoes, earthquakes, floods, droughts, extreme heat, and heavy
rainfall. It found that the safest city—the one least likely to suffer any of those natural
disasters—is Corvallis, Oregon, a small town in northwestern Oregon (and home to
Oregon State University).

SAFEST PLACE DURING AN EARTHQUAKE. When the ground starts shaking and
you're inside, it's most important to make sure nothing shakes free of a wall or ceiling
and hits you on the head. Experts say to get under something heavy and sturdy, like
a big table. If you don't have that, get in the bathtub and cover your head. If you're
outdoors, think of your head and use your head: Avoid trees (they fall) and power lines
(they fall…and can electrocute you).

Chimichanga is the Spanish equivalent of the word "thingamajig."

ARE YOU SMART ENOUGH TO WORK FOR EDISON?

We learned in school that Thomas Edison invented the first practical incandescent light bulb, the phonograph, and motion pictures. One invention he's less famous for: "The Edison Test," an odd collection of 150 questions job applicants had to answer before he would hire them to work in his labs.

HELP WANTED

Thomas Alva Edison was one of the most prolific inventors in history. He was awarded more than a thousand patents in his lifetime—the most that the U.S. Patent Office has ever issued to a single individual. And yet for all his genius, he had almost no formal education. Already hard of hearing by the age of seven, he was "dreamy," easily distracted, and he doodled in his school notebooks. All of this drove Mr. Crawford, his instructor at the Family School for Boys and Girls in Port Huron, Michigan, crazy. Edison was just three months into his first year at the Family School in 1854 when Crawford told Edison's mother that her boy was "addled" (confused). That made Mrs. Edison so angry that she pulled her son out of the school. Thomas was largely self-taught after that, his learning guided in his early years by his mother, who had once worked as a teacher.

For the rest of his life, Edison took a dim view of formal education and the kinds of people turned out by American colleges and universities. Over the years, he had repeatedly hired scientists and engineers who'd been educated in the best schools, only to be shocked at how little they actually knew—at least as far as he was concerned—and how poorly they performed on the job. By the 1920s, he'd grown so frustrated that he added a 150-item questionnaire to the employment application for his lab. If an applicant answered 90 percent or more of the question correctly, they were offered a job. Everyone else was shown the door.

TAKE THE QUIZ

The questionnaire was strange even by the standards of the 1920s, but Edison justified it by explaining that the two things he valued in an employee were 1) curiosity, which would cause them to learn the answers to many of the questions on the test; and 2) a strong memory, which would enable them to retain the information once they'd learned it. "Of course I don't care directly whether a man knows the capital of Nevada...or the location of Timbuktu. But if he ever knew any of these things and

Most popular musical instrument in North Korea: the accordion.

doesn't know them now, I do very much care about that in connection with giving him a job. For the assumption is that, if he has forgotten these things, he will forget something else that has direct bearing on his job," Edison said in 1921.

Edison tried to keep the contents of the questionnaire secret; the only reason we know what the questions are is because someone who flunked the test (and was not offered a job) was nonetheless able to recall 146 of the questions from memory. He leaked them to the *New York Times*, which published them, along with the answers. Are you ready to take the test? Many of the questions have become outdated in the decades since Edison asked them. The answers to "What is the price of 12 grains of gold?" (57¢) and "What country is the greatest textile producer?" (Great Britain) are not what they were in 1921. But here is a sample of questions whose answers have not changed. To qualify for a job with Edison, you need to answer 33 of the 37 questions correctly. Good luck! (The answers are on page 500.)

1. What countries bound France?

3. Where is the River Volga?

9. Is Australia greater than Greenland in area?

10. Where is Copenhagen?

12. In what country other than Australia are kangaroos found?

14. Who was Bessemer and what did he do?

17. Who was Paul Revere?

20. Who was Hannibal?

32. Where was Napoleon born?

34. Who invented logarithms?

35. Who was the Emperor of Mexico when Cortez landed?

37. What and where is the Sargasso Sea?

42. Rhode Island is the smallest state. What is the next and the next?

46. Of what state is Helena the capital?

59. What causes the tides?

70. Where is Kenosha?

71. What is the speed of sound?

72. What is the speed of light?

73. Who was Cleopatra and how did she die?

75. Who discovered the law of gravitation?

76. What is the distance between the earth and sun?

79. What is felt?

85. Who discovered radium?

86. Who discovered the X-ray?

92. Who composed "Il Trovatore"?

93. What is the weight of air in a room 20 by 30 by 10?

98. Who discovered how to vulcanize rubber?

101. Who invented the cotton gin?

105. Of what is glass made?

110. What is a foot pound?

121. Who wrote "The Star-Spangled Banner"?

125. Who wrote *Don Quixote*?

126. Who wrote *Les Misérables*?

129. Who made *The Thinker*?

130. Why is a Fahrenheit thermometer called Fahrenheit?

133. What insect carries malaria?

134. Who discovered the Pacific Ocean?

During a March 1989 solar storm, the northern lights were visible as far south as Cuba.

DUDE, WHERE'S MY CAR?

Forgetting where you parked your car and wandering around, sometimes for hours until you find it, is a common experience. But not finding it for days? Weeks? Longer? That's what happened to these folks.

Dude: Gavin Strickland, a 19-year-old who drove his 2015 Nissan Versa sedan from Syracuse, New York, to a Metallica concert in Toronto in July 2017

Where's My Car? Strickland parked his car in a downtown garage and took an $8.00 taxi ride to the concert. To help him find his way back, he made a mental note that his garage was near a Starbucks and a construction site. It was only after the concert that he realized that there were Starbucks and construction sites all over downtown. He looked for his car late into the night, but never found it. The following morning he took a bus back to Syracuse.

Strickland's dad posted an ad on Craigslist asking for help. "Our doofy son parked the car in an indoor parking garage…but that garage cannot now be located," the ad read, noting that the car had Florida license plates, a Canadian flag on the door frame, and a Bernie Sanders bumper sticker. Reward: $100 to the finder and another $100 to their favorite charity.

Found It! The ad not only attracted interest from Craigslist readers in Toronto, but also from newspapers, radio, and television stations all over Canada. "Apparently like a search party went out. Basically like a scavenger hunt, which I thought was pretty cool," Gavin said.

Three days later a woman named Madison Riddolls found the car at Toronto Dominion Centre after searching several garages downtown. Bonus: the garage waived the four-day parking fee and gave Gavin a Bluetooth device that will help him find the car the next time he loses it. "I love Canada, and I think I just love how the city got together to help me out," he told the throngs of reporters who met him when he stepped off the bus in Toronto.

Dude: An embarrassed Scotsman whose name—for obvious reasons—was not released to the press

Where's My Car? What could be worse than forgetting where you parked your car? In June 2016, this man borrowed his *friend's* car—a pricey BMW—and drove it from Scotland to Manchester, England, to go to a Stone Roses concert. He must have had a pretty good time, because by the time the concert was over, he couldn't find his way back to the car. He'd parked it in a multistory garage in the center of

---

The Colorado River *should* flow to the Gulf of California, but from 1998 to 2014, it didn't.
(It ran dry before it got there.)

Manchester, but there were a lot of garages in downtown Manchester and they all looked the same to him. He spent five days looking for his friend's car…and then gave up. His friend e-mailed the police and parking companies for more than a month, hoping his car would turn up. It didn't. In August he reported it stolen.

Found It! Six months later, in December 2016, police came upon an "abandoned" car in a Manchester parking garage, right where the man had parked it. They ran the license plate, found it was a car that had been reported stolen, and notified the owner that it had been found. Estimated cost of storing a car in an expensive downtown parking garage for six months: £5,000, or about $6,200.

Dude: Antonio, a 44-year-old Italian factory worker who declined to give his last name

Where's My Car? In the fall of 2013, Antonio drove his silver VW Golf from northern Italy over the Tyrolean Alps to Munich, where he planned to spend the day at Oktoberfest, the city's famous beer festival. He parked on a city street miles from the festival and hopped a tram that took him the rest of the way. "It was a small street without any particular features, close to a bus stop," he later told reporters.

By the end of the day, he'd forgotten the name of the street *and* which tram line he'd taken. It might have been the No. 15…or the No. 16. Or maybe not. Before you blame the beer, consider that Antonio claims he didn't touch a drop. "I was just there for the rides," he said.

Antonio went back over the Alps and returned to Italy, but without his car. On his days off from work, he made several trips over the Alps *back* to Munich and rode various tram lines, hoping he'd spot his car, or at least something that would jog his memory. No such luck.

Found It! After weeks of searching, Antonio's plight eventually attracted the notice of Munich's *Abendzeitung* newspaper, which ran a story about him. Someone who read the article spotted Antonio's car and told the newspaper where it was parked. Antonio made one last trip over the Alps to pick it up, five weeks after he parked it.

Dude: An embarrassed German man, not named in news reports

Where's My Car? Like Antonio, in 2010 this man parked his car in Munich. Unlike Antonio, this man admits he was in town for a night of drinking and revelry. The next day he went back to the neighborhood where he thought he'd parked the car…but there was no sign of it. He searched the surrounding streets for hours and when he found nothing, he assumed his car had been stolen. He promptly reported the theft to the police.

Americans eat 21,000 slices of pizza every minute.

Found It! Two years later, traffic police came upon a car whose inspection stickers had expired. When they ran the plates, it turned out to be the man's car, still parked where he'd left it, two and a half miles from where he *thought* he left it. Still in the trunk: the man's $51,000 worth of power tools. "The weird thing is that it turned up so far away," a spokesperson for the Munich police told reporters, "even though the owner was pretty sure of where he'd left it."

Dude: What is it about people losing their cars in Germany? This time it was a 56-year-old man, also not named in news reports.

Where's My Car? In 1997 the man parked his car in a multistory garage in the city of Frankfurt. When he went back to get it, he either went to the wrong garage, or to the wrong floor of the right garage. When he didn't find his car where he thought he'd left it, he assumed it had been stolen and reported the theft to the police.

Found It! *Twenty years later,* in 2017, the man's car was found right where he'd parked it. Somehow it had gone unnoticed by the staff of the parking garage the entire time. It was only discovered when the parking structure was closed, emptied, and prepared for demolition, and no one came to get the car. The demolition company reported it to the police, who traced it back to the owner, now 76, through his 1997 stolen car report. "Unfortunately," said a spokesperson for the Frankfurt police, "the car cannot be driven anymore and will be sent to the scrap heap."

* * *

GAME OF DRONES

According to the Federal Aviation Administration, if you want to fly a drone, you need to follow these guidelines:

- Fly at or below 400 feet above the ground.
- Always fly within line of sight; if you can't see it, bring it in.
- Stay away from airports.
- Stay away from airplanes—they have the right of way in the air.
- Do not fly over people.
- Do not fly over or close to sports events or stadiums.
- Do not fly near emergency situations such as car crashes or building fires.
- Do not fly in national parks.
- Do not fly under the influence.
- Be aware of controlled airspace.

Why do gum chewers fart more than other people? They swallow a lot of air.

MOUTHING OFF

STRANGE CELEBRITIES

Do you enjoy reading wise quotations? You won't find any on this page.

"Every great story seems to begin with a snake."
—Nicolas Cage

"I actually don't like thinking. I think people think I like to think a lot. And I don't. I don't like to think."
—Kanye West

"I've been noticing gravity since I was very young."
—Cameron Diaz

"I took so many driving tests because I was so out of it. On one occasion I nodded off during the test. When I woke up there was a note on the seat saying, 'You have failed.'"
—Ozzy Osbourne

"For years I was be-hated, and now I'm beloved."
—Barry Manilow

"In the studio, I do try to have a thought in my head, so that it's not like a blank stare."
—Cindy Crawford

"Actually, you can trademark anything. If nobody objects, I can own every breath of air you take."
—Gene Simmons

"I don't want to be alone. The aloneness is so alone."
—Kate Gosselin

"I'm not a hero. A hero is a sandwich and I'm on a low-carb diet."
—Shaquille O'Neal

THE LAST VHS TAPE

We never know we've come to the end of an era while it's happening—we have to wait until we can look back. In the world of electronics, eras end fairly quickly, but here's what you'll see when you look back.

Last movie released on Betamax: In the first home video "format war" of the 1980s, JVC's widespread VHS technology beat Sony's proprietary Betamax. But hard-core Beta enthusiasts refused to give up their players, insisting the picture quality was better. So studios kept releasing movies for this audience well into the 1990s. The last one came off the line in 1996: *Mission: Impossible*, starring Tom Cruise.

Last VHS movie: DVDs were introduced in the late 1990s, but it took a while for them to completely eliminate VHS. Reason: most people had been watching movies at home for nearly two decades. So until 2006, movie studios put out movies on both VHS and DVD. The last VHS tape available: the Viggo Mortensen mob drama *A History of Violence*.

Last LaserDisc: Film purists didn't mind dropping a few thousand bucks on a LaserDisc player. The discs were the size of a vinyl LP and offered DVD quality… in 1983. The size and cost of LaserDiscs (especially compared to VHS) meant the product never reached more than a small niche audience. Philips and MCA stopped selling the players in 2001, shortly after the last new movie was produced on LaserDisc—the Arnold Schwarzenegger thriller *End of Days*.

Last Blockbuster Video video: The last company-owned Blockbuster Video, in Hawaii, stopped renting out movies on November 9, 2013, in anticipation of shutting down completely a few weeks later. The final customer of the night rented, appropriately enough, the Seth Rogen comedy *This Is the End*.

Last HD DVD: There was another smaller, briefer home video format war in the mid-2000s. Two high-definition movie systems aimed to succeed the DVD: Blu-ray, championed by nine electronics companies, including Sony, Panasonic, and Philips; and HD DVD, created by Toshiba. Blu-ray won, and Toshiba discontinued HD DVD production. The last movie available in that format was Quentin Tarantino's *Death Proof*, in 2008.

Last book on tape: They're technically called audiobooks, although a lot of people still call them "books on tape." That's in spite of the fact that publishers ditched

The sparklemuffin is a brightly colored "peacock spider" that lives in Australia.

cassettes for CDs and downloadable files long ago. The last major book on tape actually released on tape was James Patterson and Howard Roughan's 2008 novel *Sail*.

Last cassette: Small labels continue to make tapes, as do bands that self-release their music, but the big record labels phased them out entirely in the 2000s. One of the last big albums on the format was *The Last Kiss*, a 2009 album by the rapper Jadakiss.

Last major eight-track: The oh-so-'70s format had its last hurrah in 1988, courtesy of a definitively 1970s band. The final eight-track released by a major record label was Fleetwood Mac's *Greatest Hits*.

Last CD in a longbox: Thanks to iTunes and services like Spotify, compact discs don't sell the way they did back in the 1990s. The last major change to affect CDs was the elimination of the longbox. In the late 1980s and early 1990s, CDs were sold in long rectangular packages decorated with an album's art. The reason for this nasty waste of paper: longboxes were tall, and record stores could display them in the bins that had once held LPs. Customers hated them—they reportedly added a dollar to the cost of a CD, and they produced about 18 millions pounds of extra trash. In early 1993, record companies said they'd stop using them as of April of that year…just before Earth Day. The last album to come in one of those unnecessary pieces of garbage was LL Cool J's March 1993 release *14 Shots to the Dome*.

Last Atari game: The video game craze of the early 1980s led to an industry crash in 1983. Atari barely survived, and as the decade wore on, companies like Nintendo introduced games with more advanced graphics. Amazingly, Atari kept producing games for its flagship 2600 system until the end of the decade. Its last release in North America was *Secret Quest* in 1989.

Last NES game: The dominant home video game console of the late 1980s and early 1990s was the Nintendo Entertainment System. It was unseated from its perch in 1991 by…the *Super* Nintendo Entertainment System. But there were plenty of holdouts who liked their original NES, and Nintendo kept making games for them until 1994. That year it released *Wario's Woods* in North America for the NES, a game featuring Mario's evil doppelganger, Wario.

Last SNES game: The SNES was supplanted in 1996 by the Nintendo N64. Super Nintendo games kept being made until 1998. The last one available: a remake of the classic early video game *Frogger*.

Sure, but why? Scientists figured out how to store video in the DNA of bacteria.

BALANCE YOUR RACK

If you ever graduate from playing Scrabble with family and friends to entering big-time tournaments, here are some terms that will help you sound like a P–R–O.

BINGO

Any word that uses all seven letters on the rack (you earn an extra 50 points).

NATURAL BINGO

A bingo made with no blank tiles. ("Blank bingos" are made using one or more blank tiles.)

NONGO

When you have a Bingo on your rack, but there's no room for it on the board. Also called a Dingo (short for "Din' go anywhere").

STEMS

Five- and six-letter tile combinations that are especially useful for forming bingos.

CLOSED BOARD

A board on which there are few or no remaining opportunities for bingos or other high-scoring plays.

PALMING

Concealing an unwanted tile in the palm of your hand in order to slip it back into the bag when reaching for new tiles (it's against the rules).

HOOK/HOOK LETTER

A letter that spells a new word when it's added to the beginning or end of a word already on the board.

EXTENSION

Like a hook, but with two or more letters that create a new word when added to a word already on the board.

BLOCKER

A word that's difficult to hook or extend ("vug" or "fez," for example).

POLECAT PASS

Discarding an unplayable Q when the game is nearly over.

Q-GAME

A close game that is decided by which player gets stuck with the Q.

ALPHAGRAM

When the tiles on your rack are arranged in alphabetical order.

HEAVY TILES

Consonants with high point values (Q and Z are the heaviest tiles: they're worth 10 points each).

Most favorite color: 40 percent of people say they like blue the best.

BRAILING

Feeling the surface of the tiles when your hand is in the bag, in order to grab a blank tile or one that has the letter you want (it's against the rules).

TYPO

An uncommon word that looks like a common word that has been misspelled. They can be used to trick opponents into challenging words that are valid. ("Sycosis," for example, is a real word that looks like "psychosis" misspelled.)

COFFEE-HOUSING

Any behavior, such as chatting, drumming your fingers, etc., that distracts your opponent (this is against the rules in tournament play).

ENDGAME

When there are fewer than seven tiles remaining in the draw bag.

OPEN SCRABBLE

A variant of the standard game in which all tiles are played faceup.

RACK BALANCING

Playing your tiles in a way that leaves letters on your rack that are likely to help you score well in your next turn.

STUTTERER

A word that ends in duplicate letters ("baa," "too," etc.).

TURNOVER

When a player plays as many tiles as possible in order to draw the maximum number of new tiles from the bag.

POWER TILES

The ten most advantageous tiles (the two blanks, the four Ss, and the J, Q, X, and Z), either because of their high point value or the ease with which they can be used to make words.

TRACKING

The Scrabble equivalent of counting cards—studying the letters on the board to get a sense of what letters are still in the bag or on an opponent's rack.

BLOWOUT/GRANNY

A game so lopsided (one player gets all the good tiles) that even your granny couldn't lose. Also called a No-Brainer.

FAST-BAGGING

If a player wants to challenge whether a word is real or not, they must do it before the player in question draws their tiles from the bag, ending the turn. Drawing tiles immediately after a word is played can deny opponents the opportunity to challenge it.

FISHING

Playing only one or two tiles, in order to hang on to five or six tiles in the hope of playing a high-scoring word in the next turn.

Luc Besson wrote and directed *The Fifth Element* at age 38, based on an idea he had when he was 8.

WOULD YOU BUY SNEAKERS FROM THIS MAN?

Many athletes get the bulk of their earnings not from their salary, but from endorsements. Which makes it all the worse when they blow these sweet gigs.

MICHAEL VICK

What happened: The Atlanta Falcons quarterback was indicted on charges of sponsoring a dog fighting operation in 2007. At the time, the speedy passer was one of the most famous and most recognizable athletes in America. But days after his indictment, his lengthy list of sponsors fled. That included Nike, Reebok, Rawlings, Hasbro, Upper Deck, Coca Cola, EA Sports, and AirTran Airways. Vick ended up spending 21 months in federal prison and declared bankruptcy. But after signing with the Philadelphia Eagles in 2009, Vick began to get his life back on track. He played for seven more seasons, paid back $17 million he owed to creditors, sponsored a federal law imposing new misdemeanor penalties for dog fighting, and even became the first athlete that Nike re-signed after once being dropped.

Value of the lost endorsements: Unknown—probably close to $50 million

TIGER WOODS

What happened: Over Thanksgiving weekend in 2009, the world learned that Tiger Woods had been in a minor car accident. While many suspected he must have been taking drugs at the time, the truth was a lot more shocking: He crashed after being chased by his golf club–wielding wife, who had just learned he'd had scores of affairs with different women, from famous porn stars to cocktail waitresses. After Woods announced that he was taking a break from golf to repair his personal life, he lost endorsement deals from Gillette, AT&T, Gatorade, and Tag Heuer. The scandal affected more than his pocketbook—his game has never been quite the same, either. Almost 10 years later, sports fans have gone from predicting when Woods would break Jack Nicklaus's record of 18 major championships to wondering if he'd ever win a tournament again.

Value of the lost endorsements: $22 million

An Olympic gold medal is mostly silver...and less than 1% gold.

MICHAEL PHELPS

What happened: There have been countless feats of athletic brilliance in the last 100 years of sports, but few come close to those of swimmer Michael Phelps. Over the course of his Olympic career, Phelps set the all-time record for medals (28) and gold medals (23) won by an athlete. This brought him worldwide fame, but also greater scrutiny for his mistakes. In 2004 Phelps was arrested for driving drunk, and after a 2009 photo of him holding a bong went viral, Kellogg's cereal decided to drop him from their roster. His other sponsors, including Speedo, Visa, Subway, and Omega watches, stood by him, even after a second DUI arrest in 2014 that resulted in Phelps seeking treatment at a rehab center.

Value of the lost endorsements: $250,000

ADRIAN PETERSON

What happened: The Minnesota Vikings running back burst onto the scene in 2007, when he set the NFL's single-game rushing record. In 2012, his sixth season, Peterson won the MVP award and came within eight yards of breaking the single-season rushing record. But his 2014 season came to an end after just one game when he was indicted on charges of abusing his four-year-old son. Photos leaked by TMZ showed welts on the back of his son's leg, caused by Peterson whipping his son with a "switch" from a tree. As the sports world erupted in a generational debate about domestic corporal punishment, the NFL responded by suspending Peterson for the entire season, and Peterson lost deals with Nike, Castrol Oil, and Wheaties. Though Peterson returned to the league the following year (with Adidas as a sponsor), he never regained the dominance he once had over the sport.

Value of the lost endorsements: $4 million

JON JONES

What happened: In the early 2010s, it seemed like nothing could stop the Ultimate Fighting Championship's meteoric rise into the mainstream. But the sport's popularity soon slowed, and it's no coincidence that Jon Jones's fall from grace played a major part. Once ranked the #1 pound-for-pound fighter in mixed martial arts, Jones was also Nike's first MMA fighter signed to an international endorsement deal. But a 2012 DUI arrest was the first in a string of incidents for the rising star. On top of that, Jones has tested positive for performance-enhancing drugs three times and for cocaine use once. It gets worse: In 2015 Jones was convicted of a hit and run in which he crashed into a

Is that how you get double pneumonia? Viruses can be infected by other viruses.

car driven by a pregnant woman. Jones was stripped of his championship titles three times (he regained the title twice) and lost all of his sponsors. He is currently facing a four-year suspension and it is unlikely he will ever fight in the UFC again.

Value of the lost endorsements: Unknown

LANCE ARMSTRONG

What happened: It shouldn't surprise you that professional cyclists make most of their money from sponsorships. They race in events all over the world, not in front of 40,000 ticket holders for months at a time. And no cyclist suffered a bigger loss of endorsement than the most recognizable cyclist of all time, Lance Armstrong. He famously won the Tour de France seven straight times…after beating cancer. But when years-long doping investigations finally ended in a lifetime ban from cycling and his being stripped of all his titles, Armstrong's sponsors—including companies like Nike, 24 Hour Fitness, and Anheuser-Busch InBev—canceled their lucrative deals with him.

Value of the lost endorsements: $150 million

* * *

ACTUAL & FACTUAL RANDOM FACTS

- How to respond to a sneeze in six foreign countries: Norway and Sweden: *Prosit!* (May it help!). Luxembourg: *Gesondheet!* (Health!). Switzerland: *Salute!* (To health!). Portugal: *Santinho!* (Little saint!). Turkey: *Cok yasa!* (Live long!).

- Niacin, also known as vitamin B3, was first extracted from nicotine and was originally called nicotinic acid. The name *niacin* was created (*ni-* from *nicotinic*, *-ac* from *acid*, and *-in* from *vitamin*) to avoid the perception that any foods with nicotinic acid contain nicotine, or that cigarettes contain vitamins.

- Rarest blood type in the world: hh, also known as Bombay blood, where it was discovered in 1952. Four people in every million have it—it's so rare that people who have it need to bank their own blood in case of emergency.

- On April 27, 1792, Captain George Vancouver sailed past what is now Ocean Shores, Washington, without stopping. Today the city commemorates the non-event with "Undiscovery Day." Among the festivities: at midnight, citizens gather on the beach and shout, "Hey, George!"

A one-acre parcel of land, on average, is home to about 50,000 spiders.

YOU'VE BEEN ELIMINATED

Every competitive reality show has an "elimination catchphrase"—a line that the host delivers each week to the contestant who's been voted out. It's one of the few scripted parts of the show and, as a group, they're pretty funny.

"The tribe has spoken."
(*Survivor*)

"Please pack your knives and go." (*Top Chef*)

"You've been evicted."
(*Big Brother*)

"You're terminated!"
(*The New Celebrity Apprentice with Arnold Schwarzenegger*)

"Your check is voided, it's time for you to bounce."
(*I Love Money*)

"You must leave the chateau." (*Joe Millionaire*)

"Auf Wiedersehen."
(*Project Runway*)

"Now, sashay away."
(*RuPaul's Drag Race*)

"Your time's up."
(*Flavor of Love*)

"Give me your jacket."
(*Hell's Kitchen*)

"Your banner must fall."
(*America's Best Dance Crew*)

"I have to ask you to leave the mansion."
(*Beauty and the Geek*)

"This was your final cut."
(*Shear Genius*)

"America has spoken."
(*American Idol*)

"You have fired your last shot." (*Top Shot*)

"Don't call us, we'll call you." (*The Starlet*)

"You've been eliminated from the race."
(*The Amazing Race*)

"For you, it's game over."
(*The Pickup Artist*)

"You're out of style."
(*The Cut*)

"The verdict is in—you are out." (*The Law Firm*)

"You are not the biggest loser." (*The Biggest Loser*)

"You're not tough enough."
(*WWE Tough Enough*)

"You bombed out!"
(*BOOM!*)

"You are the weakest link!"
(*The Weakest Link*)

"Membership denied!"
(*From G's to Gents*)

"You were no sweet genius."
(*Sweet Genius*)

"This is the final rose."
(*The Bachelor*)

"You're just a tool."
(*Tool Academy*)

"You're not on the list."
(*I Want to Be a Hilton*)

"You've been clipped."
(*The Assistant*)

"You're headed to the dog pound." (*Dog Eat Dog*)

"You can't always get what you want."
(*Kept*)

"Goodbye." (*The Apprentice: Martha Stewart*)

"Please turn in your apron." (*Worst Cooks in America*)

"You're fired!"
(*The Apprentice*)

"Your tour ends here."
(*Rock of Love with Bret Michaels*)

"Today is not your day."
(*Abby's Ultimate Dance Competition*)

More than 40 skyscrapers in New York City have their own ZIP codes.

PARKING TICKET NEWS

There's nothing more mundane (and infuriating!) than
getting a parking ticket. Except when it's not.

INSULT, MEET INJURY. In August 2015, a man who was parked in a parking lot in Ammanford, Wales, returned to his car to find a parking ticket on the windshield. (Amount of parking fine in U.S. dollars: about $90.) Enraged, he grabbed the ticket from the windshield, threw it to the ground, and drove off. Someone saw him throw the ticket on the ground and reported him to authorities. Result: The man was issued a ticket for littering. (Amount of littering fine: about $110.)

OOPS! The City of New York changed the code number of one of its traffic violations in April 2017. The violation concerned drivers who failed to properly display parking meter receipts in paid-parking zones. The original code number for that violation: 4-08h10. The new code number: 4-08h1. In case you missed it, the difference is a zero at the end of the code. Bad news: In July 2017, someone noticed that tickets issued for the violation still had the old code listed on them. That meant all the tickets issued with the wrong number were invalid. New York City was forced to refund the fines paid for all 400,860 tickets issued during that period. Total cost: about $18 million. (And about $8 million more in tickets that had not yet been paid were canceled, bringing the parking fine fiasco's total cost to more than $26 million. Plus all the administrative costs involved.)

A POLISH JOKE. In June 2007, a police officer in the traffic division of the Republic of Ireland's Garda police force noticed something funny: A Polish person named Prawo Jazdy had somehow accumulated dozens of parking and speeding fines—without a single conviction. Then the officer noticed something else funny: "Prawo Jazdy" appears in the top right corner of *all* Polish drivers licenses—because it's Polish for "drivers license." Officers issuing fines to the drivers were mistaking "Prawo Jazdy" for the drivers' first and last names. The officer who discovered the mistake issued a memo that was sent out to officers across the country, alerting them of the error.

LATE FEES MAY APPLY? In November 2011, a man walked into the office of the chief of police in the small town of York, Nebraska, and told a clerk that he had found an unpaid parking ticket in his mother's belongings while cleaning out her home. He then handed a package to the clerk and left. In the package was the unpaid parking ticket, mounted in an antique wood-and-glass picture frame. Date on the ticket: July

Families of the *Titanic's* orchestra members were billed for
the cost of their uniforms after the ship went down.

13, 1954. Amount of the fine: 10 cents. The man, whose name was not released to the press, paid that fine by taping a dime to the ticket. York Chief of Police Don Klug said he planned to hang the framed ticket on the wall of his office.

THEY SHOULD HAVE COPPED TO IT. A parking officer in Chicago issued a ticket to an illegally parked minivan one afternoon in May 2006. The driver of the minivan: Chicago police officer Robert Reid, who had parked the vehicle while responding to a call. Angry to find the parking ticket on his car, Officer Reid, accompanied by three other officers, started berating the parking officer. The supervisor of the city's Traffic Management Authority, Jacqueline Fegan, happened to be nearby, and she intervened on the traffic officer's behalf. Officer Reid wasn't having it. He demanded that Fegan cancel the ticket. She refused, and Reid and the other officers responded by arresting her, placing her in handcuffs, and throwing her into the back of the minivan. Fegan, who claimed her wrist was permanently injured during the incident, sued the officers and the city for false arrest, false imprisonment, battery, and more. In 2009, after three years of litigation…she won. Final cost to the City of Chicago for the $50 parking fine: $1.5 million—which is what the jury awarded Fegan.

HE AIN'T HEAVY / HE'S MY DAIHATSU. In September 2016, a woman in the city of Fremantle, West Australia, posted an angry rant on her Facebook page, regarding a parking ticket she'd received. The woman, named "Sally," posted a photo of the parking ticket, showing she had been fined $50 for failing to park between the lines of a parking bay in one of the city's parking lots. She also posted a photo of the supposedly illegally parked car, with one tire just barely touching one of the lines. When news of the seemingly unfair fine started to spread, the City of Fremantle posted a picture of their own—one that the parking officer took as evidence when he issued the fine in the first place. It showed Sally's car clearly taking up two marked car spaces. It seemed Sally had moved her car before she took her own photo, in a dishonest attempt to get out of paying the fine. So the story ended… until Sally came up with a new story: A friend of hers had seen "four big guys" actually pick up her car and move it the night she was fined. She asked the City of Fremantle if there was any CCTV coverage of the parking lot. There was! And the city agreed to view it. What did it show? Sally's car, clearly taking up two bays in the parking lot—and then "four big guys" picking up the car and moving it so they could fit their own car into one of the spaces. The time on the CCTV showed that they'd moved Sally's car just minutes after she received the fine. So it turned out that Sally *hadn't* lied when she posted her photo—but she had parked illegally in the first place. (So she still had to pay the fine.)

That won't do, pig: After playing Farmer Hoggett in the
1995 hit film *Babe*, actor James Cromwell became a vegan.

CHILD LABOR LOWS

Jolly old England wasn't so jolly for the poor boys and girls who had to work jobs that could easily top the list of the most disgusting and painful jobs in history. Think your job is tough? Consider these.

BARBER'S APPRENTICE

The job of a barber's apprentice had more to do with mopping up blood and disposing of amputated limbs than styling hair. After 1540, when the Fellowship of Surgeons merged with the Company of Barbers, barber-surgeons extracted teeth, performed enemas, dispensed medicine, performed bloodletting (with leeches) and surgery, tended the wounds of soldiers…and cut hair. In 1745 the surgeons split from the barbers, which decreased the amount of blood and gore in the barber's apprentice's life.

MATCHGIRLS

In the 1800s, more than 1,400 girls and young women at Bryant and May's match factory in London worked from 6:00 a.m. until 10:00 p.m. dipping wooden matchsticks into highly flammable (and very poisonous) white phosphorous. The girls were fined a day's wages if they talked, dropped a match, or went to the bathroom during those 16 hours. But worse than the long hours was the disease—phosphorous necrosis, also called "phossy jaw"—a cancer that destroyed the girls' lower jaws. The London matchgirls' strike of 1888 brought the plight of the "phossy girls" into the public eye, and working conditions improved, but it took 12 more years for match factories to stop using phosphorous.

CLIMBING BOYS

Chimney sweeps in the 1700s and 1800s used "climbing boys" to squeeze up the chimney stacks and scrape the soot off the walls. Climbing boys were as young as three, and no more than eight or nine years old. Because a chimney averaged 9 x 14 inches but could be as small as 7 inches square, the boys had to be tiny. To ensure that they stayed small, chimney sweeps would keep them on a near-starvation diet. Climbing boys often fell and broke legs and ankles. Their lungs were damaged from breathing soot, and many suffered from "chimney sweep's cancer," which was caused by poisonous chemicals rubbing into their body's open sores. In 1788 Parliament passed a law that no boy younger than eight could be apprenticed to a sweep, which saved kids from three to seven, but it was still a deadly job for the eight- and nine-year-olds.

Q. What was George Washington's middle name? A. He didn't have one.

TOOTH DONORS

The British upper classes consumed a lot of sugar in the 1700s. Add excessive amounts of wine and rich food to the sugar and you have a recipe for rotting teeth. The solution: replace the rotted stubs with healthy "donor" teeth. The donors were usually desperately poor children who were paid a pittance to have their tooth pulled without painkillers. The tooth was immediately inserted into the wealthy person's mouth. It wasn't really a transplant because donor teeth rarely took root. The discovery that syphilis could be transmitted by the teeth made this custom go out of fashion quickly.

MUDLARKS

During the 18th and 19th centuries, young children would stand knee-deep in sewage along the river Thames at low tide, searching through human waste and the corpses of dead animals for something they could sell. Called "mudlarks," these children scavanged bits of rope, copper nails, rags (for making paper), driftwood, and—on a lucky day—coins. The children were always in danger of being washed into the Thames or getting stuck in the mud. The tradition isn't over; children still work as mudlarks in some developing countries.

CROSSING SWEEPERS

In the 1800s, young children, armed with brooms, helped wealthy clients cross the carriage-filled streets by running just ahead of them and sweeping all of the horse manure and muck out of the way.

FLOUR MILL DAMSEL

Until the 1900s, mills used pairs of big, round stones to grind wheat into flour. The mill damsel was a young girl of six or seven who spent ten hours a day making sure that wheat was always passing between the two stones. If she fell asleep, took a lavatory break, or simply got distracted, the action of two dry stones being rubbed together could cause a spark and set the mill on fire.

GONG SCOURER'S BOY

"Gong" was slang used to describe toilets and their contents from the 1400s through the 1700s. A gong scourer was a person who cleaned the excrement from indoor privies, cesspits, and outdoor toilets. They often spent most of the workday up to their waists, and even necks, in waste, sometimes passing out from noxious fumes. A gong scourer's boy crawled into the tightest places to clean out the sludge and then hauled buckets of sewage to the top of the pits. If that job wasn't bad enough, the boys had to work from 9:00 p.m. to 5:00 a.m. so that the public wouldn't have to witness the process or smell the contents of their toilets being excavated and hauled away.

About a third of Americans have their fingerprints on file with the FBI.

THOUGHTS FROM THURBER

James Thurber was one of the most famous humorists of the mid-20th century, and there's an annual award given out by his estate—the Thurber Prize—to the funniest American book of the year. Here are some quips from the man himself.

"Humor is emotional chaos remembered in tranquility."

"There is no exception to the rule that every rule has an exception."

"Sixty minutes of thinking of any kind is bound to lead to confusion and unhappiness."

"The most dangerous food is wedding cake."

"Boys are beyond the range of anybody's sure understanding, at least when they are between the ages of 18 months and 90 years."

"The past is an old armchair in the attic, the present is an ominous ticking sound, and the future is anybody's guess."

"It is better to know some of the questions than all of the answers."

"There is no safety in numbers, or in anything else."

"The laughter of man is more terrible than his tears, and takes more forms hollow, heartless, mirthless, maniacal."

"Progress was all right. Only it went on too long."

"All men should strive to learn before they die, what they are running from, and to, and why."

"You can fool too many of the people too much of the time."

"A word to the wise is not sufficient if it doesn't make sense."

"The only rules comedy can tolerate are those of taste, and the only limitations those of libel."

"Let us not look back in anger, nor forward in fear, but around in awareness."

"The dog has got more fun out of Man than Man has got out of the dog, for the clearly demonstrable reason that Man is the more laughable of the two animals."

"The things we laugh at are awful while they are going on, but get funny when we look back. And other people laugh because they've been through it, too. The closest thing to humor is tragedy."

"There are two kinds of light: The glow that illuminates, and the glare that obscures."

When the (laboratory) conditions are just right, liquid water can boil and freeze at the same time.

THE ABCs OF RPS

Put that competitive instinct and that deep-seated pathological need to win to the test: Here are some ways to increase the likelihood you'll win at that classic battle of weapons and wits: Rock, Paper, Scissors.

THE MIND-CONTROL METHOD

Most people are just casual Rock, Paper, Scissors players. If you're going to take the game seriously, then you've already got an advantage over a relative novice…and you can exploit their newness, because it's a weakness. If your adversary is a newbie, explain the game; if they're a casual RPS'er, give a refresher course. As you do, use hand gestures to demonstrate your point. For example, when you mention that rock defeats scissors, make the scissors sign with your hand. Then, explain that scissors beats paper. Once again, make the scissors sign. That back-to-back repetition of scissors will stick in your opponent's head, and they're much more likely to throw a scissors the first time you play for real. Expecting that, throw rock. You win.

KNOW YOUR STATISTICS

According to the experts, "rock" is the most commonly thrown first move. Knowing that, you should throw paper. If the odds are in your favor, your paper covers their rock. You win. Rock is an even more common initial move among men, while casual female players statistically choose scissors on their first go-around. If you're playing against a novice lady competitor, throw rock. You win.

WATCH FOR PATTERNS

Many players will try to get into *your* head by throwing down the same thing two times in a row—two rocks, two papers, or two scissors. However, studies show that the likelihood of a player going for the same play *three* times in a row are slim. That means you can mentally eliminate the thing they did twice from the possibilities of what they'll throw on round three. For example, if they did scissors, and then scissors again, they're probably going to go for paper or rock at that point, so throw accordingly (scissors or paper, respectively). You win. (Or tie.)

THE HUBRIS FACTOR

Experienced players, such as anyone who's read this cheat sheet, are unlikely to throw a rock first—they're too prideful. Only rookies go for a rock on the first time. So that's one of three possibilities that can be eliminated already. But pride factors in once more.

Hot and cold water sound differently when poured. Hot water has a lower pitch.

Because the experienced player is so confident in their abilities, they'll assume everyone else is a newbie, which means they assume you're going to throw rock. That means *they* will throw a victorious paper…except you knew that, so you go for scissors. You win.

DISARM THEM WITH A LIE

Here's a trick that will bewilder your opponent regardless of their skill level: Tell them what you're going to throw before you throw it. And then do something else? Nope—stick to your word. They'll think that you're messing with them, which you are, but not the way they assume. They'll think that by announcing "rock," for example, it means you're going to play something else. Predicting you'll give them scissors or paper, they'll throw rock or scissors to win. But then when you actually do throw rock, you either beat their scissors or tie with their rock.

LET THEM "TELL" YOU

Just like most poker players have a "tell" when they've got a good hand, Rock, Paper, Scissors players may demonstrate some kind of physical indication that can be used to predict what they're going to throw. It's all about the way they hold their hand. Does it look like they're holding their hand in a loose fist? That's a hint they're looking to make their hand go flat fast for paper. Do they have their thumb resting on top of their fist? That looks like a rock. A hand with the first two fingers held loosely is an almost surefire tell that the opponent will pick scissors.

GET THEM ANGRY

If you use all of these tricks and just keep beating your opponent no matter what they throw, they're likely to get frustrated. And when they throw their next hand, they're likely to throw rock—it's subconsciously and psychologically the most aggressive option. But then, you knew they were going to do that, and you've got paper ready. You win.

* * *

UNLIKELY RELATIVES

Dr. Henry Heimlich, inventor of the Heimlich maneuver that's saved countless people from choking, was the uncle of Anson Williams, the actor who played Warren "Potsie" Weber on *Happy Days*.

As a teenager, famous sex therapist Dr. Ruth Westheimer was a sniper in the Israeli army.

WE ♥ OUR WORKERS

*Big companies can be challenging to work for because they don't
value their employees, do they? Well, these companies do.*

IN-N-OUT BURGER

Years before the "Fight for $15" movement to raise the minimum wage started gaining
traction, the West Coast's beloved In-N-Out Burger chain was way ahead of the curve.
California increased its minimum wage to $10.50 per hour in 2017, but In-N-Out was
paying its workforce $10.50 long before it became mandatory. Employees, including
part-time workers, get benefits like paid vacation, free meals, flexible hours, and a
401K plan—perks that are unheard of from fast-food giants whose revenues dwarf
In-N-Out's. In one of the most exploitative business sectors in the United States,
In-N-Out stands out as a "roll" model.

COSTCO

Walmart, the world's biggest retailer, typically pays minimum wage, caps pay for
veteran workers, cuts hours to prevent workers from qualifying for health care, and
uses its resources to prevent unionization. Costco, the world's second-biggest retailer,
does the opposite. In 2013 Costco's CEO publicly supported raising the federal
minimum wage to $10.10 and started workers at $11.50. More than 88 percent of
Costco's workers have health insurance through the company (compared to Walmart's
50 percent). By not spending money on advertising, Costco can pass on the savings
to employees. Most important, Costco does not participate in union busting and has
allowed tens of thousands of its workers to unionize. Costco proves you can make a
profit while not pushing your workers onto government assistance.

NVIDIA

If you play PC games, there's a good chance your computer has a Nvidia GPU
(graphics processing unit). But smaller tech companies now have to compete with
companies like Facebook and Google for the brightest workers. So how well is Nvidia
doing against these tech behemoths, known for their amazing benefits? Well, according
to *Forbes'* 2017 ranking of the top companies to work for, Nvidia came in at #3 overall
out of the 1,000 companies they surveyed. If you're a recent college graduate, Nvidia
will contribute $6,000 a year toward your student loans for five years. New moms get
22 weeks of paid parental leave. Trying to *become* a new mom or dad? Nvidia offers
reimbursement for in vitro fertilization and adoption expenses. Of the seven categories
Forbes used to determine overal rankings, Nvidia came in at #1 for worker treatment.

Brazil discontinued the one-cruzeiro banknote in 1958. (Each one cost 1.2 cruzeiros to print.)

"I'M SERINDIPIDATING"

If you haven't been "on the market" in a while, you'll be amazed at how much dating lingo has changed, thanks largely to smartphones and social media. Here are some terms for you to learn…just in case you need them someday.

Benching/backburnering: When you don't want to date someone, but you string them along to keep them from looking for someone else. (Similar to athletes who are on the team, but never leave the bench.)

Fire dooring: When someone contacts you via text or social media, but doesn't respond to your replies. (Fire doors open from the inside but are locked on the outside.)

Catfishing: Creating a fake online persona, complete with fake photos and phony details, and pretending to be that person while flirting online.

Kittenfishing: Like catfishing, but using your own exaggerated information and doctored images to create the impression that you're smarter, younger, wealthier, or better-looking than you really are.

Cushioning: Keeping in contact with one or more prospects just in case your current relationship sours, so that they will cushion your fall when you do break up.

Window shopping: Interacting with someone on social media without any intention of meeting them in person.

Mooning: Setting your phone to send a particular person straight to voicemail whenever they call. (The "Do Not Disturb" icon on an iPhone is a moon.)

Catch and release: Someone who's more interested in landing a date with someone than continuing to see them afterward. As soon as they "catch" someone, they "release" them.

Emergency call: Arranging for a friend to call you in the middle of your date, so that if it's going badly you can pretend the call is an emergency and end the date. ("I have to go! My dog is sick!")

Serindipidating: Repeatedly putting off a date with someone, in the hope that someone better will come along.

Cricketing/R-bombing: When you read a message someone sent to you (some apps, like Facebook Messenger, notify the sender you've read it), but don't respond. The sender can tell you're ignoring them.

Flexting: Boasting online to impress someone you're hoping to date.

Monkeying: Moving from one relationship to another without pausing in between—like a monkey swinging from one rope to another.

Turkey dump: When a freshman home from college for Thanksgiving dumps their hometown boyfriend/girlfriend because long-distance relationships are too difficult (or because they have a new "friend").

Small houseflies do not grow up to be big houseflies. They emerge from the larval stage fully grown.

THE SOCIAL LIFE OF TREES

Earth is home to more than 3 trillion trees—about 422 trees for every person on Earth—and, far from being silent witnesses, they have a social life that scientists are just beginning to understand.

TREE TALK

A 1997 research study conducted by forest ecologist Suzanne Simard turned our understanding of plants and fungi upside down. She discovered that trees are social and actually communicate with each other through a kind of living internet of fungi. When you see a mushroom in the forest, you're only seeing the tip of the iceberg. Below the ground is where the real action is. That's where the mycelia—a tangled mass of threads and the largest part of the fungi body—are busily running around connecting with as many trees as possible.

Certain common fungi have symbiotic relationships with plants. Because fungi cannot photosynthesize (remember, plants need light and chlorophyll for photosynthesis), the mycelium explore the soil for nutrients and water, which they then exchange with their host plants for food—up to a third of the tree's production of sugar. For this exchange to take place, the mycelium colonizes the roots of the plant at a cellular level to form the mycorrhiza, or fungal connection. Mycelia are not shy about their needs: they will hook up with multiple plants of varying species to ensure an adequate food supply.

HACKING THE WOOD WIDE WEB

This is where Simard's research comes in. While doing research for her doctoral thesis, Simard discovered that tree seedlings (mostly Douglas firs in her study) used the underground fungi network not only for the nourishment they receive from the fungi but also to communicate with other trees. She found that when a weak tree in the network needed help, a stronger tree would respond by sharing its resources—and it didn't matter if they were from different species. The fungi network connects 90 percent of all land plants and has been nicknamed the "Wood Wide Web."

Plants also use the fungi network to warn each other. In a 2010 study, researcher Ren Sen Zeng of South China Agricultural University found that when tomato plants were infected with harmful fungi, the plants sent out chemical signals to their neighbors, which gave them time to mount a defense. And in a 2013 study at Scotland's University of Aberdeen, researchers discovered that when broad bean seedlings were under attack by aphids, the plants that were connected to the fungi network were able to activate anti-aphid chemical defenses.

The size of a pair of socks refers to the length, in inches, of the sock from heel to toe.

Standing at the hub of a forest's fungi network are the biggest and oldest trees—the "mother trees." Their extensive root systems allow them to make the most fungal connections to the greatest number of trees and plants in the forest. In a single forest, a mother tree can be connected to hundreds of trees. Suzanne Simard's later research indicates that mother trees not only *recognize* family members, but they use the network to *nurture* them. "Mother trees colonize their kin with bigger mycorrhizal networks. They send them more carbon below ground. They even reduce their own root competition to make elbow room for their kids." Mother trees know that simply plugging into the fungi network will help their family survive.

CROWN-SHYNESS

There is a phenomenon that happens with certain tree species, such as eucalyptus, Sitka spruce, or Japanese larch, in which the uppermost branches of neighboring trees will not touch each other. It's known as crown-shyness. To an observer on the ground, the phenomenon looks like what one writer describes as "a giant, backlit jigsaw puzzle." Some scientists theorize that a tree can "feel" when it is approaching another tree and it reins in its branches to ensure that light can penetrate the forest canopy and photosynthesis can continue.

Another explanation for crown-shyness is that the gaps between the tree crowns become part of a forest-wide defense system against the spread of leaf-eating insects. But the simplest theory may be the most likely—the trees don't want to hurt themselves. By giving each other space, it is less likely their branches will collide or get wedged together with those of their neighbors during high winds. Crown-shyness is most common among the same types of trees, but it can occur between trees of different species.

THE REDWOOD INTRANET

Like all trees, coastal redwoods are connected to the fungi network, but they also have their own intranet—a private network of rings of interconnected roots, used to communicate and to share food. Coastal redwoods reproduce by seed, but unlike any other conifer, they use the rings to clone exact copies of themselves by sending out new sprouts from their bases and from fallen limbs.

Redwood cloning works most of the time, but every so often a mother tree will produce an albino—a ghost tree. Sightings of albino redwoods have been recorded since 1866, though they are exceedingly rare. As of 2017, there were fewer than 500 known ghost trees in the entire world. Their colors range from white, bright yellow, pale green, to mottled and variegated. (There are even "chimeric" ghost trees—trees that are part normal, part albino.) Because they lack chlorophyll—the one thing all trees need for photosynthesis—most ghost trees are small and weak, about the size of bushes. They grow

Fetuses can get hiccups. They can be observed on ultrasound images and even felt by the mother.

connected to a larger, healthy parent tree and have long been considered parasites—they were even called vampire trees. But recent research indicates that far from being parasitic, the albino redwood may play an important role in the health of redwood forests.

Research botanist Zane Moore discovered that a ghost tree acts like a liver or kidney for the forest. In exchange for the food they need to survive, ghost trees filter and store toxins from the soil, which results in keeping the poisons away from healthier redwoods. "It seems like the albino trees are just sucking these heavy metals up out of the soil," Moore said. "They're basically poisoning themselves." There are ghost trees living in Los Angeles, Portland, and Seattle, but the best place to see them is Muir Woods National Monument or Humboldt Redwoods State Park.

TREE KILLERS

The fungi web has its own "Dark Net"—plants that use the network for nefarious purposes. Acacia, American sycamore, and black walnut trees cannot stand competition and will dump chemicals into the web to harm their rivals. Another culprit, the phantom orchid, does not have chlorophyll and cannot photosynthesize, so it uses the network to steal food from nearby trees. And then there are fungi networks that are tree killers, such as the honey fungus. The honey fungus kills in slow motion by starving and dehydrating the tree to death. The most famous example of this parasite is "the Humongous Fungus" located in Oregon's Blue Mountains. It is 2.4 miles across and is considered to be the largest organism on Earth. It has been killing trees for more than 2,500 years.

KILLER TREES

In Africa, acacia trees employ a multi-tiered defense system to keeps animals from eating their leaves. First, they have long thorns that are the equivalent of barbed wire and help keep intruders away. Second, if herbivores are able to get past the thorns and start nibbling on the leaves, it takes less than 15 minutes for the acacia to pump large amounts of poison (tannins) into those leaves. The acacia will also release warning chemicals (ethylene) into the air. The chemicals drift to other trees downwind, and those trees start pumping poison into *their* leaves.

Giraffes know the acacias are potential killers. Solution: To avoid being poisoned, a giraffe will graze gently on the uppermost young leaves of an acacia tree before moving some 50 to 100 yards upwind to another tree. But giraffes aren't the only ones. In 1990 Wouter Van Hoven, a wildlife management expert from the University of Pretoria, was asked to investigate the sudden deaths of 3,000 kudu (a type of antelope) on commercial game ranches in South Africa. His discovery: acacia trees were to blame. Unlike the giraffes, the kudus were fenced in, with only the acacias to eat. The acacias defended themselves from overgrazing by killing the kudu.

No U.S. coin shows its denomination in numeral form.

FILIBUSTER? MORE LIKE BLADDER BUSTER

*It's a loophole that is used in many legislatures and parliaments around the world:
when a lawmaker wants to block or at least delay a piece of legislation from coming
to a vote, they can talk it to death using a tactic known as the filibuster. Often the
only limit on how long they can talk is how long they can go without…going.*

BLAH BLAH BLAH

In the U.S. Senate, the rules permit senators to speak as long
as they want, on as many subjects as they want, unless and
until "three-fifths of the Senate duly chosen and sworn" vote
to bring the debate to a close. Three-fifths of the Senate means
60 senators, unless some Senate seats are unoccupied due to
the death or resignation of a senator. Getting 60 senators to
agree on anything can be pretty difficult, which makes the
filibuster a powerful weapon for delaying or killing legislation.

**His staff also
stationed a lowly
intern with a bucket
in the Senate
cloakroom, just
off the floor of
the Senate.**

But there's a catch: no breaks are allowed. If more than one senator is in on
the filibuster, they can switch off, giving each other time for meal and bathroom
breaks. But if a senator is filibustering alone, the filibuster only lasts as long as their
physical stamina lasts. The weak link in a person's endurance is often their need
to pee, and that means that senators—and members of *any* legislative bodies that
allow filibusters—will go to great lengths to stretch out the time they can go without
bathroom breaks. For example:

Elected Official: U.S. senator Strom Thurmond

Filibuster: Thurmond, a segregationist, filibustered the Civil Rights Act of 1957 in
an attempt to prevent it from becoming the first federal civil rights law passed since
Reconstruction.

How He Did It: Thurmond managed to get a break about three hours into his filibuster,
on a technicality: Arizona senator Barry Goldwater asked him to yield the floor so that
Goldwater could insert something into the Congressional Record. Thurmond used
the time to race to the bathroom, but he got no more breaks after that. He prepared
for the filibuster by taking steam baths in the days leading up to his filibuster, using
the theory that if he started out dehydrated, his body would absorb liquids instead of
needing to eliminate them. His staff also stationed a lowly intern with a bucket in the
Senate cloakroom, just off the floor of the Senate, so that in an emergency he could

take one step into the cloakroom and relieve himself into the bucket while keeping the other foot on the Senate floor. But Thurmond never did use the bucket, and ended his filibuster after 24 hours, 18 minutes. The Civil Rights Act was later approved by the Senate, and was signed into law on September 9, 1957.

Elected Official: St. Louis, Missouri, alderwoman Irene Smith

Filibuster: The U.S. Senate isn't the only institution that permits filibustering—many state and local governments allow it too. So in 2001, Smith filibustered a ward-redistricting plan that she feared might cause her to lose her seat.

How She Did It: Smith spoke until she had to pee, then asked for a bathroom break. When informed that the break would end her filibuster, aides shielded her with a sheet, a quilt and a tablecloth while she relieved herself into a trash can. Result: Smith was charged with public urination, which had a maximum penalty of up to 90 days in jail, and a $500 fine, or both. But she was acquitted when prosecutors were unable to *prove* she'd actually peed. (Video footage of the incident, which had aired on public access television, was ruled inadmissible at trial because the TV director was out of the room taking a bathroom break when Smith was *in* the room taking hers. "What I did behind that tablecloth is my business," she said at the time. She did not admit publicly to relieving herself into the trash can until 2009.)

> Meier wore an "astronaut bag" (use your imagination) strapped to his leg underneath his trousers, and thus was able to relieve himself in mid-filibuster, without having to take a bathroom break.

Elected Official: Texas state senator Bill Meier

Filibuster: In 1977 Meier set the American record for the longest filibuster in any U.S. legislature when he tried to block a bill he believed would undermine Texas's open records law.

How He Did It: Meier wore an "astronaut bag" (use your imagination) strapped to his leg underneath his trousers, and thus was able to relieve himself in mid-filibuster, without having to take a bathroom break. The sympathetic lieutenant governor pitched in with procedural interruptions whenever Meier needed to empty the bag; that gave him just enough time to pop into a nearby women's restroom to complete the disgusting task.

Texas Senate rules forbid sitting or leaning against furniture or anything else during a filibuster, so two sergeants-at-arms accompanied Meier into the women's room to make sure he didn't lean on anything or sit down while emptying his astronaut bag. He lasted 43 hours, about as long as it takes to drive from New York City to San Francisco nonstop…but the bill passed anyway. As the reigning U.S. record holder for filibusters, Meier says he still gets calls from other elected officials hoping to break his record. "I tell them, 'Call me after you've finished 24 hours,'" he says.

Lost in translation: In Germany, the Rice Krispies characters say, "Knisper! Knasper! Knusper!" In Sweden: "Piff! Paff! Puff!" In South Africa: "Knap! Knaetter! Knak!"

Elected Official: Texas state senator Wendy Davis

Filibuster: In 2013 Davis, who is pro-choice, filibustered a bill that would have radically restricted access to abortion in the state.

How She Did It: Davis is, shall we say, anatomically "disadvantaged" in that she cannot be fitted with an astronaut bag (again, use your imagination) quite as easily as a man. So she fitted herself with a catheter. To prevent fatigue, she also wore a back brace and running shoes. She spoke for 11 hours on the last day of the legislative session, all the way up to the midnight deadline for the end of the session. That kept the bill from passing in that legislative session…but when it was brought up for a vote in the next session, it passed.

* * *

ACTUAL & FACTUAL FACTS ABOUT SODA POP

- The generic name for a soft drink varies by region: In New England and the Southwest, it's generally called "soda," in the Midwest and Pacific Northwest, it's generally "pop," and in Texas and the South it's called "Coke" (even if it isn't Coca-Cola).

- If you ever see a two-liter bottle of Coca-Cola at the store with a yellow cap, it's a special formula—it's kosher, brewed up for Passover.

- Faygo is a popular soda (or pop) in the Midwest, produced in Michigan. It offers super-sweet flavors like Cotton Candy and Grape because the company's founders were previously bakers, and based the flavors on frosting flavors.

- In the 1960s, Dr Pepper was losing business in the winter. So it started a marketing campaign to teach consumers to drink Dr Pepper warm with a slice of lemon, like tea.

- Worldwide, Coca-Cola produces about 3,500 different varieties of beverage.

- It costs soda companies less to manufacture their product in plastic bottles than glass ones, but glass ones work better. Carbon gas can slowly escape through the plastic, leading to less fizz over time, and a far shorter shelf life.

- When Nazi Germany was placed under trade embargoes during World War II, the country couldn't get Coca-Cola. So the country's local Coke bottler created orange-flavored Fanta. (After the war, Coca-Cola adopted the drink worldwide.)

- Soda with the most caffeine: Diet Pepsi Max, with 69 milligrams per 12-ounce serving. Legal FDA-imposed caffeine limit for soft drinks: 71 milligrams per 12-ounce serving.

What do elephants, hippos, rhinos, and sloths have in common? They can't jump.

BATHROOM MUSIC

Ideas can strike at any time, even when you're in the bathroom. Or, as these stories about songwriters prove, especially when you're in the bathroom.

"The Way I Feel Inside" The British group the Zombies had a string of dreamy, romantic, keyboard-driven singles in the 1960s, like "She's Not There," "Time of the Season," and "Tell Her No." "The Way I Feel Inside" came to keyboardist Rod Argent in 1964 while the Zombies were on tour with the Isley Brothers. "Rod wrote one of the songs on the toilet," said Zombies bassist Chris White. "I think it was 'The Way I Feel Inside,' ironically enough." Argent reportedly got so wrapped up in crafting the ballad that he almost missed the band's departing tour bus.

"The Sound of Silence" This slow-building ballad was one of Simon & Garfunkel's biggest hits (it reached #1 in 1966) and became further entrenched in popular culture when it was featured in the 1967 film *The Graduate*. Paul Simon started working on it years earlier, in 1963. "I wrote it in the bathroom in my parents' house," Simon says, "because the room was tiled, so there was an echo."

"Hole Hearted" The rock band Extreme is best known for its acoustic ballad "More Than Words," which hit #1 in 1991, and its follow-up, "Hole Hearted," which reached #4. The band's guitarist, Nuno Bettencourt, wrote the tune immediately after the very first 12-string guitar he ever owned arrived at his house. "I got kind of excited...and it made me want to go to the toilet," he said. "I sat down, took my time and, dare I say, the ideas just came pouring out."

"You Were on My Mind" The San Francisco pop rock band We Five had its biggest hit in 1965 with "You Were on My Mind." It was originally recorded a year earlier by the Canadian folk duo Ian & Sylvia. Sylvia Fricker wrote the song while holed up in a bathroom at the Hotel Earle in New York City's Greenwich Village. Why the bathroom? "It was the only place the cockroaches would not go," Fricker said.

"She Came in Through the Bathroom Window" One of the few songs in rock history that's explicitly about the bathroom was inspired by a real bathroom incident. (No, not *that* kind of bathroom incident.) Paul McCartney wrote it about obsessive Beatles fans who hung around outside the band's recording studios by day...and outside their homes at night. One of those fans, Diane Ashley, admitted to breaking into McCartney's London home. "We found a ladder in his garden and stuck it up at the bathroom window which he'd left slightly open. I was the one who climbed up and got in," Ashley said.

Jellico, Tennessee, was supposed to be called Jericho, but a misspelling... and then a typo of that misspelling...led to Jellico.

Q&A: ASK THE EXPERTS

*Here are more answers to life's important questions
from the people who know—trivia experts.*

PIT STOP

Q: *How do NASCAR drivers pee?*

A: "Traveling at tremendous speeds for hundreds of laps and accumulating hundreds of miles simply cannot be done without stopping. Tires need to be changed, fuel needs to be replenished, and other quick repairs need to be made—that's what pit stops are for. When the race car pulls in for a pit stop, a crew of seven snap to and work in unbelievable synchronicity to do whatever needs to be done as fast as possible. Most pit stops last from 15 to 23 seconds. The length of a pit stop can be the difference between winning and losing—every second counts. Thus, drivers often try to make pit stops during a caution flag so they don't lose too much fast racing time. The main thing that separates real-life driving from race-car driving is that the drivers don't pee at the pit stops. They don't pee for the whole race, in fact." (From *The Smart Girl's Guide to Sports*, by Liz Hartman Musiker)

OH, FUDGE

Q: *Why do stores in vacation towns always sell fudge and taffy?*

A: "Saltwater taffy and fudge are practically synonymous with the beach and summer vacations—in almost any resort town, you can count on a local purveyor to feature one or both of the sticky confections. But how did these chewy treats become so closely associated with summer destinations? A mix of situational appeal, entertainment value, savvy branding, and the magnetism of nostalgia. On vacation, people are more willing to indulge in sweets on the pretext of a 'special occasion,' and this craving may be enhanced by salty air. There's also a performance aspect to these candies' creation—perfect for travelers seeking a mindless thrill. Plus, candy-makers highlight the fresh, handmade quality of the sweets, convincing tourists they would make excellent souvenirs, and they also market the treats as emblems of a simpler time." (Lisa Wong Macabasco, *Slate*)

LIGHTS OUT

Q: *How do trick candles keep relighting after you blow them out?*

A: "With a normal candle, a burning ember in the wick causes a ribbon of paraffin smoke to rise from the wick. That ember is hot enough to vaporize paraffin but it is

Singing a song burns about two calories.

not hot enough to ignite the paraffin vapor. The key to a relighting candle, therefore, is to add something to the wick that the ember is hot enough to ignite. The most common substance: magnesium. Magnesium is a metal, but it happens to burn rapidly at an ignition temperature as low as 800°F (aluminum and iron both burn as well, but magnesium lights at a lower temperature). Inside the burning wick, the magnesium is shielded from oxygen and cooled by liquid paraffin, but once the flame goes out, magnesium dust is ignited by the ember. If you watch the ember you will see tiny flecks of magnesium going off. One of them produces the heat necessary to relight the paraffin vapor, and the candle flame comes back to life!" (From *How Much Does the Earth Weigh?* by Marshall Brain)

> **DID YOU KNOW?**
>
> A magnesium fire is difficult to extinguish. Adding water introduces hydrogen, which only makes the fire burn more. Carbon dioxide won't work either, because that also fuels a magnesium burn. Only a "Class D" fire extinguisher can end a magnesium fire. It uses powdered sodium chloride.

GONE GIRL

Q: *How did magician David Copperfield make the Statue of Liberty disappear in 1983?*

A: "Copperfield had a setup of two towers on a stage, supporting an arch to hold the huge curtain that would be used to conceal the statue. The TV cameras and the live audience only saw the monument through the arch. When the curtains closed, David waxed poetic while the stage was…slowly…and imperceptibly…turned. When the curtains opened, the statue was hidden behind one of the towers, and the audience was looking out to sea. Voilà! The Statue of Liberty has disappeared! Even if the stage hadn't completely hidden the statue, the towers were so brightly lit that the audience would be blinded. Copperfield had also set up two rings of lights—one around Lady Liberty, and another set up somewhere else. When the trick 'happened,' his assistants simply turned off the lights around the statue and turned on the other set for the helicopters to circle around." (Cecil Adams, *The Straight Dope*)

YOU'VE GOT TO START SOMEWHERE

Q: *How do seedless watermelons grow if they don't have any seeds?*

A: "They mess with their chromosomes, that's how. The first seedless watermelon was created in 1939. By crossing a diploid watermelon plant (having the normal two sets of chromosomes) with a tetraploid plant (having four sets of chromosomes), a fruit with triploid seeds (three sets of chromosomes) will result. How do they get tetraploid plants? They treat unpollinated flowers with *colchicine*, a poisonous alkaloid derived from the autumn crocus, that inhibits mitosis [cell division]." (From *Why Do Donuts Have Holes?* by Don Voorhees)

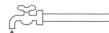

Are you a *lychnobite?* You are if you work at night and sleep during the day.

MOUTHING OFF

"JUST BE YOURSELF"

Uncle John says that's the best advice he ever got, so he wanted us to share it with you. And it turns out he's not alone.

"*This above all: to thine own self be true.*"
—**William Shakespeare**

"Do your thing and don't care if they like it."
—**Tina Fey**

"NEVER APOLOGIZE FOR WHAT YOU FEEL. IT'S LIKE SAYING SORRY FOR BEING REAL."
—**Lil Wayne**

"Some people say you are going the wrong way, when it's simply a way of your own."
—**Angelina Jolie**

"Follow your inner moonlight; don't hide the madness."
—**Allen Ginsberg**

"A fella who accepts himself and is relaxed into who he is—that appeals to people."
—**Jeff Bridges**

"**The hardest thing to do is to be true to yourself, especially when everybody is watching.**"
—**Dave Chappelle**

"*The most lies we will ever tell in our lives will be to ourselves.*"
—**Carla H. Krueger**

"To be natural is such a very difficult pose to keep up."
—**Oscar Wilde**

"You were born an original. Don't die a copy."
—**John Mason**

SPITE HOUSES

*Most houses are built to provide comfortable lodgings for their occupants.
But a few were designed for…revenge! These houses are commonly
called "spite houses." Here are some of our favorites.*

House: The Tyler Spite House, Frederick, Maryland

Background: In the 1810s, a prominent physician named John Tyler lived in a house off of Courthouse Square in Frederick. He also owned the vacant lot next to the house. In 1814 he was upset to learn that the city was about to build a road through the lot to connect Record Street to West Patrick Street.

Revenge! At the last minute, Dr. Tyler discovered a law that said that if a building either existed or was being built on the site of a proposed roadway, the road could not be built. So he raced out and found a building contractor who was willing to begin construction on a house that night. The following morning, when the road builders showed up to build the road, the other workers were already there, building the foundation for the house. Steps away, sitting in a chair on his front porch, "spiteful, self-satisfied" Dr. Tyler savored his victory. The Tyler Spite House still stands, and it's easy to find: just follow Record Street until it comes to a dead end.

House: The Hollensbury Spite House, Alexandria, Virginia

Background: In 1830 a Virginian named John Hollensbury lived next to an alley frequented by loiterers and horse-drawn wagons.

Revenge! Hollensbury was annoyed by the noise coming from the alley, which was so narrow that the hubs of wagon wheels scraped along the wall of his house. He finally got so fed up that he hired workers to build brick walls at both ends of the alley to block it off; then he topped it off with a roof. In the process he created what, at seven feet wide and two stories tall, is believed to be America's skinniest house. At last report the structure, which has just 325 square feet of floor space, was in use as a private residence for a family of three. In the kitchen and living room observant visitors can still see the indentations in the brick walls where the wagon wheels scraped past.

House: Carbisdale Castle, in the Scottish Highlands

Background: In 1889 George Sutherland-Leveson-Gower, the third Duke of Sutherland, married his second wife, Mary Caroline. He died three years later, and in his will he left a sizable portion of his estate to Mary Caroline. The fourth Duke of Sutherland—the third duke's son by his first wife—contested the will, and the fight became so nasty that Mary Caroline spent six weeks in jail for destroying evidence.

Sweet ride! Most cars in Brazil run on ethanol fuel made out of sugarcane.

The dispute was eventually resolved in the fourth duke's favor, and as part of the settlement, he agreed to pay Mary Caroline a substantial sum of cash, and also to pay for the construction of a castle for her to live in, provided that it was not built on Sutherland lands.

Revenge! The fourth duke probably wished that he'd insisted that the castle not be built *near* Sutherland lands either, or at least not in sight of them, because Mary Caroline bought land on a prominent hilltop just across the river from the fourth duke's country seat, and built her castle there. The duke could not help but see it when he traveled to and from his home. When completed in 1912, the "last castle built in Scotland" had 40 bedrooms, a billiards room, a ballroom, and, famously, a four-sided clock tower with clocks on only three sides. Why leave the clock off of the fourth side? It faced the Duke of Sutherland's estate—and Mary Caroline did not want to give her stepson "the time of day." The "castle of spite" still stands; it was a youth hostel from 1945 to 2014, when the high cost of repairs forced the Scottish Youth Hostels Association to sell it. At last report, the castle was being turned back into a private residence.

House: A three-story townhouse in the exclusive Kensington neighborhood of London

Background: In 2012 a property developer named Zipporah Lisle-Mainwaring outbid a neighboring property owner named Niall Carroll and bought the townhouse for £4.75 million (about $6.4 million). When she filed plans with the local government to demolish the house and build a larger one in its place, Carroll and other neighbors lodged a protest and in May 2015 succeeded in blocking the work from going forward.

Revenge! Lisle-Mainwaring retaliated by painting bright red and white vertical stripes on the front of the townhouse, giving it the appearance of a candy cane or a circus tent. "This has been done, so I understand, not because she likes the stripes, but purely to infuriate her neighbors," one member of the Kensington council's planning commission told the *Guardian* newspaper. The neighbors went to court and in April 2015 obtained a ruling forcing Lisle-Mainwaring to remove the stripes, but she appealed the ruling and won. The stripes stayed up…until September 2017, when Lisle-Mainwaring won final approval to demolish the building. Only then did the stripes, and the townhouse they were painted on, finally come down.

* * *

"I've learned that people will forget what you said, people will forget what you did, but people will never forget how you made them feel."

—**Maya Angelou**

Not quite the same: The songwriters of "Silver Bells" almost called the tune "Tinkle Bell."

THE JEFF ABIDES

These laid-back, off-kilter quotes might sound like they came from the brain of Jeff "the Dude" Lebowski, but they were actually uttered by the Dude's real-life counterpart, Jeff "the Actor" Bridges.

"Wake up in the morning, go to the bathroom, pee, brush your teeth, look in the mirror, and laugh at yourself. Do it every morning to start off the day."

"If you're going to wait to get all the information you think you need before you act, you'll never act because there's an infinite amount of information out there."

"Being alive, you have to do something. Not doing anything is also some kind of action."

"Well, there are all kinds of gutters. Life will supply you with gutters."

"I'm rooting for (President Trump) as a human being to do the cool thing."

"There's kind of a Zen aspect to bowling; the pins are either staying up or down before you even throw your arm back."

"So I have this word for much of what I do in life: 'plorking.' I'm not playing and I'm not working, I'm plorking."

"Your part can be the king, but unless people are treating you like royalty, you ain't no king, man."

"Hope's interesting, isn't it? I can't turn hope off—it's hopeless."

"You don't want to vilify your ego."

"In some way, my saying that I'm not here now feels sort of like an acknowledgment that I am here now, only feeling that I'm not."

"The more space and emptiness you can create in yourself, then you can let the rest of the world come in and fill you up."

"Sometimes I think about retiring but not stopping work. Just 're-tiring'—put on some new tires and go on to do something else."

"There are so many things that pop up. If you are paying attention, you can learn every second of the day. Life is my guru."

About six Australias could fit inside of Asia.

A WHALE OF A TALE

If you ever find yourself in Gothenburg, Sweden, be sure to pop into the Natural History Museum and have a look at the star attraction: the "Malm whale," the only taxidermied blue whale anywhere on earth.

RUN AGROUND

On October 29, 1865, a blue whale calf beached itself near the city of Gothenburg, Sweden. The whale was only about seven months old, but it was already more than 50 feet long, and it probably weighed about 70 tons. If such a whale were to beach itself today, most bystanders would probably try to help the whale free itself or, if nothing else, try to keep it wet until the rising tide enabled it to free itself and swim away. But this was 1865, and Gothenburg was a fishing and whaling port, so the calf was killed by a local fisherman named Olof Larsson and his brother-in-law.

Normally the two men would have cut up the whale and harvested the whale oil, the meat, the blubber, and, if there were any, the ambergris, a very valuable waxlike substance found in whale intestines that is used to make perfume. But before they could, August Malm, a zoologist and the curator of Gothenburg's Natural History Museum, arranged to buy the whale intact. He wanted to display it in the museum.

DIRTY WORK

It took three steamships and two coal barges to tow the dead whale to the slipway boat ramp nearest the museum. There, Malm, who was also a taxidermist, photographed and carefully measured the whale as it lay on its side. He only measured the one side because the whale was too heavy to roll over.

When he finished, a team of "ten sturdy butcher boys," aided by 20 assistants, set to work cutting the whale into pieces. By that point the unfortunate creature had been dead for about a week and decomposition was well underway. The stench was so overpowering that Malm had to bribe the workers with liquor—all they could drink—to get them to complete the disgusting task. After the rotting whale was cut into sections small enough to move, the pieces were transported to the museum, where the skin was removed and the blubber scraped away. The organs were preserved in barrels, and the whale's skeleton was boiled, then cleaned so that it could be reassembled and displayed in the museum alongside the taxidermied whale, creating two interesting and educational displays from the single whale.

While the skin was being tanned with repeated applications of sawdust and salt, Malm used the measurements and photographs he'd taken to make a life-size, whale-shaped, wooden form to serve as the body of the taxidermied whale. Because he planned to take the whale on tour, he designed the form so that it could be broken into four sections and shipped from place to place in pieces. And because the interior of the form was tall enough for people to stand up in, Malm designed the whale's upper jaw to open on hinges so that it could serve as a doorway to the interior of the beast. "Many people might find it interesting to penetrate all the way into the abdomen," he reasoned.

Malm had steps installed inside the whale's mouth, and had a room built inside the body, running nearly the entire length of the whale. He covered the wooden floor with a carpet, installed bench seating on either side of the whale, and decorated the walls with fabric.

BRASS TACKS

When the whale's skin was ready, workers stretched it over the outside of the wooden form and nailed it into place with rows of some 30,000 zinc and copper nails. The nails were visible (and remain visible to this day), giving the whale a stitched-together, Frankenstein-like appearance if you looked too closely.

When the taxidermied whale was finished, it was exhibited in Gothenburg for a time, then it toured Europe for several years before being reinstalled in the museum next to the skeleton. It has been the main attraction of the museum's whale exhibit ever since.

A LITTLE TOO MUCH FUN

For many years, climbing inside the whale was the highlight of a visit to the Gothenberg Natural History Museum; no trip to the place was complete without it. People were even allowed to purchase food and drinks and take them inside the whale to eat. When VIP guests visited, tables were set up and banquets served; as many as 20 people at a time could dine in style inside the whale. But the party ended in the 1890s when an amorous couple was caught in flagrante di-whale-o (we made up that word, but you probably get the meaning), and that ended the fun for everybody. The whale's mouth has been kept closed—and people kept out—ever since. The only exceptions are certain holidays and special occasions, such as national elections, which are held every four years. Only then is the mouth opened and people allowed inside. (Unrelated fact: valdagen, the Swedish word for "election," also translates as "whale day.")

More than 150 years later, the Malm whale is still the world's only taxidermied blue whale. Reason: Artificial whale models are cheaper and easier to make, much easier to preserve, and—ironically—they're more lifelike than the genuine article, even when the genuine article isn't held together with 30,000 zinc and copper nails. So if you want to climb inside a real blue whale, or at least inside the skin of a real blue whale, you have to go to Gothenburg. Just be sure to plan your visit on a holiday or during the national elections, or you'll find yourself on the outside of the whale looking in.

Gross fact: Some flea larvae feed on dried blood emitted from adult fleas' butts.

THE "ANDY GRIFFITH" SHOW

The late Andy Griffith is best known for playing small-town sheriff Andy Taylor on The Andy Griffith Show in the 1960s. But when a real-life guy named Andy Griffith tried to be a small-town sheriff, he found himself in need of a lawyer (and Matlock wasn't around).

NEW SHERIFF IN TOWN

People running for office will sometimes do whatever it takes to win. Even in small places, and for positions like sheriff, the candidates employ dirty tricks—negative ads, smear campaigns, etc.—anything to get some kind of advantage in voters' hearts on Election Day. In 2006 a candidate running for sheriff of Grant County, Wisconsin, tried to manipulate voters, too, but in a *positive* way. He wanted to associate his name with happy times, safety, and nostalgic good feelings.

So just before he filed his paperwork to get his name on the ballot, 42-year-old William Harold Fenrick made a stop at another government office…and had his name legally changed to Andy Griffith. That, he hoped, would remind voters of Griffith in his role of Sheriff Andy Taylor on the 1960s TV classic *The Andy Griffith Show*.

SURPRISE, SURPRISE, SURPRISE

Fenrick, er, Griffith, played up his name on the campaign trail, trying his best to make voters think he'd be as good a sheriff as Griffith's character had been, or at least one as folksy. During a campaign rally, he promised to get rid of speed traps in Grant County, arguing that "they never did unethical stuff like that in Mayberry!" One refrain he constantly repeated on the campaign was, "See, that's the thing about Andy Griffith. He was honest and straightforward and people respected him for that." Griffith also printed up T-shirts, hats, keychains, and other promotional items bearing the name "Andy Griffith" for sheriff—which cost him a few thousand dollars, paid for out of his own pocket—and gave them away in an attempt to secure votes.

Then Election Day 2006 arrived. When the results came in, it turned out that ten-year veteran sheriff Keith Govier won reelection with 8,452 votes. In second place was challenger Doug Vesperman with 6,985 votes. In third place: Andy Griffith, with just 1,248 votes.

NIP IT IN THE BUD

That wasn't the end of the new Andy Griffith's life as Andy Griffith. The day after the election, attorneys representing the real Andy Griffith—the actor—filed a lawsuit in the U.S. District Court in Madison, Wisconsin. The suit alleged that "Andy Griffith's"

Q: What well-known novel had the working title *First Impressions*? A: *Pride and Prejudice*.

name change, his publicity stunt, and his unsuccessful political campaign had violated trademark laws, copyright laws, and the personal privacy of the real Andy Griffith. TV Griffith's lawyer, Jim Cole, said that the former William Fenrick had changed his name with "the sole purpose of taking advantage of Griffith's notoriety in an attempt to gain votes." Griffith and Cole demanded that the defendant in the suit go back to using the name William Fenrick, and issue a public apology in local newspapers explicitly stating that he is not the actor Andy Griffith.

Not-Sheriff-Griffith called the lawsuit "incredibly absurd," saying his campaign was all in good fun, and that nobody in Grant County actually believed he was TV's Andy Griffith. "For such an American icon, it's a pretty un-American thing to do to me," Fenrick/Griffith told reporters.

FINAL EPISODE

Six months after the suit was filed, U.S. district judge John Shabaz dismissed the case. In his decision, Shabaz wrote, "There is no evidence that anyone believed that [Griffith] sponsored or approved [Fenrick's] candidacy. There is not a scintilla of evidence that anyone thought [Griffith] was running for Grant County sheriff or that [Griffith] was backing [Fenrick's] campaign for sheriff."

Wisconsin's Andy Griffith held on to the name Andy Griffith for about another year...and then changed it back to William Fenrick in 2008.

*   *   *

PAPER ROUTE

With nearly everyone using a computer these days, you'd think the world was ready to go paperless, but the opposite is true. Global consumption of paper has increased by 50 percent since 1980. Here's what happens in a single year:

- Two billion books, 350 million magazines, and 24 billion newspapers are published.
- The United States uses 68 million trees to produce paper and paper products.
- The average office worker uses 10,000 sheets of paper.
- The average college student uses 300 pounds of paper.
- The average North American uses 700 pounds of paper products.
- The U.S. Post Office delivers more than 100 million pieces of junk mail.
- Landfills receive 26 million tons of paper.
- Enough paper is thrown away to make a 12-foot wall from New York to California.

Ironic fact: Vincent van Gogh painted *The Starry Night* during the daytime.

THE BUMHOLE RESUSCITATOR

Ever hear the expression "I'm not just blowing smoke up your a**"?
(Uncle John hears it from his writers all the time.) Here's
where that cheeky turn of the phrase comes from.

FIRE IN THE HOLE

Accidentally falling into any river can be shocking, but imagine taking a nosedive into London's sewage-filled river Thames in the 1700s. Now picture total strangers dragging your drowned body out of the water, stripping off your clothes, and pumping warm tobacco smoke into your rectum using a set of bellows and a length of ivory tubing.

The "bumhole resuscitator," as it was called, was invented in 1774 by Drs. William Hawes and Thomas Cogan. They were concerned that of the 123 people who had drowned in London in 1773, some may have been incorrectly identified as dead and ended up being buried alive. Their invention was a way to revive the nearly dead with stimulation from tobacco juice and smoke. The doctors formed the Society for the Recovery of Persons Apparently Drowned (which later became the Royal Humane Society) and had resuscitator kits placed along the Thames at regular intervals, like life preservers. They also placed the kits in coastal towns. The society also offered rewards to the rescuer, as well as to any shopkeepers who allowed the drowning victim to be stripped and resuscitated on a table on their premises (pubs included).

SMOKE SIGNALS

The idea of a tobacco-smoke enema can be traced back to Native Americans who had discovered that tobacco juice and smoke were powerful irritants to the body's insides and could shock a drowned person back to life. They passed this information to early American settlers, who spread the word back to Europe. At that time, the ancient theory that a person's health depended on balancing their four "humors"—choleric, sanguine, phlegmatic, and melancholic—was still widely accepted. A drowning victim would have had too much water in their humors and could only be put back in balance by introducing warm and stimulating air into to the body. Up until the 1830s, many Londoners had home resuscitator kits, which also included tubing for injecting tobacco smoke into the lungs, stomach, and rectum.

Microwave tip: Place thicker, longer-to-cook parts of food near the outside.

CODE BLUE

By 1903 doctors had moved to the other end of the body and were using chest compressions on a drowned patient. Mouth-to-mouth resuscitation came into favor in the 1950s, and by 1960, Drs. Peter Safar and James Elam had invented cardiopulmonary resuscitation (CPR), which combined both.

Today, England's Community Resuscitation Steering Group, working with the National Health, has placed more than 14,000 public-access defibrillators in towns and cities across the UK, so that anyone can administer a high-energy shock to the heart of a person experiencing cardiac arrest. However, there are still wilderness first-aid guides that recommend shocking an unconscious, or possibly deceased, person back to life by spraying cold water on their most sensitive body part, the anus.

* * *

MAGICIANS ON MAGIC

A few thoughts from magicians that apply to the world of illusion, and beyond.

"Magicians are the most honest people in the world.
They tell you they're going to fool you, and then they do it."
—James Randi

"For a professional magician, a stack of playing cards is as good as a stack of money."
—Amit Kalantri

"Practice until it becomes boring, then practice until it becomes beautiful."
—Harry Blackstone Jr.

"If it sounds too good to be true, it always is."
—Ricky Jay

"If I produce a 450-pound Bengal tiger, it's going to create a lot more wonder than if I produce a rabbit."
—Doug Henning

"The magician and the politician have much in common: they both have to draw our attention away from what they are really doing."
—Ben Okri

"No man should regret dying because of a good act. In fact, it's a privilege."
—Harry Houdini

Cleopatra took baths in donkey milk. Each bath required the milk of 700 lactating donkeys.

ATTACK OF THE DRONES

With more and more drones in the skies, there are bound to be more drone mishaps on the ground, and in the trees, in airplanes, in helicopters, at TGI Fridays, at the White House…

RIGHT OF WAY

It had to happen someday. That day was October 12, 2017—the first time an unmanned aerial vehicle (UAV), better known as a drone, hit a passenger plane in North America. The collision occurred about three miles from the Jean Lesage International Airport in Quebec City, Canada. The small plane, carrying eight people, was flying at an altitude of 1,500 feet when the pilot saw the drone for a split second before the plane's left wing clipped it and knocked it out of the sky. "That drone should not have been there," said Canadian Transport Minister Marc Garneau, adding that it was flying five times higher than is legally allowed, and much too close to the airport. Garneau also pointed out the plane's occupants were extremely lucky that the UAV didn't hit the engine or the cockpit. The plane landed safely, suffering only scratches on its wing. Neither the drone nor its owner were ever located.

DON'T DRINK AND DRONE

One night in 2015, a Washington, DC, government worker (name not released to the press) had too much to drink and ended up flying a drone at around 3:00 a.m. from his apartment balcony. When the drone failed to come back, the man panicked; he was only a few blocks away from the White House. Sure enough, the next day, the news broke that a "mysterious drone crash-landed on the White House lawn." As newscasters wondered if it was a botched terror attack, the worker called the Secret Service and turned himself in. It's unclear whether he was reprimanded, but the mishap did raise a serious question: how is it possible that a common quadcopter bought at RadioShack could fly undetected right up to one of the most heavily guarded buildings in the world?

BACK TO NATURE

UAVs are prohibited at national parks. Here's one of the reasons why: In 2014 Theodorus Van Vliet of the Netherlands crashed his drone into one of nature's most awesome spectacles—the Grand Prismatic Spring at Yellowstone National Park in Wyoming. The largest hot spring in the United States—at around 300 feet in diameter—the Grand Prismatic is known for its steaming turquoise waters. It's also

"Snoezelen rooms" stimulate the senses of Alzheimer's patients using sound, smells, colors, and images. Patients are less likely to wander off afterward.

a fragile ecosystem that, luckily, wasn't seriously affected by the impact. Van Vliet, however, was banned from the park for a year and fined $3,200. His drone sank into the steaming cauldron and was never seen again.

UNMANNED INCENDIARY VEHICLE

While national parks are a no-no for drones, there are no such restrictions in flying them in national forests…yet. In March 2018, a drone landed on dry grass in Arizona's Coconino National Forest. Then the drone caught fire. Then the grass caught fire. By the time firefighters arrived, the blaze had grown to 50 acres, and they were unable to start containing it until it had reached 335 acres. The drone operator's identity and whereabouts remain unknown.

HEAD SHOT

A Miami Beach photo shoot with a swimsuit model named Jess Adams came to an abrupt end when she got hit in the face by a drone. She was standing on a rock facing the ocean but looking back at the camera when the quadcopter got caught in a wind gust and blindsided her. Adams was fortunate that none of the four spinning rotors inflicted much damage. Despite a few scratches and a bruise under her left eye, she was okay. In fact, she seemed pleased that the crash was caught on video. "If you're gonna get hit in the face with a drone," she wrote on her Instagram page, "better at least be able to watch it and die laughing."

BLACK HAWK DOWNER

Two U.S. Army Black Hawk helicopters were flying at 500 feet over New York City in September 2017 when one of the pilots spotted a drone coming right at him. It was too late to take evasive action, and the Black Hawk's rotor smashed the drone into tiny pieces, several of which got lodged in the helicopter's hull. The pilot maintained control and made an emergency landing in New Jersey. Meanwhile, two and a half miles from the point of impact, Vyacheslav Tantashov was wondering what happened to his DJI Phantom 4 drone. He'd been filming the New York City sunset when the video feed suddenly blipped out. He figured that his drone—which had a low battery and was on the way home—had run out of power and crashed in the Hudson River. Tantashov learned otherwise a few days later when he received a call from the National Transportation Safety Board asking if he'd lost his Phantom 4. (They obtained a serial number from a drone part that got lodged in the Black Hawk.) It turned out that Tantashov was flying in violation of "temporary flight restrictions" due to a presidential visit to the United Nations. But Tantashov had an app that was supposed to tell him if his drone entered illegal airspace, and even it didn't know that.

Myth-nomer: "Styrofoam" cups are made from expanded *polystyrene,*
*not Styrofoam (*extruded *polystyrene).*

After a National Transportation Safety Board investigation, Tantashov was found to be at fault. It's unclear from press reports whether he was charged with a crime or fined, but either way, he's out one drone.

THE STUFF OF NIGHTMARES

"FIRST-EVER DRONE SWARM ATTACK." That scary headline from January 2018 told of the 13 weaponized drones that Syrian militants flew up to two Russian military bases at sunset. Even though the bases' defense systems were able to take out the enemy drones—which were equipped with small bombs—without sustaining much damage, a Russian official told the *Washington Post*, "They thought the base was secure, but now it seems it is vulnerable."

WHO NOSE?

In December 2014, a TGI Fridays in New York City held "Mobile Mistletoe" night. It went like this: an employee flew a drone—adorned with mistletoe—from table to table, prompting couples to kiss. Flying a UAV with exposed blades indoors poses certain risks, and a *Brooklyn Daily* photographer covering the event felt the effect of those risks when a drone cut off the tip of her nose. It also took out a bit of her chin. "Thank God it didn't go anywhere under my eye," said the photographer, Georgine Benvenuto. "That is my livelihood." Interestingly, the drone operator blamed the photographer, claiming that she flinched when the drone hovered close to her face. "He's the one controlling it," said Benvenuto. "He needs to be more careful."

> **DID YOU KNOW?**
>
> In 2018 the Siberian town of Ulan-Ude invited reporters to witness the premiere flight of Russia's first-ever "postal drone." The $20,000 hexacopter (six propellers) rose off the ground while carrying a parcel… and seconds later smashed into the wall of a nearby apartment building.

OUT ON A LIMB

In February 2018, a Rogersville, Tennessee, man watched helplessly as his drone got stuck near the top of a tall tree in Crockett Creek Park, "a botanical garden containing a variety of protected trees that is used for educational purposes." After a short deliberation, the drone operator decided to try and climb up and retrieve his expensive toy. Bad move. Roughly 10 minutes later, the Rogersville Fire Department received a call from the man, who told them he was stuck in the tree 40 feet above the ground. The firefighters had to use a ladder truck to get to him. In the process, they had to cut away some limbs from the protected tree. What happened to the drone? "As far as I know," said firefighter Lee Sexton, "the drone is still there."

The first gold rush in America was in the state of North Carolina (1799).

VEXED BY TEXTS

Have you ever sent a text, not heard back from the person you were texting, and wondered if they'd received it? If you're like us, it wouldn't be long before your paranoia took over and you assumed you'd sent it to the wrong person…like these folks.

TEXT: In September 2017, Harvey Whitney of West Melbourne, Florida, received a text from a phone number he didn't recognize.

> Hey Jen lmk if u need any

the text read. Whitney had a pretty good idea what the green tree emoji stood for, but he replied to the text with "?" just to be sure. Soon a second text arrived, explaining that the tree stood for "bud"—marijuana. In other words, the sender of the text was offering to sell "Jen," whoever that was, some pot if she needed any.

VEXED! Whitney is an officer with the West Melbourne Police Department; the texter—obviously—had sent the text to the wrong number. Whitney did what any good cop would do: he set up a deal to buy $50 worth of marijuana from the dealer later that day in Palm Bay, where the dealer lived, and then alerted the Palm Bay Police Department to the planned buy.

At the appointed time and place, the Palm Bay Police arrested 20-year-old Hasan Burke when he showed up to make the drug deal. At last report, Burke was out on a $3,000 bond and facing charges of possession of marijuana, possession of drug paraphernalia, and possession with intent to sell, a felony in Florida. "What are the chances that a wrong number would be the number of an on-duty police officer?" the West Melbourne Police Department posted on Facebook following the arrest.

TEXT: In June 2017, Amy Santora, a woman living in Pittsburgh, Pennsylvania, received a text message to "Julianne" from a number she wasn't familiar with. The texter was offering to give Julianne four free tickets to watch the Pittsburgh Penguins play the Nashville Predators in game 2 of the Stanley Cup Finals that very evening.

Santora had no idea who Julianne is, but she and her husband Mike are huge Penguins fans, so it was with a heavy heart that she called the number and informed the sender that he had texted the wrong person. The man thanked Santora for her honesty.

NOT VEXED! Five minutes later, the man texted Santora again. This time he explained that Julianne (whoever she was) only needed two of the four tickets. Amy and her husband Mike were welcome to the other two, which the man would leave at the will-call window for them to pick up. Santora and her husband drove to the hockey arena half-believing that the whole thing was a joke and that they would spend the evening watching the game on the big screen outside the arena, just like everyone else who didn't have a ticket. But when they went to the will-call window, the tickets were there. Great seats, too: close to the goal, with a face value of $329 apiece, more than the Santoras could have afforded on their own. To this day, they still don't know the identity of the texter who gave them the tickets. "Whoever you are," Santora said, "thank you."

TEXT: In November 2016, a woman named Wanda Dench texted her grandson, inviting him over for Thanksgiving. "Dinner is at my house on November 24 at 3 p.m. Let me know if you're coming," she said. But her grandson had changed his phone number, and the text went to the new owner of the old number, 17-year-old Jamal Hinton, a senior at Desert Vista High School.

"Who is this?" Hinton texted back. "Your grandma," Dench answered. "Can I get a picture?" Hinton asked. Dench replied with a selfie, and when Hinton got it he sent Dench one of his. (He doesn't look anything like Dench's grandson.)

> You're not my grandma. Can I still get a plate tho?

he added, probably half-jokingly, because he already had plans for Thanksgiving.

NOT SO VEXED! Dench texted back, "Of course you can, that's what grandmas do… feed everyone." Hinton made time that Thanksgiving day for two dinners: his family's and Dench's. At 3:00 p.m. sharp he arrived at Dench's house and was the honorary guest—and grandson—at the festivities. "I'd never seen her before and she welcomed me into her home. That shows me how great of a person she is, I'm thankful for people like that," Hinton said.

WELL, A LITTLE VEXED: When Hinton posted a screen shot of his text conversation with Dench on Twitter, the post was shared more than 200,000 times…and Dench got more than 600 texts asking for invites to Thanksgiving. So many, in fact, that she had to change her cell phone number. But she doesn't regret what happened—she had Hinton back to her house for Thanksgiving in 2017, and plans to welcome him back each year.

Ronald Reagan once had a job as a hamburger cook.

THE "BARBRA STREISAND EFFECT"

Psst! Have you ever tried to keep something private, only to have it become widely known because you tried to keep it private? That's the Barbra Streisand Effect.

CAMERA SHY In 2002 a retired Silicon Valley software engineer named Kenneth Adelman embarked on an ambitious project to photograph every inch of California's 1,150-mile coastline from a helicopter. He did it to document the condition of the coast and to help preserve it from degradation. He snapped the photos as his wife Gabrielle piloted their helicopter parallel to the coast 500 feet over the Pacific Ocean.

Adelman uploaded more than 12,000 of the images to a website called the California Coastal Records Project. He made the website interactive, allowing people to download the photos and even add captions to identify structures and landmarks in the pictures. And that's what got him into trouble. At some point in either 2002 or 2003, someone accessed image #3850, a photograph that included a mansion sitting atop a bluff overlooking the Malibu coastline, and added a caption that read "Streisand Estate, Malibu."

If you've ever driven past Barbra Streisand's house in Malibu, you probably didn't know you were doing it, because like a lot of celebrities, Streisand values her privacy. There's nothing on the street outside her home that identifies who lives there, and her home, guest home, and other structures are not visible from the street.

> Someone accessed image #3850, a photograph that included a mansion sitting atop a bluff overlooking the Malibu coastline, and added a caption that read "Streisand Estate, Malibu."

PHOTO FINISH But they're clearly visible from the ocean side of the property, and when Streisand learned that the photograph identified the mansion as her home and that it could be downloaded from the website, she filed a $50 million lawsuit against Adelman, demanding the photo be taken down. The lawsuit alleged that publication of the photograph invaded her privacy, violated California's anti-paparazzi law, sought to profit from her name, and threatened her security.

The case was eventually thrown out of court and Streisand was ordered to pay Adelman more than $150,000 to cover his legal fees. Even worse for Streisand, her attempt to prevent people from seeing the photograph backfired badly: before her lawsuit, image #3850 had been downloaded

The smallest dog on record is a 3.8-inch-tall Chihuahua from Puerto Rico named Milly.

exactly six times, and two of those times were by Streisand's own lawyers. Few people other than Streisand, her lawyers, and the caption writer even knew it was there. But in the month after her lawsuit made headlines, more than 420,000 people visited the California Coastal Records Project website, many of them just to look at image #3850 and see what all the fuss was about. (No word on how many of them downloaded it.) The photo was published in newspapers and magazines, broadcast on television, and posted on countless websites.

Had Streisand simply kept quiet, the photo would likely have remained unnoticed by the public. But she didn't, and her Malibu mansion became, for a time at least, one of the most famous celebrity homes in the world.

IN THE CAN A similar incident occurred three years later when a visitor to the Marco Beach Ocean Resort in Marco Island, Florida, took a photograph of one of the resort's urinals and posted it to the Urinal.net website, claiming that the urinal was visible from the lobby. When the resort learned of the posting, their attorneys sent a cease-and-desist letter to the website, demanding that the post be taken down. Once again, a largely unnoticed photograph was pushed into the public eye by an attempt to suppress it, generating plenty of bad press in the process.

A journalist named Mike Masnick covered the story for a website called Techdirt. "How long is it going to take before lawyers realize that the simple act of trying to repress something they don't like online is likely to make it so that something that most people would never, ever see (like a photo of a urinal in some random beach resort) is now seen by many more people? Let's call it 'the Streisand Effect,' " he wrote, and a name for the phenomenon was born.

JOIN THE CLUB

Here are some other folks who have fallen prey to the Streisand Effect:

- **Toronto Pearson International Airport.** The airport is another organization that did not appreciate having a photograph of its men's room urinals posted on Urinal.net. When the Greater Toronto Airports Authority (GTAA) learned in 2003 that the photo had been posted to the site, their lawyer threatened legal action if the airport's name was not scrubbed from the site. Rather than fight, Urinal.net complied, but also stated that it had taken the name down at the GTAA's request. The GTAA didn't like that, either, and told Urinal.net that they couldn't even post the GTAA's *name*...so Urinal.net changed the listing to: "The [facility in question] has been [Canada's largest city's] main international [aircraft take-off and landing facility] since 1939 when it was first known as Malton [facility]," and added that the "Gee-Tee-Aye-Aye" did not

Boustrophedon ("turning like oxen" in Greek) is a term for writing alternate lines of text in opposite directions: from left to right, then right to left.

allow them to identify the airport by name. All of which drew lots of attention to the fact that the Gee-Tee-Aye-Aye didn't want the attention.

- **Axl Rose.** Like a lot of folks, the Guns N' Roses singer weighs quite a bit more in his 40s and 50s than he did in his mid-20s, when he was at the peak of his fame. In 2010 Boris Minkevich, a photographer with the *Winnipeg Free Press*, took some unflattering photos of Rose performing onstage. They began circulating around the internet under the hashtag "Fat Axl" with captions like "Welcome to the Jungle / We've got lots of cake," and "Sweet Pie of Mine." The Fat Axl meme was winding down in 2016 when Rose's attorneys filed what is known as a DMCA (Digital Millennium Copyright Act) takedown request with Google, stating that "no permission has been granted to publish the copyright image."

> They began circulating around the internet under the hashtag "Fat Axl" with captions like "Welcome to the Jungle / We've got lots of cake," and "Sweet Pie of Mine."

Bad move: All the takedown request did was call attention to the fact that Rose was trying to suppress the photos, and that caused them to go viral again, even more than before. Worse for Rose, the copyright for the photos belonged to the *Winnipeg Free Press*, not to Rose, since Minkevich worked for the paper. And as the *Free Press* pointed out, the photos had been downloaded from the paper's website and circulated without its authorization. "The *Winnipeg Free Press*...has not approved any third party usage," the paper said in a statement. "We were only recently made aware of these memes, and while we ethically don't approve, viral media is impossible to regulate. Welcome to the jungle."

- **The Union Street Guest House.** In 2014 this hotel in Hudson, New York, had a draconian policy of fining wedding parties $500 for every negative review that any wedding guest posted on Yelp! or any other website. The fines were deducted from the bride and groom's security deposit, and were refunded if and when the bad review was taken down. When the *New York Post* ran a story on the hotel and its no-bad-reviews policy, more than 3,000 people posted negative Yelp! reviews in 24 hours; thousands more trashed the guest house on Facebook.

The next day the hotel rescinded the policy and apologized...sort of: Owner Chris Wagoner claimed on the guest house's Facebook page that the fine "was originally intended as a joke and never something I told employees to enforce...I now realize this joke was made in poor taste and not at all funny. This is no longer a policy of Union Street Guest House and we have taken it off of our website." (The comment was later deleted.) So how has business been lately? As of April 2018, Yelp! advises on its website: "Yelpers report this business has closed."

Amateur astronomer Gary Hug has discovered 300 asteroids
and one comet using his backyard telescope.

LAST ONE STANDING

These stores and eateries once dominated the American retail and restaurant landscape. But time marched on, and they faded from popularity until only one was left.

NEWBERRY'S

J. J. Newberry's was one of the last of the major five-and-dime, or "variety" stores. Similar to Kresge's or Woolworths, these fixtures of Main Street sold a little bit of everything, from pharmaceuticals to home goods, greeting cards, stationery, clothes, toys, books, and magazines. Many even had a lunch counter or soda fountain on the premises. But starting in the late 1960s, the rise of "big box" chain stores, which sold everything variety stores did, along with groceries, furniture, and TVs, made places like Newberry's seem quaint and old-fashioned. Peaking with 565 stores in the early 1960s, Newberry's lasted all the way until 1992, when it filed for bankruptcy and started shutting down its more than 300 remaining locations within five years. The last one stood in downtown Portland, Oregon, until December 2001.

HOWARD JOHNSON'S

Before fast-food restaurants could be found at every off-ramp in the country, there was one national chain that travelers could count on to serve up familiar, reliable meals: Howard Johnson's. At its peak in the 1950s and 1960s, there were more than 600 orange-roofed HoJo's dotting the American highway system, where millions of families stopped in for hot dogs, clam rolls, 3-D burgers, and ice cream. Howard Johnson's did so well that many other companies jumped into the ring, inspiring the rise of fast food as we know it: McDonald's, Subway, Arby's, Taco Bell, etc. But these places also offered easy-in, easy-out, drive-through service, with most menu items made in advance, so customers could be on their way in a hurry. Howard Johnson's was dine-in only. By the 1980s, most Howard Johnson's were gone, although the name continued to be used by a chain of similarly orange-roofed motels. The only Howard Johnson's restaurant—in the resort town of Lake George, New York—closed in 2017 after the owner was arrested, charged with harassing a female employee.

BURGER CHEF

There are a lot of national fast-food burger joints today, mostly inspired by the rise of McDonald's in the 1950s. But before there was a Burger King or a Wendy's, the first true competitor to the industry leader was a chain called Burger Chef. It was

Drinking alcohol can contribute to a deficiency of vitamin A.

responsible for developing many of the technologies and practices still used by other fast-food companies: It employed mass production techniques with automatic burger makers that could churn out hundreds of burgers per hour, and it invented the kid's meal (called the "Fun Meal") and the value meal (burger, fries, and a drink for 45 cents). General Foods bought the chain in 1968, and by the 1970s, Burger Chef operated more than 2,000 locations…and that's what killed the company. General Foods wasn't able to manage the growth and sold the business to a Canadian company. The last remaining Burger Chef, in Danville, Illinois, flamed out in 1996.

SAM GOODY

The way people buy music has changed dramatically in the last 15 years or so. Today, buying music takes a few clicks and a download off iTunes. Or they don't buy it at all—they pay a monthly fee to subscription services like Spotify or Apple Music and use their phones or home computers to stream all the music they want. Before the 21st century, music had to be purchased on a CD, a tape, or a vinyl record, and those were purchased at music stores. One of the main outlets was a mostly mall-based chain called Sam Goody. The chain, started by a New York record store owner named Sam Gutowitz in 1951, grew to more than 800 outlets at its peak in the 2000s. As of 2018, just four remain: one each in Tennessee, Ohio, Texas, and Oregon. They still sell some CDs, but mostly DVDs, posters, and video games.

BLOCKBUSTER

Blockbuster boasts one of the most spectacular rises—and falls—in the history of American business. They were the first large video-rental chain, with more than 9,000 stores from coast to coast at its peak in 2004. In the 1980s, before VCR owners could "make it a Blockbuster night," the vast majority of video rental stores were small mom-and-pop operations. But they couldn't keep up with the local Blockbuster, which offered a huge selection and was much more likely to have the big hit movies and new releases in stock on a Saturday night. Another feature of Blockbuster: exorbitant late fees, which customers hated, but what choice did they have? None…until cheaper, more convenient, video-rental-by-mail services like Netflix arrived in the late 1990s and $1-a-day rental kiosks like Redbox started popping up in the early 2000s. Vanquished, Blockbuster filed for bankruptcy protection in 2010, and Dish Network bought around 1,700 of its locations before closing them down over the next few years. Today, only nine independently owned and operated stores bearing the Blockbuster name still operate. They're mostly in rural areas of Oregon, Alaska, and Texas, where internet service isn't good enough for video streaming.

Studies show: Silver cars are the least likely to be involved in a serious accident.

JAMES THE [BLEEP!]

Let's face it: Not every Alexander gets to be remembered as "the Great." Here's a look at some little-known historical figures who weren't as lucky as Alexander was when the nicknames were being handed out. More rulers with odd nicknames are on page 382.

ARNULF the UNLUCKY (c. 1055–1071)

Arnulf was 15 years old when his uncle, Robert the Frisian, killed Arnulf's father, Count Baldwin VI of Flanders, in a dispute over the titles and territories that each inherited from their father. On Baldwin's death, Arnulf became Count of Flanders, with his mother Richilde ruling in his name as regent until he came of age. But Uncle Robert wanted his nephew's countdom for himself. So in February 1071, Robert's forces met Richilde's at the battle of Ravenshoven, near Kassel in modern-day Germany. Richilde was defeated; Arnulf, then 16, was killed.

JUSTINIAN the SLIT-NOSED (c. 668–711)

When his father, the Byzantine emperor Constantine IV, died in 685, 16-year-old Justinian II succeeded him. During his reign, he alienated his subjects with religious persecution, high taxes that funded his extravagant lifestyle, and land policies that threatened the aristocracy. In 695 his subjects deposed him. To ensure that he could never reclaim the throne, they cut off his nose. Byzantine emperors receive their authority from God, who was perfect, the thinking went. Any facial disfigurement that rendered them less than perfect disqualified them from the job. At least that was how it was supposed to work. But Justinian replaced his nose with a gold prosthesis and in 705 he raised an army in Bulgaria, marched on Constantinople, and reclaimed the throne for himself…and that proved to be his undoing. He was so brutal in exacting revenge against his enemies that in 711 he was toppled again, this time for good. Both Justinian and his six-year-old son (and co-emperor), Tiberius, were executed.

MICHAEL MINUS-A-QUARTER (c. 1050–1090)

Michael VII Doukas, another teenage Byzantine emperor, inherited the throne in 1067 at the age of 17. Like a lot of people his age, he preferred to shirk his adult responsibilities, leaving the actual running of the empire to his mother and uncle for several years. Even when he assumed full control, he relied heavily on ministers, who instituted disastrous policies such as high taxes, profligate spending, and neglect of the

If you shove a red sea sponge through a sieve to break it up into pieces, the pieces will re-form into a new sea sponge.

army, whose subsequent mutinies cost the empire great swaths of territory in Italy and Asia Minor (modern-day Turkey). During one such military revolt in March 1078, Michael decided to abdicate rather than fight to keep his throne, and took vows to become a monk. By that time his disastrous policies had caused the Byzantine currency to lose so much value (about a quarter of its value, one would assume) that he became known as Michael Parapinakes—"minus a quarter."

HENRY the IMPOTENT (1425–1474)

If you thought Henry IV of Castile, in north-central Spain, gets his unfortunate nickname because he was a weak and ineffective leader, think again. He was a weak and ineffective leader, but he really may have been impotent. His first marriage, to his cousin the infanta, or princess, Blanche, when he was 15, was annulled 13 years later on the grounds that Henry was unable to consummate the marriage. He blamed his problem on a curse.

The annulment freed Henry to marry another of his cousins, Joana of Portugal, the sister of the Portuguese king, in 1455. That marriage produced a daughter, Juana, in 1462…or did it? Rumors circulated that Juana's real father was Joana's lover, the Duke of Albuquerque. The story became more credible when Joana had two more children with another lover, the nephew of a bishop. Henry eventually divorced his wife, and bowed to pressure to disinherit Juana in favor of his half-sister, Isabella. She became the queen of Castile when Henry died in 1474. Does the name sound familiar? She's the same Isabella who married Ferdinand II of Aragon, united Castile and Aragon in 1479 to form the kingdom of Spain, and financed Christopher Columbus's voyages to the New World. (She also established the Spanish Inquisition…but that's another story.)

JAMES the S**T (1633-1701)

James II was the last Catholic monarch of England, Scotland, and Ireland. He was deposed in 1688 when his Protestant nephew and son-in-law, William of Orange, ruler of the Netherlands, invaded England in what has become known as the Glorious Revolution (because there was very little bloodshed). Afterward, James fled to France, but in 1689 he returned to Ireland in an attempt to regain the throne. In July 1690, James met William, now King William III, at the Battle of the Boyne, 30 miles from Dublin. When James's forces were defeated, he fled back to France, deserting his Irish allies and leaving them to fight on without him until their final defeat in 1691. His abandonment of the Irish earned him the nickname Séamus an Chaca—"James the S**t."

In Finland, Cinderella is sometimes called Tuna, which is a diminutive form of Christina.

APOLLO INSURANCE COVERS

Q: How hard is it for an astronaut to get life insurance? A: It's not rocket science!
(Note: That joke worked better after a couple of beers.) Now, a cool story about the
creative life insurance programs created for our early astronauts.

SPACEMEN

In the summer of 1969, Neil Armstrong, Michael Collins, and Buzz Aldrin were
preparing for one of the most historic journeys ever: the *Apollo 11* mission to land on
the Moon. All three astronauts knew what they were getting into. There was a good
chance they wouldn't be returning. Just two years earlier, astronauts Gus Grissom, Ed
White, and Roger Chaffee died on the *Apollo 1* rocket, and they never even made it
off the ground. They were killed when a fire broke out in the rocket's cabin during a
rehearsal launch at Cape Kennedy.

All three *Apollo 11* astronauts were married and had children, and they were
naturally worried about the fate of their families if the same kind of tragedy were to
befall them. Taking out life insurance policies would have been the normal way of
addressing such a problem, but when you're about to fly a rocket into space, insurance
companies might be (understandably) reluctant to offer you a policy, and even if
they did, the premium would probably be higher than the astronauts could afford. So
someone came up with a creative way of tackling the problem: they created a bunch of
memorabilia called "covers."

GOT YOU COVERED

"Covers" is a term used by stamp collectors, and they're simply envelopes, usually with
addresses, commemorative images, and canceled stamps on them. (If you've never
sent a letter, "canceled" means they've been marked as "used" by the post office.) In
this case the envelopes had space-related images on them—NASA badges, rockets,
etc.—and each one was signed by all of the astronauts during their preflight quarantine
period before the launch. After all the covers were signed, stamps were affixed to them
(they were special-issue NASA stamps), and the covers were stored until the most
important days of the *Apollo 11* mission—the day of the launch (July 16, 1969), and
the day they touched down on the Moon (July 20), and so on—at which time they
were taken to post offices, where the stamps were canceled with those dates.

After being canceled, the envelopes were delivered to the astronauts' families for
safekeeping. These were those families' life insurance policies; if Armstrong, Collins, and
Aldrin did not return from their mission, the historic autographed covers would in all

likelihood be worth significant amounts of money. And because the men had signed so many of them, they could be held for years, or even decades, and sold only when needed.

TOUCHDOWN

The *Apollo 11* mission was, of course, a success, with Neil Armstrong and Buzz Aldrin becoming the first humans to walk on the Moon. The trio of astronauts returned home safely and, thankfully, the insurance covers did not need to be used. They did, however, become collectors' items, and you can still find them for sale today. (One fetched almost $60,000 at an auction in 2017.) Here are some more fun facts about the Apollo insurance covers:

- The Apollo insurance cover scheme was repeated for the next several missions. It was discontinued after the *Apollo 16* mission in 1972.

- Years after the Apollo missions, it was discovered that while the astronauts truly could not afford life insurance on their fairly meager NASA salaries, they did in fact have life insurance policies: NASA couldn't purchase policies for them, but big businesses, such as oil companies and banks, did contribute funds that went toward the purchase of polices for astronauts on all of the Apollo missions.

> **DID YOU KNOW?**
>
> Buzz Aldrin's real name…is Buzz Aldrin. He had it legally changed (from Edwin) in the 1980s.

- Want an Apollo insurance cover of your own? Look on eBay—they show up there on a regular basis.

* * *

20 FICTIONAL CHARACTERS WITH STARS ON THE HOLLYWOOD WALK OF FAME

1. Snoopy
2. Lassie
3. Rin Tin Tin
4. Big Bird
5. Donald Duck
6. Woody Woodpecker
7. Bugs Bunny
8. Mickey Mouse
9. Minnie Mouse
10. Winnie the Pooh
11. Kermit the Frog
12. The Muppets
13. Rugrats
14. Shrek
15. Godzilla
16. Strongheart
17. The Munchkins (from Oz)
18. Tinker Bell
19. Snow White
20. The Simpsons

"Raise" and "raze" are homonyms (they sound the same) and antonyms (they have opposite meanings).

THE MINECRAFT STORY

Do you play the video game Minecraft? *If you don't, your kids or somebody close to you probably does. Not since* Pac-Man *has a single video game been this popular. Here's a look into the origins and impact of this cultural behemoth.*

PRESS ANY KEY TO START

- Markus Persson was born in Sweden in 1979. As a child, he exhibited a natural talent with computers, and he was fortunate to grow up in a time when they were starting to become both accessible and affordable. Using a computer language called BASIC and his family's Commodore 128, he started learning computer coding at the age of seven…and was making games to play with his friends by age eight.

- He stuck with it as he grew up, and when it came time to start planning for life post-graduation, Markus told his high school guidance counselor that he wanted to design video games for a living. The counselor told Markus that his dream was just that—a dream, and it was *never* going to happen.

- Undaunted, Markus kept making small, simple games for himself, while he worked as a programmer for various companies in Sweden, including King, a software developer that made web-based games, and Jalbum, which makes digital photo sharing software.

READY PLAYER ONE

- But Persson soon grew bored with his programming job, and started to spend all of his free time building his most complex game to date. He decided to call it *Cave Game*, and it would be a game of simple graphics (resembling Nintendo games from the 1980s) that centered on a player going on a mystical quest, exploring caves, and fighting off mythical beasts.

- But then he changed his mind. He decided to lose the plot and have the game be an open world full of endless possibilities with no clear objective. And he changed the name to *Minecraft*.

- The "mine" part: players could dig in the ground (and seas, and underground, and other "biomes") to look for wood, iron, gold, emeralds, and other materials. With those, they could build simple structures or fantastic towers…they just had to look out for the skeletons, zombies, and other bad guys hanging around. The worst villain of all: the Creeper, a green monster that would approach players' hard-built structures…and blow them up.

The Golden Gate Bridge is the most photographed bridge in the world.

GAME ON

- In 2009 Persson (who started going by the name "Notch," a nickname he used in online video game forums) released the original, not-quite-polished "alpha" version of *Minecraft* online. Length of time it took him to design it: six days.

- While a lot of video games receive a huge, multimedia push, this wasn't that kind of game. The only reason anyone knew it existed was because Notch wrote on the video game forum TIGSource that he'd released a game called *Minecraft* on his website (Minecraft.net—it's still live). "It's an alpha version," he added, "so it might crash sometimes."

- Notch's plan: Sell the game to a small video game company for enough money so that he could quit his job and then design another game. Then he'd sell that one, and repeat the process. That's not exactly what happened.

EXTRA LIVES

- Most of the most popular video games in history—*Pac-Man, Super Mario Bros., The Sims*—were developed by huge software companies, and designed, programmed, and marketed by armies of employees. Remarkably, *Minecraft* was a one-man operation. Notch designed, programmed, and released the game literally by himself. That also meant he got every last penny from its sale.

- From that single post on TIGSource, the popularity of *Minecraft* grew—its appeal was in its simplicity and open-ended format. By the summer of 2010, tens of thousands of people around the world had downloaded *Minecraft*. The way they paid for the game was as humble as the game itself: they sent Notch a few bucks via PayPal.

- When Notch's personal PayPal account reached over $760,000, the service locked his account—they thought he was doing something suspicious, maybe even illegal.

- Having made almost a million dollars, Notch decided to quit his job at Jalbum to devote himself to *Minecraft* full-time. He resigned on his 31st birthday.

LEVEL UP

- Part of devoting himself to *Minecraft* meant expanding the operation to keep up with demand. To continue adding elements to the game and issuing updates to its growing army of players (something that was impossible for the manufactured disc or cartridge segment of home video games), Notch had to delegate the business side of things to other people. He formed a company called Mojang (the Swedish version of "whatchamacallit") and hired six people to help with programming and processing payments.

- As *Minecraft* grew, so did attention from beyond just the people who were playing it. And *a lot* of people were playing it—by the end of 2010, it had sold 500,000 copies, and "Minecraft" was YouTube's top search of 2014, and Google's #2 search.

- Notch started getting offers. The video game publisher Valve wanted to buy *Minecraft* or hire Notch and other Mojang staffers, but Notch resisted. Nevertheless, in 2011 he announced that he'd be leaving the company and his game. Reason: He'd created and shared his game, and said he was ready to move on to something else.

- A few months after Notch announced his departure, Microsoft bought Mojang and *Minecraft*. Price tag: $2.5 billion. Bill Gates's software giant beat offers from video game companies like Valve, Electronic Arts, and Activision, as well as a $1 billion offer from an anonymous tech giant, rumored to be Google.

MINECRAFT BY THE NUMBERS

- Despite being less than a decade old, *Minecraft* is already the second-best-selling video game of all time. More than 120 million copies have been sold worldwide. (It trails only *Tetris*.)

- *Minecraft* is the most-played online game. Fifty-five million people hop on the internet to play it each month. That's quadruple the number of people that play the second-most-popular online game, *World of Warcraft*.

- Markus Persson now lives in the United States full-time, in an expensive estate in Beverly Hills. How expensive? He paid $70 million for it—making it the priciest home in the pricey L.A. suburb. (He outbid Jay-Z and Beyoncé for it.)

- *Minecraft* remains the best-selling independently produced game of all time. That means it wasn't published by a huge video game company, the way nearly every other video game is.

- *Minecraft* is also the fourth-most-lucrative thing to ever come out of Sweden, trailing only Volvo, IKEA, and the band ABBA.

- Did Microsoft get its money's worth? In the year before the corporate giant bought the rights to *Minecraft,* the game generated $81 million. In the year after the Microsoft purchase, it made $237.7 million.

Human perspiration is odorless—at least at first. The pungent smell comes from bacteria that invade it after it exits your body.

FOR YOUR EYES ONLY

Who has appeared in the most James Bond films? Sean Connery? Guess again.
Roger Moore? No, not him either. Turns out there's someone who's
been in more Bond films than Connery and Moore combined.

HOME FROM SCHOOL

In the summer of 1964, a 22-year-old law student named Michael G. Wilson visited his stepfather, film producer Albert R. Broccoli, on location at Fort Knox, Kentucky. Broccoli was there filming scenes for *Goldfinger,* the upcoming James Bond film. He needed an assistant, so Wilson signed on for three weeks. His responsibilities consisted mostly of running errands and doing odd jobs, but when a particular scene—Bond villain Auric Goldfinger's raid of the United States Bullion Depository—called for lots of extras, Wilson suited up as a soldier and appeared in the scene.

After graduating from law school and practicing law for several years, Wilson joined Broccoli's production company. In 1976 he assisted his stepfather in filming *The Spy Who Loved Me.* He must have enjoyed appearing as an extra in *Goldfinger,* because he made an appearance in this movie too, this time as a member of the audience watching an evening light show in Egypt, near the Sphinx. (He's the man with glasses and a beard sitting behind Agent Triple X, played by Barbara Bach.)

CATCH HIM IF YOU CAN

Wilson has been involved in the production of all but one of the Bond movies made since then (1983's *Never Say Never Again,* which wasn't produced by Broccoli), and he's made cameos in every film he worked on. In some films he appears in more than one scene; in others his "appearance" is limited to his voice being heard over a loudspeaker or from another room. To date, he has been coproducer or executive producer for 14 different Bond films, five of which he has also cowritten, which makes him one of the most important people on the set. But part of the fun of his cameos is that he doesn't pick the parts he plays—the crew members pick them. For many 007 aficionados, trying to spot Wilson's scene in each new Bond film is as much fun as trying to spot director Alfred Hitchcock or M. Night Shyamalan's cameos in their films. Here are the appearances he's made…so far:

***Moonraker* (1979).** He's a tourist strolling past the Venini Glass factory with a young boy in Venice, Italy. Later, he's standing on a bridge in the background as Bond hands a vial of poison gas to M, the head of the British counterintelligence agency MI6. Near the end of the film, Wilson plays a technician at the U.S. Air Force base tracking Bond villain Hugo Drax's space station. (He's the guy who hands a piece of paper to a general and says, "It doesn't look good at all. It's over 200 meters in diameter.")

For Your Eyes Only **(1981).** The priest at a wedding on the Greek island of Corfu.

Octopussy **(1983).** Early in the film, he's the man with the camera on the tour boat when Bond is pulled out of the water. Later on, he's the man seated at the far left during the meeting of the Soviet security council.

A View to a Kill **(1985).** He's heard, but not seen, from behind a door as Bond and a female character, geologist Stacey Sutton, walk down a hallway to the file room in San Francisco City Hall.

The Living Daylights **(1987).** He's a member of the audience enjoying an opera performance in Vienna. Wilson is sitting two seats to the left of Saunders, Bond's ally in MI6.

License to Kill **(1989).** Again Wilson is heard but not seen. This time he's the voice of a DEA agent as a private jet lands on a runway. Wilson's dialogue begins with him saying, "He's landing at Craig Key. Advise Key West Drug Enforcement."

GoldenEye **(1995).** A member of the Russian defense committee that listens to the report from General Ourumov. Wilson is the man with the mustache seated in the foreground on the far left side of the screen.

Tomorrow Never Dies **(1997).** He plays media executive Tom Wallace. In the scene where Bond villain Elliot Carver threatens to blackmail the president of the United States with a compromising video, Wallace is shown on a large video screen telling Carver, "Consider him slimed."

The World Is Not Enough **(1999).** He's a man wearing a tuxedo, standing in the background at the casino in Azerbaijan.

Die Another Day **(2002).** First, a man in a white shirt and straw hat leaning against a car when Bond is in Cuba, and later, U.S. Air Force General Chandler.

Casino Royale **(2006).** He's the corrupt chief of police who is arrested in an outdoor restaurant in Montenegro and taken away.

Quantum of Solace **(2008).** He plays a man sitting in a chair reading a newspaper as Bond collects a briefcase from the front desk clerk at the hotel in Haiti.

Skyfall **(2012).** He's the guy in the doorway behind the coffins of the slain British agents when M pays her respects.

Spectre **(2015).** Wilson is seen shaking hands with C in the background, as M, walking down a hallway, approaches them. And who's the younger man standing next to him? It's the film's associate producer, Wilson's son, Gregg Wilson.

About 6 million years ago, otters were the size of wolves.

YOU'RE FIRED!

You show up at work expecting it to be like any other day, and then about a half hour after lunch you're called into the boss's office and—BOOM!—your life has completely changed.

"If you aren't fired with enthusiasm, you will be fired with enthusiasm."
—**Vince Lombardi**

"Most people work just hard enough not to get fired and get paid just enough money not to quit."
—**George Carlin**

"My career is inexplicable to me. So far I've just been not getting fired despite being myself."
—**Nick Offerman**

"Getting fired is nature's way of telling you that you had the wrong job in the first place."
—**Hal Lancaster**

"Sometimes I wish I could get fired."
—**Matt Stone**, who has been making *South Park* since 1997

"I mean, there's no arguing. There is no anything. There is no beating around the bush. 'You're fired' is a very strong term."
—**Donald Trump**

"From getting cut from the high school basketball team, to getting fired from jobs, getting credit cards rejected and cut up. Rejection has only been a distraction, not a roadblock. 'Every no gets me closer to a yes' is the saying I use."
—**Mark Cuban**

"You can get fired from a job, but you can't get fired from your gift. So find your gift and you will always work."
—**Anonymous**

"My agent said, 'You aren't good enough for movies.' I said, 'You're fired.'"
—**Sally Field**

"No one wants to get fired, so everyone's scared to take a chance."
—**Billy Eichner**

"If you don't win, you're going to be fired. If you do win, you've only put off the day you're going to be fired."
—**Leo Durocher**

"I didn't see it then, but it turned out that getting fired from Apple was the best thing that could have ever happened to me. The heaviness of being successful was replaced by the lightness of being a beginner again, less sure about everything. It freed me to enter one of the most creative periods of my life."
—**Steve Jobs**

"Getting fired can produce a particularly bountiful payday for a CEO. Indeed, he can 'earn' more in that single day, while cleaning out his desk, than an American worker earns in a lifetime of cleaning toilets. Forget the old maxim about nothing succeeding like success: Today, in the executive suite, the all-too-prevalent rule is that nothing succeeds like failure."
—**Warren Buffett**

"Be willing to get fired for a good idea."
—**Spike Jonze**

The hard way to make gold: Find two neutron stars and smash them into each other.

RESCUE ANNIE

This is the story of how one mysterious woman who drowned in Paris became the most kissed face of all time.

SLEEPING BEAUTY

In the late 1800s, the unidentified body of a young woman was pulled from the Seine River at the Quai du Louvre in Paris. It was the custom at the time to place unknown corpses on display on marble slabs in the window of the morgue behind Notre Dame in the hope that someone would recognize them. No one was able to identify the young woman, but the Paris morgue's pathologist was so taken by her beautiful, tranquil expression—a serene smile that looked almost happy in death—that he commissioned a plaster death mask of her face.

Word of the mysterious woman's beauty spread, and soon casts of the beautiful white mask hung in art studios and salons across Paris. As entrancing as her beauty was, the mystery of her identity and how she died was even more intriguing. Some suspected she committed suicide because of a broken heart. Others guessed murder, though her lifeless body was blemish-free. She soon became known as *l'inconnue de la Seine*—"the unknown woman of the Seine." French author Albert Camus called her "the drowned Mona Lisa" because of the hint of a smile on her lips.

AMUSED

"Annie, are you okay? Are you okay, Annie?"

The image of this French Ophelia spread across Europe and America, where novelist Vladimir Nabokov and painter Man Ray were two of many artists inspired by her beauty and mysterious story. She was a muse to German author Rainier Maria Rilke, whose poem "Washing the Corpse" described laying out the body of an unknown woman. Englishman Richard Le Gallienne wrote the novella *The Worshiper of the Image*, about a poet who was obsessed with wanting the mask to open its eyes. But when it does, a moth emerges from her mouth with the face of death between its wings. This story was the inspiration for the now-iconic image used on posters for the 1991 movie *The Silence of the Lambs*.

CALL ME ANNIE

In 1950 Norwegian toymaker Asmund Laerdal gave the mysterious lady a name: Anne. Laerdal had attended a conference where Dr. Peter Safar, the inventor of cardiopulmonary resuscitation (CPR), was speaking about the importance of training people in this new system that combined mouth-to-mouth resuscitation and chest compression. Safar asked Laerdal to design a life-size mannequin for use in CPR training. Laerdal, whose own son had needed to be resuscitated after nearly drowning at the age of two, was happy to take the job. The toymaker chose to make the human-size doll a woman because he thought men would feel awkward practicing mouth-to-mouth on a male doll. Laerdal had heard stories of the drowned Mona Lisa and chose her image to be the face of the plastic doll he called Resusci Anne, or "Rescue Anne."

THE KISS OF LIFE

Since 1960, more than 400 million people have learned to breathe life into Rescue Anne's lifeless body asking, "Annie, are you okay? Are you okay, Annie?" as they practice CPR and shake the body, checking to see if the victim is reviving. And Anne's legacy continued even after that. In 1984, nearly 100 years after the mysterious girl was pulled from the Seine River, Michael Jackson took a CPR course and was inspired to incorporate the phrase, "Annie, are you okay?" into the lyrics of his song "Smooth Criminal," which appeared on Jackson's 1987 album *Bad* and hit #7 on the Billboard Hot 100 chart in 1988.

* * *

2 RANDOM LISTS

5 Celebrities with Patents
Prince: "Portable electronic keyboard"
Marlon Brando: "Drumhead tensioning device"
Jamie Lee Curtis: "Disposable infant garment"
Zeppo Marx: "Cardiac pulse rate monitor"
Michael Jackson: "Anti-gravity illusion"

Top 5 Most Valuable Christmas Records
1959: Johnny Horton, *They Shined Up Rudolph's Nose* (picture sleeve), $400
1971: The Beatles, *The Beatles' Christmas Album*, $500
1971: John Lennon, *Happy Christmas* (promotional copy), $750
1957: Elvis Presley, *Blue Christmas* (white label promotional copy), $3,000
1957: Elvis Presley, *Elvis' Christmas Album* (red vinyl), $15,000

Ancient Roman catapults were often constructed using ropes made from human hair.

NAME THAT SOUP

*Ever wonder who put the "strone" in "minestrone"? The "owder" in "chowder"?
The "ho" in "pho"? (Careful, there, soup boy! This is a family soup book!)
Then sit thee down at the Table of Label—and read all about the
name origins of several well-known soups.*

MINESTRONE

Minestrone originated in simple vegetable and bean-based soups and stews made by
the people who inhabited the area around Rome more than 2,000 years ago. Those
early soups evolved as new ingredients became available—notably tomatoes, which
were introduced into Europe from South America during the Age of Exploration—
eventually becoming the thick vegetable, bean, and pasta (and sometimes rice) soup
we know today. The name "minestrone" derives from *minestra*, the Italian word for
"soup." The *-one* ending makes it mean something along the lines of "big soup."
The word entered the English language in the 1870s. (Note: *minestra* is "soup," but
it literally means "that which is served," from the Italian verb *minestrare*, meaning
"to serve," which in turn comes from the Latin *minister*, meaning "servant." Which
explains why "minestrone" has the same etymological origins as the word "minister.")

BORSCHT

Borscht is the name used for a wide variety of sour soups of eastern European/Slavic
origin. There are many varieties, including red and white borschts, some of them
served hot, but the best known is the red, beet-based, served-cold borscht whose
origins are Ukrainian. The English word "borscht" dates to the 1880s, and comes from
the Yiddish name for the soup. That, in turn, is derived from *borshch*, the Russian
name for the common hogweed plant (also known as "cow parsnip"). The pickled
flowers, stems, and leaves of the common hogweed were once the basis of this soup,
which was how it got its sour taste.

PHO

Pho, pronounced "fuh," is a brothy Vietnamese soup made with rice noodles, herbs,
and usually with thin slices of beef or chicken. It is hugely popular in Vietnam, and is
sold by street vendors and in restaurants nationwide. Most common time to eat pho:
breakfast, although it is also eaten for lunch or dinner. And it's a relatively young
dish, believed to have originated in the early 20th century, in the country's north,
not far from Hanoi. There are two main theories as to the origin of the name of this

First CGI movie sequence: a two-minute scene in *Westworld* (1973).

soup—and neither are Vietnamese. The first is that "pho" was derived from the French word *feu*, meaning "fire," or more accurately from *pot de feu*, literally "pot on the fire," the name of a thick French beef stew. Vietnam was a French colony at the time pho was developed, and because the French are credited with making beef popular in the country, this is the version most etymologists support. The second theory is that "pho" was derived from the Cantonese word *phan*, meaning "noodles." Either way, it came to English as the name of this tasty soup in 1931.

BISQUE

Bisque is a smooth and creamy crustacean-based soup of French origin. (It is most famously made from lobster, but can also be made from crab, crayfish, or shrimp.) The name "bisque" was probably derived from the name of the region where the soup was first made: the area around the Bay of Biscay, in southwestern France and northern Spain. Some historians believe the word came from *bis cuites*, meaning "twice cooked," referring to the fact that the crustaceans involved are first cooked separately, then again with the other ingredients—butter, flour, carrots, celery, onion, wine, and brandy. If this is true, then *bisque* has the same origin as *biscuit*, which is known to have been named for its original two-part cooking method. Still another possible origin of the term: "bisque" was derived from *bisco*, a word in the French Provençal language meaning "small, beveled pieces," referring to the crustacean pieces in the soup. Wherever this name came from, it first arrived in English in around the 1640s. (Bonus fact: The original French use of "bisque" referred to soup made from the meat of game birds. It only got the *crabby* meaning in the 17th century.)

*   *   *

YOU'RE MY INSPIRATION

- Buddy Holly's 1957 hit "That'll Be the Day" was the first song ever played on *American Bandstand,* and later became the first song recorded by the Quarrymen (who later changed their name to the Beatles). The idea came to Holly while he was watching a Western called *The Searchers*, and a character tells John Wayne, "I hope you die," to which the Duke replies in his distinctive delivery: "That'll be the day."

- In 2013 actor Alyssa Milano was approached to host a documentary about Disney's 1998 animated film *The Little Mermaid*. At first Milano (*Who's the Boss?, Charmed*) wasn't sure why they'd chosen her, but she said yes. Then she found out why, and it suddenly made sense: "It came out that the drawing and likeness of the Little Mermaid [Ariel] was based on pictures of me from when I was younger, which is so cool!"

During World War II food rationing in England, cardiovascular disease rates dropped…

CAT-IDATES FOR PUBLIC OFFICE

*Everyone seems to agree that the world of politics is going
to the dogs. One irrefutable sign: the number of cats who
have been candidates for public office in recent years.*

Cat-idate: Tuxedo Stan, a black-and-white cat whose markings made him look like he was wearing a tuxedo

Running For: Mayor of Halifax, the capital of Nova Scotia

Campaign Notes: Stan, a feral kitten, was adopted by a veterinarian named Hugh Chisholm and his wife Kathy in 2010. Halifax has a large population of feral cats, thanks in part to the fact that local laws require the spaying or neutering of dogs…but not cats. In 2012 the Chisholms decided to call attention to the problem by entering Stan as a candidate for mayor on the Tuxedo Party ticket. All proceeds generated from the sale of campaign merchandise (lawn signs, T-shirts, campaign buttons, etc.) went to help low-income families spay or neuter their cats.

Stan never quite made it onto the ballot. (Municipal law requires that candidates for public office have birth certificates.) Not that a little thing like that slowed his popularity: his campaign was endorsed by both Ellen DeGeneres and Anderson Cooper, and he attracted 17,000 followers on Facebook. After the election, the Halifax city council awarded a $40,000 grant in his name to the Halifax SPCA to fund a low-cost spay and neuter clinic for cats. "Stan was a true politician," Dr. Chisholm told Canada's *National Post* newspaper in 2013. "He lived up to his promises."

> Stan never quite made it onto the ballot. (Municipal law requires that candidates for public office have birth certificates.)

Cat-idate: Hank, a 10-year-old Maine coon cat owned by two Virginians, Matthew O'Leary and Anthony Roberts

Running For: State senate and, later, the U.S. Senate

Campaign Notes: O'Leary hated the way lawn signs clutter up the landscape during campaign season, and that gave him and Roberts the idea to have Hank run for a seat in the state senate. At least those lawn signs (and T-shirts and bumper stickers) would be fun to look at, they figured. On election day, they were shocked to see that Hank had actually received nine write-in votes—enough to encourage O'Leary and

...Reason: People ate lots more vegetables, because they weren't rationed.

Roberts to enter Hank in the 2012 race for the U.S. Senate. "As a typical politician, what do you do when you fail? You run for the next highest seat," O'Leary explains. Hank's opponents: Former governor (and future vice presidential candidate) Tim Kaine, a Democrat; and former senator George Allen, a Republican. Hank ran as an independent.

On election day, Tim Kaine beat Allen by more than 224,000 votes. More than 7,000 write-in votes were cast in the race, and although Virginia does not release tallies for the various names that were written in, O'Leary and Roberts believe, without evidence, that the lion's share of the votes probably went to Hank. If true, that would have made him the third-place finisher. Even better, Hank managed to raise more than $60,000 in campaign contributions, which O'Leary and Roberts donated to animal rescue organizations.

Cat-idate: Limberbutt McCubbins, a 30-pound tabby cat living in Louisville, Kentucky

Running For: President of the United States

Campaign Notes: The U.S. Constitution requires that to be sworn in as president, a candidate must have been born in the United States and be at least 35 years of age. But it doesn't say anything about who can *run* for the office. That's what two duPont Manual High School students, Isaac Weiss and Andrew Valentine, learned in 2015 when they tried to file a "statement of candidacy" with the Federal Elections Commission for their friend Emilee McCubbins's cat, Limberbutt. The FEC had to accept their paperwork because there is no rule prohibiting filing on behalf of a cat. (Limberbutt McCubbins was one of 459 candidates for president in 2016—no word on how many others were cats.) Limberbutt, a "Demo-cat," ran on a platform of better veterinary care for animals—the "Affordable Cat Act"—and including cats on any future trips to the moon. His campaign slogan: "Meow Is the Time."

Limberbutt's name never made it onto the ballot. The hurdles for that are much higher than merely filing papers with the FEC. The fat cat lost to Donald Trump in a landslide, but Emilee McCubbins is philosophical about her candidate's defeat. "We certainly identify with Trump's campaign, if not his beliefs," she told NBC's *Today Show*. "A large part of the American public views us as a joke, and yet, we remain surprisingly serious."

To see more odd candidates who filed statements of candidacy with the FEC to run as candidates for president, turn to page 415.

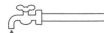

A plant-eating insect called the issus is born with interlocking gears on its body.

FORGET PARIS

Every city wants to be like Paris, one of the most beautiful and magical cities in the world.
Here are some cities that have been nicknamed the "Paris" of their country or region,
either by the consensus of visitors and residents…or (more likely) tourism bureaus.

The Paris of the Pacific:
San Francisco, California

The Paris of the West:
Cincinnati, Ohio

The Paris of the Pacific Northwest:
Port Townshend, Washington

The Paris of the East:
Warsaw, Poland; Riga, Latvia;
Prague, Czech Republic; Istanbul,
Turkey; Saigon, Vietnam; Hanoi,
Vietnam; Kabul, Afghanistan

The Paris of the Mayan World:
Copan, Honduras

The Paris of the Middle East:
Beirut, Lebanon

The Paris of the Orient:
Shanghai, China

The Paris of the Plains:
Kansas City, Missouri

The Paris of Central America:
Granada, Nicaragua

The Paris of the Midwest:
Detroit, Michigan

The Paris of the South:
Savannah, Georgia;
Asheville, North Carolina

The Paris of North America:
Montreal, Quebec, Canada

The Paris of South America:
Buenos Aires, Argentina

The Paris of Siberia:
Irkutsk, Russia (Seriously?)

The Paris of West Africa:
Dakar, Senegal

The Paris of the Prairies:
Saskatoon, Saskatchewan

The Paris of the Mississippi:
New Orleans, Louisiana

The Paris of the Caribbean:
Havana, Cuba

The Paris of the North:
Newcastle, UK; Dawson City,
Yukon, Canada; Aalborg,
Denmark; Tromso, Norway

The Paris of Appalachia:
Pittsburgh, Pennsylvania

Weird MLB rule: If a ball gets stuck in the umpire's mask, all baserunners move forward one base.

THE SAYINGS OF LAO-TZU

Was Lao-Tzu, the Chinese philosopher who said, "A journey of a thousand miles begins with a single step," an actual historical figure, or merely a compilation of Taoist sayings? Either way, he (or they) had a lot of interesting things to say.

"Being deeply loved by someone gives you strength, while loving someone deeply gives you courage."

"Nature does not hurry, yet everything is accomplished."

"A good traveler has no fixed plans, and is not intent on arriving."

"Mastering others is strength. Mastering yourself is true power."

"He who does not trust, will not be trusted."

"He who obtains has little. He who scatters has much."

"One cannot reflect in streaming water. Only those who know internal peace can give it to others."

"If you do not change direction, you may end up where you are heading."

"Respond intelligently even to unintelligent treatment."

"Life and death are one thread, the same line viewed from different sides."

"Love is of all passions the strongest, for it attacks simultaneously the head, the heart, and the senses."

"Man's enemies are not demons, but human beings like himself."

"Nothing is softer or more flexible than water, yet nothing can resist it."

"One who is too insistent on his own views, finds few to agree with him."

"Surrender your self-interest. Love others as much as you love yourself. Then you can be entrusted with all things under heaven."

"A scholar who cherishes the love of comfort is not fit to be deemed a scholar."

"An ant on the move does more than a dozing ox."

"He who knows others is wise. He who knows himself is enlightened."

"Govern a great nation as you would cook a small fish. Do not overdo it."

"The more laws and order are made prominent, the more thieves and robbers there will be."

"The snow goose need not bathe to make itself white. Neither need you do anything but be yourself."

"The wicked leader is he who the people despise. The good leader is he who the people revere. The great leader is he who the people say, 'We did it ourselves.'"

"The wise man does not lay up his own treasures. The more he gives to others, the more he has for his own."

"The words of truth are always paradoxical."

"There is no greater offense than harboring desires. There is no greater disaster than discontent. There is no greater misfortune than wanting more."

"Those who have knowledge, don't predict. Those who predict, don't have knowledge."

The first color a baby can distinguish: red.

THEY DIED ONSTAGE

You don't usually think of being a musician as a potentially fatal profession, but hey, we've all got to go sometime and you don't get to decide how or where. At least these folks died doing what they loved: performing.

NICK MENZA

Nick Menza was a pretty "metal" guy. He was the drummer for the popular heavy metal band Megadeth throughout the 1990s, and played in other loud and furious bands such as Fear Assembly, Orphaned to Hatred, and Chodle's Trunk. While sitting behind the drum kit with a band called OHM in May 2016, the 51-year-old musician's heart stopped just three songs into a show in a club in Studio City, California. Menza was rushed to a nearby hospital, where he was pronounced dead from congestive heart failure.

SIMON BARERE

Barere was one of the most renowned concert pianists in the world in the 1940s, so it was a big deal when the Philadelphia Orchestra booked him as a featured musician in 1951. For the first few minutes of the concerto they performed together, Barere's playing was masterful, but then his tempo slowed, and he started playing wrong notes. Then he stopped playing altogether and slumped forward, his head smashing into the piano's keyboard on his way to the floor. Fortunately there was "a doctor in the house," who carried Barere backstage and tried for 30 minutes to revive him. Unfortunately, he couldn't revive the 54-year-old pianist, who, it was later determined, had been felled by a stroke.

ONIE WHEELER

Wheeler is one of the great sidemen from the classic 1950s and 1960s era of country music. He played guitar and harmonica behind such legends as George Jones, Roy Acuff, Johnny Cash, and Lefty Frizzell. In the 1970s, Wheeler left the grind of touring and settled in Nashville, where he made a comfortable living as a session musician and performer at the city's iconic Grand Ole Opry. It was there, in 1984, while recording the Reverend Jimmy Snow's radio show *Grand Ole Gospel*, that Wheeler suffered a fatal heart attack at age 62 in front of the audience, both in person and listening at home.

IRMA BULE

Bule was a pop singer in her native Indonesia who had an elaborate stage act that involved dancing around the stage with a live cobra. She used a variety of different

Don't eat it! The *Hapalopilus* mushroom causes liver and kidney failure and turns urine purple.

snakes over the years, trusting that the hired snake handlers were employing the use of defanged and or de-venomized cobras. They did…until they didn't. Two songs into a show in Karawang, Indonesia, in 2016, Bule was dancing with a snake when it bit her on the thigh. She figured it was just a skin puncture, and continued on with the show. But that snake had not been neutralized. Less than an hour later, while still performing, Bule began vomiting and then had a seizure. An hour later, the 26-year-old was pronounced dead at a local hospital.

SIB HASHIAN

Hashian was a member of Boston, the arena rock band that sold 17 million copies of their 1976 self-titled debut album. Hashian, highly recognizable for his gigantic Afro hairstyle, played drums for the band during its heyday. After he left music in the early 1980s, he went on to own and operate a chain of tanning salons in the Boston area, but still played the occasional gig. His last was the March 2017 Legends of Rock Cruise, an entertainment extravaganza at sea that included performances by members of bands like Foreigner, Kansas, the Beach Boys, and, of course, Boston. While playing on the ship's stage with his band, Dirty Water, 67-year-old Hashian collapsed and died from a heart attack.

BARBARA WELDENS

This 35-year-old French singer was a rising star when her life was cut short in 2017. Weldens, who sang in the traditional French pop style, was one of the headliners at the Léo Ferré Festival, in Gourdon, France. After she put on what was reportedly a tremendous show, the crowd gave her a standing ovation…and that's when she suddenly flopped to the ground. According to news reports, Weldens, who performed barefoot, stepped on a poorly grounded electric wire, and the shock was so powerful that it stopped her heart.

BRUCE HAMPTON

The guitarist played in so many Grateful Dead–like bands from the 1960s onward (Quark Alliance, Late Bronze Age, Hampton Grease Band) that he earned the nickname "the Grandfather of the Jam Band Scene." His many friends and musical collaborators gathered at Atlanta's Fox Theatre in May 2017 to celebrate Hampton with an all-star 70th birthday jam session called "Hampton 70: A Celebration of Col. Bruce Hampton." Toward the end of the night, members of the bands Widespread Panic and Blues Traveler played a song called "Turn on Your Love Light" with Hampton, unaware that the legend had fallen to his knees and braced himself against a speaker to stay upright. Banjo player Jeff Mosier noticed that Hampton was doing a

It certainly feels like more: Airplane turbulence typically causes a drop of only about 10 to 20 feet.

"we're not worthy" gesture to teenage guitar prodigy Taz Niederauer during his solo. He wasn't—he'd collapsed. He died later that night in an Atlanta hospital.

LEONARD WARREN

Operas are almost always tragic—even when one of the performers *doesn't* die in front of the audience. In March 1960, legendary American baritone Leonard Warren, 49, was singing the part of Don Carlo in Verdi's *Forza del Destino* with New York City's Metropolitan Opera. Right after he sang the aria "Urna fatale del mio destino," or "Fatal Urn of My Destiny," Warren suffered what was later revealed to be a massive cerebral vascular hemorrhage and immediately died right there on the stage.

JANE LITTLE

This double-bass player with the Atlanta Symphony Orchestra set all kinds of records. As one of the youngest professional American symphonic musicians ever, she joined the ASO in 1945 when she was only 16 years old. And she never left. Just a few months after *Guinness World Records* recognized Little in February 2016 for the longest career of an orchestral musician—71 years—Little, 87 at the time, played her huge stringed instrument in a pops concert called "Broadway's Golden Age," an evening of show tunes. Little collapsed while playing the bass and was carried backstage, where she passed away. The song she was playing when her body gave out: "There's No Business Like Show Business."

* * *

THE MOST POPULAR AMERICAN DOG NAMES IN 2017
(ACCORDING TO THE AMERICAN KENNEL CLUB)

Males:	Females:
1. Max	1. Bella
2. Charlie	2. Lucy
3. Cooper	3. Daisy
4. Buddy	4. Luna
5. Jack	5. Lola
6. Rocky	6. Sadie
7. Oliver	7. Molly
8. Bear	8. Maggie
9. Duke	9. Bailey
10. Tucker	10. Sophie

Not as catchy: Vin Diesel's real name is Mark Sinclair.

SPORTS ONE-HIT WONDERS

We often think of "one-hit wonders" as a music thing—bands or singers who score one smash hit and then disappear forever. But it's certainly possible for people in other fields to have one big success…and only one big success.

DON LARSEN

It's a remarkable achievement for a Major League Baseball pitcher to throw a perfect game. "Perfect" means they pitch the whole game and don't allow the other team to get on base—no hits, no walks, no errors, no batters hit by pitches. Over 140 years and roughly 200,000 major league games, it's only been accomplished 23 times. Of those, only one time did a pitcher throw a perfect game when it *really* counted. Don Larsen did it in game five of the 1956 World Series, shutting down the Brooklyn Dodgers and getting the win for the New York Yankees, who went on to win the championship in seven games. Larsen was named World Series MVP on the strength of his performance in game five, the only game in which he played. It was also—by far—the best game of Larsen's otherwise lackluster career. In 1954, as a member of the Baltimore Orioles, he led the American League in losses with a 3–21 record. In 1957 he racked up a decent 10–4 record for the Yankees, then floated around the major leagues, playing for eight different teams over his career until retiring in 1967, finishing with a career total of 81 wins and 91 losses.

BUSTER DOUGLAS

By 1990 Mike Tyson had been fighting professionally for just five years, but sportswriters were already comparing him to all-time greats like Muhammad Ali. "Iron Mike" had the record to back it up: He'd never lost a bout, and had won his first 19 fights by knockout—12 of them in the first round. In 1988 he knocked out heavyweight champion Michael Spinks just 91 seconds into the first round; nobody had lasted more than five rounds against Tyson since 1987. Tyson, it seemed, was unstoppable—so much so that most Las Vegas bookmakers wouldn't even allow betting on the 1990 title fight at the Tokyo Dome between Tyson and his competitor, James "Buster" Douglas. Only one casino, the Mirage, cooked up odds, and they were ridiculously in Tyson's favor: 42 to 1. But somehow, someway, Douglas hung in there against the champ, even overcoming a knockdown and a nine-second count at the end of the eighth round. Douglas kept pummeling Tyson and finally knocked him out in the tenth round. That

New Zealand is the above-water portion of a submerged landmass called Zealandia.

wasn't just Tyson's first loss and his first knockout—it was the first time he'd ever been knocked *down* in the ring. Eight months later, Douglas defended his newly acquired title against up-and-coming boxer Evander Holyfield…and got knocked out in three rounds. Douglas retired after the fight, but came back in 1996, fought nine bouts over the next three years, and then retired again in 1999, this time for good.

IAN WOOSNAM

Born in Wales in 1958, Woosnam is considered one of the "Big Five" of his generation of golfers—he was born right around the same time as other, better European golfers, including Seve Ballesteros and Nick Faldo. Over his 20-year career, Woosnam was competitive on the European circuit, leading eight straight Ryder Cup teams to victory in the 1990s. But on the American PGA circuit, Woosnam just couldn't break through. The only two tournaments he managed to win in the United States, both in 1991, were the USF&G Classic…and the Masters—the most prestigious title in golf, which he won by one stroke.

BOB BEAMON

Robert Beamon was skilled and talented enough to make the 1968 U.S. Olympic Track and Field Team. Specializing in the long jump, he was heavily favored to win the gold medal based on his accomplishments in high school, where he had the second-longest jump in the country, and in college, where he earned a silver medal in the Pan American Games. In the lead-up to the Olympics, Beamon entered 23 track meets, and won the long jump contest in 22 of them. Beamon ultimately did win the Olympic gold medal for the long jump in Mexico City in 1968, as expected, but it's how he did it that was remarkable. On his first jump in the final round, he soared 29 feet, 2.5 inches through the air—a new Olympic record…by a span of nearly 22 inches. When the results were called out and his coach converted the metric measures to inches, Beamon realized what he'd just done and was so overwhelmed that his knees gave out. Sportscasters quickly coined a new word in Beamon's honor to describe unbelievable athletic achievements: "Beamonesque." Unfortunately, that was about the only Beamonesque thing Beamon ever did in sports. His world record long jump stood until 1991, but Beamon never came close to that distance again. He was drafted by the Phoenix Suns in the 15th round of the 1969 NBA Draft, but never played in a game. Instead, he returned to college, where he earned a degree in sociology.

Blue eyes only go back about 10,000 years.

LOST IN SPACE

Space exploration has risks. The old adage "what goes up must come down" isn't always true. Some things never make it back.

SPACE CADETS. On December 11, 1998, NASA launched the *Mars Climate Orbiter* on a 416-million-mile mission to orbit Mars and study its climate, atmosphere, and surface changes. Unfortunately, the NASA engineers and Lockheed Martin engineers who were in charge of navigation once the orbiter reached Mars were using different types of measurement—the metric system (newton-seconds) and the American system (pound-seconds)—but didn't know it. (Two navigators noticed the discrepancy, but they were ignored.) So after traveling nine months to get to Mars, the spacecraft never made a single orbit. Instead, the $327.6 million orbiter headed straight into the red planet's upper atmosphere, where it disintegrated.

BULL'S-EYE! In 2001 NASA realized it was a waste of money to send up a manned space shuttle on a repair mission every time a satellite broke down. So agency scientists created a robotic space repairman called DART (Demonstration of Autonomous Rendezvous Technology)—a full-fledged repair satellite, capable of doing much of its job without guidance. Unfortunately, on its maiden flight in 2005, multiple failures of DART's propellant and navigation systems sent it crashing into a communications relay satellite—the very satellite it was sent up to repair.

GENESIS'S EXODUS. *Genesis* was a NASA space probe designed to collect solar wind particle samples and bring them back to Earth. In 2001 it was launched into space on the back of a Delta II rocket, and it spent 850 days collecting particle samples. Its mission accomplished, *Genesis* headed back toward Earth. NASA had feared that a regular parachute landing might damage the samples, so it came up with an alternate reentry plan. Once the space probe's parachute was deployed, a helicopter was supposed to hook the chute mid-air and gently lower the probe to Earth. Unfortunately, *Genesis*'s parachute never opened and the $264 million probe slammed into the Utah desert at nearly 200 mph.

TIM-BER! On September 6, 2003, the National Oceanic and Atmospheric Administration's $239 million *N Prime* satellite was being repositioned at the Lockheed Martin factory in Sunnyvale, California. As the team was turning the satellite into a horizontal position, they found out (the hard way) that the 24 bolts that were supposed to hold it in place had been removed by a technician—and the action was undocumented, so nobody (except the technician) knew they were missing.

Rhubarb grows so fast that if you listen closely, you can hear it popping.

Result: the 18-foot satellite toppled over like a Christmas tree and crashed to the floor. Cost of repairs: $135 million.

FLYING LEFTOVERS. In 1965 the first American astronaut to walk in space, Ed White, lost a glove that is now orbiting Earth. Since that time, more than 500,000 items have joined White's glove traveling around the planet. This space junk includes pieces of old rockets and satellites, bags of trash, various tools and equipment—such as a camera, pliers, and a spatula (nicknamed "spatsat")—and a lucky rabbit's foot. Traveling at over 17,500 mph, these items can do major damage to a spacecraft. But who would guess that a load of human waste could wipe out a satellite? That's what happened to an Indonesian communications satellite, prompting NASA to discontinue the practice of flushing the contents of astronauts' toilets into space. Now they bring it back to Earth.

ONE SMALL MISSTEP FOR MAN. The images of astronaut Neil Armstrong's first step on the Moon are arguably the most important video footage in history. The July 20, 1969, video of *Apollo 11*'s mission commander bounding across the lunar surface proved to the world that the United States had "won" the space race, that the Moon's gravity really was different from Earth's, and that the *Apollo 11* team had really made, as Armstrong memorably declared, "one giant step for mankind." So imagine how you'd feel if you were the guy who erased the original footage of the entire *Apollo 11* mission. Apparently there was a shortage of videotapes at the space center in the 1980s, so it was common practice to tape over old footage, the same as people did with sitcom reruns. And *someone* made the mistake of taping over the most important video of all time. It took 35 years for NASA to discover the gaffe. Luckily, they made copies.

* * *

AMERICAN MOVIES THAT WERE RENAMED IN CHINA

Dumb and Dumber ☞	*Two Stupid Stupid People*
Ghostbusters ☞	*Super Power Dare-to-Die Team*
Nixon ☞	*The Big Liar*
Anchorman ☞	*Ace Announcer*
Knocked Up ☞	*One Night, Big Belly*
The Full Monty ☞	*Six Naked Pigs*
The Naked Gun ☞	*The Gun Died Laughing*
Guardians of the Galaxy ☞	*Interplanetary Unusual Attacking Team*
Solo: A Star Wars Story ☞	*Ranger Solo*
As Good as It Gets ☞	*Mr. Cat Poop*

The "Red Carpet" at the Oscars is colored a patented shade of garnet red.

FISH AND PZZA

What are stock ticker symbols? They're the official two-, three-, or four-letter codes that companies use for trading on the New York Stock Exchange, or other markets. IBM's stock ticker code, for example, is, well, IBM. Sometimes companies don't just pick an abbreviation of their name and have a little F-U-N with their I-P-Os.

Ticker symbol: **FUN**
Company: Cedar Fair, operator of amusement parks

Ticker symbol: **EAT**
Company: Brinker International, parent company of Chili's

Ticker symbol: **CAR**
Company: Avis Budget Rent-a-Car

Ticker symbol: **BID**
Company: Sotheby's, an auction service

Ticker symbol: **FAN**
Company: First Trust Global Wind Energy

Ticker symbol: **TAP**
Company: Molson Coors Brewing Company

Ticker symbol: **GRR**
Company: Asia Tigers Fund

Ticker symbol: **PZZA**
Company: Papa John's Pizza

Ticker symbol: **ZEUS**
Company: Olympic Steel

Ticker symbol: **EYE**
Company: National Vision Holdings

Ticker symbol: **FIZZ**
Company: National Beverage Corp., owner of Shasta and other soda brands

Ticker symbol: **CAKE**
Company: The Cheesecake Factory

Ticker symbol: **FOIL**
Company: iPath Pure Beta Aluminum

Ticker symbol: **BUD**
Company: Anheuser-Busch InBev

Ticker symbol: **WOOD**
Company: Global Timber & Forestry

Ticker symbol: **BOOM**
Company: Dynamic Materials, explosives manufacturer

Ticker symbol: **BEN**
Company: Franklin Resources

Ticker symbol: **MMM**
Company: 3M

Ticker symbol: **TAN**
Company: Guggenheim Sola

Ticker symbol: **HOG**
Company: Harley-Davidson

Ticker symbol: **PBJ**
Company: Dynamic Food & Beverage

Ticker symbol: **COOL**
Company: Majesco Entertainment, a video game publisher

Ticker symbol: **COW**
Company: Ishares Global Agriculture

Ticker symbol: **ROCK**
Company: Gibraltar Industries

Ticker symbol: **MOO**
Company: Vectors Agribusiness

Ticker symbol: **JOB**
Company: General Employment Enterprises, a staffing and recruiting company

Ticker symbol: **WOOF**
Company: VCA Inc., which runs a chain of veterinary hospitals

Ticker symbol: **FISH**
Company: Azure Midstream Partners (Get it? You find fish in a stream.)

Only woman to found a major American city: Julia Tuttle, the "Mother of Miami, Florida" (1874).

ESCAPE FROM MONKEY ISLAND

Silver Springs, Florida, is home to the largest artesian spring in the United States, and Florida's oldest tourist attraction. But many tourists who visit aren't there to see the water—they're there to see the monkeys.

GO WITH THE FLOW

In the 1860s, a businessman named Samuel O. Howse bought up nearly 250 acres of land surrounding Silver Springs, the natural spring that serves as the headwaters of Florida's Silver River. The spring is located in a giant cavern, and more than 500 million gallons of fresh water flow out of it daily, making it the largest natural spring in the United States. The water is crystal clear to depths of 80 feet or more, affording visitors excellent views of the plant and animal life in the river, including alligators, turtles, and many types of fish.

Capitalizing on the region's natural beauty, Howse developed the land into a tourist attraction. The first visitors came to the springs via steamboat up the Silver River; when the railroad arrived in the late 1870s, the number of tourists began to grow steadily. For 100 years before Walt Disney World opened, Silver Springs was *the* place to visit in the state. Like the Statue of Liberty or Ellis Island in New York, no trip to Florida was complete without a visit to Silver Springs.

SOMETHING NEW

As the years passed, new businesses sprang up in and around the park. A glass-bottom boat concession was one of the first, and in 1929 a reptile exhibit with an alligator wrestling show opened its doors. In the early 1930s, a man named Colonel Tooey created a Jungle Cruise boat ride on the Silver River.

What's a Jungle Cruise without monkeys? A few years later, Tooey decided to find a way to add primates to his attraction. On a bend of the river called Devil's Elbow, about a mile from the springs, he dredged mud from the riverbed and piled it in one spot in the middle of the river to create an artificial island. He built a monkey house and planted some trees, then ordered three breeding pairs of Asian rhesus macaque monkeys from an exotic animal dealer in New York.

Tooey thought that his "Monkey Island" would be the perfect way to showcase the animals. Monkeys can't swim, he reasoned, and that meant there would be no need to keep them caged. The island *was* the cage. Tourists would be able to watch the monkeys roaming freely in something approximating their natural habitat.

About 4 percent of the sand on Normandy Beach is made from disintegrated D-Day shrapnel.

BEST LAID PLANS

On the day the monkeys arrived from New York, three boatloads of tourists were waiting offshore from Monkey Island for Tooey to open the crates and release the macaques onto their new island home.

According to one eyewitness, the monkeys explored the island for about ten minutes. Then, one by one, they scampered to the top of a tree at one end of the island, swung out over the water on one of the branches, let go, and splashed into the river. Then they swam away. It was a painful lesson for Tooey: not only *can* macaques swim, they're actually pretty good at it.

The *island* was a flop, but the monkeys still managed to serve Tooey's purpose, because they didn't wander very far. The miles of swampy, forested wilderness that surround Silver Springs provided plenty of shelter for the macaques and plenty of plants and insects for them to eat. They also came to associate the Jungle Cruise boats with food: When the boats came by, the macaques would congregate at the water's edge to beg for peanuts and whatever else the tourists had to share.

When the movie *Tarzan Finds a Son!* was filmed nearby in 1939, the macaques developed a new mystique as the "monkeys left over from Tarzan." It wasn't true, but it was a good story and it stuck. Soon more people than ever were coming to Silver Springs to see "Tarzan's monkeys."

HOME SWEET HOME

A few years later, Tooey ordered more macaques from New York to replace some of the original monkeys that had died. The introduction of new males into the colony spurred reproduction, as the new males competed with the old ones for mates. Soon there were dozens of monkeys in and around Silver Springs, then more than a hundred.

As the colony grew, younger monkeys would break away from the group to form new colonies, and as they did, the macaques' territory increased as well. As long as they lived in the forest, they were more or less ignored by humans—except for the tourists, who continued to feed them. But by the mid-1980s the population had grown to nearly 400 monkeys and their territory butted up against surrounding communities. The number of monkey-human conflicts grew. Rhesus macaques can weigh as much as 20 pounds, and when threatened or angered they will hurl their poop or even bite. They also raid garbage cans and steal pet food, and there were also reports of small pets being killed by the macaques. Even worse, it was estimated that roughly half of the macaques were carriers of simian herpes-B. Since the disease's discovery in the 1930s, there have only been 50 cases where it was transmitted to humans worldwide, and none involving the Florida monkeys. But 21 of the 50 cases were fatal.

At least one of them is pork: There are 70 ingredients in a McRib.

...NOT SO FAST

Because the macaques are an invasive species, state law does not protect them and they can be trapped or hunted at will. In time, pressure from the state—which was in the process of creating a new Silver River State Park on land surrounding the privately owned park—grew to the point where the operators of the private park began taking steps to bring the macaque population under control.

Trappers were brought in and they caught about 200 of the monkeys. But if the park operators thought removing the monkeys would be easy, they soon learned otherwise. After all, the macaques were one of the park's biggest draws, and disease carriers or not, they were popular with many locals as well as tourists. When word got out that so many monkeys had been trapped—and, even worse, that some of them had been sold to labs for use in medical research—the public outcry was so great that the trapping program was shut down.

STATE FARM

In 1993 the State of Florida bought the privately owned park; eventually it would be incorporated into the state park, which was renamed Silver Springs State Park.

Now the monkeys were the state's problem, and in 1994 Florida's Fish and Wildlife Conservation Commission recommended that the monkeys should all be euthanized. Ironically, though the state has the power to implement the recommendation, as of 2017 it still hasn't. There are no private landowners to pressure the state anymore, and no real mechanism for the state to bring pressure upon *itself*. The only political pressure that does exist comes from local voters, and they overwhelmingly support leaving the monkeys alone. One petition circulating in Marion County in 1993 collected 25,000 signatures in favor of the monkeys—and those 25,000 people made up about a quarter of the electorate in the local state representative's district.

Someday Florida may try to reduce the population by trapping and sterilizing the monkeys, then leaving them to live out the rest of their lives in the wild. But that won't be easy. The population is now believed to exceed 1,000 monkeys, and their numbers are still growing, as is the size of their territory. Macaques have now been spotted 100 miles from Silver Springs. For the foreseeable future the monkeys will likely remain what they have been for many years now: the largest and only free-ranging population of rhesus macaques anywhere in the United States.

* * *

"I am always surprised at what movie studios think people will want to see.
I'm even more surprised at how often they are correct."
—Mindy Kaling

In Switzerland, it's illegal to own a single guinea pig. (They get lonely, so you have to buy two.)

THE NAKED TOOTH

What time should you go to the dentist? Tooth hurty.

- 300 different species of bacteria live in the plaque that's between your teeth.

- Ideal tooth brushing regimen: two to three minutes, two to three times a day.

- Along with coffee, wine, and soda, one of the most common tooth stainers is sour candy—it contains citric acid, which can stain and weaken teeth.

- The hardest substance in the human body: tooth enamel. (But if it's damaged, enamel won't heal or grow back.)

- Beneath the enamel is a layer of calcified tissue called dentin. It's naturally yellow, and it's what turns teeth yellow. When enamel weakens, it becomes translucent, allowing the dentin to be visible.

- Priorities: Americans spend $1.5 billion each year on tooth-whitening products, and about half as much on toothbrushes.

- In China, September 20 is "Love Your Teeth Day."

- Most common childhood disease: tooth decay. It's five times more common than asthma and seven times more common than hay fever.

- Teeth aren't considered bones. The main difference: bones contain collagen; teeth don't.

- Shark's teeth are actually scales, which means they can grow them back if they get damaged or lost.

- Taurine is a powerful stimulant used in energy drinks like Red Bull. It's also added to cat food as a supplement to help them keep their teeth for their entire lives.

- In South Korea, wisdom teeth are called "love teeth" because they often come in around the same time that someone experiences their first love (which, like having one's wisdom teeth extracted, is painful).

- Maybe don't try this, but under the right circumstances, a tooth that's been knocked out can be saved by jamming it back into its socket. But only if it's done within five minutes.

- In 2014 dentists in Mumbai treated a 17-year-old boy named Ashik Gavai. They removed 232 teeth from his mouth.

- "Baby teeth"—a person's first set of teeth—are also known as milk teeth and deciduous teeth. (That makes sense—trees that lose their leaves are called deciduous trees.)

- A Norwegian agency called the Mother and Child Cohort Study is building a research bank of baby teeth. So far, 13,000 kids have donated their lost teeth to the agency, which studies them to determine the effects of environmental and nutritional factors on children's health.

IT'S THE ANT'S PANTS!

Thanks to evolving concepts, new technology, and people too lazy to type full phrases, new words are added to the dictionary regularly. You don't have to be on wacky tobacky to think these additions are the ant's pants.

Abandonware: Software that is no longer sold or supported by its creator. Examples: Windows XP and the game *Tetris* for DOS.

Al desko: Eating a meal at one's desk.

The ant's pants: An outstandingly good person or thing.

Snowflake: A derogatory term for someone who is overly sensitive or easily offended; often applied to liberals (by conservatives).

Broflake: A derogatory term for a man who is offended by feminist or progressive attitudes.

Brogrammer: From *bro* and *programmer*, it's a stereotypically masculine or macho computer programmer.

Bunny: In basketball, an easy shot taken close to the basket.

Clicktivism: The use of the internet to organize protests, promote boycotts, sign petitions, or take other action to achieve a political or social goal.

Ghost: To abruptly cut off all contact with someone, especially a romantic partner.

Conlang: A constructed language, usually invented for a book, movie, or TV series. Examples: Klingon (*Star Trek*) and Dothraki (*Game of Thrones*).

Dog whistle: A statement that has a secondary meaning intended for a specific group of people; politicians use dog whistles in their speeches to resonate with certain voters.

Fatbergs: The solid masses of congealed cooking fat and personal hygiene products that are increasingly found in sewers.

Fitspiration: A combination of *fit* and *inspiration*—the person or event that motivates you to get fit.

FOMO: Fear of missing out (what your friends feel if they don't have a copy of this book).

Kompromat: From a Russian term—compromising material used in blackmail.

Listicle: An article that's presented as a list, such as "Thirteen Rockers Who Happen to Be Die-Hard Fans of *Star Wars*."

ICYMI: In case you missed it.

Strange but true: Serial killer Ted Bundy once worked a suicide hotline.

Lolcat: A picture of a cat with a funny caption that's often misspelled or grammatically incorrect. The writing style is called *lolspeak*.

Hazzled: Chapped or dried, especially by the sun.

Microbead: A tiny plastic orb found in some toothpastes and exfoliating body washes.

Rando: A stranger, especially one who behaves suspiciously. Short for "random."

Schneid: A losing streak, especially in sports. Example: "With their first-ever Super Bowl win, the Philadelphia Eagles officially broke the schneid."

Truther: A conspiracy theorist who believes that the truth about an event is being intentionally concealed.

Snollygoster: A shrewd and unprincipled person, especially a politician. The 19th-century word was considered obsolete and was dropped from *Merriam-Webster* in 2003…but reentered in 2017.

TL; DR: Too long; didn't read.

Wacky tobacky: Marijuana.

Supercentenarian: A person who is at least 110 years old.

Throw shade: To publicly disrespect, criticize, or express contempt for someone.

Milkshake duck: A person who is adored by the public at first, but is then found to be deeply flawed, causing a sharp decline in their popularity; the phrase came from a Twitter post by Ben Ward, an Australian cartoonist: "The whole internet loves Milkshake Duck, a lovely duck that drinks milkshakes! *5 seconds later* We regret to inform you the duck is racist."

Mahoosive: Exceptionally big.

MORE WORDS THAT WERE RECENTLY ADDED TO THE DICTIONARY

- bestest
- binge-watch
- butt ugly
- cat café
- face-palm
- humblebrag
- ride shotgun
- sriracha
- troll
- woo-woo
- Seussian
- yowza
- first world problem

* * *

"Language is the road map of a culture. It tells you where its people come from and where they are going."

—Rita Mae Brown

Disneyland serves up 2.8 million churros a year.

THE FATAL GLASS OF BEER

*Some American presidents have had a reputation for drinking
to excess, but Abraham Lincoln wasn't one of them.
Even so, alcohol played a role in his untimely end.*

ON GUARD

Five days after Robert E. Lee surrendered to Ulysses S. Grant at Appomattox
Courthouse in April 1865, effectively bringing the Civil War to an end, President
Lincoln and his wife decided to enjoy a rare night out. They went to see a performance
of the comedy *Our American Cousin* at Ford's Theatre, a few blocks from the White
House. That evening the president's regular bodyguard, Colonel William Crook,
was off duty, so a Washington, DC, policeman named John Parker accompanied the
Lincolns to the theater in his place. After the Lincolns and their guests, Major Henry
Rathbone and his fiancée, Clara Harris, settled into the presidential box, Parker,
armed with a revolver, stationed himself in the passageway outside.

He didn't stay there long. At some point during the play, he left his post and went
next door to the Star Saloon for a tankard of ale. (Parker later claimed that Lincoln
had released him from his responsibilities until the end of the play.)

STRANGE BEDFELLOWS

The owner of the Star Saloon, Peter Taltavull, later testified that at around 10:00 p.m.,
while Parker was drinking his ale, John Wilkes Booth walked into the saloon, ordered
some whiskey, then asked for a glass of water. After downing both, he left money on
the bar and walked out. He proceeded directly to Ford's Theatre and at 10:13 p.m.
fired the shot that killed Lincoln. Parker was still in the saloon drinking beer when
word drifted in that the president had been shot.

Mary Lincoln laid much of the blame for Lincoln's death at Parker's feet. So
did Lincoln's regular bodyguard, Colonel Crook: "Booth had found it necessary to
stimulate himself with whiskey in order to reach the proper pitch of fanaticism," he
wrote. "Had he found a man at the door or the president's box with a Colt's revolver,
his alcohol courage might have evaporated."

After the assassination, Parker, who had a history of being drunk on duty and
visiting brothels during work hours, remained on the force. He was even assigned to
guard Mary Lincoln. ("So you are on guard tonight, on guard in the White House after
helping to murder the president," she screamed before ordering him from her sight.) In
1868 Parker was thrown off the force after he was caught sleeping on the job.

There are more digits in a number called a googolplex than there are particles in the universe.

MOUTHING OFF

WISE WOMEN

Some thought-provoking words on how to thrive in a challenging world.

"I have learned over the years that when one's mind is made up, this diminishes fear. Knowing what must be done does away with fear."
—Rosa Parks

"The secret ingredient that drives hard work and excellence is passion."
—**Kelly Ayotte**

"Always be more than you appear and never appear to be more than you are."
—Angela Merkel

"I used to want the words 'She tried' on my tombstone. Now I want 'She did it.'"
—Katherine Dunham

"I would always rather be happy than dignified."
—Charlotte Brontë

"There are no hopeless situations; there are only men who have grown hopeless about them."
—Clare Booth Luce

"It isn't where you come from; it's where you're going that counts."
—Ella Fitzgerald

"A wise woman puts a grain of sugar into everything she says to a man, and takes a grain of salt with everything he says to her."
—Helen Rowland

"We are all born to die—the difference is the intensity with which we choose to live."
—Gina Lollobrigida

"Big egos are shields for lots of empty space."
—Diane Black

STRANGE CRIME: TATTOO EDITION

A tattoo can be an expression of your personality, or it can be a commemoration of a unique event in your life…or it can be a way for witnesses to identify you after you commit a crime.

STATE PRIDE. In July 2009, a man staged an armed home invasion of a mobile home in Riverview, Florida. He broke in at 5:00 a.m. and forced the residents into a bathroom while he looted the house looking for electronics, cash, and prescription drugs. The perpetrator, Sean Roberts, was later picked up by police, and was easily identified by the victims. Roberts, it turned out, had neglected to conceal his face during the invasion, and the mobile home residents remembered him for his prominent tattoo—a map of the state of Florida on his left cheek.

THE NAME GAME. A Twin Falls, Idaho, man named Dylan Contreras was wanted by police on some outstanding warrants. One night in 2012, a police officer spotted Contreras and some friends acting suspiciously, and walking down the middle of the street. As he asked the group to move to the sidewalk, he sensed that Contreras might flee, so he asked him for ID. Contreras told the cop that his name was Emiliano Velesco—but the officer didn't believe him. Reason: he had the name "CONTRERAS" tattooed on his forearm.

THE ODD NAME GAME. Two Billings, Montana, police officers were working a case when they happened to walk past a guy on the street with an odd tattoo: the word "Wolfname" was tattooed on his head. Other than the fact that face tattoos are relatively unusual, they wouldn't have thought much of it…except that they remembered having heard "Wolfname" before. It was the name of a suspect in a fatal assault case in nearby Wyoming. Police arrested the man, whose name was…Sterling F. Wolfname.

YOU CAN RUN BUT YOU CAN'T HIDE. In August 2017, a man from Thailand saw an elderly guy sitting, shirtless, on a Bangkok park bench and took a photograph of him. The photographer admired the man's elaborate and extensive tattoos depicting Japanese warriors and dragons, and he uploaded the pictures to Facebook. The photos quickly went viral, and were seen by thousands of people, including police in Japan… who quickly recognized the tattoos as ones normally sported by members of the Yakuza, the notorious "Japanese Mafia." Thai authorities were alerted, and they tracked down the man, 74-year-old Yakuza crime lord Shigeharu Shirai. He'd fled in 2003 to escape prosecution for the alleged murder of a rival. He was arrested and deported back to Japan, where he is expected to face trial.

Bone dry? Your skeleton is actually covered in a thin layer of moisture.

THE SECRET LIVES OF AUTHORS

Writers aren't always bookish and nerdy. Many of history's greatest authors lived lives of high adventure and low crime…before they wrote great works of literature.

Jack London. He felt the "call of the wild" and was his own boss when, as a teenager, he worked as an oyster pirate. He stole them from San Francisco oyster farms and then sold them at markets on the other side of the bay, in Oakland.

Charles Dickens. The reason the author's works were so sensitive to the plight of the working poor during England's Industrial Revolution was that Dickens put in his time in those factories himself. At the age of 12, he worked 10 hours a day in a boot polish factory, pasting labels onto bottles.

George Orwell. In 1922, 19-year-old Eric Blair (that's his real name) joined the Indian Imperial Police and worked as a cop in Burma. He later returned to his native England, where he conducted "experiments" and wrote about them. Example: he lived on the streets of London and Paris just to see what being homeless felt like.

Agatha Christie. During World War I, the mystery author spent four years working as a nurse's aide at a military hospital. In 1917 she was promoted to pharmacist assistant, a job she held until the end of the war, a year later.

Jack Kerouac. It should come as no surprise that the author of *On the Road* lived the same itinerant lifestyle he championed as the unofficial leader of the Beat generation. Among Kerouac's low-paying gigs: dishwasher, gas station attendant, deckhand, train brakeman, and night watchman.

Arthur Conan Doyle. In the 1880s, Doyle served as a ship's doctor before establishing a private practice in Southsea, England. Doyle based his most famous character, Sherlock Holmes, on a colleague from those days.

Harper Lee. The author of *To Kill a Mockingbird* financed her literary ambitions in the 1950s by working the ticket counter for Eastern Airlines. In 1956 a wealthy friend gifted her with one year's salary so that Lee would be free to write full-time. She used the year off to write *To Kill a Mockingbird*.

First online food ordering: Pizza Hut set up an experimental service called PizzaNet in 1994.

William S. Burroughs. Upon his discharge from the army for psychiatric concerns in 1942, Burroughs moved to Chicago and found work as an exterminator.

Herman Melville. *Moby-Dick* was informed by Melville's five years at sea. In 1839 he joined the crew of the *St. Lawrence* as a cabin boy and sailed from the East Coast to England, then worked for several ships that sailed the Pacific Ocean. Among his adventures: He was part of a mutiny (for which he was briefly jailed) and he lived among a tribe of cannibals in Polynesia.

J. D. Salinger. In 1941 the author of *A Catcher in the Rye* worked as the activities director on the *Kungsholm*, a high-end cruise ship.

Daniel Defoe. He popularized the English-language novel with *Robinson Crusoe* in 1719, but his life up to that point was the stuff of literature. In the late 1600s, he got a job as a traveling hosiery salesman, which took him to the Netherlands, Spain, and France. (It was during this time that he changed his name—from "Foe" to "Defoe," believing the prefix made him sound French and wealthy.) In 1688 he befriended William of Orange, the newly crowned English monarch, who put Defoe to work as a spy.

Fyodor Dostoyevsky. At age 15, Dostoyevsky's parents forced him into a military school that specialized in engineering. The future author of *Crime and Punishment* hated the school, but stayed in the program; upon graduation, he took a job as an engineer.

Robert Frost. Frost published his first poem in 1894, "My Butterfly: An Elegy." At the time, he was working on a factory assembly line, placing filaments inside of light bulbs.

James Joyce. Just after the turn of the 20th century, Joyce taught English in Croatia and Italy, and worked as a nightclub pianist before returning to his hometown—Dublin, Ireland—in 1909 to run the city's first movie theater.

Joseph Conrad. Born Józef Teodor Konrad Korzeniowski in 1857 in what is now the Ukraine, he joined the French merchant marines at age 16 to avoid getting drafted. He sailed for five years, but amassed huge gambling debts along the way… and attempted suicide to escape them. But he lived, and a wealthy uncle paid off his creditors. After he lost his job with the merchant marines, he joined an English fleet, changed his name to Joseph Conrad, and sailed to the Caribbean, India, Australia, South America, and Africa. His journey into the interior of Africa to transport a prominent Belgian trader named Georges Antoine Klein directly inspired his novel *Heart of Darkness*.

Every county in Utah contains at least part of a U.S. national forest.

ALL THAT AND A BAG OF CHIPS

Nowadays when you hear the term "chip maker," it conjures up images of silicon wafers and companies like Intel and Motorola. But those chips aren't nearly as tasty as the kind you buy in the supermarket. Here's a look at some of the folks who brought some of our favorite snack foods into being.

WILLIAM KITCHINER

Kitchiner, an Englishman, was the author of a best-selling 1817 cookbook called *The Cook's Oracle*. It contains the oldest known recipe for homemade potato chips, which he called "Potatoes Fried in Slices or Shavings":

> Peel large Potatoes, slice them about a quarter of an inch thick, or cut them in shavings round and round, as you would peel a lemon; dry them well in a clean cloth, and fry them in lard or dripping. Take care that your fat and frying pan are quite clean; put it on a quick fire, watch it, and as soon as the lard boils, and is still, put in the slices of potato, and keep moving them till they are crisp. Take them up and lay them to drain on a sieve: send them up with a very little salt sprinkled over them.

WAS IT GEORGE CRUM...

In the 1850s, Crum was a "tough old codger," part African American and part Native American, who was the cook at a restaurant called Moon's Lake House on Saratoga Lake in upstate New York. He had a hot temper and hated it when people criticized his cooking. As C. R. Gibbs writes in *The Afro-American Inventor:*

> The few who did complain and returned their orders to the kitchen were rewarded with the most indigestible substances the chef could concoct. His somewhat irascible nature made him commit mayhem on many a returned meal. It pleased him to watch their reaction, which ranged from disbelief to a hurried departure.

According to popular legend, that's what happened one day in 1853 when a customer sent back an order of fried potatoes sliced "very thin" because they weren't sliced thin enough, and then sent back a *second* plate when these, too, weren't thin enough to his liking. That did it! Crum grabbed a potato peeler and peeled a potato directly into

One more thing to worry about: If you were to inhale a pea, it could sprout into a new pea plant inside your lung.

a skillet filled with hot oil. He fried the paper-thin slices until they were too crispy to pierce with a fork, which was how fried potatoes were usually eaten, and sprinkled them with so much salt as to make them inedible (or so he thought). Then he sent his fried insults back out to the customer, who ate every chip…and then ordered a second helping. Why fight it? Crum added "potato crunches," later called "Saratoga Chips," to the menu. They became one of Moon's Lake House's signature dishes, and the first potato chips sold commercially instead of being made at home.

…OR CRUM'S SISTER, CATHERINE WICKS

The George Crum tale has long been the *official* story of how potato chips were invented, but in the 1930s some members of Crum's extended family claimed in interviews that his sister, Catherine Wicks, was the true inventor. According to this version of events, she invented them by accident, with a little help from George: Wicks was peeling a potato near the stove when a piece fell into a pan of hot fat. She fished the fried peel out and set it on a plate. That's when Crum walked by and popped the morsel into his mouth, not realizing it was destined for the garbage. Yummy! "We'll have plenty of these," he said.

Just as Mexican restaurants put out tortilla chips for customers, Moon's Lake House began putting bowls of Saratoga Chips out for its customers. They proved so popular that owner Cary Moon began selling "Original Saratoga Chips" as takeout food, so that people who craved them could have them even when they weren't dining in the restaurant. Moon served them in rolled-up paper cones to people who wanted to eat them right away, and in takeout boxes for customers to take home.

LAURA SCUDDER

In the early 1920s, Laura Scudder and her husband Charles owned a gas station in Monterey Park in Southern California. When a car Charles was working under fell on him and left him disabled, Laura took over the running of the business. To boost profits, she began making and selling potato chips. Scudder later sold the gas station and focused on making chips full time. In those days potato chips were sold in bulk, usually in barrels or bins, to grocery stores. When a grocery customer wanted some chips, the grocer scooped chips from the barrel into a brown paper bag. The customer took them home and typically warmed them in the oven before serving them.

Have you ever heard the expression "bottom of the barrel"? When the chips at the top of a barrel were scooped out, the chips farther down often got crushed and became stale. Nobody wanted these chips, so they were thrown out.

Scudder wanted to find a better method of packaging her potato chips, and hit on the idea of making sealed moisture-proof bags out of wax paper. Each night she sent the employees of her potato chip factory home with sheets of wax paper to iron into

---

No kidding: *Ephebiphobics* have a fear of young people.

potato chip bags. The following morning the employees brought the finished bags to work, and filled them with the potato chips they made that day, and ironed them shut to keep the chips fresh. Filling the bags with extra air (eventually nitrogen gas, to increase shelf life) helped to cushion the chips against crushing.

Another innovation of Scudder's: using *two* bags inside of a larger bag, so that customers could eat half of their potato chips without the other half going stale. Scudder's bags turned potato chips into a mass-market snack food; by the time she sold her company for $6 million in 1957, more than half of all the potato chips sold in California were Laura Scudder's Potato Chips.

JOE "SPUD" MURPHY

Until the 1950s, potato chips came in one flavor—potato. That's when Murphy, founder of Tayto's Crisps potato chip company in the Republic of Ireland, developed the first mass-production technique for adding flavoring to potato chips as they were being made. Ireland's first flavored chips were Cheese & Onion and Salt & Vinegar. The first flavor in the United States: barbecue.

FRED BAUR AND ALEXANDER LIEPA

Laura Scudder may have liked her potato chip bags full of air, but there's nothing more frustrating that opening a big bag of chips and seeing how much air, and how few chips, are actually in there. Potato chips are also greasy, and even in the most carefully handled bags of chips, plenty will still be broken. The consumer products company Procter & Gamble saw these flaws as an opportunity: they figured that if they could make less greasy, unbroken chips and package them in a container that wasn't full of air, the public would eat them up. In the late 1950s they assigned a chemist named Fred Baur to come up with just such a chip. He nearly succeeded, inventing a chip made from dehydrated, processed potato dough. He gave his chips a saddle shape that allowed the chips to be stacked inside a specially built can, which he also invented.

But Baur's chips tasted terrible, and his work was shelved until the mid-1960s, when P&G assigned Alexander Liepa the task of improving their flavor. He finally succeeded and the chips were introduced under the brand name Pringles (named for Pringle Drive in Cincinnati) in 1967. They were marketed as "potato chips" until 1975, when the U.S. Food and Drug Administration ruled that they were not actually chips. Since then they've been sold as "crisps." (Fred Baur was so proud of his Pringles can that when he died in 2008, his body was cremated and his ashes were buried inside a Pringles can, purchased by his family at Walgreens on the way to the funeral home. "My siblings and I briefly debated what flavor to use, but I said, 'Look, we need to use the original,'" Baur's son Larry told *Time* magazine in 2008.)

China used more cement between 2011 and 2013 than the U.S. did in the entire 20th century.

STAR WARS, STARRING JODIE FOSTER

Some roles are so closely associated with a specific actor that it's hard to imagine he or she wasn't the first choice. But it happens all the time. Can you imagine, for example…

CHER as MORTICIA ADDAMS (*The Addams Family*—1991)

When word got out around Hollywood that producer Scott Rudin was making a big-screen adaptation of *The Addams Family*, a number of actresses wanted the part of the mysterious, elegant, black-clad Morticia Addams, memorably played in the 1960s TV series by Carolyn Jones. Cher, having recently won an Academy Award for her role in *Moonstruck*, reportedly relentlessly pursued Rudin for the part. While she did have the right look for the character, Rudin didn't think she was quite right for it. Besides, he already someone in mind—someone he'd had in mind for the part from the beginning: Anjelica Huston.

HUGH JACKMAN as JAMES BOND (*Casino Royale*—2006)

In 2002 Pierce Brosnan starred in *Die Another Day*, his fourth outing as British superspy James Bond. Then he walked away from the extremely popular franchise, sending both the British film industry and Hollywood into a frenzy to find the next actor to play 007. The relatively unknown actor Daniel Craig got the gig, but he wasn't the producers' first choice. They really wanted Hugh Jackman, at the time best known for portraying Wolverine in the *X-Men* movies. But the Australian actor turned down the chance to be Bond. Reason: He thought the last few 007 movies hadn't been very good. "I just felt at the time that the scripts had become so unbelievable and crazy, and I felt like they needed to become grittier and real," Jackman later told *Variety*. When he found out he would get no creative input into the films, he passed.

SEAN "PUFFY" COMBS as a BOTTLE OF ALCOHOL (*Sausage Party*—2016)

Combs is primarily a rapper. But he also acts on occasion, so actor/writer Seth Rogen recruited Combs for a small role in his raunchy 2016 animated comedy *Sausage Party*. The movie is set in a grocery store at night when there are no humans around and the products come to life. Combs agreed to play a bottle of Courvoisier cognac (a nod to the 2002 Busta Rhymes hit "Pass the Courvoisier, Part II," which features Combs,

Pick-me-up: Until 1948, 7-Up contained lithium, a powerful antidepressant.

billed as "P. Diddy"). Amazingly, Combs backed out of the movie when he found out that he'd only be providing the voice of an animated character. In other words, Combs thought it was a live-action movie, and that he'd be wearing a Courvoisier costume. Rogen instead used *SNL* star Bill Hader to voice a bottle of whisky.

EMMA WATSON as MIA (*La La Land*—2016)

It took writer-director Damien Chazelle six years to get *La La Land* made. The musical about jazz and romance in modern-day Hollywood wasn't seen as very commercial, and it took Chazelle's 2014 movie *Whiplash* getting nominated for a Best Picture Oscar to get studios interested. Before *La La Land* went into production, Chazelle lined up two big stars to play the lead roles of pianist Sebastian and actress Mia: Miles Teller (the star of *Whiplash*) and Emma Watson (Hermione in the *Harry Potter* movies). But it took too long for the project to start. By the time production got going, both Teller and Watson had moved on to other projects. So Ryan Gosling came onboard to play Sebastian, and Emma Stone played Mia. Good move: She won an Academy Award for her performance.

JODIE FOSTER as PRINCESS LEIA ORGANA (*Star Wars*—1977)

Carrie Fisher was just 20 years old when she took on the iconic role of Princess Leia in the first *Star Wars* movie. That's young, but not as young as the actress she edged out for the part: 14-year-old Jodie Foster, who'd just been nominated for an Oscar for *Taxi Driver*. In 2015 Fisher told the *Daily Beast* that final casting came down to her, Foster, and Amy Irving.

CHARLES BRONSON as SUPERMAN (*Superman*—1978)

Bronson is most associated with the role of Paul Kersey in the *Death Wish* movies, a disillusioned architect who gets medieval on the world after his wife is killed by street thugs, and starts cleaning up New York's mean streets by brutally killing as many random criminals as possible. The *Death Wish* series was extremely popular, which won Bronson some consideration when producers were casting the big-budget *Superman* movie set for release in 1978. But Bronson was well over 50 at the time and, in addition, producers thought he looked "too earthy."

* * *

"If evil be spoken of you and it be true, correct yourself; if it be a lie, laugh at it."

—Epictetus

Sea monkeys breathe through their feet.

UNCLE JOHN'S PAGE OF LISTS

Random bits of information from the BRI's bottomless files.

First 4 Communications Satellites

1. *Sputnik* 1 (1957, USSR)
2. *Project SCORE* (1958, USA)
3. *TIROS-1* (1960, USA)
4. *Echo 1* (1960, USA)

7 Items Banned from Disney Parks

1. Selfie sticks
2. Wrapped gifts
3. Folding chairs
4. Drones
5. Pets
6. Balloons
7. Straws

6 Vegetables That Are Varieties of the Wild Mustard Plant

1. Brussels sprouts
2. Cabbage
3. Kale
4. Broccoli
5. Cauliflower
6. Kohlrabi

11 Items That Often Contain Cow Byproducts

1. Asphalt
2. Drywall
3. Tires
4. Paint
5. White sugar
6. Lipstick
7. Fireworks
8. Crayons
9. Dice
10. Piano keys
11. Surgical sutures

5 Country Songs About Drinkin'

1. "You Look Like I Need a Drink" (Justin Moore)
2. "Chug-a-Lug" (Roger Miller)
3. "Red Solo Cup" (Toby Keith)
4. "The Whiskey Ain't Workin'" (Travis Tritt)
5. "There's a Tear in My Beer" (Hank Williams Jr.)

4 Things Lay's Potato Chips Are Called Abroad

1. Walker's (UK)
2. Sabritas (Mexico)
3. Tapuchips (Israel)
4. Chipsy (Egypt)

8 Rap Names for Insane Clown Posse co-founder Joseph William Utsler

1. Shaggy 2 Dope
2. Guy Gorfey
3. Gweedo
4. Ham'd Burglah
5. Mr. Club
6. Southwest Strangla
7. Bazooka Joey
8 Stretch Nuts

First 8 Countries to Celebrate the New Year

1. Samoa
2. Tonga
3. Fiji
4. New Zealand
5. Australia
6. Japan
7. South Korea
8. North Korea

If your eyes were digital cameras, they'd be 576 megapixel cameras.

MOUTHING OFF

WE ARE NOT A FAN

Doesn't everybody like Star Wars and the Beatles? Apparently not.

"As entertainment, the film would benefit from the deletions."
—John C. Flinn Sr., *Variety,* on *Gone With the Wind*

"Coffee isn't my cup of tea."
—Samuel Goldwyn, movie producer

"I think he was a bad man, a man who forced the country into an unnecessary war and conducted it with great inhumanity."
—Lyon Gardiner Tyler, historian, on Abraham Lincoln

"Mother Teresa has consoled and supported the rich and powerful, allowing them all manner of indulgence, while preaching obedience and resignation to the poor."
—Christopher Hitchens

"I DON'T LIKE PIZZA. I NEVER HAVE AND PROBABLY NEVER WILL. THE EXCESSIVE GREASE AND SHEER QUANTITY OF CHEESE IS OFF-PUTTING, AND IT MAKES ME NAUSEOUS."
—Marisa Guido, *Teen Vogue*

"The only way that *Star Wars* could have been interesting was through its visual imagination and special effects. Both are unexceptional."
—Stanley Kauffman, the *New Republic*

"The rhino is now more or less extinct, and it's not because of global warming or shrinking habitats. It's because of Beyoncé's handbags."

—Morrissey

"The Beatles are not merely awful. They are so unbelievably horrible, so appallingly unmusical, so dogmatically insensitive to the magic of the art that they qualify as crowned heads of anti-music."

—William F. Buckley Jr.

"Christmas is a baby shower that went totally overboard."

—Andy Borowitz, the *New Yorker*

"Strip *Star Wars* of its often striking images and its highfalutin scientific jargon, and you get a story, characters, and dialogue of overwhelming banality."

—John Simon, *New York* magazine

"They were the worst musicians in the world. Paul was the worst bass player I ever heard. And Ringo? Don't even talk about it."

—Quincy Jones, music producer, on the Beatles

"I don't care for *Seinfeld*. I'm bothered by the character of Kramer. I find it hard to watch shows where there is one character that is so obnoxious that no one would hang out with him."

—Senator Barney Frank

"The picture leaves one cold, or disturbs one by its paradoxical, unfeeling, and grotesque unconcern for the beholder. This is the group to which Picasso belongs."

—Carl Jung

MURDER, HE WROTE

Considering how many texts people send to each other every day, it stands to reason that some of them will get sent to the wrong person. Here's the story of a wayward text that, if it could be believed, was a matter of life and death.

THE TELLTALE TEXT

In February 2017, a Monroe, Washington, businessman (name not released in news reports) received a disturbing text that was not intended for him. Addressed to someone named Shayne, it read:

> Hey Shayne hows it going. You remember you said that you would help me kill my wife. I'm going to take you up on that offer. [Wife's] life insurance is worth 1 million and if you want a bounes [sic] you can kill [daughter]. Her life insurance is 500k. I go to work 5 in the morning. [Wife] goes to work at 2:00pm so if you can make a robbery gone wrong or make it a accident she works at walmart she gets off at 11:00. I'll split everything with the insurance 50/50. Please call or text me please.

The message could not have been clearer. Luckily for the business owner, he recognized the phone number as one belonging to a former employee, a 42-year-old man named Jeffery Scott Lytle. The business owner reported the text to the Snohomish County Sheriff's Office, which went into action.

JUST THE FACTS

The sheriff's deputies assigned to the case were concerned for the safety of Lytle's wife, so they visited her during her shift at Walmart and asked her to confirm some of the information contained in the text. She told the deputies that she and Lytle had been married for seven years, and that they had a four-year-old daughter. Their finances were tight because Lytle was unemployed.

The wife admitted that like any couple, she and her husband had their problems, but she expressed shock that any marital troubles they had would be enough for her husband to want to kill her. She said that she thought she and her husband might have life insurance, but she was unable to provide the deputies with details. She

Amelia Earhart and Eleanor Roosevelt skipped a state dinner
in 1933 to take a spontaneous flight to Baltimore.

denied knowing anyone named Shayne, which wasn't surprising: Not many people know the hitman who has been hired to kill them.

A LIKELY STORY

When the deputies finished speaking to Lytle's wife, they drove to Lytle's residence to question him. He confirmed that the cell phone number was his, and that he had worked for the businessman who received the text. But Lytle denied sending the text. Under further questioning, he admitted that he had written the text, but he said he wrote it months earlier. He claimed it was a work of fiction, something he'd made up to blow off steam following an argument with his wife (she'd gotten mad at him for talking to another woman). Lytle denied sending the text to anyone, though he admitted saving copies of it on his phone.

Lytle also denied hiring a hitman, and denied knowing anyone named Shayne, hitman or not. That was just a name he came up with when he wrote the text, he told the deputies. And he denied having any insurance policies on his wife or his child, so he had nothing to gain financially by having them murdered.

So if he didn't send the text, who did? Lytle speculated that his four-year-old daughter may have sent it by accident while playing with his phone.

BOOK 'EM

Naturally, the deputies didn't buy a word of it. They took Lytle in for further questioning, and later that day they arrested him. He was charged with two counts of first-degree investigation of criminal solicitation for murder. That evening the sheriff's office passed the case to the Monroe Police Department, and they served a search warrant on Lytle's home to confiscate his cell phone and any records relating to life insurance policies.

The following morning Lytle was brought before a judge, who found that probable cause existed to believe he was guilty of the crimes. He ordered Lytle held in custody pending a trial. Bail was set at $1 million.

STRANGER THAN FICTION

Lytle was taken into jail on February 8, 2017…and walked out again on March 27. Not because he'd made bail, but because the police were unable to find any evidence that he really had tried to hire a hitman to kill his family. His crazy story about the text being a figment of his imagination suddenly didn't seem so crazy after all.

The police had scoured his phone and his phone records for any evidence that Lytle had made calls or sent any other texts to anyone named Shayne. He hadn't. And the police found no life insurance policies on his wife and daughter, so there was no evidence of a financial motive, either.

A kidney "transplant" is usually a kidney *addition*—surgeons implant the new one, but leave the old one in place.

When Lytle was released from jail, the Snohomish County Prosecutor's Office issued a statement saying the investigation was ongoing, but in May 2017 they dropped all charges against Lytle. After a month and a half more of searching, the investigators still hadn't found any evidence that a hitman named Shayne existed anywhere other than in Jeffery Lytle's imagination. "In all likelihood this case will never be fileable. If Shayne is fictional then there cannot be a conspiracy with a fictional person," the prosecutor's office said when it announced that all charges were being dropped. "Since we cannot prove Shayne is real, and cannot corroborate this disturbing text from Lytle in any way, we cannot prove a crime occurred."

> **"Since we cannot prove Shayne is real, and cannot corroborate this disturbing text from Lytle in any way, we cannot prove a crime occurred."**

The news of Lytle's release came as a shock to everyone except Lytle's wife, who never doubted her husband's innocence. "She adamantly asserts that…she is '110%' sure that Lytle would never hurt her," the Snohomish County Prosecutor's Office noted in its statement, adding that "she claims to be the assertive one in the relationship."

So what's the moral of the story? Never text your hitman, not even if he's fake.

* * *

GETTING HOOKED

Ever seen an old movie or cartoon where a bad comedian or singer gets pulled off the stage by a long crook with a hook at the end, pulled by an unseen stagehand until the offending performer is gone from the audience's view? That's called "getting the hook," a phrase that's come to describe any time someone fails, like when someone gets fired from a job or when a pitcher gets removed from a baseball game. This was actually something that happened in the world of vaudeville, the live theatrical variety shows that were a common form of American entertainment in the late 1800s and early 1900s. It started at an amateur night at Miner's Bowery, a New York vaudeville theater, in 1903. A reportedly terrible singer tried to sing an aria, and kept singing even as he was being drowned out by the crowd's boos. Owner Tom Miner wanted to end the miserable performance, so he told his stage manager, Charles Guthinger, to hide in the wings and use a prop left behind by a previous act—a comically oversized, crook-handled cane—to yank the singer off the stage. Vaudeville theaters all over the country soon started using "hooks" of their own. The famous singer and actor Eddie Cantor claimed that his energetic performance style of jumping around the stage originated when theater operators tried to give him the hook…and he dodged it.

When you swallow a teaspoon of water, you are swallowing eight times as many atoms as there are teaspoons of water in the entire Atlantic Ocean.

TODAY IS *WHAT* DAY?

There are 1,500 "National Days" per year, which averages out to 4.1 holidays every day. Here are some odd ones.

JANUARY 1: National Bloody Mary Day. Nursing a New Year's Eve hangover? Take today to remember Ferdinand "Pete" Petiot, the bartender who invented the Bloody Mary at Harry's Bar in Paris in 1921. His original name for the drink: "Bucket of Blood."

JANUARY 21: National Squirrel Appreciation Day was founded by wildlife rehabilitator Christy Hargrove as a day for people to see past squirrels' reputations as pests, vermin, and "tree rats." There are more than 200 squirrel species worldwide. Largest: the Indian giant squirrel of Southeast Asia. It can grow to be three feet long.

FEBRUARY 5: National Weatherperson's Day. Expect this holiday to be partly fun with a slight chance of learning something about weather forecasters. For example, did you know that John Jeffries, born on this day in 1745, was one of America's first weather observers? His other claim to fame: While accompanying Jean-Pierre Blanchard on his historic balloon flight across the English Channel in 1785, Jeffries dropped a letter over London, which is considered the oldest piece of airmail in existence.

MARCH 1: National Pig Day was established by sisters Ellen Stanley and Mary Lynne Rave in 1972. Their mission: To help others see pigs as they saw them—as "intelligent and domesticated animals." (If you're not interested in celebrating pigs' intelligence, consider the first Monday of September—National Bacon Day.)

APRIL 6: Plan Your Epitaph Day was created by Lance Hardie, author *How to Write Your Own Epitaph—and Live Long Enough to Enjoy It.* You can also celebrate this holiday on November 2, which coincides with the Day of the Dead. Either way, Hardie encourages you to write your epitaph before it's too late.

MAY 14: National Underground America Day. Do you not celebrate National Underground America Day? "That's just the way it should be," said Malcolm Wells. This holiday, he declared, is only for the 6,000 people across North America who live in some type of underground or "earth-sheltered" dwelling. Wells's hope is that, on every May 14, "Hundreds of millions of people all across this great land will do absolutely nothing about the national holiday I declared in 1974."

MAY 14: National Dance Like a Chicken Day honors the "Chicken Dance" song that Swiss accordionist Werner Thomas wrote in the 1950s.

Year the first computer was installed in the White House? 1978.

In 2010 chicken dancers set a world record in Mandan, North Dakota, for the longest "chicken dance line," which covered 24 city blocks. (But they didn't do it on National Dance Like a Chicken Day, so should the record really count?)

JUNE 1: National Go Barefoot Day. Kick off your shoes and enjoy the feel of the soft grass between your toes. This holiday was started by Soles4Souls, a nonprofit organization that provides shoes to underprivileged children. Afraid of stepping on a piece of glass? Skip this holiday and celebrate National Shoe the World Day in March or National Two Different Colored Shoes Day in May.

JULY 3: National Eat Your Beans Day. We love beans because they…are good for your heart (*and they make you fart!*). But the founders of this holiday want to remind you that there's more to beans than the music they make. For example, did you know that there are 40,000 varieties of beans around the world? And that in Nicaragua, people give newlyweds a bowl of beans for good luck? And that approximately 71,089 people in the world have the last name Bean? Bean facts. Bean farts. Equally entertaining.

AUGUST 23: National Ride the Wind Day celebrates Paul MacCready, who, on this day in 1977, debuted the first human-powered aircraft capable of controlled and sustained flight. He flew a figure-eight course, cruising at only 11 mph (roughly the same speed that a mouse can run).

OCTOBER 12: National Freethought Day celebrates the separation of church and state, scientific advancement, and freedom of speech. Why October 12? That marks the anniversary of the *end* of the Salem Witch Trials in 1692.

NOVEMBER 20: National Absurdity Day. Get weird! Celebrate things that make no sense! We like to celebrate by sharing absurd facts. Here are two: 1) During the Great Emu War in 1932, the Australian military tried to curb the population of emus by shooting them; the emus won. 2) The first incident of "mooning" took place in 66 AD, when a Roman soldier mooned a group of Jewish pilgrims. The mooning caused a riot, and thousands were killed.

DECEMBER 4: National Sock Day honors all of those special sock pairs that accomplish the near-impossible feat of staying together after countless washings and dryings. What about lonely single socks? May 9 is National Lost Sock Memorial Day, a day to throw them away, guilt-free.

More strange-but-real "holidays"
January 3: National Drinking Straw Day
April 2: National Ferret Day
May 27: National Grape Popsicle Day
July 12: National Paper Bag Day
August 7: National Lighthouse Day
September 16: National Play-Doh Day
October 1: National Fire Pup Day
November 4: National Candy Day
December 16: National Chocolate-
   Covered Anything Day

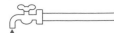

All German pet shelters are no-kill pet shelters.

FOOD FOR THOUGHT

*How much good can a single hungry schoolkid
accomplish with a little grit, determination
…and a website? More than you'd think.*

THE CRITIC

Martha Payne was a nine-year-old girl at Lochgilphead Primary School on the west coast of Scotland. She liked to write and she was also interested in nutrition, so in the spring of 2012 her father helped her set up a website called NeverSeconds, where she could critique the lunches served at school. Each day Martha rated her meals on a scale of 1 to 10 for both taste ("food-o-meter") and healthiness. She also counted the number of mouthfuls, as well as the number of hairs she found in her food, and she posted a picture of each meal on her site.

Martha was frank about what she liked and didn't like about her lunches. On May 8, 2012, for example, she was served a small slice of cheese pizza, a muffin, a single croquette (similar to a tater tot), and a few spoonfuls of sweet corn on a food tray that looks half empty. Martha gave it a food-o-meter score of 6, and a health score of 4. The pizza was "alright," she wrote, but the meal was too small. Mouthfuls: "forgot to count but not enough!…I'd have enjoyed more than one croquette. I'm a growing kid and I need to concentrate all afternoon and I can't do it on one croquette. Do any of you think you could?"

FOOD FIGHT

School lunches vary in quality and quantity from one part of the UK to another, but Martha's reviews suggested that primary schools in Scotland clearly had some catching up to do. School officials were embarrassed. About a month after Martha started her reviews, she was pulled out of class by the head teacher and told that the local Argyll and Bute government council, which runs the school, had banned Martha from taking any more pictures of her lunches.

When Martha reported the development on her website in a post titled "Goodbye" and announced that she was ending her school lunch reviews, the BBC and other news outlets covered the story; within hours it began spreading virally on Facebook and other social media sites. Over the next 24 hours, Martha's website received more than

> **Over the next 24 hours, Martha's website received more than 2 million visits from people all over the world. Many expressed outrage over the fact that Martha had been silenced.**

2 million visits from people all over the world. Many expressed outrage over the fact that Martha had been silenced.

That was all it took: The next day, after being pressured by Mike Russell, Scotland's Education Secretary, the Argyll and Bute council reversed itself and allowed Martha to resume taking pictures of her lunches. The school had already announced that students would be allowed unlimited servings of fruit, vegetables, and bread with their lunches (though it claimed that this had always been the policy).

"Well my friends and I never knew that," Martha wrote. "It must have been a well-kept secret."

LUNCH MONEY

Bonus: When Martha launched the NeverSeconds website in April 2012, in the upper right corner she posted a link to a fund-raising page for Mary's Meals, a charity that provides food aid to schools in developing countries. When the photo ban caused visits to her website to soar, donations to the charity also climbed, from £2,000 (about $2,700) before the controversy to more than £90,000 ($125,000) in just a few days. That was more than enough to build a new kitchen at an elementary school in the African nation of Malawi.

Martha continued posting her lunch reviews until the end of the 2012 summer school term. After that, she posted less frequently. Like most nine-year-olds, she had lots of interests and was eager to move on to other things. But she invited schools around the world to continue contributing their own photographs and posts, so that kids everywhere could see what their peers in other countries were eating.

Martha's last post was in February 2014, when she reported that her website had received its 10-millionth hit, and had raised more than £131,000 ($183,000) for Mary's Meals. And that's enough money to feed 12,300 schoolchildren in Malawi for an entire year.

* * *

TONY'S TONYS

The Tony Awards are named after American Theatre Wing cofounder Antoinette Perry. Three Tonys have won Tonys: costume designer Tony Duquette (for *Camelot* in 1961), scenic designer Tony Walton—three times, for *Pippin* (1972), *The House of Blue Leaves* (1986), and *Guys and Dolls* (1992)—and playwright Tony Kushner, who won for Best Play twice, for each part of *Angels in America*: 1993's *Millennium Approaches* and 1994's *Perestroika*.

The person who said "previously on *Lost*" on *Lost* was ABC chairman Lloyd Braun...

FRIGHT WHITE

Many horror stories told around the campfire end with the victims being so terrified that their hair instantly turns white. Is that just a scary story or can it really happen? Read on...

MEDICAL MYSTERY

For centuries, the idea of a person's hair turning white overnight was thought to be a myth, but there are now enough medical professionals who have witnessed and documented the phenomenon that it has earned an official name: *canities subita,* or "sudden hair blanching." Researchers agree that the condition can be caused by extreme stress from fear, grief, or traumatizing medical events. What is not quite clear is how hair turns white from root to tip. (One possibility: a sudden infusion of air into the hair shaft caused by an adrenaline rush.)

Proof that it really does happen is no clearer than in the case of Alexander Littlejohn, a first-class steward on the *Titanic.* As the ship was sinking, Littlejohn was helping women and children board Lifeboat 13 before he was ordered to get in and row the boat. A photo taken just before Littleton boarded the *Titanic* shows a dark-haired, mustached man of 40. A second photo, taken just six months after he survived the disaster, reveals that not only did his hair turn white—his eyebrows, eyelashes, and mustache were also bleached of color.

OFF WITH HER HEAD!

Sudden whitening of hair is also known as "Marie Antoinette syndrome," named after the French monarch and wife of King Louis XVI. Marie Antoinette was the poster girl for the excesses of the nobility, which led to the French Revolution in 1789. Placed under house arrest, she tried to escape in 1791 but was recaptured and sentenced to die by the guillotine. Observers at the execution reported her auburn hair had turned white overnight. Both Sir Thomas More in 1535 and Mary, Queen of Scots in 1587 were also reported to have had their hair turn white as they waited for the chopping block, but it was the last queen of France for whom the fright-white syndrome was named.

POST-TRAUMATIC TRESS DISORDER

The numerous recorded instances of sudden whitening of the hair include:

- In 1631 the hair of the Mughal emperor of northern India, Shah Jahan, turned white from grief after his favorite wife, Mumtaz Mahal, died in his arms. (He built the Taj Mahal to house her tomb.)

- In 1851 the *Boston Medical and Surgical Journal* published a report of a gambler whose hair turned completely white overnight after he staked his entire fortune on a single card in a poker game. (He must have lost.)

- In 1975 a college student loaned her Toyota Corona to two friends so they could move their belongings to a new apartment in New Jersey. A day later, she got a call that her car had been found upside down in a stream near the Raritan River. Her friends, unable to open the doors or break the glass, drowned. When the car's owner went to identify their bodies, the hair of both victims had turned white.

- An article in the 2013 *International Journal of Trichology* (a peer-reviewed medical journal in India) reported that researchers identified 196 cases of sudden whitening of the hair that involved not only scalp hair but also beards, eyelashes, and other body hair.

- In 1902 the *British Medical Journal* reported the case of a 22-year-old girl who witnessed a woman's throat being cut. Following this ghastly fright, the pubic hair on only the right side of her body turned white.

- Anne Jolis, reporter for the *Atlantic*, published a personal account in 2016 about hearing a series of prolonged gunshots outside her hotel window in Dagestan. Terrified, she hid under her bed for 15 minutes…until she finally realized it wasn't a gun battle, it was a wedding celebration. But the damage was done. The next morning when the 30-year-old Jolis looked in the mirror, she discovered that the dark "mustache" hairs on her upper lip—which had been the bane of her existence—had all turned white.

- In 1882 two doctors actually observed a 38-year-old woman suffering from violent neuralgia to the scalp transform from a brunette to a platinum blonde over the course of five hours.

THE WHITE HOUSE

It's often been noted that the graying of a U.S. president's hair is directly related to the amount of stress he faces. Barack Obama took office months after the 2008 financial meltdown, which is why on March 4, 2009, the *New York Times* wrote: "Well that didn't take long. Just 44 days into the job and President Obama is going gray." Barbara Bush, wife of President George H. W. Bush, was as well known for her bright white hair. It wasn't a fashion choice—when Mrs. Bush was just 28, the couple lost their three-year-old daughter, Robin, to leukemia. The future First Lady's reddish-brown hair turned white practically overnight.

Southjaws: Left-handers also chew their food on the left side of their mouths.

THE FUNGUS AMONG US

If you buy mushrooms at the supermarket, you're probably familiar with button mushrooms, portabellos, maybe even oyster, shiitake, or porcinis. But there are hundreds of varieties of mushrooms—some edible, some poisonous…and almost all weird. Here's a sampling.

Fungus: Indigo milk cap

Found In: North America and East Asia

Details: Also called the blue milk, it's one of the few naturally occurring blue objects in nature. It's found in the wettest parts of forests and looks like a standard and familiar white mushroom… except for a slight blue tint. Turn it upside down and the underside of the cap is covered in thick, deep-blue gills.

Edible? Yes.

Fungus: Brain mushroom

Found In: Eastern Europe

Details: Usually found under coniferous trees. Along with a nondescript light brown stem, it's got a cap that's large, reddish-brown, and wrinkled. In other words, it looks just like a tiny little brain growing on the forest floor.

Edible? It's lightly poisonous—if you eat it raw, you'll get sick, but some people say it's fine, even a delicacy, if it's cooked properly. (Nevertheless, it's banned from sale in Spain.)

Fungus: Lobster mushroom

Found in: North America

Details: It's not exactly a mushroom— it's a parasitic fungus that grows on certain edible mushroom species. It completely overtakes them, turning the host mushroom a reddish-orange color that's the exact same shade as a cooked lobster.

Edible? Yes and, oddly, lobster mushrooms have a taste that's similar to lobster.

Fungus: Bleeding tooth

Found In: North America, Europe, Iran, and Korea

Details: It's a mushroom that's bright white with a funnel shape that resembles a human tooth. That's not all—it's covered in pores, and when the mushroom is young, a red fluid oozes out. It looks like, well, a bleeding tooth.

Edible? No. It's not toxic, but it tastes terrible.

Fungus: Texas star

Found In: Texas and Japan

Details: It's not a star at first. As it grows, it takes on the shape of a cigar—a cylindrical capsule with a rounded end, colored brown. But when it's time to reproduce, the "cigar" splits open into a six-sided, orange-colored star, sending its spores into the air. And when it does burst open, it whistles.

Edible? Unknown—probably not.

At any given moment, there are an average of 9,728 planes up in the air.

Fungus: Mycena chlorophos

Found In: Japan and Polynesia

Details: In the daylight, these look like a lot of other fungi. They've got inch-wide caps that are brownish-gray and sticky to the touch. But when the sun goes down, something magical happens: They glow in the dark, emitting a peculiar shade of lime green. In Japan, they are called *yakoh-take*, or "night-light mushroom."

Edible? No, but they're *bioluminescent!*

Fungus: Puffballs

Found In: North America

Details: Imagine a balloon made out of mushrooms. It's a very thin-skinned ball found in fields and meadows. They're usually only an inch or two wide, but some as large as five feet across have been found.

Edible? Most are, but some varieties closely resemble toxic mushrooms such as death caps, so experienced mushroom hunters cut them lengthwise and examine them carefully to determine whether the interiors have white flesh (good) or gills (bad).

Fungus: Basket stinkhorn

Found In: Africa, Asia, Europe, and North and South America

Details: As the name suggests, this globe-shaped mushroom grows in a lattice pattern that looks like a wicker basket or a cage; the interior is hollow. Found on decaying trees, the basket stinkhorn looks like a bunch of Cheetos melted together. Like the anemone fungus, it smells like rotting meat.

Edible? No.

Fungus: Lion's mane

Found In: Asia, Europe, and North America

Details: Also called the bearded tooth, satyr's beard, or the pom-pom mushroom, the meaty part of this 'shroom is covered in long, thick tendrils that make it look like a wizard just left his beard on the side of a log. It grows on the sides of hardwood trees.

Edible? Yes. Reportedly, it tastes a lot like fried shrimp.

Fungus: Anemone fungus

Found In: Australia and New Zealand

Details: Sea anemones live in shallow ocean water, and look like starfish, but with stubbier appendages and a bigger hole in the middle. The anemone fungus is bright red and looks like somebody dropped a sea amemone onto a grassy area or a pile of garden mulch, which is where they usually grow. It's covered in brown slime, which attracts flies. The flies then pick up the mushroom's spores and spread them. Another attractant for flies: the anemone fungus's distinctive odor of rotting carrion, which also accounts for its other name: anemone stinkhorn.

Edible? No.

STRANGE TALES OF SLEEPWALKING

Sleepwalking, or somnambulism, is a fascinating phenomenon. While the body is for all intents and purposes asleep, the brain tells it to get up, walk around, and do things. That can get an unconscious person into an awful lot of trouble.

PUT YOUR MIND AT ZZZZZZZS

The British Royal Navy is one of the oldest and most prestigious military operations in the world, which apparently means there's no place on board its many ships for sailors who wander around in their sleep. In 2015 five different men were given medical discharges after each was found to be sleepwalking. Among the possible dangers: hitting their heads, trying to fire weapons, or falling overboard. The UK Ministry of Defence would not reveal how the five sailors were discovered sleepwalking, but it updated its official policy—anyone with a diagnosis of sleepwalking can no longer join the Royal Navy.

GATOR AID

James Curren of Palm Harbor, Florida, had a long history of sleepwalking, but he'd never experienced anything like this. In November 1998, the 77-year-old got up in the middle of the night and walked into a pond near his home. When he came to, he found himself standing in three feet of water, stuck in the thick mud…and surrounded by alligators. But Curren walks with the use of a cane, which he'd somehow managed to grab as he sleepwalked out of his home. He used the cane to fend off the gators while he yelled to his neighbors for help.

MIDNIGHT DELIGHT

The drug *zolpidem*—sold under the brand name Ambien—is one of the most commonly prescribed sleep aids on the market. Because it so thoroughly shuts down an awake brain, it stands to reason the drug would be linked with a number of sleep disorders, including sleepwalking. Among the adverse reactions noted by the UK's federal drug regulation agency: A woman on Ambien awoke outside of her house with a brush in her hand, and discovered she'd just painted her front door. Another woman gained 50 pounds over the seven months she was taking the drug, which she couldn't explain until she

> A woman on Ambien awoke outside of her house with a brush in her hand, and discovered she'd just painted her front door.

woke up in the middle of the night eating food while standing in front of her open refrigerator.

OPEN ALL NIGHT

In March 2017, police in Aberdeen, Scotland, responded to a call from a local ASDA supermarket at 2:30 a.m. regarding a barefoot woman acting strangely. Clad only in a nightgown, the woman was trying to buy a watermelon. Police woke up the 23-year-old, who, amazingly, had walked a mile and a half from her home to the all-night grocery store, all while her brain kept sleeping. "Thanks to the very kind ASDA staff who warmed me up and gave me shoes, socks and a cup of tea," the woman told reporters, "and to the lovely police officers who deposited my very confused self back in bed."

> **DID YOU KNOW?**
>
> What do sleepwalkers look like? Sleepwalkers don't look the way they do in cartoons, with their arms extended out in front of them like zombies. They move and act completely normally— a sleepwalker may even have their eyes open.

THE BEST DEFENSE

In 2003 a sleepwalking woman in Colorado managed to drink half a bottle of wine and take her car out for a spin, dressed in only a nightshirt to help brave the 20-degree temperature. Not surprisingly, she crashed her car…and then got out and relieved herself on the road. Police officers immediately spotted her and tried to arrest the woman, who resisted by punching and kicking. Citing the "sleepwalking defense" (which is apparently a real thing), the woman pled guilty to a single charge of reckless driving. Because she wasn't awake for all of her misdeeds— driving while intoxicated and public urination—the court agreed that she couldn't be held fully accountable for them.

SLEEPWALK CHECKLIST

At about 6:00 a.m. one morning in 2015, the parents of 19-year-old Taylor Gammel of Arvada, Colorado, reported their daughter missing. Local police used bloodhounds to try to track her down in the area surrounding her house, but to no avail. Then, a couple of hours later, the Gammels received a call—it was Taylor. She was at her uncle's house…nine miles away. Gammel says she woke up while walking. "It took me a minute to realize I wasn't dreaming, but that I was actually walking." She recognized the area as her uncle's neighborhood and went to his house to let her parents know she was all right. Clad only in pajamas and socks, Gammel said she noticed soon after waking up that her feet and legs were sore. That makes sense, considering that she walked *nine miles*. "It's a shock to me that I made it that far," she told a reporter.

Bobby Leach is the second person to go over Niagara Falls in a barrel…

ALL IN THE FAMILY

What's the most influential TV show of all time? Star Trek? Seinfeld? The Twilight Zone? The Sopranos? They're all great shows, but don't forget this one. It made us laugh…and it brought something new to prime-time television: relevance.

PICTURE THIS. Picture the United States in 1970: In the thick of the Vietnam War, President Nixon secretly invades Cambodia, setting off massive protests on college campuses across America. Four protesting students at Kent State University are shot and killed by the Ohio National Guard. The Chicago Seven are found guilty of inciting to riot at the 1968 Democratic National Convention. Now picture the landscape of American television at this moment: an array of mindless sitcoms like *Bewitched* (a suburban man marries a witch), *The Beverly Hillbillies* (bumpkins strike oil and move to Beverly Hills), *I Dream of Jeannie* (an astronaut finds a sexy genie in a bottle), and *Hogan's Heroes* (wisecracking Allied prisoners help win World War II while held in a German POW camp). Enter *All in the Family*, an intelligent series that combined comedy with real-life issues—bigotry, gay rights, the Vietnam War, women's liberation.

ARCHIE MEETS WORLD. *All in the Family*'s storylines centered on the daily lives of the Bunker family of Queens, New York.

• Archie, the patriarch played by Carroll O'Connor, was a loading-dock worker who raged about the changes that were happening in America, at work, and in his own home. He had a derogatory name for everyone, especially those who he felt were directly responsible for keeping hardworking white guys like him down: "spades," "spics," and "Heebs."

• Archie's flighty wife, Edith ("the dingbat"), played by Jean Stapleton.

> Gloria Stivic: "Hi Dad, where's Ma?"
> Archie Bunker: "I don't know, she flew out of here like a dingbat outta hell."

• Their daughter, Gloria, played by Sally Struthers, and her college student husband, Mike Stivic ("Meathead"), played by Rob Reiner, lived with them, much to Archie's dismay. Mike was as liberal a 'do-gooder' as Archie Bunker was prejudiced and closed-minded. Their heated arguments fueled much of the comedy in the series, allowing Archie to pontificate on "the women's lubrication movement," the "infernal revenue," and "pinko commies making suppository remarks about our country."

IN THE BEGINNING. In the late 1960s, veteran TV writer/producer Norman Lear and director/producer Alan "Bud" Yorkin had the idea to buy the rights to the BBC

…years later, he died of injuries sustained from slipping on an orange peel.

hit series *Till Death Us Do Part*. The show featured a middle-aged, working-class man named Alf Garnett, who lived with his family in London's East End. Alf spouted racist, antisocialist views at his wife, daughter, and son-in-law, reminding Lear of his own father, who his family called "King Lear" because of the way he ruled their roost.

Lear pitched an American version of the comedy to Mickey Rooney, hoping he could entice him to play the lead role. But when Rooney heard that the main guy was a bigot who used words like "spade" and "fairy," Rooney immediately turned it down, saying, "Norm, they're going to kill you, shoot you dead in the streets."

IT'S CHEMISTRY, STUPID. Directors often say "Casting is everything," and *All in the Family* proved that to be true. Carroll O'Connor was invited to read for the role of Archie because Lear liked the way he'd played the outrageous but likable General Max Bolt in the 1966 movie *What Did You Do in the War, Daddy?* And, as Lear later reported, "Carroll had the role by the third page." Jean Stapleton, who had recently appeared on Broadway in the musicals *Damn Yankees* and *Funny Girl*, instantly won the role of Edith. The problem was finding the right actors to play Gloria and Mike (who was originally named Dickie). They shot two pilots for ABC, each with different actors in those roles. The first program was called *Justice for All*, a reference to the family's original surname, Justice. The second was called *Those Were The Days*. ABC wasn't interested because there was no chemistry between the kids and the parents. The determined producers, Lear and Yorkin, then went to CBS with a third pilot, this time with Struthers and Reiner as Gloria and Mike. It worked. CBS, anxious to shake up their lineup of "rural comedies," as they called shows like *Mayberry R.F.D.*, *Petticoat Junction*, and *Green Acres*, decided to take a risk and give *All in the Family* a try.

ON THE AIR AT LAST. The show premiered on January 12, 1971. CBS was so worried that *All in the Family* might upset TV audiences, it hired telephone operators to field calls from angry viewers. They even posted this disclaimer before the first episode:

"The program you are about to see is *All in the Family*. It seeks to throw a humorous spotlight on our frailties, prejudices, and concerns. By making them a source of laughter, we hope to show—in a mature fashion—just how absurd they are."

But very few calls came in. And each week, as *All in the Family* shone a light on so many subjects that were previously taboo, the audience got bigger and bigger.

GAME CHANGER. In the first season alone:

- Archie is outraged to hear a black family is moving into his neighborhood and leads a protest, only to discover it's the family of his friend Lionel Jefferson.
- Mike and Archie send dueling letters to President Nixon about his leadership and the Vietnam War.

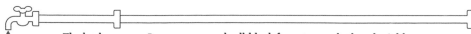
The hacker group Anonymous sends all-black faxes to people they don't like.
Reason: To drain their ink cartridges.

- Gloria moves out, demanding that Mike stop being a chauvinist and treat her as an equal.

- Archie, who refers to gays as "fairies," discovers that his best friend is gay.

And while the Bunkers held frank and funny exchanges about current events and everyday problems of working people, toilets flushed in the background, Archie burped in the foreground and Mike and Gloria enjoyed an active sex life upstairs. By the end of the first season, *All in the Family* had become the number one show on television.

SURPRISE ENDING. Instead of disliking Archie, television audiences actually embraced him and his "Bunkerisms." During the 1972 presidential campaign, "Archie Bunker for President" bumper stickers appeared on many TV fans' cars. President Nixon, who was *not* a fan, can even be heard discussing several episodes of the 1971 show on one of the infamous Watergate tapes. Over its award-winning nine-season run (1971–79), *All in the Family* continued to address such taboo subjects as abortion, integration, rape, Watergate, gun control, and prejudice, setting the bar high for all the shows that followed and earning it the distinction of being one of the greatest television series of all time.

> Archie Bunker: "They just wanna get rid of us old guys over 50, that's all, and put us out to pasture. Well, I ain't ready to be pasteurized."

FAMILY FACTS

- *All in the Family* was videotaped in front of a live studio audience. Canned laughter was never used.

- It's the first sitcom for which all of its main actors won Primetime Emmy Awards.

- Archie Bunker was partially based on Norman Lear's father, who called him "Meathead" and "the laziest white kid I know." Like Archie, the elder Lear called his wife "Dingbat," and when he wanted her to stop talking, he'd order her to "stifle herself." He also had an armchair reserved for his use only.

- Harrison Ford was originally offered the role of Archie's son-in-law Mike Stivic, but turned it down.

- Penny Marshall was almost cast as Gloria Stivic, which would have been interesting, considering she later married Rob Reiner.

- Even though *Those Were the Days* didn't work as the series title, it worked perfectly as the theme song that Carroll O'Connor and Jean Stapleton sang at the start of every show (including the pilot).

- The chairs used by Archie and Edith Bunker are on display at the Smithsonian National Museum of American History.

Oscar-winning actress Natalie Portman has published two papers in scientific journals, one of them when she was in high school.

ROBOTS IN THE NEWS

*One day, they'll enslave and/or kill us all. Until then, let's just
enjoy these stories about (mostly) friendly robots.*

IT'S GOT A GOOD BEAT AND YOU CAN RISE UP AGAINST THE HUMANS TO IT

Electronic dance club music sounds like it was made by robots, so why have a DJ up onstage pressing buttons on a computer when a robot could just as easily handle the task? That's the thinking of the management at the Karlovy Lazne Music Club in Prague, Czech Republic. They've had DJ KUKA, a former car factory robot, dropping beats at the venue since late 2017. The club's owners hired a local robotics firm to create the robotic arm with a pincer on the end. The robot takes CDs from a rack and puts them into a player, scratches records, and even dances. So far, club regulars aren't particularly fond of the electronic entity's style. "It can't feel what the people want to dance to," one human told reporters. "There is no emotion behind the music."

CITIZEN BOT

The signature droid of a Hong Kong-based company called Hanson Robotics is Sophia, a robot that looks like a human female and can make a variety of realistic facial expressions. Because Sophia can accomplish tasks while seemingly empathizing with humans, Hanson thinks "she" has a big future replacing customer service workers… and getting humans more used to humanoid robots. Saudi Arabia is already embracing the future. In October 2017, the Middle Eastern nation (where women have been allowed to vote only since 2015) made Sophia a citizen—the first robot to ever get citizenship anywhere in the world.

WHERE'S THE EXIT?

In 2018 researchers at Scotland's Heriot-Watt University put their robotic "shopping assistant" to work at a Margiotta supermarket in Edinburgh. The first robotic store clerk in the UK—nicknamed "Fabio"—was programmed to know the locations of hundreds of items in the store, and direct customers when asked. Fabio also offered high fives, hugs, and jokes on command. (It greeted some customers by saying, "Hello, gorgeous!") "We thought a robot was a great addition to show the customers that we are always wanting to do something new and exciting," store owner Elena Margiotta told reporters. She misjudged her clientele. They found the robot, which resembles a toddler in an all-white robot costume, off-putting. Very few asked it for help, and those

that did got terrible directions. One customer asked where the beer was, and rather than directing them to the correct aisle, Fabio told them that the beer was "in the alcohol section." The robot's creators chalked it up to too much ambient background noise, but after just three days on the job, Fabio was demoted to handing out samples.

ROBOT ARMY

A few years ago, high-tech organizations Android Technics and the Advanced Research Fund began work for the Russian government on a highly advanced, humanoid rescue robot. Once they got going, however, all parties realized that their project, FEDOR—short for Final Experimental Demonstration Object Research—had much more practical military applications. FEDOR's finger-like appendages have remarkable dexterity. It's able to change a light bulb, handle small tools, and, most alarmingly, fire semiautomatic firearms with remarkable accuracy. Anticipating exactly what everyone is thinking, Russia's deputy prime minister of defense, Dmitry Rogozin, said, "We are not creating a Terminator, but artificial intelligence that will be of great practical significance in various fields."

WATCH THIS

As hundreds of martial arts movies and Michelangelo from the Teenage Mutant Ninja Turtles have demonstrated, the Japanese weapon known as *nunchucks*—two heavy sticks connected with a short chain—are pretty cool. It takes a skilled fighter to handle them—to fend off bad guys and simultaneously manage to avoid hitting yourself in the head. Or you could get a robot to do it. Roboticists at the New Jersey Institute of Technology taught a small robotic arm how to wield nunchucks. An army of nunchucking robots may sound like bad news, but that wasn't the NJIT team's goal. They were developing new ways to quickly "teach" robots new tasks by using motion sensors to have a robot "watch" a human do something. Lead researcher Cong Wang taught himself how to use nunchucks over the course of two months, then he let the robot watch for two hours...by which point it was a master.

* * *

LIKE THE MOVIE? READ THE BOOK! (AGAIN)

In 1992 Francis Ford Coppola directed *Bram Stoker's Dracula*, based on the classic novel by Bram Stoker, of course. To promote the movie, Signet Books released *Bram Stoker's Dracula: A Francis Ford Coppola Film*. It's a novelization of the movie... which was based on a novel.

FIGHTING THE GOOD FIGHT

*Even if you don't know it by name, you've probably familiar with "Lucha Libre,"
the Mexican form of professional wrestling where the fighters wear facemasks.
Here's the story of one of the most unusual people ever to take up the sport.*

MEAN STREETS Sergio Gutierrez Benitez was a kid growing up in a tough
neighborhood of Mexico City in the 1950s. By age ten he'd already joined a gang,
committed petty crimes, and started using drugs—marijuana at first, then harder drugs.
Finally, after years of gang violence and drug addiction, he hit rock bottom in his early
20s and went to a local church to get help. As he told the BBC in 2018, the response
he got was not what he expected:

> The priest said, "Have you come to confess or what?" And I said, "No, I want
> you to help me. I'm a drug addict." He said, "This is not a rehabilitation center
> here, so get out!" The priest took me by one ear and threw me out. When he
> kicked me out of the church, I turned around and insulted his mother. And
> from that moment, my idea to become a priest was born.

Benitez thought that if there were more "cool and laid-back priests" who understood
what it was like to grow up in poverty, they'd be better able to help troubled young
people like himself turn their lives around. He decided that he would be that kind
of priest. He checked into a drug rehabilitation facility, where they detoxed him
using a primitive technique: they tied his arms and legs to a table until the drugs
left his body. Then he entered a seminary, and after several
years of study he was ordained a Catholic priest in Veracruz,
Mexico, in 1973.

> **Father Benitez was
> going to have to
> come up with the
> money himself…
> but how?**

KID STUFF Father Benitez says he found his true calling
by chance one day when he came across an orphan who
was living under a bridge in Veracruz. He took the child
in, and asked his superiors for permission to build an orphanage. When they refused,
he moved to Teotihuacan, northeast of Mexico City, where the bishop was more
welcoming. There, using donations from the community, he opened his orphanage and
began taking in street children.

Benitez never turned away a child in need. Soon he had dozens of kids in his care,
more than he had money to feed. But the diocese was poor and the bishop didn't have
the money to support the orphanage. Father Benitez was going to have to come up
with the money himself…but how?

In 1923, jockey Frank Hayes died of a heart attack mid-race…and his horse still won.

The inspiration turned out to not be too far away. Benitez thought back to two wrestling movies made in the 1960s that were still shown on TV—*El Señor Tormenta (Mister Storm)*, and *Tormenta En El Ring (Storm in the Ring)*. They both had the same storyline: a priest becomes a masked *lucha libre* ("free fight") wrestler to support a struggling orphanage. It worked in the movies—why not give it a shot? "I decided to make the fantasy come true," Father Benitez says.

> "I decided to make the fantasy come true," Father Benitez says.

LEARNING THE ROPES It took a while for Benitez to find a wrestler who took him seriously enough to teach him how to wrestle. He eventually found a wrestler named *El Líder* (The Leader), who taught him some moves, and also agreed to wrestle Benitez in his first match, in the mid-1970s. "The Leader must not have taught me everything. I lost," he later joked.

Benitez took the name *Fray Tormenta*—"Friar Storm," and wrestled The Leader wearing a homemade costume that consisted of yellow tights and T-shirt, both trimmed in red; red shorts with yellow stripes on the sides; and a gold mask trimmed with red around the eyes and mouth. Printed on the front of his T-shirt: "FT," framed with lightning bolts on either side.

Father Benitez admits that when he started wrestling, he imagined he'd be able to make a quick fortune and get out after a year or two. He soon found out that the job paid as little as $20 a fight. But he kept at it, being very careful not to let anyone know that "Friar Storm" was really a priest. *Luchadores* live and die by their athletic skill and artistry in the ring; how many fight promoters would have been willing to believe that a priest had the goods? In those early years when Benitez was trying to establish himself, he was helped by the fact that lucha libre wrestlers never remove their masks in public. Nobody knew what he looked like or had any idea who he was.

UNMASKED Fray Tormenta's identity might still be unknown today, had a wrestler named Hurricane Ramirez not attended a wedding that Father Benitez performed and outed him after recognizing his voice. That got Benitez in trouble with his bishop, a man named Magin Torreblanca, who ordered him to give up wrestling. When Benitez explained that he did it to raise money for the orphanage, Bishop Torreblanca gave him his blessing...sort of: "Officially, I have not given him permission to continue wrestling, but I overlook it, because I consider his skills a gift from God," he told the *Los Angeles Times* in the 1980s.

THE BIG LEAGUES Being exposed as a priest not only didn't hurt Benitez's career, it helped it. He built up a huge following of fiercely loyal fans who admired him

If you can read this, you don't have it: *Optophobia* is a fear of opening your eyes.

for going to the mat—literally—for his kids. People began showing up at his fights with donations of cooking oil, rice, beans, and other foods for him to take back to the orphanage. They also brought pots and pans—not to cook in but to bang on as encouragement during Fray Tormenta's fights. "Luchadores were afraid to fight me, not because of my strength or skill but they were afraid of the fans," he told the Slam! Wrestling website. "They would shout out, 'You can't fight a priest!' and they would throw tomatoes, garbage and even coins at them!"

Father Benitez quickly moved from being just another obscure regional fighter to signing with the biggest lucha libre promotion agency in the business, which put him in bigger fights not just in Mexico but also in the United States, where he toured 70 times, and Japan, where he made 14 trips to fight professional wrestlers there. The days of $20 fights were over: the bouts in Japan paid $5,000 apiece, and even the fights in Mexico paid hundreds of dollars—sometimes even thousands. If the fights were far from Mexico City, money for airfare and hotels was included. But rather than use the money for that purpose, Father Benitez would drive to his fights in an old camper truck, sometimes traveling 15 hours or more to get there, fight a 20-minute bout, and then drive home again, sleeping on the road and saving the money for the orphanage. "To accept luxury would be taking food out of the mouths of the children," he told *Sports Illustrated* in 1987.

> "They would shout out, 'You can't fight a priest!' and they would throw tomatoes, garbage and even coins at them!"

FOR WHOM THE BELL TOLLS Benitez wrestled in more than 4,000 bouts in a career lasting more than 20 years. In 1998 health issues forced him into semi-retirement, and he made only occasional appearances in the ring. In 2011 the 66-year-old quit for good, though he still makes personal appearances in his mask and refuses to be photographed without it.

Over the course of his career, Benitez broke his nose and his ankle, cracked three ribs, mangled several of his fingers, and dislocated his shoulder in the ring. (As you may have guessed, he's the inspiration for the 2006 film *Nacho Libre*, starring Jack Black.) But rather than think about all that he's been through, Benitez prefers to focus on the more than 2,000 homeless kids that his wrestling has saved from a life on the streets. Many have gone on to lead fulfilling lives as doctors, lawyers, accountants, computer technicians, and other professions. At least one became a priest, and several, including Fray Tormenta Jr., Tormenta II, Infernal-Face, and Krypton, have followed him into the ring.

A big galaxy can absorb a smaller galaxy—astronomers call it "galactic cannibalism."

A STORE IS BORN

You've probably never heard of Joe Coulombe, but there's a good chance you've shopped at the chain of grocery stores he founded. Even if you haven't, it may just be a matter of time until you do.

ORIGINAL JOE

In 1957 the struggling Rexall drugstore chain hired a young Stanford University MBA named Joe Coulombe to run a project that the company hoped would stem its losses. At the time, Rexall was being hammered by discount drugstore chains like Thrifty Drug and Eckerd. The head of company, Justin Dart, had recently been to Dallas, Texas, where he'd seen a new kind of retail business: a "convenience store" called 7-Eleven that opened early, closed late, and stocked a limited selection of grocery basics like milk, bread, and eggs for people who shopped after hours or who didn't want the hassle of going to a big store when they just needed a few things.

There weren't any stores like 7-Eleven in Los Angeles, where Rexall had recently moved its headquarters, and Dart wanted Coulombe to open some for Rexall. The first location opened in Pacific Palisades in 1958. Called Pronto Market, it was a mini-mart/drugstore that also processed photographs, sold paperback books, and stocked lots of Rexall health and beauty products.

CHANGE OF PLANS

Over the next four years Coulombe opened half a dozen Pronto Markets around L.A. and they were making money. But then his bosses told him to sell the stores. Reason: Justin Dart had recently purchased the Tupperware Corporation, and he wanted to free up money to invest in *that* business. At the time, Coulombe was due for a vacation, so he went to the Caribbean to clear his head and think about what he wanted to do next. By the time he returned, he'd decided that rather than stay with Rexall, he wanted to buy the Pronto Markets and run them himself.

He and Rexall agreed on a price, and over the next few years Coulombe doubled the size of the chain to twelve stores. His company was making money, but then 7-Eleven muscled into the Southern California market. Coulombe knew that if he tried to compete directly against them, it was just a matter of time until they drove him out of business. He had to think of a way to differentiate Pronto Market from the competition.

Coulombe was a voracious reader, and he'd recently read an article in *Scientific American*, of all places, that helped him decide on a strategy. The article pointed out that 60 percent of Americans who were eligible for college were taking advantage of that opportunity, up from 2 percent in the 1930s, when the country was still mired in

They're evolving! Whales have been born with legs.

the Great Depression and hardly anyone could afford a college education. He'd also read that Boeing was introducing the 747, an enormous new jet that was predicted to drive down the cost of air travel, making it possible for people with even modest incomes to see the world. "I wanted to appeal to the well-educated and people who were traveling more," he told *Forbes* magazine in 1989, "like teachers, engineers and public administrators. Nobody was taking care of them."

WHAT'S IN STORE

This was not a generation that wanted Salisbury steak TV dinners with Jell-O and Cool Whip for dessert, so Coulombe began adjusting the selection in his Pronto Markets toward more exotic and international foods. Then he began phasing out many of the drugstore offerings that were holdovers from the Rexall days. And because he'd read an article about a correlation between the number of years a person spent in school and the amount of alcohol they consumed, he stocked his stores with a wide variety of beers, wines, and liquor.

By then he'd also adopted the strategy of renting existing buildings in less-than-prime locations to save money. One early store in Pasadena, for example, was in a building that had once been a bottling plant. These locations were larger than his original Pronto Markets, and they gave him plenty of room to expand his offerings.

Coulombe wanted his stores to be fun places that customers looked forward to visiting. He thought back to his vacation in the Caribbean and thought a South Seas/tiki theme would be interesting, so he gave his stores a makeover and changed the name to Trader Joe's.

The next big change came in 1970, when Coulombe read an issue of *Scientific American* that sparked his interest in health food and vitamins. He began incorporating these products into the store's offerings, and rejiggering existing products to make them healthier, turning Trader Joe's into a "health food on top of a liquor store," as he put it.

MOVING ON

By the late 1970s, the Trader Joe's chain had grown to 27 stores in and around Los Angeles. Its low prices and unique offerings had developed a cult following among the "overeducated, underpaid" clientele that Coulombe sought. But Trader Joe's was still a strictly Southern California phenomenon. It might have remained so forever, were it not for the fact that Coloumbe had started thinking about his own mortality. He was pushing 50, and he'd already lost friends to heart attacks. He realized that if he were to die suddenly, inheritance taxes might eat up as much as half of his business. That was more than he could stand, so he decided to sell Trader Joe's.

Part 2 of the story is on page 327.

Paul Winchell, voice of Tigger, held 30 patents, including one for an artificial heart.

THE GÄVLE GOAT

Here's the story of the only Christmas tradition that involves arson (that we know of).

If You Build It...

Beginning on Advent, which marks the beginning of the holiday season by some Christian churches, members of the Southern Merchants (local businesspeople) in Gävle, Sweden, build a 43-foot-high yule goat out of straw over a metal skeleton. It spends the month of December in the Slottstorget, a historic square located in the center of the city. A yule goat, by the way, is a centuries-old Christmas symbol in northern Europe, kind of like Santa. Its most common incarnation is as a Christmas tree ornament.

The gigantic goat tradition goes back to 1966. The story goes that a local Gävle advertising guru named Stig Gavlén convinced a local businessman named Harry Ström to put up the money. Then Gavlén convinced his brother, the local fire chief, to build it. That first goat was over four stories tall and weighed 6,000 pounds. It took dozens of firefighters several days to complete it.

Setting the goat ablaze took only a minute or two.

...They Will Burn It

For some unknown reason, an arsonist destroyed the first Gävle Goat within mere hours of its dedication ceremony. Ström (the businessman) demanded his money back. Fortunately, the goat was insured. Unfortunately, the prank kicked off another annual tradition: The Southern Merchants try to keep the goat safe; arsonists try to destroy it. And more often than not, the arsonists win. Despite this, the Southern Merchants dutifully build a new goat in Slottstorget every Advent...and hope he doesn't go up in flames. "It's not fair," said one of the townspeople. "All the children are always sad. It's a sad feeling around the town."

This macabre cycle of birth and destruction has become something of a spectacle around the world. Will the Gävle Goat survive Christmas? To keep tabs, you can watch his progress on a 24-hour webcam (courtesy of Gävle's tourism board). He's even got his own Twitter account and Spotify list. (Favorite songs: Elton John's "I'm Still Standing" and the Bee Gees' "Stayin' Alive." Least favorite songs: anything with the words "fire" or "burn" in the title.)

Goat-and-Mouse

As of December 2017, the goat's been damaged 37 times since 1966. If he meets his

Technically, escaping from prison isn't illegal in Germany.
(But if they catch you, they will send you back.)

doom prior to Saint Lucia, a holiday on December 13, he's rebuilt. After that date, the city makes do without the goat until the following year. This game of cat-and-mouse gets more elaborate every year. Some highlights:

- In 1976 a student drove his Volvo through the goat's back legs, collapsing him. Since then, he's been protected by a metal barrier.

- One particularly cold winter night, the goat's security team decided to warm up at a nearby tavern. They'd only just received their drinks when they looked out the window and saw the goat ablaze.

- In 2005 two men dressed as Santa Claus and the Gingerbread Man took out the goat Rambo-style with a flaming arrow.

- In 2010 one of the goat's security guards told an interesting tale: He was approached by two pranksters who offered him 50,000 kronor (about $6,000) to abandon his post for a few minutes. Their plan was to "kidnap" the goat with a helicopter and fly him to Stockholm and drop him in a public square.

- In 2011 organizers sprayed the goat with water, assuming it would freeze and keep the goat safe. When the weather warmed up, the ice melted, and the goat was burned down on December 2.

- A few hours after the dedication ceremony on opening day of the Gävle Goat's 50th anniversary in 2016…someone burned it down. Despite the St. Lucia rule, frustrated organizers refused to build another one, so some high school students put up a smaller goat. That one only lasted until the wee hours of December 5, when it too was destroyed.

- If you're wondering if all this goaticide is legal, it isn't. In 2001 an American tourist named Lawrence Jones found that out the hard way when he got drunk and burned down the goat with his cigarette lighter. He told the arresting officer that his Swedish "friends" had told him it was a perfectly legal tradition. Jones spent 18 days in jail and was given a hefty fine. His lighter was confiscated as well.

A Christmas Miracle

After 2016's opening day debacle, organizers pulled out all the stops to prevent a repeat. "The Gävle Goat lives a dangerous life," goat spokesperson Maria Wallberg told *National Geographic* in 2017. "But we are full of hope that he will survive this year." To ensure this, the goat's straw was coated with a strong fire protectant; two menacing fences encircled him, and he was guarded around the clock by ex-cons from the Swedish reality show *X-Cons*. Lo and behold, the Gävle Goat made it all the way to January 2, when he was peacefully disassembled.

Will he survive next year? Stay tuned.

Sperm whales sleep by pointing themselves toward the surface and bobbing around.

THE FINAL ISSUE

These magazines were once publishing powerhouses…until they folded.
Here's who or what was on the cover of their very last print issues.

Newsweek (December 31, 2012)

As a nod to its past, the editors ran a vintage photo of its old offices, a Manhattan skyscraper called the Newsweek Building. As a nod to its future (as an online publication), the headline read, "#LASTPRINTISSUE."

Life (May 2000)

The photo-based weekly newsmagazine ended its 36-year run on December 29, 1972, with an appropriate cover story: "The Year in Pictures 1972." *Life* returned as a monthly in 1978. The last issue of that magazine featured a striking image of two adult hands holding a tiny premature baby—in other words, *Life* ended showing life beginning.

Nintendo Power (December 2012)

The first issue of *Nintendo Power* back in 1988 featured a scene from the video game *Super Mario Bros. 2*, rendered in clay. The scene: Mario stomping on a mushroom and running away from his nemesis, King Koopa. The final issue featured a re-creation of the image from the first issue, except that the clay renderings were more lifelike.

George (January 2001)

John F. Kennedy Jr. was a celebrity from birth. Gossip columnists tracked his every move, and there was widespread speculation about what the handsome young playboy would eventually do with his life. After working as an assistant district attorney in New York for a while, Kennedy made his move: In 1995 he launched a glossy magazine called *George,* which combined political news and opinion with humor. (It was sort of like *The Daily Show* or *Real Time* before either of those TV shows existed.) Then Kennedy died in a plane crash in 1999, and the magazine couldn't weather the loss of its leader—it folded a little over a year later. Its final cover: a photograph of John F. Kennedy Jr.

Playgirl (Winter 2016)

The internet revolutionized (or eliminated) a lot of industries, notably the pornography business. Anyone who wants to see pictures of naked people can easily obtain them on the internet, saving themselves the embarrassment of getting dirty

What's *jamais vu?* It's the opposite of *déjà vu:* when something familiar feels unfamiliar.

magazines at a newsstand or in their mailbox. *Playgirl*, which featured images of naked men, began publication in 1973 and went out of business 43 years later, in 2016. Its final cover story (and image) was "Campus Hunks: the Boys of Ft. Lauderdale."

Spin (September 2012)

New York indie rapper Azealia Banks, who had become nationally known after self-recording and releasing several singles, was on the cover. The power and scope of computers and the internet enabled Banks to do that…and competition from free-to-read music blogs on the internet sunk the print edition of *Spin*.

Self (February 2017)

As the internet became more mainstream, fewer people wanted to pay for health/beauty/fitness content when they could get it for free online. *Self* was a victim of that trend, and its ominous final cover model was Iskra Lawrence, a model who achieved fame via Instagram.

Jet (June 23, 2014)

One of the few general-interest magazines geared toward an African American audience, *Jet* ended its print edition after 63 years. On the cover of the final issue: a collage of 38 classic Jet covers that featured Nelson Mandela, Marvin Gaye, Prince, Jesse Jackson, Aretha Franklin, Spike Lee, Michael Jordan, and others, along with the headline "An American Icon."

PC Magazine (January 2009):

The last issue of this major computer magazine offered a cover story about the latest and greatest PC operating system to date: Windows 7.

Photoplay (June 1980)

From the 1910s through the 1960s, *Photoplay* was one of the most popular movie fan magazines, publishing movie stills and Hollywood gossip. (It was a precursor of magazines like *People* and *Us Weekly*.) By 1980 far fewer people were going to the movies than in the 1940s, choosing to stay home and watch TV instead. It's fitting, then, that gracing the cover of the last *Photoplay* were Charlene Tilton and Victoria Principal, stars of *Dallas*, the most popular television series at the time.

National Lampoon (November 1998)

Appropriately enough, it was "The Failure Issue."

Did you know? Tonsils are lymph nodes.

THE SCRABBLE SCANDAL

One of the most entertaining parts of a Scrabble game is bluffing your opponents by playing a made-up word to see if they'll challenge it and look it up in the dictionary to see if it's really there. It turns out that one of the biggest Scrabble fights ever was over which words should, and should not, appear in The Official Scrabble Players Dictionary.

WORDPLAY If you're a serious Scrabble player and you played in the 1970s, you may remember that in those days, *Funk & Wagnalls Standard College Dictionary* was the reference work that American Scrabble tournaments used as a guide to which words were acceptable for play, and which ones weren't. If a word appeared in *Funk & Wagnalls*, it was acceptable; if it didn't, it wasn't—as simple as that.

But *Funk & Wagnalls* had its problems, the most glaring of which was that many common words, such as "surreal" and "busload," weren't in it. "Smart" was in the dictionary, but "smarter" wasn't. Foreign words aren't allowed in the English-language version of Scrabble unless they've actually entered the English language—words like "chauffeur" and "sushi." But quite a few foreign words appeared in *Funk & Wagnalls*, such as *ja* and *bitte* in German ("yes" and "please"), and *oui* in French ("yes"). That meant that these words were playable in Scrabble, but "smarter" was not. Idiosyncrasies like these drove hard-core Scrabble players nuts, and as Scrabble tournaments grew in seriousness and number throughout the 1970s, the need for a better dictionary became acute.

> If a word appeared in *Funk & Wagnalls*, it was acceptable; if it didn't, it wasn't.

DO-IT-YOURSELF Selchow & Righter, the company that owned Scrabble, decided to create their own dictionary, and they worked with Merriam-Webster to do it. Their plan was to consult five different collegiate dictionaries—published by Funk & Wagnalls, Merriam-Webster, American Heritage, Webster, and Random House—and use them to compile a list of words and definitions for what became known as *The Official Scrabble Players Dictionary*. Any English word that appeared in at least one of the dictionaries would make it into the Scrabble dictionary and would therefore be acceptable in gameplay. The first edition of *The Official Scrabble Players Dictionary* was published in 1978.

The approach was straightforward, but the execution, it turns out, was flawed. Rather than hire a professional staff to compile the word list, Merriam-Webster relied heavily on lists created by members of the National Scrabble Association. These amateurs made plenty of mistakes, and so did Merriam-Webster staffers. Obscure

The horses on Disneyland's King Arthur Carrousel are repainted every two years.
Each horse takes 40 hours to paint.

words were misspelled, some foreign terms made it in, and some English words, like "granola" and "meltdown," were left out, even though they appeared in all five of the dictionaries consulted. One dedicated Scrabble player named Joe Leonard eventually compiled a list of 5,500 words that should have made it into the Scrabble dictionary, but for some reason had not.

SLURRED SPEECH The second edition of *The Official Scrabble Players Dictionary*, published in 1991, was a big improvement, but it ran into its own problems in 1993, when a Virginia woman named Judith Grad was playing with some friends who were Scrabble fanatics. They pointed out that both the old dictionary and the new one contained the word "jew." Not as a proper noun meaning "Jewish person," because proper nouns are not playable in Scrabble, but as a verb meaning "to bargain with someone in a miserly or petty way." In other words, as an ethnic slur.

It turned out that there were plenty of other racist words in the dictionary—"wetback" and "spic," for example—and that made Grad angry. She wrote to both Merriam-Webster and Milton Bradley, the division of Hasbro that had bought the American rights to Scrabble in the mid-1980s, to complain. They thanked her for her concern but refused to remove the offending words. "Slurs are part of the language, and reputable dictionaries record them as such," Merriam-Webster replied.

> **"Slurs are part of the language, and reputable dictionaries record them as such," Merriam-Webster replied.**

Grad didn't see the Scrabble dictionary as just another dictionary. It existed to support a game played by families, and also by children in schools, and she felt that ethnic slurs and other offensive terms had no business in such a book. She started a letter-writing campaign to get the dictionary changed, and as groups like the Anti-Defamation League joined the campaign, it eventually caught the attention of Hasbro chairman Alan Hassenfeld, who had fond memories of playing Scrabble with his mother. She would not have allowed the use of such words in their Scrabble games, and he didn't see why his company should be in the business of promoting them, either. On his own, without consulting either Merriam-Webster or the National Scrabble Association, he announced that the offending words would be removed.

FIGHTIN' WORDS When the third edition of *The Official Scrabble Players Dictionary* was published in 1996, 167 offending words had been taken out. Not just the ethnic slurs, but other words like "boobie," "bazooms," "nooky," "fatso," "peeing," "fart," "turd," "gringo," and even "jesuit."

Most serious Scrabble players hated the changes: They saw Scrabble as just a game about words, and felt the sanitized dictionary as an arbitrary form of

Silent, and silenced: 75% of American silent movies are considered permanently lost.

politically correct censorship that accomplished nothing. They began their own letter-writing campaigns to get the words on the "poo list," as it would come to be known, reinstated. "There are huge numbers of words which may be offensive to one or another group. However, a book purporting to be a dictionary cannot pretend that these words do not exist," one petition written by a woman named Hilda Siegel read.

> **167 offending words had been taken out. Not just the ethnic slurs, but words like "boobie," "fatso," "peeing," "fart," and even "jesuit."**

Why stop at 167 offensive words? What about the word "cripple?" Why was that still in the dictionary? It was certainly offensive to disabled people. What about "gyp"? The term, which means "to cheat or swindle someone," is offensive to Gypsies. Why wasn't it taken out?

Many players threatened to drop out of the National Scrabble Association or boycott officially sanctioned tournaments if the offending words weren't put back in. Things came to a head at the 1994 national tournament, when hundreds of players demonstrated against the changes with specially printed T-shirts and signs.

SOOTHING WORDS Executives at Hasbro thought they had diffused a controversy by removing the offending words, but it was now clear that they had created a new one in the process, perhaps even larger than the one they had tried to address. So they blinked. Before the 1994 national tournament ended, it announced that from now on there would be two official word lists: the still-expurgated *Official Scrabble Players Dictionary*, which would be marketed to the public and would be suitable for families and schools, and an uncensored *Official Tournament and Club Word List*, which would have the 167 offending words put back in.

To avoid controversy, the *Official Tournament and Club Word List* (called OWL for short) would not be sold to the public. It would be made available only to National Scrabble Association members, and only upon request. And it was a word list only, with no definitions whatsoever, not even of words that weren't deemed offensive.

(NOT) AS SEEN ON TV The OWL list has been used in official tournament play in the United States, Canada, Thailand, and Israel ever since. (But nowhere else—and that's a story for another time.) The only time it isn't used is when the final round of the National Scrabble Championship is broadcast on TV. Reason: FCC rules prohibit the broadcasting of offensive words on TV. In the early (untelevised) rounds, the offensive terms are allowed, but on the night before the final, the two players are each given a list of excluded words to peruse, and if they have any questions during play about whether a word is permitted or not, they are allowed to consult an official.

Heroin was originally marketed as "a morphine substitute for cough suppressants."

MAINE MEN

Ever been to Maine? The local accent and the local vernacular can make Maine-speak sound almost like a foreign language. In case you need it, here's our Maine slang decoder guide.

Buggin': Lobster fishing.

Finest kind: The absolute best.

Ayuh: Yes.

Crittahs: Animals.

Cunnin': Cute.

Down cellah: A basement.

Italians: What Mainers call submarine sandwiches.

Yow'un: Kids or teenagers.

Numb: Dumb.

Gawmy: Awkward.

Spleeny: Annoying and wimpy.

Prayer handles: Your knees.

Right out straight: When a Mainer is this, it means they're very busy.

From away: If you're not from Maine, you're "from away."

Chout: A contraction of "Watch out!"

Dooryard: The area in front of someone's house.

The County: The northernmost and most rural part of Maine—Aroostook County, where there's a large French-speaking population (it's close to Quebec).

Dite: A small amount of something.

I know it: The equivalent of "You can say that again!"

Kife: To steal.

Lozenger: A cough drop.

Put on a corn sweat: To try extremely hard.

Ugly: Angry.

Puckahbrush: Vacant, undeveloped land covered in weeds.

Out in the Willie-Wacks: To be out in the wilderness or the middle of nowhere.

Rugged: Stocky or thick of build (and meant as a compliment).

Stove-up: To wreck or destroy something.

Savage: Anything that's fantastic or appreciated.

RUSSIA 1.0

Russia's purported interference in the 2016 United States presidential election has fueled a lot of heated discussion in the press. But reporters use a lot of terms that might be unfamiliar to average folks, so here is Uncle John's cheat sheet on Russian history and terminology. Now you too can join in the argument.

TSAR (OR CZAR)

What is it? The emperor of Russia before 1917. The term "tsar" is derived from the Latin *caesar*.

The story: The reign of the tsars began in 1547 when Ivan, the 17-year-old grand prince of Moscow, was crowned tsar of all Russia. "Ivan the Terrible," as he became known, was infamous for his fits of rage and brutality, even killing his first-born son and heir. Ivan created the first official secret police of Russia—the Oprichniki, who dressed in black and rode black horses, and terrorized all who opposed the tsar. Tsars ruled Imperial Russia for the next 370 years until 1917, when Nicholas II was executed in the Bolshevik Revolution and Russia's royal dynasties came to a bloody end.

BOLSHEVIK

What is it? The majority wing of the Russian Social Democratic Workers' Party. *Bolshevik* is Russian for "one of the majority."

The story: In 1914, when World War I broke out, Tsar Nicholas II forced millions of Russian farmers and workers to join the army and fight under horrible conditions. The soldiers had no training or food. Many were barefoot and without weapons, and millions were killed. Three years later, in October 1917, the people revolted en masse and the Bolsheviks, led by Vladimir Lenin, seized control of the Russian government.

LENIN

What is it? Vladimir I. Lenin (1870–1924), leader of the Bolshevik Revolution, founder of the Russian Communist Party, and first leader of the Soviet Union.

The story: A lifelong revolutionary, Lenin was guided by his belief in the writings of German philosopher and political theorist Karl Marx, whose *Communist Manifesto* called for an end to the class system. Lenin led the 1917 Bolshevik Revolution, declaring the need for a government led by the people, with Lenin becoming supreme leader of the newly formed Communist Party. But not everyone was on his side. During his first years, Lenin led the "Red Russians" (the Bolshevik revolutionaries) in a fierce civil war against the "White Russians" (the anti-communists). He ordered his

Each year, an average of 600 patients catch fire during surgery in the U.S.

secret police, the Cheka, to kill anyone who spoke out against the government. Lenin instituted a policy called "war communism," seizing all the food grown by the peasants and doling it out to his Red Army. This policy created a horrific food shortage. By 1922 more than five million Russians had starved to death and 30 million were undernourished. But this cruel policy ultimately helped Lenin win the civil war, and he established the Union of Soviet Socialist Republics (USSR), the first communist country in the world.

Side note: Lenin's birth name was Vladimir Ilyich Ulyanov. He took Lenin from the river Lena in Siberia, where he had been exiled, serving three years in a prison camp for publishing a communist newspaper called *The Workers' Cause*.

COMMUNISM

What is it? A political and economic system in which productive resources like mines, factories, and farms are collectively owned by the public or the state. Money is divided equally among citizens according to an individual's need.

The story: In 1848 Karl Marx and Friedrich Engels published *The Communist Manifesto*, the most influential book (it was actually a pamphlet) in the history of the socialist movement. The manifesto described a vision of a society without class divisions or government, in which the production and distribution of goods would be based upon the principle "from each according to his ability, to each according to his needs."

STALIN

What is it? Joseph Stalin (1878–1953), the brutal dictator of the USSR from 1924 to 1953. He is responsible for an estimated 20 million deaths during his rule.

The story: After Lenin's death, Joseph Stalin became sole leader of the Soviet Union, and began moving the USSR from being an agricultural nation to an industrialized one. He expanded the powers of the secret service and encouraged citizens to spy on each other. To show his zero tolerance for resistance, Stalin created a man-made famine in which millions starved to death. Millions more were executed or sent to slave labor camps. After World War II, Stalin began taking over Eastern European countries that he had "saved" from the Nazis, which started the Cold War between the East and the West. In 1949 Stalin detonated an atomic bomb, taking the Soviet Union into the Nuclear Age and sending fear into the hearts of Americans who worried which superpower—Russia or the United States—would push the "red button" first.

Side note: Stalin's real name was Iosif Vissarionovich Dzhugashvili. He chose the surname Stalin because it means "Man of Steel."

Do you get mosquito bites? That means you're allergic to mosquito spit. (Nearly everyone is.)

SPUTNIK

What is it? *Sputnik* was the world's first man-made satellite. It was a battery-powered metal sphere the size of a beach ball that weighed 184 pounds and emitted radio waves. *Sputnik* is Russian for "fellow traveler."

The story: On October 4, 1957, the Soviet Union launched *Sputnik I* into orbit. Ninety-eight minutes later, *Sputnik* completed its first orbit of Earth. It continued to orbit for three months, finally burning up in the atmosphere on January 4, 1958. With *Sputnik*, Russia claimed the first significant victory in the "space race" between the United States and the USSR.

PRAVDA

What is it? The official newspaper of the Communist Party. *Pravda* means "the truth," but the newspaper was really just a propaganda machine for the party.

The story: From 1912 to 1991, *Pravda*'s daily mission was to skew the news to fit the party's view and encourage readers to toe the party line.

KGB

What is it? The secret police of the Soviet Union from 1954 to 1991. It was the largest spy and state security machine in the world. KGB stands for *Komitet Gosudarstvennoy Bezopasnosti*, which means "Committee for State Security."

The story: The KGB's mission was to serve as the "sword and shield" of the Communist Party—in other words, to protect the regime. The KGB suppressed dissidents and quashed revolts through the use of "active measures"—disinformation, propaganda, surveillance, physical harassment, sexpionage, imprisonment, psychological harassment, psychiatric commitment, exile, and assassination. At its peak, the KGB had infiltrated every major Western intelligence operation and placed agents of influence in almost every major capital.

Side note: During the U.S. civil rights movement in the 1960s, the KGB is believed to have spread pamphlets that claimed black Americans were attacking Jews and looting Jewish-owned shops in New York. The fake pamphlets implored their readers to fight against "black mongrels."

We're not done nyet. To learn more about Russian words and phrases, go to page 358.

Fear-o-vision: Your eyesight improves slightly when you're frightened.

UNCLE JOHN'S STALL OF FAME

Ordinarily, when a filmmaker says their movie is "in the can," they mean that it's finished. But in the case of the Indian film Toilet: A Love Story, *"in the can" means something else entirely.*

HONOREES: Shree Narayan Singh, director of the 2017 film *Toilet: Ek Prem Katha* ("Toilet: A Love Story"), and the actors Akshay Kumar and Bhumi Pednekar, who star in it.

CLAIM TO FAME: Making a feature film that calls attention to one of India's biggest sanitation problems—lack of available toilets.

DETAILS: More than 1.3 billion people live in India, and according to one United Nations estimate, 564 million of them do not have access to a toilet and must relieve themselves out in the open. The problem is especially vexing for women living in rural areas. Because they risk being sexually assaulted while relieving themselves, the custom in many places is for the women of a village to rise before dawn and walk together out into the fields, sometimes traveling more than a mile from their homes, so that they can answer the call of nature together, as a group. Afterward they return home, and wait until the evening before heading out together after dark to relieve themselves gain.

Holding it in all day and all night like this is not healthy. Pregnant women especially are at risk of developing urinary tract infections, and women who don't have access to a toilet are more likely to give birth to children with low birth weights. In some places there is considerable cultural resistance to putting a toilet inside the home, where there is a kitchen and a prayer room. Relieving yourself in the open air is considered cleaner and healthier than answering nature's call indoors.

> **She is shocked to discover they do not have a toilet.**

HOORAY FOR BOLLYWOOD: Shree Narayan Singh tackles these issues in *Toilet: A Love Story.* In the film, which is based on a true story, Akshay Kumar plays Keshav, a man who falls in love with a woman named Jaya, played by Bhumi Pednekar. Jaya was raised in a home with a toilet, but after she marries Keshav and returns to the home that he shares with his parents, she is shocked to discover they do not have a toilet. At 4:00 a.m. she is woken up by the women of the village, who invite her to accompany them out into the countryside to relieve themselves. She goes with them

Both the Mayans and Aztecs used cocoa beans as money.

but can't work up the nerve to do her business in that fashion. Afterward she returns home, and after arguing with her husband, she moves back in with her parents and tells Keshav that she will not return to live with him until he builds her a bathroom.

Keshav's father objects to building a bathroom in the front courtyard of their house. "How can we build a toilet in the same courtyard where we worship?" he says. When Keshav builds one anyway, his father and his friends start tearing the building down while Keshav is asleep, but he wakes up in time to stop them from destroying it entirely.

SPOILER ALERT: Though Jaya loves her husband, she resigns herself to the fact that he will never be able to build her a toilet, and files for divorce. Not long afterward, Keshav's mother slips and falls early one morning while on her way out to go relieve herself. Her injury prevents her from joining the other women on their morning ritual, which leaves Keshav's father with no choice but to assist his wife in using the damaged but still-functioning bathroom in the courtyard. The experience teaches him the value of having a bathroom in their home. He permits Keshav to repair the toilet, Jaya calls off her divorce, and everyone lives happily ever after.

FLUSHED WITH SUCCESS: *Toilet: A Love Story* wasn't exactly a darling with the critics. One reviewer wrote that "Akshay Kumar's film stinks to high heaven." But Indian filmgoers loved it. It grossed more than $33 million, blockbuster numbers for a Bollywood film. And now that Indian audiences have shown that they are receptive to films that deal with difficult topics, films tackling other sensitive issues, such as menstrual hygiene and erectile dysfunction, are now in the works. (Films dealing with politics are still taboo.)

> **One reviewer wrote that "Akshay Kumar's film stinks to high heaven."**

For Akshay Kumar, one of Bollywood's biggest stars and a celebrity ambassador for the Indian government's Clean India campaign to build 45 million new public toilets by 2020, the impressive box office receipts are beside the point. "I don't know how many people will watch the film eventually," he told the *Los Angeles Times* in 2017, "but even if five percent helped build toilets, I will feel my film is successful."

* * *

"It is far more impressive when others discover your good qualities without your help."
—Judith Martin

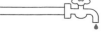

Studies show: The later it gets, the weirder your dreams get.

GONE COASTAL

In England, it's a common tradition for people to name their houses. We do it in the United States too, but usually only with beach homes. Here are some of the funniest ones we found.

Latitude Adjustment	Fantasea	Sea Renity
Sol Mate	Anchors Away	2 If By Sea
Once Upon a Tide	Gimme A Break	Sunny Daze
At Last	Baydream Believer	Sunnyside Up
Victoria's Sea-Cret	Surf 'N Sound	Vitamin Sea
The Reel World	Dock Holiday	Sea Forever
Sandy Bottoms	Dune Our Thing	Deja Blue
Sea-Esta	Fiddler on the Reef	Feeling Tip-Sea
Gone Coastal	Bay Hoovs Us	Hide 'N Sea
Looney Dunes	Hip Nautic	Good Times & Tan Lines
What's Up Dock	Seanior	A Wave From it All
Shore Thing	Decks 2 Sea	Wait 'n Sea
Waite 'n Sea	Hook Wine & Sinker	Bikini Bottom
Seas the Day	Seal La Vie	Bikinis & Martinis
Family Tides	Shore Fun	Just For The Halibut
After Dune Delight	Seabatical	Porpoise of Life
Beachy Keen	Seaclusion	Shore to Please
All Decked Out	Slo-N-EZ	Baywatch
Sand Castle	Beach Nuts	Something Fishy

Think before you ink: 1 in 7 people with a tattoo regret the tattoo.

A BAKER TO REMEMBER

One of the most unusual true-life stories to come out of the Titanic *disaster
is one that barely made it into James Cameron's 1997 blockbuster
film: the fascinating story of the ship's head baker.*

RUDE AWAKENING

When the *Titanic* struck the iceberg at 11:40 p.m. on the night of April 14, 1912,
Charles Joughin, 33, was resting in his bunk in his cabin on E Deck, amidships on the
port side (the left side) of the ship. Like most people on board, Joughin had no idea
that the *Titanic* was doomed. It wasn't until 12:05 a.m., when Captain Edward Smith
ordered the lifeboats uncovered and the passengers were instructed to head to the Boat
Deck, that Joughin realized something was seriously wrong.

When the order to "provision boats," or fill them with food, reached him, Joughin
instructed the 13 bakers who worked under him to grab as much bread as they could
from the kitchens and deliver it to the lifeboats. After seeing that this had been done, "I
went down to my room for a drink," he told the British government inquiry investigating
the sinking of the *Titanic*. For members of the crew, drinking alcohol was forbidden, but
Joughin had a bottle of whiskey hidden in his room. Why let it go to waste?

READY OR NOT

At about 12:30 a.m., Joughin finished drinking and went up to the Boat Deck, where
women and children were being loaded into the lifeboats. He was assigned to Lifeboat
10 on the port side aft, or to the rear of the ship, so that's where he went. To prevent
panic, the passengers had not been told that the ship was sinking, or that there were
only enough lifeboats for about half of the approximately 2,200 people on board.
Many of the women and children did not understand the urgency of the situation
and, understandably, were reluctant to leave the safety of the "unsinkable" *Titanic*
and climb into the lifeboats to be lowered down the side of the ship into the sea. The
fact that they were being ordered to do so without their men coming along with them
made them even more resistant.

When persuasion no longer worked, Joughin and other crewmembers resorted to
force, as he testified to the British inquiry:

> We got [Lifeboat 10] about half full, and then we had difficulty in finding ladies
> for it. They ran away from the boat and said they were safer where they were...I
> myself and three or four other chaps went on the next deck and forcibly
> brought up women and children...We threw them in...Eventually it was filled—
> pretty well filled anyway.

Don't hold your breath: It's possible to inflate a balloon with your ear.

Joughin was assigned to be the captain of Lifeboat 10. But he was a baker, not a sailor, and when he saw that three members of the crew were already in the boat, he gave up his spot and remained aboard the *Titanic*. "It would have set a bad example if I had jumped into the boat. None of the men felt inclined to get into the boat," he testified.

JUST A DROP

By now it was about 1:20 a.m., and the *Titanic* had only an hour left. Joughin made another trip down to his cabin and drank some more whisky. He initially claimed he had just "a drop of liqueur," but under further questioning he admitted to drinking "a tumbler, half-full" of "spirits"—whisky. Half a tumbler may have been as much as a fifth of whisky or more; added to what he'd had to drink earlier, it was probably enough to get him good and drunk.

Joughin remained in his cabin for about 25 minutes, until the seawater flooding into his cabin was up to his ankles. No word on whether the alcohol in his system had anything to do with it, but Joughin didn't understand where the water had come from, and he wasn't particularly concerned about it, either. "If it had been higher I should have thought something about it, but under the circumstances I thought it might have been a pipe burst," he testified.

THE CHAIR MAN

At about 1:45 a.m., Joughin stumbled out of his cabin and made his way back up to the Boat Deck. There he saw that all of the lifeboats (except for the collapsible boats) were down and away. So he headed down to the promenade on B Deck, and began throwing deck chairs overboard so that people in the water could use them as flotation devices.

Joughin estimated that he threw about 50 deck chairs overboard, which wore him out and made him thirsty. So he made his way to the pantry on the starboard side of A Deck and got a drink of water. There he heard a crash "as if something had buckled... as if the iron was parting," followed by the sound of people on the Boat Deck above him rushing toward the rear, or stern, of the ship. The crashing noise he heard may have been the sound of the *Titanic* breaking in half at the middle, separating the stern from the bow.

His thirst quenched, Joughin went up to the Boat Deck and followed the crowd to the stern of the ship. He made it as far as the Well Deck when the *Titanic* suddenly started listing toward the port side, knocking everyone over—everyone, that is, except Joughin. He kept his balance, even as the list became so great that the *Titanic* was practically laying on its port side, with the stern rising high into the air. No longer able to stand on the deck, Joughin clambered over the side of the ship onto the hull. Holding onto the ship's rail, he climbed upward along the hull to the stern of the ship, which had risen 150 feet out of the water and was now nearly vertical.

Rapper Tupac Shakur died in 1996 and was cremated.
His friends claim they smoked his cremains....

FINAL DESCENT

There, standing at the highest point on the *Titanic*'s stern like a man on a mountaintop, Joughin had just enough time to tighten the straps on his life preserver and check his watch—it was 2:15 a.m.—before the ship began its final descent into the sea. He rode the stern all the way down, as if it were a slow-moving elevator, then simply stepped off into the water as the *Titanic* slipped gently beneath the waves. "I do not believe my head went under the water at all. It may have been wetted, but no more," he testified at the inquiry.

> He rode the stern all the way down, as if it were a slow-moving elevator.

Though a precise count is not possible due to discrepancies on the passenger list, only about 700 of the 2,200 passengers and crew aboard the *Titanic* made it into the lifeboats before the ship went down. The rest, some 1,500 people, were now floating in the icy waters of the North Atlantic.

It's estimated that the temperature of the water that night was 28°F. The sudden shock of immersion in water that cold—the *Titanic*'s second officer, Charles Lightoller, described the sensation as like being stabbed by "a thousand knives"—kills some people in as little as a minute or two. Nearly everyone dies from hypothermia within 30 minutes, as their core body temperature drops so low (below 80°F) that their heart begins to beat irregularly, causing blood flow to slow or stop altogether, resulting in death. That is precisely what happened to the people in the water: with the exception of the dozen or so people who were pulled into lifeboats, nearly everyone in the water was dead within 30 minutes. *Nearly* everyone, but not Charles Joughin.

IRON MAN

After Joughin went into the water, he was unable to see any lifeboats nearby, so he started paddling around in no particular direction, just trying to keep afloat. It was "no trick at all," he later told Walter Lord, author of *A Night to Remember*, a best-selling account of the *Titanic* disaster published in 1955.

Joughin, who seemed unaffected by the cold, paddled from 2:20 a.m. until the first light of dawn, sometime around 4:00 a.m., when he saw what looked like a large piece of floating wreckage in the distance and swam toward it. The "wreckage" turned out to be Collapsible Boat B, which was overturned. Some 30 survivors were standing on it in two columns, swaying back and forth to counteract the rocking motion of the waves and keep the boat level. The lifeboat, which had a wooden floor and canvas sides, was submerged and slowly sinking under the weight of so many people. The water was up to their knees already, and there was no room for Joughin to climb aboard. So he paddled around to the other side, where a cook named Isaac Maynard recognized Joughin and held his hand to keep him from drifting away.

Joughin floated alongside Collapsible Boat B for about half an hour until Lifeboat 12 floated into view. When it came within 50 yards, someone on it yelled that they had room for ten more people. On hearing this, Joughin let go of Maynard's hand and *swam* the 50 yards to Lifeboat 12, this after floating in the icy water for nearly two and a half hours—water so cold that it had killed 1,500 other people in minutes.

Maybe the alcohol was finally starting to wear off, or maybe Joughin had just gone numb after so much time in the water, but it wasn't until he was pulled into the lifeboat that he really felt a chill. "I felt colder...after I got in the lifeboat," he told the British inquiry.

Investigators looking into the *Titanic* sinking wondered if drunkenness was what kept Joughin alive.

ALL ABOARD

Meanwhile, the RMS *Carpathia* had been steaming toward the *Titanic*'s last known position since picking up its distress signals shortly after midnight. It arrived in the area at about 4:00 a.m. and began picking up survivors, who were scattered over a wide area in 19 different lifeboats. (By now everyone standing on Collapsible Boat B had been transferred to Lifeboat 12 or Lifeboat 4.) Joughin and the others aboard Lifeboat 12 were the last to be picked up; they were taken aboard the *Carpathia* at about 8:15 a.m. By then his feet were so swollen that he had to climb the ladder up the side of the *Carpathia*'s hull on his knees.

Even in 1912, the investigators looking into the *Titanic* sinking wondered if drunkenness was what kept Joughin alive. "My suggestion is...I think his getting a drink had a lot to do with saving his life," an examiner named Mr. Cotter stated during the inquiry.

Mr. Cotter may have been right: ordinarily, alcohol increases the rate that a person succumbs to hypothermia, because it causes blood vessels to dilate, allowing warm blood to flow away from the vital organs where the heat is needed most. This can cause a person's body temperature to drop more quickly, speeding death. But that's in cold air. In cold water, the shock of sudden immersion may cause the blood vessels to constrict sharply, overwhelming the dilation effect of the alcohol and keeping body heat near the vital organs, prolonging life.

JUST RELAX

Add to that the fact that alcohol is a depressant that slows the activity of the central nervous system, and it's possible that the whisky may have prevented Joughin's body from overreacting to the physical stress of sudden immersion in icy-cold water. Two common responses to such immersion are involuntary gasping and hyperventilation, which can cause a person to inhale water and drown. Joughin didn't experience either of these reactions, perhaps because the alcohol had depressed his central nervous system.

9,000 years ago, an ear of corn was about one-tenth the size it is today.

Being drunk may have also made it harder for Joughin to feel the cold, while also giving him "liquid courage." Thrashing around the water in a panic can speed the rate at which heat leaves the body, but Joughin didn't panic; he paddled calmly for more than two hours until he was finally pulled into Lifeboat 12.

(If Joughin *was* saved by drunkenness, he's got lots of company. In one 2012 study of shooting and stabbing patients admitted to Illinois trauma centers, researchers found that the likelihood of a patient surviving their injuries was directly proportional to the level of alcohol in their bloodstream. The drunkest patients were nearly 50 percent more likely to survive their injuries than patients who were sober when they were shot or stabbed.)

BACK TO WORK

Charles Joughin survived the sinking of the *Titanic* with little to no lasting effect on his health, either physical or psychological. And he wasn't fired from the White Star Line, even though drinking alcohol aboard the *Titanic* was a fireable offense. He continued working on ships until his retirement in 1944. According to his obituary, he was aboard the SS *Oregon* when it sank, but at least three ships by that name sank during Joughin's career, and it's not clear which one he was on (or how much he drank). He lived just long enough to be interviewed by Walter Lord for *A Night to Remember*, then passed away the following year at the age of 78.

The next time you watch James Cameron's 1997 film *Titanic*, look for the scene near the end where Rose (Kate Winslet) and Jack (Leonardo DiCaprio) are holding onto the stern rail just before the ship goes down. Rose looks over at a man with a mustache who's dressed all in white, and he looks back at her. That's Joughin, played by Liam Tuohy. Just as in real life, he rides the *Titanic* all the way into the water.

Joughin also appears in another scene three minutes earlier, again at the stern rail, this time just after the stern has risen up out of the water. In this scene he pulls a flask out of his pocket and takes a big swig. Other than a few other scenes where he's in the panicked crowd as it surges toward the stern, that's all you see of him. If you want to see more, have a look at the 1958 film *A Night to Remember*, based on Lord's book. That film is considered a more accurate version of events, and in it Joughin gets a lot more screen time. You even get to see him in his cabin, enjoying his bottle of whisky.

For another story related to the Titanic *that's mostly forgotten today,*
paddle over to "Sunk by the Titanic*" on page 495.*

* * *

Random Fact: More time elapsed between when Stegosaurus and Tyrannosaurus rex lived than when Tyrannosaurus rex died out and human beings came along.

First European colony in America: San Miguel de Gualdape, near Georgetown, SC.
It failed after three months (1526).

WEIRD DEATHS

When you gotta go, you gotta go…even if it's a really, really strange way to go.

DEATH BY MAGNETS

In 2018 Rajesh Maru, 32, went to Nair Hospital in Mumbai, India, and died there…but not the way people usually die at a hospital, like from an illness or a traffic accident. No, Maru was visiting a relative who was at the hospital for an MRI scan, and a hospital employee asked him to bring the relation's oxygen tank into the MRI room. That's when the MRI machine's powerful magnetic field pulled in the metal oxygen tank along with Maru, who was holding it. His hand got pinned between the MRI machine and the oxygen cylinder, opening its valve. Maru breathed in a fatally high dose of oxygen and died instantly of a collapsed lung.

DEATH BY ATTACK FISH

In 2016 a Tanzanian fisherman named Robert Mwaijega was doing what he'd done hundreds of times before: standing on the riverside, fishing for a native species known locally as *perege*. Mwaijega and his friends had caught several, placing them into a plastic basin and letting them flop around until they died. One small fish flopped extremely hard, sending it high up into the air, and then down, right into Mwaijega's mouth. From there it wiggled down the man's throat and into his chest, where it became lodged, cutting off Mwaijega's air flow. He died at a hospital before doctors could surgically remove the fish.

DEATH BY ESCALATOR

Xiang Liujuan was shopping at a mall with her two-year-old son in the Chinese province of Hubei one day in 2015. She was riding an ascending escalator when the paneling that covered the landing area at the top of the machine suddenly broke away, exposing the grinding machinery beneath. There was no way Xiang could get off the escalator, but she thought fast and tossed her toddler to a mall employee…as she was sucked into the escalator's workings. Evidently, a maintenance crew had recently worked on the escalator but hadn't secured the floor plate properly.

DEATH BY WHIPPED CREAM

Rebecca Burger was a 33-year-old French lifestyle blogger who demonstrated the results of her exercise and diet tips as an online model—her Instagram account had more than 160,000 followers by early 2017. That's when Burger died. Cause of death:

Workers at Sweden's Epicenter Co. can be implanted with microchips that open doors and buy drinks at the company store.

a whipped-cream dispenser. Burger was using her Ard'Time *siphon de cuisine* when a nitrous oxide capsule exploded, flew out of the device, and struck her in the chest so hard that she went into cardiac arrest and died the next day.

DEATH BY DEAD SNAKE

Two things you might not have known about cobras:

1) People eat them. Cobra flesh soup is a traditional dish in some Asian countries, particularly China.

2) Like most snakes, a cobra can bite and spread its venom even after it has been dead for as long as an hour.

Peng Fan, a chef in Foshan, China, definitely didn't know fact #2. In 2014 he was working in a restaurant chopping up an Indochinese spitting cobra for soup, and had set its head aside. About 20 minutes later, he grabbed the head to throw it in the garbage…and it bit him. Diners heard screams coming from the kitchen as Peng Fan died from the fast-acting venom.

* * *

6 JOKES THAT MIGHT GET YOU FIRED

Q: How is a workplace like a septic tank?
A: The biggest lumps rise to the top.

Q: Why's it so hard to work at McDonald's?
A: Because the boss is a clown.

Q: What's the difference between a boss and the pope?
A: The pope only wants you to kiss his ring.

Q: How many bosses does it take to change a lightbulb?
A: Why don't you think about it, and we'll circle around later with an action plan at tomorrow's meeting?

Q: Why is Christmas like a day at work?
A: You do all the work and some guy in a suit takes all the credit.

Q: What do a boss and a bottle of beer have in common?
A: Both are empty from the neck up.

Pointed up, a horseshoe over your door supposedly catches luck.
Pointed down, it pours luck on those who enter.

MOUTHING OFF

CELEBRITY ADVICE?

As the existential philosopher Eddie Murphy once said, "The advice I would give to someone is to not take anyone's advice."

"Talk to your children, at least once a week. If you've got time, do it two or three times a week."

—Will Ferrell

"IF YOU WANT TO BE A ROCK STAR, LOOK OUT THE WINDOW, STARE AT THE CLOUDS, AND DO LOUD FARTS."

—Liam Gallagher, to a group of schoolkids

"It detoxes you, and it's good for your skin."

—Jessica Simpson, on drinking cow urine

"You get clean kitty litter, mix it up with hot water, apply it for 10 minutes, and your face will be as smooth as a baby's butt."

—Snooki

"It's okay to have beliefs, just don't believe in them."

—Guy Ritchie

"We're human beings and the sun is the sun—how can it be bad for you? I don't think anything that's natural can be bad for you."

—Gwyneth Paltrow

"I think the more positive approach you have to smoking, the less harmful it is."

—Sienna Miller

"You don't want to show it all off on the first date, you know? Dress fancy, but go to McDonald's. Her world will be so rocked."

—Adam Levine

"Parenting Tip: If your child is crying, hold it close and whisper, 'You don't have a clue what horrors this world holds.'"

—Rob Delaney

RUN, GOBI, RUN!

*Once an animal lover forms a bond with a critter, they'll do almost
anything for it. Don't believe it? Check out this unlikely story
of a man and his furry little friend.*

ON YOUR MARK

In March 2016, Dion Leonard, a 41-year-old ultramarathon runner from Edinburgh,
Scotland, flew to western China to participate in a long-distance race known as
the Gobi March. It is one of four annual endurance races set in the world's most
inhospitable locations—the Gobi Desert of China, the Sahara Desert of North Africa,
the Atacama Desert of South America, and the "desert" of Antarctica, parts of which
are so dry that they receive less than an inch of snow a year.

The Gobi March is divided into six daylong stages, each of which is so grueling
that only the most serious long-distance runners make their way to this remote, barren
part of western China to compete in it. The starting line of the 2016 race was located
near a village outside of Urumqi, the capital of Xinjiang Province, and as the runners
and race officials gathered before the race, a pack of stray dogs showed up to see what
the fuss was about and to scrounge for food.

GET SET...GO!

When the race started, a number of the dogs chased after the runners. Usually in races
like this, the dogs lose interest after a short distance and go back to wherever they
came from. And that was the case this day, with one exception: a light brown female
dog, apparently a terrier mix of some kind and only a year or two old, ran the entire
course. She kept pace with the runners all day, and when the first leg of the race was
over she followed them into camp. She sat with the runners into the evening, sharing
their dinner, and remained in the camp after they went to bed.

The next morning, the little dog was still there, and ready to run again. And her
interest had focused on a particular runner: Dion Leonard. To this day, Leonard is not
sure why she chose him, because he didn't give her any more attention than the other
runners did. Maybe the dog was attracted to the gaiters that he wore over his running
shoes to keep out the dust, or perhaps she liked the way he smelled. Whatever the
case, as he stood near the starting line waiting for the race to begin, the dog ran up to
him. Then when the race started, she chased after him, nipping playfully at his gaiters
some of the time, and running ahead or falling back at other times, but never straying
too far. Just as she had the day before, the little dog ran the entire 23-mile leg of the
race, which included a climb of more than 20,000 feet into the Tian Shan mountains

The 1911 Reeves OctoAuto was 20 feet long with eight wheels.
It flopped. So did a six-wheeled version.

before dropping down into the desert. That night, Leonard said, "she came into camp, she followed me straight into my tent, laid down next to me and that was that—a bond had been developed." From then on the two were inseparable. The dog needed a name, so Leonard named her after the desert they were running through: Gobi.

TAKING A BREAK

The following morning Gobi was ready to go again. Just as she had before, she ran the entire course with the runners, except for the parts of the course where the runners had to wade across rivers in waist-deep water. On those stretches, Leonard carried her across the water. But three days of long-distance running had taken their toll: Gobi was limping by the time she crossed the finish line, and shortly after crossing it, she barfed. The race doctors found nothing seriously wrong with her, but it was clear that she needed a rest. Leonard decided she would sit out the next two stages of the race, when the daytime temperature was expected to climb as high as 125°F. On these days Gobi hitched a ride to the end of the course in a race officials' vehicle and was there, tail wagging, to greet Leonard as he crossed the finish line.

Three days later, Gobi joined Leonard again as he ran the sixth and final stretch of the 155-mile race; Leonard estimates that the pup ran about 80 miles of it over the four days that she'd been allowed to run. Leonard came in second overall in the Gobi March. By the time the race was over, Gobi had become its unofficial mascot, and when she and Leonard crossed the finish line, race officials had a surprise for her: after they placed the silver second-place medal around Leonard's neck, they produced an identical medal and placed it around Gobi's neck.

GRAND PRIZE

The biggest prize was yet to come. There was little doubt that Gobi was a stray, and Leonard was distressed at the thought of leaving the little dog to fend for herself after he returned home to Scotland. "As soon as I got back to the hotel after the race, I rang my wife and said to her, 'Do you think our cat will mind if I bring Gobi home?' "

It's not easy bringing stray dogs into the United Kingdom: cases of rabies are so rare on the British Isles that dogs and cats are not vaccinated against the disease, which leaves them vulnerable if rabies ever does appear. To prevent this from happening, the British government places very strict restrictions on bringing animals into the country. For Gobi, this meant months of quarantine in China under veterinary supervision to ensure that the dog was healthy. It also meant at least £5,000 ($6,300) in expenses for Leonard, plus mountains of paperwork that would have to be completed before Gobi would be allowed to enter the UK. He made arrangements to board Gobi in China with a race official who had taken a liking to the dog, and then he flew home to begin the arduous task of bringing his new friend to live with him in Scotland.

Good news, bro! A fist-bump spreads one-twentieth the bacteria that a handshake does.

A few days later, Gobi's keeper called Leonard with bad news: Gobi was gone. She'd slipped out a door that had been left ajar, and had disappeared into the streets of Urumqi, which is home to three million people. There's a good chance that she'd run off in search of Leonard.

Leonard flew to Urumqi the very next day and began to search for Gobi. He used the Chinese equivalents of Facebook, Twitter, and other social media sites to circulate information and photos of Gobi to the citizens of Urumqi and to recruit volunteers to help in the search. Then, working from 6:00 a.m. until midnight, he and the volunteers canvased the city, distributing flyers, visiting dog shelters, public parks, and other places they thought Gobi might have gone.

Leonard admits now that he didn't hold out much hope of ever finding Gobi. The city was too big, Gobi was too small, and time was too short—he only had about a week to look for the dog before he would have to return to the UK. But he felt he had to try.

DOG-LE-GANGERS

After several days of searching, Leonard and his volunteers found no trace of Gobi. They did receive numerous calls from people who'd seen dogs that looked like Gobi, but none of them were her. Then on about the fifth day of the search, they received a call from a man who'd seen one of the "missing dog" flyers, and while he and his son were walking their own dog in a park in Urumqi, they found a stray dog that kind of looked like Gobi. The man brought the dog home with him and texted a photo to Leonard. The picture wasn't great: it had been taken in dim light and Leonard didn't think the dog looked much like Gobi. But he couldn't tell for sure, so he drove out to the man's house to see for himself. He had little hope that it was Gobi, and with only a day or two left before he had to return to the UK, he was preparing for the worst.

When Leonard arrived at the man's house, he never got a chance to look the dog over to see if it was Gobi, because "Gobi spotted me as soon as I walked in," he recounted in the *Washington Post*. "Literally, she was running up my leg and jumping all over me and squealing with delight. It was just mind-blowing to think that we had found her."

HOME RUN

Gobi had a nasty gash on her head and she walked with a limp, but after a trip to a veterinarian she was on the mend. The rest of her quarantine period, which she spent at a kennel in Beijing, passed without incident. When the four months were up, Leonard flew out to Beijing and brought her home. "The whole journey took 41 hours and throughout the whole thing it was like it was us back at the race," Leonard told the BBC in January 2017. "I kept saying to her, 'Just believe in me, we're going to have a great life when we get to Edinburgh.' And I'm looking forward to sharing that with her."

Botanist and "plant wizard" Luther Burbank (1849–1926) developed white blackberries.

BIG SCREEN 👍
LITTLE SCREEN 👎

*Some movies, such as M*A*S*H, Buffy the Vampire Slayer,
and Fargo, have been successfully adapted into long-running
TV series. Others, like these, didn't fare as well.*

WORKING GIRL

In the 1988 movie version of *Working Girl*, Melanie Griffith played Tess McGill, a woman with a "head for business and a bod for sin." The satire of 1980s corporate culture earned Griffith an Oscar nomination, and in 1990 NBC execs felt it could easily be adapted into a workplace sitcom. Even though Griffith wouldn't reprise her role as McGill, the network went ahead with the series, even after they couldn't get Nancy McKeon from *The Facts of Life* to star. Instead, producers cast Sandra Bullock in one of her first major roles. *Working Girl* was canceled after just eight episodes.

PARENTHOOD

The bittersweet 1989 comedy film starring Steve Martin, Keanu Reeves, Joaquin Phoenix, and others as members of a multigenerational family enduring the trials and tribulations of life was successfully adapted into a prime-time soap opera that ran on NBC from 2010 to 2015. But that was NBC's second attempt. Twenty years earlier, the network had tried to turn it into a sitcom starring Ed Begley Jr. in the Martin role, and David Arquette and Leonardo DiCaprio in the Reeves and Phoenix roles. The show had good writers—Lowell Ganz and Babaloo Mandel (who'd written the movie), and Joss Whedon—and it earned critical raves, with *USA Today* and the *New York Post* calling it the best movie-to-TV adaptation since M*A*S*H. NBC executives were so excited that they almost ran it two nights a week. Viewers apparently didn't read the reviews. Low ratings doomed *Parenthood* to just 12 episodes.

A LEAGUE OF THEIR OWN

A *League of Their Own* entertained and educated moviegoers in the summer of 1992. It told the little-known story of the World War II–era All-American Girls Professional Baseball League, starring Oscar winner Geena Davis, Madonna, Rosie O'Donnell, and Tom Hanks as the team's drunkard coach who whined that there was "no crying in baseball." CBS had a TV version ready for the start of baseball season in the spring of 1993. But despite looking just like the movie—thanks to the involvement of the film's

During his career with the Who, Pete Townshend smashed 136 guitars.

director, Penny Marshall—the cast of mostly unknown actors didn't bring in much of an audience. (They also ran out of ideas pretty quickly—one of the first episodes was about a wacky chimp that becomes the baseball team's mascot.) *League* was benched after five episodes.

FERRIS BUELLER

When NBC brought the classic Matthew Broderick teen movie *Ferris Bueller's Day Off* to TV in 1990, it came with the complicated premise that the series was actually about the "real life" people that the 1986 movie had been about—clever, smarmy Chicago teen Ferris Bueller and his family. It wasn't a reality show, of course, but a comedy shot like a documentary, with characters addressing the camera (sort of like *Modern Family* or *The Office*). Beyond that set-up, the show was a standard sitcom about a cool teenager (Charlie Schlatter) and his antagonistic sister, Jeannie (portrayed in the movie by Jennifer Grey; future superstar Jennifer Aniston got the part on TV, one of her first roles). *Ferris Bueller* the show was not as well-received as *Ferris Bueller* the movie and lasted just 13 episodes.

DELTA HOUSE

Nationals Lampoon's Animal House was a hugely popular movie in 1978. Not only did it make a movie star out of *Saturday Night Live* cast member John Belushi, it also turned the humor magazine *National Lampoon* into a brand name for films. But more important for Hollywood, *Animal House* cost $3 million to make, and took in over $141 million at the box office—more than half a billion in 2018 dollars. All three TV networks promptly came to the conclusion that a ribald comedy set in a college fraternity would make a fine premise for a weekly sitcom. ABC and *National Lampoon* collaborated on *Delta House*, which hit the air in January 1979. Stephen Furst (Flounder), Bruce McGill (D-Day), and John Vernon (Dean Wormer) all reprised their movie roles, while Josh Mostel got the difficult job of replacing John Belushi, portraying "Blotto," the brother of Belushi's character, "Bluto." A few weeks later, NBC and CBS debuted *Animal House* knockoffs: *Brothers and Sisters* and *Co-Ed Fever*, respectively. Audiences didn't like any of them. *Delta House* and *Brothers and Sisters* lasted half a season; *Co-Ed Fever* was canceled after a single airing.

* * *

RANDOM ORIGIN: THE SPIKED DOG COLLAR

Adding sharp spikes to a dog collar goes all the way back to Ancient Greece.
Why spikes? To protect the dog from attacks by wolves…
which went straight for the neck first.

An adult male giraffe weighs about as much as a Toyota Prius (3,000 pounds).

CLASSROOM ORIGINS

Close your eyes and think back on your school days. Picture that chalkboard and the hand-cranked pencil sharpener, and that soft pink eraser in your desk. Here's where all that stuff came from.

PENCIL SHARPENER

What's the old-fashioned way to sharpen a pencil? Whittling away at the tip with a knife until it was fine. That was time-consuming, inexact, and, for children, potentially dangerous. In 1828 a French mathematician named Bernard Lassimone received a patent for the *taille-crayon*—literally, "pencil cutter." A system of tiny metal files was ensconced in a block of wood, a pencil was inserted, and, as the pencil was slowly turned, the files whittled away at the pencil tip's sides. It was safer than a knife, but apparently not much faster or cleaner. Inventors in Europe and North America kept trying to improve on Lassimone's design until the 1840s when French inventor Therry des Estwaux came up with the idea to make the "pencil insertion chamber" conical and lined with blades—that way, when a pencil went in and was turned, every side was shaved down equally and all at the same time.

PINK ERASERS

The Faber-Castell Company had been making pencils in Bavaria since the 1760s. Fourth-generation operator John Eberhard Faber took over in the 1850s and moved the company to Greenpoint, Brooklyn, where he opened America's first pencil factory in 1861. Soon after, the company secured a contract to make a line of pencils to be sold at Woolworth department stores. Marketed under the name Pearl Pencil, they were topped with erasers that combined rubber and pink pumice—volcanic ash imported from Italy. The erasers worked so well that Faber started making stand-alone erasers (for all those mistake-prone kids who wore out their pencil erasers before they wore out their pencils).

BLACKBOARD

There's archaeological evidence that students used something akin to individual blackboards as far back as ancient Babylonia. They didn't have paper and pencils (or pens), so they took notes and wrote lessons on smooth clay tablets with a clay stylus. They'd erase the tablets by wiping them down with water, or writing could be made permanent with a simple bake in a kiln. Over the centuries and around the world, by the 18th century, clay tablets had evolved into "slates" in the West—tablet-sized

First "smart" appliance: a Carnegie Mellon University Coke machine that could be checked...

writing surfaces made out of either actual slate or wood painted with slick, washable paint. Pro: They were cheap and reusable. Con: Teachers had no way to demonstrate a group lesson—they had to go from student to student to show them, for example, a math problem. In 1801 James Pillans, the headmaster of Old High School in Edinburgh, Scotland, came up with a solution: He hung a very large piece of slate on the wall at the front of his classroom and wrote on it with a piece of chalk. The idea spread through Europe and then to the United States, where black slate was especially cheap and plentiful thanks to slate mining operations across the Eastern seaboard. The blackboard remained mostly unchanged until the 1960s, when a green-colored board—a steel plate coated with green porcelain enamel paint—was introduced. The new green boards were easier to read than blackboards from the back of a classroom, and chalk dust erased more efficiently. (But they were still called blackboards.)

BLACKBOARD ERASER

All those blackboards had to be wiped clean with something. At one time, teachers used an old damp rag. But there were some downsides to that method: 1) it took the board a long time to dry, 2) it was messy, and 3) it left behind a lot of chalk dust. In the early 1860s, John Hammett, the owner of a Rhode Island school supply store that sold mostly slates and chalk, figured out a better way. A piece of cheap, dry felt was much more efficient than a wet rag. He commissioned an easy-to-handle, felt-wrapped item, and the first eraser that his team came up with is pretty much unchanged today.

AN APPLE FOR THE TEACHER

The origin of this custom is not definitively known, but here's one reasonable theory: As settlers laid down roots in the American Midwest in mid-1800s, they opened small, one-room schoolhouses to teach the children. It was the responsibility of the community to find a teacher—almost always a young unmarried woman. And because they couldn't afford to pay much, if anything at all, the community took care of the teacher's basic needs as best they could. Someone might donate a home, for example, while parents of other kids might help keep her fed. An apple for a teacher was an outgrowth of that—a sweet treat for a job well done (in lieu of salary). But why apples and not, say, peaches or corn? Kids may well have brought those, too, later in the year. Apples may be the iconic gift for teachers because the beginning of the school year coincides with peak apple season in September.

*   *   *

"When life gives you lemons, squirt someone in the eye." —**Cathy Guisewite**

...via the Internet to see if it had any Cokes in it, and whether they were cold (1982).

WHAT WOULD *YOU* TAKE?

If a firestorm were sweeping toward your home and you had to get out fast, what would you take with you? The following responses—taken from Facebook posts and newspaper reports related to recent fires in California and Canada—are our favorite answers to the question "What random thing did you grab when you had to evacuate?"

"My black lab and my Tony Bennett tickets."—Tim N.

"Wife took my bear head off the wall. Nothing for me to wear, but got me bear head."—Rodney T.

"Grabbed all my crystals and tarot cards but forgot checkbook and underwear." —Beth S.

"I packed a bottle of ketchup but not one pair of pj's for my 4 year old! In my defense, he likes ketchup better than pj's anyways!"—Kayla M.

"My 22-year-old son grabbed his combat-ready light sabers and I grabbed a toothbrush that could be replaced the second I walked into my planned evacuation shelter (my dental office)." —Shana V.

"My Hawaiian shirt collection."—Peter S.

"The braided 28-inch ponytail I recently cut off and haven't donated yet."—LaDahn G.

"Processed cheese slices and snow pants (in May)."—Jennifer K.

"A basket of empty picture frames." —Shelly H.

"Half a blender and a watermelon." —Vanessa L.

"The keys to my son's car that we left parked in front of our house!"—Ginger G.

"My wife brought dog poop bags and we don't have a dog."—Greg B.

"A digital projector and a bottle of Fogbelt Del Norte IPA."—Justin R.

"A container of zip ties."—Kelley E.

"Forgot all toiletries but did manage to remember eyelashes and self-tanner...not my brightest moment."—Renee H.

"An antique potato peeler. I have two new ones that aren't worth anything. They just don't make things like the used to." —Dave J.

"I packed a doll I'd had since I was two and yogurt and one sock."—Rehta K.

"Bags of Flaming Hot Cheetos." —Angela B.-D.

"One of our laptop chargers. But not the laptop."—Nichole M.

"My daughter's Smile Safe ID card (in case kids go missing) from when she was 9. She's 21 now and lives in the northeast." —Denise L.

"Every key to every vehicle we ever owned. No socks, no underwear, no food but I have keys. And house and current vehicle I am driving are keyless entry." —Winston E.

"My husband has no underwear but he brought a pie plate!"—Danielle D.

The first "March Madness" NCAA basketball pool was at Jody's Club Forest Bar on Staten Island in 1977.

TOTALLY (YOU)TUBULAR

Stop watching cat videos on YouTube for a second and check out these amazing facts about the internet's most entertaining waste of time, YouTube.

▶ Founding Fathers: Three former employees of PayPal, Chad Hurley, Steve Chen, and Jawed Karim. When eBay bought PayPal, they used their bonuses to start YouTube in February 2005.

▶ The initial idea for what became YouTube: a video dating site called Tune In Hook Up.

▶ The founders got the idea to host videos because of two specific events in 2004: 1) Karim wanted to see footage of Janet Jackson's notorious "wardrobe malfunction" at the Super Bowl, but couldn't find it anywhere, and 2) Hurley and Chen wanted to send a short video of a dinner party by email, but couldn't because of attachment size restrictions.

▶ First YouTube video: "Me at the zoo" by a user named Jawed (a.k.a. co-founder Jawed Karim) in April 2005. It was 19 seconds long and it shows Karim at the San Diego Zoo talking about elephants.

▶ First YouTube comment: In 2005 Marco Cassé typed "LOL!!!!!!!" in response to a video called "Good Times!!!"

▶ You'll never watch them all. Every minute, about 100 hours of video are uploaded.

▶ Not counting people who watch but don't have accounts, there are a billion registered users on YouTube—a third of all internet users worldwide.

▶ The first video to amass a billion views on YouTube was the 2012 music video for "Gangnam Style," the worldwide smash hit by South Korean rapper Psy. View counters on YouTube only had six digits at the time, forcing an update to the code.

▶ Psy's record has long since been surpassed. In 2018 Puerto Rican singer Luis Fonsi hit number one in the United States with "Despacito." Within a year of its release, the video for the song hit 4.7 billion views.

▶ You can "like" or "dislike" videos on YouTube. Most disliked ever: the 2010 music video for "Baby" by Justin Bieber. As of March 2018, more than 8 million people have given it a thumbs-down.

One horsepower is defined as the amount of power needed to lift
550 pounds one foot (off the ground) in one second.

▶ Lots of music videos have scored a few billion views, but the most popular non-musical video is a 2012 episode of the Russian cartoon *Masha and the Bear*. It's been viewed by nearly three billion people.

▶ If you make YouTube videos and do pretty well at it—like get 10,000 subscribers—the company lets you use a production studio in Los Angeles to make your videos, free of charge.

▶ The most popular search engine on the internet is Google, but number two is YouTube. More people search for things on YouTube each day than they do on Bing, Yahoo!, and Ask put together.

▶ Just 18 months after YouTube went live, Google bought it for $1.65 billion.

▶ Soon after YouTube launched in 2005, a website called utube—the online home of the Universal Tube & Rollform Equipment Company of Perrysburg, Ohio—started getting millions of new visitors. Utube sued YouTube, on the grounds that the similar name was hurting their business. (The suit was dismissed and utube changed its domain name to utubeonline.com.)

▶ YouTube is available around the world; after the United States, the country that watches the most videos is Saudi Arabia. That nation—where Facebook Messenger is blocked—racks up 190 million views every day.

▶ YouTube's many user-generated "tutorial" videos are a great way to learn how to do something. The two most popular topics: how to kiss, and how to tie a tie.

▶ It's not just a waste of time, it's a waste of energy, too. A three-minute live-action YouTube video uses up about 30 megabytes of data, which requires about three AA batteries' worth of energy.

▶ Worldwide, humans spend about a billion hours every day watching YouTube videos.

▶ Ever had to watch a slideshow of somebody's vacation pictures? In 2011 a guy named Jonathan Harchick made a video slideshow out of his pictures of a vacation to Chile. It lasted 571 hours, 1 minute, and 41 seconds—over 23 days. It's the longest video ever uploaded to YouTube. (It's since been taken down, thankfully.)

First woman to die in the electric chair: Martha Place, for murdering her stepdaughter (NY, 1899).

PIRATES OF THE FRONT PORCH

Nearly 26 million Americans had a holiday package stolen from their doorstep or front porch by "porch pirates" in 2017. (Did you?) The number has been growing in recent years. Here's what some folks have been doing to fight back. Some are nice, and others…well, let's just say you might want to talk to a lawyer before following in their footsteps.

Nice Pirate Fighter: Jason Ennor of Castle Rock, Colorado

Fighting Back: Ennor is at home during the day when many of his neighbors are at work. Package theft had been a problem in his neighborhood, so in December 2016, Ennor let his neighbors know via social media that he was starting a one-man pick up and delivery service. Here's how it works: neighbors share their FedEx, UPS and U.S. Postal Service package tracking information with him, and as soon as he receives a text notifying him that a package has been delivered, he rushes out to collect it before porch pirates can steal it. Then when the neighbors return home, he delivers their packages in person. He charges $5 for the service. "At the moment, being Christmas, it's especially a focus," he told Denver's Channel 7 News. "Who wants to buy something and then have it not be there?"

Not-So-Nice Pirate Fighter: Angie Boliek of Hillsboro, Oregon

Revenge! It's a Christmas tradition in the Boliek household to photograph all the kids in the new pajamas that Santa brings each year, but in 2017 someone stole the package containing the pajamas off her doorstep. She decided to get some payback. She stuffed an Amazon box with 15 of her four-month-old son's soiled diapers, along with a note reading "Enjoy this you thief!" (How disgusting were the boy's diapers? "Well, he's been sick the last week, so we'll just leave it at that.") She put the package on her doorstep on a Sunday morning. "It was gone by Monday afternoon," Boliek says. "The police thought it was hilarious…and awesome."

Nice Pirate Fighter: The Package Guard

Fighting Back: The Package Guard is a device that looks kind of like a frisbee and functions similar to a bathroom scale. You install it on your front porch where you want your packages to be delivered. A message reading "PLACE PACKAGE HERE" is printed on top, and when a package is set upon it, the weight triggers the device to alert you via e-mail, text, or the included app that the package has arrived. If anyone tries

Dr. Seuss's inspiration for the Grinch who stole Christmas: himself "on a bad day."

to lift your package off the Package Guard without entering the correct code into the smartphone app, the device gives off a shriek that's as noisy as a car alarm. Price: $79.

Not-So-Nice Pirate Fighter: Jaireme Barrow of Tacoma, Washington

Revenge! Barrow had so many packages stolen from his doorstep that he invested in a video surveillance system for his front door. All that got him was footage of several more people stealing his packages, but no arrests. In 2016 he rigged up a 12-gauge shotgun "blank" in a cardboard box that he leaves out on his doorstep. When porch pirates lift the box, they get a large BANG!…and Barrow gets hilarious footage of the terrified porch pirates running for their lives. He posts the videos on YouTube… and sells his "Blank Boxes" on his website for $50–$70, plus $4.99 for five extra shells.

Barrow swears his Blank Boxes are legal, but the Tacoma Police disagree. Who's right? The final verdict may have to wait for the outcome of a future lawsuit (assuming one is ever filed) brought by someone who gets injured while trying to steal Barrow's packages. Till then, he says he's having a blast…so to speak. "It's instant karma," he says. "Someone is trying to commit a crime, and you are able to get back at them instantly. It's a satisfaction I can't describe."

Nice Pirate Fighter: Terry Bohlan of Campbell, California

Fighting Back: After Bohlan's home security system recorded a porch pirate stealing packages from his doorstep, he reported the theft to the police department…and volunteered his own doorstep as a place where police could leave "bait" packages to catch porch pirates. The bait packages contain items, such as laptops, that are commonly shipped through the mail, plus a GPS tracking device that allows police to follow the thieves and arrest them. Now when porch pirates come to Bohlan's doorstep, instead of nabbing his belongings, *they* are nabbed by the police. (A similar program in Arcadia, California, has resulted in more than 100 arrests for theft.)

Not-So-Nice Pirate Fighter: Tom Mabe, a comedian in Louisville, Kentucky

Revenge! Why limit yourself to boxes filled with poop or exploding rounds when you can have both? After Mabe and his neighbor Bob had packages stolen from their front doorsteps, Mabe rigged up a box with "four-day-old poop," presumably (and hopefully) from a pet, and some kind of small explosive charge. He left the box out on his front doorstep. Four days later, his security camera recorded someone stealing the package and driving off in a car. They didn't get far: When the car reached the end of the block, the package, triggered by a 40-second timer, detonated inside the car, which came to a sudden stop. The poop-sprayed porch pirate quickly exited the car and appeared to vomit on the sidewalk.

New Year's Eve tradition for kids in the Philippines: jump up and down 12 times at midnight.

NAMING CANADA

*Here's how each of the Great White North's provinces and territories
got their names. (Well, all except for the Northwest Territories—
we assume you can figure that one out for yourself.)*

BRITISH COLUMBIA. When western Canada was under British rule, the large portion of the Pacific Northwest that surrounded (and was drained by) the Columbia River was called the Columbia District. By 1848 the area had been split into British and American control, and so Queen Victoria decreed that her portion be called British Columbia. (The rest was the Oregon Territory.) The Columbia River was named after the *Columbia Rediviva*, the first American ship to circle the globe and which was used to ship furs caught and processed in the region.

ALBERTA. Alberta broke apart from the Northwest Territories to become an official province in 1905, and took the name Alberta, after Victoria's fourth daughter, Princess Louise Caroline Alberta. The princess had other Canadian connections: She was married to the Marquess of Lorne, who served as Canada's governor general (a figurehead representative of the Crown) from 1878 to 1883.

PRINCE EDWARD ISLAND. Here's another person who got their name on something Canadian because of his relationship to Queen Victoria. Prince Edward (the Duke of Kent and Strathearn) was the fourth son of King George III, and father of Victoria. In 1763, after the Seven Years' War between England and France, England took control of what is now Nova Scotia, including the small island formerly known as St. John's Island. In 1799 the land was renamed Prince Edward Island in honor of the prince, who was stationed with an army regiment in Canada at the time.

MANITOBA. The native Ojibwa tribe called the waterways that feed into the province's massive lake (now known as Lake Manitoba) *manidoobaa*, which means "the straits of Manitou, the Great Spirit."

ONTARIO. This province also gets its name from its large, signature body of water. Lake Ontario (one of the five Great Lakes) comes from one of two words used by indigenous peoples. The Wyandot called the Great Lake *ontarí:io*, or "great lake." The Iroquois called it *skandario*, which means "beautiful water."

SASKATCHEWAN. The Cree called the Saskatchewan River *kisiskāciwani-sīpiy*, which means "swift flowing river." European settlers named the region after the river.

Sea otters sleep on their backs, floating in the water, in large "rafts" of 100 otters or more.

QUEBEC. The Algonquin once ruled the province, which they called *kébec*, or "where the river narrows." That referred specifically to the land surrounding what is now Quebec City. It's there that the St. Lawrence River narrows.

NEW BRUNSWICK. The maritime province was once part of Nova Scotia, but it was partitioned off in 1784—separating the French settlers on Nova Scotia from the English on New Brunswick. They named it New Brunswick, because there are a lot of places in England named "Brunswick." That's the anglicized spelling and pronunciation of Braunschweig, the northern German city from which King George III's family came.

YUKON. This territory in western Canada gets its name from the great Yukon River which flows through it. "Yukon" comes from the local Gwich'in tribe's name for the waterway, *chųų gąįį*, which translates to "pale water."

NEWFOUNDLAND AND LABRADOR. While typically referred to as just "Newfoundland," the full name of the eastern Canadian province encompasses both major land areas that comprise it: Newfoundland (an island) *and* Labrador (part of mainland Canada, adjacent to Newfoundland). While most of Canada has a lot of influence from English, Scottish, and French settlers, the name of this province remembers the Portuguese explorers who set foot there in the early 1500s. Portugal's Gaspar Corte-Real and Miguel Corte-Real (they were brothers) charted the area, which was named *Terra Nova*, or "New Land" in both Latin and Portuguese. Translated into English, roughly, that becomes "Newfoundland." The settlement of Labrador is named after another Portuguese explorer, 15th-century navigator João Fernandes Lavrador.

NOVA SCOTIA. The first Europeans to settle in the maritime island province were the French in the 1600s, who called it Acadia, after *arcadia*, an ancient Greek term for "idyllic land." The British conquered it in 1710 and French settlers slowly started to move out, with the remainder forced out in 1755. In the 1760s and 1770s, vast numbers of Scottish Highlanders were evicted from their homes and farms in the British Isles (their land was essentially stolen by governments) and settled en masse in what was soon named Nova Scotia, Latin for "New Scotland."

NUNAVUT. There's no such thing as "Eskimos." The indigenous people who live in Canada's deeply cold, Artic Circle–approaching territories are more accurately referred to as the Inuit. From their language (called Inuktitut) comes Nunavut, the name of Canada's newest "official territory"—it separated from the Northwest Territories in 1999. In Inuktitut, *nunavut* means "our land."

Two common ingredients in dust: human skin flakes and dust mite skeletons.

YOUR 1981 GROCERY LIST

Uncle John's family never throws anything away. (Hey, you never know what might make a good Bathroom Reader page!) He was recently helping his sister clean out her apartment and came across a Grand Union supermarket circular from 1981. (She actually had two copies.) So we used it to make this shopping list for a family of four. Times—and prices—sure have changed.

PRODUCE

Head of romaine lettuce (1)	39¢
Tomatoes (2 pounds at 39¢/pound)	78¢
Potatoes (5 pounds)	89¢
Onions (5 pounds at 39¢/pound)	$1.15
White grapefruit (bag of 5)	99¢
Carrots (1-pound bag)	49¢
Red Delicious apples (3-pound bag)	$1.19

DELI AND DAIRY

Butter (1 pound)	$1.99
Eggs (dozen)	90¢
Milk (gallon)	$2.25
Philadelphia Cream Cheese (8-ounce package)	69¢
Sliced ham (1-pound package)	$2.99
Bologna (1-pound package)	$1.39
Swiss cheese (1-pound package)	$1.59
Hot dogs (1 package)	$1.19
Oscar Mayer sliced bacon (1 pound package)	$1.89
Knockwurst (12-ounce package)	$1.29

FROZEN

Downyflake Waffles (12 count)	79¢
Frozen peas (1-pound package)	89¢
Frozen baked ziti (10-ounce package)	89¢
Orange juice concentrate (1)	$1.29

One of the sounds used to make the dinosaur noises in *Jurassic Park:* recordings of tortoises mating.

BAKERY

English muffins (8 count)	59¢
Bread (2 loaves)	98¢
Hot dog buns (1 package)	89¢

BUTCHER

Sirloin tip steak (2-pound package)	$5.18
Chuck for stew (3-pound package)	$5.97

HOUSEHOLD ITEMS

Charmin toilet paper (4 rolls)	89¢
Paper napkins (1 package)	79¢
Paper towels (3 rolls at 69¢ each)	$2.07
Kitty litter (1 bag)	$1.19
Joy dish detergent (1 bottle)	$1.69
Crest toothpaste (1 tube)	$1.29
Ziploc sandwich bags (1 package)	$1.45
Cat food (12-ounce bag)	$2.69

CANNED AND PACKAGED

Instant oatmeal (1 box of 8 packets)	$1.19
Maple syrup (1 bottle)	$1.89
Kellogg's Corn Flakes (18-ounce box)	$1.25
Ground coffee (1 pound)	$1.49
Instant cocoa (1 box of 8 packets)	69¢
Wishbone Italian dressing (1-pint bottle)	$1.39
Velveeta (1-pound box)	$1.99
Spaghetti (2 pounds at 59¢ each)	$1.18
Spaghetti sauce (2-pound jar)	$1.49
Rice-A-Roni (6-ounce box)	$1.29
Peas (17-ounce can)	59¢
Beans (16-ounce can)	39¢
Cookies (1 package)	89¢

TOTAL COST: $67.30

Chicago's Wrigley Field didn't get electric lights until 1988.

PRESIDENTS WHO PARTOOK

*American presidents are just like anyone else—some of
them drink a little…and some of them drink a lot.*

FRANKLIN PIERCE (1804–1869)

- Pierce, who took office in 1853, was one of the heaviest drinkers ever to occupy the White House. When he ran for president, his opponents derided him as "the hero of many a well-fought bottle."

- Pierce endured more than his fair share of tragedy in life and may have been seeking refuge in liquor. All three of his children died in childhood: Franklin Pierce Jr. died when he was just three days old in 1836, and four-year-old Frank Robert Pierce died from typhus in 1843. Benjamin "Benny" Pierce, 11, died two months before his father's inauguration in 1853 when the train he and his parents were riding in derailed and tumbled down an embankment. Both Franklin and his wife, Jane Appleton Pierce, watched their son die; neither ever got over it. Mrs. Pierce, who also suffered from tuberculosis, was so distraught that she did not attend her husband's inauguration, and was unable to fulfill her social duties as First Lady. She deferred to an aunt, Abby Kent-Means, who served as White House hostess while Mrs. Pierce hid upstairs in her room writing letters to her dead son.

BAD TIMING
- Pierce also held office at a difficult period in American history: the country was deeply split over the issue of slavery and sliding toward civil war, which was eight years away. Pierce was a pro-slavery Northerner, which pleased no one, giving him another reason to drink. By 1856 he was so unpopular that he felt compelled to hire a full-time bodyguard, the first president to have one.

- After losing the Democratic Party's nomination for a second term, Pierce supposedly exclaimed, "There's nothing left but to get drunk." He fought a losing battle with alcoholism for the rest of his life and died from cirrhosis of the liver in 1869.

ANDREW JOHNSON (1808–1875)

- Johnson's reputation as a drunkard dated to the day he was sworn in as Abraham Lincoln's vice president in March 1865. Johnson, who was the military governor of Tennessee at the time, was recovering from typhoid fever and had begged off attending the inauguration, but Lincoln insisted. Already in a weakened state,

100 percent humidity doesn't necessarily mean rain. It just means that
the air is saturated with moisture and can't absorb any more.

Johnson had had too much to drink at a party given in his honor the night before the inauguration. Then on the morning of the inauguration, already hung over from the night before, Johnson drank two or three more shots of whiskey to steady his nerves. Disheveled, red-faced, and reeking of liquor, he delivered a rambling 15-minute inaugural address that shocked the assembled dignitaries. "It was lucky you did not come to the inauguration," Congressman (and future president) Rutherford B. Hayes wrote to his wife Lucy: "Andy Johnson's disgraceful drunkenness spoiled it."

- Johnson never lived down the incident. For the rest of his career, his opponents derided him as "the drunken tailor" (his former profession) and "Andy the sot." Just six weeks after the inauguration, Lincoln was assassinated and the drunken tailor became president.

- In August 1866, President Johnson embarked on a 2,000-mile speaking tour of the northern states to drum up support for his policies. His behavior at many stops, as he angrily shouted down hecklers, once again invited speculation that he was under the influence. One journalist wrote that Johnson appeared "touched with insanity...stimulated with drink," and U.S. Senator John Sherman complained that he had "sunk the Presidential Office to the level of a Grog House."

ALL IN THE FAMILY
- All three of his Johnson's sons were drunks. His eldest son Charles, a Union Army surgeon during the Civil War, became addicted to "medicinal" alcohol and died in 1863 after he was thrown from his horse. He was 33.

- Johnson's second son, Robert, a Union Army colonel, was forced out of the army during the Civil War due to drunkenness. Johnson then hired Robert as his personal aide, and brought him to the White House when he became president. There Robert's drinking continued; he brought scandal to his father's administration by openly consorting with prostitutes in the White House. He was also linked to a "pardon broker" named Mrs. L. L. Cobb, who used her feminine wiles to obtain presidential pardons for former Confederates. A few months after his father left office in 1869, Robert, 35, committed suicide.

- In 1874 ex-president Johnson delivered a speech in Nashville after winning reelection to the U.S. Senate. He was drunk again. "It was a pitiful sight to see him standing there," one witness remembered, "holding onto the iron railing in front of him and swaying back and forth, almost inarticulate with drink. It was a sight I shall never forget—the bloated, stupid, helpless look of Mr. Johnson, as he was hurried away from the balcony to his rooms by his friends and led staggering

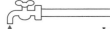

In the two days following a Daylight Saving Time switchover, there's an 8% increase in the rate of strokes.

through the corridors." A few months later, Johnson suffered a series of strokes and died in 1875 at the age of 66. (Four years later, Johnson's third son, Andrew Jr., died from alcoholism and tuberculosis. He was 27.)

ULYSSES S. GRANT (1822–1885)

- Grant battled alcoholism his entire adult life. A West Point graduate, his drinking derailed his military career in 1854 when he was forced to resign from the army due to drunkenness. The outbreak of the Civil War in 1861 was likely the only thing that saved him from a life of poverty and obscurity. He rejoined the army and rose quickly through the ranks; by 1864 he'd been promoted to lieutenant general and was commander of all the Union armies. The surrender of Confederate General Robert E. Lee at Appomattox Court House in 1865 made Grant a national hero, and in 1868 he was elected president.

- Grant was a binge drinker who succumbed to temptation when bored and away from his wife Julia. Luckily for him, the presidency kept him occupied and close to his family. He was careful not to overimbibe, at least not when people were watching. How much he drank when away from the White House and socializing with friends in private clubs is open to speculation.

ON THE ROAD
- The most colorful account of Grant's drinking to excess took place after he left office in 1877 and embarked on a two-year, around-the-world trip. During a stop in India in 1879, the viceroy of India, Lord Lytton, claimed that at one dinner, "Grant, who got drunk as a fiddle, showed that he could also be as profligate as a lord. He fumbled Mrs. A, kissed the shrieking Miss B—pinched the plump Mrs. C black and blue—and ran at Miss D with intent to ravish her. Finally, after throwing the female guests into hysterics by generally misbehaving like a must elephant, the noble beast was captured [and]...deposited in the public saloon cabin, where Mrs. G[rant] was awaiting him...This remarkable man satiated there and then his baffled lust on the unresisting body of his legitimate spouse, and copiously vomited during the operation. If you have seen Mrs. Grant you will not think this incredible."

  To be fair, his biographers "have rightly found this story to be suspect," historian Ron Chernow writes in *Grant*. "Grant had no history of groping women, much less his wife, and Lytton left Calcutta the day before the dinner in question. Still, one wonders whether this patently embellished story, obviously based on hearsay, may have had a kernel of truth. This was the sole allegation of Grant's getting drunk on his extended trip, despite numerous temptations."

18th-century British kids went door-to-door on Valentine's Day singing songs and begging for treats.

TERRIBLE TYPOS

Typos are a dish best served clod.

In a Reebok ad that was
apparently written too quickly:

**Not Eveything Needs to be
Done in a New York Minute**

On the door of a
credit union in Wales:

**Due to the weather we are closed
Sorry for any incontinence**

On a "No Parking" sign
(with a happy ending):

**Violators Will Be
Towed and Find $50**

On a sign outside an
elementary school:

LETERACY NIGHT

On a sign outside another school:

**Congradulation
Spelling Bee Winners**

On a billboard advertising
ABC Children's Academy:

ABC Chilren's Academy

Seen in a Power Point presentation
(and posted on Reddit):

**The Average North American
Consumes more than 400 Africans.**

On a McDonald's sign:

Over 10 Billion Severed

Outside a Louisville,
Kentucky, auto dealership:

We Bye Used Cars

On a wedding invitation:

Love is Sweat

On a sign at a cake shop
(not a great advertisement):

Cake Writting $2.00

In a textbook:

**Beethoven was in a flurry
of musical writing. Being
dead did not stop him in the
slightest from recovering
quickly and going on
with his music.**

(Beethoven was deaf—not dead.
The dead part came later.)

In a TV station's on-screen
graphic for a story about the Lance
Armstrong doping scandal:

Report: Armstrong Used Rugs

On a restaurant awning
(in the Sahara?):

Cakes & Other Deserts

In a TV weather report's
on-screen forecast:

**Warming Up,
Not Ass Cold**

On a restroom door:

**Toilet ONLY for
Disabled Elderly
Pregnant Children**

Another sign that missed the mark:

No Skatedoarbs

In a dialogue box that popped up
on a computer screen:

**Are you sure you
want to exist? Yes   No**

The sides of the head are called "temples" because the hair there is often...

WANTED: PLANETARY PROTECTION OFFICER

Here's a mind-blowing fact: Every time a space vehicle visits another planet, it runs the risk of accidentally delivering bacteria that will cultivate new colonies and change that world forever. And every time it returns, we face the possibility that it's bringing some alien bacteria that could wipe out our entire planet. Luckily, there's someone at NASA whose sole job is to keep us safe.

MEETING OF THE MINDS

In the years following World War II, the scientific community was well aware that outer space had to be the next frontier. So in 1956—a year before Russia launched Sputnik, the world's first artificial satellite—scientists from around the world gathered in Rome to discuss the possible dangers that went along with space exploration. In 1958 the United Nations and the Committee for Space Research (known as COSPAR) suggested a code of conduct for protecting Earth and other planets. The job of Planetary Protection Officer was created by the U.S. government after the UN General Assembly adopted the Outer Space Treaty of 1967, which states that the international signers of the treaty who pursue "studies of outer space, including the moon and other celestial bodies" promise to do so only for peaceful purposes.

OUT-OF-THIS-WORLD JOB

The Planetary Protection Officer, who receives an annual salary of $187,000, visits NASA's ten space centers, checking planet-bound robots and probes to make sure they are sterilized and have a less than a 1-in-10,000 chance of contaminating an alien world. If any aliens or alien microbes enter our biosphere, the officer works to develop plans, like quarantine programs, to protect Earth. Astrobiologist Dr. John Rummel, who served for 17 years as NASA's Planetary Protection Officer, puts the potential danger in historical context by comparing it to our own experience with the exploration of North and South America: "We brought smallpox to the new world when the Europeans came over, and they took home syphilis."

NO-GO ZONES

NASA and the commercial company SpaceX are now making plans to send a manned mission to Mars, causing scientists to worry about alien microbes that could sicken astronauts or cause infections if brought back to Earth. Part of the Planetary

...the first to go gray, marking the passage of time—*tempus* in Latin.

Protection Officer's job is to map out "no-go zones"—areas of Mars to be avoided, such as streams of water, because they are most likely to harbor Martian life-forms. Because of this worry, scientists are considering the possibility of astronauts landing on Mars's moon Phobos and exploring Mars with robots.

ONLY EARTHLINGS MAY APPLY

The job has been around since the 1960s, but when NASA posted the want ad for Planetary Protection Officer on their website in 2017, it generated a lot of excitement. As would be expected, being the person in charge of protecting not just Earth but all of the planets in our solar system has some pretty stiff requirements. According to the job listing at NASA, the Planetary Protection Officer must have an advanced degree in physics, engineering, or mathematics. The candidate must have at least one year of experience as a top-level civilian government employee, and have experience "planning, executing, or overseeing elements of space programs of national significance." But the job has such a "wow" factor that even those tough requirements didn't stop a number of unusual people from applying, including Jack Davis of New Jersey, who submitted this application:

> Dear NASA,
>
> My name is Jack Davis and I would like to apply for the Planetary Protection Officer job. I may be nine but I think I would be fit for the job. One of the reasons is my sister says I'm an alien. Also I have seen almost all the space and alien movies I can see. I have also seen the show *Marvel Agents of Shield* and hope to see the movie *Men in Black*. I am great at video games. I am young, so I can learn to think like an Alien.
>
> Sincerely, Jack Davis
> Guardian of the Galaxy
> Fourth Grade

NEW SHERIFF IN TOWN

On January 19, 2018, NASA announced that Lisa Pratt, an astrobiologist from Indiana University, had been hired as the new Planetary Protection Officer. In an official statement, Dr. Pratt said, "I am excited about the opportunity to contribute to the mission of planetary protection at a defining moment in human evolution and the advancement of science. We are on the verge of becoming a spacefaring species, and I feel privileged to be invited into an extraordinary conversation, pushing the frontiers of science, exploration and discovery at NASA. This position plays a direct role in seeking evidence to address a profound question: Are we alone?"

A photon would take 40,000 years to travel from the sun's core to its surface—but only 8 minutes from there to Earth.

REAL ESTATE "HOLDOUTS"

Sometimes when a developer wants to build a big building, such as a skyscraper or a shopping mall, they have to buy out a number of smaller property owners to get the land to do it. If the price is right, they usually succeed, but every once in a while there's a holdout: someone who refuses to sell.

Holdout: Austin Spriggs, an architect who operated his business out of a town house on Massachusetts Avenue between Fourth and Fifth Streets in Washington, DC

Details: Like a lot of places in the mid-2000s, real estate in Washington, DC, was booming. Several developers made offers to buy Spriggs's town house so that they could build condo and office buildings on the entire block. Spriggs apparently was willing to sell, but not for the price the developers were willing to pay. Even when one developer offered him $2 million, he held out for more.

What Happened: The developers finally decided to build around Spriggs's 1,800-foot parcel, and soon 10-story glass-and-steel buildings were built right up to the property line on three sides of his two-story house. That turned his property into "an essentially undevelopable" lot, and the offers dried up. By 2010 the boom was over and Spriggs's building was on the verge of being foreclosed on, so he put it on the market for $1.5 million. No takers—and the building went into foreclosure. In 2011 some investors bought the townhouse from the lender for $750,000. They fixed it up and sold it for $3.88 million in 2016. Today it's home to a restaurant and a gym.

Holdout: Vera Coking, owner of a vacation home in Atlantic City, New Jersey

Details: Coking and her husband paid $20,000 for the house in 1961. In the mid-1970s, *Penthouse* magazine publisher Bob Guccione bought up the parcels around the Cokings' property so that he could build a *Penthouse*-themed casino and hotel on that block. He offered the Cokings $1 million for their place. Not a bad return on their $20,000 investment…but the Cokings said no.

What Happened: In 1978 Guccione went ahead and started building his casino anyway, wrapping the seven-story structure right around the Cokings' three-story home. But Guccione only got as far as building the steel framework before the project ran out of money. The unfinished building sat there, rusting, until 1993 when it was torn down. Donald Trump bought the property to turn it into a parking lot for the Trump Plaza and Casino, located nearby. He wanted Vera Coking's house, too, but again she refused to sell. The city supported Trump's project and tried to take Coking's property by eminent domain, but she fought the action in court and won. She remained in the house for another 12 years until she moved into a retirement home. Her daughter sold the house for $583,000 in the summer of 2014, and it was demolished that November. But it had outlived the money-losing Trump Plaza and Casino, which went under in September.

Holdout: Robert H. Smith, proprietor of a dry-goods store near the old Macy's department store at 14th Street and Sixth Avenue in New York City

Details: In the early 1900s, Sixth Avenue between 14th and 23rd Streets was one of the hottest shopping districts in the city. A company called Siegel-Cooper had a huge department store there (between 18th and 19th Streets), the largest in the world at the time. Macy's was smaller and a few blocks away. Founder Rowland H. Macy decided to steal Siegel-Cooper's thunder by building an even bigger department store near Herald Square at 34th and Broadway. He started buying up properties on the block and managed to get all of them except one: the five-story building on the corner. Robert Smith snapped that one up for $375,000 before Macy could buy it. He is believed to have been working on behalf of Siegel-Cooper, which either hoped to block the Macy's building entirely, or wanted to trade the corner building for a lease on Macy's old building.

What Happened: Whatever the case, rather than cut a deal, Macy's built their huge department store *around* Smith's building. In 1911 he sold it to another buyer for $1,000,000, an astronomical price at the time, and one that earned the building the name "Million Dollar Corner." Siegel-Cooper is long gone, but Macy's flagship store is still there. So is Smith's building: Macy's never did buy it, but today they lease the exterior, which they have covered with billboards that make it look like a giant Macy's shopping bag.

Holdout: Jean Herman, who lived at 134 East 60th Street in New York City in the 1980s

Details: Herman is the rare example of a *renter* who was able hold out against real estate developers. In 1981 a real estate company bought every building on her block, including the five-story 1865 brownstone where she lived in a rent-controlled ($168 per month) fourth-floor walk-up apartment. But the rent control laws in New York are so strong that the real estate company was unable to evict her, not even after she turned down an a reported $650,000 to pack up and move away. Herman felt the owners had a duty to find her an even nicer rent-stabilized apartment in the same neighborhood (she lived right across the street from Bloomingdales). "I already like where I live, so if they want me to get

> They demolished the back half of the brownstone behind Herman's apartment and the entire fifth floor above her, then built their 31-story skyscraper flush up against the rear of the building.

out, they're going to have to do me one better," she told the *New York Times* in 1986. When none of the two dozen apartments they showed her were suitable—at least as far as she was concerned—she stayed put.

What Happened: The developers had no choice but to work around her. They demolished the back half of the brownstone behind Herman's apartment and the entire fifth floor above her, then built their 31-story skyscraper flush up against the rear of the building. Herman lived out the rest of her life in her apartment, and passed away in 1992 at the age of 69. Today the building serves as office space.

Holdout: The owners of a charcoal company in Osaka, Japan

Details: In 1983 the city made plans to build a new stretch of the Hanshin Expressway through the area, and began buying out local landowners and demolishing buildings to create room. They wanted to put the Umeda exit ramp on the land occupied by the charcoal company, but the owners refused to sell. They thought they could make more money by building an office building on the property.

> The government would run the Hanshin Expressway right *through* the building on those floors.

What Happened: The government refused to issue the permits to build the office building, so it wasn't built. But the property owners refused to sell the land, so the expressway wasn't built, either. The stalemate dragged on for five years, until the two parties agreed to a compromise: The property owners would be issued permits to build their office building if they agreed to "rent" the fifth, sixth, and seventh floors to the government, which would run the Hanshin Expressway right *through* the building on those floors. The 16-story Gate Tower opened its doors in February 1992; 13 floors contain offices, the other three house the expressway. In the elevators, there are no buttons for the fifth, sixth, and seventh floors. Instead, a sign reads simply: "Hanshin Expressway."

* * *

STREET FIGHTER: THE GAME BASED ON THE MOVIE BASED ON THE GAME

One of the most popular video games of the 1990s: *Street Fighter*, in which players used colorful characters to engage in violent, hand-to-hand combat. It was so popular that it was adapted into a 1994 film starring Jean-Claude Van Damme and Raul Julia. A tie-in Super Nintendo game called *Street Fighter: The Movie* was released, a remake of the original *Street Fighter*, but with the original characters removed and replaced with ones that looked more like the actors from the film.

Maximum penalty for cheating on a college exam in China: 7 years in prison.

DNA KIT DISCOVERIES

DNA ancestry kits are one of the biggest fads in years. For about $100, you spit into a tube (really), send it off, and then, a few weeks later, you get a complete workup of your genetic, racial, and even family history. Only drawback: it's really messing with some people's sense of identity.

GOODBYE, FAMILY

A biologist named George Doe (not his real name) gave his parents a DNA kit as a gift, intending to find out about any possible genetic health problems. There was nothing particularly frightening on that front, and Doe's family's racial background was what they all figured it would be. But Doe's online results also asked if he wanted to see if there were any genetic matches in the database. He checked yes, and learned that he had a 22 percent genome match with a man named "Thomas." Doe asked his father if he knew who this Thomas was. He didn't, but then they checked the "see matches" on the dad's profile. Thomas showed up again, this time with a 50 percent match. What does that mean? Doe's father was also Thomas's father—George and Thomas were half-brothers. News of the secret child tore the Doe family apart. The parents, for whom the DNA test had been a gift, wound up getting divorced.

TWISTED SISTERS

Wendy Garrett, 29, decided to take a DNA test in 2015 to try and find her biological relatives. She was adopted through an agency when she was a baby, and through that organization, she learned that somewhere out there, she had a brother. She lived in Pennsylvania, but she'd grown up in California. And that's where a 28-year-old woman named Lisa Olivera lived. Olivera was also adopted as a child (she'd been abandoned on a beach in California the day she was born), and she was also taking a DNA test. Result: The DNA testing company connected the two people when a genome match revealed that they were sisters. Amazingly, both have the same middle name (Anne), play the banjo, and love to camp. They met up in June 2016 and camped in Yellowstone National Park together. (No word on whether they took their banjos.)

YOU'VE BEEN SERVED

Cleon Brown worked as a police officer in Hastings, Michigan, for years with little incident, getting along well with his fellow members of the force. In December 2016, Brown submitted an ancestry test and found out that while he identified as white, his DNA was 18 percent of African ancestry. (In other words, he was part black.) When

The "Hello Girls" were female soldiers stationed on the front lines during WWI to operate…

he shared that information with his coworkers, Brown says they immediately began taunting him with abusive comments and racial slurs. The mayor, the chief of police, the city manager, and a police sergeant all allegedly said racist things to Brown. A lawsuit he filed against the city, citing a hostile work environment, is still pending.

MORE THAN FRIENDS

Walter MacFarlane was born in 1943 and raised in Nu'uanu, Hawaii. His best friend since sixth grade has been a guy named Alan "Robi" Robinson. They were both star players on their high school football team—MacFarlane at tight end and Robi at tackle—and they did everything together. More than 60 years later, they still live near where they were raised and they're still inseparable. In 2017 MacFarlane's children bought him a DNA testing kit for his birthday. He sent in his info, and the testing company told him he matched with someone in his area: Alan "Robi" Robinson. It turns out the friend who was like a brother to him really was his brother. (They have the same mother. Robi was adopted; MacFarlane was raised by his grandparents.) MacFarlane said the possibility never crossed his mind, though "there [were] times when I did think, 'I look like Robi a little bit.'" MacFarlane shared the news with Robinson at a family Christmas party, to which he was invited as a "new" member of the family. "I've never gotten a Christmas present this good," Robinson said.

> **DID YOU KNOW?**
>
> For decades, police hunted "the Golden State Killer," wanted for 12 murders in the 1970s and '80s. In 2018, using publicly available DNA evidence, they found a match to genetic material recovered from crime scenes, leading to the arrest of a 72-year-old ex-cop named Joseph DeAngelo.

* * *

8 APPS THAT COST $999.99

- CyberTuner (piano tuner)
- QSFFStats (flag football stats)
- vueCAD Pro (CAD viewer)
- Vizzywig 4K (video camera/editor)
- Agro (farming app)
- Alpha-Trader (trading and investing money)
- BarMax CA (bar exam review course)
- app.Cash ("stylish cashier system" for rich people)

CARD GAME PHRASE ORIGINS

Do you become a "wild card" "when the chips are down"? We're "calling your bluff."
Here are some other phrases you might not realize came from card games.

READ 'EM AND WEEP

Meaning: To produce evidence while gloating

Story: This phrase is generally used when someone presents physical proof to win an argument, and it comes from poker—in the 19th century, players would say it when they laid down an undeniably winning hand on the table. It implores other players to "read" the cards, see that the hand is unbeatable, and then "weep" because they just lost the game (and presumably money). It was used in poker games so often that by the early 20th century it was being used in other walks of life. In 1919 some newspaper ads for stores began with the phrase to imply that the sale prices were so good that the reader would weep tears of joy after seeing them.

TO HAVE SOMETHING IN SPADES

Meaning: To have something of an unusually high degree

Story: In the game of bridge, the highest-ranking and most valuable cards are of the spade suit. It's a very lucky player who has a lot of spades.

STRONG SUIT

Meaning: A personal strength

Story: Another phrase from the game of bridge. A player has a "strong suit" (also called a "long suit") when their hand of 13 cards contains five or more cards in one of the four suits—five spades, five hearts, and so on. It means they've got what it takes to win the game.

SHOOT THE MOON

Meaning: To take a big risk

Story: Over the last 50 years, the phrase became associated with the U.S. space program. In the 1960s, NASA *literally* shot for the Moon, and succeeded in 1969. In a broader sense, the phrase means to take a chance and try to reach a lofty goal, and it comes from taking a big risk in the card game hearts. The goal of the game is to collect the fewest penalty points. Each heart is worth one penalty point, and the queen of spades is worth 13. Players try to avoid getting these cards. A much bolder (and riskier) play is to try to amass *all* the points. If a player is successful, they get zero penalty points and their opponents get 26. That play is called "shooting the moon."

If you shave your eyebrows off, it will take 64 days for them to grow back.

THE *CANDID CAMERA* HIJACKING

Here's one from our "Strange Crime" files: In 1969 an Eastern Air Lines flight headed for Miami was hijacked by terrorists. Or maybe it was hijacked by a camera crew pulling off an elaborate prank. Adding to the confusion: a celebrity passenger known for pranking people.

THE UNFRIENDLY SKIES

Between 1968 and 1972, heightened political tensions between the United States and Cuba led to dozens of airplane hijackings for reasons ranging from extortion to mental illness to political asylum. In January 1969, for example, a man named Alan Sheffield hijacked a flight departing from San Francisco because he was "tired of TV dinners and tired of seeing people starve in the world." The hijackings became so common that it became sort of an odd fad. Johnny Carson often made fun of hijackers on *The Tonight Show.*

That might explain the relaxed mood during the hijacking of a Newark-to-Miami flight in February 1969. Another reason for the relaxed mood: Allen Funt was on the flight—the same Allen Funt who was famous for *Candid Camera,* the long-running TV show that featured elaborate hidden-camera pranks and the catchphrase "Smile, you're on *Candid Camera!*" When the captain announced that they were being diverted to Cuba, many of the passengers thought it was a joke.

NO JOKE

One problem: Funt wasn't doing *Candid Camera* anymore. The show had been off the air for two years. He was working on a film at the time, but it had nothing to do with hijacking planes. He was on a trip with his wife and two of his kids. Accounts vary as to what actually happened during the flight, but, as Funt later wrote in an Associated Press article, he saw a "fat, little man" grab a stewardess and hold a knife to her throat while pulling her toward the cockpit. So when the pilot made the announcement, Funt knew it was serious. A few minutes later, as Funt's daughter Juliet (who was two at the time) recalled during a 2015 interview, a woman jumped up from her seat and told everyone that the hijacking was just a staged stunt for *Candid Camera.* As proof, she pointed to Funt.

Then a party broke out. Several passengers swarmed Funt and asked him to autograph their air sickness bags. Stewardesses popped open bottles of champagne while some passengers started dancing in the aisles. Funt tried to convince everyone

Q. Can you name the six NFL teams that don't have cheerleaders?
A. The Bears, Bills, Browns, Giants, Packers, and Steelers.

that this was not his doing, to no avail. "Looking back at the experience," he wrote, "the unbelievable thing is the way everybody took it as one big joke. We saw the knife, but everybody was cool and calm, just a little annoyed at the delay. It is strange how you can be so close to danger and not feel it."

At one point, a hijacker popped his head out of the cockpit to find out what the commotion was about and the passengers started applauding him. That's when Funt tried to hatch a plan to take down the hijacker himself…only to have his wife talk him out of it. A few hours later, the Miami-bound plane landed in Havana.

ON FOREIGN SOIL

By that point, as the Cuban military surrounded the plane, the passengers had come to the grim realization that this was no hidden-camera prank. According to Juliet, several passengers turned their anger on Funt for "tricking" them into assuming that it was all a gag.

In the 11 hours that followed, the Funts and the other passengers were transported by bus to Varadero, a town along Cuba's northern coastline. They were treated well, but no one was allowed to phone their relatives. Eventually, they were loaded onto another plane and flown back to the United States.

"The biggest joke," wrote Funt, "was how much the whole thing looked like a bad movie. Nobody looked the part. The hijackers were ridiculous in their business suits."

The incident concluded with no injuries, and the terrorists were reportedly never prosecuted. Hijacking airplanes wasn't officially declared a crime in Cuba until the 1970s.

* * *

10 METROPOLITAN AREAS LARGER THAN THE ENTIRE STATE OF RHODE ISLAND

1. New York City

2. Tokyo

3. Chicago

4. Atlanta

5. Philadelphia

6. Boston

7. Los Angeles

8. Dallas

9. Houston

10. Detroit

One purpose of the egg white: to keep bacteria away from the developing chick.

POLITICAL ANIMALS

*Ordinarily, the term "political animal" refers to a person who has politics
in their blood. But every once in a while, the political animal
really is an animal—a critter that's running for office.*

Candidate: Duke, a seven-year-old Great Pyrenees dog living in Cormorant, Minnesota
Running For: Mayor of Cormorant
Campaign Notes: Cormorant is a small township, and the mayor's job is purely
ceremonial. That probably had a lot to do with David Rick, a resident of the township,
entering his dog Duke in the mayor's race in 2014. How small is Cormorant? So
small that only about a dozen people voted in the election…and at least seven of
them voted for Duke—enough votes for him to beat his human opponent, Richard
Sherbrook, and become mayor. Sherbrook says that even he voted for the hound after
deciding it would be "pretty cool" to have a dog as mayor. "There's no question that
he'll do a good job representing the community," Sherbrook told ABC News. "He's
a sportsman and he likes to hunt. He'll really protect the town." (Cormorant holds
mayoral elections every year, and Duke won reelection in 2015, 2016, and 2017.)

Candidate: Giggles, a nine-month-old pig owned by Michael Ewing, a Flint,
Michigan, defense attorney
Running for: Mayor of Flint
Campaign Notes: Ewing decided to enter Giggles in the 2015 mayoral campaign
after election officials publicized the wrong date as the filing deadline for the mayoral
primary. The *actual* filing deadline was earlier than the publicized date, causing every
single candidate to miss it. Result of the snafu: *no* candidates' names would appear on
the ballot, turning them all into write-in candidates. Ewing thought this made the
campaign less transparent, which was a big problem considering that one candidate
had served nearly 19 years in prison for murder, and another had been convicted of
driving drunk the wrong way down the highway on four flat
tires. "Giggles was sitting next to me while I was reading
reports about the candidates and I said to her, 'You would
make a better candidate than these people.' So I did what
any normal person would do—I ran her for mayor," Ewing
told the *Huffington Post* in May 2015.

A month later, when state officials passed a special law
that allowed the (human) candidates' names to appear on the
ballot, Ewing announced that Giggles was pulling out of the

> **"Giggles was sitting
> next to me while I
> was reading reports
> about the candidates
> and I said to her, 'You
> would make a better
> candidate than these
> people.'"**

But who would want to? Urine can be used as a yeast substitute.

race. Which of her opponents did she endorse? None of them. "She's not voting for anyone because she's a pig, and that's really the only good excuse for not voting in an election that is this important," Ewing said.

Candidate: Saucisse ("Sausage"), a Dachshund living in Marseilles, France
Running For: Mayor of Marseilles and president of France
Campaign Notes: Saucisse was the office dog of L'Écailler du Sud, a publishing house that specializes in detective novels. When Serge Scotto, one of the publisher's authors, started featuring the wiener dog in his detective novels, Saucisse found his first measure of fame. Then in 2001, Scotto entered him in the mayor's race.

Saucisse came in sixth, beating the Rally For France candidate by nearly a percentage point. Not a victory, but not bad! So the following year, Scotto registered Saucisse as a candidate in the *presidential* election. The dog lost again and retired from politics after that, but continued to make regular appearances on TV and in Scotto's detective stories. He even had a wine named after him—Cuvée Chien Saucisse—and lived to the ripe old age of 16 before passing away in 2014.

Candidate: Crawfish B. Crawfish, a boiled Louisiana crawfish (similar in appearance to a lobster, but smaller)
Running For: President of the United States
Campaign Notes: When Louisiana governor Bobby Jindal announced in June 2015 that he was running for president, someone who was definitely *not* one of Jindal's admirers created a Facebook group called "Can This Crawfish Get More Supporters Than Bobby Jindal?" and uploaded a photo of a boiled crawfish to the page. So many people clicked "like" on the photo that the creator decided to enter C.B. in the presidential race, where he continued to take shots at Jindal. (Jindal's campaign slogan: "Tanned. Rested. Ready." C. B. Crawfish's: "Red. Boiled. Ready.")

Jindal's popularity in-state and out was at a low point when he launched his presidential campaign; being dogged by a dead, well-cooked, smart-alecky "Claw and Order candidate" didn't help. Jindal never rose above 1 percent in the polls and in one Fox News survey trailed dead last behind "None of the above." His campaign never caught on and in November 2015 he threw in the towel. One of the few bright spots in the race: he accumulated more than 250,000 followers on Facebook…and C. B. Crawfish topped out at 25,000.

* * *

A BAD JOKE FROM THE 1970s

Q: How do you punish a Pet Rock?
A: You hit rock bottom.

Only U.S. state to host both the Summer Olympics and the Winter Olympics: California.

FARTS IN THE NEWS

This just in: Phbblbbttt!

FART HEALTHY

According to a recent study, farts can "reduce the risk of cancer, heart attack, strokes, arthritis, and dementia." British researchers at the University of Exeter made the discovery after "feeding" cells tiny amounts of hydrogen sulfide, the smelly part of farts. "Our results indicate that if stressed cells are treated with [hydrogen sulfide], mitochondria are protected and cells stay alive." (So the next time you let one rip in public, remind everyone to thank you for extending their life.)

FART FIGHT

In February 2018, not long after takeoff, passengers on a Dubai-to-Amsterdam flight heard the sound of uncontrolled flatulence, as a foul-smelling aroma permeated the cabin. Two men who were sitting next to the perpetrator asked him to stop, but he refused and kept on farting. He wouldn't even apologize. Several passengers complained to the flight crew, but they couldn't get the man to stop farting, either. By this point, the two men were threatening violence, so the pilot came out and told everyone to calm down. A few minutes later the man farted again. That was it: fists flew, people scattered, and the pilot made an emergency landing in Austria, where police with dogs boarded the plane. In the end, four people were thrown off the flight—the two men who started the brawl, and two women sitting nearby (who had nothing to do with the fight and later sued the airline). As for the unapologetic farter, he was allowed to remain on the plane.

THE RIGHT TO FART

In 2017 a German man, identified in press reports as Christoph S., was being given a routine identity check on a Berlin street when he let out two loud farts in front of two female police officers. Perceiving the flatulence as an insult, the Berlin police department fined Christoph 900 euros ($1,100). Perceiving the fine as a violation of his rights, Christoph hired a lawyer and appealed. "It is one thing if the leader of a police unit sees his colleague's honor as being injured by a fart," argued the lawyer, "but it is quite another if prosecutors and the judiciary agree. That is a failure of the state." Verdict: You have a right to pass gas in public. Christoph's fart was ruled perfectly legal and the fine was thrown out.

Each year, over a thousand tons' worth of diamonds rain down on Saturn.

VIRTUAL FARTS

To promote the 2016 release of its fart-themed video game *South Park: The Fractured But Whole* (read it out loud), the game's developer, Ubisoft, debuted an interesting accessory they called the Nosulus Rift. It's a mask you wear while playing the game that "transfers the smell of the fart directly into your nose." If you want to buy a Nosulus Rift for yourself…well, that's weird. Anyway, you can't. Ubisoft only demoed the fully functional fart mask at trade shows—it's not for sale. Fortunately, it shouldn't be too difficult for gamers to fill their dens with fart smells on their own.

FARTASAURUS

In the summer of 2017, Canada's Manitoba Museum allowed visitors an opportunity to smell the past. As part of the World's Giant Dinosaurs exhibit, one of the lifelike "robosaurs" (a Dilophosaurus) was designed to fart loudly and odiferously, by way of a cartridge that emits a malodorous scent. (Another roboosaur, the Protoceratops, urinated into a pond.) "We want to give the impression of every aspect of dinosaur life," said exhibit designer "Dino" Don Lessem (who was an advisor on 1993's *Jurassic Park*). "There's a scientific point to all of this stuff, but really above all, have fun."

FART STORM

Until recently, Neptune's atmosphere was home to a massive cyclone composed primarily of hydrogen sulfide, the same stinky gas people emit when they fart. Astronomers using the Hubble Telescope discovered the storm in 2015 and studied it for three years as it slowly fizzled out of existence. At the fart storm's greatest intensity, it had a diameter of more than 2,000 miles. To put it another way, it was a fart the size of China.

"FARTS OF BEAUTIFUL WOMEN"

"All 120 million fart fans across the country: Back by popular demand, 'Everyone Listen to the Farts of Beautiful Women Party Vol. 2' will be held! Buff! Puu! Buree! Buha! Psuuuu!" Those are the opening lines of a press release for an event that was held in Tokyo in 2018. Apparently, the first annual "Farts of Beautiful Women" was such a success that they held a second one. It's pretty much what the name implies: scantily clad ladies walk across a stage…and fart. But do they really pass gas, or are the farts simulated? According to this disclaimer, "Please understand that, depending on the physical condition of the performers, farts may not come out."

* * *

"In the Age of Information, ignorance is a choice." —**Donald Miller**

No computers were used to animate the 1988 film *Who Framed Roger Rabbit?*
The nearly two million drawings were made by hand.

DANGER EVERYWHERE!

*So many seemingly benign things are working toward your demise that it's a
miracle you're sitting there reading this. Here are just a few silent killers.*

MICROBES

How They Seem Harmless: Microbes, tiny organisms that include viruses, bacteria,
and fungi, are everywhere. They're in the water, the air, the Earth's crust, and in every
living thing, including your body. They are so numerous that if you gathered them all
up, they'd form a layer around the planet five feet deep. Most microbes are harmless,
and many are helpful. Humans need certain bacteria, for example, to maintain healthy
immune systems and to help them digest food. But some microbes are dangerous.

How They Can Kill You: Even though less than 1 percent of bacteria strains can
cause illnesses, that 1 percent includes pestilent diseases such as tuberculosis and the
bubonic plague. And bacteria are continually evolving. The problem (for humans)
is microbes' ability to adapt. According to one expert, "Every once in a while, they
evolve into something our bodies can't handle very well. Think SARS...or Zika."
Or Ebola—the virus that killed more than 11,300 people during a recent outbreak in
Africa. And microbes are practically eternal. They've been on Earth longer than any
other organisms, and they can adapt to any conditions. So, if you're betting on who'll
win the battle between microbes and humanity, put your money on the microbes—just
like microbes are on your money.

SALTY FOOD

How It Seems Harmless: Salt is an essential part of the human diet, when consumed
in the proper quantities. Adults require about 1,500 milligrams of sodium, or ¾
teaspoon, of salt per day. Your cells need it to regulate your body fluids and prevent you
from getting dehydrated.

How It Can Kill You: The problem is when people eat too much of it. For a 200-
pound person, eating as little as four tablespoons of salt all at once can send them to
the morgue. When there's too much sodium in the bloodstream (a condition called
hypernatremia), water moves out of the cells and into the blood to balance out the
sodium. But that leaves cells dehydrated. In extreme cases of overconsumption, the
cells shrink, bleed, and die, causing seizures, coma, or death. In 2013 a Virginia college
student, John Paul Boldrick, spent three days in a coma after he drank a quart of soy
sauce (which contains about ¾ cup of salt) on a dare. He survived, but only barely. In
a baby, just two teaspoons of salt can be fatal. In 1962 a hospital in Binghamton, New

Hematidrosis is a medical condition in which the patient sweats blood.

York, fed 14 newborns formula that had accidentally been prepared using salt instead of sugar, and six of the babies died.

Even when consumed in nonlethal doses, eating too much salt can shorten your life by damaging your kidneys and causing heart attacks and strokes. According to the Centers for Disease Control, 90 percent of Americans ingest too much sodium, and if they reduced their intake, tens of thousands of lives would be saved each year.

CARBON DIOXIDE

How It Seems Harmless: When animals exhale or organic matter decomposes, carbon dioxide (CO_2) molecules are released. Without it, all plants and animals would die.

How It Can Kill You: Carbon dioxide levels that are too high have the potential to destroy much of life on Earth, and unfortunately, those levels are soaring. According to the National Oceanic and Atmospheric Administration (NOAA), the concentration of CO_2 in the air before the year 1800 was 280 parts per million (ppm), but today it exceeds 408 ppm. That's because CO_2 is emitted when coal and other fossil fuels are burned to run cars, factories, and power plants.

The problem is that CO_2 in the atmosphere acts like a blanket, trapping heat that would otherwise escape into space. Having too much of it makes the planet warmer. According to NOAA, the average global temperature has risen at least 2°F since 1880, when researchers first began tracking it. "Something as simple as elevated carbon dioxide levels in our atmosphere," says Professor Doug Haywick, "could easily wipe out a large proportion of life on the planet because of the associated increase in temperature. It likely happened before and is one theory about what killed the dinosaurs 65 million years ago." What we don't know is which threat will destroy us first: the violent storms associated with global warming, starvation from widespread droughts, or floods from melting ice. Whatever the case, expect the death toll to rise until CO_2 levels are reduced…but don't hold your breath. (Actually, that might help.)

HOT SPRINGS

How They Seem Harmless: Hot springs form when water that's heated deep in the earth rushes to the surface fast enough to retain its heat. People soak in the mineral-infused water to improve blood circulation, skin conditions, joint pain, and more.

How They Kill You: Next time you visit a hot spring, try not to think about the presence of hydrogen sulfide, which can be lethal if you inhale enough of it. The stinky gas with the rotten egg smell is produced by bacteria that feed off sulfide minerals in the springs, or when decaying matter mixes with standing water in sewers or swamps. Hot springs deaths are rare, but near the springs of Rotorua (nicknamed "Sulphur City") in New Zealand, at least 13 people have died from hydrogen sulfide

More people live in India than in Africa, South Korea, and the UK combined.

poisoning since 1946. If you do take a dip in a hot spring, pay attention to what your nose tells you: the stronger the odor of rotten eggs, the more hydrogen sulfide there is. If it becomes overpowering, get out!

Other risks associated with hot springs are the high temperature and the pH level of the water. If the pH level is too high (alkaline) or too low (acidic), the water can be deadly. In 2016 a 23-year-old Oregon man visiting Yellowstone National Park ignored warning signs against "hot potting," or soaking in certain dangerous springs. When he reached down to check the temperature of one particular hot spring, he fell in and died. He was probably killed by the temperature of the water, which can be as much as 200°F on the surface and even hotter a few feet farther down. But the acidity of the water was also so high that by the time a rescue crew was able to attempt to recover the body the following morning, there was no body left to recover: all that remained of the man were his wallet and his flip-flops. Everything else had dissolved into the hot spring.

POT BELLIES

How They Seem Harmless: Most people think of fatty tissues as dormant and a mere annoyance, if they think about body fat at all. And it does serve a purpose: visceral fat wraps itself around internal organs, which protects them from injury.

How They Kill You: Belly fat can make you go belly up if there's too much of it. Visceral fat tissues, found deep in your belly, are not stagnant—they're active. They produce chemical responses in the body; they trigger the release of hormones (like organs do) and inflammatory chemicals (like a tumor does). That's because visceral fat bombards organs with chemicals called cytokines, which lead to inflammation that can accelerate aging, cause terminal diseases such as cancer, and increase the risk of death.

As part of a vicious cycle, visceral fat works hard to keep us fat. For one thing, it infiltrates muscles, where it forms a cushion between muscle fibers and slows down the actions of muscle cells. (No wonder you feel sluggish.) Belly fat also interferes with hormones that regulate appetite and weight. Incredibly, the more visceral fat you have, the more it signals your brain to eat, and the slower your metabolism becomes. That, in turn, will raise your risk of heart attack, liver disease, dementia, depression, and diabetes. And if you think you're safe because you're thin, think again. According to a Mayo Clinic study, people who are a normal weight but have too much visceral fat are *twice* as likely to die prematurely than overweight people who don't have much belly fat. If you measure your waist (without sucking in your gut), on average it should be less than 35 inches if you're female, or less than 40 inches if you're male. More than that, and you're at higher risk for health problems.

The Mickey Mouse Club and *Captain Kangaroo* both premiered on the same day: October 3, 1955.

More everyday items that could kill you:

- Vending machines. They're a mortal threat for about 13 people each year, when they try to rock the machines but get crushed when they topple over.

- The fuzzy *Lonomia obliqua* caterpillar, found in South America. It looks harmless, but each of those fuzzy "hairs" is actually a stinger with its own supply of a powerful venom, which can be lethal in sufficient quantities. There are more than 500 confirmed fatalities that were caused when people touched the caterpillars.

- Bouncy castles. There have been multiple reports of poorly anchored bounce houses or inflatable slides blowing away with people inside when they are hit by high winds. In 2016 one person was killed and 41 were injured in China when a bouncy castle flew 164 feet into the air and hit a phone line. Serious and even fatal injuries are another risk: In the United States, more than a dozen people have perished from 1990 to 2010 due to bounce house accidents.

- Clothes dryers and lint. In the United States, there are nearly 2,900 fires caused by clothes dryers each year, and they cause an estimated five deaths, 100 injuries, and $35 million in property damage. Thirty-four percent of these fires are sparked by built-up dryer lint blocking the vent that users didn't clean out after each load.

* * *

EVERY KNOWN NAME FOR THAT GAME WHERE YOU THROW BEANBAGS THROUGH A BOARD WITH HOLES IN IT

- Cornhole
- Bag toss
- Bags
- Tailgate toss
- Backyard toss
- Lawn toss
- Soft horseshoes
- Corn toss
- Hillbilly toss
- Baggo
- Chuck-O
- Doghouse
- Dadhole
- Dummy boards

There are no nuts in Honey Nut Cheerios. It has a nut flavoring made from ground peach pits.

GROANERS

What do you call a belt made of watches? A waist of time…like this page of bad jokes.

Q: Why do scuba divers fall backwards out of the boat?
A: Because if they fell forward, they'd still be in the boat.

I'd like to get a job cleaning mirrors. It's something I could really see myself doing.

Jay: "I got you this elephant for your room."
Brian: "Thanks."
Jay: "Don't mention it."

This just in: A dog gave birth to puppies on the sidewalk and was cited for littering.

Q: What's unthinkable?
A: An itheberg.

I can't stand those Russian dolls. They're so full of themselves!

Q: How many optometrists does it take to change a light bulb?
A: Is it one, or two? One… or two?

An artist friend of mine asked me to critique his self-portrait. I told him that it was good, except the eyebrows are too high. He seemed surprised.

"This job isn't for everyone," said the scarecrow, "but hay, it's in my jeans."

Q: Did you hear about the fisherman magician?
A: He says, "Pick a cod, any cod!"

Q: How do you find Will Smith in the snow?
A: Follow the fresh prints.

Q: What do you get when you cross a joke with a rhetorical question?

Q: Why did the little cookie cry?
A: Because his mother was a wafer so long.

Q: How was Rome split in two?
A: With a pair of Caesars.

A man was crushed by a pile of books. He only had his shelf to blame.

Q: What's the difference between a hippo and a Zippo?
A: One is really heavy, and the other is a little lighter.

What's so great about Switzerland? Well, the flag is a big plus.

Man, I bought these shoes off a drug dealer. I don't know what he laced them with, but I've been tripping all day!

It said my password had to be eight characters long, so I picked Snow White and the Seven Dwarfs.

Christmas present idea: give them a refrigerator and watch their face light up when they open it.

I watched hockey before it was cool. They were basically swimming.

Q: What did the pirate say when he turned 80 years old?
A: "Aye matey!"

Did you hear Chef Boyardee died? He pasta way.

Who cares if I don't know what "apocalypse" means? It's not the end of the world.

A man walks into a bar and orders a fruit punch. The bartender says, "If you want a fruit punch, you'll have to stand in line." The man looked around, but there was no punchline.

ONE LAST HIT

Most singers and bands record music for many decades, sometimes to the bitter end. That doesn't mean people are still listening, though. Here are some of the most popular musicians of all time…and their last song to hit the Billboard *top 50 chart.*

BING CROSBY

Crosby dominated American music during the 1930s and 1940s—he placed more than 300 songs on the *Billboard* pop chart over the course of his long career. Many of them became standards of American music, including "Pennies from Heaven," "You Must Have Been a Beautiful Baby," and "Swinging on a Star." But then along came Elvis Presley and rock 'n' roll in the mid 1950s, and Der Bingle suddenly became passé. The only ones still regularly heard are his holiday classics, such as "Mele Kalikimaka (Hawaiian Christmas Song)" and "White Christmas." So it should be no surprise that the last time Crosby hit the top 50 was with "Adeste Fideles" (also known as "O Come All Ye Faithful"), which reached #45 in 1960. (He died in 1977.)

THE BEE GEES

Sure, the Gibb brothers defined the 1970s with disco hits like "Stayin' Alive'" and "Night Fever," but that was their comeback phase. Before that, they were a rock band with nine top-20 hits from 1967 to 1971. Among them was "How Can You Mend a Broken Heart," which reached #1 in 1971 and was their last big success…until they reinvented themselves as a disco group with "Jive Talkin'" in 1975. After disco died, the Gibb brothers dove into songwriting and production. Barry Gibb coproduced Barbra Streisand's 1980 hit album *Guilty*, and in 1983 the brothers wrote Kenny Rogers and Dolly Parton's #1 hit "Islands in the Stream." As a group, however, the Bee Gees enjoyed two more (brief) comebacks. In 1989 their synth-pop ballad "One" hit #7, and in 1997 "Alone" squeaked into the top 30.

THE BEATLES

The Beatles are the most famous rock band ever—they landed 48 songs in *Billboard's* top 50, including 20 #1 hits (such as "I Want to Hold Your Hand," "Hey Jude," and "Help!"), which is still more than any other act in history. The Fab Four broke up in 1970 and fans' hopes for a reunion ended in 1980, when John Lennon was assassinated. However, the other three Beatles did reunite—briefly and only in the studio—in the mid-1990s. ABC aired a documentary miniseries called *The Beatles Anthology*, which premiered around the same time that a trilogy of Beatles rarities,

All tortoises are turtles, but not all turtles are tortoises.

called *Anthology 1, 2,* and *3,* was being released. To entice fans to check out both projects, Paul McCartney, George Harrison, and Ringo Starr laid down new vocal and instrumental tracks over two old John Lennon demos—"Free as a Bird" and "Real Love." Released in 1995 and 1996, the songs hit #6 and #11, respectively.

BILLY JOEL

Billy Joel's first hit: The 1973 song "Piano Man," about his time as the house pianist playing in an L.A. bar. That was just the first of a long string of hits for Joel. He had a whopping 34 top-50 hits, including karaoke favorites such as "Uptown Girl," "The Longest Time," and "My Life." In 1999 the Piano Man abruptly announced that he would stop recording pop albums. Two years later, he released *Fantasies & Delusions,* a collection of original, classical-style piano compositions. Joel soon returned to touring and playing his old hits, but he no longer actively makes new pop music. The last time he had a hit single: 1997, when he covered Bob Dylan's "To Make You Feel My Love" for a greatest hits collection. It reached #50 on the pop chart.

MICHAEL JACKSON

Jackson's nickname was the "King of Pop," and that would be pretty obnoxious if it wasn't true. Not even counting his work with the Jackson 5, Jackson sold about 350 million albums (more than 100 million of those were *Thriller,* the best-selling album ever) and more than 40 hit singles ("Beat It," "Billie Jean," "Rock with You," "Smooth Criminal," and "Black or White," to name just a few). After he became increasingly isolated, and known as much for his weird behavior and appearance as his music, Jackson's popularity started to fade. At the time of his death in 2009, he was planning a comeback in the form of a Las Vegas residency show. But Jackson's death triggered a nostalgia-driven explosion of interest in his music. The King of Pop's old albums sold millions more copies, spurring producers to dig up old, unreleased and unfinished songs. "Love Never Felt So Good," a demo Jackson made in the 1980s, was dusted off, Justin Timberlake added some vocals, and the song hit #9 in 2014. (While Jackson was alive, his last hit was the 2001 single "Butterflies," which reached the top 20.)

DARYL HALL AND JOHN OATES

According to *Billboard,* Hall & Oates are the most successful duo in pop music history, racking up 28 top-40 hits in the 1970s and '80s, including "Sara Smile," "Rich Girl," "Private Eyes," "I Can't Go for That (No Can Do)," and "Maneater." Appropriately, as the 1980s ended, the big-in-the-'80s act had their last big hits: "So Close" hit #11 in 1990, and the follow-up "Don't Hold Back Your Love," which peaked at #41.

ABBA

The Swedish dance-pop band remains popular in the 21st century thanks to the success of *Mamma Mia!*, a Broadway musical (and then a movie) built around some of ABBA's more than a dozen hit songs, like "Dancing Queen," "S.O.S.," and "Mamma Mia." The group consisted of two married couples, and when the couples broke up in the early 1980s, so did the band. ABBA disbanded in December 1982, vowing never to reunite. When all was said and done, their last hit was "When All Is Said and Done," which reached #27 in late 1981.

CARPENTERS

Carpenters (no "the"—just Carpenters) countered all the social turmoil of the 1970s, and the bombastic soul, funk, arena rock, punk, and New Wave that came out of the radio during that decade. They were a squeaky-clean brother and sister act from suburban California who sang gentle songs about love, romance, and heartbreak. Richard Carpenter played piano and wrote the songs, while Karen Carpenter played the drums and sang. They virtually invented the genre of "soft rock" (still called "easy listening") in the 1970s with catchy, mellow tunes, including "(They Long to Be) Close to You," "Rainy Days and Mondays," and "Top of the World." The duo made it to the higher levels of the pop charts more than 20 times before fading from relevance and popularity in the early 1980s. The band last hit the charts in 1981 with the top-20 hit "Touch Me When We're Dancing," and never would again, because of the untimely death of Karen Carpenter in 1983.

ELTON JOHN

John is still very much in the public eye, playing concerts around the world, making movie soundtracks, writing Broadway musicals, making cameos in movies, and appearing on talk shows, but he doesn't record all that much music anymore. He doesn't need to—he has a huge catalog of hits to draw from when he plays live. Over the course of a career that's lasted more than 50 years, John has amassed an amazing 61 top-50 hits. Examples: "Crocodile Rock," "Rocket Man," "Daniel," "Levon," "Don't Go Breaking My Heart," "I'm Still Standing," "Sacrifice," "Philadelphia Freedom," and "Candle in the Wind," which was originally written in the 1970s to memorialize Marilyn Monroe, and rewritten in 1997 for his friend Princess Diana. (John performed it live at her funeral.) It went on to become the second-best-selling single of all time (behind Bing Crosby's "White Christmas"). That was just about the last time John made an impact on the pop chart. In 2000, "Someday Out of the Blue" hit #49, Elton John's last big appearance on the *Billboard* Hot 100.

Second largest air force after the U.S. Air Force: the U.S. Navy and Marines (combined).

QUEEN FOR A DAY

*As of 2018, the UK's Queen Elizabeth has been on the throne (so to speak)
for 66 years—longer than any other monarch in British history. Here
are some leaders whose reigns were quite a bit shorter than that.*

Ruler: "Unnamed daughter" of Emperor Xiaoming of the Chinese kingdom of
Northern Wei (528–?)
Reign: A few hours
Details: Xiaoming was only five years old when he inherited the imperial throne
in 515. Because of this, his mother, Empress Dowager Hu, ruled as regent in his
name. But when the boy came of age, the empress dowager refused to surrender
power. That led to a struggle between Hu and Xiaoming that ended only when she
poisoned Xiaoming. By then the 18-year-old had fathered a daughter with one of
his concubines, but because the child was female, she was ineligible to inherit the
throne. Undeterred, the empress dowager passed off the child as a boy, and thus the
new emperor, so that she could maintain power by serving as the child's regent. A
few hours after proclaiming the child emperor, she realized the ruse was not going to
work, so she admitted the "boy" was a girl and proclaimed Xiaoming's two-year-old
male cousin, named Yuan Zhao, emperor instead. These shenanigans did not impress
a general named Erzhu Rong. He marched on the capital, captured both the dowager
empress and Yuan Zhao, and drowned them in the Yellow River.

Ruler: Pope Stephen (II) of the Roman Catholic Church (752)
Reign: Four days
Details: Stephen suffered a stroke three days after he was elected pope, and died
the following day—before he could be consecrated as pope in a special ceremony. In
those days, popes weren't considered popes until the consecration took place, so for
centuries the church did not recognize him as a pope. Only later, when being elected
pope came to be seen as what counted, did the church add his name to the official list.
Subsequent popes who took the name Stephen have two numbers beside their name:
one number that doesn't include Pope Stephen (II), and one (in parentheses) that
does. The last was Pope Stephen IX (X), who ruled from 1057 to 1058.

Ruler: King John I "the Posthumous" of France and Navarre (1316)
Reign: Five days
Details: When King Louis X (Louis the Quarreler) died in 1316, his wife was four
months pregnant with their unborn child. Louis already had a daughter, Joan, but if
the unborn child turned out to be male, he—not Joan—would inherit the throne.

Closest U.S. state to Africa: Maine. Its easternmost point is 3,154 miles west of El Beddouza, Morocco.

While the realm waited for the child's birth, Louis's brother, Philip the Tall, ruled as regent. On November 15, 1316, a baby boy was born. He was proclaimed King John I, but died five days later. His was the shortest reign in French history, and he was the only king born a king. So...did Joan become the queen after John died? Nope—Philip the Tall muscled in and claimed the thrones of both France and Navarre (a small kingdom between Castille and Aragon in northern Spain) for himself. When Joan protested, he called her paternity into question and raised other issues that kept her from ever becoming the queen of France. But she did become the queen of Navarre in 1328, and reigned there until her death in 1349.

Ruler: Czar Alexei II of Russia (1904–1918)
Reign: Just shy of nine hours
Details: World War I was only three days old when Germany declared war against Russia on August 1, 1914. The war went badly for Russia, and after Czar Nicholas II assumed personal command of the army in 1915, much of the blame fell on him. By March 1917, the country was near collapse. Revolution broke out in the capital, and on the 15th, Nicholas abdicated in favor of his 12-year-old son, Alexei.

The moment that Nicholas signed the abdication papers at 3:00 p.m., Alexei became the czar. Nicholas initially assumed that because Alexei was a minor, the boy's uncle, Grand Duke Michael, would rule in his name until he came of age, and Nicholas would be allowed to raise his son in Russia. But after speaking with advisors, Nicholas realized that he would likely be sent into exile, without the boy czar. Making the situation more painful, Alexei suffered from hemophilia, a life-threatening and, at the time, untreatable blood disorder. Nicholas decided it would be cruel to permit his son to be raised away from his family. Shortly before midnight, he signed a second set of abdication papers, back-dated to 3:00 p.m., passing the throne to Grand Duke Michael instead.

Ruler: Czar Michael II of Russia (1878–1918)
Reign: Less than a day
Details: When Grand Duke Michael awoke on the morning of March 16, 1917, he was handed a telegram informing him that his brother, Czar Nicholas, had abdicated and that *he* was now the czar. Representatives of the provisional government were already on their way to meet with him; the discussions that followed lasted well into the afternoon. By the time they ended, Michael had decided to abdicate. He said he would be willing to return to the throne if a democratically elected government asked him to. But that never happened: in November the Bolshevik Party (later renamed the Communist Party) seized power and abolished the Russian monarchy. In the months that followed, Michael, Nicholas, his wife Alexandra, their son Alexei, their four daughters, and a dozen other members of the royal family were executed by the Bolsheviks to prevent them from ever returning to power.

UPS trucks are painted a trademarked color called Pullman Brown. It was formerly used on...

BEST SPORTS OWNERS

You can choose your team, but you can't choose your owner.
For fans of these teams, that's not a problem.

MARK CUBAN

Most billionaires who buy sports teams do it because no matter how poorly the team does, its value will grow thanks to lucrative TV deals. But bartender-turned-billionaire Mark Cuban bought the Dallas Mavericks for another reason: he's a rabid sports fan. When Cuban bought the Mavs in 2000, the team was the laughingstock of the NBA. In the 17 years since, they've made the playoffs 15 times and won one NBA title. But winning isn't the only reason Cuban is beloved by players and fans. From day one, Cuban has taken the heat off his players by berating referees and opponents from his courtside seat (he attends nearly every game) to the cost of more than $2 million in fines since buying the team. This endeared him to fans, who could email him their thoughts and complaints—and actually get a response back. Cuban didn't just create a winning team, he created a winning culture with a blueprint that has since been copied by other owners.

JERRY BUSS

The late Dr. Jerry Buss was such an outsized Hollywood character that the team he bought instantly took on his personality. Originally a chemistry professor at USC, Buss switched to investing in Los Angeles real estate when he realized the vast fortune he could make. In 1979 he struck a deal with Los Angeles Lakers owner Jack Kent Cooke to buy the team and its Inglewood arena, the Forum. But it wasn't just the Lakers' five championships in the 1980s that made Buss a beloved figure among Angelenos. With Buss's playboy reputation and Hollywood stars in the seats, the Lakers became the hottest ticket in town. The Lakers didn't just win, they won with a flashy style that became known as "Showtime." And everything related to the team, from Magic Johnson's no-look passes to the scantily clad Laker Girls, could be traced back to the culture Buss imbued into this franchise. When Buss passed away in 2013, Angelenos mourned the loss but were grateful that the owner, who was just as much a family man as he was a ladies' man, passed the team down to his children, led by his daughter and protégée, Jeanie Buss.

ROCKY WIRTZ

To say Chicago Blackhawks owner Bill Wirtz was disliked by his fans is a bit of an understatement. Thanks to decades of penny-pinching on contracts and upholding the ridiculously anachronistic policy of not airing home games on TV, he was one of the most hated men in Chicago. So much so that when the team requested a moment

...Pullman railroad cars. UPS adopted it because it's "easy to keep clean."

of silence after his 2007 passing, the United Center erupted in boos. Bill's son, Rocky, inherited the team and decided to take a markedly different approach. Besides obvious changes like allowing fans to watch all 82 regular-season games on TV, Rocky rebuilt relationships with former Blackhawk greats and spent on current players and fan amenities in a way befitting a team in America's third-biggest market. The result: three Stanley Cup titles (2010, 2013, 2015) after a 49-year championship drought.

PETER MAGOWAN

The San Francisco Giants have one of the most beautiful stadiums in all of sports and won three World Series in the 2010s. However, younger fans might be surprised to know that the San Francisco Giants were on the verge of moving not just once but twice. Unlike the Los Angeles Dodgers, their longtime rivals who also moved from New York to California in 1958, the Giants did not build a baseball-only park. Instead, the City of San Francisco built a baseball-football hybrid—Candlestick Park—in Bayview Heights, ensuring cold and windy conditions, and awful sight lines. With decades of low ticket sales and nearly zero interest from free agents, owner Bob Lurie, who bought the team in 1976 to stop their move to Toronto, was close to selling the team to a St. Petersburg, Florida, group. Thankfully for the Bay Area, an investment group led by Safeway CEO Peter Magowan stepped in and stopped the team from leaving. Magowan made an instant change to the team's culture by signing Barry Bonds, a superstar and Bay Area native whose father Bobby and godfather Willie Mays both played for the team. Then Magowan built a brand-new stadium, using no public funds. While Magowan stepped down as principal owner in 2008 prior to San Francisco winning their three World Series titles, every Giants fan knew that Magowan was the reason they still had a team.

GREEN BAY PACKERS INC.

The Green Bay Packers are the only major professional American sports team to be owned by the community it plays in. Sports fans may know that the team got its name in 1919 when co-founder and head coach Curly Lambeau solicited funds from the Indian Packing Company for uniforms and equipment. Lambeau continued to have financial trouble, which led to the formation of the Green Bay Football Corporation (later reorganized as Green Bay Packers, Inc.). Starting with a 1923 stock sale in which 1,000 shares were offered at $5 each, the Packers now have 360,584 stockholders. Unlike traditional stock, this stock doesn't include an equity interest or pay dividends, so the lucky "cheeseheads" who own a piece of the team aren't doing so to make a profit—they're doing it purely out of their devotion to the Pack. While Packers Inc. does have an executive committee and board of directors to ensure that little Tommy from Kenosha can't fire their head coach, this unique ownership structure ensures that the small town of Green Bay will forever keep its historic football team.

What do sodium, lithium, and potassium have in common? 1) They're all metals. 2) They all float.

TALK PIDGIN "TALK STORY"

In 2015 the U.S. Census Bureau finally added Pidgin to its list of official languages in the state of Hawaii. It was about time—Hawaiian Pidgin had been around since the 1850s.

WHAT IS PIDGIN?

Linguists use the term to describe a simplified blend of multiple languages spoken by communities of people who do not share a common language. Hawaiian Pidgin English originated as a means of communication between English-speaking Americans, Hawaiians, and non-English speaking immigrants (Japanese, Portuguese, Cantonese, Filipinos, Koreans, and Puerto Ricans) on the sugar plantations. When the children of pidgin-speakers learned it as their native language, Hawaiian Pidgin evolved into its own language, with a fully developed vocabulary, pronunciation, and grammar.

To pass the time telling stories is called "talk story" in Hawaiian Pidgin. Maui author Serena Leilani Shipp recently translated these well-known opening lines from literature into Hawaiian Pidgin for *Uncle John's Bathroom Reader*.

A Christmas Carol, by Charles Dickens
English: Marley was dead: to begin with.
Pidgin: Marley stay ma-ke-die-dead.

Invisible Man, by Ralph Ellison
English: I am an invisible man.
Pidgin: I stay one buggah' dat you no'can see.

Anna Karenina, by Leo Tolstoy
English: Happy families are all alike; every unhappy family is unhappy in its own way.
Pidgin: Dem happy ohana stay all da' same; an' da kine unhappy ohana stay all buss up in dea own special kine way.

A Good Man Is Hard to Find, by Flannery O'Connor
English: The grandmother didn't want to go to Florida.
Pidgin: Da Tutu no like go fo' Florida.

Adventures of Huckleberry Finn, by Mark Twain
English: You don't know about me without you have read a book by the name of *The Adventures of Tom Sawyer*, but that ain't no matter.
Pidgin: You no can know na'ting 'bout me if you nevah reed da kine book da *Adventures of one haole braddah, Tom Sawyer*, but no worries.

Another Roadside Attraction, by Tom Robbins
English: The magician's underwear has just been found in a cardboard suitcase floating in a stagnant pond on the outskirts of Miami.
Pidgin: Da magician's unda'wea stay found in one cardboard suitcase in one ma-ke pond on da side of da kine Miami.

Dandelion, milkweed, and sagebrush all contain rubber.

A Tale of Two Cities, by Charles Dickens
English: It was the best of times, it was the worst of times, it was the edge of wisdom, it was the age of foolishness, it was the epoch of belief, it was the epoch of incredulity, it was the season of Light, it was the season of Darkness, it was the spring of hope, it was the winter of despair.
Pidgin: It stay da bes' foa' times, it stay da' wors' foa' times, it stay da' edge fo' wisdom, it stay da age fo' foolishness, it stay da epoch fo' belief, it stay da epoch fo' da kine incredulity, it stay da sea'sin fo' Light, it stay da sea'sin fo' Darkness, it stay da spring fo' hope, it stay da winta' fo' despeah'.

The Catcher in the Rye, by J. D. Salinger
English: If you really want to hear about it, the first thing you'll probably want to know is where I was born, and what my lousy childhood was like, and how my parents were occupied and all before they had me, and all that David Copperfield kind of crap, but I don't feel like going into it, if you want to know the truth.
Pidgin: If you like fo' hea' 'bout it fo' real, guarantee da firs' ting you like try know is where I stay born, how bunk life was when I stay one keiki, an' what da kine parents did befoa' dey make me, an' all da kine David Copperfield crap, but I no' like foa' talk story about it, if you like know da trut'.

The Stranger, by Albert Camus
English: Mother died today. Or maybe yesterday; I can't be sure.
Pidgin: Mada ma-ke tade'. O' maybe she ma-ke yestade'; No can be sure.

The Old Man and the Sea, by Ernest Hemingway
English: He was an old man who fished alone in a skiff in the Gulf Stream and he had gone eighty-four days now without taking a fish.
Pidgin: He stay one old buggah dat try fish alone in da kine skiff in da Gulf Stream an' he go eighty-foa days an' nevah even take one fish.

On the Road, by Jack Kerouac
English: I first met Dean not long after my wife and I split up. I had just gotten over a serious illness that I won't bother to talk about, except it had something to do with the miserably weary split-up and my feeling that everything was dead.
Pidgin: I firs' fo' meet da braddah Dean afta' ma' wahine an' I stay split up. I get one serious illness dat I won' boddah you wit, but I stay all sick ovah how ma' wahine an' I no stay togeda no moa', an' da kine feeling dat every'ting is ovah an' ma-ke-die-dead.

Murphy, by Samuel Beckett
English: The sun shone, having no alternative, on the nothing new.
Pidgin: Da sun kep' shining, having na'ting else foa' to do, on da na'ting new.

Paradise, by Toni Morrison
English: They shoot the white girl first.
Pidgin: Dey shoot da haole gurl firs'.

DID YOU KNOW?

In Hawaiian, Pidgin is called ōlelo pa i ai, which means "pounding-taro language."

There are 200 times as many chickens as people in Delaware.

YOUR MIND IS A SEWER

When Uncle John was a boy, whenever he said something his mother thought was distasteful or offensive, she would say to him, "Your mind is a toilet!" Little did she know just how right she was.

NOTHING TO SNOOZE AT

If you live to be 100 years old, you'll spend some 33 years of that time fast asleep. And yet for all the time humans spend sleeping, the process remains very mysterious, like the brain itself. One area where scientists have gained considerable insight in recent years is in understanding the mechanism that your brain uses to refresh itself when you sleep.

Every living cell in your body functions like an engine, consuming fuel as it performs whatever task it is designed to do. The fuel is contained in your blood, and delivered to each individual cell via the blood vessels that are an important part of your circulatory system.

As your cells work, just like an automobile engine they create waste products, such as ammonia and certain proteins, that accumulate over time. The more work that a cell does, the more waste it produces and deposits into the spaces between individual cells.

So how is all this waste disposed? In most (but not all) of your body, it's removed through a parallel network of vessels similar to blood vessels called the *lymphatic system*. These vessels collect the waste products from the spaces between your cells and deliver them to the bloodstream, which transports them to the liver. From there they exit the body by way of the kidneys, in the form of urine.

> Although your brain accounts for just 2 percent of your body mass, the electrical activity that takes place there consumes about 25 percent of your body's energy supply.

ANOTHER STORY

That's how cellular waste is disposed of in most of your body—but not in your brain. There are no lymphatic vessels in your skull, which is remarkable considering that although your brain accounts for just 2 percent of your body mass, the electrical activity that takes place there consumes about 25 percent of your body's energy supply.

Your brain cells consume that much energy because they do a lot of work—and that means they produce a correspondingly large amount of waste. Like other cells in your body, they dump this waste in the spaces between individual cells. Scientists believe that you experience the accumulation of these wastes as fatigue. The longer

A Nintendo Entertainment System console from the 1980s had twice the computing power as the computers that put a man on the Moon.

you are awake, the more wastes accumulate and the more tired you become, until finally at the end of the day you have to go to sleep.

INSIDE AND OUT

So how does your brain get rid of all the waste it produces without making use of lymphatic vessels? It turns out that the blood vessels in your brain perform double duty: Inside the vessels, blood containing fuel and oxygen is transported to every individual cell in your brain. And *outside* the vessels—along the outer surface—a fluid called *cerebral spinal fluid* is pumped from outside the brain into the spaces between the brain cells. This fluid flows in, collects the waste products that have accumulated there, then flows back out again, taking the waste with it. From there, the fluid transports the waste to your bloodstream, where it is removed from the body via the liver and kidneys.

All of this activity occurs when you are sleeping. It's as if the brain lets the waste products accumulate while it's busiest; then when you're asleep and your brain has less to do, it has time for housekeeping. It literally *flushes* itself clean while you sleep. Then, after the waste has been removed, you awaken refreshed.

In studies of living mice, their brain cells shrink by as much as 60 percent when they sleep. This creates more space between the brain cells for the cerebral spinal fluid to flow, and the amount of fluid moving through the brain increases nearly twentyfold. The same process is believed to take place in human brains during sleep, and scientists at the Oregon Health and Science University in Portland are conducting similar research with human subjects to determine if this is the case.

> It's as if the brain lets the waste products accumulate while it's busiest; then when you're asleep and your brain has less to do, it has time for housekeeping. It literally *flushes* itself clean while you asleep.

TIGHT QUARTERS

So why did the brain develop its own waste-removal system when the rest of the human body makes use of the lymphatic system? One theory: doing away with a network of lymphatic vessels inside the skull frees up more room for the brain, allowing it to grow larger than it would have been able to otherwise. This extra space, now occupied by extra brain cells instead of lymphatic vessels, may be what makes us human, or at least more human than we would be if we had smaller brains.

All of the planets in the solar system could fit inside the distance between the Earth and the Moon.

SWEET HISTORY

The short and sweet histories of some of the world's most delicious desserts.

BAKED ALASKA

Description: Ice cream over layers of sponge cake in a pie plate, topped with a dome of meringue (whipped egg whites and sugar, usually with an acidic element such as cream of tartar to help the meringue stiffen). The dessert is kept frozen until serving, then put in a hot oven for a few minutes to brown the meringue before serving.

Sweet History: Baked Alaska was invented in 1867 by Charles Ranhofer, the French chef at New York City's renowned Delmonico's restaurant. Original name: Alaska-Florida, for the hot-and-cold elements of the dish. (Alaska was a popular subject in 1867—the year the United States purchased the territory from Russia.) The dish became known as "Baked Alaska" some years later.

Note: Ranhofer is believed to have based his creation on a similar dish that was popular in Paris. The Parisian desert also had a geography-inspired name—*Omelette Norvégienne*, or "Norwegian Omelet."

HUMMINGBIRD CAKE

Description: A spice cake made with pineapples, bananas, and pecans (or walnuts), topped with cream cheese frosting

Sweet History: Cakes made with pineapples and bananas have been popular since the Great Depression. The hummingbird cake has been especially popular in the American South for decades, but that's not where it comes from. The cake was first created, without cream cheese icing, in the Caribbean island nation of Jamaica, probably around the late 1960s. It was named after Jamaica's national bird, the swallow-tailed hummingbird (known as the "doctor bird"). Variations of the Jamaican recipe started showing up in Southern newspapers and cookbooks by the early 1970s, under names like "Doctor Bird Cake" and "Tropical Treat Cake." In 1978 a recipe for the "Hummingbird Cake" (with its now-familiar cream cheese frosting) was published in *Southern Living* magazine and it became a Southern standard.

LINZER TORTE

Description: A torte is a multilayered cake with rich filling between the layers. In a Linzer torte, the "cake" is a crumbly pastry made with ground nuts (usually hazelnuts or almonds), filled with preserves or jam, and covered with lattice pastry strips.

Can you name the two fears you were born with? 1) Falling. 2) Loud noises. You had to learn the rest.

Sweet History: The Linzer torte was named after the town of Linz, Austria (*Linzertorte* means "torte from Linz"), and food historians say it's one of the oldest modern cake recipes still in use. A recipe for an early version of this dessert was found in the personal cookbook of a Countess Anna Magarita Sagramosa, in the library of Admont Abbey, a Benedictine monastery in the Austrian Alps. Date the recipe was written: 1653. The cake was first mass-produced in Austria in the 1820s and became popular across Europe in the ensuing decades.

Bonus: A 1965 article in *American Heritage* magazine credits the Linzer torte's introduction in the United States to one Franz Holzlhüber:

> In 1856 Holzlhüber, an enterprising young Austrian from the vicinity of Linz, started for America. He had very little money but was equipped with a zither, a sketchbook, some education in the law and in draftsmanship, and the promise of employment in Milwaukee as conductor of an orchestra. Somewhere between New York and Wisconsin, he lost both his luggage and the letter confirming his job, which, it turned out, was no longer available. Nothing daunted, he went to work as a baker—introducing (so he said) the Linzer Torte to America...

ROCKY ROAD

Description: A mix of chocolate ice cream, nuts (usually almonds), and marshmallows

Sweet History: It was first concocted in 1929 by William Dreyer, founder of Dreyer's Grand Ice Cream (originally known as Edy's Grand Ice Cream, after Dreyer's partner, Joseph Edy) in their Oakland, California, ice cream factory. Dreyer's original recipe used walnuts, an idea he got from Edy, who had used walnuts and marshmallows in a candy recipe. How did they come up with the name "Rocky Road"? According to Dreyer's official history, they picked the name after the start of the Great Depression in October 1929, "to give folks something to smile about" in the face of the economic disaster.

Uh-oh, Another Story: Fentons Creamery, an ice cream parlor in San Francisco, claims Rocky Road was invented by their candymaker, George Farron. The Fentons story goes that Farron used the same ingredients in a candy bar and later added them to a batch of chocolate ice cream. Dreyer, says Fentons, stole Farron's recipe and called it his own. Fentons still claims to be the inventor of Rocky Road ice cream.

> **DID YOU KNOW?**
>
> What's the difference between ice cream and gelato? Gelato is an Italian version of ice cream. The name comes from the Italian word for "frozen," and it's usually made with milk instead of cream. It's thicker and creamier because, unlike ice cream, very little air is whipped into the mixture.

How did dairying ants get their name? They "farm" aphids for the sugary substance...

MISSED IT BY THAT MUCH

Here's a piece of history you probably didn't learn in school: Were it not for bad weather and bad behavior on the high seas, the United States might have adopted the metric system way back in the 1790s.

BASKET CASE

One important item of business that America's founders needed to address after winning independence from England was designating a standard of weights and measures that every state could use. At the time, different states used different systems, and that made trade between the states difficult.

New York, for example, had been a Dutch colony called New Amsterdam until the English captured it in 1664. It still used the Dutch system of weights and measures. But the neighboring New England states used the traditional English system. The bushel used by the state of New Jersey to measure dry goods was larger than the bushel used by Connecticut; a New Jersey bushel basket was large enough to hold 32 pounds of grain, but a Connecticut bushel basket held only 28 pounds. There were already 13 states in the Union, and with more territories moving toward statehood, the problem was only going to get worse unless the federal government did something about it.

THE JEFFERSONIAN SYSTEM

Thomas Jefferson, then George Washington's Secretary of State, had given some thought to the matter, and invented a decimal-based system of weights and measures that he thought would do the job. Decimal-based systems use units of measure that are divisible by ten. In Jefferson's system there were ten inches in a foot, and ten feet in a "decade." Each inch was divisible into ten "lines." There were 10,000 feet in a mile.

Jefferson devised decimal-based measures of volume and weight as well, and when the new U.S. Congress met in 1789, he presented his system and proposed that it be adopted as the new standard of weights and measures for the United States. Congress considered Jefferson's proposal…and did nothing. Americans were left to muddle along as they always had.

PRESENT TENS

On the other side of the Atlantic, the French government was also considering moving to a decimal-based system. In 1790 the National Assembly asked the French Academy of Sciences to devise a system that the entire world could use. The following

…they produce, even "milking" the aphids by stroking them with their antennae.

year, members of the academy returned with a proposal for a system that used a base unit of length called a "meter," which was defined as one ten-millionth the distance from the North Pole to the equator.

And unlike Jefferson's system, which used unrelated terms like "line" and "decade" as well as "rood" (100 feet) and "furlong" (1,000 feet) as names for multiples and divisions of the foot, the French system used standard prefixes like *milli-*, *centi-*, and *kilo-* to designate multiples and divisions of the meter. There are 100 centimeters in a meter, for example, and there are 1,000 meters in a kilometer.

Measures of area, volume, and mass could also be derived from the meter. The weight of one cubic centimeter of water was called a *gram*, and the volume of one thousand cubic centimeters of water was called a *liter*, which weighed exactly one *kilogram*.

SETTING SAIL

This new "metric" system, as it would eventually become known, was simple, elegant, and smart. When Thomas Jefferson learned about it, he wrote a letter to the French government asking for more information.

Remember, France was a longtime rival of the English, and it had a strategic and economic interest in luring the United States away from the hodgepodge of English weights and measures used in many American states. If the United States adopted France's metric system, that would make trade with France easier, and trade with the English more difficult. So rather than reply to Jefferson's request with a letter, in 1793 the French government dispatched an aristocratic scientist named Joseph Dombey to the United States to explain the metric system to Jefferson in person.

TROUBLED WATERS

When Dombey set sail for America, he brought with him a metal rod that was exactly one meter in length, and a cylindrical copper weight called a "grave" that weighed exactly one kilogram. Had he made it to the United States, it's possible that he and Jefferson might have been able to persuade President George Washington and the U.S. Congress to adopt the metric system.

But Dombey didn't make it. When he was in the middle of the Atlantic, a storm blew his ship far to the south and into the Caribbean Sea, where privateers—private ships that were commissioned by England to harass French shipping—seized Dombey's ship and sailed it to the island of Montserrat, southeast of Puerto Rico. There he was imprisoned and held for ransom. But Dombey died soon after he arrived, so the ransom was never paid.

Harvard University (established in 1636) is older than calculus (1660s).

COMING UP SHORT

When France learned of Dombey's death, they sent another metric system emissary to the United States in 1794, but the moment had passed. By then Thomas Jefferson had resigned from Washington's cabinet after losing too many battles to his rival, Secretary of the Treasury Alexander Hamilton. The new Secretary of State, Edmund Randolph, wasn't as interested in the metric system, and it went nowhere.

Over the years, the U.S. government has been gradually embracing the metric system. In 1875 it was one of 17 countries that signed the Treaty of the Meter, which set up an international system for administering the metric system. It has long been taught in American schools, and is used widely in commerce and science. But the traditional English system of weights and measures has never been abandoned, and remains the standard for ordinary Americans. Unlike almost every other country in the world, Americans drive miles, not kilometers; measure distances by the foot, not the meter; and buy bananas by the pound, not the kilogram. We will continue to do so for the foreseeable future, and we may have the pirates—well, privateers—of the Caribbean to thank for it.

* * *

UNCLE JOHN'S STRANGE CRIME BLOTTER

- In February 2018, closed-circuit TV cameras captured footage of a Taiwanese woman breaking into a claw machine. In the video, which went viral in Taiwan, a bit of the woman's butt crack can be seen, hence her nickname, "Butt-Crack Babe." The agile toy thief managed to squeeze inside the claw machine and—over the course of an hour—steal all the toys. According to press reports, she was "bitter that she couldn't win any toys legitimately." When police finally caught up with the Butt-Crack Babe a week later, she told them she'd given all the toys to neighborhood kids. They arrested her anyway.

- The stocks, a favorite colonial method of punishment, were invented in 1643 by a Boston carpenter named Edward Palmer. When he charged too much for his work, he became the first person sentenced to spend time in the stocks.

- In 1902 a man was sentenced to 20 years in the Ohio State Penitentiary for attacking his father-in-law with a knife. While there, he improved the prison's electric chair by adding iron restraining clamps. Released in 1910 for "exemplary service to the state," he murdered a man a few months later and in 1911 was executed in his improved electric chair. The man's name: Charles Justice.

Frosted Flakes originally had two mascots: Tony the Tiger and Katy the Kangaroo.

OOPS!

*It's always nice to hear about people screwing up even more than
you are. So go ahead and feel superior for a few moments.*

IN THE BAG

In February 2018, Duncan Robb, an Irishman living in Chesterfield, England, was
surfing the Internet when he read that the Red Hot Chili Peppers were going to play a
rare show in Belfast, Ireland. And tickets were only £30 ($42)! An incredible bargain,
Robb thought. So he quickly bought two tickets for himself and his girlfriend, who's a
huge fan of the legendary California funk band. Then he booked a flight and a hotel
room for a romantic Valentine's weekend in Belfast. They were so excited! Then, a
few days before the concert, Robb's girlfriend remarked that she hadn't heard anything
about the Chili Peppers playing in Ireland, so he took a closer look at the tickets and
realized he'd actually bought tickets to see the Red Hot Chili *Pipers*, a bagpipe band
that bills itself as "the most famous bagpipe band on the planet." The couple laughed it
off and went anyway. When asked what they thought of the bagpipe band, Robb said it
was "an experience."

KLAW ECAPS

In 2018 two Russian cosmonauts endured a space walk that lasted 8 hours, 13 minutes
in order to upgrade an old antenna on the International Space Station. The good
news: they set a record for the longest space walk in Russian history. The bad news:
they set that record because they installed the antenna backward and had to spend
an extra two hours trying to fix it. According to the *Daily Mail*, "The pair watched
in dismay as the antenna got hung up on the Russian side of the complex and could
not be extended properly." In order to get it back into place, the two cosmonauts
had to push on the antenna while the flight controllers tried to rotate the dish. It
finally popped free, but they still couldn't get it to point in the right direction. "Is it
working?" asked one of the exasperated cosmonauts. "Or are we just wasting our time?"

"It's being evaluated," responded Mission Control in Houston. At last report, a
NASA spokesperson said that the "antenna is in good shape and is operating, in spite
of pointing in the wrong direction by about 180 degrees."

BREAKFAST OF CHAMPIONS

How many eggs does it take to feed 109 Olympic athletes and their support staff? The
Norwegian chefs at the 2018 Olympics in Pyeongchang calculated 1,500. So that's
how many they ordered from the South Korean food supplier. But something got lost

Eyelash mites exist. There are probably some on your face right now.

in translation, and the truck arrived at the Norwegian compound with *15,000* eggs. "It was unbelievable," said team chef Stale Johansen. "There was no end to the delivery." The goof was blamed on the host country's "complex counting system." According to the *Guardian*, "It is common for restaurants to buy eggs by the crate in multiples of 30 in South Korea, but changing one syllable would mean the difference between 1,500 and 15,000."

THE NUCLEAR OPTION

The U.S. Department of Defense (DOD) carries the heavy burden of defending America against a nuclear attack, which is what makes its Nuclear Posture Review so important. The review provides a comprehensive report of several nations' nuclear stockpile and ambitions. The 2018 review caused a great amount of concern, not just because there are some serious threats but also because no one at the DOD seems to know how to read a map. According to CNN, the agency "was forced to correct several mistakes…after an initial version of the report…labeled Taiwan as part of China and included the disputed Kuril Islands in a chart depicting Russia. An earlier draft version of the report…included a graphic that superimposed the North Korean flag over an image of the entire Korean peninsula." Said one Pentagon official: "I imagine it led to a very awkward phone call with our Asian allies."

THINKING INSIDE THE BOX

A six-year-old boy named Mason got stuck inside a claw machine at the Beef O'Brady's restaurant in Titusville, Florida. No one could figure out how he got in, nor could they get him out. (Only the vendor had the key.) Ten minutes later, firefighters arrived and had to break the plexiglass to free him. Apparently, this kind of thing happens fairly often; over the past few years there have been similar reports of little kids getting trapped inside claw machines in Maryland, Nebraska, Tennessee, Texas, Minnesota, Kentucky, Ireland, England, and Australia, and in each case, after the children were freed, they got to keep a toy.

NOT TOO SHARP

In December 2017, John Gomes, an 51-year-old amateur swordsmith from Cohoes, New York, attempted to bend a piece of metal just like he saw them do on the History Channel show *Forged in Fire*. Lacking a foundry, the man started a barrel fire in his backyard…on a very windy day. Yada yada yada. "This is the worst disaster our city has ever seen," lamented Cohoes mayor Shawn Morse. "We often tell people we don't allow open burns in the city and they say, 'What's the worst that could happen?' Well, this open burn just caused millions of dollars of damage and destroyed half our downtown."

What do you have to do to join the Sun City Poms, a cheerleading squad in Arizona? Be at least 55.

WATCHING THE DETECTIVES

Uncle John loves detective TV shows. Some of his favorite series were made overseas. If you're a fan and you haven't seen these shows yet, they may help solve the mystery of what you're going to binge-watch next.

JOHNNY STACCATO (U.S.)

John Cassavetes plays Staccato, a Greenwich Village jazz musician who moonlights as a private eye. Or is he a private eye who moonlights as a jazz musician? Guest stars who went on to greater fame include Mary Tyler Moore, Martin Landau, and Cassavetes's wife, actress Gena Rowlands. (NBC: 27 episodes, 1959–60)

PRIME SUSPECT (UK)

Academy Award winner Helen Mirren stars as Jane Tennison, a detective chief inspector with London's Metropolitan Police. She investigates murders and other high-profile crimes while battling sexism in the police force *and* trying to find a balance between work and her personal life. She also drinks too much. (15 episodes, 1991–2006)

MAIGRET (France)

This series, which is based upon the novels of the best-selling Belgian author Georges Simenon, features Jean Richard and later Bruno Cremer as Commissaire Maigret of the National Police. When Simenon created Maigret, the character was purely fictional, but as he developed a friendship with France's greatest living police detective, Chief Inspector Marcel Guillaume, he based more and more of Maigret on Guillaume. The French TV series is best, but if you can't stand subtitles, there are three British series as well, starring Rupert Davies, Michael Gambon, and Rowan Atkinson, respectively, and one TV movie starring Richard Harris. (144 episodes in the French series, 1967–2005)

DA VINCI'S INQUEST (Canada)

Nicholas Campbell is Dominic Da Vinci, the chief coroner of Vancouver, British Columbia, who teams up with his ex-wife, chief pathologist Patricia Da Vinci, and Vancouver Police detectives Leo Shannon, Mick Leary, and Angela Kosmo to get justice for the victims of foul play in the cases he investigates. The Da Vinci character was based on real-life chief coroner Larry Campbell (no relation to Nicholas), who,

Nineteenth-century slang for sex: "horizontal refreshment."

like Da Vinci, eventually became mayor of Vancouver. *Da Vinci's Inquest* aired for seven seasons, five of which won the Gemini Award for Best Dramatic Series in Canada (91 episodes, 1998–2005)

INSPECTOR MONTALBANO (Italy)

Salvo Montalbano, played by Luca Zingaretti, is the chief inspector of police in the fictional Sicilian town of Vigàta. Inspector Montalbano is hot-tempered and doesn't suffer fools gladly, but he's a friend to the people he trusts—and that's a good thing, because he often needs their help solving crimes. The show is so popular in Italy that it inspired a spinoff show, *The Young Montalbano*. (30 episodes so far, 1999–2017)

ANDY BARKER, P.I. (U.S.)

Conan O'Brien's talk show sidekick Andy Richter stars as Andy Barker, a certified public accountant who rents office space vacated by a retiring private detective. When a prospective client who's looking for the detective agency mistakes Barker for the detective, he decides to take the case. Barker gets help from the retired detective, a video store owner who's seen too many detective films, and other characters. The show won praise from critics but never found an audience, and was canceled after just four weeks. (6 episodes, 2007)

THE SNIFFER (Ukraine)

Kirill Käro stars as *Nyukhach* "the Sniffer," a man with a sense of smell so powerful that he can use it to assist his childhood friend, Major Victor Lebedev of the Special Bureau of Investigations, in solving crimes. One of the most popular television shows ever to come out of Ukraine, *The Sniffer* airs in 60 different countries, including the United States, where it has been available on demand from both Amazon Prime and Netflix. (24 Russian-language episodes so far, 2013–2017)

THE UNDERTAKER (Switzerland)

Luc Conrad, played by Mike Müller, was a police detective until his father's death forced him to take over his family's funeral home…just as he's being investigated for murder. Conrad's police background enables him to notice things that other undertakers don't, and soon he's investigating the deaths of his funeral home's clients, to the exasperation of his former colleagues on the force. (34 episodes so far, 2013–2018)

Bird is the word: In Spanish, *paloma* means both "dove" and "pigeon."

MIRACLE FEET

Ever heard of "clubfoot"? Probably not, thanks mostly to this guy.

MADE IN SPAIN

In 1944 a 30-year-old Spanish physician named Dr. Ignacio Ponseti joined the faculty of orthopedic medicine at the University of Iowa's medical school. One of his early assignments was to review the case histories of all the surgeries that had been performed to cure "clubfoot" at the university since 1921. That was the year that another faculty member, Dr. Arthur Steindler, developed a surgical procedure to treat the crippling birth defect, in which a child is born with a foot turned inward and upward. The condition gives the foot an appearance similar to a golf club. If left untreated, the child will be unable to stand with the foot flat on the ground; instead they must learn to walk on their ankle or on the side of the foot. In about half of all such cases, both feet are clubfooted.

As Ponseti reviewed the case files, he made a startling discovery: In many cases, Dr. Steindler's procedure hadn't really cured the disability—the surgery just postponed it until later in the patient's life. Clubfoot occurs in about one of every 800 births. It is caused when the tendons on the inward side of the foot and calf are too short, pulling the foot in an abnormal direction. Dr. Steindler's procedure lengthened the tendons, restoring a more normal appearance to the foot. But the scar tissue that resulted often left the foot stiff and weak. Painful arthritis frequently set in when the patient reached their early twenties, making the disability far worse.

A DIFFERENT APPROACH

Ponseti had served as a medical officer in the Spanish Civil War in the mid-1930s. He spent much of his time treating traumatic injuries, including setting many broken bones. Under wartime conditions, surgery wasn't always possible, but Ponseti found that he often got good results using only braces and plaster casts. He knew that the limbs of newborn babies are soft and flexible compared to those of adults, and he wondered if it might be possible to treat clubfoot the same way.

He wasn't the first person to think of treating clubfoot with plaster casts. But earlier physicians had not paid enough attention to the anatomical structure of an infant's foot. "They did not know how the joints moved," Ponseti explained to an interviewer in 2007. "They just tried to smash the bones into position."

STEP BY STEP

Ponseti took a more careful approach when developing what became known as the

"Ponseti method." He carefully studied the anatomy of infant feet. When treating his tiny patients, he used this knowledge to gently straighten and rotate the affected foot to a more normal position, adjusting it only as much as the baby's comfort would allow. Then he placed the leg in a plaster cast to hold the foot in that position.

This "adjust-and-cast" process was repeated five to seven times over several weeks. After each new cast was removed, the foot was massaged and stretched to a new, more desirable position, then placed in another plaster cast to hold it there. In as little as a month, the tendons were stretched enough to return the foot to a completely normal position.

To prevent the tendons from tightening back to their original shape, which would cause the clubfoot to return, the next step was to fit a patient with special shoes mounted on a metal bar that held the feet in the correct position. The shoes were worn 23 hours a day for three months, then overnight and during naps for four to five years.

> Some patients, such as Troy Aikman, Kristi Yamaguchi, and Mia Hamm, went on to live very athletic lives.

After the five years were up, 95 percent of the children Ponseti treated were completely cured of clubfoot, with no further action required. They went on to live full and active lives—and for some patients, such as Troy Aikman, Kristi Yamaguchi, and Mia Hamm, very athletic lives—with none of the negative outcomes that resulted from surgery.

THANKS...BUT NO THANKS

The University of Iowa's medical school soon adopted the Ponseti method, and not a single clubfoot surgery was performed anywhere in the state after 1948. But outside of Iowa the medical world was slower to adopt the procedure. Poor results from earlier attempts to cure clubfoot using plaster casts left many medical professionals wary of the Ponseti method, and orthopedic surgeons were suspicious of any technique that didn't involve surgery. "Surgeons love their little knives," Ponseti told the *Chicago Tribune* in 2006. People even joked that his method only worked on kids born in Iowa.

As the years passed, Ponseti promoted his procedure by publishing articles in medical journals and training physicians in teaching clinics around the country. But by the time he retired in 1984 at the age of 70, surgical correction was still the preferred treatment everywhere except in Iowa.

In the early 1990s, Ponseti came out of retirement and returned to treating clubfoot cases at the University of Iowa a few days a week. By this time the university had treated more than 2,000 cases of clubfoot dating back to the 1940s. "I have follow-ups of thirty, forty years, and those patients have normal feet," Ponseti would tell anyone who would listen. "Often they don't know which foot was the clubfoot."

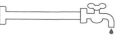

Viagra added to the water in a vase of flowers will make them stand up and live an extra week.

By that time Ponseti, nearing 90, had spent decades living with the knowledge that he'd found a simple, effective cure to a cause of considerable human suffering, but was being ignored. Thousands of people had gone through unnecessary, ineffective surgery over the years, and were living with the consequences. There was little he could do about it.

WEBBED FEET

It was at about this time that things finally began to change. Not because of anything Ponseti did, but because the parents whose children had been restored to full mobility without surgery were suddenly able to sing his praises far and wide, using the power of the internet.

Before the internet, parents of children with clubfoot could go to their doctor for information, get a second opinion from another physician, or go to the library. If they were lucky, they might know another family with a child who had clubfoot. That was it. Then in the early 1990s, the parents of one of Ponseti's patients started an internet mailing list dedicated to clubfoot and the Ponseti method. Now anyone with an e-mail address had easy access to information. After the development of the World Wide Web and search engines in the mid-1990s, parents who searched for information about clubfoot quickly found their way to websites describing the Ponseti method, including many set up by parents of the kids he treated.

TIME FOR A CHANGE

Instead of showing up at their doctor's office with little or no information of their own, parents now arrived well-informed and determined to use the Ponseti method, whether their physician liked it or not. If the physician refused, the parents went elsewhere—if necessary, to Iowa, where the number of children treated at Ponseti's clinic increased tenfold over the next few years. As time passed and demand for Ponseti's method continued to soar, interest in surgery plummeted. In 2006 the American Academy of Pediatrics endorsed the Ponseti method as the standard of care in the United States; by 2010 the number of clubfoot surgeries performed in the United States had declined by more than 90 percent.

Ponseti lived long enough to witness the revolution he created: He was still seeing clubfoot patients in 2009 when he suffered a stroke in his office and passed away at the age of 95. By then his method had been endorsed by the United Nations, and charities with names like MiracleFeet had sprung up, dedicated to bringing the Ponseti method to the developing world, where 80 percent of clubfoot cases occur, and where five out of six cases still go untreated.

But not for much longer.

Ancient rap battles: Vikings engaged in "flyting," or exchanging insults rapidly in verse.

THE FIRST VIRAL VIDEO?

*Even if you don't recognize the video clip "badday.mpg" by name,
there's a good chance you've seen it. It began circulating around
the internet in the late 1990s, when circulating around the
internet was not such an easy thing to do.*

YOU'VE GOT MAIL

If you're old enough to have had an e-mail account in 1997, you probably remember those dark, pre-Facebook, pre-Instagram, and pre-Twitter days when the only way to share something odd and entertaining with your friends was to send it as an e-mail attachment. It's also a pretty safe bet that back then someone e-mailed you a video called "badday.mpg attached." (And in those innocent times, you would have felt perfectly comfortable opening an attachment titled "badday.mpg.")

The 26-second video appears to be security camera footage from an office filled with cubicles. In the cubicle nearest the camera, a chubby man with a mustache sits typing at his desktop computer. Suddenly he slaps the side of his computer monitor with his left hand. The person in the neighboring cubicle peeks over the divider to see what's going on, then sits back down. A few seconds later the first man pounds repeatedly on the keyboard with his fists; then he gets up, grabs his keyboard like a baseball bat and swings it at the monitor, knocking it off the desk and onto the floor just outside the cubicle. Then, as his neighbor peeks up again, the man walks over to the monitor and kicks it some more.

WORD OF MODEM

By today's standards, the video file wasn't big—only five megabytes in size. But in 1997, five megabytes was a lot. On a dial-up computer modem it could take 20 minutes—or longer—to download such a file. But when people received it as an e-mail attachment sent by a friend, they took the time to download it. Then after watching it, they were so entertained that they sent it to other friends, who sent it to their friends.

"Badday.mpg" was one of the first videos to spread around the world this way. When people saw it, they must have wondered who the man was, and where and when the footage was taken. But hardly anyone wondered why the man was so angry. Who hasn't wanted to kill their computer at one time or another? Especially their work computer? This guy appeared to be actually doing what so many office workers have fantasized about doing during their careers. That's why the video spread virally—it spoke to people and provided them with a sense of catharsis. And it was funny.

P. T. Barnum asked a NY paper to run his obit before he died so he could read it. (They did.)

OFF THE HOOK

Some fans of badday.mpg built websites devoted to it; others studied it frame by frame, zooming in carefully to study any detail that caught their interest. And when they did, they began to notice things about the video that seemed a little fishy. The monitor did not appear to be connected to the computer, for one thing. When the man knocked it off the desk, the monitor's cable should have pulled the computer off the desk with it. But it didn't...so was it really attached? If not, why was the man working on a computer that wasn't even hooked up?

Also, when the man walks over to kick the monitor, he pauses briefly and appears to look directly at the camera. Some people thought it looked like he was smirking or smiling. If he really was as angry as he appeared, why was he smiling?

Lots of people had questions, but no one had answers, at least not for about a year. Then in 1998, someone must have forwarded "badday.mpg" to a friend who worked at Loronix Information Systems, a company in Durango, Colorado. They had all the answers, because it was their video.

REVELATION

Loronix sells video surveillance systems and the software that's needed to operate them. When they were preparing marketing materials in the mid-1990s, they decided they needed a few short videos that demonstrated the kinds of activities the security cameras were designed to detect. Rather than go to the trouble of hiring actors, the company's chief technology officer, Peter Jankowski, made the videos in-house. He filmed his shipping manager, Vinny Licciardi, in various scenes, such as getting cash from an ATM, stealing inventory from a warehouse, and—of course—attacking the computer in his cubicle. And just as some viewers had noticed, he didn't destroy an actual working computer. Instead, Jankowski set a defective monitor on top of an empty computer case, then put a broken keyboard in front and let Vinny go to town. (The video you see is the second take: the first take was unusable because everyone burst out laughing.)

The videos were never intended to be seen by the public. They were distributed on CDs at trade shows along with a brochure promoting Loronix's product line. Someone must have enjoyed the video so much that they pulled it off of the CD and e-mailed it to a friend, who forwarded it to their friend, and so on, starting a ball rolling that continues rolling to this day. "Badday.mpg" may be the very first video to spread virally via e-mail, and it certainly is one of the longest-lived. It still pops up on Facebook, Twitter, and other places from time to time. "I'm kind of amazed it's still going around as much as it is, but I think everyone can relate to that moment," Vinny Licciardi told *Wired* magazine in 2018. "They're so ticked off because their software is not working, or there's some glitch, and everybody's wanted to do that at one point in their life."

There is no official language of the United States.

"KEEP PANICKING"

You've probably seen an inspirational poster hanging in an office cubicle or behind a guidance counselor's desk. It's usually a quote about following one's dreams or aiming higher, superimposed over a powerful image of nature, like a sunset or a waterfall. Well, someone designed a program called InspiroBot that generates "inspirational" phrases and pairs them with stock photos to create an endless series of robot-designed—and very bizarre—inspirational posters. It doesn't seem like the bots will replace humans any time soon. Here are a few of InspiroBot's stranger (and funnier) creations.

"If you open your heart to respect, you cannot open your heart to victims."

"Thou shalt attract what idiots think of as unattractable."

"Artists lost their inspirations."

"Tragedy creates empathy for the elitists."

"Before inspiration comes the slaughter."

"If you want to get somewhere in life, you have to try to be dead."

"Basing your everyday on science creates loneliness."

"Make yesterday your rival."

"When you understand how to steal her, you understand how to talk about her."

"Fearful men hide boredom."

"Quality time and collective deception are two sides of the same coin."

"Knowing what you are is what makes you feminine."

"Every day can be as beautiful as a princess in the morning."

"The decline of civilization kills the snake in the garden."

"Forget the art. Remember the player."

"There's a connection between popularity and simply being annoying."

"Try to be yourself or stick a finger in the back of your throat."

"Life is what we do when we're not dying."

"Pregnancy is just a word."

"Don't blame the abuse. Blame the abuse."

"Get embraced."

"Lie about what you know."

"A chicken kills you."

"Now. Now."

"Keep panicking."

"Try to tell yourself that you are horrible."

"You don't need tea in order to raise the dead."

"After the universe comes the big bang."

"Pains are just erotic fantasies on drugs."

"Don't depend upon your enemy's feelings, just be a grown-up."

"Keep calm and stay ugly."

"Remain inbred. Feast on wheat grass."

"Reality is an accident waiting to happen."

"Don't enjoy. Punish."

It's illegal to own rabbits in Queensland, Australia...unless you're a scientist or a magician.

"ALO! SOLLUNGA!"

It may seem natural to say "hello" when answering the phone, but that's just because we've been taught that. Many countries around the world have their own cultural norms for how to greet a caller.

France: *"Allo, qui est a l'appareil?"* ("Hello, who's calling?")

Mexico: It's a Spanish-speaking country, so *"diga"* is used sometimes, but not as often as *"bueno."* It literally means "good," but it's also an idiom that means "I can hear you." In the mid-20th century when phone reception in the nation was poor, *"bueno"* meant the signal was good, or clear enough, to hear the person on the other line.

Italy: *"Pronto,"* which means "I'm ready." Then the caller asks, *"Chi parla?"* or "Who is speaking?"

Polish: *"Cześć,"* an informal greeting similar to "hi." Another way is to say *"Tak, słucham,"* which translates roughly to "Yes, I'm listening."

Dutch: In the Netherlands they say *"met,"* and then their name. It means "You're speaking with…"

Germany: It's customary to clearly state one's last name only.

India: In the southern region where Tamil is spoken, people say *"Alo, sollunga,"* which means "Hello, speak!"

Japan: *"Moshi moshi,"* the polite verb form of "I'm going to talk," said twice.

Spain: *"Diga,"* which means "speak."

Arab countries: A telephone exchange may involve a long string of pleasantries from both parties. Something like this is realistic:

> ANSWERER: May your morning be good.
> CALLER: May your morning be full of light.
> ANSWERER: Praise God, your voice is welcome.
> CALLER: Welcome, welcome.
> ANSWERER: How are you?
> CALLER: Praise God.
> ANSWERER: Praise God.
> CALLER: What news? Are you well? Is your family well?
> ANSWERER: Praise God. How are you?
> CALLER: All is well. All is well. Welcome. Welcome.

And *then* the conversation can begin.

Denmark: Danes answer the phone by saying their first and last name.

Brazil: *"Fala,"* which is an invitation to "talk."

Russia: Reportedly because of widespread phone-tapping during the Soviet era, most Russians still don't say anything when they answer…and let the other person speak first.

Gross fact: Porcupines crave salt, and have been known to sneak into outhouses to suck it up from urine-soaked floorboards.

TOY ORIGINS

A look into how some all-time favorites came to be.

MY LITTLE PONY

Bonnie Zacherle grew up in Japan—her father was a veterinarian with the U.S. Army who watched over quarantined and abandoned animals during the post–World War II occupation. Bonnie's favorite animal: a chubby, short-legged pony from Korea named Knicker. The family returned to the United States, and Bonnie grew up to get a degree in illustration from Syracuse University, which led to a job designing toys for Hasbro in 1978. Many times over the course of three years, Zacherle pitched the idea of a pony doll—small, soft, and cuddly with a tail and mane kids could comb. The bosses cited research that said kids, girls in particular, didn't want pony toys, so she gave up... until one executive asked her to design a *different* pony toy. He wanted it to be huge— about the size of a cat—made of hard plastic, and with a lever that made its ears wiggle, eyes wink, and the tail move. That toy, My Pretty Pony, sold about a million units when it was released in 1981, but a Hasbro executive thought they could do better. He asked his wife how she would improve the toy, and she suggested they make it smaller and softer, with comb-able hair. In other words...just like Zacherle's original idea. In 1982 Hasbro revamped My Pretty Pony as a line of six soft vinyl ponies with manes and tails that kids could brush, and called it My Little Pony.

COZY COUPE

Pedal cars for kids have been around almost since the birth of "real" cars. In the 1970s, a former auto industry worker named Jim Mariol came up with a new idea. The ex-Chrysler designer wanted to make an immersive make-believe car for kids, so he created the Cozy Coupe—a toy car that, unlike most other kid-size vehicles, had a roof and working doors. He had the money for those elements because the Cozy Coupe had no pedals. Taking inspiration from Fred Flintstone's car, no motor skills were required, and with no pedals to operate, it was perfect for younger kids. First released by Little Tikes in 1979, the Cozy Coupe was selling 500,000 units a year by the early 1990s... which was more than any "real" American-made car at the time.

FIDGET SPINNER

In early 2017, teachers were besieged by kids carrying cheap, three-pronged plastic devices that spun on a ball bearing. The "fidget spinner," as it was nicknamed, purportedly helped channel kids' nervous energy, thereby allowing them to focus on

Why is chocolate is associated with Valentine's Day? One theory is that doctors in the 1800s prescribed chocolate to heartbroken people.

their classwork. Whether it really did was beside the point—for a few months, the fidget spinner was the hottest toy in the world, available in stores everywhere for just a couple of bucks. It was based on a device designed by an IT worker named Scott McCoskery. He got so bored during meetings that he created a Torqbar, a metal top-like object that he'd hold in one hand and spin around with the other to pass the time. Figuring other people were probably as bored as he was, he started selling the Torqbar online in 2014. Cost: $300…and yet he couldn't keep up with demand. By late 2016, other companies started making Torqbar knockoffs, and for the much more attractive price of $5 or less. McCoskery filed for a patent, but it was too late. By the time the fidget spinner fad started to fade in late 2017, McCoskery's patent still hadn't been approved.

BETSY WETSY

It's probably an apocryphal story, but the official Ideal Toys company line on how it came up with the idea for one of the most popular dolls ever made involved a frustrated mother talking to a company designer at a party. The woman said that her preschool-aged daughter felt miffed whenever mom had to go and change her newborn baby's diaper. She suggested Ideal come up with a lifelike doll so that little girls could play with it and work right alongside their mothers. This was in the early 1930s, and it took Ideal a while to develop the perfect plastic—it had to be submergible in hot water (if a kid gave the doll a bath), and the company wanted it to really drink and "wet" itself. In 1934 Ideal debuted Betsy Wetsy, one of the first "realistic" toy dolls, made out of soft latex. It drank water, cried tears, and left a wet mess in a diaper. It didn't really take off in sales until after World War II, but was the best-selling doll of the 1950s and remained in production until the early 1980s. (Why was it named Betsy? That was Ideal executive Abraham Katz's daughter's name.)

* * *

WHAT IT'S CALLED IN CANADA

- DiGiorno frozen pizza is called Delissio.
- In Quebec, signage must be printed in both English and French by law. In French, KFC is known as PFK, because "Kentucky Fried Chicken" translates to "Poulet Frit Kentucky."
- Exxon used to be known in the U.S. as Esso, until it was changed in 1972. It's still Esso in Canada.
- Mr. Clean's French Canadian cousin: Monsieur Net.

Indonesian wedding tradition: Newlyweds get a tooth filled to "seal" their negative qualities.

RECIPES TO DIE FOR

Uncle John's mom had a secret recipe for pecan bars that she wouldn't share with anyone. "Over my dead body!" she'd say. When she died, the pecan recipe went with her. But it doesn't have to be that way: some folks have found a unique way to share beloved family recipes—whether they're secret or not—after they pass on.

ETCHED IN STONE

When Maxine Menster died in 1994 at the age of 68, her family searched for a way to honor her warmth and generosity of spirit in a way that was "specific to her," her daughter Jane says. One memory that came quickly to mind was the smell of the Christmas cookies that she baked each year using a recipe passed down in her family for generations. On the day she made them, the kitchen would be filled with cookies cooling "over every surface—the counters, the tables, the chairs—there were cookies everywhere," family friend Charlie Becker told the *Cedar Rapids Gazette*. "She loved to bake."

The cookie recipe was hardly a secret; Maxine shared it with anyone who asked. So why not continue that tradition and share it with the world? That's just what the Mensters did: When they ordered the tombstone for Maxine's grave in the Cascade Cemetery in Cascade, Iowa, they had the recipe carved into the back side of the marker.

> ## MOM'S CHRISTMAS COOKIES
>
> Cream: 1 cup sugar
> ½ cup oleo [margarine]
>
> Add: 2 beaten eggs
> 1 tsp. vanilla
>
> Add: 3 cups flour
> 3 tsp. baking powder
> 1 tsp. salt
>
> *Add alternately with 1 cup cream. Chill and roll out with flour. Bake 350 degrees oven, and frost.*

FOOD FOR THOUGHT

Carving a loved one's favorite recipe into their tombstone is hardly a fad. But now that nearly everyone has a smartphone with a camera built in, whenever someone stumbles across a recipe in a cemetery, they tend to take pictures, and soon those photos begin circulating on the internet. Only problem: the recipes usually take up so much space that they appear on the back side of the marker, and either the person taking the picture neglects to photograph the side with the name, or the picture of the side with the name doesn't circulate as widely as the one with the recipe. Either way, it makes it difficult to determine where the picture was taken and who is being memorialized. But that doesn't make the recipes any less tasty!

A snake with "king" in its name means it will kill and eat other snakes.

Here are some other examples of recipes so good that they've literally been carved into stone:

SEEN ON: A grave in a cemetery in Nome, Alaska (identity of the deceased unknown)

CHOCOLATE OATMEAL COOKIES (NO BAKE) EVERYONE'S FAVORITE

2 Cups of Sugar
½ Cup of Milk
¼ Cup of Cocoa (Swiss Miss)
¼ Cup of Margarine (1 Stick)
Bring to a Full Boil In a Sauce Pan.
Remove From Heat and Let Stand for 5 Minutes
Then Add
3 Cups of Quick Oats
2 Tablespoons of Peanut Butter
2 Teaspoons of Vanilla

Drip on Wax Paper And Let Set Until Firm

(The grave is also decorated with an image of a tub of Cool Whip, which presumably was dolloped onto the finished cookies.)

SEEN ON: The grave of Jacob and Mina Toper in the Kibbutz Na'an in Israel

YANKELE'S YEAST CAKE

1 kilo flour,
50 grams yeast,
A pinch of salt,
3 eggs,
7 spoons sugar,
Margarine, 200 grams,
A cup and a half milk,
Cinnamon to taste.

SEEN ON: The grave of Kathryn Kirkham Andrews and Wade Huff Andrews, Logan City Cemetery, Logan, Utah

KAY'S FUDGE

2 Squares Chocolate
2 Tbs. Butter
Melt On Low Heat
Stir In
1 Cup Milk
Bring to Boil
3 Cups Sugar
1 Tbs Vanilla
Pinch Salt
Cook to Softball Stage
Pour on Marble Slab
Cool & Beat & Eat

Where Ever She Goes There's Laughter

Why did Mr. Rogers announce he was feeding his fish on his show?
A blind child who worried about the fish...

STALL OF FAME: "THE TINDER POO DATE"

It's a sad fact of life: if you're old enough to go on dates, you've probably had at least one "date from hell." But can you top this one? It took place in Bristol, England, and went so badly that it made headlines and earned the unfortunate couple a spot in our Stall of Fame.

ON A ROLL

In the summer of 2017, a Bristol University graduate student named Liam Smith, 24, met a woman (unnamed in news reports, for reasons that will become clear in a moment) using the dating app Tinder. He liked her and she liked him, so they agreed to go for dinner and drinks at Nando's, a popular Portuguese restaurant in Bristol. That part of the date went well—so well, in fact, that the happy pair went back to Smith's flat to watch a movie on Netflix. About an hour into the movie, the woman excused herself to use the bathroom. That's when the trouble started: The woman had to go "number two," and it was only after she did so that she realized that Smith's toilet was malfunctioning. It would not flush.

Had the pair known each other even a little bit better, the story would probably have ended there. One of them would have found a way to fix or flush the toilet, and the unfortunate occurrence would be quickly forgotten. But remember, this was their first date—and the woman panicked.

> Remember, this was their first date—and the woman panicked.

THE PLOT THICKENS

Rather than admit to her new friend that she had a problem, the woman wadded up some toilet paper and used it to—carefully—pluck her poo out of the toilet, then she wrapped the offending item in more toilet paper and tossed it out the bathroom window, which opened at the top. That's how she learned that the bathroom window was no ordinary bathroom window.

"Unfortunately, owing to a design quirk of my house, the toilet window does not in fact open to the garden, but instead into a narrow gap of about a foot and a half, separated from the outside world by another (non-opening) double-glazed window," Smith writes. "It was into this twilight zone that my date had thrown her poo." Apparently, the outer window was so clear—or Smith's date was so panicked—that she did not realize the second window was there until her

…wrote in and said, "I can't see if you are feeding them, so please say you are feeding them out loud."

TP-wrapped poo bounced off of it and landed between the two windows, where it was clearly visible from inside the bathroom.

The gap between the two windows was narrow and deep—so deep that when the woman tried to reach down to retrieve her imperfectly jettisoned poo, she found that her arms were too short to reach it.

THERE'S SOMETHING YOU SHOULD KNOW

At this point the woman decided to fess up. She exited the bathroom and "with a panicked look in her eye," told her date what happened. ("It was one of the hardest things I've ever had to say," she later admitted.) Trying to be helpful, Smith suggested they just smash the window and retrieve the poo that way. But his date had another idea: she was an experienced gymnast, and she thought she could climb through the opening at the top of the inside window and lower herself upside down between the two windows, grab the poo, and with a little help from Smith, pull herself back out again without breaking any glass.

They decided to try it. The woman climbed through the opening at the top of the window and lowered herself into the gap. She reached for the poo…and couldn't quite get it. So she lowered herself a little further into the gap. She still couldn't reach her poo. So she lowered herself still further into the gap and…success! She reached the poo and, with a plastic bag covering her hand, bagged it, and handed it up to Smith. He dropped it into the toilet and was able to get the toilet to flush.

A TIGHT SPOT

Now all that remained was to remove the upside-down woman from the narrow gap between the two windows. No such luck: "My hips were wedged in the window," the woman explained online. Smith spent 15 minutes trying to free her before he gave up and called firefighters, who arrived a short time later and freed her by breaking the window. The woman spent a total of about 30 minutes wedged upside down, and other than a few scratches—and a lot of embarrassment—she was fine.

> **"My hips were wedged in the window."**

The story might not have spread any further than the couple, the firefighters, and their friends were it not for the fact that Liam Smith is a starving grad student. He didn't have the £200 (about $350) that he figured he was going to need to fix the window so that his landlord wouldn't evict him. So he took the woman out on a second date, and over drinks they decided to launch a GoFundMe campaign to raise the money to fix the window. On his GoFundMe page, Smith gave a full account of the incident. He also posted pictures of the windows—with and without the woman wedged upside down in the gap between

Dublin, Ohio, is home to an art installation called Cornhenge:
It's 109 six-foot-tall concrete ears of corn.

them—and a photo of the firefighters working to free her. If ever a story was tailor-made to spread quickly across the internet, this was it. Within hours the tale of the "Tinder Poo Date" had tongues wagging all over the world. The BBC contacted the Avon Fire and Rescue service, which confirmed the story. They had indeed "received a call and freed a woman trapped between external and double glazing," and that "a window was broken in the process."

ALLS WELL THAT ENDS WELL

The GoFundMe campaign raised more than $3,500— more than ten times the amount of money needed to replace the window. Smith and his date donated the excess money to two charities: one that supports firefighters in the Bristol area, and another called Toilet Twinning, which builds toilets in the developing world.

At last report the Tinder Poo Date woman was still safely anonymous, and she is remarkably philosophical about what she has been through. "It's not something I'm proud of, but people are laughing, and if I'm making people happy then I'm not going to complain," she says. Whether she'll find love with Liam Smith is another question. "As for a third date," she told the BBC, "I'm not sure."

*   *   *

FOOD (NOT) FOR THOUGHT

The concept of throwing food at lousy stage acts predates tomato cultivation. (Tomatoes were introduced to Europe in the 16th century, but many people thought they were poisonous and they didn't catch on as a popular food until the 19th century.) The first printed reference to pelting speakers with produce is from 63 AD, when Roman emperor Vespasianus Caesar Augustus tried to calm a rioting crowd… and was greeted with a barrage of turnips. At London's Globe Theatre—where William Shakespeare presented many of his plays in the 17th century—people in the cheap seats (directly in front of the stage) threw rotten eggs at performers. Shakespeare reportedly figured it was because they were getting bored, so he started to write his plays differently, placing serious or emotional scenes just before and after crowd-pleasingly funny, sexy, or violent scenes. The first known instance of a tossed theatrical tomato wasn't until 1883 in Hempstead, New York. The *New York Times* reported that while performing in a vaudeville show, a tumbler named John Ritchie was unable to complete a somersault because "a great many tomatoes struck him, throwing him off his balance and demoralizing him." One tomato hit Ritchie between the eyes and knocked him to the ground. He hightailed it off the stage, dodging tomatoes as he ran.

Sea otters have a pouch under their arms. That's where they carry the rocks they use to crack open shellfish.

THE MAYOR OF FLAVORTOWN

Food Network star and restaurateur Guy Fieri may not be known for being a great chef, but he sure can whip up a fantastic word salad.

"If it tastes really good and it's funky, it's funkalicious."

"I wanna be the ambassador to Chimichanga Flavortown."

"That's dreamy *and* creamy."

"That's a lean, mean pinto bean."

"The flavor jets just turned on. They're trying to shut down the flavor fire I've got going on in my mouth."

"Holy-moly, Stromboli!"

"They make a porchetta you won't forgetta."

"I just want to smear this all over me."

"His seafood is so fresh it'll slap ya!"

"I could put this on a flip-flop and it would taste good."

"The crust is just bomb-dot-com flaky."

"You're like a blackjack dealer at the Flavortown Casino."

"Those are the culinary buoys in the shipyard of Flavortown."

"So much salami, call my mommy!"

"These ribs are like the hub on the flavor wheel of life."

"I'm gettin freaky with your tzatziki."

"Shut the front door, son of Tatum O'Neal, that's dynamite."

"That's slamma jamma in Alabama."

"Dude, I've been stricken by chicken."

"You're takin' the gobble full throttle."

"Do you have a garden hose? Something I can clean up with?"

"Peace, love and taco grease!"

Not that George Washington. Belgium's George Washington invented a process for making instant coffee in 1906.

DUSTBIN OF HISTORY: CHALMERS GOODLIN

Some people make history. Others nearly do, and spend the rest of their lives wishing they had. Say hello to Chalmers "Slick" Goodlin.

THE WALL

In the early 1940s, while America was still fighting World War II, the U.S. government began looking into the possibility of supersonic flight. At the time, it wasn't clear that such a thing was even possible. During the war, when fighter pilots in the heat of battle were forced to dive at top speed, as they approached Mach 1—the speed of sound (about 760 mph at sea level)—their planes became very unstable. The flight controls stopped functioning, the planes shook violently, and many times the aircraft disintegrated in midair, killing everyone on board. This led to the belief among many aeronautical engineers of the day that the speed of sound was an actual physical barrier—a *sound barrier*—beyond which humans would never fly.

Other engineers weren't so sure. It was difficult to reproduce the conditions of supersonic flight in a wind tunnel, and this, in turn, made it difficult to design planes that would fly properly at supersonic speeds. That, these engineers reasoned, was why so many planes broke apart when they approached the speed of sound. They believed that once the flaws were corrected it could be possible to fly faster than Mach 1.

BULLETPROOF

One object that was known to travel smoothly and stably at supersonic speeds was the .50-caliber bullet fired from Browning machine guns. So when the Bell Aircraft company landed a U.S. Army Air Forces contract in 1945 to build a test plane that would attempt to fly faster than the speed of sound, designing it in the shape of a "bullet with wings" seemed like a good place to start.

The test pilot Bell Aircraft hired to fly the rocket-powered plane, soon to be known as the X-1, was a man named Chalmers Goodlin. The 23-year-old was hired because he had been one of the best combat pilots in the war. Also in his favor: he was a Hollywood casting agent's dream of what a fighter pilot should look like. He was tall, dark, handsome, and he had a swashbuckling charm about him that—along with his skill as a pilot—had earned him the nickname "Slick." Though the X-1 program was a secret, Bell's public relations department made no secret of the fact that the company

Georgia peach? South Carolina produces more peaches than Georgia does.

had a dashing young test pilot in its employ. He even appeared in Gillette razor ads that billed him as the fastest man alive. "You couldn't open a magazine without reading about Slick," another test pilot remembered. And unlike U.S. Army Air Force pilots, who made less than $10 a day, Goodlin's pay was very generous, with lucrative "risk bonuses" for really dangerous flights.

HITTING TURBULENCE

On October 11, 1946, Goodlin made his first unpowered flight in the X-1. It was dropped from the bomb bay of a modified B-29 Superfortress bomber and Goodlin had to glide in to a runway below. After a few more such flights were completed, the powered flights began. There were more than 20 in all, and on each flight Goodlin increased the airspeed by 0.02 Mach, nudging ever closer to the speed of sound.

And just as the World War II pilots had experienced when they dove at too high a rate of speed, Goodlin reported that as he approached the speed of sound, the X-1 began to buffet wildly and the flight controls became unresponsive. One reason for having so many flights was to allow the engineers to modify the X-1 from one flight to the next, and in the process improve the plane's performance in the process. But even with the changes, the flights remained an extremely jarring experience.

> This led to the belief among many aeronautical engineers of the day that the speed of sound was an actual physical barrier—a *sound barrier*—beyond which humans would never fly.

Perhaps a little *too* jarring for Goodlin: after 26 test flights in two different models of the X-1, he told his superiors at Bell Aircraft that he wanted to be paid a $150,000 bonus (equivalent to more than $1.5 million today) if and when he flew faster than the speed of sound. Considering that he was risking his life in an experimental aircraft that, in spite of all its modifications, still performed poorly in a task that many people believed was impossible to begin with, $150,000 may not have been unreasonable compensation. But Bell balked at paying the bonus, and when they did, he refused to make any more flights until he received the money.

GOVERNMENT TAKEOVER

The Army Air Force was already frustrated by the slow progress of the X-1 program, and when they learned that Goodlin was refusing to fly, they took away control of the program from Bell Aircraft and looked for a military test pilot to fly the X-1. The pilot they chose was 24-year-old Chuck Yeager, who'd flown 61 combat missions during the war and downed 11 enemy planes. He'd been working as an Army Air Force test pilot since the end of the war, making $283 a month…and his pay did not increase when he agreed to fly the X-1.

Lowest temperature recorded in the continental United States: -70°F at Rogers Pass, Montana (1954).

Yeager had only a high school education. That hadn't hurt his military career so far, and now his limited education may have even given him an advantage because, unlike many aeronautical engineers with advanced degrees, he didn't quite grasp the concept of a sound barrier, and didn't believe it existed.

During the war and as a test pilot, Yeager had flown many different kinds of aircraft, but he had never flown a rocket plane. So he asked Slick Goodlin to brief him on the X-1. No dice: "Slick said he'd be glad to check me out in the X-1 as soon as the Air Corps made out a thousand-dollar contract," Yeager recounts in his 1985 autobiography. "I told him, 'Well Slick, if you flew that thing, I guess I can too.'"

WILD BLUE YONDER

The scuttlebutt around Muroc Army Air Field (now Edwards Air Force Base) in California, where the X-1 test flights were being conducted, was that Slick Goodlin had gotten out just in time. So many people were convinced that Yeager would die trying to break the sound barrier that they nicknamed his test flights "Slick Goodlin's Revenge."

But the naysayers were wrong. After several test flights of his own, on October 14, 1947, Yeager was dropped from the belly of a B-29 Superfortress aboard the X-1, then he lit the rocket engines and soared into the history books as the first person to break the sound barrier, proving in the process that the sound barrier wasn't really a barrier after all. Yeager

> He didn't quite grasp the concept of a sound barrier, and didn't believe it existed.

realized what he'd accomplished when his Machmeter needle twitched briefly at Mach 0.98, then pegged off the right side of the scale. "I thought I was seeing things. We were flying supersonic! And it was smooth as a baby's bottom." The turbulence that materialized as a plane approached the speed of sound disappeared at speeds greater than Mach 1, and in the years to come better aircraft designs would eliminate it even at subsonic speeds.

INTO THE DUSTBIN

Yeager remained anonymous for another eight months while the Air Force (which had become an independent branch of the military a few weeks before Yeager's flight) worked to keep the X-1 program a secret from America's Cold War rival, the Soviet Union. But word leaked out within weeks of the flight, and in June 1948 the Air Force made it official. Overnight, Yeager became the most famous pilot since Charles Lindbergh, a fame that would not be eclipsed until Alan Shepard became the first American in space in 1961. Even today Yeager is more famous than all but a handful of most prominent NASA astronauts.

Wood you believe? America's first water pipes were made from hollowed-out logs.

As for Slick Goodlin, he faded into obscurity, his fame never again reaching the heights he'd known when he appeared in Gillette razor ads. He held a variety of jobs in the aviation industry for the rest of his career, including working as a test pilot for the fledgling Israeli Air Force and running a company that bought and sold used aircraft. He grew bitter at having missed his chance at history, and he feuded publicly with Yeager repeatedly over the years. He even denied refusing to fly the X-1 unless he received $150,000. According to Goodlin's version of the story, Bell Aircraft agreed to pay him the money, "but the Air Force wanted a man in uniform to break the sound barrier—better PR. And to make Yeager look like a hero, they made up the story about me refusing to fly," he told *Air & Space* magazine in 1989.

Goodlin continued to fly airplanes into the 1990s, when he suffered a stroke and had to surrender his pilot's license. He avoided flying on commercial airlines—he was convinced that commercial jets were death traps. He died in 2005 at the age of 82, having never flown faster than the speed of sound, though he did consider flying to Europe aboard the Concorde supersonic passenger jet. But he never did, not because he thought the Concorde was dangerous (though he probably believed that too), but because the tickets cost too much.

* * *

17 ATHLETES WHO CHANGED THEIR NAMES

Cassius Marcellus Clay Jr.	Muhammad Ali
Walker Smith Jr.	Sugar Ray Robinson
Eldrick Woods	Tiger Woods
Ron Artest	Metta World Peace
Mike Stanton	Giancarlo Stanton
Jon Koppenhaver	War Machine
Lloyd Bernard Free	World B. Free
Maybyner Rodney Hilário	Nenê
Ferdinand Lewis Alcindor Jr.	Kareem Abdul-Jabbar
Edson Arantes do Nascimento	Pelé
B. J. Upton	Melvin Upton Jr.
Milton Henderson Jr.	J. R. Sakuragi
Robert Earl Moore	Ahmad Rashād
Shammgod Wells	God Shammgod
Mark Duper	Mark Super Duper

Chad Johnson ☞ Chad Ochocinco ☞ Chad Johnson

Sharmon Shah ☞ Karim Abdul-Jabbar ☞ Abdul-Karim al-Jabbar

Prodigy: Prince wrote his first song at age 7. It was called "Funk Machine."

FOOD MYTHS

Read on, and eat with a little more confidence.

Myth: We need to consume dairy products for strong, healthy bones.

Truth: Chalk this one up to decades of advertising and public relations from trade organizations like the National Dairy Council. Many kids were raised to drink milk with every meal, told that it's packed with calcium to help them grow up big and powerful, with strong bones. While it's true that milk has calcium, it's not the only food that has calcium. Dark leafy vegetables like collard greens, mustard greens, bok choy, and kale all contain calcium levels similar to milk, and they also contain vitamin K, a nutrient that promotes bone health…and which isn't found in dairy products at all.

Myth: People with high cholesterol should avoid eating eggs because they're loaded with cholesterol.

Truth: While one egg does contain a lot of dietary cholesterol, a human's blood cholesterol levels aren't much affected by what's in eggs, or most other foods for that matter. What raises a person's cholesterol levels are foods high in saturated fat and trans fat. Eggs have very little saturated fat (and no trans fat), so they're not really dangerous.

Myth: Chinese food makes people feel lousy because it's loaded with MSG.

Truth: MSG (short for *monosodium glutamate*) is a crystalline food additive that enhances the flavor of food, adding an extra-savory quality. It was discovered in 1908 by a Japanese chemist, and it quickly became a component of cooking throughout Asia. By the 1950s, it was widely used in the United States in packaged foods and also in the many then-exotic Chinese restaurants popping up around the country. In 1968 the *New England Journal of Medicine* published a piece from a doctor who complained that he experienced weakness, pain in his limbs, and palpitations every time he ate at a Chinese restaurant. He *theorized* that it was MSG or too much salt, and the notion that the culprit was the strange and foreign MSG (as opposed to good old salt) caught on with the general public.

Suddenly, millions of people claimed to have what the media soon dubbed "Chinese food syndrome." Chinese restaurants posted signs in their windows proclaiming their food to be "MSG free," to keep customers coming in, assuring them that eating there wouldn't lead to achy bones, a rapid heartbeat…or insomnia, sluggishness, or intense headaches. Numerous studies have since completely debunked the idea that MSG leads to those symptoms (except for a very small percentage of

The chocolate that's in between the cookie layers of a Kit Kat bar contains ground-up Kit Kat bars.

the population that *is* allergic to glutamate, a naturally occurring protein). So what's to blame for people who felt so awful after a Chinese meal? After "Chinese food syndrome" became a thing, it was probably just the power of suggestion. Or maybe the fact that the food in many Chinese restaurants tends to be extremely salty, extremely sugary, and loaded with fat and calories. (Mmm, good!)

Myth: Adding salt to water makes it boil faster.

Truth: On a grand scale, yes, that's true—adding a huge amount of salt to water will change its chemical makeup and thus lower its boiling point from its standard 212°F. But that would take almost an equal amount of salt to water, which would give you unpalatable salt water. Sprinkling a dash of salt into a boiling pot of water actually raises the boiling point slightly…but it doesn't make it boil any quicker.

Myth: You burn more calories digesting celery than there are in the celery itself.

Truth: A large celery stick has only around 10 calories. Celery is mostly water, and most of its calories come in the form of cellulose—a type of fiber that passes through the body almost entirely undigested. All of that digestive work, not to mention the effort it takes to chew the stuff, led to the idea that celery has "negative" calories, meaning the body uses more calories to process the celery than are present in the celery. It doesn't: chewing and digesting a stalk uses about the same amount of calories found in a stalk. If there's a calorie deficit, it's minuscule.

* * *

ART IMITATES LIFE (AND DEATH)

The 2017 film *Three Billboards Outside Ebbing, Missouri* tells the story of a fictional character named Mildred Hayes (Frances McDormand). She's a grieving mother who rents three billboards to shame the local police into solving her daughter's murder. They read: "Raped while dying." "And still no arrests?" "How come, Chief Willoughby?" The idea came to writer/director Martin McDonagh about 20 years earlier when he was taking a bus through Rose City, Texas, and saw signs with a similar message. (The first one read "Raped while dying.") McDonagh recalls that they "flashed by and it stuck in my mind, just bubbling away…the pain and rage and sadness of the person who would put that out there…calling out the cops, and graphic about the crime. I decided it must have been a mother. So Mildred literally just popped out, fully formed—that pain and the bravery to go out of your way to stand up to the police publicly." He was close; the signs were put up by a grieving father, who still believes that his son-in-law killed his daughter, but the case was never solved.

In 2015, researchers at the University of California invented a process for un-boiling an egg.

SAVE FERRIS!

Take the day off and enjoy these behind-the-scenes facts about one of the best teen movies ever made: Ferris Bueller's Day Off (1986), the story a clever Chicago teen, his girlfriend, and his best friend, who just want to skip school and have fun.

★ *Ferris Bueller's Day Off* takes place over the course of about ten hours. Writer-director John Hughes wrote the screenplay in just six days.

★ Hughes took the name Bueller from his childhood friend Bert Bueller.

★ John Candy wanted to play the role of Ferris's best friend, Cameron Frye, but Hughes thought the 36-year-old Candy was too old for the part. It went to Alan Ruck…who was 29 at the time of filming.

★ Other casting close calls: Molly Ringwald, who'd starred in Hughes's *The Breakfast Club* and *Pretty in Pink*, wanted to play Ferris's girlfriend, Sloane, but Hughes wouldn't let her. Emilio Estevez (*The Breakfast Club*) turned down the role of Cameron.

★ Matthew Broderick (Ferris) and Alan Ruck (Cameron) were friends before filming started. They had worked together on Broadway in Neil Simon's *Biloxi Blues*. When Cameron calls the school and berates the principal, pretending to be Ferris's father, the deep voice he uses is his impression of Broderick doing an impression of the play's director, Gene Saks.

★ Economist and former Richard Nixon speechwriter Ben Stein won the small role of a boring high school economics teacher. ("Bueller? Bueller?") John Hughes asked Stein to deliver a real economics lecture, so he improvised one— everything he says is legitimate.

★ Stein later called *Ferris Bueller's Day Off* "the most life-affirming movie possibly of the entire postwar period."

★ Throughout the movie, Cameron Frye wears a Gordie Howe Detroit Red Wings jersey—an odd and bold move in a movie set in Chicago, home to the Red Wings' rival, the Blackhawks. According to actor Alan Ruck, John Hughes did that on purpose. He'd decided that while Cameron didn't get along with his father, he got along great with his grandfather, who lived in Detroit and took him to Red Wings games. The dad is a Blackhawks fan, so Cameron wears the jersey to spite him.

Cost of a Bugatti sports car: $2 million. Cost of a Bugatti oil change: $20,000.

★ Ferris complained about getting a computer when he really wanted a car, but he could have sold his state-of-the-art keyboard to get a car. The synthesizer he uses to fake voices and snoring is an E-mu Emulator II. Used by 1980s synth-pop bands like New Order and Depeche Mode, it cost about $8,000 in 1986.

★ The car belonging to Cameron's dad—stolen (and destroyed) by Cameron and Ferris—is a 1961 Ferrari GT250. They didn't really wreck a classic car for the movie, or even drive one. It was too expensive for the filmmakers to buy or rent one, so they made three fiberglass replicas, each on an MG chassis.

★ The fancy French restaurant Ferris talks his way into is called Chez Quis. In French, it means essentially nothing: "the house of whom." It was a subtle joke. Said aloud, "Chez Quis" sounds like "Shakey's," the name of a once-popular pizza chain.

★ Lyman Ward and Cindy Pickett played Ferris Bueller's parents. Shortly after filming on the movie ended, they got married in real life.

★ Similarly, Matthew Broderick and Jennifer Grey (who played Ferris's sister, Jeannie) started dating and became engaged (briefly).

★ In 1990 First Lady Barbara Bush delivered the commencement address at Wellesley College. "Find the joy in life," she told graduates, "because as Ferris Bueller said on his day off, 'Life moves pretty fast. If you don't stop and look around once in a while, you could miss it!' "

★ A lot of weird "fan theories" about the secrets of what's *really* going on in movies have floated around the internet, but one of the first was the "*Ferris Bueller/ Fight Club* Theory." It suggested that cool and free Ferris Bueller isn't real—he's merely the figment of sad-sack Cameron's imagination…much the way that free spirit Tyler Durden is imagined by the narrator in *Fight Club*.

★ For a few years after filming wrapped, Hughes and Broderick discussed making a sequel, but they never came up with an idea they thought was worth doing. Hughes ultimately felt a sequel wouldn't work because the first movie was "about a singular time in your life."

★ In 2011 an amateur filmmaker named Rick Rapier wrote a *Ferris Bueller 2* script that he released on the internet, and it went viral. The film never got made, but it had an intriguing premise: Ferris Bueller grew up to be a motivational speaker (like Tony Robbins), but he's so overworked that his business manager (Cameron Frye) arranges for a day off.

Odds that a billionaire didn't finish college: 1 in 3.

MOUTHING OFF

WHAT THE FACT?

What is a lie? What is the truth? What is the difference?
Here are some clear thoughts on a fuzzy subject.

"Telling the truth is less demanding than telling a lie."

—Eraldo Banovac

"Lies can't grow. Once plucked they can only wither. But every truth, once planted, grows into a tall, noble tree."

—Stefan Emunds

"Every man has a right to his opinion, but no man has a right to be wrong in his facts."

—Bernard M. Baruch

"Facts do not cease to exist because they are ignored."

—Aldous Huxley

"Lies sound like facts to those who've been conditioned to misrecognize the truth."

—DaShanne Stokes

"The best lies stay close to the truth."

—Cornelia Funke

"Atticus told me to delete the adjectives and I'd have the facts."

—Harper Lee, *To Kill a Mockingbird*

"The wisest in council, the ablest in debate, and the most agreeable companion in the commerce of human life, is that man who has assimilated to his understanding the greatest number of facts."

—Edmund Burke

"A MAN IS HIS OWN EASIEST DUPE, FOR WHAT HE WISHES TO BE TRUE HE GENERALLY BELIEVES TO BE TRUE."

—Demosthenes

NOT COMING TO A THEATER NEAR YOU

You'd be surprised by how many films in Hollywood are started...without ever being finished. Here's a look at a few that will probably never make it onto the big screen.

🎞 *AT THE MOUNTAINS OF MADNESS*

GREAT IDEA: Director Guillermo del Toro has created some of the most visually stunning movies in recent memory, including *Pan's Labyrinth*, *Hellboy*, and *The Shape of Water*. Hs passion project, however, was a film version of H. P. Lovecraft's classic science-fiction novella *At the Mountains of Madness*. Published in 1936, it's the spooky tale of a geological expedition to Antarctica that uncovers the preserved ruins of ancient cities, and the remains of monsters thought to be dead or mythological. That sounds like the ingredients for a perfect blockbuster, and Universal Studios agreed. In the early 2000s, the company budgeted a whopping $150 million to make the movie.

KISS OF DOOM: Del Toro insisted that the movie be as dark as Lovecraft's book. That would have meant an R rating, and Universal Studios balked. PG-13 movies have much better commercial prospects...simply because more people can go see it in the theater. Del Toro refused to compromise his vision, and Universal pulled the plug.

🎞 *UNCLE TOM'S FAIRY TALES*

GREAT IDEA: Before Richard Pryor became the incendiary, profane, political comedian he's known as today, he did tame observational comedy. That all changed around 1968. And while his stage material was changing, Pryor was writing, producing, and starring in a movie about race in America called *Uncle Tom's Fairy Tales*—a dark satire about what happens when a white man is put on trial for assaulting an black woman.

KISS OF DOOM: Reportedly, Pryor was so obsessed with the film—his first—that his wife, Shelley Bonis, became enraged because he wasn't spending enough time with her. When she confronted him, they got into a fight and he spitefully tore up the only negative of the movie. It was never released, of course, but a few clips showed up in a 2005 retrospective on Pryor hosted by the Directors Guild of America. Where'd they come from? Turns out *Uncle Tom's Fairy Tales* director Penelope Spheeris found a print in her possession at some point...but there are still no plans to release the still-unfinished film.

🎞 *MIDNIGHT RIDER*

GREAT IDEA: There have been a lot of great rock 'n' roll movies, like *The Buddy Holly*

About 18,000 people have been successfully hidden by WITSEC, the witness protection program.

Story, *The Doors*, and *La Bamba*. *Midnight Rider* could have joined that canon. The film biography based on singer Gregg Allman's memoir, *My Cross to Bear*, began filming in 2014. Filmmakers started shooting with a sequence of a train traveling along a trestle in rural Georgia, standing in for Allman's home state of Tennessee.

KISS OF DOOM: There was a deadly accident on that first day of filming. The trestle scene called for the train to crash into a hospital bed that was resting on the tracks. The collision caused debris to fly through the air. Some of it struck a camera assistant named Sarah Jones, knocking her into the oncoming train. She died instantly. Not only was the movie canceled, but the film's director, Randall Miller, was convicted of involuntary manslaughter. It also turned out that the railroad company had actually denied *Midnight Rider* filmmakers permission to use the trestle because it was unsafe.

🎞️ EI8HT

GREAT IDEA: In director David Fincher's 1995 crime saga *Se7en*, cops Somerset (Morgan Freeman) and Mills (Brad Pitt) hunt down serial killer John Doe (Kevin Spacey), who has murdered five people, each inspired by one of the seven deadly sins (greed, lust, gluttony, etc.). The movie was a critical and commercial smash, so the studio, New Line Cinema, bought the rights to a crime thriller called *Solace*, hired screenwriters to insert Morgan Freeman's character (who now had psychic abilities) into the story, and retitled it *Ei8ht*.

KISS OF DOOM: Fincher didn't want to do it. When asked by a reporter about *Ei8ht*, Fincher said he "would be less interested in that than I would in having cigarettes put out in my eyes." New Line dropped the idea, removed Detective Somerset and all the other *Se7en* references it had wanted put in, and instead produced *Solace* in its original form, starring Anthony Hopkins, and released it in 2016. It was a box-office flop.

🎞️ THE GODFATHER PART IV

GREAT IDEA: *The Godfather Part III* wasn't nearly as well-received (by critics or fans) as the first two entries in Francis Ford Coppola's mafia film saga. But it made $67 million at the box office and received seven Oscar nominations, so neither Coppola nor his screenwriting partner, Mario Puzo, were quite ready to let go of the Corleone family. Result: in 1990, shortly after filming on *Part III* wrapped, the two got together and hammered out a basic story for *The Godfather Part IV*. It had two main plotlines: 1) the rise of Vincent Corleone (Andy Garcia), and the fall of Michael Corleone (Al Pacino), filling in the time between *The Godfather Part II* and *Part III*.

KISS OF DOOM: Upon rereading the material later, neither Puzo nor Coppola thought either plot trajectory was very good. Puzo's death in 1999 and Coppola's semiretirement from filmmaking (to focus on his winery) ultimately killed the project.

Pope Francis once worked as a bouncer at a Buenos Aires nightclub.

NAME THE PLACE

Everything has a name, and a lot of things are named after the place where they originated. Sometimes those things are so important or successful, they become a lot more famous than where they came from. Here are some of those things.

JALAPEÑO. These mildly spicy, deep green chilies were unknown outside of Mexico before the 1930s. They originated (and were cultivated) in the city of Jalapa (also sometimes spelled Xalapa), the capital city of the southeastern Mexican state of Veracruz. When the chili peppers were exported, they were called *jalapeños*, which means "from Jalapa" in Spanish.

DUFFEL BAG. Today a duffel bag is synonymous with a laundry bag or a gym bag—a large, floppy, over-the-shoulder cloth carryall. But it used to refer to a very specific kind of bag, both the style of the bag and the material from which it was made. Duffel is a town in Belgium where a thick, durable woolen cloth—*duffel*—has been manufactured for more than a hundred years. A bag made of duffel—like one carried by soldiers—was known as a Duffel bag…and then just a duffel bag.

BADMINTON. There's a village in Gloucestershire, England, called Badminton. Settled around the year 1000 under the Middle English name of *Badimyncgtun*, it means "Beadmund's farm." As the English language evolved, Badimyncgtun became Badminton. In the 17th century, a fancy Gloucestershire estate called Badminton House was acquired by the Earl of Worcester. It is there that an ancient racket-based game, brought back from India by British colonials, became popular in the late 1800s. Before long, the sport was known as badminton, too.

VARNISH. The first use of this wood-preserving paint in the Mediterranean region was in the Roman city of Berenice (present-day Benghazi, Libya), probably before the ninth century. Tree resins were used to make it, and the finished product was shipped throughout the Roman Empire. The Latin name for Berenice: *Vernix*, and "varnish" is an Anglicization of that.

GEYSER. A geyser is a naturally occurring hot spring that bubbles and shoots water from underground up onto the surface. Iceland is dotted with thousands of these springs, among them one called Geysir, which gets its name from *geysa*, the Icelandic word for "gusher."

First American city with electric streetlights: Wabash, Indiana (1880).

WISEGUYS AND WHALES

Whether you're a casual gambler or a Vegas regular, it pays to know the language spoken in casinos. How else are you going to spot the mechanics and the mushes?

Arm: A craps player who's so skilled at throwing the dice that they can increase their chances of winning

Steaming/On Tilt: Placing reckless bets in fear or anger, in the hope of winning back money that has been lost

Crossroader: An old-time term for a cheat (casinos used to be built at major crossroads)

Square: A casual gambler (the opposite of a sharp)

Playing the Rush: Playing more aggressively (or sloppily) after winning a bunch of money

First Base: The position at a blackjack table immediately to the left of the dealer (and thus the first to be dealt cards)

Third Base: The position to the immediate right of the blackjack dealer (the last position to be dealt cards)

Black Book: The list of gamblers (cheats, etc.) who are banned from every casino in the state of Nevada

Racino: A racetrack that also has casino gambling

George/Real George: A player who tips the dealer generously

Fish/Pigeon: An unskilled, money-losing player

Flea: A small-stakes player who still expects the casino to "comp" them free drinks, free meals, etc.

Spooking: Standing behind the blackjack to peek at the hole card, then signaling to an accomplice placing bets at the table

Coat-tailing: Copying the bets of someone who is winning money

Beard: Someone who places bets for another gambler

Mush: A gambler who is unlucky to be around

Automat: A gambling establishment that offers nothing but electronic games—no dealers required

Shiner: Something with a reflective surface that a cheater uses to see a card that has been dealt facedown

Honeymoon Period: Beginner's luck

The good news: Only 1.5% of Earth's 9 million insect species are harmful to humans. The bad news: 1.5% of 9 million still comes to 135,000 species.

Color Up: To exchange smaller-denomination chips for higher-denomination chips (of a different color)

Barber Pole: A stack of chips with more than one denomination, and thus more than one color

Carpet Joint: A high-end casino

Eye in the Sky: Video surveillance cameras installed in casino ceilings above the gaming tables

Mechanic: A casino dealer who cheats; it can also mean a gambler who uses sleight of hand to cheat at cards or dice

Crack the Nut: When a casino makes enough money off of losing gamblers to cover its expenses and turn a healthy profit

Camouflage: Any techniques (disguises, feigning drunkenness or inexperience, etc.) that a highly skilled gambler uses to appear unskilled or impaired

Firing: Placing one big bet after another

Sharp: A professional gambler

Silver Mining/Slot Walking: Checking unattended slot machines for coins that have been left behind by other gamblers

Whale: A player who bets in increments of at least $1,000 (a "high-roller" bets $100 or more per round)

Grinding It Out: Gambling consistently over time, often when the grinder understands the probabilities of the game

Burn Cards: Cards that are removed from the top of the deck and removed from play after the deck is shuffled and cut

Sawdust Joint: A low-end casino

Card Washing: Shuffling the cards by laying them facedown on the table and spreading them around the surface of the table with both hands in a manner that looks like they're washing the tabletop

Scared Money: The money a gambler can't afford to lose

Skinning the Hand: When a card cheat gets rid of their extra cards

*   *   *

UNINTENDED CONSEQUENCES

"Being fired has some of the advantages of dying without its supreme disadvantages. People say extra-nice things about you, and you get to hear them."

—**Howard Zinn**

The geographical center of the United States is located near the Nebraska/Kansas border.

HERE COMES BOATY MCBOATFACE!

Here's what happened when the British government let the internet name a $287 million polar research ship.

SEEMED LIKE A GOOD IDEA

In March 2016, England's Natural Environment Research Council (NERC) launched a competition to name the new Royal Research Ship (RRS) that was scheduled to set sail in 2019. The bright red, 15,000-ton, 423-foot-long vessel includes a helipad, a crane, and onboard labs. It has the ability to deploy subs and can host as many as 90 research scientists who will study ice sheets, ocean currents, and marine life. In the name-that-ship competition, NERC said it was looking for "something inspirational" that would exemplify the magnitude of the ship's work.

The British, who are known for their dry, absurd, Monty Pythonesque sense of humor, immediately submitted inspirational names like *What Iceberg?* and *It's Bloody Cold Here*. One submission, *Clifford the Big Red Boat*, inspired BBC presenter James Hand to toss his idea for a name into the ring: *Boaty McBoatface*. His submission immediately went viral and within 48 hours it received 8,000 votes and crashed the NERC website.

VOTES ARE IN

Though more inspirational suggestions—such as RRS *Henry Worsley*, after the explorer who died trying to cross Antarctica alone, and RRS *Poppy-Mai*, after a brave young girl who died from a rare form of brain cancer—received quite a few votes (15,231and 34,371), *Boaty McBoatface* was the absolute favorite with 124,109 votes.

AND THE WINNER IS

Much to the dismay of the voting public, Science Minister Jo Johnson said it would be inappropriate to give a joke label to the ship. "Its title should fit the mission and capture the spirit of public endeavor," he said. Johnson reminded voters that NERC had reserved the right in the competition rules to have the final say on the name. So the polar research ship was named RRS *Sir David Attenborough* in tribute to the great broadcaster and natural scientist. Some Brits suggested that in the interest of

> ### NO, THEY'RE NOT
>
> "We are excited to hear what the public has to suggest and we really are open to ideas."
>
> —NERC official

The 19th Amendment to the U.S. Constitution, giving women the vote, took 42 years to ratify (1878–1920).

democracy and humor, Sir David should change his name to Sir Boaty McBoatface…
but no such luck.

IT'S BAAACK

The joke would not die.

- One month after the Boaty vote, Google released a natural language parser that they called Parsey McParseface.

- That August, the Cartoon Network's series *The Regular Show* broadcast an episode titled "Spacey McSpace Tree."

- A character on BBC Three's popular online series *Pls Like* was named Vloggy McVlogface.

- Later that year, a new salt-spreading truck in the UK was named Salty McSaltface.

- Sweden's Stockholm-Gothenburg rail line named one of their engines Trainy McTrainface.

- A new ferry in Sydney, Australia, was dubbed *Ferry McFerryface*.

- The first Humboldt penguin to hatch in the UK's Sea Life Sanctuary was named Fluffy McFluffyface.

- And as a consolation prize for NERC voters, the yellow submarine on the RRS *Sir David Attenborough* was named Boaty McBoatface.

* * *

TWO TERRIBLE TYPOS

A special Google home page banner replaced the second "g" with a g-shaped strawberry, but the typesetter deleted the "l" as well and forgot to put it back, so for an entire day Google's home page said:

Googe

Fact 1: The 2018 Winter Olympics were held in PyeongChang, South Korea.
Fact 2: P. F. Chang's is an Asian-inspired restaurant chain with more than 200 U.S. locations. Those two facts collided in the Olympics logo that Chicago's WLS News displayed on its screen during a story about the PyeongChang games:

P.F. Chang 2018

Dam! North American beavers used to be as big as bears.

SPORTS LASTS

You can make the sports history books by being the first to do something…or by being the last to do something.

Last baseball team to integrate: In 1947 Jackie Robinson of the Brooklyn Dodgers became the first African American player in the major leagues, integrating baseball. Other teams slowly added black players to their rosters. The final holdout: the Boston Red Sox, who signed Elijah "Pumpsie" Green in 1959.

Last East Coast team to head out west: In 1955 the Philadelphia Athletics moved to Kansas City. Three years later, the Brooklyn Dodgers and New York Giants became the Los Angeles Dodgers and San Francisco Giants, respectively. In 1960 the NBA's Minneapolis Lakers headed to Los Angeles, followed shortly by the Philadelphia Warriors heading to San Francisco in 1962. That brought professional sports to the far west, and the end of that particular moving bonanza. The *very* last time it happened, however, was in 1978. The NBA's Buffalo Braves moved to California and became the San Diego Clippers. (Six years later, they headed north and became the Los Angeles Clippers.)

Last time a team won a championship and then immediately folded: In the early 1990s the Canadian Football League expanded into the United States, bringing its distinct style of play into pro football–starved cities such as San Antonio, Birmingham, and Memphis. The experiment ended in 1995 after two seasons; all of the American franchises went out of the business. That included the Baltimore Stallions, who in November 1995 became the first and only American team to win the CFL's Grey Cup. The NFL returned to Baltimore the following year with the birth of the Ravens.

Last Heisman Trophy winner who didn't turn pro: Awarded at the Downtown Athletic Club in New York City since 1935, the Heisman Trophy is the most prestigious player award in college football. Being named the winner of the Heisman almost guarantees the recipient will be selected high in the NFL Draft and go on to a career in the pros. (Some past Heisman winners turned Pro Football Hall of Famers: Barry Sanders, Marcus Allen, and Roger Staubach.) In the mid-20th century, college football was far more popular than pro football, so many early Heisman winners opted for a non-football life after college. Upon graduating in 2005, Jason White, the 2003 Heisman-winning University of Oklahoma quarterback, was not drafted. He got a tryout from the Kansas City Chiefs, and was signed as a free agent by the Tennessee Titans, but he walked away from football because multiple knee injuries left him feeling like he couldn't make it in the NFL.

There's currently a black hole traveling through space at a speed of 5 million miles per hour.

Last pitcher to win 30 games: Nowadays, winning 20 games in a season is an achievement that will often nab a pitcher a Cy Young Award. It's difficult to win much more than that because most teams employ a five-man rotation (some are even beginning to toy with a six-man rotation). But during the 1960s, baseball was dominated by pitchers…and some teams had *four*-man rotations. The last time a pitcher won 30 games or more: 1968, when Denny McLain won 31 for the Detroit Tigers, winning both the American League Cy Young and MVP Awards.

Last player-coach in the NBA: Who knows how to coach basketball better than somebody who played basketball? Somebody who *still* plays basketball. In the first few decades of the NBA, player-coaches were not uncommon, as coaches frequently demonstrated stuff out of the playbook by leading by example. The process fell out of favor in the 1960s, and the last player-coach in the league was the Boston Celtics' Dave Cowans in the 1978–79 season.
Bonus fact: The last player-manager in baseball was Pete Rose. During the 1986 season, "Charlie Hustle" managed the Cincinnati Reds and also occasionally stepped in to play several infield positions.

Last NHL goalie to play without a mask: Helmets were optional in the NHL for decades. Some players refused to wear them—even after Bill Masterson of the Minnesota North Stars died from an on-ice head injury in 1968—because they thought it made them appear to be "sissies." It was a different story for goalies. That position involved the most high-speed pucks flying toward the face, so by the 1960s, most goaltenders opted to wear protective masks (like the one made famous by killer Jason Voorhees in the *Friday the 13th* movies) over their faces. But they still didn't *have* to wear one, and a journeyman goalie named Andy "Fearless" Brown opted to go without, claiming that the safety gear blocked his vision. By the time he left the NHL in 1977, he was the only goaltender in the league with an uncovered face. (Two years later, the NHL made helmets and masks mandatory, though players who'd signed NHL contracts prior to June 1, 1979, could continue to play helmetless if they so desired.)

Last American League pitcher to get a hit before the DH rule: Major League Baseball has long been split into two leagues—the National and the American Leagues. Gameplay was essentially the same in both leagues…until 1973. That's when the American League, in an effort to add more offensive excitement to the game, stopped sending pitchers up to bat. Instead, AL teams started using a designated hitter, who would bat in place of the pitcher but not take the field to play defense. The last pitcher who batted in the pre-DH era in a regular-season AL game and got a hit: rookie New York Yankees hurler Larry Gowell, on October 4, 1972. He pitched in a total of seven innings in a grand total of two big-league games, and got to bat once. But he made it count, hitting a double. (That gave him a perfect career batting average of 1.000.)

Weird MLB rule: If a player tries to catch a ball with his hat, the batter gets to take third base.

"TWO CHICKENS TO PARALYZE"

*What's a mondegreen? A woefully misheard or misunderstood phrase...
or song lyric. Here are some of the funniest ones we've collected.*

Song: "Mama Said," by the Shirelles
Actual lyric: "There'll be days like this, my mama said"
Misheard as: "There'll be days like this, my marmoset"

Song: "Hit Me With Your Best Shot," by Pat Benatar
Actual lyric: "Hit me with your best shot"
Misheard as: "Hit me with your pet shark"

Song: "Another Brick in the Wall," by Pink Floyd
Actual lyric: "No dark sarcasm in the classroom"
Misheard as: "No *Dukes of Hazzard* in the classroom"

Song: "I Just Want to Celebrate," by Rare Earth
Actual lyric: "I just want to celebrate"
Misheard as: "I just wanna salivate"

Song: "Like I Love You," by Justin Timberlake
Actual lyric: "You're a good girl, and that's what makes me trust you"
Misheard as: "You're a good girl, and that's what makes me Justin"

Song: "Blank Space," by Taylor Swift
Actual lyric: "Got a long list of ex-lovers"
Misheard as: "Got along with Starbucks lovers"

Song: "Rock You Like a Hurricane," by Scorpions
Actual lyric: "Here I am, rock you like a hurricane"
Misheard as: "Here I am, rock you like I'm Herman Cain"

Song: "Pet Sematary," by the Ramones
Actual lyric: "I don't wanna be buried in a pet sematary"
Misheard as: "I don't wanna meet Barry in a pet cemetery"

Song: "Bizarre Love Triangle," by New Order
Actual lyric: "I feel a shot right through like a bolt of blue"
Misheard as: "I feel a shot right through like a butt of poo"

Song: "Mercy," by Duffy
Actual lyric: "You got me begging you for mercy"
Misheard as: "You got me begging you for birdseed"

A seabird called an arctic tern can live up to 34 years. In that time, it can travel up to 1.5 million miles.

Song: "Message in a Bottle," by the Police
Actual lyric: "A year has passed since I wrote my note"
Misheard as: "A year has passed since I broke my nose"

Song: "Drive," by the Cars
Actual lyric: "You can't go on thinking nothing's wrong, uh-uh"
Misheard as: "You can't go on thinking nothing's wrong, pork pie"

Song: "Two Tickets to Paradise," by Eddie Money
Actual lyric: "I've got two tickets to paradise"
Misheard as: "I've got two chickens to paralyze"

Song: "Let My Love Open the Door," by Pete Townshend
Actual lyric: "Let my love open the door"
Misheard as: "Let Milo open the door"

Song: "Behind Blue Eyes," by the Who
Actual lyric: "No one knows what it's like to be the bad man"
Misheard as: "No one knows what it's like to be the Batman"

Song: "Every Time You Go Away," by Paul Young
Actual lyric: "You take a piece of me with you"
Misheard as: "You take a piece of meat with you"

Song: "Stairway to Heaven," by Led Zeppelin
Actual lyric: "And as we wind on down the road"
Misheard as: "And there's a wino down the road"

Song: "Higher Love," by Steve Winwood
Actual lyric: "Bring me a higher love"
Misheard as: "Bake me a pile of love"

Song: "Hurts So Good," by John Cougar
Actual lyric: "Sometimes love don't feel like it should"
Misheard as: "Sometimes love is gonna feel like s**t"

Song: "Bohemian Rhapsody," by Queen
Actual lyric: "I sometimes wish I'd never been born at all"
Misheard as: "I sometimes wish I'd never been boiled in oil"

Song: "Jet Airliner," by the Steve Miller Band
Actual lyric: "Big ol' jet airliner"
Misheard as: "Put old Jeb in the lineup"

Song: "Panic," by the Smiths
Actual lyric: "Hang the D.J."
Misheard as: "Hank the D.J."

Song: "I Wanna Be Sedated," by the Ramones
Actual lyric: "I wanna be sedated"
Misheard as: "I want a piece of bacon"

Deadliest job in WWII: serving on a German sub. It had a 75% fatality rate.

MOOS IN THE NEWS

If you've herd any these stories before, you might want to steer clear of this page.

COW ISLAND

In January 2018, a Polish farmer identified in news reports as "Mr. Lukasz" attempted to get a cow into his truck to take it to its final destination: the slaughterhouse. Seemingly aware of its fate, the cow broke free of human handlers (breaking one farmhand's arm), crashed through a metal fence, and headed for the nearby Lake Nyskie. That's when Mr. Lukasz saw the cow dive into the lake and start swimming away. The cow reached a small island in the middle of the lake and took up residence there. Lukasz tried for a week to get to the cow with the aid of a fire department's boat…which prompted the cow to swim farther away to a nearby peninsula. Lukasz finally gave up, and now just has food delivered to make sure his cow survives on its new home.

I JUST WANNA GRAZE IN GRASS ALL NIGHT

KISS bassist Gene Simmons has one of the most distinctive looks in rock 'n' roll history. For more than 40 years, Simmons has worn his stage makeup in a certain pattern: face painted white, with what resembles black bat wings painted over his eyes and a black Bela Lugosi widow's peak extending down from his hairline. In July 2017, a baby cow on a ranch north of San Antonio, Texas, was born with almost the same patterns on its face, leading some reporters to suggest that Simmons and the calf are from the same "gene pool." The calf's owners, the Taccetta family, say they'll raise the cow as a pet. They named her Genie.

GOLD, FRANKINCENSE, AND MOO

Since 1973 the Old First Reformed United Church of Christ in Philadelphia has staged a live nativity scene each Christmas season. Their re-creation of the first Christmas features real donkeys, sheep, and cows, and there was never an incident until 2017. On December 14 at around 2:30 a.m., one of the nativity cows—named Stormy—escaped from the animal enclosure in the churchyard, fled the scene, and walked to the on-ramp of a nearby highway. That's where police surrounded Stormy with squad cars, then tied a rope around her and led her back to the nativity scene. A few hours later, police received a report that Stormy had escaped *again*. This time, she made it to the top floor of a downtown Philadelphia parking garage before police took her back to church. Stormy was subsequently replaced by her "understudy"—a cow named Ginger.

Give or take: The Chinese census has a 2% margin of error. That comes to about 26.7 million people.

ANNE FRANK, RECONSIDERED

Historians have long wondered who it was that betrayed Anne Frank's family in Amsterdam. But were they really betrayed? A new theory could explain how their hiding place was discovered.

IN HIDING

The story of Anne Frank and the diary she kept while she and her family were hiding from the Nazis is perhaps the most familiar story to emerge from the Holocaust. Children all over the world read her diary in school, and it has also been made into a play, an Academy Award–winning 1959 film, and numerous television dramas. The details of her life hardly need repeating: During the Nazi occupation of the Netherlands in World War II, Anne, her parents, her sister Margot, and four other Jews went into hiding in a "Secret Annex" hidden behind a bookcase in the building where her father, Otto, ran his business.

Four trusted employees kept the people in the Secret Annex supplied with food they purchased with black market ration cards. During the two years and one month that Anne lived there, she made regular entries into her diary describing everyday life in hiding. Then on August 4, 1944, three days after Anne's last diary entry, the building was raided by the Nazis and the eight people hiding in the Secret Annex were arrested and taken away to concentration camps. Only Otto Frank survived; he was the one who arranged for Anne's diary to be published after the war.

WERE THEY BETRAYED?

One question that has remained unanswered for more than 70 years is how the Franks and the others in the Secret Annex were discovered. Otto Frank was certain that they must have been betrayed by someone who tipped off the Nazis to their hiding place. He spent the rest of his life trying to discover who the betrayer was, and after his death in 1980, the foundation that operates the Anne Frank House continued the search. The Dutch government launched two investigations of its own into the matter, one in 1948 and another in 1963. It questioned both the surviving police officials who participated in the raid, and numerous people who worked in the building, all in an attempt to find out who, if anyone, was responsible.

> One question that has remained unanswered for more than 70 years is how the Franks and the others in the Secret Annex were discovered.

Otto Frank suspected a man named Willem van Maaren, who began working in the warehouse on the ground floor of the building in 1943. He hadn't been told that

Jews were hiding in the building, but he suspected as much, and he set several "traps" to try to find out if people were moving around the building at night: "He places books and bits of paper on the very edges of things in the warehouse so that if anyone walks by they fall off," Anne wrote in her diary on April 25, 1944. Van Maaren also sprinkled potato flour on the floor to see if anyone would walk through it and leave footprints.

Another suspect was Lena Hartog, who cleaned the building and was married to a man who worked in the warehouse. According to this theory, Hartog had learned somehow that Jews were hiding somewhere in the building; fearing for her safety and her husband's if the Jews were discovered, she reported them to the Nazis. A third suspect was a member of the Dutch National Socialist Party named Tonny Ahlers. To date, very little evidence has surfaced to suggest that any of these suspects, or any of the others that have been proposed over the years, were actually responsible for betraying the Franks and the others hiding in the Secret Annex.

A NEW THEORY

In December 2016, Dr. Gertjan Broek, a historian affiliated with the Anne Frank House, published an article in which he suggests that there may not have been a betrayer after all. He argues that it is possible that the Secret Annex was discovered by accident, when Nazi police officials searched the building while there on another matter.

One piece of evidence is the timing and the nature of the police raid. The Nazis arrived at the building sometime around 11:00 a.m. on the morning of August 4, 1944. While they were there, people were allowed to enter and leave the building freely. This suggests that they weren't looking for people, Dr. Broek argues, because if they had been, no one would have been allowed to leave.

Jan Gies, one of the people who arrived at the building a short time after the Nazis did, left as soon as he realized they were there. He went to a nearby bridge and observed the scene from that safe vantage point, and was still there at 1:00 p.m., when the Franks and the other Jews who had been hiding in the Secret Annex were taken away. That means the raid took nearly two hours. If the Nazis were there to arrest the people in the Secret Annex, Dr. Broek asks, why did it take them two hours to do it? He suspects that the Nazis did not know that the Secret Annex was there, or that anyone was hiding in it, until they stumbled across it by accident.

"B" AND "D"

Another potential clue comes from the pages of Anne Frank's diary. On March 10, 1944, five months before the raid, she notes that the Nazis arrested "B" and "D," two men who dealt in illegal ration cards, "so we have no coupons to buy food with." B and D were Martin Brouwer and Pieter Daatzelaar, two salesmen who worked in the

Your body has enough DNA to reach from the sun to Pluto and back—17 times.

building and who also trafficked in ration cards on the side. Neither of them knew about the Secret Annex or the people hiding there—Anne Frank writes elsewhere in her diary that when Brouwer and Daatzelaar were in the building, she and the others in the Secret Annex had to be very quiet to avoid detection.

FOLLOW-UP

Typically when traffickers like Brouwer and Daatzelaar were arrested, the information was forwarded to a Nazi-controlled police agency called the Special Unit of the Central Investigation Division, which was set up in 1941 to investigate "illegal distribution of ration coupons and meat," Dr. Broek writes. One of the collaborators who assisted the Nazis in the August 4 raid was a Dutch policeman named Gezinus Gringhuis—who worked for the Special Unit of the Central Investigation Division. A second collaborator, an Austrian policeman named Karl Silberbauer, was assigned mostly to property crimes, not to ferreting out Jews in hiding.

All of this information leads Dr. Broek to suspect that when the Nazis raided the building, they were there to follow up on the arrests of the ration card traffickers Brouwer and Daatzelaar, who worked there. The Nazis searched the building thoroughly for nearly two hours looking for evidence of ration card fraud, and when they got to the bookcase that hid the Secret Annex, the fate of Anne Frank and the other people hiding there was sealed.

But Dr. Broek admits that it's just a theory: "The possibility of betrayal has of course not been entirely ruled out by this, nor has any relationship between the ration coupon fraud and the arrest been proven. Clearly," he writes, "the last word about that fateful summer day in 1944 has not yet been spoken."

*   *   *

9 U.S. STATES WITH A BALD EAGLE ON THEIR FLAG

1. Illinois
2. Iowa
3. Michigan
4. Missouri
5. New York
6. North Dakota
7. Oregon
8. Pennsylvania
9. Utah

The film shoot of *Grease* went through 100,000 pieces of bubble gum.

BRANDED

Do names have power? Certainly. And in the case of brand names, they have the power to help part consumers from their hard-earned money.

WHAT'S IN A NAME? The cost for a pharmaceutical company to name and brand a new drug can go as high as $3 million. But the pharmaceutical market is a $450 billion business in the United States alone, so there's a lot at stake, financially, and if the name is right, the investment is worth it. That's why drug companies don't give the naming job to a few clever people who sit around a big table, order pizza and beer, and write ideas on a whiteboard, but to "branding agencies"— companies whose entire purpose is to name and brand new products. The process can be complicated because prescription drugs must have three different names: the chemical name (ibuprofen), the generic name (NSAID: nonsteroidal anti-inflammatory drug) and the brand name (Advil).

Major branding agencies, or "naming companies," such as Catchword, Zinzin, and the Brand Institute, go through an intense yearlong process of picking just the right brand name for a new drug. First the agency must understand the drug's purpose. Then they compile a list of hundreds or even thousands of possible names, which is condensed to a dozen finalists. Those names are crosschecked in databases to make sure the name hasn't already been taken. Then the company checks foreign language databases to make sure the name doesn't translate into something shocking in another country, which is what happened to the soft drink Coca-Cola. In Chinese, "cocacola" roughly translates to "bite the wax tadpole," which is why the company wisely changed its Chinese brand name to *Kekoukele*, which means "tasty fun."

NO ROOM FOR ERROR. The rules of the U.S. Food and Drug Administration (FDA) and the European Medicines Agency are strict. To avoid the possibility of a prescription error, the name cannot contain any medical modifiers, prefixes, suffixes, or numbers that could be confused for a dosage. According to the Institute of Medicine, at least 1.5 million Americans are sickened, injured, or die every year because of mistakes made in prescribing or dosage. Naming companies work to prevent these errors by having many test subjects write out the brand name to make sure it can't be confused for a different drug because of sloppy handwriting.

> **DID YOU KNOW?**
>
> Drug names cannot promise a result, which is why Rogaine, the popular drug for hair loss, had to change its name from Regain, which appeared to promise hair growth.

THE WOW FACTOR. Interbrand is the world's leading branding company. In 1987 it took Eli Lily and Company's new product—an antidepressant with the chemical name of *fluoxetine hydrochloride*—and gave it the brand name Prozac, which they said sounded positive, professional, and "full of zap." Scott Piergrossi, vice president of creativity at the Brand Institute, was so impressed that he said, "Prozac is what I call the big bang of pharmaceutical naming. It came out of nowhere, it means absolutely nothing, and it really just said, 'Wow! Okay, now this is blockbuster naming in the drug world.' " Since the launch, Prozac has been prescribed to more than 55 million adults and children. It has even been given to dogs, cats, parrots, elephants, and polar bears.

THINK UP! Arlene Teck, creative director at ixxéo Healthcare, is a rock star in the product branding business for naming the drug that treats erectile dysfunction, or ED. In 1992 she ran a focus group with urologists to discuss this condition. She asked one of the doctors what it felt like for a man when his ED was cured. He told her to visualize a "strong stream." With that image in mind, Teck combined the words "vigorous" and "Niagara" and came up with Viagra.

WE TRY HARDER. With Viagra as king of the erectile dysfunction market, how did other drug companies offering similar drugs compete? They had to be just as clever in their naming process, so if Viagra was addressing the "action" resulting from taking the drug, pharmaceutical giant Eli Lilly and Company decided its ED drug should describe the "feeling." They started with the word *ciel*, which means "sky" in French, and added the word "bliss" to get Cialis. Bayer and GlaxoSmithKline partnered to offer a third contender in the impotence market: Levitra. The name is designed to make consumers think of words like "lever," "levitate," and "leverage." (The creative team must have decided to overlook the fact the LEV stands for "low-emission vehicle" in the automotive industry.)

YOU COULD DIE. The average broadcast television viewer is over 60 years old. This could explain why the TV networks run back-to-back commercials for medications to treat heart disease, diabetes, COPD, incontinence, and erectile dysfunction. But what explains the 15 seconds spent on describing the *benefits* of the drug versus the 45 seconds spent listing the *horrific side effects?* You might think hearing of the possibility of shortness of breath, nonstop diarrhea, erections that last more than 48 hours, and sudden death would be a deal-breaker for consumers, but it's exactly the opposite. According to a study reported in the *New York Times,* the fact that a drug could have such dire side effects actually makes potential users more confident in its power to cure.

> The fact that a drug could have such dire side effects actually makes potential users more confident in its power to cure.

A CURE FOR INSOMNIA

Can't sleep? One of these weird cures might help…or not—some of them are so gross, they might actually keep you awake thinking about how gross they are.

- 16th-century Italian mathematician Gerolamo Cardano developed many important theories, including the probability theorem. He was also a doctor who told patients who had trouble sleeping to rub a dog's earwax on their teeth.

- Old Japanese folk remedy for sleeplessness: Eat the entrails of a sea slug just before bed.

- Old French folk remedy for sleeplessness: Eat fried lettuce just before bed.

- Ancient Egyptians had another lettuce-based insomnia cure. They drank *lactucarium*, a powerful, opium-like narcotic made out of extracts of different leafy greens. (So it probably worked.)

- Charles Dickens claimed to have cured his sleep troubles by making sure his bed was pointed to the north.

- In 1621 English doctor Robert Burton wrote in *The Anatomy of Melancholy* that foot massages could cure insomnia. Specifically, foot massages in which the fat of a dormouse was rubbed on the soles of the feet.

- The health page of an 1898 issue of Scotland's *Glasgow Herald* told insomniacs to soap their hair with yellow soap and "rub it into the roots of the brain until it is lathered all over," then tie up the wet hair in a towel, wash it out the next morning, and repeat the process daily for two weeks.

- In modern-day Japan, "sleep concerts" are a thing. Held in large rooms or theaters, attendees sit in big chairs or lie in sleeping bags while live bands play slow, relaxing music.

- In Babylonia, conventional wisdom held that insomnia was a result of one being haunted by the uneasy spirits of dead relatives. To get to the root of the problem, insomniacs had to sleep with the relative's skull for a week. That was thought to clear things up, as long as the person also licked the skull each night.

- Hemlock is a poison—the ancient Greek philosopher Socrates had to drink it to fulfill his death sentence. And yet in 1879 the *Canadian Journal of Medicine* advocated small amounts of hemlock to sleep for just a little while. (Take too much and you'll "sleep" for a lot longer.)

TELEVISION BY THE NUMBERS QUIZ

Guess which character we left off of these TV show casts. (Answers on page 501.)

1) Which of the eight *Eight Is Enough* Bradford kids is missing?
David, Mary, Joanie, Nancy, Elizabeth, Tommy, Nicholas

2) Of the seven Camden kids on *7th Heaven,* which one isn't here?
Sam, David, Ruthie, Lucy, Mary, Simon

3) Which of the six Brady kids from the *The Brady Bunch* isn't listed?
Bobby, Marcia, Cindy, Greg, Peter

4) There were five Huxtable kids on *The Cosby Show*. Who's missing?
Sondra, Denise, Rudy, Vanessa

5) Of the eight Walton children that survived infancy on *The Waltons,* who did we forget to say "good night" to?
John-Boy, Jason, Mary Ellen, Ben, Erin, Elizabeth

6) There were four Conner kids on *Roseanne*. Who got left out?
Becky, D.J., Darlene

7) *Seven Brides for Seven Brothers* was a musical film *and* a TV show. Which TV brother is missing?
Ford, Crane, Adam, Daniel, Guthrie, Evan

8) Hey, hey, hey! Which one of Fat Albert's seven friends from the Junkyard Band isn't here?
Dumb Donald, Weird Harold, Bill, Russell, Rudy, Bucky

9) Who's the fifth member of the Archies on *The Archies?*
Archie, Betty, Veronica, Reggie

10) Which kid living in the house on *Full House* got left off this list?
D.J., Michelle, Alex, Nicky

11) Who's the missing kid from the 1990s blended family sitcom *Step by Step?*
Dana, Mark, Brendan, Karen, J.T.

12) There were six "Angels" throughout the run of *Charlie's Angels*. Who's not here?
Sabrina, Tiffany, Julie, Kelly, Kris

13) Which member of the Partridge family did we forget?
Shirley, Keith, Laurie, Danny, Chris, Tracy

14) In the large extended family on *Modern Family*, which kid is missing?
Haley, Alex, Luke, Joe, Lily

15) Of all these hosts of *The Tonight Show*, who did we neglect to include?
Steve Allen, Johnny Carson, Jay Leno, Conan O'Brien, Jimmy Fallon

Comic book creator Stan Lee's first writing job: writing advance celebrity obituaries for a newspaper.

WRITER'S BLOCK!

Uncle John's surefire cure for writer's block: Writing about other people who've suffered from writer's block.

VICTOR HUGO (1802–1885)

Claim to Fame: French author of *The Hunchback of Notre Dame*, *Les Misérables*, and other works

Blocked! Like a lot of writers, Hugo spent a lot of time cooped up indoors, writing plays and novels when he would rather have been outside having fun. Sometimes when the temptation to play hooky grew too great, Hugo would strip naked and order his valet to hide his clothes. Then he would lock himself in a room containing nothing but a writing desk, a pen and some paper, and a blanket (in case he got cold), and start writing. Whether this improved his productivity is open to speculation; *Les Misérables*, published in 1862, took him nearly 20 years to finish.

RAYMOND CHANDLER (1888–1959)

Claim to Fame: One of the giants of "hard-boiled" detective fiction, Chandler wrote seven novels and numerous short stories that are considered classics of the genre.

Blocked! Chandler also wrote movie screenplays. In 1945 he was hired by Paramount Pictures to rush out a script for Alan Ladd, one of the studio's biggest stars, who was about to be called up for military service. Chandler came up with a story called *The Blue Dahlia*, in which a navy aviator's cheating wife is murdered the night he returns home from the war. The police suspect he's the killer; his only hope of proving his innocence is to go on the lam and catch the murderer himself.

That was a nice beginning, but four weeks after filming got underway, Chandler still hadn't come up with an ending. A recovering alcoholic, he decided that the only path to breaking his writer's block was by drinking alcohol. He told the studio that he needed to work at home instead of on the Paramount lot, which was usually not allowed. And he needed to be provided with six secretaries "in three relays of two" to be available around the clock to support him whenever he was sober enough to work. He also needed "two Cadillac limousines, to stand day and night outside the house with drivers" to fetch his doctor, take finished pages to the studio, or run whatever errands needed running, plus "a direct telephone line open at all times" to producer John Houseman's office by day and the Paramount switchboard at night.

Paramount agreed to the terms and Chandler relapsed into his alcoholism. A few

Walruses inflate their *pharyngeal pouch* to keep themselves floating while they sleep.

weeks later he finished work on the story that the *Hollywood Reporter* called "a kick-em-in-the-teeth hit," and that earned him his second Academy Award nomination for Best Original Screenplay. (But he lost.)

SERGEI RACHMANINOFF (1873–1943)

Claim to Fame: Russian pianist, composer, and conductor

Blocked! When Rachmaninoff's Symphony no. 1 was performed in public for the first time in 1897, it was conducted by a man named Alexander Glazunov, who may have been drunk at the time. The performance was not well received by critics, one of whom compared it to the ten biblical plagues of Egypt. Though Rachmaninoff denied that he cared about what the critics thought, he slipped into a depression that lasted for three years. In that time, he was able to compose only a few short pieces of music and had to support himself by giving piano lessons. Even a visit from the writer Leo Tolstoy, one of Rachmaninoff's favorite authors, failed to improve his spirits. It wasn't until 1900, when Rachmaninoff began receiving psychotherapy and hypnotherapy treatments from a physician and friend named Nikolai Dahl, that his depression began to lift and he was able to compose again. His Piano Concerto no. 2, which he completed in April 1901, is dedicated to Dahl. Fortunately for lovers of his music, Piano Concerto no. 2 received good reviews, spurring Rachmaninoff on to further work.

DONALD LAU (1948–)

Claim to Fame: For more than 30 years, Lau was the CFW (chief fortune writer) at Wonton Foods of Brooklyn, New York, which bakes 4.5 million fortune cookies a day and is the largest fortune cookie baker in the United States. There's a very good chance that the last fortune cookie you ate was baked in Brooklyn by Wonton Foods.

Blocked! Lau, who is now Wonton Foods' chief financial officer, was assigned the job of writing fortunes in the early 1980s when the company, originally a noodle maker, bought a small bakery in New York's Chinatown and expanded into fortune cookies. The bakery's catalog of fortunes was small and dated to the 1940s; many were old-fashioned and no longer relevant. As Wonton Foods ramped up production, the company realized it didn't have enough fortunes for all the cookies it planned to bake. Lau says he got the job by default, since he was the one that spoke the best English. Writing three or four new fortunes a day when he wasn't tending to his other responsibilities, over time he built up a rotating catalog of some 10,000 fortunes. But by 2017, Lau was out of gas. His case of writer's block proved incurable, so he turned his fortune-writing duties over to James Wong, a nephew of the company's founder. His advice for Wong and other aspiring fortune writers: "Don't have too complicated a mind," he says. "Think in ten-word sentences."

Figs aren't vegan—when wasps pollinate them, they get trapped inside the fruit. (By the time...

THE PAPER CHASE

Next time you ball up a piece of stationery and toss it in the trash, consider what the ancient Egyptians went through more than 5,000 years ago just to write a simple letter.

3,000 BC

Long before the paper we use today was invented in China, Egyptians from the First Dynasty were using the papyrus plant to make a thick yellow paperlike material that they used for accounting, recording history and sending important messages. The plant's inner stalk was cut lengthwise into strips, which are laid out next to each other. Water from the Nile was then spread on that layer. More strips were laid crisscross over the first layer and put in a press. Then the sheet was beaten with a mallet, polished with a shell, and rubbed with cedar oil. Ten to twenty sheets would be glued end to end and rolled around a stick to create a scroll. When the process was complete, an Egyptian scribe would write on the papyrus with a reed brush dipped in ink made from charcoal and water.

Papyrus paper was produced all around the Mediterranean in Egypt, Rome, and Greece. Romans used papyrus as late as the third century and had different names for it, depending on the quality. *Augustus* (named after the first Roman emperor) was the premium quality, while *emporitica* (packing paper) was a coarser product, used to wrap fish. Rolls of papyrus were made in large quantities in the city of Byblos, Phoenicia, one of the oldest cities in the world. The Greeks took their word for book, *biblios*, from the city's name, and that's where the word *bible* comes from.

105 AD

Cai Lun, a court eunuch for Emperor He of China's Han Dynasty, was observing wasps build nests by chewing plant fibers and shaping them into a thin paper. He came up with a way of imitating the wasps' process by suspending felted sheets of fiber made from cotton, rags, and plants in water, and then draining the water, creating a thin matted sheet of paper. Until then, the Chinese had used costly silk or heavy bamboo for writing messages, but from that time on, paper was the stationery of choice for the Chinese…and then the world.

1806

For generations, Henry Fourdrinier's family had been in the papermaking business in France, as engravers and stationers. In 1806 Henry and his brother, Sealy Fourdrinier, patented the first modern papermaking machine, which made paper in a variety of sizes and in rolls. Their machine became the model for all future papermaking machines.

...the fig is ripe enough to eat, the wasp has been completely absorbed.)

1844

1857

Joseph Gayetty invented toilet paper.

1896–1950s

1896

In 1838 Charles Fenerty was working in his father's lumber mill in Nova Scotia when he heard that a local paper mill was having trouble finding the rags required for making quality paper. The enterprising 17-year-old began experimenting with making paper out of wood pulp from the mill. Six years later, on October 26, 1844, Fenerty delivered a letter to the top newspaper in Halifax, Nova Scotia, the *Acadian Recorder*. The letter said: "The enclosed piece of paper, which is as firm in its texture as white, and...as durable as the common wrapping paper made of cotton, hemp and ordinary materials of manufacture is actually composed of spruce wood."

Pulped wood paper began to be adopted by paper mills in Canada, the United States, and Europe, using steam-driven papermaking machines. Only problem: conventional paper was so expensive that only the elite were able to afford stationery or books. Charles Fenerty changed that when he invented a process for producing "newsprint" paper and, in doing so, he launched an entire industry: "the pulps"—affordable newspapers, magazines and novels printed on cheap newsprint. After the pulps were introduced, magazines printed on higher-quality paper were called "glossies" or "slicks."

Not all European printers were eager to switch from rags to wood pulp. On April 17, 1896, Menzel & Company's paper manufactory in Austria conducted a public demonstration to prove that making paper from wood pulp was the best choice because it was cost effective and, above all, speedy.

7:35 a.m. Menzel's men fell three trees in the presence of a notary. The trees are carried to his factory, cut in pieces 12 inches long, then peeled and split. The split wood is ground into pulp and the pulp is poured into a vat of chemicals. The treated pulp is sent over the hot rollers of the paper machine.

9:34 a.m. The first finished sheet of paper appears. Menzel, still accompanied by the notary, takes a few sheets of the paper to a printing office two and a half miles away.

10:00 a.m. A copy of the printed paper is placed in the hands of the notary, proving that a standing tree could be converted into a newspaper in two hours, 25 minutes.

10:10 a.m. Nagged by a few unforeseen delays, Menzel declares, "I'm certain I can shorten the process by 20 minutes!"

First HDTV broadcast: the 1998 launch of the space shuttle *Discovery*.

DAIRY QUEEN:
THE "BUTTER-COW LADY"

If you've ever been to the Iowa State Fair, you know that one of the must-sees is the "Butter Cow," a life-size cow sculpted from butter. For more than 40 years, they were carved by the "Butter-Cow Lady," a local celebrity in her own right.

MOOVING STORY

In the summer of 1959, 30-year-old Norma Lyon and her husband, both dairy farmers, showed their family's cows at the Iowa State Fair. During a break in the festivities, Lyon took some time to tour the other exhibits, including the fair's famous "Butter Cow," a life-size cow sculpted out of butter churned from the milk of Iowa cows. The sculptures had been a tradition at the fair since at least 1911.

The fair's most recent sculptor had retired the year before, so this year's cow was the work of a new sculptor, a man named Earl Dutt. Lyon was not impressed with Dutt's work. His cow was more a caricature than a realistic sculpture, she thought. Lyon had a background in animal science and had spent years working with cows on her dairy farm. She'd also studied sculpture in college. She was convinced she could do a better job, and when she met with the organizers of the state fair, she told them so. She offered to sculpt the cow for the following year's fair. "If I can't make a better one, I'll eat it," she said.

BUTTERFINGERS

The fair organizers hired Lyon to sculpt the cow for the following year. She had six children then, and by the time the fair came around, she was pregnant with her seventh. But she still honored her commitment to sculpt the 1960 butter cow.

The process took three days. Lyon started with a wooden frame covered with metal wire mesh that formed the rough outline of a cow. Then, working with a single handful of butter at a time, she kneaded it and rolled it into a ball in her hands until it was soft enough to press onto the wire mesh. She applied one handful after another until the entire frame was covered with about 600 pounds of butter, enough for 19,200 slices of toast. Then, using chisels for broad strokes and dental tools for finer work, she proceeded to sculpt what was perhaps the most lifelike cow ever produced for the Iowa State Fair. The organizers invited Lyons back the next year, and the year

> **The entire frame was covered with about 600 pounds of butter, enough for 19,200 slices of toast.**

Ants breathe, but they don't have lungs. (No insects do.)

after that, and though she had her hands full raising what would eventually be nine kids and helping run the dairy farm, she returned to the state fair to sculpt the butter cow each year for the next 46 years.

AS SEEN ON TV

The butter Jerseys, Holsteins, and Guernseys sculpted by Lyon were created with a serious purpose in mind: to promote Iowa's dairy industry. But the quaint peculiarity of life-size buttery bovines proved to be irresistible viewing on the relatively new medium of television. In time, Lyon developed a measure of fame in her own right. In 1963 she made an appearance on the game show *To Tell the Truth,* where celebrity panelists had to guess which of the three mystery contestants on the show was the real Butter-Cow Lady. Lyons proved so knowledgeable about dairy cows that all of the panelists correctly picked her.

> Her interpretation of Leonardo da Vinci's *The Last Supper* required more than a ton of butter to sculpt the 13 figures seated at the table.

Lyon's fame grew to the point that where once people had come to see her butter cows, now they came to see the cows and the Butter-Cow Lady who made them. The exposure prompted other state and county fairs and other agricultural exhibitions to hire her to sculpt cows—and other animals. One pork association commissioned her to sculpt a pig out of pork lard. In 1984 she made an appearance on *Late Night with David Letterman,* and presented Letterman with a cow sculpted from cheddar cheese (cheese is sturdier than butter, easier to transport, and it doesn't melt as easily under hot TV studio lights).

CATTLE CALL

Beginning in 1984, Lyon started sculpting other objects for the Iowa State Fair in addition to butter cows. One year she sculpted a horse and foal; in another she sculpted country singer Garth Brooks. In subsequent years her subjects included rustic barns, birthday cakes, motorcycles, Smokey the Bear, John Wayne, and Charlie Brown and other *Peanuts* characters. Her most complicated composition was probably her interpretation of Leonardo da Vinci's *The Last Supper,* which required more than a ton of butter to sculpt the 13 figures seated at the table.

Lyon kept at it year after year, not stopping even after she suffered a stroke in 1996. She recovered in time to sculpt a cow for the 1997 fair, plus one of her most popular figures ever: a 6-foot-tall butter Elvis, which fairgoers lined up by the hundreds to see. (Lyon wanted to do the King in beef tallow, which would have given him an ivory color, but the beef industry representative at the fair "didn't want anything to do

Gulp? There's a 1 in 5 chance your coffee mug contains a trace of fecal matter.

with it. They're so down on fat, they almost had a fit. I knew the butter people would jump on it," she told an interviewer in 1997.)

MOOVING ON

Lyon retired in 2006. (Her figures for that year's fair included a cow—of course—and Superman.) She then turned her responsibilities over to her assistant, Sarah Pratt, who has sculpted every butter cow since then.

By the time she retired, Lyon's fame was such that when Barack Obama, then a junior U.S. senator from Illinois, came to Iowa in 2007 during his campaign for president, he sought her endorsement for the state primary…and got it. "He knows our kids need opportunity here in Iowa so they don't have to leave home to follow their dreams, even if that dream is 500 pounds of butter shaped like a cow," Lyon said in a 60-second radio ad she recorded for the Obama campaign. Did it help? Obama's surprise victory in the January 2008 Iowa caucus established him as a serious contender for the Democratic nomination for president.

> One of her most popular figures ever: a 6-foot-tall butter Elvis.

Lyon passed away in 2011 at the age of 81, survived by her husband Joe (still hard at work overseeing the family's herd of more than 400 dairy cows), their nine children, 23 grandchildren, and five great-grandchildren. She also lives on in the hearts of many of the millions of people who visited the Iowa State Fair over the years.

PRESSING THOUGHT

More than a few fairgoers have wondered what the state fair did with all the butter used to make each cow after the fair was over. In the early years, the butter was sent off to a pet food factory, where it was used to make dog food. In later years the butter was collected, frozen, and saved until the next year's fair, when it was used to make another cow. (No word on how many years the butter lasted before it had to be replaced with fresh butter.)

*   *   *

YOU DON'T KNOW "JACK"

You've probably heard the phrase "jack of all trades, master of none." It derisively refers to someone who can do a little bit of everything, but isn't excellent at any of them. The full version of the phrase actually means the complete opposite: "jack of all trades, master of none, but better than a master of one."

No. 1 movie at the box office the weekend *Star Wars* opened in 1977: *Smokey and the Bandit*.

"TOTAL LOSS OF TONGUE"

In 1863 the United States Congress passed the Civil War Military Draft Act in order to draft as many young men as possible for the Union Army. If you were a pacifist (or rich), you could avoid the draft by finding someone to take your place or by paying a $300 fee. The only other way to get out of service: if you had one of these conditions, as listed in an official circular issued by the War Department's Provost Marshal General's Office on November 9, 1863.

"Stammering, if excessive."

"Total loss of nose; deformity of nose so great as seriously to obstruct respiration."

"Habitual and confirmed intemperance, or solitary vice, which has so materially enfeebled the constitution as to leave no doubt of the man's incapacity for military service." (That means an addiction to "pleasuring" oneself.)

"Tumors or wounds of the neck."

"Abdomen grossly protuberant."

"Pain, whether simulating headache, neuralgia in any of its forms, rheumatism, lumbago, or affections of the muscles, bones or joints."

"Artificial anus" (the 1800s equivalent of a colostomy).

"Stricture of the rectum" (an overly narrow passage which results in painful bowel movements).

"Total loss or nearly total loss of penis."

"Old and ulcerated internal hemorrhoids."

"Total loss of a thumb."

"Urinary fistula" (a hole in the urinary tract).

"Stone in the bladder, ascertained by the introduction of the metallic catheter" (that means if a man thought he had a bladder stone, the military doctor would poke around with a metal tool to see if he really did).

"Loss or complete atrophy of both testicles from any cause."

"Total loss of the index finger of the right hand."

"Varicose veins of inferior extremities, if large and numerous, and accompanied with chronic swellings or ulcerations."

"Total loss of a great toe."

"Club feet."

"Loss of a sufficient number of teeth to prevent mastication of food."

"Total loss of tongue."

"Epispadia or hypospadia" (a malformed male organ).

"Excessive obesity."

"Manifest imbecility."

Tea was invented in 2737 BC. The tea bag was invented in 1904 AD.

A WEEK OF NAKED NEWS

Was there a full moon or something? All of the following incidents occurred just days apart in February 2018.

ROAD TRIP

On February 23, 2018, a Wilmington, North Carolina, man named Derrick Anthony Dunbar, 33, crashed his car while driving at speeds of over 100 miles per hour. According to witnesses, after the crash he jumped out of the car, fired several rounds from a handgun, then stripped naked and ran into the woods. A few minutes later, he returned to the car and was putting his clothes back on just as New Hanover County Sheriff's deputies arrived on scene. They arrested him for indecent exposure, unlawful discharge of a firearm, and "going armed to the terror of the public." (Dunbar says that his behavior was "out of character" and that someone gave him something that had him "trippin' out.")

JOIN THE CLUB

On February 24, a new nightclub called Klubb Naket opened on the island of Södermalm in Stockholm, Sweden. Just as the name suggests, the club encourages its patrons to strip naked; people who do shed their clothes don't have to pay the cover charge. The club hasn't impressed Lennard Torebring, the pastor of the nearby Södermalmskyrkan Church. He denounced it as "a breeding ground for depression and broken souls." "Doing what you want is not good for you. We don't need less boundaries just because we get older," he told the StockholmDirekt website. In spite of Pastor Torebring's protests, the club opening went off without a hitch as about 400 people jammed the venue. The bare facts, according to Eddie Eneqvist, who works at the club: "It was around 50/50 naked, with great respect and understanding."

> **"It was around 50/50 naked, with great respect and understanding."**

ALL-TERRAIN, NO CLOTHES

On February 25, a naked man stole an all-terrain vehicle and led police on a 90-minute chase through the streets and freeways of Kansas City, Missouri, including a wrong-way run down a stretch of I-435. The chase ended when he crashed his vehicle on some railroad tracks and was taken into custody while trying to run away. Johnathon A. Menth, 27, was charged with burglary, tampering, property damage, and sexual misconduct (his genitals were showing). In a statement to police, Menth

Calendar rule of thumb: If March starts on a Thursday, so will November.

admitted to being under the influence of drugs, and said he "freaked out" when the police spotted him. "Some elements of the incident, including the reason Menth had no clothes on, remain a mystery," wrote the *Kansas City Star*. At last report, Menth was still being held in the Clay County Detention Center on a $50,000 bond. One of the terms of his release, if he ever makes bail, is that he "not go out in public unless fully dressed." A video of the naked police chase was uploaded to Facebook; it was viewed 2.3 million times in two days.

NEITHER SNOW, NOR RAIN...

On February 26, the residents of the clothing-optional Eden RV Resort and City Retreat in Hudson, Florida, went public with their beef against the U.S. Postal Service. The problem: A substitute mail carrier, who fills in pretty regularly, refuses to deliver packages inside the resort because she is offended by the sight of naked people. The resort's mail is usually delivered to a "centralized delivery unit"—a bank of curbside mailboxes and parcel lockers outside the resort, which is hidden behind a tall fence. But if a package is too big for the parcel lockers—or even if it isn't, some residents complain—this mail carrier refuses to bring it inside the resort. "She marks it undeliverable, whether it fits in the box or it doesn't, so we don't get the mail that day," resident Eileen Hudak told WFLA TV News. "And sometimes the mail is important. Like with our neighbor, it's her medication sometimes." In a statement, the U.S. Postal Service said the mail carrier was completely within her rights to stay outside the nudist resort. "Carriers are not required to deliver beyond the centralized delivery units. We can assure all customers that mail and packages are being delivered according to national centralized delivery requirements."

JUNK MAIL

In December 2010, a Whitefish Bay, Wisconsin, mail carrier was arrested and charged with lewd and lascivious behavior after he admitted to stripping naked to deliver mail to a law firm. According to the police report, when David A. Goodman, 52, observed one afternoon that a female employee at the firm seemed to be "stressed out," he decided to "make her laugh" by delivering the law firm's mail in the nude. But "after [the woman] let him in, he could immediately see that he had upset her and immediately felt bad and stupid. He apologized, left the office, and got dressed," the report states. Police responded to the call of a naked postal carrier in the building, but Goodman was gone by the time they got there. They caught up with him about a week later. The citation carried a $681 fine, but Goodman faced no jail time for his "special delivery."

The western border of South Dakota was supposed to be a straight line, but it isn't. The southern...

PET TECH

It used to be that all a pet needed was a bowl, a collar, and a toy or two. But pet products have become a $70 billion industry…so maybe it's gotten a bit out of hand.

Product: SmartPult

Details: Dogs love playing "fetch," and humans often get tired of the game long before the dog does. Enter the SmartPult, a pitching machine that shoots mini tennis balls a reasonable distance and low to the ground, allowing dogs to play fetch by themselves.

Cost: $189

Product: PetChatz

Details: It's a videophone…for pets. PetChatz is a box containing a camera, monitor, speaker, and treat dispenser, mounted on the wall—down low, at pet-eye-level. You activate a ring tone from your phone or computer and your dog or cat comes to the PetChatz, where it can see you on the built-in HD screen. (There's even a wireless, paw-shaped floor pad that your pet can stomp on to "call" you.) Once you have the pet's attention, you can use the PetChatz app to send dispense a treat or release calming aromatherapy scents. Bonus: you can stream DOGTV's dog-oriented video on PetChatz, making it, according to the marketing team, a viable alternative to doggie daycare.

Cost: $379

Product: Petzi

Details: Like PetChatz, Petzi is a way to see your dog or cat and give them a handful of treats when you're away from home. Unlike PetChatz, this "treat cam" doesn't have a video monitor built in, so your pet can hear you but not see you. And no DOGTV. But it does dispense treats, so your dog probably won't miss the video.

Cost: $170

Product: WonderWoof

Details: People use "activity trackers" like a FitBit or Apple Watch to count their steps, calculate calories burned, and gather other information to help them meet their fitness and weight-loss goals. The WonderWoof is exactly the same thing, only for dogs. It's a collar (not a wristband) with a tracker in the shape of a bow tie (available in a wide array of fashionable colors!). The dog can go about its business and each day, a summary of its activity is sent to its master, who can use the data determine if Fido is getting enough exercise.

Cost: $45–$65

…portion jumps about a mile to the west at the Montana-Wyoming border, due to a surveyor's error.

Product: Soft Claws

Details: One of the most annoying parts of pet ownership—for both human and pet—is nail trimming. The animal hates being held down and having its claws clipped, which makes the human hate it, too. But it has to be done, both for the animal's health and to make sure floors and furniture don't get all scratched up. Soft Claws purports to be a workaround—"nail caps" that slip over a dog or cat's nails or claws (good luck getting those on) and prevent household damage. Bonus: they come in a variety of bright colors, making it look like your pet has painted fingernails.

Cost: $19 a set

Product: Hefty Cat

Details: The obesity epidemic hasn't affected just humans—our pets are getting heavier, too. More and more cats out there are becoming so Garfield-esque that they're too big to use regular cat products, such as cat doors. Ideal Pet Products has come up with a solution. Diet food? No, Hefty Cat—an extra-large cat door for your extra-large cat.

Cost: $30

Product: Poop Tent

Details: We humans take bathrooms for granted. When nature calls, we can retreat there and close the door and do what we need to do in privacy and peace. Dogs don't have that luxury. We just take them outside, find a spot, and make them do their business in public for all the world to see. Apparently being on display like that is mortifying to dogs. That's why the folks at Benji Ventures came up with the Poop Tent: to offer protection for the discreet doggy. Poop Tent is a "puppy port-a-potty" that gets set up over a patch of grass or dirt. Doggy simply goes inside…and relieves itself with dignity. Bonus: It's waterproof, so it's also great for dogs who don't like to go in the rain.

Cost: $10

> **DID YOU KNOW?**
>
> There are companies in New York, New Jersey, and Los Angeles that offer "bark mitzvah" services—like a bar mitzvah, the traditional Jewish coming-of-age ceremony…but for dogs. It is performed when a dog turns either 13 months or 13 years old (as is done for boys in the Jewish community). Dogs are outfitted in a ritual prayer shawl and a yarmulke.

* * *

Random Fact: One of the most commonly misspelled words is "misspell."

In 1920 Missouri levied a "bachelor tax" on unmarried men aged 21 to 50.

A LONG, STRANGE TRIP

The earth's oceans are connected to one another, so it's actually possible to sail around the world without ever setting foot on land. But the continents are not connected, and you can't drive around the world…at least not in a conventional vehicle.

ODD DUCK

Ben Carlin was an Australian engineer who served in the Indian army during World War II. After the war ended, he was stationed at an air force base in the Indian state of West Bengal. It was there one day in March 1946 that he and a friend, British RAF officer Mac Bunting, stumbled across an odd-looking vehicle while walking through a military salvage yard. The vehicle they spotted was a Ford GPA, an amphibious version of a standard American army GP (General Purpose) vehicle, better known as a "jeep."

The GPA, sometimes called a "seep," looked a little bit like a regular jeep with a boat built around it. The vehicles were pretty rare, and for good reason: they were lemons. Designed and thrown together in a hurry using as many standard jeep parts as possible, the vehicles weighed in at nearly 900 pounds more than military specifications called for. This made them very slow. It also caused them to sit low in the water, which made them prone to sinking, especially when overloaded. The army was so disappointed with the GPAs that it canceled production after one year.

> "You know, Mac, with a bit of titivation [upgrading], you could go around the world in one of these things."

EYE OF THE BEHOLDER

As Carlin looked over the battered old jeep, he didn't see a flop, he saw opportunity. He said to Bunting, "You know, Mac, with a bit of titivation [upgrading], you could go around the world in one of these things."

"Nuts!" Bunting replied.

But months passed and Carlin could not get the idea out of his head. An around-the-world trip in an amphibious vehicle "would be difficult enough to be interesting," he recalled years later, "a nice exercise in technology, masochism, and chance—a form of sport—and it might earn me a few bob." He figured such a trip would take about a year.

By the time Carlin was released from military service in 1946, he'd decided to attempt the around-the-world trip. He booked passage to the United States, where he planned to buy a surplus amphibious jeep. On his way there he passed through Hong Kong, where he renewed a romance with an American Red Cross nurse named Elinore Arone. Carlin

All in the family: Salvador Dalí believed he was his dead brother, reincarnated.

had intended to make his around-the-world attempt by himself, but when he told Arone about it, she wanted to come along. Ben consented, and then he continued on to the United States alone, with Elinore to follow when she finished her work in Hong Kong.

CAR-BINGERS

In January 1947, Carlin bought a battered old Ford GPA for $901 at a government auction near Washington, DC How battered was it? It took Carlin two days to drive the 70 miles to the boatyard where he planned to work on it, because it was literally falling to pieces. Undaunted (or maybe just unwilling to take the hint), he spent the next nine months preparing the jeep for its around-the-world voyage.

Carlin added a new bow (front end), extending the vehicle's length and creating extra room for fuel tanks. An additional "belly tank" was strapped to the bottom of the vehicle when it was in the water; the tank could be removed when the jeep drove on land. Carlin also built a 5-by-10-foot cabin, creating an enclosed living space about as long and wide as a prison cell, but not nearly as tall. There was enough room in the cabin for the two front seats and a single bench seat in the rear that served as a sleeping cot, though it wasn't long enough to stretch out on. The only way in or out of the cramped cabin was via a watertight hatch in the ceiling.

Near the ceiling above the cot, Carlin mounted a two-way radio. Beneath the passenger seat, he installed a marine toilet. It was accessed by lifting the passenger seat cushion, which served as a second toilet lid. When completed, the vehicle was 18 feet long, 5 feet wide, and had top speeds of about 3 knots (3.5 mph) at sea and 25 mph on land. Carlin named it the *Half-Safe,* after a slogan in an Arrid deodorant radio commercial: "Don't be half-safe, use Arrid to be sure."

By October 1947, the vehicle was ready for its first sea trial. Carlin embarked on what he thought would be a trip of a few days, traveling up Chesapeake Bay from Annapolis, then overland across Delaware to Delaware Bay. From there he planned to sail along the New Jersey shoreline until he reached New York City. But on the fourth day of the trip, he was incapacitated when exhaust fumes filled the cabin, nearly killing him and causing him to run aground in Delaware Bay. That brought the sea trial to an abrupt end.

IF AT FIRST YOU DON'T SUCCEED...

By now any sensible person would have thrown in the towel. But what sensible person would have attempted the trip in the first place? For the next ten months, Carlin lived in a Manhattan flophouse and scraped by on his meager savings as he fixed the problems that had arisen during the sea trial. Then when Elinore joined him in New York in June 1948, the two got married. "It was a formality that the press agent they'd hired to promote their forthcoming journey had suggested," James Nestor writes in his

What are your arrector pili muscles for?
They give you goose bumps and make your hair stand on end.

book *Half-Safe*. "In the late 1940s, a pair of adventurous newlyweds setting out on a honeymoon across the Atlantic in a jeep would be an easy story to sell."

FALSE START(S)

In June of 1948, everything was ready...or so Ben and Elinore thought. Over the next two months they made four attempts to cross the Atlantic, and suffered mechanical failures each time. The fourth attempt, in early August, ended after eight days when the propeller shaft jammed and Ben was unable to fix it. By then the *Half-Safe* was nearly 300 miles out into the Atlantic; they drifted helplessly for ten days until an oil tanker saw them signaling SOS with a flashlight and came to the rescue.

At that point, the Carlins were completely broke. It took them another 13 months to earn enough money to make their fifth try at crossing the Atlantic, which they attempted in September 1949. In the intervening months, Ben had realized that the *Half-Safe*'s fuel tanks weren't large enough to carry all the fuel they would need to cross the Atlantic. His solution to this problem wasn't to give up—never!—nor would he look for a bigger vehicle with more room for fuel. Instead, he decided to drag two bulky 500-liter fuel tanks (about 130 gallons each) behind the *Half-Safe*. Bad idea: When the Carlins set sail from New York that September, they made it just 35 miles out to sea before the tanks smashed against each other with such force that one tank ruptured and the other was lost at sea. Without the extra fuel, there was no point in continuing, so they turned around and headed back to port again.

SIXTH SENSE

Ten more months passed before the Carlins were ready to try again; by now they'd spent more than two years trying—and failing—to complete the first leg of an around-the-world trip that they had assumed would, in its entirety, take them about a year to complete.

Ben Carlin reasoned that the fifth attempt had failed because he'd towed *two* tanks behind the *Half-Safe*; if he dragged just one larger tank behind the *Half-Safe*, it would have nothing to bang into. So that's what he did. Starting the trip on land in Montreal, he and Elinore drove to Halifax, Nova Scotia. There, on July 19, 1950, they drove the *Half-Safe* into the water and set sail across the Atlantic towing a 280-gallon fuel tank behind them on a rope, as a crowd of onlookers gawked in amazement. ("Grizzled waterfront veterans eyed the jeep and said it should have been called Unsafe," the Calgary Herald reported.) Their first stop: the Azores, an island chain in the North Atlantic, some 2,000 miles away.

If you've ever been on an ocean trip—on a cruise ship, a sailboat, or a motor yacht—rest assured your experience was nothing like the Carlins' as they suffered through what they assumed would be about a two-week trip across the Atlantic in

It pays to live in paradise: Hawaii is the state with the longest life expectancy, at 82.4 years.

their jury-rigged, amphibious jeep. For one thing, the tight confines of the cabin were made even tighter by the six weeks' worth of food (mostly canned), water, beer, and other supplies that they jammed into the tiny space. There was no view to speak of, because Ben decided it would be safer to travel with the windows covered with canvas to keep out the seawater and the rain. The only time they could see much of anything at all was when they poked their heads out of the hatch.

RATTLE TRAP

The *Half-Safe*'s engine was noisy and it caused the entire boat to rattle like it was going to shake apart. The air inside the claustrophobic cabin stank with a foul mixture of gasoline, exhaust fumes, and human sweat, not to mention vomit whenever Ben or Elinore were seasick, which was often. Add to that the smell of human waste whenever rough seas caused the marine toilet to spill its contents. And if you value privacy, remember that the toilet was located underneath the passenger seat, so whenever Ben or Elinore had to relieve themselves, they did so in full view of the other person, who was usually sitting in the driver's seat. There was no place for either of them to escape to—after all, they were crossing the Atlantic in a jeep.

While one person peeked through an opening in the canvas and drove, the other person kept watch or napped. Naps were about all Ben and Elinore ever got. They lost so much sleep during the journey that both of them hallucinated frequently. The food they ate didn't help: their diet was limited mostly to the canned goods they'd brought with them, plus the single fish they caught during the crossing. As *Life* magazine reported in 1950, the Carlins "were accompanied almost all the way by some dolphins, one of which they caught and ate. They cooked it by wrapping it around the *Half-Safe*'s exhaust pipe. Part was burned, part uncooked. Only [a] sliver in the middle was edible." (The magazine described their voyage as "certainly the most foolhardy and possibly the most difficult transatlantic voyage ever made.")

The *Half-Safe* putt-putted its way across the Atlantic at an average speed of 3 knots (3.5 mph) for the first week. Then engine trouble forced the Carlins to reduce their speed. Several times they had to shut the engine off entirely so that Ben could perform repairs. As a result, their voyage to the Azores, which was supposed to take a little over two weeks, dragged on for 32 days. They were out of radio contact for much of the trip, and when they failed to arrive in port, many people gave them up for dead. But on August 19, 1950, they finally spotted Flores, the westernmost island in the Azores chain, and limped into the harbor a few hours later. Unlike everyone else who has ever visited Flores, they arrived by car.

For part II of the story, float over to page 395.

Egg storage tip: If you want them to last longer, store them toward the back of the fridge, not on the door. (They're vulnerable to changes in temperature.)

REMEMBER ME

*Lots of animals are loved, but only a select few
are ever memorialized with statues.*

Animal: Old Bet, the first circus elephant brought to the United States

Honored With: A statue in Somers, New York, a town famous for being "the cradle of the American circus"

Details: Old Bet isn't just the first American circus elephant, she actually inspired the creation of the first American circus. She was living in a menagerie in 1808 when a cattle dealer named Hachaliah Bailey bought her with the intention of putting her to work on his farm. So many townspeople dropped by to see the elephant at work that Bailey realized he could make more money with a traveling animal act than he could with the farm. So he bought more animals, including pigs and a dog that did tricks, and began touring. The Bailey Circus—later to become part of the Ringling Brothers and Barnum & Bailey Circus—was born.

On July 24, 1816, the Bailey Circus was touring near Alfred, Maine, when a local farmer named Daniel Davis brought his rifle to the circus and shot Old Bet, apparently in the belief that circuses were a sinful waste of the public's money. Old Bet was dead, but Bailey wasn't done cashing in: nine years later he built the Elephant Hotel in Somers, where he lived. In front of the hotel he erected a tall granite pedestal and placed a wooden statue of an elephant on top of it. Both the building and the monument are still there, but today the Elephant Hotel serves as the Somers Town Hall.

Animal: Tombili ("Tubby"), a stray cat who lived in the Kadiköy district of Istanbul, Turkey

Honored With: A piece of bronze sidewalk art

Details: The chubby, friendly stray was popular with the residents of Kadiköy, and he had a favorite spot on a step next to the street where he would sit for much of the day. But unlike most cats, he sat *upright* on his rump, while reclining against a raised brick and resting on it with one elbow (or whatever you call an elbow on a cat). It was a remarkably human pose, and when someone snapped a photo and posted it on social media, Tombili shot to worldwide fame.

In the summer of 2016, Tombili fell ill; he died on August 1. Not long afterward, his admirers started circulating a petition asking the city to memorialize him with a life-size bronze statue of the cat slouching on his favorite step. After the petition collected 17,000 signatures, the city agreed, and in October 2016 the statue was installed in Tombili's favorite spot in a ceremony presided over by Istanbul's deputy

From the time it was discovered in 1930 to the time it was "demoted" to the status of dwarf planet, Pluto never fully orbited the Sun.

mayor and witnessed by hundreds of the cat's admirers. If you ever get a chance to visit Kadiköy, be sure and look for the statue. It won't be hard to find, since it's usually surrounded by candles, cat food, and other offerings left by fans.

Animal: Macaco Tião ("Tiao the Monkey"), a cranky chimpanzee who lived at the Rio De Janeiro Zoo in Brazil

Honored With: A life-size bronze statue

Details: The Rio Zoo has had lots of primates over the years, but only Macaco Tião has his own memorial. It's not because he was nice—it's because he was nasty, and in a way that was very entertaining to the people, especially children, who came to see him: He liked to hurl his poop at visitors. And the more important the visitor, it seemed, the more angrily he threw his poop. He seemed to have a special hatred for politicians, and in 1988 that prompted a Brazilian magazine, *Casseta Popular*, to suggest him as a candidate for mayor of the city.

> The more important the visitor, the more angrily he threw his poop. He seemed to have a special hatred for politicians.

The magazine was joking, but some 400,000 people wrote in Macaco Tião's name on their ballots, enough that he came in third out of a field of twelve. When he died in 1996 at the age of 34, the zoo lowered its flags to half-staff, the city government declared a three-day mourning period, and the bronze memorial was installed at the zoo. Sadly, it doesn't hurl poop, but it has become a popular attraction to visitors who remember Macaco Tião.

Animal: Mrs. Chippy, a cat aboard the sailing ship *Endurance* during the ill-fated Shackleton 1914 expedition to the South Pole

Honored With: A memorial on her owner's grave

Details: Mrs. Chippy belonged to Harry "Chippy" McNish, a carpenter on the Shackleton expedition, which ran into trouble when the *Endurance* was crushed by pack ice, stranding the crew on Elephant Island off the coast of Antarctica. Shackleton, McNish, and four other crew members made a daring journey by small boat over nearly 800 miles of open sea to South Georgia Island to summon help from whaling ships. Their voyage was a success, and all of the crew members on Elephant Island were rescued. But Mrs. Chippy was not: soon after the *Endurance* was crushed, Sir Ernest Shackleton, believing the cat would not survive the harsh conditions on Antarctica, gave orders for her to be shot. McNish never forgave him. McNish died in 1930 and was buried in Karori Cemetery in Wellington, New Zealand. In 2004 a bronze sculpture of Mrs. Chippy was added to his grave so that the two could be reunited in death as they had not been in life.

THE OCCUPATIONAL NAME QUIZ

Can you guess the names of these famous people if we give you a clue about their lives…and the lives they could lead if they took on the job or hobby that correlates to their last name? (Answers are on page 501.)

1. He starred in *The Hangover*…and he can also build you a nice barrel, if you need one.

2. She played drums and sang easy-listening tunes in the 1970s with her brother…when she wasn't making furniture, that is.

3. He created *King of the Hill* and *Beavis and Butt-head*…and he decides whether criminals go to jail or go free.

4. She was the prime minister of a major western European nation…and could also fix your rustic, old-fashioned roof.

5. He starred in four *Lethal Weapon* movies…and he also kept the crew's hands warm.

6. He ground up politicians and celebrities as a talk show host and *Weekend Update* anchor…and then ground grain into flour.

7. He can tell you what hot new gadgets Apple has in development…and then he can whip up a batch of applesauce.

8. He was a star NFL running back… and now he can take a little off the top and give you a shave.

9. She's an actress from *The Last Picture Show* and *Moonlighting*…and she also moonlights as a steward of sheep.

10. He made his legacy by finding hundreds of uses for peanuts…but he could also craft a statue, if need be.

11. He portrayed a villainous Scottish professional wrestler in the 1980s… and he could also play the traditional instrument of his "homeland."

12. Perhaps the most glamorous movie star in Hollywood history, she won two Oscars, had violet-colored eyes…and could make a suit for you, too.

13. He's an R&B superstar…who will show you to your seat.

14. She's best known for *Raising Arizona*, *The Piano*…and tracking down deer in the wilderness.

15. He played the coach on *Friday Night Lights*. "Clear eyes, full hearts"…and expertly made candles.

16. Along with Frank Sinatra and Dean Martin, he was part of the famous "Rat Pack"…and he came in handy when it came time to absolve everyone's sins.

Cold cash: The flu virus can live on a dollar bill for as long as two weeks.

WILLIAM HENRY HARRISON, RECONSIDERED

President William Henry Harrison lives on in trivia contests across the United States: His 31 days in office is the shortest presidency in American history—supposedly cut short by a cold that he caught on a frigid Inauguration Day. But is that really what killed him? Some historians have their doubts.

LONG AND SHORT

William Henry Harrison (1773–1841) is the rare example of a president whose inauguration is better remembered than the things he did in office. Inauguration Day, March 4, 1841, was a miserably cold and wet day, and the 68-year-old Harrison was, at the time, the oldest person inaugurated as president. (Ronald Reagan and Donald Trump later beat that record.) Nevertheless, Harrison declined the offer of a closed carriage and instead rode to his inauguration on his horse. He delivered a nearly two-hour inaugural address, the longest in U.S. history, outdoors in the freezing cold, without putting on a hat, gloves, or overcoat. Afterward, he climbed back on his horse and rode in the inaugural parade. The hours spent outdoors in cold, wet clothing, the story goes, gave him a chill that turned into a cold and then pneumonia, killing him a month after he took office.

Historians have accepted that version of events because Harrison's physician, Thomas Miller, cited the cause of death as "pneumonia of the lower lobe of the right lung, complicated by congestion of the liver." But Miller himself admitted that he chose a pneumonia diagnosis as a matter of expediency as much as anything else. "As this was the most palpable affection, the term pneumonia afforded a succinct and intelligible answer to the innumerable questions as to the nature of the attack," he wrote.

A NEW THEORY

Not everyone believes that Harrison was killed by the cold. In 2014 Jane McHugh, a writer, and Dr. Philip A. Mackowiak, a physician on the faculty of the University of Maryland School of Medicine, published an article in the medical journal *Clinical Infectious Diseases* that reexamined the case with a modern scientific eye.

Dr. Miller left a detailed account of Harrison's final illness. He reported that the president first complained of anxiety and fatigue, not a cold, on March 26, 1841, three weeks after his inauguration—likely too late for bad weather on Inauguration Day to have played any part in his illness. Miller told the president to go to bed; then when

Baboons have been known to kidnap dogs.

he checked on him later that evening, Harrison reported feeling much better. But the next day he complained that he had a severe chill and constipation. The doctor prescribed laxatives and other treatments, including a medicine called Mars Hydrarg, which contained mercury.

Over the next several days, Harrison's condition deteriorated. He became feverish, he developed severe gastrointestinal pain, and he developed breathing problems made worse by a cough that was sometimes wet, sometimes dry. Miller prescribed enemas, more laxatives, and opium to control Harrison's pain, but nothing seemed to work.

By April 3, Dr. Miller noted, Harrison was near death, his "pulse sinking; extremities blue and cold." He lingered throughout the day, then at half an hour past midnight on the morning of April 4, "without a groan or a struggle, he ceased to breathe."

GUT INSTINCT

In their 2014 article, McHugh and Mackowiak note that while Harrison's lungs were clearly impacted by whatever it was that afflicted him, "his pulmonary symptoms didn't arise until the fifth day of his illness and were intermittent rather than progressive thereafter. His gastrointestinal complaints, by comparison, began on the third day of the illness and were relentless as well as progressive." Based on this, they conclude that Harrison's pneumonia was a "secondary diagnosis," not his main affliction.

Their candidate for what killed Harrison: either typhoid fever or paratyphoid fever, both of which are caused by exposure to strains of salmonella bacteria in drinking water contaminated by human waste. Collectively, these diseases are known as *enteric fevers* because they cause tremendous gastrointestinal distress like that suffered by Harrison.

One of the tools that McHugh and Mackowiak used in their diagnosis was an 1846 street map of Washington, DC In those days, Washington had no sewage-treatment system whatsoever. The sewage pipes of some public buildings emptied their contents onto vacant land not far from the White House, where it stagnated in pools. Other buildings in the city were served by waste collectors, who carted what was called "night soil" to a dumping ground just seven city blocks from the natural springs that provided water to the White House. Seven blocks *uphill* from the natural springs, which meant that if any of the waste in the dumping ground contained the salmonella bacteria, it could easily have flowed downstream, either above or below ground, and contaminated the White House's source of drinking water.

HEARTBURN

One way or another, McHugh and Mackowiak believe that President Harrison ingested contaminated water and fell ill. Ordinarily he might have escaped getting sick, because the body's stomach acid acts as a "gastric barrier" that destroys the

bacteria before it reaches the small intestine, which is where salmonella enters the system and sickens an infected person.

But it happens that Harrison suffered from indigestion, and in those days one of the remedies was an antacid called "carbonated alkali," which relieved the symptoms of indigestion by neutralizing stomach acid. In neutralizing the acid, however, it also impairs the body's ability to destroy harmful bacteria. Instead of being destroyed in the stomach, the bacteria passes through to the small intestine, where it can infect the patient. Once stomach acid has been neutralized, it takes only a small amount of salmonella to make someone sick.

ADDING INSULT TO INJURY

Though Dr. Miller didn't realize it at the time, some of the treatments he administered to Harrison may have made it *more* difficult for his body to fight off the infection. The opium he prescribed to ease Harrison's pain has a side effect of impairing bowel function, which makes it hard for the body to expel the salmonella bacteria from the small intestine. And the longer the bacteria stays in the body, the greater the risk that it will be absorbed into the bloodstream.

Enteric fevers also cause inflammation in the lower intestine, placing it at greater risk of perforation. In such cases, enemas are *not* advised because the risk of perforation is too great. But Miller didn't know this, and he prescribed one enema after another to his suffering patient. McHugh and Mackowiak believe that somehow, either naturally or through a perforated intestine, the salmonella bacteria spread to Harrison's bloodstream, causing a condition called *septic shock*, which would explain the sinking pulse and cold, blue extremities that Dr. Miller noted in the hours before Harrison's death.

BUT WAIT, THERE'S MORE...

It's possible that Harrison wasn't the first U.S. president killed by enteric fever.

☠ Zachary Taylor died just 16 months into his presidency in 1850, reportedly after consuming large amounts of raw fruit and iced milk on the Fourth of July. Afterward, he fell ill from an undetermined digestive ailment accompanied by a fever, and died five days later.

☠ President James K. Polk suffered a similar gastrointestinal ailment during his term of office. He recovered and served out the remainder of his presidency, only to die from cholera, another disease caused by drinking contaminated water, in 1849.

"In all three cases," write McHugh and Mackowiak, "the illnesses were likely a consequence of the unsanitary conditions that existed in the nation's capital during most of the nineteenth century."

In the years after Hurricane Katrina, the rate of babies named Katrina dropped by 85%.

THE SOUND OF MOVIES

Here are some fun things to listen for the next time you see these movies.

Jaws (1975)

We Hear: At the end of the film, when (spoiler alert) the shark is blown up, it sinks to the bottom of the sea. Right before it lands, it lets out a high-pitched scream.

Actual Sound: It's the scream sound effect from the 1954 horror classic *Creature from the Black Lagoon. Jaws* director Steven Spielberg first used the *Black Lagoon* scream in his 1971 thriller *Duel*, when a truck drives off a cliff. Then he used it again for the shark's untimely end.

Fast & Furious 6 (2013)

We Hear: Car crashes—lots and lots of car crashes.

Actual Sounds: "We spent a lot of time abusing metal," explains sound designer Peter Brown. "Everything from taking a crane and picking cars up about 80 feet in the air and dropping them onto other cars, to attaching weird pieces of metal (including washing machines and refrigerators) to the back of a truck and dragging them all around the airport on various roads and over dirt." To record the crash sounds, the film crew rented an airport in the middle of the Mojave Desert, where they could make as much noise as they wanted and—more important—not have their recordings ruined by all the background noises you hear in more populated places.

Mad Max: Fury Road (2015)

We Hear: The "War Rig" roaring down Fury Road. The heavily armored tractor-trailer was stolen by Furiosa (Charlize Theron) to escape the evil clutches of Immortan Joe (Hugh Keays-Byrne).

Actual Sound: Whales. According to sound designer Mark Mangini, "I had this notion that the truck itself was an allegory for *Moby-Dick*." And he viewed Immortan Joe as Captain Ahab "hell-bent on killing the great white whale—the War Rig." So when it came time to providing the sounds for the truck, "we wanted to personify it as this giant, growling, breathing, roaring beast. It had to be grounded in reality, but we wanted it to be more than that, so we designed whale sounds to play underneath all those truck sounds to embody the real sounds and to personify it." (The allegory goes beyond sound design: at the end of the film, the bad guys are literally throwing harpoons at the War Rig.)

There's more water in our atmosphere than there is in all the rivers on Earth combined.

Terminator 2: Judgment Day (1991)

We Hear: The liquid-metal T-1000 (Robert Patrick) oozing his way through steel bars.
Actual Sound: Wet dog food being poured out of a can.

The Transformers movies (2007–present)

We Hear: The wheezing of Megatron, the main villain who (like Darth Vader in the *Star Wars* series) has a breathing problem.
Actual Sound: A tiger with emphysema. "Most of Megatron is voiced by Hugo Weaving," said sound editor Ethan Van der Ryn, "but there were moments when we wanted to get more animalistic with him—a little more violent. We went to this animal park just hoping to get cool sounds from animals…and the tiger just happened to have, lucky for us, emphysema. It had this crazy kind of asthmatic wheeze that ended up working well. A lot of the times in our business, some of the best things come from happy accidents." (Not so happy for the tiger, though.)

The Arrival (2016)

We Hear: The aliens' logograms. Their way of communicating is to use "ink" to make circular pictographs that represent words and phrases.
Actual Sound: The film's Foley artist, Nicolas Becker, blended a lot of disparate elements together to create the squishy sounds of the alien writing: "We basically played with vegetables that we put in water, and also rice. Then we worked with plastic boards. We took metal brushes and scratched them across the plastic board. All of those sounds were combined and treated and that's how we made the logograms."

Caddyshack (1980)

We Hear: The gopher's squeaky voice as it wreaks havoc above and beneath the golf course.
Actual Sound: The squeaky voice of a dolphin. And not just any dolphin, but the same dolphin sound effect that was used for the 1960s TV show *Flipper*.

Star Wars: The Force Awakens (2015)

We Hear: The rumbling of a many-tentacled rathtar chasing Han Solo (Harrison Ford) down a corridor in a spaceship.
Actual Sound: A Honda Civic coasting down a gravel road. That sound effect was created by legendary sound designer Ben Burtt for *Raiders of the Lost Ark* when a giant

Payback: Pirates captured Julius Caesar and held him ransom for 38 days…

boulder chases Indiana Jones (Harrison Ford) through a cave. *The Force Awakens* sound designer David Acord used the sound as an homage to Burtt, but also because it really fit the scene.

The Lord of The Rings: The Fellowship of the Ring (2001)

We Hear: The screams of the Nazgul, long-dead kings hell-bent on finding the One Ring. Their screams are so evil that anyone who hears them has to cover their ears in agony.
Actual Sound: Two plastic beer cups being rubbed together.

Godzilla (1954)

We Hear: The monster's famous roar
Actual sound: A double bass. There are two broad categories of sounds that Foley artists have to re-create: those that exist in the real world, and those that don't. Godzilla is a good example of the latter, and it took the filmmakers a while before they got a roar that worked. They first tried several different animal sounds, but they all sounded too…real. So they turned to the movie's composer, Akira Ifukube, who came up with Godzilla's iconic roar by "dragging a resin-coated leather glove along the loosened strings of a double bass."

Godzilla (2014)

We Hear: The monster's famous roar
Actual Sound: Unknown. The filmmakers refuse to say how they came up with Godzilla's voice for Gareth Edward's remake. The sound designers, Ethan Van der Ryn and Erik Aadahl, explained their reasoning to NPR. "If we tell everybody exactly how we did it," said Aadahl, "people will think of that when they hear the roar, and we want them to think of Godzilla." And that gag order came all the way from the top of the movie studio: "We actually were sworn to take it to our graves with us," said Van der Ryn.

The X-Men films (2000–present)

We Hear: The "SNIKT" sound of Wolverine's (Hugh Jackman) adamantium claws springing out of his fist.
Actual Sound: Like most superhero sound effects, this one combines a real-world sound—a metal blade being pulled from a sheath—and something extra to give it a "hyper-reality." What was the extra something? According to sound designer Craig Berkey, it was a turkey carcass being torn apart.

…after his release, he personally commanded the brigade of ships that caught and killed those pirates.

HEN-SCARTINS WITH A CHANCE OF BLENKY

The Brits and Scots have hundreds of unusual (to us) words to describe the weather. Scotland alone has 421 different words for snow, including feefle (swirling snow), spitters (small drops of wet snow), and skelf (a large snowflake). Here are some more.

AMMIL

Origin: Devon, England

Definition: A thin layer of sparkling ice that glosses trees, leaves, and grass when a freeze follows a partial thaw.

Sentence: "The Snow Queen waved her wand and *ammil* covered the grass and trees, glittering like diamonds."

APRICITY

Origin: Exeter, England

Definition: The warmth of the sun in winter.

Sentence: "Mary looked skyward, and basked in the *apricity* of that perfect January day."

GRIMLINS

Origin: Orkney Islands, Scotland

Definition: That time of a midsummer night when dusk blends into dawn.

Sentence: "On the summer solstice, we stayed up through the *grimlins*, watching the sky turn from deep purple to glowing gold."

BLENKY

Origin: Devon, England

Definition: To snow very lightly. Derived from *blenks*, which describes cinders.

Sentence: "It *blenkied* last night and the whole yard looks like it's been dusted with ash."

BLACKTHORN WINTER

Origin: Rural England

Definition: A sudden cold snap in early spring when the blackthorn blossoms.

Sentence: "The April snow ushered in a *blackthorn winter*."

FLAN

Origin: Scotland

Definition: A gust of wind.

Sentence: "The ladies at the military tattoo giggled when a *flan* lifted the piper's kilt."

> **OTHER WORDS FOR ICICLES**
>
> **Daggler** and **clinkerbell** (Hampshire), **ickle** (Yorkshire), **shuckle** (Cumbria), and **tankle** (Durham)

HEN-SCARTINS

Origin: Northumberland, England

Definition: Long, thin streaks of clouds that forecast rain. It means "chicken scratches."

Sentence: "Judging by the *hen-scartins*, I'd say we're in for a wet one."

SMIRR

Origin: Scotland

Definition: A continuous mist of rain that is so fine, it looks like smoke when seen from a distance.

Sentence: "*Smirr* is the worst, 'cause you hardly know it's there. You step outside for a few and suddenly you're soaked to the bone."

DREICH

Origin: Scotland

Definition: Really nasty, gloomy, dismal, wet weather.

Sentence: "We were so looking forward to our vacation, but the weather was such gray *dreich*, we never left the house."

YOWE-TREMMEL

Origin: Scotland

Definition: A week of cold, windy, wet weather at the end of June.

Sentence: "Don't pack away your winter woolies yet. We're in for one helluva *yowe-tremmel*."

FIZMER

Origin: Fenland District, Cambridgeshire, England

Definition: The whispering sound of wind in reeds or grass.

Sentence: "As the hunter crossed the field, the only sound he heard was the soft *fizmer* of the reeds."

AQUABOB

Origin: Kent, England

Definition: An icicle

HOOLIE

Origin: Orkney Islands, Scotland

Definition: A strong wind or gale.

Sentence: "Strike the mainsail, it's blowin' a *hoolie*!"

POOTHY

Origin: Fenland District, Cambridgeshire, England

Definition: Close, hot, muggy weather.

Sentence: "This *poothy* is suffocating. I'm just sitting here sweating buckets."

ROARIE BUMMLER

Origin: Scotland

Definition: A fast-moving bank of storm clouds.

Sentence: "Get inside before you get drenched! A *roarie-bummler* is speeding across the northeastern sky."

More salt is used for de-icing roads than for seasoning food.

MOUTHING OFF

CELEBRITY WISDOM

Random thoughts from famous folks.

"I wish I could trade my heart for another liver so I could drink more and care less."

—Tina Fey

"In every circle of friends there's always that one person everyone secretly hates. Don't have one? Then it's probably you."

—Will Ferrell

"There is no sunrise so beautiful that it is worth waking me up to see it. "

—Mindy Kaling

"One person's craziness is another person's reality."

—Tim Burton

"If you know you're going to fail, then fail gloriously!"

—Cate Blanchett

"One of my goals in life is to have the biggest residential pool on the planet."

—Drake

"Well, I try to keep to 'Thou shalt not kill.' The rest of them I'm kind of shaky on."

—Willie Nelson

"You laugh at me because I'm different; I laugh at you because you're all the same."

—Lady Gaga

"LUCK IS ABOUT NINE-TENTHS OF IT."

—Woody Harrelson, on his success

"I broke something, and realized I should break something every week to remind me how fragile life is."

—Andy Warhol

WEIRD CANADA

O, Canada: where the mountains are capped with snow, the maple trees and beavers are abundant, and the news stories are really, really strange.

NOSEY NEIGHBORS

David and Joan Gallant moved in next door to Lee and Shirley Murray's farm in Indian Mountain, New Brunswick, in 2001. Everyone was friendly with everyone until late 2013, when Lee Murray left a massive load of cow manure on his lawn. (Estimated size of the poop pile: 18 by 14 meters, or 59 by 46 feet.) *That* much manure tends to stink to high heaven, and it drove the Gallants mad. They asked many times to clear the waste away, but the Murrays apparently refused, at one point telling the Gallants that it would freeze over and stop smelling once winter came. Meanwhile, the manure mountain started to slip…and run into the Gallants' property. David Gallant enlisted a local farm board to help, and after 11 months, the Murrays finally got rid of the cow poop, but then they accused the Gallants of trespassing, which sent the whole thing to court. (A judge ruled in favor of the poor Gallants.)

FIRE AND ICE

Late one night in January 2018, a fire raged throughout the small Saint-Gabriel-de-Valcartier Hotel outside of Quebec City, Quebec. The hotel was almost completely booked, with guests asleep in 13 of the structure's 14 rooms. Nobody was killed or seriously hurt, but several patrons reported minor smoke inhalation. What's so weird about this? The Saint-Gabriel-de-Valcartier is an ice hotel, meaning it's made completely out of frozen blocks of water. Amazingly, the fire didn't melt the hotel, which reported no structural damage, although the lack of windows left a strong smoky smell in the hotel for a few days.

THE MONEY PIT

Leston Lawrence worked at the Royal Canadian Mint in Ontario up until 2016, when he was convicted of taking his work home. Between 2014 and 2015, Lawrence smuggled 22 solid gold disks (called "pucks," because this story took place in Canada) out of the mint. Total worth of the pucks: about $190,000, although he sold most of them for $130,000, which he sold to build a house and buy a boat. So, how did Lawrence get those pucks out of the mint, and fool the metal detectors in place to prevent this exact crime? He hid them in his rectum. Lawrence was sentenced to 30 months in prison and a fine of $190,000 by an Ontario provincial judge. Bonus: The judge's name was Peter Doody.

Spy hard: Before he was an actor, Bruce Willis was a private detective.

BEARLY LEGAL

Innisfail is a small town in rural, southern Alberta. Its biggest attraction: an animal refuge and theme park called Discovery Wildlife Park. The center's most notable resident is a young Kodiak bear named Berkley, whose videos have gone viral. One clip depicted Berkley leaning out of the driver's-side window of a pickup truck so she could eat ice cream and cake right out of the hands of a Dairy Queen employee working the drive-through. "We've got Berkley in the drive-through testing out some ice cream so she can pick out her birthday cake," a man named Mark says in the video. Two days later, Discovery posted another video showing Berkley licking the frosting off an ice cream cake. In the same video, a park employee notes that in addition to cake, Berkley also enjoys peanuts and "Kraft Dinner," which is what Canadians call boxed macaroni and cheese. These are just two more examples of questionable behavior by Discovery Wildlife Park, which has led to an investigation by Alberta's Environment and Parks department. The agency has previously received complaints about the park after its Facebook page depicted photos of children standing by the bears, and adults allowing the bears to kiss their faces.

FOR THE BIRDS

Police were sent to a home in Brighton, Ontario, one evening in 2016 when neighbors, fearing a violent domestic dispute, overheard what they believed to be the couple who lived there screaming at one another. According to police records of the call, the man was yelling things like "I hope you die." But it wasn't the couple yelling at each other. "We located the male of the household alone in the house," Constable Steve Bates said. The man had apparently been "screaming at his pet parrot who had been 'beaking off' at him" (at least that's what the man told police). Fortunately, the bird had not been physically abused, and, unsurprisingly, the man had been drinking. No charges were filed, although Bates said, amazingly, "These are the kinds of stories that police run into all the time."

FREEDOM FROM INFORMATION ACT

In 2018 Michael Dagg, a researcher from Ottawa, filed a request with Library and Archives Canada for access to 780,000 documents that related to a mid-1990s police investigation into money-laundering and corruption. The national request program allows any Canadian to request government information for a $5 fee. It usually takes about 30 days. But in this case, the federal department told Dagg it would take a little longer. How much longer? About 290,000 days…roughly 800 years. Dagg then received another email informing him that the first email had been in error. It wouldn't take 800 years to get the documents—it would take only 80 years.

In the 19th century, the Egyptian "mummy trade" was so booming that tourists could buy them from Cairo street vendors.

TYPO-RRIFIC!

What blood type is Uncle John? Typo. Now, some typo stories you might apprecihate.

THERE'S A TYPO IN YOUR SENTENCE

In 1987 a jury in California found Bruce Wayne Morris guilty of first-degree murder in the death of a hitchhiker he'd picked up in Sacramento. During the sentencing phase of the trial in 1987, the judge sent the jury a note informing them that they had a choice of sentencing Morris to death or life in prison *without* the possibility of parole. Except that the judge mistakenly wrote *with* the possibility of parole. The jury, thinking their choice was between a death sentence and the possibility of Morris walking the streets again, chose death. Morris's attorneys appealed the case, and in 2001—14 years of litigation later—the death sentence was overturned by a federal appeals court, on the basis of the judge's typo. The case was sent back to the original court for a new sentencing hearing; the death sentence was vacated.

ABOUT TIMES!

On January 20, 1853, the *New York Times* published an article about Solomon Northup, a former slave who had written a memoir titled *12 Years a Slave*. Except they spelled his name wrong…twice: they spelled it "Northrup" in the article's headline, and "Northrop" in the article itself. The *Times* was informed of the error and issued a correction…161 years later. A Twitter user alerted them of the typo in 2014, after the film adaptation of *12 Years a Slave* won the Oscar for Best Picture at the Academy Awards.

LESUS!

In October 2013, the Vatican issued a commemorative medal to celebrate Pope Francis's first year as head of the Catholic Church. Around the rim of one side of the coin was a phrase in English, reportedly a favorite of the pope, that said, "Jesus, therefore, saw the tax collector, and because he saw by having mercy and by choosing, He said to him, 'Follow me.'" Except the most important word in the phrase—Jesus—was spelled "Lesus." All 6,000 of the medallions, which had been minted in gold, silver, and bronze, and which had already been sent out to retailers, were recalled and destroyed. (Italian media reported at the time that four of the medallions were actually sold to collectors before the recall—meaning those collectors now own some extremely valuable "Lesus" medals.)

The *subclavius* muscle, located between the shoulders and under the clavicle,
serves little purpose after you learn how to walk.

TAKING IT TO THE STREETS

Here's a look into the history and namesakes of some of the most famous roads, streets, and avenues from around the world.

Street: Champs-Élysées (Paris, France)

Details: This tree-lined boulevard runs from the Arc de Triomphe to the Place de la Concorde, and it's one of the most popular places to hang out and sightsee in the City of Light. Fancy shops, restaurants, bars, theaters, hotels, museums, and the Eiffel Tower are all within walking distance.

Origin: It was a vacant expanse of fields to the west of the Tuileries Gardens until King Louis XIV called for its development into a grand avenue. Designed by France's premier landscape architect, André La Nôrte, it was completed in the late 1600s and named the Grand Cours, or "Grand Promenade." In 1709 it was renamed with the French translation of "Elysian Fields"—the heavenly paradise of Greek mythology where warriors went after they died.

Street: Beale Street (Memphis, Tennessee)

Details: Memphis is one of the world's great music cities—it's where the blues developed in the 20th century at the many African American–owned clubs, bars, and outdoor performance areas in the city's Beale Street district.

Origin: Developer Robertson Topp got the contract to build up the area, which is adjacent to the Mississippi River, in 1841. Who's Beale? No one knows for sure. The official line from the City of Memphis is that Topp named the street (originally Beale Avenue) after a forgotten war hero, but his full identity has been lost to time.

Street: Downing Street (London, England)

Details: Like many streets in London, it's crammed full of rows of well-kept town houses. What makes Downing Street different is that it's where the UK government is headquartered, and where the prime minister lives—at 10 Downing Street, to be exact. (The second-most-powerful person, the Chancellor of the Exchequer, lives at 11 Downing Street.) "Downing Street" has become a catchall to refer to the British government, similar to the way that "the White House" is shorthand for the American government.

Origin: The area where Downing Street now sits was once the site of a large estate called Hampden House, and before that, a brewery. Sir George Downing, a diplomat who served under King Charles II, bought the land in 1654 and began developing it into a residential street in the 1680s.

In 1520 England's King Henry VIII challenged France's King Francis I to a wrestling match. (Henry lost.)

Street: Carnaby Street (London, England)

Details: In the mid-to-late 1960s, "swinging London" was based around Carnaby Street. Young, edgy clothing designers like John Stephen and Mary Quant set up studios and shops there to sell their brightly colored suits, psychedelic and paisley shirts, and scandalously short miniskirts.

Origins: Before London urbanized, the land where Carnaby Street sits was occupied by a huge mansion called Karnaby House, which gave way to Karnaby Market in the early 1800s. The market's gone, but the name lives on.

Street: Lombard Street (San Francisco, California)

Details: Lombard is a major thoroughfare in San Francisco, but the street is most famous for a one-block section known as "the crookedest street in the world." In a city known for its steep hills, Lombard Street runs atop one of the steepest, so the designers who built it in the 1920s figured a good way to break up the grade was installing eight tight turns. Drivers have no choice but to take it slow—but just in case they don't think Lombard is all that steep, there's a 5 mph speed limit.

Origins: In 1847 Irish-born explorer Jasper O'Farrell was named the first official surveyor for the City of San Francisco, which means he had a big hand in designing the city. He also got to name a lot of streets, such as Market, Chestnut, and Valparaiso Streets. O'Farrell named Lombard Street after a street by the same name in Philadelphia. Reason: O'Farrell thought Philadelphia was America's greatest city, and he aimed to make San Francisco just as great.

Street: Bourbon Street (New Orleans, Louisiana)

Details: New Orleans has a lot of French influence. The place to be to drunkenly celebrate Mardi Gras ("Fat Tuesday," the last day before the self-denial of Lent begins) is the city's Bourbon Street.

Origins: While a lot of drinking happens on Bourbon Street, it's not named after bourbon the spirit. The House of Bourbon was a European royal family that ruled France in the 16th century. France still controlled what's now New Orleans when Rue Bourbon was first constructed in 1721.

* * *

STAMPED OUT

Conductor Jean-Baptiste Lully liked to stamp out the beat on the floor with a staff. During a performance in 1687 celebrating the recovery of King Louis XIV from illness, he struck his foot by accident. The foot got infected, and he died.

In 1997 the American chicken population passed 240 million, outnumbering American humans for the first time ever.

FAT CLUB

The first rule of Fat Club: Tell everybody about Fat Club, or rather "fat men's clubs" that were popular among America's heavyset elite in the early 1900s.

THE BIG IDEA

In the late 19th century in New York City, there were dozens of "gentlemen's clubs." Finally: places where wealthy, well-connected white men could be themselves. They'd drink, smoke cigars, network, and make big political and business deals… and eat. At least that was what the Fat Men's Association of New York City did at their meetings. So did other organizations, such as the Jolly Fat Men's Club, the United Association of the Heavy Men of New York State, the Fat Men's Beneficial Association, and the Heavy Weights. These were early examples of "body positivity" movements—overweight guys admitting that they were overweight, and then celebrating it by getting together to gorge on rich, sumptuous banquets of food.

Those New York clubs were a novelty and they didn't last long. However, they made a comeback and became a small cultural phenomenon in the northeastern United States a few years after the turn of the 20th century. At a tavern in Wells River, Vermont, one night in 1903, owner Jerome Hale was talking with 10 traveling salesmen, all of whom were regular patrons of the establishment. Like Hale, they were all husky men, each weighing more than 200 pounds. The group started talking about their struggles to lose weight…and how they'd prefer to just forget it and stay overweight, because eating was far preferential to starving themselves. Hale, unaware of the New York fat men's clubs from a generation earlier, suggested that they form a "fat men's club." The salesmen loved the idea and quickly came up a name—the New England Fat Men's Club—and a slogan: "We're fat and we're making the most of it."

LARGE AND IN CHARGE

The group also established some ground rules. Members of the New England Fat Men's Club had to weigh a minimum of 200 pounds, learn a secret handshake and password, and were expected to attend twice-yearly club meetings—announced with plenty of advance notice, just in case members had dipped below 200 pounds and needed to get back up to that magic number.

The traveling salesmen quickly spread the word. In the fall of 1904, just a little over a year after the New England Fat Men's Club had first been proposed, the organization welcomed hundreds to a meeting, which took over Wells River for a long weekend. Here's a contemporary account from the *Boston Globe:*

More good news: There are more bacteria in your mouth than there are people on the planet.

"This village is full of bulbous and overhanging abdomens and double chins tonight, for the New England Fat Men's Club is in session at Hale's Tavern. The natives, who are mostly bony and angular, have stared with envy at the portly forms and rubicund faces which have arrived on every train."

MASSIVE SUCCESS

Entry into a "meeting" cost $1.00. It wasn't so much a meeting as it was a sumptuous bacchanal. Attendees began the day with a huge group breakfast, then they headed outdoors for strength and stamina contests. They played games like leapfrog, they ran footraces, and they competed to see who could jump the farthest. Not every sport was successful. At the 1904 meeting, Jerome Hale won a potato-sack race in which three other competitors fell down, including 377-pound F. C. Dignac of New Hampshire, who couldn't get back up in time to finish. Pole-vaulting events were called off when no one could find a pole that wouldn't snap in half. The tug-of-war was nearly canceled after the rope broke, only to be replaced with a chain.

However, all of that physical activity was merely an excuse to work up an appetite, because after the sports came a gigantic dinner. One New England Fat Men's Club dinner was a multicourse affair consisting of oyster cocktail, cream of chicken soup, boiled snapper, beef filet with mushrooms, roast chicken, suckling pig, shrimp salad, steamed pudding in brandy sauce, cakes, cheese, ice cream, coffee, and cigars. The men reportedly stayed up until well after midnight, all the while eating, smoking, drinking, and laughing.

The New England Fat Men's Club held "meetings" like this twice a year for more than a decade. At one point, the Fat Men's Club counted regular membership of around 10,000 portly guys who dutifully weighed in before each official organization banquet, clambake, picnic, or gala. And unlike many other elite activities of the era, these events weren't held in smoky rooms away from view—the Fat Men's Club ate and exercised in public. Meetings were announced in newspapers, and spectators were invited to gawk at club members as they ate themselves under the table.

THROWING THEIR WEIGHT AROUND

Fat men's clubs were a celebration of both rotundity and wealth—which were equated with one another. The early 20th century was the last time that being overweight was widely considered attractive, simply because having extra meat on one's bones indicated that a person was wealthy enough to be properly nourished.

Beyond the privileged circles of the Northeast, fat men's clubs sprung up in small towns in places like Nevada, Utah, and Tennessee. (In those locations, the

Alfred Hitchcock wanted to film a movie at Disneyland. Walt Disney said no.
(He thought *Psycho* was "disgusting.")

clubs operated more like the Rotary or the Better Business Bureau—places where community leaders could meet up and network.) Members' approval was even sought out by politicians. William Jennings Bryan actively campaigned at fat men's clubs during his 1908 presidential run, and President William Howard Taft was offered membership in the New England Fat Men's Club. He declined to join, but he did attend one of their raucous meetings—or at least he tried to. When he arrived in Wells River, the car that came to pick him up couldn't move after the 340-pound president got in. So he got back on the train and returned to Washington, DC.

LOSING IT

Changing attitudes toward weight and beauty standards, along with more advanced food production and preservation techniques brought about by the Industrial Revolution, chipped away at membership in fat men's clubs and the "fat pride" that led to their creation. Around 1910, doctors and actuaries started to suggest that being extremely overweight was also extremely unhealthy. The New England Fat Men's Club held its last meeting in 1924. Where 10,000 men had once gathered, this time only 38 showed up…and none of them met the 200-pound weight minimum rule.

* * *

THE HONEST TRUTH ABOUT…TRUTH AND HONESTY

"Men in general are quick to believe that which they wish to be true."
—Julius Caesar

"The brightest flashes in the world of thought are incomplete until they have been proved to have their counterparts in the world of fact."
—John Tyndall

"He who dares not offend cannot be honest."
—Thomas Paine

"The cure to eliminate fake news is that people stop reading 140-character tweets and start reading 600-page books."
—Piero Scaruffi

"All control, in essence, is about who controls the truth."
—Joseph Rain

Miniskirt inventor Mary Quant named it after her favorite car, the Mini Cooper.

A GOOD PLACE TO GET BOMBED

*Whether you're looking for protection against nuclear holocaust,
asteroids, or the Rapture, these do-it-yourself bunkers will
keep you (and your 50 pounds of ramen) safe.*

ATLAS SURVIVAL SHELTERS

Atlas Survival Shelters was founded by Ron Hubbard (no, not *that* Ron Hubbard) in the Los Angeles suburb of Montebello, and advertises itself as the everyman's shelter. With a round corrugated pipe shape, it is described as "the only bunkers...tested against the effects of the nuclear bomb." Hubbard's shelters provide a much nicer living environment than fallout shelters of the 1950s, and at a decent price. Hubbard, who calls himself the "modern Henry Ford," sells consumer-friendly bunkers that start at "only" $25,000. Like most of the bunkers on this list, Atlas Survival Shelters are buried underground either next to your home or in a location of your choice. They start as small as 10 x 13 feet and go as big as you want. (They'll even build you barracks!) They come equipped with essentials such as air-filtration systems, blast doors, and indoor plumbing, but also offer upgrades like hardwood floors and marble kitchen counters.

VIVOS

Vivos (Latin for "living") is the name of a company that offers a community-based survival experience. While most bunker companies have a standard practice of *not* sharing the location of their customers' bunkers, Vivos takes applicants for their sites in South Dakota and Indiana, the latter of which holds dozens of massive shelters built during the Cold War. And like a gated community, Vivos has underground common areas, giving you the opportunity to have neighbors over during a nuclear holocaust. To secure one year of bunker living at their South Dakota site, home to 500 brand-new mini shelters, approved applicants pay $5,000. Reserving one of their older Indiana bunkers costs $25,000 (up front, of course). But at least you won't have to pack your bags, as each bunker is stocked with food, supplies, survival gear, and all the amenities (and appliances) of normal life. The threat of nuclear war must be good business. Vivos recently opened Vivos Europa, which provides 34 private shelters built in a former Soviet military base that's located under a mountain.

You didn't have your first dream until you were about 3 or 4 years old.

ULTIMATE BUNKER

If you buy a shelter from Ultimate Bunker, you're not looking to skimp out when the apocalypse comes. These bunkers start at $60,000 and can cost up to $619,900 (although for that price, you get to design it). But Ultimate also touts itself as the go-to bunker manufacturer for customers who plan to bring along their own weapons arsenals. Ultimate Bunker specializes in custom gun vaults with huge Fort Knox–style doors. You're not going to bring just one jug of water down to your bunker, so why would you pack only one rifle?

SUBTERRA CASTLE

Located on a 34-acre estate in the pastoral Kansas hills 25 miles west of Topeka, Subterra was once an ICBM site with a four-megaton warhead housed deep underground. In 1994 Edward and Dianna Peden bought the land and have converted it into a series of survival shelters. Unlike other shelter companies, Subterra focuses less on doom and gloom and more on what they call "a vision of a healthy, healing, community environment, nurturing Body, Mind, and Spirit." The Pedens have lived underground since they purchased the site and now offer six different home types in their reclaimed nuclear weapon sites. But just because they're preparing for the end of the world, that doesn't mean they aren't capitalists: Their bunkers go for as much as $3.2 million.

* * *

THEY MADE THEIR MARKS

- Pro baseball player Germany Schaefer's odd claim to fame: stealing first base from second base, "to confuse the pitcher." He played from 1901 to 1918; in 1920 a rule was passed stating that if a player runs the bases in the wrong direction, the umpire must declare him out.

- When herring is salted and smoked, it turns red and pungent. In 1807 a British journalist named William Cobbett wrote about how he used red herrings to lay a false scent trail for some hunting dogs he was training. From his story, the expression "red herring" came to mean a distraction created to divert attention from the real issue.

- Two settlers in northern Oregon in 1845 couldn't agree on a name for their settlement. Asa Lovejoy, from Massachusetts, wanted Boston. Francis Pettygrove, from Maine, wanted Portland. They flipped a coin (best two out of three). Who won? Here's a hint: Today the coin is on display in a museum—in Portland, Oregon.

Scientists say: Bacon is addictive in much the same way that cocaine is (but it's not as bad for you).

UNCLE JOHN'S STALL OF FAME

*Uncle John is amazed—and pleased—by the unusual ways
people get involved with bathrooms, toilets, and so on.
That's why he created the "Stall of Fame."*

HONOREE: Peter Freuchen (1886–1957), an Arctic explorer from Denmark

NOTABLE ACHIEVEMENT: Saving his own life with a "stool tool."

TRUE STORY: In 1912 Freuchen was a member of the First Thule Expedition, which sought to test American Arctic explorer Robert Peary's belief that a sea channel separated Peary Land, the northernmost part of Greenland, from the rest of Greenland.

It was while trekking across more than 600 miles of this forbidding territory that Freuchen got caught out in the open in a blizzard. He took what shelter he could beneath his dogsled, but was soon buried under several feet of snow that had frozen into hard ice.

Freuchen didn't have any sharp tools on him that he could use to dig his way out, and he had to go to the bathroom. Why not kill two birds with one stone? Freuchen pooped, waited for the poop to freeze, then used it as a "dagger" to dig his way to freedom. By the time he made it back to base camp, his left leg was so badly frostbitten that it had to be amputated, but he completed the expedition and proved that Peary Land is not separate from the rest of Greenland.

> Freuchen didn't have any sharp tools on him that he could use to dig his way out, and he had to go to the bathroom. Why not kill two birds with one stone?

HONOREE: Jumpy, a border collie–blue heeler mix owned by Omar von Muller, who bills himself as a "dog trainer to the stars"

NOTABLE ACHIEVEMENT: Knowing a bathroom trick that many *human* males have yet to master.

TRUE STORY: Jumpy is very talented. He knows how to paint, do backflips, ride skateboards and wakeboards, and has more than 30 acting credits to his name. But the thing that lands him in the Stall of Fame is a YouTube video titled "Jumpy Leaving His Mark at the Chandler Valley Center Studios." In it, Jumpy lifts his leg and pees into a men's room urinal without spilling a drop onto the floor, then stands on his hind legs and flushes the urinal. The video has been viewed more than 166,000 times. Bonus: When von Muller isn't busy with training dogs for TV and the movies, he makes his services available to the public. So if you live in L.A. "or you are willing to get on a plane with your pup," he says, he may be able to teach your dog (or the man in your life) the same trick.

HONOREE: Nina Katchadourian, a Brooklyn-based artist

NOTABLE ACHIEVEMENT: She makes artistic self-portraits in airplane bathrooms using paper towels, toilet paper, seat covers, and other items found in airplane bathrooms.

TRUE STORY: Katchadourian says she stumbled across her odd form of portraiture by chance. "While in the lavatory on a domestic flight in 2011, I spontaneously put a tissue paper toilet cover seat cover over my head and took a picture in the mirror using my cellphone." The resulting image reminded her of 15th-century Flemish portraits, she writes on her website.

Why stop at one? Katchadourian had a long-haul flight from San Francisco to New Zealand coming up in a few weeks, and she decided to spend much of that flight in the restroom, posing for as many portraits as she could. (The other passengers slept for long stretches on the 14-hour flight, so the restrooms were unoccupied.) "By the time we landed," Katchadourian writes, "I had a large group of new photographs entitled Lavatory Self-Portraits in the Flemish Style. There is no special illumination other than the lavatory's own lights and all the images are shot hand-held with the camera phone." See for yourself: Katchadourian has posted her self-portraits on her website, ninakatchadourian.com, and in some of them she really does look like a woman from the 15th century.

HONOREE: YoYo Li, a Los Angeles restaurateur

NOTABLE ACHIEVEMENT: Bringing toilet-themed cuisine to the United States.

TRUE STORY: When Li decided to go into business in L.A., the two options she considered were opening a "bubble tea" shop, or opening a toilet-themed Chinese restaurant. We've written in the past about the thriving Modern Toilet restaurant chain in Taiwan: Customers sit on toilets, eat toilet-themed foods out of bowls shaped like Western- and squat-style toilets, and drink beverages from glasses that look like urinals.

L.A. already had plenty of bubble tea joints, so Li settled on her second option. She copied the Modern Toilet concept and opened the Magic Restroom Cafe in the City of Industry suburb of Los Angeles in 2013. Menu items included "Smells Like Poop" (braised pork on rice), "Constipation" (noodles with soybean paste), "Black Poop" (chocolate sundae), and "Stinky Tofu" (stinky tofu). Want to go? If you haven't gone already, you waited too long—the restaurant closed its doors in May 2014 after just eight months. "Magic Restroom Cafe Goes Down the Toilet," read the headline in Los Angeles Magazine.

The Pop Tart is based on a Danish homemade dessert called *hindbaersnitter*.

IRONIC, ISN'T IT?

There's nothing like a good dose of irony to put the problems
of day-to-day life into proper perspective.

BURNING IRONY. A devastating wildfire tore through Santa Rosa, California, in October 2017. In one particularly hard-hit area, a local Carl's Jr. was the only restaurant left standing. That's why, on October 9, dozens of hungry firefighters showed up at the fast-food joint and ordered 165 cheeseburgers. The line cooks tried to get the burgers out as fast as they could. Unfortunately, all that charbroiling made the exhaust vents extremely hot, and a grease fire broke out and quickly caused around $75,000 worth of damage. Within 15 minutes, the firefighters—who were at that restaurant only because all the others had burned down—extinguished the fire that started because they had ordered so many burgers at once.

IRONY TAKES A PASS. In August 2017, officials at the Pinellas Suncoast Transit Authority in St. Petersburg, Florida, decided to give one of their most loyal customers, Barbara Rygiel, a lifetime bus pass. Rygiel is 103 years old.

ISN'T IT IRONIC? (IT IS NOW.) Alanis Morissette has taken a lot of flak over the years for her 1996 hit song "Ironic" because the lyrics aren't really ironic. Like this one: "An old man turned 98 / He won the lottery and died the next day." It's unfortunate, but it's not ironic. (In Morissette's defense: she was 19 when she wrote the song.) In 2013 two musicians, sisters named Eliza and Rachael Hurwitz, decided to give Morissette a helping hand by writing a corrected version of the song. Now called "It's Finally Ironic," here's that same lyric, corrected: "An old man turned 98 / He won the lottery and died the next day / from a severe paper cut from his lottery ticket."

Update: In 2016 Morissette finally copped to her linguistic faux pas while performing a parody version of the song on *The Late Late Show with James Corden*. She updated the lyrics for the social media era: "An old friend sends you a Facebook request / and you find out he's a racist after you accept." Still not ironic. But then Morissette ended the song with this line: "It's singing 'Ironic' / when there are no ironies. / And who would have thought? / It figures."

> Morissette ended the song with: "It's singing 'Ironic' when there are no ironies. And who would have thought? It figures."

IRONY GOES NIGHTY-NIGHT. In 1953 Eugene Aserinsky, a graduate student at the University of Chicago, discovered REM sleep, and went on to become one the world's most renowned sleep experts. In 2003 Aserinksy, 77, was killed when he hit a tree after falling asleep at the wheel.

IRONY ON THE SIDELINES

- Vincent T. Lombardi Middle School in Green Bay, Wisconsin—named after the NFL's most revered head coach of all time—had to cancel its football season in the fall of 2017. Reason: they couldn't find anyone willing to coach the team.

- One of college basketball's best teams, the University of Kansas Jayhawks have amassed an impressive .750 winning percentage in the 120 years since their debut season in 1898. Only one head coach in the history of the team has even had a losing record: James Naismith. If that name sounds familiar, it's because Naismith is the man who invented the game of basketball. (His coaching motto may shed light on why he lost so many games: "You can't coach basketball; you just play it.")

WARNING: IRONY AHEAD. Of all the road signs for a drunk driver to hit, none would be more ironic than one that says "REPORT DRUNK DRIVERS. CALL 911." That's the sign that a 57-year-old Aptos, California, man hit in his Jeep Wrangler one night in 2017. After demolishing the sign, the Jeep "careened up an embankment, flipped, and landed on its roof." According to the arresting officer, "He was quite intoxicated."

IRONY THAT EATS ITS OWN TAIL. Is irony dead? Some people claim it is. Who are those people? Ironic hipsters—the very same group that helped propel irony into the mainstream. They've now declared it dead because of the popularity of the phrase "hipster irony." Or, as a hipster named Peter Furia put it to NPR, "The ironic part is that hipsters' opposition to pop culture has become pop culture."

> "The ironic part is that hipsters' opposition to pop culture has become pop culture."

THERE'S AN IRONY FOR THAT. A smartphone app called The Hold is available for people who are addicted to… smartphones. It "allows users to earn rewards such as cinema tickets for not using their phone." Unfortunately, the only way to access the app is with your phone.

'TIL IRONY DO WE PART. For a Valentine's promotion in 2018, a law firm in Little Rock, Arkansas, held a contest for married couples to enter. The prize: a free divorce (a $985 value!). No word on who the lucky "winners" were.

About 50 coffee beans are used to make a single shot of espresso.

"PRINCESS TAKES A BALLET CLASS"

Movie prequels get released all the time, but songs never do. Can you guess the name of the famous song if we tell you the artist and the made-up "prequel" to that song? The answers are on page 501.

1. Ray Charles, "Now, Listen Carefully"

2. The Beatles, "Two Days Ago"

3. Elton John "I Bet We'll Be Together Forever"

4. Al Green, "Maybe We Should Break Up"

5. Elvis Presley, "Please Don't Arrest Me, Officer"

6. James Brown, "Papa Went to the Bag Store"

7. The Who, "I Hope This Fog Clears Soon"

8. Prince, "The Day the Red Clouds Met the Blue Clouds"

9. Blondie, "I Just Bought a Phone"

10. The Doors, "Two-Thirds of the Way Through"

11. Carole King, "Don't Worry, There's Plenty of Time"

12. Ramones, "I'm Uncomfortably Agitated"

13. David Bowie, "Interplanetary Travel?"

14. Eddie Cochran, "Spring Fever"

15. ABBA, "Princess Takes a Ballet Class"

16. Billy Joel, "I Need a New Apartment"

17. Cheap Trick, "You're Surrounded!"

18. Fleetwood Mac, "Heavy Rains"

19. Queen, "We Are Contestants"

20. Steely Dan, "Do It"

21. U2, "A Week After Christmas"

22. Madonna, "A Prolonged Period of Work"

23. Guns N' Roses, "An Autumnal Change of Barometric Pressure"

24. Rolling Stones, "Prime It White"

25. Talking Heads, "Pouring Gasoline on the Kitchen Floor"

26. Tom Petty, "Whoops! Forgot My Parachute!"

In the 1928 Olympics, Australian rower Bobby Pearce stopped his boat to let some ducks pass. He still won the gold medal.

MOUTHING OFF

MEAT-FREE

Words of wisdom—and advice on going vegetarian—from vegetarians.

"If slaughterhouses had glass walls, we would all be vegetarian."
—Paul McCartney

"I choose not to make a graveyard of my body for the rotting corpses of dead animals."
—George Bernard Shaw

"THOSE WHO EAT FLESH ARE BUT EATING GRAINS AND VEGETABLES AT SECOND HAND."
—Ellen G. White

"I wouldn't touch a hot dog unless you put a condom on it."
—Bill Maher

"Man is the only animal that can remain on friendly terms with the victims he intends to eat until he eats them."
—Samuel Butler

"Many refined people will not kill a fly, but eat an ox."
—I. L. Peretz

"We all love animals. Why do we call some 'pets' and others 'dinner'?"
—k. d. lang

"Perhaps a man hitched to the cart of a Martian or roasted on the spit by inhabitants of the Milky Way will recall the veal cutlet he used to slice on his dinner plate and apologize (belatedly) to the cow."
—Milan Kundera

VEGETABLES, SCHMEGETABLES

Then again, there are some people out there who think it's absurd to adopt a vegetarian lifestyle.

"VEGETARIANISM: YOU ARE WHAT YOU EAT, AND WHO WANTS TO BE A LETTUCE?"
—Peter Burns

"IS A VEGETARIAN PERMITTED TO EAT ANIMAL CRACKERS?"
—George Carlin

"I love animals, especially with barbeque sauce."
—J. Richard Singleton

"Vegetarians, and their Hezbollah-like splinter faction, the vegans, are the enemy of everything good and decent in the human spirit."
—Anthony Bourdain

"I was a vegetarian until I started leaning toward the sunlight."
—Rita Rudner

"Meat isn't murder. It's delicious."
—Johnny Rotten

"Vegetables are interesting but lack a sense of purpose when unaccompanied by a good cut of meat."
—Fran Lebowitz

"There are two types of vegetarians: Those who have beef with chicken, and those who are too chicken to have beef."
—Mokokoma Mokhonoana

NEVER EVENTS

*It's an unfortunate fact of life: even skilled professionals who hold the
lives of others in their hands can and do make really dumb mistakes.
Warning: you may find these stories slightly gruesome.*

BACKGROUND: DO NO WRONG...MOST OF THE TIME

Fifty-three million surgeries are performed each year in the United States. Of these,
it's estimated that some 4,000 of them—less than 0.0001 percent—involve "never
events." That's the term for mistakes like performing the wrong procedure, operating
on the wrong body part or the wrong patient, or leaving a foreign object (such as a
sponge or a surgical instrument) inside the patient. The good news (if it can be called
that) is that such mistakes are rare. The bad news is that they're called "never events"
because they're *never* supposed to happen. Numerous controls are put in place to
prevent them from happening, but sometimes they do. Here are some examples:

Spare(d) rib. In May 2015, Deborah Craven was having a section of her eighth rib
removed at Yale New Haven Hospital because a precancerous lesion on the bone was
causing her pain. In preparation for the surgery, radiologists marked the rib by attaching
metallic coils to it and injecting dye into the surrounding tissue to indicate to Dr.
Anthony Kim, the surgeon, and Dr. Ricardo Quarrie, a surgeon-in-training, which
rib needed to be removed. But Craven was still in pain after the surgery, so an X-ray
was performed. It revealed that the eighth rib and the metal coils were still in place.
Translation: the doctors had removed the wrong rib. Kim admitted his mistake, but
according to Craven, Quarrie tried to cover it up by telling her she needed a second
surgery because not enough of the rib had been removed. "Making the patient undergo
another surgery the same day, without owning up to the real medical reason for the repeat
surgery," Craven's lawyer, Joel Faxon, said after filing a lawsuit, "is just plain deceitful."

It *is* brain surgery. In December 2014, Michael Krabbe checked into St. Mary's
Health Center in St. Louis, Missouri, to have a "very large" brain tumor removed and
biopsied. The surgery was performed, but when Krabbe woke up from the operation,
he was unable to speak or move his right arm and leg. Krabbe alleges that the surgeon,
Dr. George Bailey, told him he'd removed the tumor, but had to perform an additional
surgery to insert chemotherapy wafers near the tumor site. That's when Krabbe decided
it was time for a second opinion. An MRI—at a different hospital—revealed that
Bailey had operated on the left frontal lobe of the brain (above the eye), not the left
temporal lobe (above the ear), where the tumor was located. He had removed healthy

"No man ever became great or good except through
many and great mistakes." —William E. Gladstone

brain tissue and left the brain tumor in place. "We have complete confidence in Dr. Bailey and the care he delivers to our patients," a spokesperson for St. Mary's Health Center said after Krabbe filed a lawsuit against Dr. Bailey and the hospital.

Anyone seen my scalpel? In 2013 Glenford Turner had his prostate removed at the West Haven Veterans Affairs Hospital in Connecticut. The procedure, which was performed by fifth-year urology trainee Dr. Jaimin Shah under the supervision of the chief of urology, Dr. Preston Sprenkle, left Turner with severe abdominal pain. But the U.S. Army veteran toughed it out…for *four years*. Finally, in 2017, the pain became unbearable and he returned to the hospital for answers. That's when X-rays revealed that a five-inch scalpel had been left inside Turner's pelvis during the surgery. Somehow both doctors failed to notice that they were one scalpel short after finishing the surgery. While Turner was recovering from surgery to remove the scalpel, Dr. Sprenkle, completely oblivious to the irony, noted that the patient "does notice the pelvic pain that has been present since his prostatectomy is now gone."

In a pinch. In April 2017, a woman named Mary Harber had surgery at Shasta Regional Medical Center in Redding, California, to remove a benign tumor from her abdomen. Recovering at home afterward, Harber suffered from back, kidney, and abdominal pain for two weeks. By May 1, the pain was so great that she went to the emergency room, where X-rays revealed that a pair of eight-inch-long surgical forceps had been left in her abdomen. In a second procedure, surgeons removed the forceps plus 18 inches of Harber's small intestine, which had "looped into one of the forceps' finger holes."

Foul ball. After experiencing pain in his right testicle for 15 years, in 2013 Steven Haines decided to see a urologist at J. C. Blair Memorial Hospital in Huntingdon, Pennsylvania. Dr. V. Spencer Long discovered that Haines's right testicle had atrophied due to scarring and damage from a previous injury. He performed surgery to remove the testicle, but when Haines woke up, the pain was still there. An examination revealed that Dr. Long had removed his healthy *left* testicle, and left the atrophied *right* testicle in place. According to Haines's attorney, Braden Lepisto, "The doctor gave an explanation that really made no anatomical or medical sense. He claimed that he removed the testicle that was on the right side of the scrotum and the testicle had a spermatic cord that led to the left side of the body. Essentially, the doctor claimed that the testicles had switched sides." At last report, Haines was still living with his atrophied right testicle and the pain that it causes him—Lepisto says he has a "debilitating fear" of receiving further treatment for his condition. (If he has the testicle removed, he'll need testosterone therapy for the rest of his life.) In June 2017, a jury awarded him $870,000 in damages for the botched surgery.

There's enough water in Lake Superior to cover all of North and South America a foot deep.

THINKING OUTSIDE (AND INSIDE) THE BOX

You probably haven't heard of Malcom McLean, but he was one of the most innovative businessmen of the 20th century and, for good or bad, one of the architects of the modern globalized economy.

GAS MONEY

Malcom McLean was like a lot of kids who graduated from high school during the Great Depression in the 1930s: He had big dreams, but his family didn't have enough money to send him to college. So he got a job pumping gas, and after a few years he saved up enough money—$120—to buy a used pickup truck. With it, he went into business for himself, hauling produce, animal feed, and empty tobacco barrels around Winston-Salem, North Carolina. He soon had more work than he could handle alone, so he brought his sister and brother into the business. Then he began buying more trucks and hiring additional drivers to operate them.

Two years later, during Thanksgiving week in 1937, McLean hauled a shipment of cotton bales to Jersey City, New Jersey, where they were going to be loaded onto a ship bound for Istanbul, Turkey. Jersey City is at least a day's drive from Winston-Salem, and when McLean arrived at the port he discovered that it was going to take at least that long for the longshoremen to unload his truck.

In those days, ships were still loaded and unloaded the same way they'd always been: by hand, once piece of cargo at a time, using manual labor. Each of McLean's bales of cotton had to be taken aboard the ship individually, by hand if it was small enough, or using a crane if it was too heavy for longshoremen to carry. Once aboard, the bale had to be secured in place with ropes, again by hand, to prevent it from being tossed about by rough waters when the ship was at sea. Only after that first bale was secured in place would the longshoremen return for the next bale, and then only if some other piece of cargo didn't need to be loaded first.

TIME IS MONEY

Loading and unloading a ship in this fashion was so inefficient and time-consuming that cargo ships typically spent half of their entire service lives stuck in port. This was the most expensive part of the journey: shipping companies spent more money moving cargo on and off their ships than they did sailing them to distant ports and back. As McLean sat there, waiting for his truck to finally be unloaded and wondering if he'd

The Internet's very first web page (info.cern.ch/hypertext/WWW/TheProject.html), which went live in 1991, is still active.

make it back home in time for Thanksgiving, it occurred to him that the process would be much quicker if his *entire truck*, along with the cargo it contained, could be loaded aboard the ship as one unit. Then when it arrived in Istanbul, the truck could be unloaded and used to drive the cotton bales to their destination.

More than 20 years passed before McLean was able to act on his intuition. He was just a truck driver, after all.

GOING TO SEA

By the 1950s, McLean and his siblings had built their business into the second-largest trucking company in the United States. In 1955 they sold the company and its fleet of 1,700 trucks for $25 million, the equivalent of more than $220 million today.

> McLean believed that if the decks of tanker ships were retrofitted to carry trucks loaded with cargo, the ships would make more money hauling the extra freight, and they would make it in both directions.

Now McLean had the seed money he needed to put his shipping ideas to the test. He'd noticed over the years that when tanker ships carried crude oil from Texas to refineries on the East Coast, they made the return trip to Texas empty, without any paying freight. No cargo was ever carried on deck, either. All of the oil was transported in huge tanks in the ship's hold belowdecks. McLean believed that if the decks of tanker ships were retrofitted to carry trucks loaded with cargo, the ships would make more money hauling the extra freight, and they would make it in both directions. He managed to sell an executive from National City Bank on the idea, and secured a $500 million loan.

ON A ROLL

McLean used $7 million to buy two old oil tankers and retrofitted them with steel platforms on their decks to hold truck trailers. At first he left the wheels on the trailers, but he soon realized that the trailers would be much more stable in rough seas if he removed the wheels and secured the trailers directly to the decks. Removing the wheels eliminated wasted space beneath each trailer, and stowing the trailers so securely made it possible to load more of them onto the ship. McLean managed to cram 58 truck trailers in a single layer onto the deck of each ship (stacking them on top of each other would come later), and on April 26, 1956, the first of them, the SS *Ideal X*, set sail from Port Newark, New Jersey, for Houston, Texas. When it arrived, the containers were quickly removed from the ship by cranes that lowered the containers onto waiting trucks and railroad cars, without any manual labor from longshoremen, in a fraction of the time it would have taken to unload the cargo by hand. The container-shipping era had begun.

Jay Leno owns a car that runs on tequila.

The *Ideal X* didn't sink from the weight of all the trailers on its decks, as skeptics had predicted, and the containers didn't fall over the side, either. But McLean's shipping company, soon to be known as Sea-Land, didn't turn a profit until 1961.

In the early 1960s, McLean talked the New York Port Authority into building the world's first purpose-built wharf for container ships in Elizabeth, New Jersey. A few years later he convinced the port of Rotterdam, in the Netherlands, to begin handling container ships as well, opening the way for the transatlantic container shipping trade. The first Sea-Land ship arrived in Rotterdam in May 1966.

HELP YOURSELF

McLean was careful to patent the designs of his shipping containers, the cranes that lifted them on and off of ships, and other technologies that he developed. But he was shrewd enough to understand that there was more money to be made from increasing the flow of goods by standardizing port facilities all over the world than there was in defending his patents against competitors. So he made them available, royalty-free, to the world. In the process he established a single international standard for containerized shipping.

His international standard.

In 1967 McLean secured a contract with the Pentagon to deliver war matériel from the West Coast of the United States to Southeast Asia during the Vietnam War. The ships made the return trip to the United States empty—at least until McLean convinced the Japanese authorities that container shipping was the wave of the future. He soon began diverting his homeward-bound ships to Japanese ports, where containers packed with cameras, transistor radios, and other goods were waiting. U.S. trade with Japan soared, helping Japanese brands like Sony, Panasonic, and Nikon establish a foothold in the United States.

MOVING ON

By 1968 Sea-Land was the largest container shipping firm in the world, with annual revenues of $227 million and a fleet of 36 ships carrying 27,000 shipping containers to and from ports all over the world. Containerized shipping was so much more efficient than the traditional method of loading and unloading cargo that other companies had little choice but to embrace the system or risk being squeezed out of the market entirely. And as the competition intensified, McLean realized that Sea-Land was going to need access to more capital to keep up.

Perhaps thinking back to his days hauling empty tobacco barrels around North Carolina, he approached the American tobacco giant R. J. Reynolds about buying Sea-Land, and in 1969 he sold the company to RJR for $530 million. His personal stake

Cheetahs don't roar—they meow.

in Sea-Land sold for $160 million, the equivalent of more than $1 billion today. Not bad for a man who got his start driving a used pickup truck, paid for with $120 that he earned pumping gas.

BRAVE NEW WORLD

Containerized shipping lowered the cost of loading and unloading ships by more than 97 percent, down from nearly $6 a ton to just 16¢ a ton. In the process, McLean unleashed economic forces that even he did not fully comprehend. As shipping companies and port facilities all over the world copied his containerized shipping methods to avoid being driven out of business, manual labor jobs on the docks all but disappeared. By 1996, 90 percent of global trade was being moved by container ships. The lost longshoreman jobs were more than offset by the explosion of jobs created by increasing global trade, but many of those jobs were created thousands of miles from American shores.

The Macy's flagship department store at Herald Square in New York City, for example, is in the city's Garment District, where clothing was designed and manufactured for decades. Clothing companies could deliver their merchandise to Macy's on foot. But the steep decline in shipping costs meant that it was now cheaper to buy cotton fabric in India or China, ship it to clothing factories Bangladesh, Thailand, or Turkey, and ship the finished clothes to Macy's in Herald Square, than it was to make the clothing in a Garment District factory across the street. As a consequence, the number of clothing manufacturing jobs in New York has declined steadily for 50 years, even though the clothing companies are still headquartered in the Garment District. They have moved nearly all of their production overseas.

The low cost of containerized shipping is the reason why Americans can buy a 32-inch Sony TV for $290 and a laptop computer for $350, but they can't get a job in a TV factory or a computer factory, even though TVs and personal computers were invented in the United States. Nearly all of the manufacturing plants moved overseas many years ago, and it's hard to imagine them ever coming back.

KARMA?

One of the casualties of the economic disruptions of the 1970s and 1980s turned out to be Malcom McLean himself, though he was more a victim of rising oil prices than declining shipping costs. Nine years after selling Sea-Land, he jumped back into the shipping business by buying the struggling United States Lines, which he hoped to turn into a strong competitor of his former company.

The price of fuel oil was one of the major expenses of shipping goods across oceans, and when the price of crude oil rose from $3 a barrel in 1972 to $34 a barrel by

Drink ice water when you're really thirsty. It will cause your stomach to constrict, forcing water into your small intestine, where it will absorb faster.

1981, the shipping companies were hit hard. McLean assumed the price of oil would remain high into the future, so he bought a dozen giant, energy-efficient container ships called "Econships" that burned less fuel, but were also slower than other ships. McLean made other big bets that assumed the price of oil would climb even higher… but it didn't. The oil crisis of the late 1970s was followed by the oil glut of the 1980s, which caused the price of oil to drop to less than $10 a barrel by 1986. McLean's slow, expensive ships couldn't compete with faster, cheaper ships; United States Lines went bankrupt in the mid-1980s, taking a good chunk of McLean's fortune with it.

SHIPPING OUT

McLean was down but he was never out. He formed another shipping company in 1992 and was still involved in running it when he passed away in 2001 at the age of 87. The revolution he first conceived of while waiting for his truck to be unloaded on the Jersey City docks is still underway. Like it or not, the global economy continues to move production to lower-cost countries, passing tremendous savings on to the consumer but eliminating manufacturing jobs in developed countries in the process. The brave new world Malcom McLean created seems here to stay, at least until someone else comes along and thinks of something even more revolutionary to replace it.

* * *

SUCKER PUNCH

In his younger days, President Rutherford B. Hayes (1822–1893) was no stranger to beer and wine, but that all stopped after he married Lucy Ware Webb in 1852. Mrs. Hayes was active in the temperance movement, which sought to outlaw all forms of liquor. When Hayes became president in 1877, he banned the serving of alcohol at White House functions.

In time, however, a rumor began to spread that certain members of the White House staff, pitying guests who had to endure long dinners and other occasions without a drop to drink, had taken to spiking the oranges in the Roman punch with rum. Anyone who needed a pick-me-up need only pay a visit to "the Life-Saving Station," as the punch bowl came to be known, and make sure that some slices of orange ended up in their cup. But as President Hayes himself later admitted in his diary, he was the one who spiked the oranges—and not with rum: "The joke of the Roman punch oranges was not on us but on the drinking people. My orders were to flavor them rather strongly with the same flavor that is found in Jamaica rum [but no rum]…This took! This was certainly the case after the facts alluded to reached our ears."

A cheetah can accelerate from 0 to 63 mph in three seconds.

TOO MUCH OF A GOOD THING

Enough of just about anything can (and will) kill you. Here's exactly how much of various items you'd have to consume or endure (assuming you're an average-size adult) in order for your body to shut down.

Oranges. The vitamin C that's plentiful in oranges is water-soluble, meaning that if you consume more than your body needs, you pee it out. But it takes the body time and energy to process that extra vitamin C. If you ate about 11,000 oranges, your body couldn't handle all that vitamin C, and you'd die of vitamin C poisoning.

Chocolate. Chocolate is derived from the cacao plant, which contains a bitter alkaloid called theobromine. It's a natural diuretic and stimulant, and too much will completely dehydrate you or make your heart beat too fast until it gives out. It would take about 1,000 milligrams of chocolate per kilogram of body weight for that to happen. For an average adult, that works out to about 85 regular-size Hershey bars.

Sugar. Consuming 10½ cups (or 500 teaspoons) of sugar all at once is too much for your body to handle. Your pancreas wouldn't be able to produce insulin fast enough to process it all, and you'd go into an instant—and probably fatal—diabetic coma.

Bananas. Too much of something good can be a bad thing. Like bananas. They famously pack a lot of potassium, a vital nutrient that your body needs. But if you were to eat around 480 of them, you could die from potassium poisoning.

Cherries. Eat the cherry, spit out the pit…immediately. A cherry pit contains a small amount of cyanide, a notorious toxin. But it's not *that* small. If you bit into just two cherry pits, that would release enough cyanide to end you.

Apples. Apple seeds, like cherry pits, contain cyanide. There's less in apples than there is in cherries, though. You'd have to eat 200 apple seeds, or 20 apple cores full of seeds, to die.

Caffeine. Too much coffee, espresso, or any other caffeinated beverage can lead to an arrhythmia, or a rapidly or irregularly beating heart. About 70 cups of coffee or 180 espresso shots would trigger that.

Salt. Similarly, consuming too much sodium too quickly would send your body's sodium levels to toxic heights. So never eat 45 teaspoons of salt all at once.

Angelina Jolie, Jeff Bridges, and Matt Damon all say they've misplaced their Oscars.

Water. Drinking too much water all at once can throw off your body's sodium levels. They would become too diluted and your organs would shut down. Amount of water it would take: chugging slightly less than two gallons.

Nutmeg. It's used sparingly in cooking because it has a strong taste…but also because more than that can be toxic. How much more? Consuming two or three full teaspoons of the spice would deliver a toxic dose of a naturally occurring psychoactive compound called *myristicin* that could bring on convulsions, severe dehydration, and intense body pain.

Black pepper. Common pepper can be deadly, but it would take around 130 teaspoons to fell an average adult. Black pepper contains capsaicin, the chemical that makes all peppers spicy. Too much can lead to severe swelling of the skin and mucus membranes, as well as vomiting, diarrhea, heart attacks, and death.

Toothpaste. Most contain fluoride, a compound that contributes to good dental health. But there's a good reason you spit out toothpaste and mouthwash that contain fluoride: it's poison. Consume enough fluoride-enhanced toothpaste and your body will react the way it reacts to most poisons: with stomach pain, intestinal blockages, vomiting, diarrhea, and difficulty breathing. Consuming 24 six-ounce tubes of toothpaste might leave you with extremely fresh breath, but it would also likely kill you.

Green potatoes. Exposing potatoes to too much light enables the growth of a toxic substance called *solanine*, which builds up as a thin green layer just underneath the skin. The flesh of the potato can be cooked and eaten even if solanine is present in the skin, but eating the skin could lead to severe stomach cramps and nausea, and if you ate 25 solanine-laden potatoes, you could die. So keep potatoes stored in the dark.

Noise. You don't eat it, but something that's too loud can actually kill you. A noise of more than 200 decibels heard up close produces enough air pressure to create a fatal arterial blockage—or embolism—in the brain. (The loudest sound ever recorded: a NASA Saturn V rocket. It reached 204 decibels.)

*   *   *

VOTING FOR DUMMIES

In 1993 the City of San Francisco voted on a ballot measure over whether or not a city police officer named Bob Geary would be allowed to take his ventriloquist dummy, "Brendan O'Smarty," on his patrol. By a squeaker of a 51 to 49 percent vote, Geary won the right to carry his doll around.

Sorry, but it's the law: In 2009 the Canadian government passed the Apology Act, which states that an apology is not an admission of guilt.

"IT'S A SITUATIONSHIP"

*More social media dating terms to help the newly single
turn their leads into accounts without getting ghosted.*

Sliding into DMs: Moving from public social media posts, which everyone can see, to direct messages, which are private and (hopefully) more intimate.

Stashing: When someone dates you but doesn't introduce you to their friends or family, or post about you on social media.

Tinstagramming: When you see someone on Tinder and you're not a match, so you contact them through their Instagram account instead.

Deep liking: Scrolling back months or even years to click "like" on someone's old posts to impress them.

Leads and accounts: Inspired by sales and marketing terms. "Leads" are people you hope to date, and "accounts" are people you've already scheduled dates with.

Textlationship: A relationship that never moves beyond the texting stage.

Situationship: A relationship that's more than a friendship…but less than a relationship.

DTR conversation: What you have when you've been seeing someone long enough to "define the relationship." Are you officially a couple, or something else?

FBO: If your DTR conversation goes well, you can update your online status and make it "Facebook Official."

Ghosting: Disappearing from someone's life by not responding to their texts and calls.

Slow fade: A gradual form of ghosting.

Ghostbusting: Continuing to text or message someone who's ghosting you.

Haunting/zombie-ing/submarining: When someone you were seeing disappears out of your life, only to suddenly return "from the dead" and pretend that there's nothing out of the ordinary going on.

Breadcrumbing: When someone seems to be pursuing you, but things never move forward. They're just leaving an occasional online breadcrumb to keep you from moving on.

Roaching: Hiding from a new love interest the fact that you're still seeing other people. (If they catch you with one of your cockroaches, they can assume there are others.)

Code 143: When someone you've started dating moves too quickly to the "I love you" stage. (The digits represent the number of letters in each word.)

IRL: When you move past online communicating to dating "in real life."

DFMO: Dance floor makeout (self-explanatory).

Talking: When you're dating someone but not ready to admit it. ("We're just talking.")

Hang up! There is 18 times more bacteria on your smartphone than on a toilet handle.

ODD-TIME RADIO

Television doesn't have a monopoly on bizarre premises. My Mother the Car? The Six Million Dollar Man? Charlie's Angels? Before there was TV, there were old-time radio shows with concepts that were just as weird as anything television had to offer...if not weirder.

It Pays to Be Ignorant (1942–1951)

Game shows on the radio—which set the style and standard for TV game shows—were so entrenched and familiar by 1942 that this game show parody became a huge (and long-running) hit. Spoofing highbrow, academic games of the era, such as *Information Please* and *Doctor I.Q.*, the show's panel of comedians aimed to give the funniest answer possible to the common knowledge questions posed. For example, quizmaster Tom Howard might ask, "Do married people live longer than those that don't marry?" and a panelist would answer, "No, but it seems longer."

Yours Truly, Johnny Dollar (1949–1962)

Private investigator stories have thrilled and delighted audiences over various media: books, movies, television, and radio. When *Yours Truly, Johnny Dollar* premiered, it was about a hard-boiled P.I. named Johnny Dollar (played by Charles Russell). That show ran for almost six years, but in 1954, it went off the air for a few months and then returned as a show about...an insurance investigator. That's a decidedly less exciting premise, but the show's announcer did his best to drum up audience interest, boasting of Johnny Dollar's "action-packed expense account." What's even more odd: the *Yours Truly, Johnny Dollar* reboot ran for another eight years and is considered by old-time radio enthusiasts to be a classic series.

Life with Luigi (1948–1953)

This CBS Radio series will probably never be rebooted as a TV series. Reason: it is "politically incorrect," and that's putting it lightly. This sitcom was about a recently arrived immigrant from Italy named Luigi Basco, and the night school citizenship classes he attended with other people who had just arrived in Chicago from around the world. Every character spoke in the broad, stereotypical accent of their home nation. (Luigi, for example, "talked a-like a-this.") When he wasn't in school, Luigi had to delicately fight off attempts by his citizenship sponsor Pasquale to get Luigi to marry his daughter— whom Luigi was not interested in because she was overweight. Another slap at Italian Americans: Luigi was played by Irish American character actor J. Carrol Naish. (Pasquale was played by Alan Reed, who later became the voice of Fred Flintstone.)

A cluster of bananas is called a hand. (It kind of looks like one.)

The Whisperer (1951)

A lawyer named Philip Gault (played by Carleton G. Young) decides to take down "the Syndicate," an organized crime ring that terrorizes his hometown of Central City. He poses as a gangster and destroys the Syndicate from the inside…even though he can only speak in a whisper due to an old college football injury.

The Gibson Family / Uncle Charlie's Tent Show (1934–1935)

For the first nine months of its life, *The Gibson Family* was a very ambitious soap opera about a musically talented family—parents Bob and Dot Gibson, daughter Sally Gibson, and their butler (named Awful). Each episode included a few original songs written for the show. But it wasn't a hit, so NBC tried to save it by revamping it as *Uncle Charlie's Tent Show*. Under the new format (which only lasted three months), a character named Uncle Charlie befriended the Gibsons in order to take them on a theatrical tour. But then, most of the Gibsons disappeared and the show became a variety series set inside a touring tent.

The Bickersons (1946–1951)

It starred Don Ameche and Frances Langford as a married couple actually named John and Blanche Bickerson. Their unusual name was the entire plot of the show: most of every episode consisted of the couple loudly (and hilariously) arguing—and often about the same things they were arguing about in the previous episode.

Crime Doctor (1940–1947)

The plot: A petty thug criminal named Benjamin Ordway (played by Ray Collins) got knocked on the head and suffered from that old fictional plot device of "amnesia." He later recovered and renounced his criminal ways…and then became a psychiatrist. Using his firsthand and academic knowledge of "the criminal mind," he served on a parole board and helped police solve crimes. Two years into the show's run, producers added in a new element. Instead of the parole board determining the fates of the criminals, Dr. Ordway would consult with a "jury," made up of members of the studio audience.

Various Edgar Bergen shows (1937–1956)

Bergen was one of the most popular and enduring stars of the Golden Age of Radio, one half of two "comedy teams" with Mortimer Snerd and Charlie McCarthy. It should be noted that both of those partners were dummies. Yes—Bergen carved out a successful career as a ventriloquist, voicing and operating puppets without moving his lips…on the radio, where nobody could see whether his lips were moving.

Zookeepers get panda breeding pairs "in the mood" by showing them videos of other pandas mating.

TURN LEFT ON UGLEY

We recently sent a scout on a tour of the UK and Ireland to find the naughtiest street and village names. We were certain he made these up...but they're all real.

East Breast
Greenock, Scotland

Pratt's Bottom
Orpington, England

No Place
Durham, England

Toot Hill Butts
Oxford, England

Effin
Limerick, Ireland

Gravelly Bottom Road
Kent, England

Bonar Bridge
Ardgay, Scotland

Matching Tye
Harlow, England

Kilmacow
Kilkenny, Ireland

Blubberhouses
Otley, England

Crapstone
Devon, England

Horney Common
Uckfield, England

Scratchy Bottom
Dorset, England

Catbrain Lane
Bristol, England

Ballinamallard
Fermanagh, Ireland

Brokenwind
Aberdeenshire, England

Crazies Hill
Reading, England

Bladda Lane
Paisley, Scotland

Great Snoring
Fakenham, England

Butt of Lewis
Western Isles, Scotland

Beer Beach
Seaton, England

Nut Tree Close
Orpington, England

Stepaside
Dublin, Ireland

Fattiehead
Banffshire, Scotland

Snotsdale Wood
Orpington, England

Thong
Kent, England

Sandy Balls
Hampshire, England

Lordsleaze Lane
Chard, England

Piddle River
Dorset, England

Wigginton Bottom
Tring, England

Nasty
Ware, England

Crackpot
North Yorkshire, England

Ugley
Essex, England

Fanny Barks
Durham, England

Bury Old Road
Manchester, England

Blue Ball Lane
Egham, England

Winkle Street
Southampton, England

Doody's Bottoms
Wicklow, Ireland

Hospital
Limerick, Ireland

Emo
County Laois, Ireland

Spittal of Glen Muick
Ballater, Scotland

Upton Snodsbury
Worcestershire, England

Jack in the Box sells an average of 1,000 tacos every minute.

THE FORCE IS NOT VERY STRONG WITH THIS ONE

Lots of people have run afoul of the law at least once in their lives (Uncle John spent a few hours in the Disneyland jail in the 1970s, but that's a story for another time). So it stands to reason that in some cases, the Star Wars movie franchise will tie in with the lawbreaking in some way.

Stormtrooper: George Cross, 40, of Lynn, Massachusetts

(Not Such) A Long Time Ago: In 2015 Cross bought a pricey stormtrooper costume—one that looks just like the ones in the movies. He put it on and went for a walk around his neighborhood. (Unfortunately for him, he also decided to take his toy stormtrooper laser gun with him.) Brickett Elementary School is nearby, and the school day was just about over. According to police, Cross said he went there and "was hanging around in front of the Brickett School because he thought the children would like the costume."

The children might have liked it had they gotten a chance to see it, but school administrators and parents picking up their kids were alarmed at the sight of a man with a mask and a gun hanging around in front of the school, even if he was dressed as a stormtrooper. The principal locked down the school and called the police.

Aftermath: Cross was arrested and charged with disturbing a school and loitering within 1,000 yards in front of the school. He was released on his own recognizance after pleading not guilty to the charges; at last report the case was still pending. "I bought a costume. I was walking through the neighborhood showing friends," he told Boston's Channel 7 News. "Like I'm a some kind of weirdo or something?"

> Cross said he went there and "was hanging around in front of the Brickett School because he thought the children would like the costume."

Jedi Knights: Two armed robbers who pulled their heists while wearing rubber Kylo Ren masks.

(Not Such) A Long Time Ago: In March 2016, the two robbers held up a pharmacy in West Deer, Pennsylvania. In April they struck again, hitting a drug store in New Alexandria, Pennsylvania. They wore different masks this time, but their methods were so similar that the police were convinced that the two robberies were committed by the same crooks. The combined haul from the two crimes was $2,000 in cash and $325,000 worth of prescription drugs.

Pick a random spot in the ocean, and it's probably about 2.3 miles deep.

Here's a tip for people considering a life of crime: If you and your partner plan to wear the same kind of mask, don't buy your masks at the same time. And if you do buy them at the same time, don't do it in a store with security cameras. When police investigators learned that the rubber Kylo Ren masks used in the pharmacy heists were sold at Target, they visited stores in the area and reviewed security camera footage shot in the days leading up to the first robbery.

> If you and your partner plan to wear the same kind of mask, don't buy your masks at the same time.

Sure enough, they found footage of a man buying two Kylo Ren masks. Police recognized him as Stephan E. Corrick, 66, who'd recently been arrested for buying drugs from an undercover officer at a local playground. Officers went to Corrick's home, where he confessed and identified his accomplice as a man named Dana L. Shipley.

Aftermath: When Shipley was picked up, he was carrying a backpack containing pills stolen from both robberies, the gun used in the robberies…and both Kylo Ren masks. The men pled guilty to felony robbery, conspiracy, firearm, and drug charges. In January 2018, Shipley was sentenced to 18 years in federal prison; Corrick was still awaiting sentencing.

Jedi: Arthur C. Roy, 18, of Helena, Montana

(Not Such) A Long Time Ago: In December 2015, Roy was Facebook friends with another young man, not named in police reports. No word on whether Roy is still friends with this guy, but probably not, because on the opening weekend of *Star Wars: The Force Awakens*, the friend went and saw the movie before Roy did, then revealed a key plot twist in a Facebook post. "_____ dies in the new Star Wars. Told you I would do it!" it reads.

Roy was so enraged by his friend's post that he threatened online to go to the friend's high school and shoot him there. He backed up the threat with a photo of himself holding a handgun that he identified as a Colt 1911 semiautomatic. (It was actually a BB gun.) The other young man was frightened enough to report the incident to the school. They locked down the school and notified the police, who went to Roy's house and arrested him.

Aftermath: Roy was charged with felony assault with a deadly weapon and lodged in jail on $10,000 bail. Prosecutors later dropped the charges as part of a deal in which the 18-year-old pled guilty to having sex with three underage girls (in an unrelated case).

Wookiee: An unidentified Ukrainian man dressed as Chewbacca

(Not Such) A Long Time Ago: Politics can get pretty tense in Ukraine, where public officials are notoriously corrupt and where Russian troops back a militant separatist

Game of Thrones films on a soundstage in Northern Ireland built on the former shipyard where the RMS *Titanic* was constructed.

movement in the eastern part of the country. Apparently, one of the ways the locals protest the sad state of affairs is by running for office dressed as Star Wars characters. In 2014, for example, 16 different Darth Vaders ran for seats in the national parliament. (They all lost.)

In October 2015, another Darth Vader ran for mayor of Odessa. On election day, he was driven to the polls by a man dressed as Chewbacca. There they were stopped by the police, and when Chewie was unable to produce a driver's license, he was arrested and taken away in a police car. Several people filmed the arrest with cellphone cameras; by the end of the day video clips of a handcuffed Chewbacca being loaded into the back of a police car were circulating all over the internet. (Darth Vader lost the mayor's race, but Emperor Palpatine won a seat on the Odessa city council with 54 percent of the vote.)

Aftermath: Chewbacca was fined 170 hryvinia (about $6) for the "administrative offense" of not carrying an ID card. That's not a very big fine, but Chewbacca said he was unable to pay because his money is "in an intergalactic bank that has no branches on this planet." Besides, as the Ukrainian police said on their official Instagram account, "Darth Vader…has already claimed this [arrest] was illegal as Chewbacca is his pet and general servant and does not require documents."

> Darth Vader lost the mayor's race, but Emperor Palpatine won a seat on the Odessa city council with 54 percent of the vote.

Jedi Knights: Members of the Star Wars Club of Norwich, England

(Not Such) A Long Time Ago: In May 2013, the club held its annual convention at the University of East Anglia. But the good times turned sour when Jim Poole, treasurer of the rival Norwich Sci-Fi Club, and three other members tried to crash the party. As soon as the members of the Star Wars Club recognized Poole, they told him and his friends to leave. But Poole refused to go, and that's when the argument got so heated that someone called the police to report that a fight had broken out. "There has been a longstanding feud between the two clubs," Poole explained to the *Daily Mail* newspaper. "We got miffed when they decided to rename their event and call it a convention."

Aftermath: The police arrived and broke up the quarrel, but made no arrests. According to a spokesperson, "After lengthy investigation, talking to witnesses and reviewing good CCTV footage, it was confirmed that there was no assault. The two rival groups were spoken to and advised to keep out of each other's way."

At last report, the Star Wars Club and the Sci-Fi Club were "having discussions about having a meeting to settle their differences amicably."

The word "onion" comes from a Latin word that means "large pearl."

Stormtrooper in Training: An unnamed employee of the Huntington Beach, California, Police Department

(Not Such) A Long Time Ago: In April 2016, a familiar name appeared on the police department's online arrest log: Harrison Ford. According to the log, Ford was arrested and booked into jail on suspicion of inflicting corporal injury on a spouse (his wife is actress Calista Flockhart) and possession of a controlled substance. An hour later, the arrest record mysteriously disappeared from the site. Was it a case of a powerful Hollywood actor using his star power to cover up his misdeeds? Nope. Harrison Ford wasn't even in the country when the crimes and arrest supposedly took place.

His name appeared in the arrest log only because the police department was training employees on how to create police records. Trainees do this by creating fake records for crimes that have not occurred. One of the trainees decided to use the actor's name when creating the record. Somehow it was mistaken for a genuine arrest record and posted online. "Of the thousands of recent training entries, one was not properly deleted, and it accidentally appeared on the public arrest log for a brief time," the department said in a statement. "No one by the name of Harrison Ford, celebrity or otherwise, was arrested by the Huntington Beach Police Department yesterday."

Aftermath: A police department spokesperson said that the department "will be more diligent in the future in catching potential errors." However, it has no plans to change its training methods.

* * *

RANDOM ORIGIN: THE DUNCE CAP

Up until the 1950s or so, acting up in class or doing poorly on an assignment might have landed you a spot in the corner of the classroom wearing a "dunce cap," a tall, conical—and embarrassing—hat. It's named for John Duns Scotus, a Franciscan priest from Scotland who, in the late 13th and early 14th centuries, was a doctor of theology in Cologne, Germany. Scotus became an influential Catholic philosopher with many theories that affected religious and secular thought. But he was also obsessed with pointy hats, and believed that they actually trapped knowledge floating around in the sky, having been sent down from God. (It came in through the tip, and was then absorbed by the captive brain below.) Followers of Duns's teachings—Dunsmen—wore *duns*, or "dunce caps," until the mid-16th century, when Duns's theories fell out of favor. Those who remained devoted Dunsmen continued to wear the pointy hats and were seen as behind the times or dumb (especially by Protestants). Dunsmen became known as "duns" or "dunces," and when kids didn't do well in class, they had to pay the price by showing everyone how "dumb" they were—by wearing dunce caps.

Top two lemon producers in the U.S.: 1. California and 2. Arizona.

DANGER: MAGNETARS

On page 187, we told you about dangers that are hiding in plain sight around you.
Here's a look at a danger that may be lurking somewhere in the Milky Way galaxy.

Magnetic Personality. When a massive star (much bigger than our Sun) reaches the end of its life span, it explodes into a supernova and turns into a neutron star. Neutron stars are dense, fast-spinning, highly magnetic masses. Some are so magnetic that they get their own special category. Called magnetars, these stars have magnetic fields up to a quadrillion times (that's 1,000 trillion) more magnetic than the Earth's. But magnetars are rare, and they last only a short while (about 10,000 years) before they decay.

Going to Pieces. Astrophysicist Paul Sutter wrote an article called "Why Magnetars Should Freak You Out" and…he wasn't kidding! If Earth were ever to come too close to a magnetar, the magnetism would destroy all computers, appliances, power lines, and compasses. "The magnetic fields," Sutter explains, "are strong enough to upset not just your bioelectricity—rendering your nerve impulses useless—but your very molecular structure. In a magnetar's field, you just kind of…dissolve."

This is all theoretical, of course. Our sun isn't massive enough to become a magnetar, and the ones that astronomers know about are too rare and too far away to endanger Earth. Or at least until December 27, 2004, when a magnetar called SGR 1806-20 experienced a "starquake"—a crack in its crust. Even though the crust probably moved only a centimeter, a magnetar is so dense (a teaspoon of its material weighs 10 million tons) and its gravity is so strong that the tiny shift caused an immense explosion. Instantly, it released the same amount of energy our sun gives off in hundreds of thousands of years, sending a flood of high-energy gamma rays and X-rays across the galaxy.

Too Close for Comfort. When the gamma rays hit Earth that day, they fried several satellites, even the ones specially designed to view the rays. The explosion even affected Earth's magnetic field and upper atmosphere. But the most unbelievable part: SGR 1806-20 is a whopping 50,000 light-years from Earth, halfway across the Milky Way galaxy. According to astronomer Bryan Gaensler, "Had this happened within ten light-years of us, it would have severely damaged our atmosphere and possibly have triggered a mass extinction." But magnetars are rare, right? Yes, but astronomers have identified about 10 in our galaxy…including one less than 10,000 light-years away. Let's hope that scientists don't discover any magnetars that are even closer to Earth. And if they do, let's hope that it doesn't have any quakes, or we could be toast, in a magnetic sort of way.

Tamerlane, a 14th-century Turco-Mongol conqueror, made towers out of his enemies' severed heads.

BOTTLES & CHOKERS

Making motion pictures is an expensive and chaotic process that forces the directors, actors, and crew to work as quickly as possible. That requires quick, clear communication that has given the industry a language all its own.

Juicer/Sparky: Electrician.

Stinger: Extension cord.

Do a Banana: When an actor walks a curved path toward or away from the camera, so that their body doesn't block the view of something important in the background.

Cashew: A short banana.

Man Maker: Any device used to make a short actor appear taller on camera.

Dead Cat: The fuzzy cover that goes on a microphone to block wind noise.

Dead Wombat: A large dead cat.

Abby/Abby Singer: The second-to-last shot of the day. Named for a production manager famous for warning the crew that they'd soon have to break down the set.

Bottle: The camera lens.

Martini: Last shot of the day (the next shot will be drunk in a bar, after work).

Legs/Sticks: Camera tripod. A small tripod used for low-angle shots is called a "baby legs."

Lewinskys: The kneepads worn by stuntmen.

Magic Hour: The period right before sunrise or right after sunset when filming in natural light produces visually striking results.

Bogie: An unauthorized person who has walked on set and into the shot.

Choker/Screamer: A tight close up of an actor, sometimes from the top of the neck up, and sometimes with just their eyes in the shot.

Picture's Up: Everything on set is ready for the filming of a scene to begin.

Flying In: When a needed person or object is on their way to the set.

Buff and Puff: Sending an actor back to the hair and makeup department for a touch-up.

Upgrade: When an actor taking a 10-1 decides they're going to need a 10-2.

Run and Gun: A film made quickly and on the cheap, with little production equipment other than the camera.

Mark: The place an actor needs to stand for the camera to be in focus; usually marked by an "X" on the floor in gaffer's tape.

Closed Set: When only the most essential cast and crewmembers are allowed on set (such as when a nude scene is being filmed).

Sausage: A raised mark, made with a roll of fabric instead of gaffer's tape, so that the actor can find the mark with their foot, without looking down at the floor while being filmed.

Golden Time: Overtime, when the crew receives double pay.

Last Looks: The call made to the hair/makeup crew to let them know the actors they're working on will be needed on set soon.

Big Eyes: Camera operators focus their cameras by zooming in on the eyes of the actor. "Big eyes" is the instruction that tells the actor to not blink or look away.

10-1: A short bathroom break ("number one"). A 10-2 is a longer bathroom break.

Some turtles breathe through their butts.

TWANTRUMS

What's a Twantrum? A Twitter tantrum. (We made up the word.) As even the least tech-savvy person now knows, Twitter is an alternate universe where anyone—from ordinary people to heads of state—can make public rants. As these stories show, the fallout can range from minor to serious, but fortunately does not include nuclear war (yet).

YOU DRIVE ME NUTS

Tweeter: Scott Bartosiewicz, account manager for New Media Strategies, a social media consulting firm

Date: March 9, 2011

Backstory: While stuck in traffic on his way to work, Bartosiewicz typed out a frustrated tweet. Unfortunately, he wasn't signed into his own account as he'd thought—he was signed into the corporate Chrysler account that he managed, which had more than 7,000 followers.

Twantrum: "I find it ironic that Detroit is known as the #motorcity and yet no one here knows how to f***ing drive."

Aftermath: Surprisingly, the company was less upset about the tweet's profanity than it was about Bartosiewicz badmouthing Detroit, because Chrysler had just launched its "Imported from Detroit" campaign. "We simply couldn't tolerate any messaging—whether or not there was an obscenity—that was denigrating to Detroit," said the company's spokesperson. Not only was Bartosiewicz fired, so was New Media Strategies.

NEWS HOUND

Tweeter: Roger Stone, former adviser to Donald Trump's presidential campaign

Date: October 28, 2017

Backstory: For the past year, Trump allies and associates had attacked CNN and other mainstream media as sources of "fake news." On October 28, CNN reported that special prosecutor Robert Mueller, who was investigating Russia's interference in the 2016 U.S. presidential election, was about to indict someone...but didn't say who. Apparently, the reports so enraged Stone that he went on an hours-long tirade directing personal insults at six CNN anchors and contributors.

Twantrum: Stone called Don Lemon a "buffoon" and a "dumb piece of sh*t," called Ana Navarro a "dumbf**k," and said Bill Kristol was "packing on the pounds" and used the hashtag #porky. To commentator Charles Blow, Stone

A "dead" Egyptian desert snail was placed on display in the British Museum in 1846...and woke up four years later.

tweeted, "YOU Lie…you fast talking arrogant fake news piece of sh*t !" He attacked investigative journalist Carl Bernstein with: "If Carl Bernstein says something the overwhelming odds are that it's false lied about Watergate lying lying now." He labeled CNN anchor Jake Tapper "human excrement" and called for Lemon to be "confronted, humiliated, mocked and punished."

Aftermath: In response, Charles Blow tweeted back a single word: "Stoned." Tapper posted a gif of a famous scene from *Raiders of the Lost Ark* showing a villain's face melting off with the comment "Watching some prominent meltdowns on Twitter. Quite a sight!" And Twitter's response: permanent suspension of Stone's account, citing the company's policy that prohibits users from engaging in "the targeted abuse or harassment of others."

JUST SAYING

Tweeter: Amanda Bynes, star of Nickelodeon's *All That* and *The Amanda Show*

Date: October 10, 2014

Backstory: The 28-year-old actor had been on a downward spiral for a few years. Bynes had been charged with two counts of hit-and-run and, in a confused state, had (accidentally) soaked her dog in gasoline while (intentionally) trying to set her neighbor's yard on fire. She'd also been arrested twice for DUIs and once for throwing a marijuana bong out of the window of her 36th-floor apartment. When her parents arranged to take her to a mental health facility, she lashed out with a series of tweets.

Twantrum: "My dad was verbally and physically abuse to me as a child," she wrote. "I need to tell the truth about my dad. He called me ugly as a child." Then she described her father's alleged lewd behavior and added, "My mom knows that my father's literally and physically incestual towards his own daughter." In conclusion, she said, "Call me what you want but please do not call me crazy or insane because that's a joke."

Aftermath: Her mother immediately released a statement in which she blamed the allegations on "Amanda's mental state…They have no basis in reality." Within hours Bynes recanted her claims, tweeting: "My dad never did any of those things. The microchip in my brain made me say those things but he's the one that ordered them to microchip me."

After-aftermath: Later that day, after getting booted from LaGuardia Airport for berating a ticket agent who refused to reroute a plane for her, Bynes was checked into a psychiatric hospital. In 2017 she announced that she is sober and is planning a comeback to TV.

It's not easy eatin' green: *Geomelophagia* is the compulsive desire to eat raw potatoes.

DROPPING THE BALL

Tweeter: Stevie Johnson, Buffalo Bills wide receiver

Date: November 28, 2010

Backstory: The Bills were the underdog in their game against the Pittsburgh Steelers but, impressively, they were holding their own. They managed to tie the score and send the game into overtime. With Johnson in the end zone, quarterback Ryan Fitzpatrick threw a pass that landed directly in his hands and would have been the game-winning touchdown…but Johnson dropped it. A half hour after losing the game, he sent a rage-tweet directed at God.

Twantrum: "I PRAISE YOU 24/7!!!!!! AND THIS HOW YOU DO ME!!!!! YOU EXPECT ME TO LEARN FROM THIS??? HOW???!!! ILL NEVER FORGET THIS!! EVER!!! THX THO…"

Aftermath: When the message was reported by news outlets, many of his fans were offended. The next day, Johnson backtracked, tweeting, "No, I Did Not Blame God…I Simply Cried Out And Asked Why? Jus Like yal did wen sumthin went wrong n ur life!"

CAN YOU HEAR ME NOW?

Tweeters: Verizon and T-Mobile

Date: February 5, 2017

Backstory: During the 2017 Super Bowl, T-Mobile aired an edgy commercial featuring comedian Kristen Schaal in a spoof of the movie *Fifty Shades of Grey.* The ad suggested that being a customer of T-Mobile's competitor, Verizon, is painful and punishing, like the BDSM relationship in the movie. The commercial ends with: "Wireless pain is fine, if you're into that sort of thing" and then promotes T-Mobile's unlimited data plan.

Twantrum: In response, Verizon tweeted, "Yes @Tmobile, we're into BDSM. Bigger coverage map, Devastating Speed, and Massive capacity." This unleashed a torrent of innuendo-laden tweets from T-Mobile, Verizon, Schaal, T-Mobile CEO John Legere, and their Twitter followers. T-Mobile posted, "Your bill should never make you feel naughty! Dont get #Punished by overages. #TheSafeWordisUnlimited." Verizon responded with: "Unfortunately no one will hear your safe word if you're on @ Tmobile." T-Mobile followed up with: "Think you've had too much? Are you close to being finished…with limits? You won't get punished with #TMobileONE."

Aftermath: While most observers found the Twitter feud funny, some people complained that it was awkward and went way too far, including one Twitter user who summed it up with: "50 Shades of Don't."

It's illegal for Indiana liquor stores to sell milk or cold soda. (Warm soda is OK.)

CABLE: THE FINAL FRONTIER

Tweeter: Sir Patrick Stewart, who played Captain Jean-Luc Picard in *Star Trek: The Next Generation*

Date: September 13, 2012 (Stardate: 90310.28)

Backstory: Celebrity status couldn't help Stewart when he ended up suffering the same slings and arrows as normal people: He spent a day and a half waiting for the Time Warner Cable guy, who never showed up to activate his cable service. So Stewart, who is esteemed for his Shakespearean acting, took to Twitter.

Twantrum: "All I wanted to do was set up a new account with @twcable_nyc but 36hrs later I've lost the will to live," he wrote in a theatric tone. Eventually, the message caught the attention of Time Warner, which asked through Twitter how they could help. Dejected, Stewart tweeted, "If that question had been asked at any time in the last 36hrs it would have been of value. But now…" leaving readers to picture him dramatically stabbing a blade through his heart.

Aftermath: To counter the potential bad publicity, Time Warner tweeted this statement: "Our Care and Social Media teams are fully engaged to make sure he's well tended to. On behalf of the many Trekkers and Sir Patrick Stewart fans across our company, I can assure you, we will make it so."

HUNG OUT TO DRY

Tweeter: Jon-Barrett Ingels, a waiter in Los Angeles

Date: July 17, 2009

Backstory: At the Barney Greengrass restaurant in Beverly Hills, Ingels got his fair share of famous customers. One day, he waited on Jane Adams, best known for her roles on the TV shows *Frasier* and *Hung*. When he brought the check, she got really embarrassed and said she'd forgotten her wallet in the car. After promising to be right back, she never returned. Surprised, Ingels wrote it off as a loss when the restaurant closed that night. But that wasn't the end. Eventually, Adams's agent called the restaurant and although he paid the bill on her behalf, he did not leave a tip.

Twantrum: "Jane Adams, star of HBO series 'Hung,' skipped out on a $13.44 check. Her agent called and payed the following day. NO TIP!!!" Six weeks later, Ingels posted an update. Adams had come in person and angrily gave him a tip. "A month later," he wrote, "she brought in $3 tip. Made big deal about $3. Bitterly said she read about it on Twitter."

Aftermath: Though Ingels had only 22 followers on Twitter when he made the first post, the story was eventually picked up by news sites. Adams and others complained about the unprofessional tweet, and Ingels was fired.

More photos are taken every two minutes than were taken in the whole of the 1800s.

Tweeter: Charlie Sheen

Date: June 21, 2015

Backstory: Charlie "Tiger Blood" Sheen is famous for his public meltdowns. But his worst was probably on Father's Day, nine years after his divorce from actress Denise Richards. Sheen was livid that Richards and their two daughters had declined his invitation to join him at a resort in Mexico. So he spent the holiday going ballistic on Twitter.

Tweet: A lot of it is too profane to include, but here are some highlights (or lowlights): "Open letter to the media: Denise Richards is a shake down piece of sh*t doosh phace & worse mom alive! A despicable charlatan." Sheen discussed co-parenting: "I have paid that Klay-Vinnik leaky diaper over 30 Mil and she calls me a DbD [dead beat dad]! see u in court you evil terrorist sack of landfill rash." (Sidenote: If you figure out what Klay-Vinnik means, please let us know.) He went on to criticize her dad, her boyfriend, and her acting ("couldn't act hot in a fire or wet in a pool.")

Aftermath: That night, Richards posted a response that was roundly praised as "classy." She tweeted: "Happy Dad's Day! @charliesheen have a great trip in Mexico! Kids were disappointed u weren't here for it- Hey we'll celebrate when u r back!" Sheen eventually deleted the tweets.

Bonus! During the tweetstorm, Sheen managed to say a few nice things about his third ex-wife, Brooke Mueller. "Brooke M is a sexy rok star whom I adore D Richards a heretic washed up piglet shame pile Happy Father's Day!!!"

*   *   *

THANKS, BUT WE'LL PASS

Anybody who was anybody in the music business during the golden days of *American Bandstand* had to make a guest appearance with Dick Clark. But there were three recording stars who hit #1 on the Billboard Hot 100 charts and were never on the show.

- Elvis Presley, whose manager, Colonel Tom Parker, wouldn't let him appear.
- Ricky Nelson, who didn't need exposure on Clark's show—he was already featured on his family's weekly TV series, *The Adventures of Ozzie and Harriet.*
- The third big act that didn't appear on *American Bandstand* probably would have liked to…but they couldn't. Reason: the "group" was actually one person— Ross Bagdasarian singing as Alvin and the Chipmunks on one of 1958's biggest hits, "The Chipmunk Song (Christmas Don't Be Late)."

Orange and green insects are those colors for a reason—
they "warn" predators that they may be poisonous (or at least taste awful).

A GIRL WITH HEART

*Here's the story of a girl who found a way to improve the lives
of people suffering with "invisible" disabilities using
sign language—restroom sign language.*

ON THE INSIDE

Grace Warnock is a 12-year-old girl living in Prestonpans, Scotland. She is one of more than 115,000 people in the UK living with Crohn's disease, a disorder in which the body's immune system attacks the digestive tract. Because of it, there are times when Grace urgently needs to use the bathroom. If the only one available is a disabled access restroom, she uses it. But when she does, she sometimes gets dirty looks from other people, because even though she has a disability, she doesn't *look* like someone who has a disability.

"People were horrible. It wasn't just me. Just after my diagnosis, I spoke to other people and we had all experienced the same thing," she told Glasgow's Evening Times in February 2018. "I thought a better restroom sign might help, so I sketched an idea for one on a napkin."

PAIR OF HEARTS

The international symbol for a restroom that's accessible to disabled people is a figure in a wheelchair. Grace added two more figures: a man and a woman, both with hearts on their chests to represent invisible disabilities. "I want people to have a heart and think before they say something rude, because not all disabilities are easy to see," she says.

When Grace wrote a letter to the Scottish Parliament telling them about her sign and asking for their help in spreading the word, they adopted it for their disabled restrooms. Since then the signs have popped up on restroom doors at schools, airports, sports stadiums, and other places all around Scotland. They've begun appearing around the rest of the United Kingdom, too. (Prince William and his brother Harry were so impressed, they invited Grace to visit them in London.) Given the amount of interest her idea has received from people in the United States, Australia, and elsewhere in the world, it's probably just a matter of time before the signs begin appearing on disabled restrooms near you.

> She gets dirty looks from other people, because she doesn't *look* like someone who has a disability.

"So many people have got in touch to congratulate Grace on her idea, telling her it is so important," Grace's mother, Judith Warnock, told the *Evening Times*. "I don't think it has quite sunk in for Grace, just how big an impact her idea has had."

Only 8% percent of Dunkin Donuts sales come from doughnuts.

NAME THAT SOUP, TOO

On page 75 we gave you a huge bowlful of soup name origins. (BURRRRRRP.) Who's up for seconds?

RAMEN

You're probably familiar with ramen—the Japanese noodle soup consisting of thin, yellow wheat noodles in a broth made from fish, pork, beef, vegetables, or chicken (or some combination of those ingredients), typically flavored with soy sauce or miso, and topped with a variety of ingredients, including scallions, sprouts, and meat. Many sources say this distinctly Japanese soup is actually Chinese: it was brought to Japan by Chinese immigrants in the late 19th or early 20th century. By the 1910s, the soup, originally known as *shina soba,* meaning "Chinese noodles," was hugely popular in Japan, and after World War II it became a global phenomenon. The Japanese name for the soup, spelled "ramen" in English, is derived from the Chinese *lamian* (or *la mian),* meaning "pulled noodles," referring to the ancient Chinese stretching and pulling method of making noodles. The first instant ramen noodle packages hit stores in Japan in 1958, the year instant noodles were invented by Japanese inventor Momofuku Ando. (They were printed in Japanese, but included the English-esque words "Chikin Ramen.") Today annual sales exceed 100 billion packages worldwide.

CHOWDER

There are lots of different kinds of chowders—clam chowder, oyster chowder, fish chowder, potato chowder, corn chowder, and more—almost all of them characterized by their cream- or milk-based textures. The dish is believed to have originated as fish chowder along the coast of France, and to have been brought to northeastern North America by French explorers and trappers in the 1700s. (Which explains how it became a traditional favorite in New England and Canada's Maritime provinces.) The most likely sources of our English word "chowder": the French word *chaudron,* for "cauldron," or *chaudière,* for "stew or cooking pot," the names of the pots the chowder was cooked in. (Non-creamy chowders include Manhattan clam chowder, Rhode Island clam chowder, and Bermuda fish chowder, which are called "red chowders" because they're tomato-based rather than milk-based.)

GAZPACHO

A cold, creamy soup of very old Andalusian (referring to a region in the south of Spain) origin that is still immensely popular in Spain and Portugal today, especially during hot

There's an estimated 3 million wrecked ships at the bottom of the world's oceans.

Iberian summers. It consists of stale bread, raw chopped or blended vegetables (typically tomato, cucumber, green pepper, onion, and garlic), and usually olive oil and sherry vinegar. According to food historians, gazpacho's culinary influences were introduced over many centuries, first during the Roman and Muslim eras in the region, and later by the many new foods imported into Europe during the Age of Exploration, especially tomatoes, which became one of gazpacho's chief ingredients. And the origin of the name "gazpacho"? Most sources say it came from the Mozarabic language, a long-defunct, Arabic-influenced, Latin-based language spoken by Christians in Andalusia during the era of Muslim rule (fifth to eighth centuries), and their word *caspa*, meaning "fragments," referring to the pieces of stale bread used to make this dish.

EXTRAS

- Rumford's soup (*Rumfordsche Suppe* in German) was developed in the German state of Bavaria around the year 1800, as an effort to develop an inexpensive and nutritious meal for the poor. Made from barley, dried peas, potatoes, and beer, it was named after its inventor, Count Rumford, a.k.a. Benjamin Thompson, an American scientist and inventor from Massachusetts. Thompson fought for the British during the American Revolutionary War, and moved to England after the British lost the war. In 1785 he moved to Bavaria, where he was made a count—and invented the soup that still carries his name.

- *Mulligatawny* is a spicy Anglo-Indian curry soup that first became popular in England during the 1700s. The name comes from the Indian Tamil language, and means "pepper-water" or "chili-water."

- According to legend, the soup known as bouillabaisse was created by fishermen in the French Mediterranean port of Marseille. Not wanting to use the best, more valuable fish for their own meals, they used the cheaper varieties, including conger eels, along with local vegetables and herbs, to create this singular and now world-renowned fish stew. The name "bouillabaisse" was derived from the French Provençal name for the soup, *bolhabaissa*, taken from the words *bolhir*, "to boil," and *abaissar*, "to simmer."

- Wedding soup is a meat and green vegetable soup found in many Italian restaurants in the United States. Why "wedding soup"? Legend has it that it was traditionally served at weddings in Italy…but that's wrong. The term really comes from a misunderstanding about the name of an Italian soup called *minestra maritata*, meaning "married soup," which was a reference to the "marriage" of the soup's ingredients.

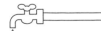

Technical name for a glob of toothpaste sitting on a toothbrush: a *nurdle*.

A STORE IS BORN, PART 2

On page 129 we told you the story of how competition with 7-Eleven helped turn a chain of Los Angeles mini-marts into the Trader Joe's franchise. But how did that franchise spread nationwide? That part of the story involves two reclusive brothers who built their own grocery chain in Germany…then split it in half following a fight over cigarettes.

OUT OF THE ASHES

When Joe Coulombe, the founder of the Trader Joe's grocery chain, decided to sell his company in the late 1970s, the person who snapped it up was a German businessman named Theo Albrecht. He and his brother Karl had built up the Aldi (short for Albrecht Discount) grocery store chain in Germany from very modest beginnings. Their father, Karl Sr., had been a coal miner, but in the early 1930s he developed emphysema and could no longer work. So their mother, Anna, opened a small food store near Essen and supported the family that way. Theo, two years younger than Karl, helped in the store and Karl got a job in a delicatessen.

After Hitler seized power in the 1930s, Karl and Theo were drafted into the military as soon as they came of age. Both men fought for Germany in World War II, and both ended up in prisoner-of-war camps when the war turned against the Nazis. After the war, they returned home to Essen. Because Essen was in Germany's industrial Ruhr area and within close range of England, it had been bombed more than 200 times during the war. Very little of the city was left standing when the boys returned home, but somehow their mother's shop had survived.

> That's when Albrecht developed an interest in a small but thriving Los Angeles grocery chain called Trader Joe's.

WHAT'S IN STORE

Theo and Karl went back to work at the store, and soon they were running it themselves. Soon they added a second store, then a third, and then a fourth.

It didn't take a genius to see what the defeated, war-ravaged, impoverished German consumers wanted from a grocery store: just the basics—bread, butter, milk, canned goods—and as cheaply as possible. That's what the Albrecht brothers gave them. Their stores were absolutely bare-boned. The few items that the store carried sat on the floor in the shipping crates they had arrived in—why waste money on shelves? Customers bagged their own groceries, using bags they brought from home; if they didn't have one they had to buy one. Shopping in an Aldi store wasn't particularly pleasant, but the prices were rock-bottom and that's what mattered.

What kind of wood do termites like best? Vibrating wood.

By 1955 the Aldi chain had grown to more than 100 stores in West Germany, and by 1960 there were more than 300. Though times were improving—the strong economic growth of the 1950s has been called West Germany's "economic miracle"— the Albrechts never changed their formula, and West German shoppers never got tired of going to Aldi. The chain kept growing.

WHERE THERE'S SMOKE...

In the early 1960s, Karl and Theo had a falling-out over whether or not Aldi stores should carry cigarettes. Not because of health concerns, but because Karl thought they'd be an attractive target for shoplifters. So the brothers split their business in two: Theo took the stores in the north (Aldi Nord), and Karl took the stores in the south (Aldi Sud). They also split the western world into territories: in the future, Theo would expand Aldi Nord into Europe; Karl would open Aldi Sud stores in the United Kingdom, Australia, and North America.

That formula worked well for the next decade or so, but by the mid-1970s Theo was eager to break into the American market. Because of his agreement with his brother, he couldn't...at least not with Aldi stores. But their deal didn't say anything about investing in other store chains...and that's when Theo developed an interest in a small but thriving Los Angeles grocery chain called Trader Joe's.

Theo was impressed with the way Trader Joe's did business: like Aldi, it placed great emphasis on selling goods at rock-bottom prices. (Unlike Aldi, the stores had character, and shopping in them was a pleasant experience. But Theo Albrecht was willing to overlook that.) In 1977 he made an offer to the company's founder, Joe Coulombe...who turned him down. But two years later, Coulombe decided to sell. For how much? The price he and Albrecht agreed upon has never been made public. When asked, Coulombe says simply he "can't remember."

TOP SECRET

If you're a fan of Trader Joe's and you're wondering why you've never heard of Theo Albrecht, it's because like his brother Karl, he was about as secretive and reclusive a businessman as has ever lived. This was partly due to his personality, but it was also out of necessity. In the 1970s, terrorist groups like the Red Army Faction were targeting German businessmen for kidnapping and assassinations, so people like the Albrechts had little choice but to keep a low profile.

In 1971 Theo himself was kidnapped while driving to work—not by terrorists, but by a lawyer with gambling debts who was aided by a burglar accomplice. When he was taken, the kidnappers demanded to see his driver's license to be sure it was really Theo Albrecht. They didn't know what he looked like, since photographs of him were

Coca-Cola sold about nine Cokes a day in 1886; today's daily sales are around 1.9 billion.

virtually nonexistent, and they could not believe that someone wearing such a cheap suit could really be one of Germany's wealthiest businessmen.

The kidnappers held Theo for 17 days, then released him after a ransom was paid. (True to his cost-cutting ways, Theo bargained the ransom down to about $2 million, then deducted the amount from his taxes as a business expense.) After he was released, he told a reporter that he was "exhausted" from his ordeal, and a photographer managed to snap a photograph. Though he lived another 39 years and built a fortune estimated at more than $25 billion, he never made another public statement, and no one ever took another picture of him, at least not one that was made public. When Theo passed away in 2010, he left this world just as privately as he had lived in it: Aldi did not announce his death until after the funeral was over and he was safely buried in his grave.

> Though he lived another 39 years and built a fortune estimated at more than $25 billion, he never made another public statement, and no one ever took another picture of him.

NO COMMENT

Today Trader Joe's is owned by Theo Albrecht's heirs through a family trust. The company has continued his tradition of secrecy: At the corporate headquarters in Monrovia, east of Los Angeles, there are no signs on the building identifying it as such. Trader Joe's does not release financial information to the public, nor does it comment on news articles about the business. Ever. They do not acknowledge that Albrecht bought the company in 1979 (that information comes from Joe Coulombe), or that his heirs have inherited the business. They don't even identify Coulombe, the founder of the company, by name on the Trader Joe's website. They refer to him simply as "Trader Joe."

IF IT AIN'T BROKE

When Theo Albrecht bought the company, it was debt-free and making huge profits. He opted to leave it alone, and paid Coulombe to stay on and run the company for another decade. Coulombe retired in 1988, just as the chain was expanding outside Southern California and opening a Trader Joe's in San Rafael, north of San Francisco.

In the years that followed, the company's growth rate soared as it opened stores in Arizona and up and down the West Coast, then the East Coast, then the states in between. By the end of 2017, there were 474 stores in 43 states and Washington, DC. It's estimated that Trader Joe's now sells more than $13 billion worth of groceries a year, but—of course—the number can't be confirmed because the company isn't talking. If you're curious to visit a Trader Joe's but live in one of the seven states that hasn't gotten a store yet, don't worry: it probably won't be long before one opens near you.

Marilyn Monroe's first taste of fame: In 1948 she was named the Artichoke Queen of Castroville, California.

BUNKERISMS

A huge part of All in the Family's *success was the "wisdom" that Archie Bunker dispensed from his armchair at 704 Hauser Street, Queens, New York. His twisted English and skewed view introduced a new phrase into the lexicon: "Archie Bunkerisms."*

On Politics and History

"Between here and Florida, ya got your original 48 states."

"We have the highest standard of living! The grossest national product!"

"That's how ya got your Chinatown, your Harlems, your Little Italy...all them grettos."

"Something's rotten in the state of Denver."

"That's what Columbus said to the Indians just before he gypped 'em out of Manhattan."

"In the words of Harry S. Truman: 'If it's too hot in the kitchen, stay away from the cook.'"

"As our president said in his renegurial address."

"Nixon's got that big house to maintain in San Clemency."

"It's a well-known hysterical fact: they gave 'em an inch of Czechoslovakia and they took Poland."

"Won by...your distinguished incrumbent."

"You wanna talk that Russian talk, take yourself back over to the USSO."

On Marriage

"I'm a man. Men have got another thing... they got whaddya call, a carnival instinct."

"Hell hath no fury like a woman's corns."

"A woman should cleave into her husband. Right here in this house is where Edith's cleavage belongs."

"Do you, Edith, take Archie Bunker to be your lawfully bedded husband?"

"Our marriage vows: till death do us part, for better for worse, in secrets and in health."

"If everything is good in the henhouse youse don't have to go out for eggs."

"Tell her I ain't crawlin' home to her with my tail between her legs."

"Birth patrol pills."

"She's loaded with, whaddya call, women's intermission."

"The sexual act was never constipated."

"The titular head—that's the mother, ain't it?"

"We're like two sheeps that pass in the night."

"All kids are trouble, Edith. And I don't wanna spend my reclining years trying to raise another one."

"It's too late Edith, my bus has sailed."

On God

"It ain't supposed to make sense—it's faith. Faith is something that you believe that nobody in his right mind would believe."

"The whole world is turning into a regular Sodom and Glocca Morra."

We should all be so lucky: Sloths poop once a week, and when they do, they lose about a third of their body weight.

"He made us all one true religion, Edith, which he named after his son, Christian—Christ, for short."

"Honor thy parents. That's one of the Lord's top ten commandments. That's right around covetin' your neighbor's cattles and wives and there."

On the Law

"Your honor, may I encroach the bench?"

"I just want to take the opportunity to express my whaddya call, gratitude and depreciation."

"Certainly I'm innocent, Edith…but of what?"

"Ifso fatso."

"Here's my last will and tentacle."

"Position is nine-tenths of the law."

"And that's the crutch of the situation."

"The dent in his car is hardly cold and he's coming over here to claim his pound of fish."

"It's a proven fact that capital punishment is a well-known detergent to crime."

Fightin' Words

"What'd ya think, you were gonna pull the wolf over my eyes?"

"I ain't in no mood to play 120 questions."

"I got bigger fish to fly."

"Up there in his ivory shower."

"Wild hornets couldn't drag me there."

"I'm gonna keep a beagle-eye on you the whole weekend."

"Maybe my mind chewed off more than the mind should bite."

"Wouldn't let 'em get in a word wedgewise."

On Health

"My doctor tells me I got a communications disease."

"They got her in the expensive care unit."

"Probably a torn filament right there in the kneecap."

"They said he had neurosis of the liver."

"Don't be hollerin' at him, will ya, you'll give him a mental sterosis."

"What ya eat ain't got nuttin' to do with how old ya are. That all depends on your ancestors. It's what they call a matter of heresy."

Advice

"I just don't want you to do nothin' on the sperm of the moment."

"It's a pigment of your imagination."

"It ain't exactly the Pope diamond."

"You don't hear me gettin' historical."

"There's an old saying: 'Ya don't keep runnin' after you catch the bus.'"

On Bigotry

"Welcome to our home. And as youse people say 'shaboom.'" (shalom).

"He was wearing a Yamaha."

"Fags…that's what ya call an ungendered species."

"For too long they've been gettin' the short end of the totem pole."

"Well, if that ain't the black calling the kettle pot!"

"Welfare incipients."

"These people know a lot about that voodoody-oh-doo-doo."

There's three times more water in the Earth's mantle than in all the oceans combined.

WHATEVER HAPPENED TO AL SMITH?

The U.S. presidency is one of the world's biggest contests. We know what happens to the winners—they become president and part of history. But what about the losers? Here's what happened to some of America's major party presidential candidates after they lost their run for the highest office in the land.

BOB DOLE

Election: Gerald Ford selected Dole, the senior U.S. senator from Kansas, as his vice-presidential running mate in the 1976 election campaign. When they lost, Dole returned to the Senate, but 20 years later he secured the Republican presidential nomination for himself. He lost again in 1996, thoroughly defeated by Bill Clinton by a margin of nine points. Dole joined Richard Nixon as the only candidates to be on both halves of a presidential ticket and lose both times. Unlike Nixon, however, Dole would never go on to win the presidency. After the election, Dole didn't have a job to return to—in order to devote the time necessary to running for president, he stepped down from his position as a U.S. senator, a job he'd held since 1969. After the election, the 73-year-old Dole retired from politics.

After: Dole had a dry, curmudgeonly, self-deprecating sense of humor that he displayed on the campaign trail and in interviews. Once decorum was no longer an issue, he really let it loose. He became a major media personality and constant TV presence. The former Senate majority leader appeared in an ad for Dunkin' Donuts, an ad for Pepsi (with pop star Britney Spears), and even in one for the new "miracle drug" Viagra, bringing the phrase "erectile dysfunction" into the English lexicon. Dole also made cameo appearances on TV sitcoms and on *Saturday Night Live,* and after Clinton left office in 2001, the two teamed up for a weekly political debate segment on *60 Minutes.* Away from TV, Dole became a Washington, DC, lobbyist, working on behalf of foreign government interests, anesthesiologists, and the chocolate industry.

AL SMITH

Election: With the economy flying high under President Calvin Coolidge, his Republican successor, Commerce Secretary Herbert Hoover easily ascended to the White House in a landslide in the election of 1928. Hoover defeated New York governor Al Smith by a vote of 444 to 87 in the Electoral College. Smith's religion may have had something to do with his unpopularity—he was the first Roman Catholic

Silly Putty was originally marketed to adults.

presidential candidate, and anti-Catholic sentiment was high in the United States, brought on by massive immigration from Europe in the late 19th and early 20th century.

After: Hoover proved extremely unpopular—the stock market crash of 1929 and the beginnings of the subsequent Great Depression happened on his watch, giving the Democrats a virtual lock of winning back the White House in 1932. Smith threw his hat in the ring again, but was easily defeated in the primaries by another former New York governor: Franklin D. Roosevelt. But probably the most interesting thing Smith did after politics: He was named president of Empire State Inc., the company that built and operated the Empire State Building, the tallest building in the world at the time. Smith was also among the first figures in the U.S. to warn of the increasingly powerful Nazi Party in Germany. In 1933 he publicly advocated for an international boycott on German-manufactured products and delivered speeches on the radio and at political rallies trying to get Americans and political leaders to pay attention to what was going on in Europe before World War II could break out. When war did break out, Smith tried to sway public opinion to American entry, a position also held by his former opponent, President Roosevelt.

WILLIAM JENNINGS BRYAN

Election: Bryan is the only politician in American history to be a major party's nominee in three different elections…and lose every time. In 1896 the Democrat ran on a platform of putting the United States on a silver standard (as opposed to gold) to cure the nation's economic ills; he lost to Republican William McKinley. (It was also the first U.S. presidential election in which both major candidates had the same first name.) The 1900 election was a rematch between Jennings and McKinley, and McKinley won again. After the popular President Theodore Roosevelt declined to run for reelection in 1908, William Howard Taft ran at the top of the Republican ticket, promising to uphold Roosevelt's policies, and he easily beat the Democratic nominee…William Jennings Bryan (the only other U.S. presidential election in which both major candidates had the same first name).

After: When Democrats took back the White House in 1912 with the election of Woodrow Wilson, Bryan's long service to the party was recognized with a plum appointment: Secretary of State. In 1915 he resigned the position because he disagreed with President Wilson, who insisted on strong sanctions against Germany after its military torpedoed the English ocean liner *Lusitania*. Bryan also dabbled in the law— such as when he argued in opposition to Darwinism being taught in public schools in the famous 1925 Scopes trial in Tennessee. The teacher on trial, John Scopes, was ultimately found guilty of the crime of teaching evolution. Just five days after the verdict, Bryan died in his sleep.

Hi Mom!

BEYOND SPITE HOUSES

On page 44 we told you about spite houses—homes that were built to intentionally annoy a neighbor. But it turns out that some folks have applied the same sentiment—revenge—to other kinds of buildings.

Building: The Sam Kee Building, 8 W. Pender St., Vancouver, British Columbia

Background: Sam Kee was a prosperous Chinese merchant who owned a parcel of land in Vancouver's Chinatown in 1912. That year, the city government decided to widen Pender Street, and to do it they appropriated a 24-foot-wide strip off Kee's lot. Only a five-foot-wide strip remained, plus a few more feet that became a sidewalk. The city and Kee's neighbors—who hoped to buy the remaining strip from him and incorporate it into their own parcel—believed there was too little left for Kee to build on.

Revenge! Kee didn't see it that way. He refused to sell what little remained of his parcel. Instead, he hired an architect to design a commercial building that was just 4 feet, 11 inches from storefront to rear on the ground floor. The basement was wider: it extended beneath the sidewalk, and the second floor extended 25 inches out over the sidewalk. *Guinness World Records* considers it the shallowest commercial building in the world…and it's still in use today.

Building: The Richardson Spite House, Lexington Ave and 82nd St., New York City

Background: In the early 1880s, a man named Joseph Richardson owned a strip of land on Lexington that was just over a hundred feet long but only five feet wide. An adjoining plot was much larger, and its owners, Hyman Sarner and Patrick McQuade, wanted to buy Richardson's parcel so that they could join it with his and build an apartment building on the enlarged parcel. They offered Richardson $1,000 for his strip, but Richardson wanted $5,000. Sarner and McQuade balked at paying that much; instead, they went ahead and built their apartment building on their lot, figuring that Richardson's five-foot-deep lot could never be built on.

Revenge! How wrong they were! Richardson built a four-story apartment building on his little strip of land, completely blocking the light and the views in Sarner and McQuade's building in the process. Richardson lived in one of the skinny apartments for the next 32 years until his death in 1897. If you were hoping to see the building the next time you're in New York, you're more than a century too late: Richardson's heirs sold the building in 1902 and it was torn down in 1915.

Building: The Edificio Kavanagh, Buenos Aires, Argentina

Background: The Kavanagh building was built in the 1930s by Corina Kavanagh, a

Odds that a glass of water you drink contains at least
one molecule that passed through a dinosaur: 99.9%.

wealthy Argentine woman of Irish descent. She is said to have built it to get back at the aristocratic Anchorena family after she fell in love with a member of the family but was blocked from marrying him because she came from "new money."

Revenge! The Anchorenas lived in a mansion overlooking the Plaza San Martin in Buenos Aires. From the mansion, they had a view of the Basilica of the Holy Sacrament, which the family built in 1916 and donated to the Catholic Church. When Kavanagh learned that a parcel of land between the mansion and the basilica was for sale, she snapped it up and commissioned a 31-story Art Deco skyscraper to be built on the spot. She instructed the architects to make sure that the building blocked the view of the basilica from the Anchorena mansion.

After the Kavanagh building was completed in 1936, Corina moved into an apartment that occupied the entire 14th floor and lived there for many years. The Anchorenas moved out, selling their mansion to the Argentine government in 1936. Today it serves as the ceremonial headquarters of the Ministry of Foreign Relations. The Edificio Kavanagh still stands, and it still blocks the mansion's view of the basilica.

Building: A house across from the Westboro Baptist Church in Topeka, Kansas

Background: The Westboro Baptist Church is infamous for its inflammatory speeches and for picketing churches and military funerals with signs containing slogans like "Thank God for 9/11," "Thank God for Dead Soldiers," and "God Hates Fags." In 2012 a nine-year-old Topeka boy named Josef Miles staged his own counterprotest near some Westboro demonstrators with a handmade sign that read "God Hates No One."

When Aaron Jackson, the co-founder of a nonprofit charity called Planting Peace, read about Josef's counterprotest, he was impressed by the boy's courage, and he was curious to get a look at the Westboro church. So he checked out the church's neighborhood on Google Street View. "I was 'walking' down the street and saw a 'for sale' sign," Jackson told the *Washington Post* in 2013, and thought "how great it would be to paint it in the colors of the gay pride flag."

Revenge! That house was no longer for sale, but the house directly across the street from the church was. So Jackson bought it for $81,000. When local painters balked at doing the job, he found a contractor—and military veteran—named Mike McKessor who agreed to paint the house in rainbow colors. "I don't like them messing with veterans," he said. Then in 2016, when the house next door to the rainbow house came up for sale, a donor named Martin Dunn stepped forward and provided the funds for Planting Peace to buy the house. Volunteers painted it the pink, white and blue colors of the transgender flag, in the process creating a "spite neighborhood" across from the Westboro Baptist Church. Who knows? As more houses in the neighborhood come up for sale, the neighborhood may grow larger.

Before buffalo wings were invented in 1964, chicken wings were used almost entirely for making soup stock.

FUN GUN FACTS

The only way to stop a bad page of gun facts is a good page of gun facts.

◈ Oldest gunmaker in the world: Beretta. They started manufacturing guns in Brescia, Italy, back in 1526.

◈ Russian cosmonauts were issued triple-barreled shotguns. In case of alien attack? Nope—if, on the trip back to Earth, they crash-landed in Siberia, they'd be able to defend themselves against bears.

◈ In 1881 Charles J. Guiteau shot President James Garfield with an ivory-handled revolver. He claimed he specifically selected that one over a wooden-handled gun because he thought it would look better in a museum.

◈ The 2005 Nicolas Cage war movie *Lord of War* features the most guns ever shown on screen: a stockpile of more than 3,000 AK-47s. Filmmakers planned to use prop guns, but it was cheaper to buy real ones.

◈ The popular Daisy BB gun of the 1940s and 1950s started as a promotional item. Daisy sold outdoor products and gave away the guns with purchase, but the guns proved more popular than any of their actual products.

◈ Silencers are technically called suppressors—they reduce the sound of a gunshot from about 150 decibels… to about 120 decibels.

◈ Weird gun law: The city of Kennesaw, Georgia, requires all households to have a gun.

◈ The reason behind that famous photo of Richard Nixon and Elvis Presley: Presley wanted Nixon to make him an official "narcotics officer," so he could legally travel with as many guns as he wanted.

◈ State with the lowest gun ownership rate: Hawaii (about 7 percent).

◈ Guns (with concealed-carry permits) are usually allowed at the political party conventions…but squirt guns are banned.

◈ TSA workers at American airports spot an average of six guns in carry-on baggage every day.

◈ Revolver inventor Samuel Colt died in 1862, just at the beginning of the Civil War, in which the United States would buy and use more than 300,000 of his guns.

◈ Real name of a bazooka: the M1 rocket launcher. Soldiers nicknamed it "bazooka" after a homemade musical instrument played (and invented) by a popular radio comedian named Bob Burns.

◈ About one in five American women claim to be gun owners.

Only two actors to receive Oscar nominations in every decade from the 1960s through the 2000s: Jack Nicholson and Michael Caine.

GOOD NEWS

Beer guzzlers, LEGO builders, nervous drivers, architects, and those who are seeking ways to ensure a cleaner, healthier planet should cheer when they see what's available right now or in the very near future!

BEER BOTTLE SAND

One of New Zealand's largest beer companies, DB Breweries, has devised a way to help that nation save its sandy beaches, which are being scooped up for use in building homes, roads, and golf courses. The company has a machine that can crush glass beer bottles into a sand substitute for construction companies and let the beautiful sand stay on New Zealand's beaches, where it belongs. You simply drop a bottle into a slot on the machine and in five seconds the plastic label is vacuumed off and the bottle is pulverized into 200 grams of sand substitute by miniature steel hammers. Beer drinkers take note: you'll need to drink and crush 5,000 DB Export bottles to create a ton of sand.

NO PLASTIC BRICKS

LEGO is going green with the release of their first plant-based LEGO elements—LEGO trees and bushes made from a sugarcane-based plastic—in 2018. The Danish toy company says its goal is to be totally sustainable by 2030.

I SEE YOU!

Unexpected obstacles that lurk around the corner—a stopped car, a dog running loose, kids playing in the street—can be deadly for a driver. To help solve this problem, researchers at Stanford University are developing a laser-based computer technology that will allow cars, particularly driverless cars, to "see" around corners by emitting laser pulses and then measuring the time it takes for the light to be reflected back.

RELEASE THE WAX WORMS

The wax worm is a caterpillar that eats beeswax. In 2016 scientists at the Institute of Biomedicine and Biotechnology of Cantabria in Spain accidentally discovered that wax worms also eat polyethylene plastic, which they metabolize into degradable ethylene glycol. There aren't enough wax worms on Earth to consume all the plastic bags that clog our landfills and waterways, but scientists are working to isolate the plastic-digesting bacteria in the wax worms' gut, and someday...

Two doughnut flavors found at South Korea Dunkin' Donuts: Kimchi and Glazed Garlic. (In Japan, you can get doughnuts filled with soy.)

SAVING THE WORLD, ONE SMART KID AT A TIME

Gitanjali Rao, an 11-year-old girl from Lone Tree, Colorado, invented a simple product to test for lead in water. Instead of using unreliable test strips or having to send water samples to a testing lab, Rao's low-cost device uses carbon nanotubes to detect lead and connects to an app on your phone to provide instant results.

THE WONKAVATOR

In Roald Dahl's book *Charlie and the Chocolate Factory*, Willy Wonka has an elevator that can go "up and down, sideways, slant ways, and any other way you can think of," which readers knew was pure fiction…until now. A German engineering company, Thyssenkrupp, has announced the invention of the MULTI, a magnetic levitation system that enables elevator cars to go up, down, and sideways. Elevators can now have horizontal offshoots to other buildings or even do loop-de-loops. Want to ride the MULTI? Be in Berlin in 2021. That's when this amazing new system is scheduled to launch.

THE WRITE STUFF

Graviky Labs at MIT has invented a product that turns air pollution into ink. AIR-INK collects the unburned carbon soot you see coming out of cars' exhaust pipes and turns it into high quality black ink. As Buckminster Fuller said, "Pollution is nothing but the resources we are not harvesting. We allow them to disperse because we are ignorant of their value."

* * *

A TON OF FUN

Charles Barkley was one of the heftier players in basketball history—in college, he was listed as weighing 252 pounds, but he was around 300 by the time he started his Hall of Fame NBA career. Along the way, he earned himself a lot of nicknames.

- Sir Charles
- The Bread Truck
- The Love Boat
- Food World
- The Crisco Kid
- Wide Load from Leeds
- Ton of Fun
- Goodtime Blimp
- Round Mound of Rebound

100 WORDS FOR SNOW

Uncle John loves sharing little-known facts, but here's a common "fact"…that's untrue.

Myth: "Eskimos" have 100 words for snow.

Truth: It seems logical. After all, Eskimos have resided in Alaska, Canada, and Greenland for centuries. Those areas are snowy, icy, frozen, and just plain cold, and it makes sense that the inhabitants would have learned to differentiate between all the slightly different varieties of weather. While the different groups that live in Eskimo country do have several different words for snow, they don't have anywhere near 100.

First of all, there is no single group of people known as "Eskimos." The name derives from a word Algonquin tribes in Quebec used for the people who lived in the northern areas of Canada. (Some experts think it meant "person who laces snowshoes.") But no tribe called themselves Eskimos. When referring to an "Eskimo," most people are thinking of groups native to the Artic and subarctic regions of North America—the Inuit, Iñupiat, or Yup'ik peoples, for example.

Second, there's no "Eskimo" language. There are several native languages in Alaska, Canada, and Greenland, including Inuktitut and Athabaskan, both spoken by tens of thousands of people. So why do so many people think "Eskimos" are a single group of people, with one language and a fixation on describing the nuances of snow?

- In 1986 Cleveland State University language professor Laura Martin traced the origin of the myth back to Franz Boas, a German-American anthropologist who in 1911 wrote about the similarities between some world languages, and casually referenced the fact that there were four words in the "Eskimo" language for snow: *aput* (snow on the ground), *qana* (falling snow), *piqsirpoq* (drifting snow), and *qimuqsuq* (a snow drift).

- The myth was expanded in the 1950s by another major linguist, Benjamin Lee Whorf, who wrote that the so-called Eskimos had seven words for snow.

- Before long, textbooks were printing the information as fact…and the number kept growing.

- In the hit 1978 Lanford Wilson play *The Fifth of July*, a character remarks that there are 50 words for snow.

- A *New York Times* article not long after said there were 100, and it just took off from there.

Even if any Native American language *did* have 100 words for snow, it wouldn't be all that weird or notable. After all, English has snow, frost, powder, blizzards, sleet, flurries, snowdrifts, freezing rain, frozen fog, snow squall, hoarfrost, whiteout…

The fastest animal on two legs: the ostrich, which can run faster than 45 mph.

THE INTERNATIONAL LEAGUE

Football is America's most popular sport, but outside of the United States its popularity is miniscule. Baseball has a lot of fans outside of the United States, but mostly in Latin America and parts of Asia. So what American sport is the most popular around the world? Thanks in part to the success of the 1992 Olympic Dream Team, it's basketball. In fact, the 2017–18 NBA season had a record 108 players from 42 other countries or territories. Here are the first players to represent their country in the NBA, and the total number who have played in the league as of 2018.

Antigua and Barbuda: Julius Hodge (2005)
1 player in the NBA

Argentina: Pepe Sanchez (2000)
12 players in the NBA

Australia: Luc Longley (1991)
17 players in the NBA

Austria: Jakob Pöltl (2016)
1 player in the NBA

Bahamas: Mychal Thompson (1978)
4 players in the NBA

Belarus: Maalik Wayns (2012)
1 player in the NBA

Belgium: D. J. Mbenga (2004)
2 players in the NBA

Belize: Marlon Garnett (1998)
3 players in the NBA

Bosnia and Herzegovina: Aleksandar Radojević (1999)
6 players in the NBA

Brazil: Rolando Ferreira (1988)
16 players in the NBA

Bulgaria: Georgi Glouchkov (1985)
1 player in the NBA

Cameroon: Ruben Boumtje-Boumtje (2001)
4 players in the NBA

Canada: Hank Biasatti (1946)
36 players in the NBA

Cape Verde: Edy Tavares (2015)
1 player in the NBA

China: Yao Ming (2002)
7 players in the NBA

Croatia: Dražen Petrović (1989)
20 players in the NBA

Cuba: Andrés Guibert (1994)
3 players in the NBA

Czech Republic: George Zidek (1995)
4 players in the NBA

Democratic Republic of the Congo: Dikembe Mutombo (1991)
5 players in the NBA

Dominica: Garth Joseph (2000)
1 player in the NBA

Dominican Republic: Tito Horford (1988)
8 players in the NBA

Egypt: Alaa Abdelnaby (1990)
2 players in the NBA

England: Chris Harris (1955)
11 players in the NBA

Estonia: Martin Müürsepp (1996)
1 player in the NBA

Finland: Hanno Möttölä (2000)
3 players in the NBA

France: Howard Carter (1983)
21 players in the NBA

Gabon: Stephane Lasme (2007)
1 player in the NBA

Georgia: Vladimir Stepania (1999)
5 players in the NBA

Germany: Frido Frey (1946)
22 players in the NBA

Greece: Jake Tsakalidis (2000)
11 players in the NBA

Guyana: Jason Miskiri (1999)
2 players in the NBA

Haiti: Yvon Joseph (1985)
4 players in the NBA

Hungary: Kornél Dávid (1999)
1 player in the NBA

Iceland: Pétur Guðmundsson (1981)
1 player in the NBA

Iran: Hamed Haddadi (2008)
1 player in the NBA

Ireland: Marty Conlon (1991)
3 players in the NBA

Israel: Omri Casspi (2009)
3 players in the NBA

Italy: Mike D'Antoni (1973)
10 players in the NBA

Jamaica: Wayne Sappleton (1984)
6 players in the NBA

Japan: Yuta Tabuse (2004)
1 player in the NBA

Latvia: Gundars Vētra (1992)
4 players in the NBA

Libya: Hesham Salem (2004)
2 players in the NBA

Lebanon: Rony Seikaly (1988)
3 players in the NBA

Lithuania: Šarūnas Marčiulionis (1989)
11 players in the NBA

Macedonia: Pero Antić (2013)
2 players in the NBA

Mali: Soumaila Samake (2000)
2 players in the NBA

Mexico: Horacio Llamas (1997)
4 players in the NBA

Montenegro: Predrag Drobnjak (2001)
6 players in the NBA

Netherlands: Swen Nater (1976)
6 players in the NBA

New Zealand: Sean Marks (1998)
4 players in the NBA

Nigeria: Hakeem Olajuwon (1984)
17 players in the NBA

Norway: Torgeir Bryn (1989)
1 player in the NBA

Panama: Rolando Blackman (1981)
5 players in the NBA

Philippines: Raymond Townsend (1978)
3 players in the NBA

Poland: Jeff Nordgaard (1997)
5 players in the NBA

Puerto Rico: Butch Lee (1978)
14 players in the NBA

Qatar: Jarvis Hayes (2003)
2 players in the NBA

Romania: Gheorghe Mureşan (1993)
1 player in the NBA

Russia: Sergei Bazarevich (1994)
12 players in the NBA

Saint Vincent and the Grenadines: Adonal Foyle (1997)
1 player in the NBA

Senegal: Makhtar N'Diaye (1999)
11 players in the NBA

Serbia: Vlade Divac (1989)
28 players in the NBA

Scotland: Robert Archibald (2002)
1 player in the NBA

Slovakia: Richard Petruška (1993)
1 player in the NBA

Slovenia: Marko Milič (1997)
10 players in the NBA

South Korea: Ha Seung-Jin (2004)
1 player in the NBA

South Sudan: Luol Deng (2005)
3 players in the NBA

Spain: Fernando Martín (1986)
17 players in the NBA

Sudan: Manute Bol (1985)
1 player in the NBA

Sweden: Jonas Jerebko (2009)
3 players in the NBA

Switzerland: Thabo Sefolosha (2006)
4 players in the NBA

Tanzania: Hasheem Thabeet (2009)
1 player in the NBA

Trinidad and Tobago: Ken Charles (1973)
2 players in the NBA

Tunisia: Salah Mejri (2015)
1 player in the NBA

Turkey: Mirsad Türkcan (1999)
10 players in the NBA

Ukraine: Alexander Volkov (1989)
9 players in the NBA

U.S. Virgin Islands: Charles Claxton (1995)
3 players in the NBA

Uruguay: Esteban Batista (2005)
1 player in the NBA

Venezuela: Harold Keeling (1986)
6 players in the NBA

DUMB CROOKS

Here's proof that crime doesn't pay.

HOUSE CALL. An off-duty police officer (name not released) from Brownsville, Texas, was awakened one November night in 2009 at 3:30 a.m. by someone knocking on his apartment door. He got up and groggily answered, and there was 19-year-old Anthony Carrazco, who asked the cop if he wanted to "buy some weed." "Be right back," said the cop. He returned a moment later with his badge and handcuffs and arrested the inebriated entrepreneur.

BEARING FALSE WITNESS. In October 2017, a 25-year-old Nebraska man named Thomas Hartman went to Omaha Police headquarters to report that his brother had stolen money from him. A quick investigation revealed that his brother had a solid alibi, but Hartman kept insisting that his brother robbed him. Officers smelled something fishy, so they held him for questioning. While Hartman was alone in the interrogation room, he suddenly realized that showing up at police headquarters with crack cocaine in his pocket was probably a bad idea, so he put a chair on the table and climbed up to try to hide the drugs above the ceiling tiles. Several officers (who were watching him via a surveillance camera) rushed in and apprehended him. Remarked one cop, "You're at the frickin' police station, man...you just tried to put a chair on the table to get up in the ceiling."

NO NAPKINS? Our new favorite headline: "Man Accused of Stealing Meatballs Had Red Sauce on His Face." The meatball robber was Leahman Potter, 48, of Sugarloaf, Pennsylvania. He snatched the meatballs from a neighbor's garage, where they were being cooled in a pot. The neighbor called police, who later found the empty pot (and a spoon) in the middle of a cul de sac not far from the house. And not far from the pot was Potter, who was arrested with red sauce on his face and clothes.

SISTER ACT. Scott Vosburgh, 50, had way too much to drink one night in February 2018, and crashed his car on the side of a road in Perth, New York. When the highway patrol gave him a breathalyzer test, his blood alcohol level was .29 percent, more than three times the legal limit. After Vosburgh was processed at the station, he called his sister Kim Ledoux, 51, to come and pick him up. A few minutes later, she showed up at the station "visibly intoxicated." (If you're keeping score, her blood alcohol level was .22 percent.) Ledoux was immediately charged with DWI, just like her brother. According the police report, "Both were released to a sober third party."

The WWII-era submarine HMS *Trident* kept a fully grown reindeer on board for six weeks...

TALES FROM THE CRYPTO. You'd think that a "criminal mastermind" who could plan a digital currency heist worth millions—complete with a fake kidnapping—would be too smart to end up in a Dumb Crooks article. Enter Louis Meza of Passaic, New Jersey. In December 2017, Meza's multifaceted plan was set into motion when he invited a wealthy business associate to join him at a Ruby Tuesday's in Times Square. At one point, the conversation turned to the valuable cryptocurrency that the associate had invested in. After the meal, Meza insisted on paying for his friend's Uber ride home, so he called for a car, and watched as the man got in the front passenger seat and rode away. Moments later, an armed "kidnapper" emerged from the back seat and demanded the associate's apartment keys, along with the password to his "hardware wallet," which, according to *Fortune* magazine, "lets users store digital currency offline and safe from hackers (though not from kidnappers)."

The victim eventually escaped. By that time, however, Meza had broken into the victim's apartment (he got the keys from the kidnapper), stole the man's hardware wallet, and transferred $1.8 million worth of cryptocurrency into his own bitcoin account. His plan was to pull off the heist without the victim even suspecting him. But Meza made three crucial errors that led detectives right to him. Goof #1: Meza didn't hide his face from security cameras in the victim's apartment building, placing him at the scene of the crime. Goof #2: The next day, he bragged to several people that he was now a "cryptocurrency player." Goof #3: According to *Fortune*, Meza "transferred the stolen funds to an account under his own name at a well-known U.S. digital currency exchange." If he had transferred the currency to his own digital wallet, it would have been nearly impossible to trace back to him. "Instead, he sent them to the cryptocurrency world's version of Chase Bank, making it possible for the DA's office to locate and seize him."

PUBLIC SERVICE ANNOUNCEMENT. In March 2016, police in Granite Shoals, Texas, posted an urgent message on their Facebook page:

> BREAKING NEWS ALERT: If you have recently purchased meth or heroin in Central Texas, please take it to the local police or sheriff department so it can be screened with a special device. DO NOT use it until it has been properly checked for possible Ebola contamination! Contact any Granite Shoals PD officer for testing.

A few days later, the police posted the mug shot of Chasity Eugina Hopson, 29, and named her "winner of the Facebook challenge." She actually showed up at the station with her meth. Good news: no Ebola! Bad news: she was arrested.

...Her name was Pollyanna, and she was a gift from Russia.

ANIMAL INVADERS

Probably the most famous "invasive species" is the cane toad. In the 1930s, when native cane beetles were ravaging Australia's sugarcane plantations, authorities brought in the toads, which ate up the beetles…and then reproduced until they numbered in the millions and overran the country. Here are some stories of other animals that wound up where they didn't belong.

Animal: European starling

Emigration: In the 1870s, New York pharmacist Eugene Schieffelin was the chairman of the American Acclimatization Society, a group whose mission was to bring plants and animals that were native to Europe to the New World. Schieffelin wanted to be more specific, and introduce all of the birds named in the works of Shakespeare to the United States, including the starling, which is mentioned—just once—in *Henry IV Part 1*, when the character Hotspur quips, "Nay, I'll have a starling shall be taught to speak nothing but 'Mortimer,' and give it to him to keep his anger still in motion." In 1890 Schieffelin arranged for 60 starlings to be shipped to his country home outside New York City…and then he let them loose in Central Park.

Result: Each year the Department of Agriculture's Wildlife Services exterminates about four million nuisance animals—mostly starlings. Today the starling population is estimated to be about 200 million, *all* descendants of Schieffelin's original 60. These aggressive foragers travel in flocks as large as 3,000 that descend on farms and swarm over (and eat) the crops, at a cost of $800 million annually. They live in pretty much every corner of the country, where they'll push other, native birds out of their nests.

Animal: Burmese python

Emigration: Exotic pets are popular in Florida, and in the 1980s one of the hottest exotic pets was the Burmese python. They're nonvenomous, but can grow up to 20 feet long, weigh 140 pounds, and they have extremely sharp teeth, so they're quite intimidating (and attractive to people who like snakes). In 1992 Hurricane Andrew destroyed a Burmese python breeding facility, sending hundreds of the gigantic Asian snakes slithering into the Everglades.

Result: An estimated 100,000 Burmese pythons now live in Florida's swamps. Not only do the reptiles have no natural predators, they'll hunt and eat just about anything (except humans), wrapping themselves around prey, squeezing it to death, and then swallowing the unlucky creature whole. A Burmese python can devour an alligator this way, as well as deer, raccoons, marsh rabbits, bobcats, and opossums. In some areas of the Everglades, populations of those animals have declined by 99 percent since 1992.

Adorably gross: Pandas poop out about 60 pounds of waste every day.

Since establishing an eradication program in 2002, state agencies have captured and killed 2,000 pythons, which isn't very many. The South Florida Water Management District pays hunters about $8.10 an hour to search for pythons in the region and grants a $50 bonus for every python at least four feet long, with $25 for each foot beyond.

Animal: Emerald ash borer

Emigration: Shipments of wood packing-crate materials from Asia arrived in Michigan in the 1990s (the region did a lot of trade with China), and unbeknownst to anyone, those crates held emerald ash borer larvae. Those larvae grow into metallic-green beetles that are no bigger than a dime, but they feast on ash trees and burrow their way through…which ultimately kills the trees.

Result: Ash used to be big business in southeastern Michigan, with millions of trees being used to make flooring, church pews, baseball bats, and guitars. In a little over 20 years, emerald ash borers have killed tens of millions of ash trees in that region alone. Result: the ash industry in Michigan is essentially over. And thanks to ash firewood that's been shipped to other parts of the United States and Canada, the bug has killed about 100 million ash trees. So far.

Animal: Indian mongoose

Emigration: In the same way that cane toads were brought to Australia to eliminate cane beetle infestations, the Indian mongoose was brought to Puerto Rico and Jamaica in the 1870s. The cute creature, about two feet long, was tasked with patrolling sugarcane plantations, protecting the crop against rats and snakes—by killing and eating those rats and snakes.

Result: The mongoose dutifully killed those pests, but then started killing what wasn't on the preapproved list—native species of birds, reptiles, and amphibians. In total, the mongoose has caused the local extinction of 12 reptile and amphibian species. Which is to say nothing of the millions of dollars in annual damage they cause to farms, where they attack chickens, killing some and spreading rabies to others.

Animal: Asian citrus psyllid

Emigration: This Asian insect was spotted in Florida for the first time in 1998. Within two years, it was present in 31 counties in the Sunshine State. Scientists think larvae found its way from Asia to the United States on imported ornamental plants.

> **DID YOU KNOW?**
>
> Burmese pythons are very adaptable. Young ones live in trees; mature ones live on the ground. But they'll also try water (such as Floridian swampland). Turns out they can stay underwater for up to half an hour without needing a gulp of air.

IRS Publication 17 states that if you steal something, you must report it as income (unless you give it back).

Result: The psyllid feeds on citrus tree sap and leaves, particularly orange trees, but carries bacteria that destroys the tree and its fruit. Once infected with the bacteria, the plant malfunctions. Roots and leaves grow deformed, and oranges drop from branches well before they're ripe. Then the tree dies. Florida orange growers have called the psyllid infestation a "cancer"—half of all citrus trees in Florida have been infected over the last two decades. Eighty percent of American not-from-concentrate orange juice comes from Florida, so if something isn't done soon, Florida orange juice could become a thing of the past.

Animal: Brown tree snake

Emigration: Ironically, when American forces liberated the Pacific island of Guam from Japanese occupation in 1944, military ships that came from Papua New Guinea inadvertently brought along a few venomous brown tree snakes. The snakes quickly began to thrive in the island's forests, rich with a diversity of animals that they could devour.

Result: Today Guam is infested with more than two million snakes in its 210 square miles; some forested areas boast a snake density of 13,000 serpents per square mile. And they sure are hungry. By the mid-1980s, the snakes had eradicated 10 of Guam's 12 native bird species, including a kingfisher that was found nowhere else in the world. The delicate ecosystem has been so thoroughly destroyed that tree growth on Guam is down by 92 percent since the arrival of the snakes. They even wrap themselves around power lines and have caused $4.5 million worth of electrical damage over the past seven years, in addition to triggering blackouts. Authorities have been working on getting rid of the snakes, and have come up with one novel solution: Tylenol. Turns out acetaminophen is deadly to brown tree snakes. In 2010 animal-control groups tried implanting the over-the-counter pain reliever into dead mice, putting tiny parachutes on them, and dropping them over forested areas from a helicopter. (Really.) The parachutes then snag on tree branches, where they dangle enticingly for brown tree snakes…who take the bait and quickly die.

* * *

PHRASE ORIGIN: PRECIOUS LITTLE SNOWFLAKE

This insult—a retort to self-help books that say that everyone is a precious snowflake—was popularized by Chuck Palahniuk in his 1996 book *Fight Club:* "You are not special. You're not a beautiful and unique snowflake. You're the same decaying organic matter as everything else. We're all part of the same compost heap. We're all singing, all dancing crap of the world."

Watch your step: The surface of Saturn's moon Titan is covered in electrified sand.

THE KID WHO STAYED UP REALLY LATE

If you've ever had to cram for a test or had an unfinished paper that was due the next day, you probably know what it's like to pull an all-nighter. Now try to imagine having to pull an 11-nighter. That's what this high-schooler tried to do. Did he make it? Read on (and please try not to fall asleep before the end).

GOING TO THE FAIR

In the fall of 1963, two San Diego high school kids named Randy Gardner and Bruce McAllister decided to enter the local science fair. One of the first ideas they came up with for their entry was a test of the effect of sleeplessness on paranormal ability—abilities that are outside the normal senses, such as mind-reading or seeing the future. Then they had second thoughts. "We realized there was no way we could do that, so we decided on the effect of sleep deprivation on cognitive abilities, like performance on the basketball court, or whatever we could come up with," McAllister told the BBC in 2018.

The boys had read that the world record for sleeplessness was set by a Honolulu disc jockey named Tom Rounds, who'd stayed awake for 260 hours during a radio station "wake-a-thon" to raise money for charity. That's just four hours shy of eleven days, so Gardner and McAllister decided to try and stay up for 264 hours, or eleven days straight. They flipped a coin to see which one of them would be the guinea pig, and Gardner won: he would make the record-breaking attempt, while McAllister observed and documented his activities in a journal.

SURE, GO AHEAD

Gardner probably wasn't the first kid to try to stay up for days on end just to see if he could, but he may have been the first one to obtain his parents' permission. Perhaps assuming that their son would doze off after just a night or two without sleep, Mr. and Mrs. Gardner gave their consent, but they did insist that Randy be monitored by a doctor to ensure that he wasn't endangering his health. Because Gardner's father served in the military, the medical professional who observed the boy was Dr. John J. Ross, a physician assigned to the U.S. Navy's Neuropsychiatric Research Unit in San Diego.

Three days after Christmas on December 28, 1963, the boys started their experiment at McAllister's house. They soon realized they were going to need some more help, because the only way that McAllister could be sure that Gardner stayed awake was to stay awake with him. "After three nights of sleeplessness myself, I woke up tipped against the wall writing notes on the wall itself," McAllister recalled. So he

---

What are *supernumerary* teeth? Extra teeth that grow in alongside
normal teeth. (It's not uncommon in humans.)

and Gardner recruited Joe Marciano, a schoolmate from Point Loma High School, to help. For the rest of the experiment, McAllister and Marciano worked in shifts, with one of them sleeping while the other stayed up with Gardner.

Each day McAllister and Marciano tested Gardner in every way they could think of, so that they could document how his physical and cognitive abilities, as well as his sense of hearing, sight, smell, taste, and touch changed over time.

Gardner stayed active to keep from falling asleep. He and his friends played basketball and pinball for hours at a time and went for lots of drives. "At night we'd go to Winchell's Donuts or down to the local jail—just for something to do. When we were at my house, we listened to a lot of surfer music: the Beach Boys, Jan & Dean, the Surfaris," Gardner told *Esquire* magazine in 2007. "It was fun for the first few days. Then it got to be a real bummer." (How did McAllister and Marciano keep Gardner from dozing off during bathroom breaks? They made him talk through the closed bathroom door the entire time he did his "business.")

ONE DAY AT A TIME

The first 24 hours were tiring but uneventful. The second day was a more difficult. After examining Gardner, Dr. Ross reported that the young man had difficulty focusing his eyes at times, and he struggled to recognize objects just by touch, one of the tests he took to measure his mental alertness. By the third day he was becoming moody, and struggling to repeat tongue twisters, another measure of alertness.

On Gardner's fourth day without sleep, his moodiness increased and he became paranoid: He was convinced that people were staring at him and talking about him. He had trouble with concentration and memory, and he began hallucinating. At one point he imagined he was pro football player Paul Lowe, who played for the San Diego Chargers. "My friends thought that was hilarious, because I weighed like 130 pounds," Gardner said. Later, when Gardner and his friends drove past a street sign, he imagined it was a person.

MEET THE PRESS

By now Gardner was beginning to attract the attention of the news media. The sleep experiment took place barely a month after the assassination of John F. Kennedy, and perhaps because of this, it received a lot of media attention. Much of the coverage treated it as just another silly teenage fad, like swallowing goldfish or cramming people into a phone booth, but the public was hungry for light news stories, and this tale of a teenager staying up for days fit the bill perfectly.

One person who took the story seriously was a Stanford University sleep researcher named William C. Dement. As soon as he learned the experiment was underway, he flew to San Diego to observe it. While he found Gardner to be tired (no surprise),

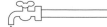

If you drilled a hole through the center of the earth and out the other side, then jumped into...

the boy didn't seem particularly impaired. Dr. Dement drove Gardner, McAllister, and Marciano around town in a rented convertible, took them out to eat, and played pinball with Gardner to test his skill. Dr. Dement observed that Gardner played well and beat him several times. Another skill that seemed unaffected by sleep loss was his ability to play basketball: Bruce McAllister says Gardner played as well without sleep as he did when he was well rested.

One thing that had changed noticeably was Gardner's sense of smell. "Don't make me smell that, I can't stand the smell," he told McAllister when presented various items during his daily sniff tests.

STILL GOING

On his fifth day awake, Gardner's hallucinations increased. Once, when staring at a wall, he saw it dissolve and turn into a forest with a path running through it.

On the sixth and seventh days, Gardner's speech began to slur as if he were drunk, and he struggled to complete sentences or even name simple objects. The hallucinations continued.

On the seventh and eighth days, "everything basically went in the toilet," he told *Esquire* magazine. "There were no more highs, just lows and lower lows. It was like someone was taking sandpaper to my brain. My body was dragging along okay, but my mind was shot." He struggled mightily to remember what he said from one moment to the next. Luckily for him, he was a 17-year-old and in great shape; anytime he seemed close to nodding off, all McAllister or Marciano had to do was get him to play basketball or pinball, or walk around the neighborhood. He also took lots of showers.

On the ninth day Gardner was battling harder than ever to stay awake. Nights were more difficult than days, because there was less to do. The hours before daybreak were worst of all.

ON THE (PIN)BALL

On the tenth day Gardner gave a radio interview, but had trouble focusing enough to answer the interviewer's questions. The experience triggered more paranoid thoughts: he believed that the interviewer was trying to make him look bad.

On the eleventh and final day, Gardner really had to struggle to remain awake. His speech was badly slurred now, he spoke in a monotone, and his face had lost all expression. His attention span was extremely short. When he was given a "serial sevens test," where the subject counts down from 100 by subtracting 7 repeatedly (100, 93, 86, etc.), Gardner only made it five rounds to 65 before he forgot what he had been asked to do.

At 2:00 a.m. on January 8, Gardner broke Tom Rounds's world record by staying awake past 260 hours; four hours later he achieved his own goal by staying awake for

...the hole, it would take you 38 minutes and 11 seconds to pop out the other side.

264 hours—11 days straight. He was examined one last time by Dr. Ross at the naval hospital, then went to sleep there in the hospital instead of at home, so that Ross could measure his brain waves as he slept. Gardner dozed for 14 hours and 40 minutes straight, and only woke up because he had to go to the bathroom. Afterward he stayed up for 23 hours, then slept for another 10 hours. After that, his sleep patterns returned to normal.

CAUGHT NAPPING

When the brain wave recordings and other data were analyzed, they revealed something that had been observed previously in combat and other situations where humans have been forced to stay awake for extended periods of time: Parts of Gardner's brain appeared to shut down and take "catnaps" to restore themselves while other parts of his brain continued to function. Once one part of his brain refreshed itself, it would resume functioning, allowing another part of his brain to rest.

Ironically, though Gardner suffered no apparent ill effects of his 11 days without sleep, when he reached his early 60s, he was plagued with terrible insomnia for more than a decade. Today he's able to sleep up to six hours a night, but no more than that. Though he loved to drink tea, today he abstains from caffeine entirely. "I'm afraid I won't be able to sleep at night," he says.

So is Gardner's insomnia a result of his 11 days of sleeplessness some 40 years earlier? No one knows. "Maybe it's karma, like the universe saying, 'Oh, you don't want to sleep? Well, there you go!'" he told the *New York Times* in 2010.

PUT TO BED

Gardner may have held the world record for sleep deprivation for only two weeks, because later that same month a California State University, Fresno, student named Jim Thomas reportedly stayed up for 266.5 hours, beating Gardner's record by two and a half hours. *Guinness World Records* used to have a category for sleep-deprivation records, but it no longer does, out of concern that people who try to set such records will harm themselves in the process. The last recognized record-holder was Maureen Weston of Peterborough, England. She stayed awake for 449 hours, or 18 days and 17 hours, while competing in a rocking chair marathon from April 14 to May 2, 1977. "Though she tended to hallucinate toward the end of this surely ill-advised test, surprisingly, she suffered no lasting ill effects," the Guinness editors noted.

What separates Gardner's attempt from all the others is the fact that his experiment was so thoroughly documented by medical professionals. This makes Gardner's experience especially useful to sleep researchers and other scientists and, as a result, his record-setting attempt is likely to remain one of the best-known cases for many years to come. (Bonus: Gardener and his friends won the science fair.)

Owl eyeballs aren't round—they're elongated and tubular in shape.

LIFE IN 1948

*Here's what the world was like 40 years before the
invention of* Uncle John's Bathroom Reader.

MAJOR EVENTS

- Israel was declared an independent nation.
- The United Nations established the World Health Organization.
- Congress approved the Foreign Assistance Act, or "Marshall Plan," providing $13 billion to rebuild Europe after World War II.

MOST ADMIRED

Beginning in 1946, Gallup conducted an annual poll to determine the "most admired person in America." In 1948 they asked respondents to vote for the most admired man *and* most admired woman for the first time. Voters' picks: President Harry S. Truman and former First Lady Eleanor Roosevelt.

TELEVISION

Only 35,000 people owned a television set in 1948, but the first big TV hit—and one that prompted millions of Americans to buy TV sets—debuted that year: *Texaco Star Theater*, starring Milton Berle.

The first nightly newscast debuted in May on CBS. *CBS Television News*, with anchor Douglas Edwards.

A variety show called *Toast of the Town* premiered in June. It was later renamed after its host as *The Ed Sullivan Show*.

DEATHS

- Jan. 30: Mahatma Gandhi, 78
- Jan. 30: "First in flight" Orville Wright, 76
- July 15: World War I general John J. Pershing, 87
- Aug. 16: Babe Ruth, 53
- Dec. 23: Hideki Tojo, 63, prime minister of Japan during World War II, was hanged for war crimes.

WHAT THINGS COST

- Average price of a new home: $7,700
- A new car: about $1,250
- A gallon of gas: 16¢

NEW! NEW! NEW!

Available in stores for the first time in 1948: Cheetos, Dial (the first antibacterial soap), Mentos, Nestlé Quik, Reddi-Wip, the Frisbee, Scrabble, and the Polaroid camera.

BOOKS

Among the most popular novels of the year: *The Big Fisherman*, by Lloyd C. Douglas (the story of Jesus's disciple Simon-Peter); *Dinner at Antoine's*, by Frances Parkinson Keyes (a murder mystery set in Louisiana); and *The Naked and the Dead*, by Norman Mailer (based on Mailer's experiences in the Philippines during World War II).

Egg-poaching tip: add salt, lemon juice, and vinegar to the water.
The egg white will coagulate faster and keep its shape.

James Michener's *Tales of the South Pacific* (which would later be adapted into the musical *South Pacific*) won the Pulitzer Prize for Fiction. Poet T. S. Eliot won the Nobel Prize for Literature.

MUSIC

According to *Billboard*, these were the top 5 hit songs of 1948:
1) "Twelfth Street Rag," by Pee Wee Hunt
2) "Mañana," by Peggy Lee
3) "Now Is the Hour," by Bing Crosby
4) "A Tree in the Meadow," by Margaret Whiting
5) "My Happiness," by Jon and Sondra Streele

1948 was also the year that Columbia introduced the long-playing vinyl record, or LP. It played at 33⅓ rpm—rather than the previous standard, 78 rpm—and could hold up to 23 minutes of music per side.

SPORTS

Both the Summer and Winter Olympics were held for the first time since 1936. (The Olympics had been suspended during World War II.) The summer games were held in London, and the winter games in St. Moritz, Switzerland.

Almost 20 years before the Super Bowl, the big football event of the year was the NFL Championship Game. During a blizzard at Shibe Park in Philadelphia, the Philadelphia Eagles beat the Chicago Cardinals, 7–0.

The Cleveland Indians won their last World Series to date, defeating the Boston Braves in six games. They were led by American League MVP Lou Boudreau, who played shortstop and was also the team's manager.

In the still obscure sport of professional basketball, the NBL (not yet the NBA) title went to the Minneapolis Lakers over the Rochester Royals.

On June 25, Joe Louis beat Jersey Joe Wolcott in 11 rounds and was named the heavyweight champion of the world for the 25th time. And then he retired.

Citation won the Triple Crown of horse racing, only the eighth horse to do so.

MOVIES

The top-grossing box office hits (U.S.):
1) *The Red Shoes*, a British movie starring Moira Shearer
2) *The Three Musketeers*, with Gene Kelly and Lana Turner
3) *Red River*, a John Wayne western
4) *The Treasure of the Sierra Madre*, directed by John Huston and starring Humphrey Bogart
5) *When My Baby Smiles at Me*, a musical starring Betty Grable

Other films of 1948: *The Snake Pit*, starring Olivia de Havilland; *Key Largo*, starring Humphrey Bogart and Lauren Bacall; *The Paleface*, starring Bob Hope and Jane Russell; *Rope*, directed by Alfred Hitchcock, starring James Stewart; *The Bicycle Thief*, directed by Vittorio De Sica; *Fort Apache*, directed by John Ford, starring John Wayne; *The Big Clock*, starring Ray Milland and Charles Laughton

Laurence Olivier's *Hamlet* won Best Picture at the Academy Awards, the only Shakespeare adaptation ever to do so.

What's "umop apisdn"? It's "upside down"...spelled upside down.

LOONIE CANADIAN LAWS

Believe it or not, these bizarre statutes are still on the books up in the Great White North.

It's illegal to whistle in Petrolia, Ontario.

Two bagpipers may not play on the street near one another at the same time in Victoria, British Columbia.

You can't drive cattle through the streets of St. John's during daylight hours. (It's fine at night.)

Also in Victoria: street performers aren't allowed to hand out balloon animals to children.

If you sneak out of a hotel in Ontario without paying, the establishment has the right to confiscate your horse and sell it to settle your debt.

If you live on the corner of a street in Souris, Prince Edward Island, you may not build a snowman taller than 30 inches.

Nationwide, it's illegal to prank the queen.

Internet speeds exceeding 56K—state of the art in 1994—are illegal in Uxbridge, Ontario.

If you live in Beaconsfield, Quebec, you can be fined for having your home painted more than two different colors.

You can't keep a cow as a pet in Newfoundland.

It's illegal to lock your car doors in Churchill, Manitoba. Reason: Just in case somebody needs to run and hide from a rampaging polar bear.

It's illegal to own more than four rats in Port Coquitlam, British Columbia.

You may not wear a snake on your shoulders in public in Fredericktown, New Brunswick.

You can get arrested in Wolfville, Nova Scotia, for unhinging someone else's front gate.

You can't fill a front yard water trough in Cobourg, Ontario, after 5:00 a.m.

In Hay River, Northwest Territories, it's against the law to ride a dogsled on the sidewalk.

In Ontario, it's against the law to drive one's sleigh on the highway without at least two bells attached to the horse's harness.

In Windsor, Ontario, you're breaking the law if you play a musical instrument in an office.

Pretending to practice witchcraft is a crime throughout Canada. (Apparently, practicing it is okay.)

You can't show a "For Sale" sign in the window of a moving vehicle in Montreal.

In the distinctly bilingual province of Quebec, it is illegal to curse in any language other than French.

It is explicitly against the law in Alberta to set someone else's wooden leg on fire.

Canada, known for its politeness, has a nationwide law against "offending a place with a bad smell."

Pretending to be a foreigner is against the law in Quebec.

The warm-blooded Atlantic bluefin tuna thrashes so hard when caught by fishermen that it can cook its own flesh.

SORRY, WRONG NUMBER

Most of the time when a person dials a wrong number, nothing
unusual happens. You hang up, and try your call again.
The recipient of the call will soon forget it, too.
But that's not what happened to these folks…

CALLS: In September 2017, Wendi Walsh of Winton, California, received a call from someone who wanted to order a pizza. A few days later she got a strange call, this time from someone asking how late the restaurant was open. Over the next few weeks, she received more and more such calls, and by early October her phone was ringing off the hook into the wee hours of the morning with callers demanding pizza.

WRONG NUMBER: Walsh learned from the callers that Rico's Pizza, a local restaurant, had been distributing promotional flyers listing her phone number as the restaurant's number. (It wasn't an easy mistake to make: the restaurant's number begins with 358 and Walsh's number begins with 812.) Rico's printed new flyers, but by then, hundreds had already been distributed. Walsh's husband says that the restaurant offered him a gift card for free pizza for their trouble…and asked him to refer callers to the restaurant's actual phone number. Nothing doing—instead, the exasperated Walshes changed their number. "I feel like they should pay a fine or maybe make a donation to a charity of our choice," Wendi says.

CALL: When Hurricane Irma struck Puerto Rico and the Florida coast in August and September 2017, the Federal Emergency Management Agency tweeted a message to homeowners with storm-damaged roofs, instructing them to call a toll-free number to receive assistance with repairs.

WRONG NUMBER: The tweet listed an 800 number, but the correct number had an 888 prefix. Callers who dialed the 800 number were connected with…a sex hotline. "Welcome to America's hottest talk line," said the recording. "Guys, hot ladies are waiting to talk to you. Press '1' to connect, free, now." FEMA quickly deleted the original tweet, sent out a corrected version, and apologized.

CALLS: In early 2017, residents of Westport, Ireland, began receiving calls from Irish viewers of Babestation, an X-rated cable TV channel headquartered in the UK, who were hoping to speak to models working for a sex chat line.

WRONG NUMBER: The callers were dialing the right number, but they probably didn't realize that Babestation operates out of the UK, and neglected to dial 00 and the UK country code—44—before dialing the number. Leaving it out when dialing the chat-line numbers, which all began with 098, routed the calls to Westport, which uses the prefix 098. Babestation apologized for the inconvenience and changed all of its chat-line numbers so that they didn't begin with 098. They also sent three Babestation models to Westport to apologize to the locals in person. "Anyone calling the UK from the Republic of Ireland should always use the prefix 00 44," said a spokesperson for ComReg, the agency that regulates telephone service in Ireland.

CALL: In January 2017, Bub and Pop's Deli in Washington, DC, got a call from someone who was angry that Donald Trump was the new president. Not surprising, considering that Bub and Pop's is just blocks away from the White House. But when more than a hundred people called the deli with similar complaints, they knew they had a problem.

> Callers "continue to rant about Trump even after being told they have the wrong number."

WRONG NUMBER: The deli's phone number, it turns out, is just one digit different from the White House public comment line—the White House number has a 6, and the deli's number has a 7. When someone tweeted out Bub and Pop's number on Twitter, it was most likely a typo, but the calls came pouring in. According to employees of the deli, many callers "continue to rant about Trump even after being told they have the wrong number."

CALL: Someone called the Donald E. Schick Elementary School in Montoursville, Pennsylvania, in October 2017, and left the following message: 'If you don't stop calling this number, I'm going to find out what your [expletive] address is and believe me, three sticks of dynamite will get rid of you and all your [expletive]." School officials decided not to evacuate the campus, but they did notify the police, who remained at the school until the end of the day.

WRONG NUMBER: The call was traced to 81-year-old Lawrence Stabler, who was arrested and charged with threatening to blow up the school. Stabler, a retired college professor, says it's all a misunderstanding. He was trying to intimidate a crank caller who had been calling *him*. "I have received a number of harassing telephone calls, whole bunch of calls, silence, deep breathing," he explained in court. His explanation didn't get him very far, though. At last report he was lodged in jail on a $25,000 bond and charged with "threatening to use weapons of mass destruction, terroristic threats, disorderly conduct and harassment."

CALL: On Christmas Eve 2015, Betty Barker, a 79-year-old grandmother who lives in West Sussex, England, received an odd call. There was a long pause, and then a man asked, "Hello, is this planet Earth?" "I thought it was somebody asking if it was a nightclub. I just said 'no' and put the phone down," Barker told the *Daily Telegraph*.

Say "cheese" in other languages: *fromage* (French), *ost* (Swedish), *chizu* (Japanese).

WRONG NUMBER: Moments later Tim Peake, a British astronaut, tweeted a message to Earth from aboard the International Space Station. "I'd like to apologize to the lady I just called by mistake saying 'Hello, is this planet Earth?'—not a prank call... just a wrong number!" Peake says he was trying to call his own family, who also live in West Sussex, but inadvertently dialed the Barker house instead. "They didn't know who I was. I blame it on my Excel spreadsheet. It had a rounding error. That's my story, anyway," he says.

CALL: In July 2017, a West Virginia man named Shannon Barbour was awakened by an early morning call asking him if his heifer was still for sale. Barbour, 19, did not have a heifer for sale. "I don't know what a heifer is," he said before hanging up the phone. (It's a young female cow that has not borne a calf.) For the rest the day Barbour was besieged by similar calls and texts asking if his heifer was for sale.

> "I'd like to apologize to the lady I just called by mistake saying 'Hello, is this planet Earth?'"

WRONG NUMBER: Barbour found out that someone with a heifer for sale on Craigslist had posted his cell phone as the contact number with the online ad. He received more than a hundred calls and texts before the ad was taken down, and responded to many of the inquires with silly answers. "Too late, just had steak for breakfast," he replied to one text; "It has been put down :(," he told another. When he posted the silliest exchanges on Twitter they were re-tweeted more than 77,000 times and received 258,000 likes, earning him his 15 minutes of internet fame. Not that it mattered: "This has been the worst morning of my life," he complained in one of his tweets. Adding insult to injury: the heifer was offered for sale for just $50, much less than the actual value of a heifer, leading Barbour to suspect that the ad may have been a prank placed by his friends.

* * *

THE TOILET BOT

Ariel and Hila Ben-Amram are parents of four children, so they really hate the one chore everybody hates—cleaning toilets. That distaste for toilet brushes, and the inspiration of autonomous floor-cleaning Roomba vacuums, led the couple to invent SpinX, "the world's first toilet cleaning robot." It consists of a self-contained plastic and metal apparatus that fits on a toilet between the lid and the seat. When closed down over the bowl and activated at the push of a button, the SpinX releases a robotic arm with a rapidly spinning toilet brush on the end, scrubbing faster than a human ever could and with the help of soap from specially made SpinX cleaning tablets. The device then cleans and dries the seat, too, as well as the brush itself. Cost: about $200.

What's an *eccedentesiast?* A person who smiles to hide their pain.

MMM...EVERYTHING

Homer Simpson's appetite knows no bounds. Over 30 years of The Simpsons,
He's devoured doughnuts, chips...and some very weird non-food items.

- Two five-pound buckets of rancid shrimp
- A sample of Lemon Time dish soap
- The remains of a ten-foot hoagie he found behind the radiator
- Fancy bath soaps
- "America Balls" (scoops of dog food with miniature American flags in them)
- Dog medicine wrapped in cheese
- 64 slices of American cheese (at once)
- A packet of gravy he found in a parking lot
- Gasoline
- A "Guatemalan insanity pepper"
- A puddle of blood and Vap-O-Rub he licked off the floor of the Kwik-E-Mart
- The "strictly ornamental" hot dogs at the Kwik-E-Mart
- 19 cans of Crab Juice
- A block of butter wrapped in a waffle
- A pie crust full of cloves and Tom Collins mix
- Lipstick
- The cat's ear medicine
- A pile of "free goo" on the street
- A jar of petroleum jelly
- Play-Doh
- The dirt under the bleachers at a football stadium
- A giant jar of pickle brine
- A waffle stuck on the kitchen ceiling, loosened with a broom handle
- His pet lobster, Pinchy
- A can of something called "Nuts n' Gum"
- A urinal cake
- A turkey he found behind a bed in a motel
- The plastic bride and groom from on top of a wedding cake
- Raw sausage
- Five pounds of spaghetti and meat sauce compressed into a handy mouth-sized brick
- Vodka poured into a jar of mayonnaise
- His own leprosy scabs (made out of oatmeal and poster paint)
- "Gum with a cracker center"
- A cup of buttermilk from 1961
- A can of Billy Beer from the 1970s
- A 15-year-old care package
- A hot dog he dropped into a kiddie pool
- A rubber mouth guard

Best argument for scuba lessons we've seen all day: There's an estimated
$60 billion in sunken treasure in the world's oceans.

RUSSIA 2.0

*On page 139 you learned the meaning of several Russian terms you
might hear on the news. Here's the second installment, comrade.*

THE COLD WAR

What is it? The post–World War II period of tension (1945–1991) between the
Western world and the Communist countries of Eastern Europe.

The story: The Cold War, so named because it wasn't a "shooting war" like World
War II, was led by the world's two superpowers—the United States and the Soviet
Union—and it dominated international affairs from the period immediately after
World War II until the Soviet Union fell in 1991. The Cuban missile crisis, the Berlin
Wall, the Vietnam War, and the threat of nuclear war were just a few of the points
of conflict between America and Russia. The two countries competed fiercely in the
"arms race" (building massive stockpiles of nuclear weapons) and the "space race" (an
intense battle to be the first to land a man on the Moon).

GULAG

What is it? The agency responsible for forced-labor camps throughout Russia and the
remote regions of Siberia and the far north. "Gulag" is short for *Glavnoe Upravlenie
Lagerei,* which means "Main Administration of Camps."

The story: First established in 1919 under Cheka, Lenin's secret police, the Gulag
served as the Soviet Union's primary penal system. The camps held perceived enemies
of the state—political prisoners, POWs, and religious dissidents along with its
population of criminals. Conditions in Gulag camps, especially in Siberia and the far
north, were notoriously deplorable, and the death rate from exposure, exhaustion, and
starvation was high.

GLASNOST AND PERESTROIKA

What is it? The policy of "openness" and "reform" in General Secretary Mikhail
Gorbachev's Soviet Union in the 1980s.

The story: In 1986 Mikhail Gorbachev wanted to modernize the USSR, so he
introduced Soviet citizens to *glasnost,* which allowed freedom of assembly, speech,
and religion, the right to strike, and multicandidate elections. His *perestroika* policies
included taking steps toward decentralizing government control over business and
establishing a semi-free market economy. While Gorbachev intended for his policies
to strengthen Soviet ideology, glasnost and perestroika actually had the opposite effect.

It goes both ways: Cats can be allergic to humans. (But most of the time
they're actually allergic to soap, perfume, or laundry detergent.)

The people were impatient and tired of the long lines, strikes, and general civil unrest. Five years later, in 1991, the USSR broke apart, leaving Russia on its own and under the leadership of President Boris Yeltsin and his successor, Vladimir Putin.

OLIGARCHS

What is it? Wealthy Russians who, because of their money and connections, have a great deal of political influence.

The story: Following the collapse of the Soviet Union in 1991, the government of Russia began to sell (and give away) its assets to the Russian public. Despite having had no experience with modern capitalism, the reformers believed that by spreading the wealth of Russia to its citizens, Russia could transition into a market economy. There was concern that if they held an open sale of state-owned assets, only a few well-connected individuals would end up with the lion's share. So the reformers created vouchers that could be exchanged for shares in the enterprises slated for privatization. This would allow the citizens of Russia to share in the wealth of Russia.

Unfortunately, most people did not understand the voucher-to-share program or were so poor that they sold their vouchers for immediate money. As a result, the exact opposite occurred: the Russian mafia, the *nomenklatura* (influential posts in government and industry), and other well-connected individuals managed to gain control of the vouchers and ownership of shares in the largest and most strategic business sectors of Russia. It was from this that the Russian oligarchs emerged.

GAZPROM

What is it? A gas company founded in 1989, owned by Russian oligarchs and the government. "Gazprom" is the combination of the first syllables of *gazovaya promyshlennost*, the Russian words for "gas industry."

The story: During the privatization of the former Soviet Union's assets, Gazprom emerged from the Ministry of Gas as a hybrid company—it makes a profit, but also advances Russia's national interests. At its peak, Gazprom was the largest natural gas company in the world, with production fields in the Arctic and western Siberia.

FSB

What is it? The FSB is Russia's new police force/spy agency and is primarily responsible for domestic civilian intelligence, border security, antiterrorism, and surveillance. *Federal'naya sluzhba bezopasnosti Rossiyskoy Federatsii* (FSB) means "Federal Security Service."

The story: Following the dissolution of the Soviet Union in 1991, the KGB was dismantled and reconstituted into several successor agencies: the Foreign Intelligence

Company founder who appeared in the most TV commercials: Dave Thomas, founder of the Wendy's hamburger chain. (He made more than 800 appearances.)

Service, the Federal Agency of Government Communications and Information, then the Ministry of Security, then the Federal Counter-Intelligence Service (FSK). In 1995 President Boris Yeltsin reorganized the FSK into the FSB and gave it the power to enter private homes and conduct intelligence services abroad. The FSB is often thought of as the equivalent of the FBI, but it is really more like a combination of the FBI and CIA. Under the direction of President Putin, the FSB is more powerful than ever, adding assassination and cyber warfare to its spy portfolio.

PUTIN

Who is he? The strongman president of the Russian Federation, elected in 2000, 2004, 2012, and 2018. Self-described as a "man's man," publicity shots of a shirtless Putin riding on horseback and fishing and hunting pitch this ex-KGB spymaster as the "Macho President."

The story: In 1999 President Boris Yeltsin named Putin, then director of the Russian spy agency FSB, to the office of prime minister of Russia. By the end of the year, Yeltsin had resigned and Putin completed Yeltsin's term. Putin was elected president in 2000 and reelected in 2004. Prevented from running for a third term because of constitutional term limits, Putin got his protégé Dmitry Medvedev elected president and got himself appointed prime minister, assuring his continued control of Russian politics. When Medvedev "retired" four years into his six-year term, Putin adroitly used Russian laws of succession to return to the presidency. Russians likened the maneuver to *rokirovka*, or castling in chess—a move in which the rook trades places with the king to save the king. Putin was reelected in 2012…and again in 2018.

FANCY BEAR

What is it? A Russian cyber espionage group that has been operating since the mid-2000s. Also known as Advanced Persistent Threat 28, Pawn Storm, Sofacy Group, Sednit, Tsar Team, and STRONTIUM.

The story: American cyber security firms CrowdStrike, SecureWorks, and ThreatConnect have reported that the Russian hackers known as Fancy Bear all work under the Russian military agency GRU and represent a constant threat to the rest of the world. Fancy Bear is said to be responsible for cyber attacks on the White House, NATO, the 2018 Olympics, and on elections in Germany, France, and the United States. The *New York Times* reported in 2016 that Russia's cyber power has proved to be "the perfect weapon: cheap, hard to see coming, hard to trace."

* * *

Directions on a bottle of One-A-Day vitamins: "Take two capsules daily."

When sunlight hits the Eiffel Tower, the metal heats up and expands, causing the tower to grow as much as 6 inches…

DON'T CALL IT THAT

"Kleenex" is probably the most famous example of a "genericized trademark"—a product so popular that people use the brand name to identify it. Here are some other brand names that have gone generic…and what, technically speaking, you should be calling them.

Epi-Pen. This preloaded syringe, trademarked by Mylan, is a life-saving device that people with severe allergies can carry with them to take in case they are accidentally exposed to a dangerous allergen. The "Epi" is short for the active ingredient, epinephrine, a hormone and neurotransmitter that occurs naturally in the body—where it's also known as adrenaline.

Aqualung. The very first commercially available piece of scuba gear was an underwater breathing apparatus patented in the 1940s by engineer Emile Gagnan and French naval officer (and future documentary filmmaker) Jacques Cousteau. The duo formed a company called La Spirotechnique to market the "Aqua-Lung," which is now often called an aqualung, but is also known by its technical name: a "demand valve" or "diving regulator." (The Jethro Tull song "Aqualung" remains unchanged.)

Freon. The chemical associated with making refrigerators and air conditioners work is the registered commercial property of Chemours, a chemical manufacturer that was spun off from DuPont in 2015. It's a refrigerant properly known as a *chlorofluorocarbon* or *dichlorodifluromethane*.

Dremel. Albert Dremel founded the Dremel Tool Company in Wisconsin in 1932, and it's now a division of the Bosch Tool Corporation. Dremel found a niche as a manufacturer of a versatile handheld motorized tool that, with a variety of attachments, could drill, grind, polish, carve, engrave, and more. Today it's commonly referred to as a dremel, but the generic term is "rotary tool."

Realtor. The terms "real estate agent" and "realtor" are often used interchangeably to describe a person who sells houses or property for a living, but there's a big difference. Not every real estate agent is a Realtor (note the capital "R"), but every Realtor is a real estate agent. "Realtor" is a trademarked word that can only be applied to members of the National Association of Realtors. When an agent calls themselves a Realtor, it's supposed to be a guarantee that they're among the best of the best in their profession.

Zeppelin. A popular form of mass travel until the *Hindenburg* explosion in 1937 ("Oh, the humanity!"), zeppelins aren't seen too much anymore, with the exception of the

…taller. (The side facing the sun expands the most, making the
tip of the tower move 7 inches away from the sun.)

Goodyear Blimp hovering over nationally televised sporting events (and Led Zeppelin on classic rock radio stations). The airborne vehicle gets its name from its inventor, Count Ferdinand von Zeppelin, who patented his designs in Germany in 1895. Only Zeppelin-designed airships are zeppelins. The rest are simply "airships."

Crock-Pot. "Slow cookers"—portable electric pots that cook food…slowly—have been around for a long time. One of the first was called the Naxon Beanery All-Purpose Cooker, sold in the 1950s by a company called Naxon Utilities. Naxon was bought out by appliance giant Rival in 1970, which rebranded the Beanery as the Crock-Pot. (A "crock" *is* a pot, so technically, "crock-pot" means "pot-pot.") The Crock-Pot has been the best-selling slow cooker ever since.

Chyron. Since the mid-1960s, most of the technology that allows TV broadcasts to lay text over moving images has been developed by a New York–based company called the ChyronHego Corporation. Their techniques were so revolutionary and innovative that the words or logos superimposed on the screen came to be known in the industry as chyrons. That's trademarked. Onscreen graphics should properly be called, well, "onscreen graphics." People in the TV industry now call words on the screen "lower third," because that's where they usually show up on the screen.

* * *

GOING IN STYLE

- Looking for an unusual way to travel to the hereafter? Trekkies can rest for eternity in a casket based on the sleek black-and-red "PhotonTorpedo" from *Star Trek II: The Wrath of Khan*. The Federation insignia is mounted on the inside, right above where the body lies.

- KISS is one of the most merchandised bands in rock 'n' roll history. Probably the weirdest piece of KISS merchandise: the Kiss Kasket. Every inch is covered in images of the members of KISS, along with band logos and other cool stuff like flames and lightning bolts.

- If you're you a graduate of one of America's 40 most popular universities, you can show that school pride forever with an officially licensed casket. Among the varieties available—in each school's official colors, of course—are "forever boxes" representing the University of Georgia, the University of Florida, and Florida State University. (If you'd rather not put such a huge investment—one costs $4,000— into the ground, school-branded urns for cremains are also available.)

Older than you thought? The first known use of "OMG" was in a letter to Winston Churchill—in 1917.

YOU'RE A WINNER *AND* A LOSER

An Academy Award is the pinnacle for any actor. All it takes is one great performance for him or her to become immortalized upon winning the iconic gold statue. Unfortunately, there's another gold statue, the Razzie (short for "raspberry"), that immortalizes the exact opposite.

SANDRA BULLOCK: In 2009 Sandra Bullock won the Best Actress Oscar for her role as a Southern foster mother in the true story *The Blind Side*. But just 24 hours earlier, she'd earned the less-prestigious Razzie for her performance in the flop *All About Steve*. This made her the first person to win both awards in the same year. Bullock was magnanimous about it, though, and made an appearance to accept her Razzie. She also accidentally walked off with the solid metal statue that's used for photo ops instead of the cheap replica that's given to winners.

EDDIE REDMAYNE: Thanks to a string of typical Oscar bait-type roles, Redmayne has been gently accused of chasing Academy Awards. And he got one, winning the Best Actor award in 2014 for his portrayal of a young Stephen Hawking in *The Theory of Everything*. Nobody ever accused him of chasing a Razzie, though. Nevertheless, for his role as Balem Abrasax in the much-maligned sci-fi flop *Jupiter Ascending*, Redmayne was awarded Worst Supporting Actor.

AL PACINO: Despite being one of the most respected actors of his generation, it took Al Pacino eight nominations to finally win an Academy Award for his role as a blind, cantankerous army officer in *Scent of a Woman* (1992). While Pacino hasn't earned an Oscar nomination since then, he's racked up two Razzies for playing himself in Adam Sandler's sibling comedy *Jack and Jill* (2011). Widely considered one of the worst movies of all time, it was nominated for a record 12 Razzies and won 10. Pacino claimed two of them: Worst Supporting Actor and Worst Screen Couple, which he shared with Sandler. In case you're wondering, the plot of the movie is that Jack, an advertising exec (played by Sandler), tries to convince his twin sister (also played by Sandler) to go out on a date with Al Pacino so that Pacino will agree to appear in a Dunkin' Donuts commercial.

HALLE BERRY: Berry made history when she became the first (and still the only) African American woman to win Best Actress for her work in 2001's *Monster's Ball*. But just four years later, she landed a Razzie for her performance in the superhero

There's a basketball court on the fifth floor of the U.S. Supreme Court Building in Washington, DC, nicknamed "the Highest Court in the Land."

bomb *Catwoman*. Compounding the insult, she didn't even get to claim the title of first African American woman to win Worst Actress at the Razzies; that went to Scary Spice for *Spice World* (all five Spice Girls actually received the award that year). However, Berry had a sense of humor about the award and even showed up to accept it…with her Oscar in one hand and the Razzie in the other.

NICOLE KIDMAN: Kidman has won a lot of awards, including the 2002 Best Actress Oscar for *The Hours*. (And she might need even more storage space after recently picking up two Emmys for HBO's *Big Little Lies*—one for acting, one for producing.) But in 2005, she and Will Ferrell starred in the critically abhorred box office bomb *Bewitched*. The filmmaker, Nora Ephron, tried to go meta by having Kidman play an actual witch who is cast in a remake of the classic 1960s sitcom. But the clever concept couldn't overcome the poor script and direction, which led to Ferrell and Kidman winning the Razzie for Worst Screen Couple.

LIZA MINNELLI: Though she was born into Hollywood royalty, Minnelli proved that her success wasn't a fluke of nepotism by winning the EGOT: an Emmy, a Golden Globe, an Oscar (Best Actress in *Cabaret*), and four Tonys. But her career hit a low point in the late 1980s when she turned her EGOT into a REGOT by winning the 1989 Worst Actress Razzie for her appearances in *Rent-a-Cop* and *Arthur 2: On the Rocks*.

MARLON BRANDO: Brando's acting prowess won him two Best Actor Oscars—for *On the Waterfront* (1954) and *The Godfather* (1972). But he must have checked his acting chops at the dock when he made *The Island of Dr. Moreau* (1996). The ill-fated shoot was covered in the documentary *Lost Soul: The Doomed Journey of Richard Stanley's Island of Dr. Moreau*, and shows Brando as being called a "monster" by the film's screenwriter, arriving on the set weighing about 300 pounds, and choosing to improvise all of his dialogue. For his role as the title character, Brando won the Worst Supporting Actor award at the 1996 Razzies.

KEVIN KLINE: Once nicknamed the "American Olivier," Academy Award winner (Best Supporting Actor in *A Fish Called Wanda*) Kevin Kline has surprisingly few acting awards in his trophy case. That could be because he's notoriously picky about the roles he chooses. But in 1999, Kline starred in the critically panned summer blockbuster *Wild Wild West* alongside Will Smith. Kline played multiple characters in that flick and, with Smith, won the Razzie for Worst Screen Couple. Kline received two other *Wild Wild West* nominations—Worst Actor for his roles of U.S. Marshall Artemus Gordon, and Worst Actress for his role as a prostitute—but he wasn't bad enough to win either.

Hello there! Prairie dogs greet each other by kissing.

HAPPY BERMUDA DAY!

We all need an excuse to celebrate. Here are a few holidays from around the world.

BERMUDA DAY. Many countries have a day named after themselves, commemorating the moment in history the country was founded or gained its independence. Canada, for example, celebrates Canada Day on July 1—the day in 1867 when three colonies merged to become the Dominion of Canada. On the tropical island paradise of Bermuda, the last Friday in May is Bermuda Day, but it doesn't commemorate freedom (Bermuda is a territory of the UK). Instead, Bermudans celebrate what's *really* important in Bermuda: summer. The holiday functions as the first official day of summer, and unofficially the first day of the year that it's socially acceptable to hang out on the beach, take the boat out, and wear Bermuda shorts.

DIA DEL MAR. Some holidays celebrate major military battles, usually victories. Bolivia's Dia Del Mar, or "Day of the Sea," is one of the few holidays that commemorates a major military defeat. In the War of the Pacific (1879–83), Bolivia and Peru fought Chile over claims to areas off South America's western coast. On March 23, 1879, Chile expelled Bolivian forces from the Port de Calama. That marked the last time the now-landlocked Bolivia had access to a seaport. Now, each March 23, thousands of Bolivians march in quiet parades. Then everybody somberly listens to nostalgic recordings of sea sounds, like ocean waves cashing on the shore, seagulls, and ship horns.

NYEPI. Most holidays involve boisterous celebration, partying, and noisemakers. Not so with Nyepi. This holiday on the Indonesian island of Bali is also called "Day of Silence"…and for good reason. Celebrants ring in the new year according to the Balinese calendar (sometime in mid to late March) without making a peep. The entirety of Bali shuts down—all lights are lowered, TVs are switched off, and nobody speaks, all so people can stay at home contemplating what they want to accomplish in the new year with no distracting noise to deter them from their quiet reflection and introspection.

BLESSED RAINY DAY. When the monsoon season ends in the tiny South Asian nation of Bhutan, it's reason to celebrate. The rainstorms ravage the country for three months a year, and once the torrential winds and rains stop, locals can get on with their lives. They begin with…more water. People simply go outside and let the last, dying waters of the monsoon purify them. Blessed Rainy Day takes place in the last week of September, but the exact hour of the cleansing ritual is the decision of astrologers. They recommend the perfect time to the Bhutanese government, and the government tells the people when to hit the showers.

More than half of the world's lakes are in Canada.

HOW WE DIE

Like it or not, death is part of life. (You probably chose "not.") If you've never lost someone close to you, you might be surprised to learn that, though every death is unique, there are three distinct stages to the end of life, and they're the same for almost everyone. How do we know? We read about it in Living with Dying: A Complete Guide for Caregivers, *by BRI stalwarts Jahnna Beecham and Katie Ortlip.*

THE LABOR OF DEATH

Nurses and hospice workers compare the process of dying to the process of giving birth. And just as women go through the different stages of labor, most of us will experience a type of labor when we die. Some people go through the labor in months, some in days, and some in hours, but there are three stages of dying: early labor, transitional labor, and active labor. Knowing what happens in each of those stages can help take some of the fear out of dying.

EARLY LABOR: 1–4 Months Before Death

I want to be alone

Whether someone is dying from a disease or simply from old age, months before, they start to lose energy and experience major fatigue. They may start taking an afternoon nap and then add a morning nap or an evening nap, or both. They begin to withdraw from the world, losing interest in outside activities and a social life, as their focus turns inward—toward themselves and what's happening to them. They may talk less, preferring to be alone.

I can't eat that

People's dietary habits will change too. The body's digestive system won't be working as well as it did before, so people stop wanting foods that are difficult to swallow or process, such as meats and vegetables. Or food may just not taste good anymore.

TRANSITIONAL LABOR: 1–2 Weeks Before Death

I'm not really hungry

The closer people get to death, the less they want to eat or drink. Not eating puts the body in a kind of starvation state, which can sound bad, but is not painful because the body releases endorphins and ketones, which are the body's natural painkillers. They cause mild euphoria and sedation, like a "runner's high."

Millionaire railroad and shipping tycoon Cornelius Vanderbilt slept in a bed whose legs were placed in dishes of salt. Reason: to ward off evil spirits.

...or thirsty

Not wanting to drink anything is also normal and may actually add to a person's comfort. As the body dehydrates, there is less fluid in the lungs and heart to cause congestion. There is also less pressure around tumors, so pain may decrease. Dehydration leads to electrolyte imbalance that causes a release of chemicals that make us sleepy and peaceful. Oftentimes loved ones, who are just trying to help, insist on feeding tubes and artificial hydration, not realizing they are interfering with the body's natural process. This can sometimes do more harm than good.

My bags are packed

In the transitional stage, people sleep a lot more, because all their energy is being used to stay alive. When awake, people may seem confused or disoriented. They may pick at the bedclothes or pluck at invisible spots in front of them. It may seem odd, but quite often people talk in travel metaphors, saying, "I have to pack" or "I've got to catch that plane" or "I have to go home." At this point they may also begin expressing heartfelt gratitude to their caregivers and loved ones as they prepare themselves for saying good-bye.

Nice to see you

It is common for them to "see" people in the room. Some see deceased relatives, others angels or Jesus, and have conversations with them. Hospice workers report that sometimes those who are dying seem to act as go-betweens, relaying messages between relatives on "the other side" and people in the room. At other times, they seem to have one foot in this world and one in another, blissfully describing that other world to those around them. One hospice nurse reports that she had a patient who told his wife, "If you could see what I see, you wouldn't be afraid."

ACTIVE LABOR: A Few Days to Hours Before Death

The end is near

In the last few days and hours, a person's breathing becomes shallow and more rapid as their body labors to die. The body's temperature can swing widely; the pulse can increase while the blood pressure decreases. In a last push, the body sends blood to its vital organs at the core of the body, which causes the person's feet and hands to become mottled and cold. A rash can form around the knees, chest, and lower back. And though the person may be asleep, their eyelids may be slightly open, because it takes too much energy to close them.

I'm ready to go

In the last hours of life, breathing can sometimes stop for up to a minute. Some people may extend their lower jaw and start *agonal*, or "guppy," breathing, which

Tip for getting a song on the radio in the 1930s: Don't use the word "do" in your lyrics. (It was considered too "suggestive.")

looks like a fish gulping for air out of water. Some, after days of sleeping, may have one last surge of energy and call out to a loved one. Even people with dementia or Alzheimer's may become lucid for a moment or two and speak very clearly for the first time in a long time—even years. One woman on hospice who had been silent for years turned to her son and said, "I'm sorry, but I can't stay any longer. I have to go now." Others search the room as if they are looking for someone in a crowd. When they finally "see" them—often in an upper corner of the room—they take their final breaths. And many get their wish of a peaceful end—they simply close their eyes, go to sleep, and are gone.

DID YOU KNOW?

Each Death Is Unique

Some hospice workers say people tend to die the way they lived. They handle the challenge of dying the way they handled other challenges in their lives.

- People who ran away from their problems tend to deny that they are dying, sometimes even up to the very end.

- People who were controlling types will orchestrate their dying down to who they want in the room, what music they want playing, and make sure it happens that way.

- Often, the protective mother will not die with her children in the room. She'll let them sit by the bedside for 24 hours, and in the few minutes that they are outside the room, she'll choose to die.

- If a person has been a fighter their entire life, challenging everyone and everything, they will probably go out fighting.

---

*   *   *

ALCOHOL(IC) ORIGINS

- There's an old expression in the South to describe someone who is extremely intoxicated: "As drunk as Cooter Brown." Who's Cooter Brown? Legend has it he lived right along the Mason-Dixon Line when the Civil War broke out in 1861. He had family in the North and the South, and he didn't want to take a side…nor did he want to fight for either side. So, Cooter Brown got too drunk to get drafted—day in and day out for the entirety of the war.

- Alcoholic drinks like vodka and whiskey are sometimes called "spirits." That's because in Europe in the Middle Ages, some people thought that evil spirits lived in the alcohol, and that they were the reason why people acted so weird when they drank. These same people believed that evil spirits hated the sound of bells, so in an attempt to neutralize the demons, they'd "clink" glasses together.

Strongest organism on Earth? Gonorrhea. The bacteria can pull 100,000 times its own body weight.

FOOD THAT'S ART & ART THAT'S FOOD

On page 259 we told you about Iowa's "Butter Cow Lady." Here are some other folks who make food the medium, or the subject, of their art.

Artist: Robin Antar, a New York artist

Medium: Stone

Food for Thought: Remember Andy Warhol's famous paintings of Campbell's soup cans? Antar does the same kind of thing, but in stone. She carves realistic soda cans, Heinz Ketchup and other condiment bottles, bags of Oreo cookies, hot dogs, hamburgers with fries, bagels with lox, out of various kinds of stones. (She also sculpts non-food items, such as shoes, pencils, boxing gloves, flowers, tubes of toothpaste, and abstract pieces as well.) "I take a raw stone most people think of as trash and express my emotions and feelings," she says.

Artist: Lucy Sparrow, a British artist working in New York

Medium: Stuffed felt

Food for Thought: Sparrow has found a unique way to call attention to the fact that gentrification and rising rents are threatening to push the ubiquitous corner grocery stores known as *bodegas* out of Manhattan. In 2017 she rented a space in the city's Meatpacking District and turned it into a bodega called "8 'till late." Only in this store everything, from the cereal to the bologna, fresh vegetables, liquor, cigarettes, and even the cash register, was made by her out of stuffed felt—more than 9,000 items in all. Every piece was for sale to the public, at reasonable prices. The felt cigarette lighters sold for $15, and a carton of Minute Maid orange juice cost $60. The exhibit was so popular that she had to close the exhibit for a few days in mid-run, just to restock the shelves. The new "merchandise" sold just as quickly; the exhibit ended nine days early because there was nothing left on the shelves.

> In this store everything, from the cereal to the bologna, fresh vegetables, liquor, cigarettes, and even the cash register, was made by her out of stuffed felt.

Artist: Amelia Fais Harnas, a New York artist

Medium: Wine and tablecloths—she makes "wine stain art"

Food for Thought: Harnas, who describes herself as an "artist who is very happy to nerd out and play scientist," hit on the idea of painting portraits on tablecloths using

Comedian Lucille Ball swore she picked up coded radio transmissions from Japanese spies in the fillings of her teeth during World War II.

wine as the "paint" in 2010. She uses a technique called batik in which she treats parts of the tablecloth with wax to prevent the wine from soaking into the fabric where she doesn't want it. "I am particularly intrigued by the challenge of trying to control the unpredictable nature of wine bleeding through fabric in order to channel the equally imprecise nature of a person's character," she says.

Artist: Song Dong, an artist who lives in China

Medium: Cookies, in art installations he calls "Eating the City"

> "When we are eating the city we are using our desire to taste it, but at the same time we are demolishing the city and turning it into a ruin."

Food for Thought: Song uses his art to call attention to the rapid pace of change in China, in which old sections of Beijing and other cities are destroyed and cleared to make way for new buildings. He builds urban skylines by piling up thousands of cookies to make skyscrapers, sports stadiums, and other city features, and then invites the public to eat them. "My city [is] tempting and delicious," he explained at a London exhibit in 2011. "When we are eating the city we are using our desire to taste it, but at the same time we are demolishing the city and turning it into a ruin."

Artist: Heide Hatry, a German-born artist who divides her time between Berlin and New York

Medium: The body parts of food animals. She uses the parts that have no economic value and are usually thrown away—pig ears, duck beaks, chicken combs, fish heads and tails, etc.

Food for Thought: In her "Not a Rose" series of photographs, Hatry, who was raised on a farm in Germany, explores "the moral, ethical, and political dimensions of meat production and consumption" by combining the animal parts to create "images of beautiful flowers from animal parts that most of us would find impossible to consume (even though we eat the flesh of those very same animals…without a thought)." She has published her deceptively realistic photographs in a coffee table book called Not a Rose that, as long as you don't read the text, is virtually indistinguishable from other coffee table books about flowers. *New York Times* columnist David Streitfeld writes that the photos push viewers "into a realm where we question our relationship with beauty, animals and dinner."

* * *

"Cooking is an art, but you eat it too." —**Marcella Hazan**

By any other name: The inventor of snowboarding almost called the sport "snurfing."

HORSE JOKES

Heard the one about the pony with the sore throat?
He was a little hoarse. (Wait. It gets worse.)

Q: What do you call an Amish guy with his hand in a horse's mouth?
A: A mechanic.

Q: Why can't horses dance?
A: Because they have two left feet.

Q: Why was the horse from Kentucky so generous to his horse friends?
A: Southern horspitality.

A horse with a bandage on its head limps into a bar. He orders a glass of champagne, a brandy, and two beers. He downs the lot and says to the bartender: "I really shouldn't be drinking with what I've got." The bartender says, "Why, what have you got?" The horse says, "About $2 and a carrot."

Q: When does a horse talk?
A: Whinny wants to.

Q: How to you make a horse a sandwich?
A: With thoroughbred.

Q: What would you name a horse with no legs?
A: Flattery, because it'll get you nowhere.

A horse walks into a bar. "Hey!" yells the bartender. "Yes please!" says the horse.

Q: What do you call a horse popularity contest?
A: A gallop poll.

Q: Why did the horse eat with its mouth open?
A: Bad stable manners.

A racehorse owner's best horse gets sick, so he takes him to the vet. Once the vet has finished his examination, the owner anxiously asks him, "Will I be able to race him again?" The vet replies, "Of course! And you'll probably beat him, too!"

Q: What did the horse say when it fell down?
A: "I've fallen and I can't giddyup!"

Q: What did the momma horse say to the baby horse?
A: It's pasture bedtime.

Q: What do you call a horse wearing Venetian blinds?
A: A zebra.

Q: Why was the racehorse named Strawberry Ice?
A: Because he's a sherbet.

Q: Which side of a horse has more hair?
A: The outside.

Just as human babies suck their thumbs, baby elephants comfort themselves by sucking their trunks.

THAT'S VERY COOL

The term cryonics *is often used interchangeably with* cryogenics, *but they're very different. Cryogenics is the study of how materials behave when subjected to extremely low temperatures, usually for industrial applications. Cryonics is the science of freezing biological tissue, and it usually refers to the process of freezing dead bodies with the hope of reanimating them later when science finds a cure for whatever killed them. (That led to a lot of confusion in January 2018 when the ice-cream manufacturer Dippin' Dots announced that it was starting a cryogenics company.) Here's everything you need to know about the exciting world of cryonics.*

DEEP FREEZE

Thinking of freezing your body when you die so you can get thawed out later and live in the future? The cryonics process is complicated (and expensive). To be properly preserved, a body must reach an internal temperature of −320°F. And for the process to work correctly, a corpse must be treated by cryonics specialists *immediately* after death. The deceased must be declared legally dead before technicians can start freezing, but they must start within two minutes of the heart stopping to meet ideal conditions. If 15 minutes pass, it's pointless, because irreversible brain death and damage have set in. If you've passed those hurdles, here's what's next:

❇ First, the body of the departed is packed in a box full of ice (or dry ice). Then it's injected with anticoagulants, which prevent the blood from clotting en route to the cryonics facility.

❇ Once the body arrives at the storage facility, it's placed in a bath of extremely cold chemicals that slowly and carefully chill the body to an internal temperature of 33°F.

❇ At that point, the blood is drained and is replaced with an injected solution that preserves organs. It consists mostly of an antifreezing substance that prevents the water in the body from turning into ice crystals, which would lead to permanent and unfixable cell damage.

❇ The body is then placed in an ice bath, where it will gradually cool down to −202°F.

❇ Then the body goes to its resting place for the next few years (or centuries): a coffinlike box that is placed into a vacuum flask called a *dewar*. (It looks like a man-sized propane tank.) The body is suspended, upright, floating in liquid nitrogen set permanently to a temperature of −320°F.

Math trick: Pick a three-digit number. Repeat the digits to form a number with six digits. It will be evenly divisible by 7, 11, and 13.

THE ICEMEN COMETH

While science hasn't yet come up with a cure for death, it has mastered the fine art of freezing a dead body. Still, as of 2018, fewer than 500 people around the world have had their bodies preserved via the method described above.

❉ First person to have themselves cryopreserved: a World War I veteran and psychology professor named James Bedford. He died of kidney cancer at age 73 in 1967, and was frozen immediately thereafter. Bedford has been in his dewar ever since…except for a few minutes in 1991 when he had his preservation liquids changed.

❉ Bedford's corpse awaits rebirth at Alcor Life Extension Foundation, a cryonics company in Arizona that is one of only four human freezing facilities in the world. The others: Alcor's second facility in Portugal, one called KrioRus in Russia, and the Cryonics Institute in Michigan.

❉ In addition to Bedford, the Arizona branch of Alcor houses about 150 human-cicles, among them Baseball Hall of Famer Ted Williams.

❉ The Cryonics Institute houses 160 patients, but claims to have a list of 2,000 people who've signed up to be frozen upon their deaths.

❉ *Family Guy* creator and star Seth MacFarlane has reportedly arranged for his body to be frozen, eventually. So has talk show host Larry King. Paris Hilton and *American Idol* judge Simon Cowell have both publicly said they're thinking about getting iced when they die.

❉ Muhammad Ali looked into it in the 1980s, but ultimately decided against it and was buried in the traditional way when he died in 2016.

ANOTHER PART OF THE STORY

❉ How far has science come on reanimating dead organs? Not very. Frozen hearts and kidneys have never been successfully transplanted.

❉ All cryonics facilities will accommodate a customer's wish to have just their heads or brains frozen, but that presents a different technological challenge. Not only will scientists have to figure out how to reanimate dead tissue, but they'll have to figure out how to jump-start a brain, and then find a way to implant it into a fresh (and brainless) human body. Scientists have actually made some head-way on this, believe it or not. In 2016 Robert McIntyre of the Massachusetts Institute of Technology became the first person to freeze and then revive a mammalian brain. He used a rabbit's, and after he brought the brain back to life, it was found to have all of its membranes, cellular structures, and synapses intact.

The snow carnival scheduled for May 1, 1953, in Sheridan, Wyoming, had to be canceled. Reason: too much snow.

❄ So how much does this kind of thing cost? It varies by location. Alcor charges $200,000 for a whole body, KrioRus charges $38,000, and the Cryonics Institute has a steal of a deal at $35,000. (Freezing just the head costs about half as much, on average.)

❄ Those are the hows, but how about when? Exactly when will the frozen dead walk among the living? According to Cryonics Institute president Dennis Kowalski…we don't know. "Cryonically bringing someone back to life should definitely be doable in 100 years, but it could be as soon as ten," he said in 2018. Kowalski added that while cryonics pioneers like his company are responsible for preserving the dead, it's up to modern medicine to revive them.

DISNEY'S FROZEN

So, is Walt Disney—or just his head—really hanging out in some liquid nitrogen–filled tank somewhere? Short answer: No. Long answer: Disney died in 1966 at age 65, just a month after doctors removed a cancerous tumor on his left lung, but the disease had spread throughout his body. According to news reports, he was cremated two days after his death and buried at Forest Lawn Cemetery outside Los Angeles. In 1972 Bob Nelson, president of the Cryonics Society of California, mentioned in an interview that while Disney was not frozen, he *had* expressed interest in the technology, but died before he could make a decision or sign a letter of intent to have his corpse frozen. Oddly, though, two weeks after Disney died, Nelson's organization froze its first body. The timing led to the notorious urban legend that Walt Disney was frozen. "If Disney had been the first," Nelson later said, "it would have made headlines around the world…and been a real shot in the arm for cryonics."

* * *

IT'S ALL ABOUT…YOU

"Always be a first-rate version of yourself, instead of a second-rate version of somebody else."
—Judy Garland

"Be true to your work, your word, and your friend."
—John Boyle O'Reilly

"Let yourself be drawn by the stronger pull of that which you truly love."
—Rumi

Ounce for ounce, grasshoppers have four times as much calcium and twice as much iron as beef.

MOUTHING OFF

MORE STRANGE CELEBRITIES

"I basically love anything that comes in a hot dog bun... except hot dogs."

—Gwyneth Paltrow

"I'M USING MY BRAIN FOR THE FIRST TIME IN A LONG TIME."

—Victoria Beckham

"[I] DON'T READ BOOKS, I ONLY READ MINDS."

—Liam Gallagher, when asked about his favorite book

"People are always like, 'Why did you get a monkey?' If you could get a monkey, well, you would get a f***ing monkey, too! Monkeys are awesome."

—Justin Bieber

"Do I have a large frog in my hair? I have the sensation that something is eating my brain."

—Joaquin Phoenix

"I feel like this year is really about, like, the year of realizing stuff. And everyone around me, we're all just, like, realizing things."

—Kylie Jenner

"I'm thinking of buying a monkey. Then I think, 'Why stop at one?' I don't like being limited in that way. Therefore, I'm considering a platoon of monkeys, so that people will look at me and see how mellow and well-adjusted I am compared to these monkeys throwing feces around."

—Robert Downey Jr.

"I fed [my 11-month-old son] Bear a tiny bit of veggies...from my mouth to his. It's his favorite, and mine. He literally crawls across the room to attack my mouth if I'm eating."

—Alicia Silverstone

"What if we spelled 'people' like this: 'peepole.' That would be funny I think."

—Kim Kardashian

GETTING IN ON THE ACTION (FIGURES)

Action figures are big business. But for every blockbuster success like Star Wars action figures or He-Man action figures, there are plenty of failures, such as these.

THE WALTONS

If the majority of a toy company's customers are already kids—who will eventually outgrow its products—how does the company acquire future consumers? By pitching products to even *younger* kids. That's a solid marketing plan, but the Mego Corportion picked the wrong toy line to execute it with. In 1976 the company secured the rights to a line of action figures based on the popular squeaky-clean family TV show *The Waltons*. But just because the TV series about a Depression-era mountain family was appropriate for kids didn't mean that kids actually liked the show...or even watched it. Apparently they didn't. Mego's line of 8-inch-tall dolls of John-Boy Walton and his kin was a total failure and was out of stores within a year.

ALIEN

Kenner Products made a lot of money in the late 1970s, when they produced the original *Star Wars* toys and action figures. So why not try a second time? In 1979 the company was offered the toy license for another science-fiction movie, and they quickly signed on. The movie: Ridley Scott's *Alien*, a massive hit and one of the top-grossing (and grossest) movies of the year. The only problem was that it was a disturbing, scary, R-rated horror movie. Not many kids were even allowed to see *Alien*, and most of those that did weren't allowed to have the centerpiece of the *Alien* toy line—an 18-inch-tall "Xenomorph," the film's villainous, goo-dripping, gigantic, terrifying alien monster. So many parents' groups complained about the toy being inappropriate for kids that Kenner had to pull the toy out of stores. Most of the rest of the *Alien* line remained on store shelves, untouched.

KOJAK

Kojak was one of many gritty 1970s cop shows. It starred bald, middle-aged Telly Savalas as a gruff, lollipop-sucking detective who solved grisly crimes. In other words, *Kojak* wasn't a kids' show. But a company called Excel Toy Corporation, which made dolls of Wild West figures like Annie Oakley and Jesse James, decided to get into the

A best-selling book in 1919, *The Young Visiters,* was written by a nine-year-old English girl named Daisy Ashford. (She misspelled the word "Visitors" in the title.)

pop culture toy market with a Kojak doll. The packaging boasted "realistic action" and a "removable costume" (so kids could see what Kojak looked like naked). It also came with a Kojak accessory (and choking hazard): tiny lollipops, just like the ones Kojak sucked on in the show. Who loves ya, baby? As far as these toys went, not many.

CAPTAIN AND TENNILLE

While 1970s kids were listening to the music of teen idols such as David Cassidy, Leif Garrett, and the Bay City Rollers, their parents were listening to smooth, easy-listening, soft rock acts like the Captain and Tennille, who sang about long-term relationships and lovemaking in "Love Will Keep Us Together" and "Do That to Me One More Time." The married, middle-aged "Captain" (real name: Daryl Dragon) and Toni Tennille didn't have much appeal to kids. Nevertheless, in 1977 the Mego Corporation released Captain and Tennille dolls as a tie-in with their TV variety show. Like the TV series, these toys disappeared quickly.

MANIMAL

Manimal is one of the most legendary flops in TV history. Debuting in 1983, this NBC action-adventure series was about an international playboy named Dr. Jonathan Chase who could turn, at will, into any animal on the planet. But he usually turned into either a hawk or a panther, probably because in those days "morphing" footage was expensive to make. The combination of poor reviews and the fact that it aired opposite CBS's extremely popular *Dallas* killed *Manimal*—it was canceled after eight episodes. Fleetwood Toys' line of *Manimal* merchandise didn't do very well either. Even though transforming technology was available (transforming toys such as Transformers were already around) there was no "action" in the *Manimal* action figures. Fleetwood released three unposable, hard plastic figures of animals—a cobra, a lion, and a panther—with slightly human features and *Manimal* branding on the package.

DOCTORS WITHOUT BORDERS

The French humanitarian organization is also known as *Medecins sans Frontieres*, and its army of volunteer doctors, nurses, and other personnel bravely head into war zones and areas affected by disaster to provide free medical services to those in need. That's more heroic than any superhero, so it's somewhat logical to produce action figures based on these good doctors. But what child would want to play doctor with action figures? French company Berchet quickly flatlined with its Medecins sans Frontieres line of toys, which included doctors and patients—one of whom was a sick, emaciated little boy named "Samba the Dying African." Really.

Spies in ancient Rome used carrier pigeons to deliver intelligence.

THE CONTRONYMS QUIZ

Contronyms (also called autoantonyms) are words that have two meanings…
which are the complete opposite of one another. Can you match the word or
phrase to its two opposing meanings? The answers are on page 501.

1. Cleave

2. Bolt

3. Fine

4. Handicap

5. Wind up

6. Blunt

7. Left

8. Game

9. Rent

10. Flog

11. Sanction

12. Trim

13. Bill

14. Fix

15. Bound

16. Peer

17. Weather

18. Quantum

19. Fast

20. Either

21. Buckle

22. Custom

23. Skin

24. Screen

25. Refrain

26. Put out

a) Barely satisfactory…and the best of the best

b) Restrained…and to jump away

c) Gone…and remaining

d) A social equal…and a member of the upper class or nobility

e) Dull (in an object)…and sharp (in words)

f) The regular or expected…and the very special

g) Bring together…and separate

h) To fasten…and collapse

i) To begin…and end

j) Paper money…and an invoice

k) To endure…and wear away

l) Firmly secure…and quickly move away

m) To display…and block

n) To authorize…and punish

o) To cover with a fine layer…and to remove a fine layer

p) A problem…and a solution

q) To remove pieces of…and add onto

r) To make…and to end

s) Quick…and immovable

t) To borrow…and loan out

u) To stop…and to repeat

v) Extremely small…and extremely large

w) One or the other…or both

x) A physical or mental disadvantage…and an advantage (in sports)

y) Ready, willing, and able…and nonfunctional

z) Relentlessly promote…and relentlessly punish

The fish known as the "sole" got its name because of its flattened appearance,
which makes it look like a sandal—*solea* in Latin.

EXTREME RECYCLING: BATHROOM EDITION

Recycling isn't just for paper, bottles, and cans anymore. Here's a look at a few folks who've come up with ideas for recycling just about everything. (Some people are going to miss the good old days...)

Recyclers: Scientists from the University of the Netherlands and the University of Amsterdam

Recycling: Used toilet paper, into electricity

Details: Western European countries treat their sewage differently than American wastewater treatment facilities do. They filter out the toilet paper and dispose of it separately, usually by drying it out and burning it. The heat produced is used to generate a small amount of electricity. But these scientists, led by Els van der Roest, have devised an improved process for generating more electricity from the toilet paper. They "gasify" the paper by feeding it into a chamber and heating it to over 1,000°F. The heat converts the paper into to ash, tar, and various gases, including methane, an odorless flammable gas.

> **If all the toilet paper in Amsterdam were converted to electricity using the process, enough energy would be generated to power 6,400 homes.**

The gases are then fed into solid-oxide fuel cells, which use chemical reactions to convert the methane into electricity. The process generates up to three times as much electricity as when the toilet paper is burned, making it about as efficient as a natural gas power plant. But it produces only about one-sixth the amount of greenhouse gases of a coal-fired power plant. The researchers estimate that if all the toilet paper in Amsterdam were converted to electricity using the process, enough energy would be generated to power 6,400 homes. (A different pilot project in the Dutch city of Alkmaar converts the toilet paper into cellulose pellets that can be added to asphalt and used to pave roads.)

Recyclers: The Park Spark Project

Recycling: Dog poop, into light

Details: After a dog does its business, that "business" releases methane gas as it biodegrades. Normally the methane escapes into the air, but the Park Spark Project, which has been installed in a dog park in Cambridge, Massachusetts, traps the methane and uses it to power a gas street lamp. Dog owners deposit the waste into a

The fictional character Cyrano de Bergerac was inspired by a real person, the French novelist Savinien de Cyrano de Bergerac (1619–1655).

large fiberglass tank called a "bio-digester" connected to the lamp, then turn a wheel on the tank to mix the new waste with the poop that's already in there. This helps to release the methane, which flows through a pipe to the lamp, where it powers an "eternal flame."

Recyclers: Sanitation and Health Rights in India, a group that builds blocks of public toilets in communities that don't have them already

Recycling: Human waste, into "safe, well-maintained and hygienic toilets"

Details: The waste that's collected in the toilets is fed into a bio-digester, and the methane that's created by the waste is used to power a pump that draws water from a well. The water is then filtered, bottled, and sold to the public for about 2¢ a gallon. The income generated pays about half the cost of maintaining the toilets and keeping them clean, increasing the likelihood that the community will put them to use.

Recyclers: GENeco, a wastewater treatment company in Bristol, England

Recycling: Household sewage and organic waste, into bus fuel

> If you want to take a ride on the "Poo Bus," as it's affectionately known, look for the one decorated with a giant mural of people sitting on toilets.

Details: GENeco collects the methane produced by decaying sewage and food waste in its wastewater plant and uses it to power its "Bio-Bus," a city bus converted to run on natural gas. The bus can travel 185 miles on a single tank, and it produces considerably less air pollution than a bus powered by fossil fuels. If you visit Bristol and want to take a ride on the "Poo Bus," as it's affectionately known, it won't be hard to find: look for the one decorated with a giant mural of people sitting on toilets, and the caption, "This GENeco Bio-Bus is powered by your waste for a sustainable future." The bus serves Bristol's Number 2 bus route. (Get it? Number 2!)

Recyclers: Norrebro Bryghus, a Danish brewery

Recycling: Urine, into what the BBC says could be "the ultimate sustainable hipster beer"

Details: In 2015 the brewery collected 50,000 liters (about 13,200 gallons) of urine from the urinals at the Roskilde Festival, northern Europe's largest music festival, held each summer in Roskilde, Denmark. They used the urine to fertilize fields where barley is grown, instead of using manure or chemical fertilizers. Then they used the barley to brew 60,000 bottles' worth of a special pilsner beer called Pisner.

"When the news that we had started brewing the Pisner came out, a lot of people thought we were filtering the urine to put it directly in the beer and we had

a good laugh about that," Henrik Vang, Norrebro Bryghus's chief executive, told the BBC. The brewery sells Pisner at the Roskilde Festival, where, presumably, it will be "beercycled" into the next batch of Pisner.

Recyclers: A research team at the University of Ghent, in Belgium

Recycling: Urine, into fertilizer, drinking water...and more beer

Details: In 2016 the researchers developed a machine that uses solar energy and a special filter membrane to process the urine. The pee is heated in a boiler using only sunlight, then it is forced through the membrane to filter out potassium, nitrogen, phosphorus, and other nutrients. The nutrients

> "We call it 'from sewer to brewer.'"

are collected for use as fertilizer, and the filtered water that's left over is safe to drink. The researchers hope to introduce the technology in developing countries where both fertilizer and safe drinking water are hard to come by. And in a nod to the Roskilde Festival, someone came up with the idea of using the recovered water to brew a batch of beer. "We call it 'from sewer to brewer,'" University of Ghent researcher Sebastiaan Derese told Reuters.

* * *

A STASH OF 'STACHE JOKES

Q: What did Sherlock say when his crime-fighting partner grew a mustache?
A: "Watson your face?"

Q: Where do mustaches go for a drink?
A: To the handle bar.

Did you hear about the guy who tried to grow a mustache? He didn't like how it felt at first, but then it started to grow on him.

Q: What has two beards and rocks?
A: ZZ Top.

This guy told everyone on the internet that he had a beard, but then he posted a picture of himself, and he was totally clean-cut. What a bald-faced liar!

We had one more mustache joke to tell you...but we had to shave it for later.

...from people on *The Bachelor* and *The Bachelorette* combined.

KING OTTO THE CRAZY

*You've heard of Ivan the Terrible, but have you heard
of Carlota, the Wench of Queluz? More rulers
with odd nicknames are on page 63.*

MICHAEL the CAULKER (1015–1042)

Today we think of caulk as the stuff that carpenters put around doors and windows to keep the cold air out (or in), but for much of history the term referred to the materials that made a ship's hull watertight. Michael gets his nickname because his father, Stephen, started out as a caulker of ships in the Byzantine Empire. (The Byzantine Empire is what the Eastern Roman Empire was called after the western half of the Roman Empire collapsed in 474). Stephen rose from that lowly position to become an admiral, and then married Maria, the sister of Emperor Michael IV.

Michael the Caulker was the product of Stephen and Maria's union, and he became a favorite of the emperor's wife, Zoe. The emperor had no children, so Zoe maneuvered to have Michael named heir to the throne. When the emperor died in 1041, Michael succeeded him as Michael V. He reigned for four months with Zoe as his co-emperor…and then he tried to banish her to the island of Prinkipo and rule the empire by himself. He found out the hard way that she was a lot more popular than he was: An angry mob surrounded the palace and forced him to restore her to power. The next day, Michael was deposed. He fled to a monastery and took vows to become a monk in an attempt to save himself, but it didn't do any good. He was captured, blinded, and castrated by an angry mob. He died a few months later.

CARLOTA, the WENCH of QUELUZ (1775–1830)

Carlota, the eldest daughter of King Charles IV of Spain, was only 10 years old when her parents arranged her marriage to her 18-year-old cousin, Prince John, the infante of Portugal, in 1785.

In 1799 John became the de facto ruler of Portugal when his mother, Queen Maria, was incapacitated by mental illness. Once he was in charge, Carlota tried to meddle in state affairs and slant the government's policies in favor of Spain. When Prince John resisted, she conspired to have him declared insane as well, so that she could rule the country in his place. But the plot was discovered and Carlota was banished to the Queluz palace (the source of her nickname) while Prince John lived in another palace.

You've got company: There are roughly 10 times as many
bacterial cells in your body as there are human cells.

Two years later, in 1807, Napoleon Bonaparte invaded Portugal and the royal family, Carlota included, fled to Brazil, then a Portuguese colony. There, Carlota schemed with Spanish officials and South American nationalists to create a kingdom of her own, either by carving out territory from what is now Argentina and Uruguay, or by overthrowing Prince John and becoming queen of Brazil. That plot failed too.

Napoleon fell from power in 1815, and in 1821 John returned home to Portugal. While he'd been away, liberal reformers had passed a new constitution limiting the king's powers, a situation that John accepted but that Carlota was determined to reverse. This time she schemed with her son, Prince Miguel, in two separate plots to depose King John and restore an absolute monarchy with Miguel as king, but John foiled these conspiracies as well. When Queen Carlota was caught plotting yet again to overthrow her husband, he finally had enough. Carlota was placed under house arrest in Queluz palace. She was still confined there when she died, possibly by suicide, in 1830.

OTTO the CRAZY (1848–1916)

Many kings and queens have battled mental illness; it's perhaps one of the unfortunate consequences of so many marriages between royal cousins. King Otto of Bavaria is an unusual example of a king who was so insane that he was never allowed to rule his kingdom at all. He was the younger brother of Mad King Ludwig (1845–1886), who ruled from 1864 to 1886. Ludwig's erratic behavior and penchant for squandering his family fortune building one castle after another (including Neuschwanstein, the inspiration for the castles in Disney theme parks) led the Bavarian government to depose him in 1886. He and his personal physician drowned under mysterious circumstances three days later.

Crazy Otto was Mad Ludwig's successor, but because of his mental illness, the Bavarian government appointed his uncle, Prince Luitpold, to rule in his name as regent until Otto was well enough to take the throne. That day never came: 26 years later, he was deposed in favor of a cousin who became King Ludwig III in 1913. Otto died three years later. Today historians can only guess at the source of his mental illness. It may have been post-traumatic stress disorder caused by his fighting in both the Austro-Prussian War of 1866 and the Franco-Prussian War of 1871. It's also possible that his condition was caused by having contracted syphilis, or that he was schizophrenic.

Odds of a perfect deal in bridge (all four players receive a complete suit):
1 in 2,235,197,406,895,366,368,301,559,999.

LARGEST AMERICAN BUSINESS LAYOFFS

These mega-companies may specialize in manufacturing, retail, and finance…but they're also industry leaders in handing out pink slips.

IBM

Big Blue's long list of business innovations is proof that they're one of the most important tech companies ever. The ATM, the PC, the floppy disk, the hard disk drive, the magnetic strip card, and the bar code are just a few of them. But the company's decision *not* to build a proprietary operating system or microprocessor in the early 1980s gave Microsoft and Intel free reign to grow, and that proved nearly fatal for IBM. The PC revolution quickly rendered IBM's core business of selling mainframe computers obsolete. By 1992, it was a bloated company of 400,000 that posted a loss of $8.1 billion. In 1993, for the first time in its history, IBM looked outside the company to hire a new CEO, Louis Gerstner. Gerstner immediately initiated the company's first-ever layoffs and axed 60,000 employees. This is still the American record for the most layoffs at one time. Now, more than a century after its founding, IBM is thriving as a smarter, leaner company…but it came at a huge cost.

CITIGROUP

The Great Recession of 2008 resulted in the worst economic crisis since the Great Depression and it spared very few, including the financial giants responsible for causing it. In November 2008, with the financial collapse of American business looking frighteningly imminent, in November, Citigroup announced that it was laying off more than 50,000 employees. Combined with previous layoffs at the start of the crisis, the financial giant eliminated nearly 15 percent of its workforce, while its stock price plummeted to less than $1 per share. To prevent further damage to the global economy, the U.S. government deemed Citigroup "too big to fail" and bailed it out with tens of billions of taxpayer dollars.

SEARS ROEBUCK

Sears was once America's largest retailer, but few people born after the 1990s even recognize the brand today. Sears's retail troubles go back to 1993. That was the year the company ended production of its famous "Wish Book"—the phone book–sized catalog that was a staple of American homes. It was also the year the company laid

Collectively, commuters in Los Angeles drive 300 million miles a day, the equivalent of driving to the Moon and back more than 600 times.

off 50,000 employees in an attempt to stave off competition from companies like Walmart. It didn't work. In 2004, Sears underwent a merger with K-Mart, which had filed for bankruptcy two years prior to the purchase. Since 2006, Sears has gone from more than 3,000 stores to fewer than 600.

GENERAL MOTORS

For years, American car companies refused to adapt to changing consumer needs and international competition. And when the Great Recession hit in 2008, the curtain nearly closed on America's automobile industry. In order to qualify for a $50 billion government bailout, in 2009 GM underwent a massive restructuring that resulted in the elimination of approximately a third of its brands and the layoffs of 47,000 employees, including 35 percent of its executives. The government's unprecedented investment in GM was a success: by 2010, the company paid back its loan, and in 2013, the federal government sold off the rest of its GM stock. While the loss of jobs was tremendous, many economists feel it was inevitable, because without the bailout, the company would not have survived.

AT&T

In 1996 AT&T announced its shocking decision to lay off 40,000 employees. The reason it was so shocking: unlike the rest of the companies on this list, AT&T was doing extremely well at the time. But the layoffs were part of the company's plan to divide its telecommunications equipment, communication services, and computer divisions into separate companies. Wall Street cheered the news as AT&T's stock went up $2.63 per share in reaction to the announcement. (AT&T's employees did not have the same reaction.)

BOEING

The 9/11 attacks forever changed the aviation industry. Air travel was limited, planes were grounded, airport security became super-tight, and people weren't flying. Boeing, which built the four planes that were hijacked by al Qaeda terrorists, was jolted immediately. Within a month of the attacks, America's largest aerospace business laid off 31,000 workers—a third of the company. Boeing wasn't alone. The attacks caused nearly every major airline to dismiss at least 10,000 employees, and the entire industry had to be bailed out by the federal government at the cost of $15 billion.

STRANGE CRIME: SELFIE-INCRIMINATION

These days, it's not enough to just accomplish a goal. People need to know about it!
That's where selfies come in handy. Hold the phone at arm's length, snap the pic,
and hit the "share" button. However, if your goal was achieved by
breaking the law, you might want to skip that last part.

ONE CLICK TOO MANY

Brazilian convict Brayan Bremer was one of over 100 inmates who escaped from prison during a 2017 riot. He's also the only one who stopped long enough to take a photo of himself and a fellow escapee giving a thumbs-up. The clicks he heard shortly after posting the selfie on Facebook weren't "likes," they were handcuffs.

OUTLAW IN-LAW

When Amanda Taylor's husband, Rex, hanged himself in 2014, she blamed her father-in-law, Charles Taylor. After all, Rex was strung out on drugs and it was Charles who had introduced his son to drug use when he was still a teen. The hate and anger built up for months until Amanda released it by stabbing her 59-year-old father-in-law in the chest with a knife so long that she claimed she barely got any blood on her clothes. The knife, however, dripped with it. How do we know? From the selfie she took next to her father-in-law's dead body. "I was just really excited," Amanda said later, "and I was like hey, I'm gonna take a picture so I can post it and show everyone." The photo earned her life in prison.

BUT...WHY?

There are some things you just shouldn't do in Thailand. That's what American tourists Joseph Dasilva, 38, and Travis Dasilva, 36, discovered when they took a selfie in front of Bangkok's Temple of the Dawn. They were arrested at the Bangkok airport while trying to board a flight to the United States, fined 5,000 baht ($154), and detained awaiting possible charges of violating Thailand's Computer Crime Act. If that seems harsh, consider that the photo was posted to their Instagram account: traveling_butts. Yes, it was a photo of their bare bottoms. The act of exposing themselves at a religious site in this conservative country could have resulted in 12 years in prison. And a second photo they'd posted, taken at another Thai temple, left no ifs, ands...or butts...about their guilt. (Lucky for them, the charges were dropped.)

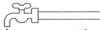

When riding in a train along a standard railroad track with 39-foot rails,
the number of rail-clicks you hear...

NOTE TO SELF

If you plan to strangle your friend with a belt, you probably shouldn't post a photo of yourself wearing the murder weapon around your waist. Brittney Gargol, 18, probably had no idea just what a killer night out she was about to have with her 21-year-old friend Cheyenne Rose Antoine. The two young Canadians got dolled up, took a few selfies (including the one with the belt), and then went to a bar in Saskatoon. Apparently, they got pretty drunk, got into an argument, and then...off came Cheyenne's belt. Unfortunately for Cheyenne, she tossed out the belt with the body when she dumped her BFF on the side of a road south of town. Though she posted "Where are you? Haven't heard from you. Hope you made it home safe" on Brittney's Facebook page to cover her tracks, an anonymous source tipped off police. That left Cheyenne with few options. She pretended she couldn't remember the crime, pleaded guilty to manslaughter, and got away with a sentence of seven years in jail.

JUST...DON'T DO IT

London drug dealer Junior Francis seems to like the Nike slogan "Just Do It." Here's what he did: First, he bullied his way into a thriving heroin and money-laundering business. Next, he took selfies showing off huge stacks of ill-gotten bills, which he then posted to Instagram. (He was wearing a "Just Do It" T-shirt.) What kind of feedback did the 33-year-old get? Along with thanks from the police for making their job easier, Francis got six years and eight months in prison. But Detective Constable Matthew Cook got the last words: "He was ultimately undone by his vanity."

KINGS OF SELFIE-DUMB

In 2015 two young men wearing black stocking caps used an iPad to video themselves fanning out $5,000 worth of hundreds at a Burger King in Houston, Texas. Then they went to Starbucks to continue the buzz by posting the video online. Too bad they didn't understand how iCloud works. The video and 17 incriminating photos they'd taken went straight to the account of the iPad's owner, Randy Schaefer, the man from whom they'd just stolen the iPad and the cash. Dorian Walker-Gaines, 20, and his partner-in-dumb, Dillian Thompson, 22, pled guilty to felony theft.

NO CLEAN GETAWAY

Posing in a tub full of cash must have seemed like good clean fun to Jeane Napoles. And posting a cash-bath selfie on social media in 2013 may have been a fun way to up the ante. Only problem: Jeane's mom, Janet Lim-Napoles, was under investigation for being the brains behind a 10 billion peso ($230 million) embezzlement scheme by members of the Philippine parliament. Jeanne reportedly liked to share her cash-rich lifestyle in

...in about 27 seconds (26.6 to be exact) is the speed of the train in miles per hour.

regular posts on Twitter, YouTube, and Instagram, believing that only 20-somethings such as herself are social-media savvy. Wrong. The Philippine Board of Internal Revenue follows the social exploits of citizens with questionable lifestyles. Jeane reported no income for the year 2013. That's why she's now facing charges for tax evasion.

SELFIE-SERVED

A human head on a plate garnished with oranges? The image could have come straight out of the 1989 dark comedy *The Cook, The Thief, His Wife, and Her Lover*. Except it didn't. It came out of a broken cell phone found on a street in Krasnodar, Russia. The phone belonged to Dmitry Bakshaev, 35, and his wife Natalia, 42, and was filled with gory selfies and images like the one described above. In the military hostel where the couple lived, police found a freezer stocked with packs of human body parts. The place reeked of ether, one of two drugs the pair used to put their victims to sleep. Reportedly, the Bakshaevs confessed to being cannibals, having killed and eaten 30 people. In shades of an even darker comedy (*Sweeney Todd*), Natalia claimed that she'd baked some of the human meat into pies and sold them to local restaurants.

THE GANG'S ALL HERE

There's nothing wrong with taking selfies with the gang...unless it's a criminal gang. For two years, the "Felony Lane Gang" conducted a nationwide operation targeting places frequented by women—day care centers, cemeteries, sporting events, parks, and gyms. Reason: when women go to these places, they often leave their purses in their cars. Purses contain valuables such as checkbooks, credit cards, driver's licenses, and Social Security cards, exactly what the gang needed to commit identity fraud and cash stolen checks. They had a good thing going until June 23, 2015, when two gang members fleeing the scene of a car break-in flipped their car. After they were arrested, police examined their cell phones, which contained selfies of gang members showing off wads of cash, and photos of stolen driver's licenses and Social Security cards. Though the gang operated throughout the country, their spree ended in Michigan. So far, the U.S. Attorney's Office in Detroit has arrested and charged 10 gang members with bank fraud; each could get up to 30 years in prison.

* * *

HE'S OUTTA THERE!

A great relief pitcher: Ernie Shore of the Boston Red Sox. On June 23, 1917, the starting pitcher walked the first batter and was ejected from the game for arguing with the umpire. Shore came in and went on to pitch a no-hitter. The starting pitcher he replaced: Babe Ruth.

In 1937 a legless man named Charles Zimmy, 44, swam down the Hudson River from Albany to New York City, a distance of 145 miles, in 148 hours.

IT'S ABOUT LYME

Chances are you don't know a lot about Lyme disease unless you've had it or know someone who has. But according to the U.S. Centers for Disease Control and Prevention, 329,000 Americans are diagnosed with Lyme disease each year— more than with breast cancer and HIV/AIDS combined. So here are some inside facts about what many have called the "quiet disease."

THE BASICS

• Lyme disease is a bacterial infection spread to humans by infected deer ticks, also called blacklegged ticks. Some (but not all) people develop a bull's-eye-shaped lesion around the bite. If caught early and treated aggressively with antibiotics, the infection can be eradicated in a month or two. But if it goes untreated, Lyme disease can become chronic and lead to years of misery.

THE HISTORY

• One of the earliest mentions of a tick-borne disease came from a Dr. John Walker, who was visiting an island off of the west coast of Scotland in the mid-1700s. He wrote of a common aliment there that causes "exquisite pain [in] the interior parts of the limbs." Walker was on the Isle of Jura, from an old Norse name meaning "Island of the Deer."

• In 1975 two doctors from the Yale School of Medicine, Allen Steere and Stephen Malawista, were sent to three small towns in Connecticut—Lyme, Old Lyme, and East Haddam—to find out why more than 50 people of all ages were suffering from what was thought to be juvenile rheumatoid arthritis. After doing blood tests and interviews, a pattern began to form: 1) Nearly all the sufferers lived on the outskirts of the towns near the forests; 2) the outbreaks occurred in early to mid-summer; and 3) 25 percent of the patients reported that, before their symptoms appeared, they were bitten by a tick and noticed a bull's-eye-shaped lesion. Steere and Malawista became convinced that the outbreak in Lyme was caused by deer tick bites, so they named it "Lyme arthritis." Over the next few years, it became clear that the symptoms go far beyond arthritis. So they changed the name to "Lyme disease."

THE SYMPTOMS

• Lyme is considered "multisystemic." According to Dr. Leo Galland, a Lyme disease specialist from New York:

Longest English words in which the letters are in alphabetical order:
almost, biopsy, chimps, chintz, begins, and abhors.

[The] symptoms involve many different organs, including your skin, nervous system, joints, muscles, heart, and eyes. In my medical practice, Lyme disease is the trigger for half my patients with chronic fatigue syndrome or fibromyalgia, most patients with painful neuropathies or autonomic nervous system disorders, 40% of people with dizziness, and 30% of patients with arthritis or autoimmune disorders. I've seen Lyme disease cause abrupt changes in personality, impaired thinking, memory loss, and panic disorder.

- In the northeast United States, where Lyme is most prevalent, doctors are more likely to suspect Lyme disease when the common symptoms are present. However, in most other regions, where Lyme is much rarer, it can be misdiagnosed as Crohn's disease, chronic fatigue syndrome, ALS, multiple sclerosis, Alzheimer's, colitis, encephalitis, fibromyalgia, fifth disease, motor neuron disease, arthritis, cystitis, irritable bowel syndrome, lupus, prostatitis, bipolar disorder, depression, Sjogren's syndrome, sleep disorders, thyroid disease, and more. That's why Lyme disease is sometimes called "the Great Imitator."

THE BACTERIUM

- The life cycle of Lyme disease doesn't begin with the tick, but with a bacterium known as *Borrelia burgdorferi* that infects the tick. This parasite was discovered in the early 1980s by Willy Burgdorfer, a researcher at the Rocky Mountain Biological Laboratory, who described it as "poorly stained, rather long, irregularly coiled spirochetes." (A *spirochete* is a wormlike bacterium known for its corkscrew shape.) And like most species of bacteria, *B. burgdorferi* has some sneaky survival mechanisms: This one produces a protein that actually fools the victim's immune system into not producing any antibodies at first. It can even tag other beneficial bacteria to be killed.

THE TICK

- These bacteria infect deer ticks (*Ixodes scapularis*). But don't the let the "deer" in the name fool you: the tiny ticks can latch onto any mammal and even some birds.

- The ticks go through three stages in their two-year life span: larva, nymph, and adult. It's usually during the nymph stage—which occurs in late spring and early summer—that *Borrelia*-infected ticks find their way to humans. Because the nymphs are only about the size of a poppy seed at this stage, they often go unnoticed. Result: they can feed off your blood for several days while infecting you with *B. burgdorferi*. Deer ticks used to be confined to the northeastern

First ship to pass through the Panama Canal (1914): the SS *Ancon*. It was carrying cement.

United States, but now they've spread across the continent, and with them, Lyme disease.

- Infected ticks can deliver more than Lyme; many also carry bacterial co-infections—most commonly *Babesia* and *Bartonella*—that come with their own set of Lyme-like symptoms. So if you think you have Lyme disease and you get a blood test, you might get a positive result for one of the co-infections, but the Lyme result is indeterminate.

TREATMENTS

- The most aggressive way to treat Lyme disease is to administer the antibiotics via an IV drip, an expensive treatment that requires going to a doctor's office for hours at a time several days a week. These intravenous treatments can cost up to $3,000 *per week*. (Most insurance plans cover the antibiotics in pill form only.)

- A popular but controversial Lyme treatment: bee venom therapy. It's said to work like this: Inject a bee-sting's worth of venom near problem joints, and the venom kills the bacteria. There are two ways to administer it: Via bee venom in a vial that was harvested without killing the bees. (It's actually quite clever— bees land on a screen, which has a slight electric charge that causes them to sting, and the venom falls through and the bees live to buzz another day.) The other method uses live bees…held by tweezers…and placed stinger-first onto your skin. (Sadly, it kills the bees.)

AN OUNCE OF PREVENTION

The best way to treat Lyme disease is to not get it in the first place.

- **Know Your Risks:** Lyme-infected ticks can exist naturally anywhere in the world except Antarctica, but some areas are more prone than others. It's best to assume that any forest or grassy meadow can have ticks, especially during the summertime.

- **Cover Up:** If you're walking through a meadow, tuck your pants into your socks, and if you're in the woods, wear a hat and other protective clothing. And always keep an eye out for ticks, remembering that they can be as small as the period at the end of this sentence. Light-colored clothes make ticks more visible.

- **Use Bug Spray:** Most Lyme disease prevention lists recommend using a spray with DEET, but according to the health website *Shape,* "DEET only works on your skin. Using a spray with Permethrin, a clothing-only repellent, kills ticks on contact before they even have a chance to reach a spot where they could

According to Finnish legend, witches roam the earth on Easter.

attach." (Another trick: bring a lint roller—you may be surprised what comes off your pants and onto the roller.)

- **Save the Tick:** If you do find a tick sucking your blood, try and save it. (You can find safe tick-removal tips online.) There are laboratories where you can send the tick, so it can be tested for Lyme. If your tick tests positive for Lyme disease, you can start treatment before your symptoms appear, greatly increasing your chances of getting over it quickly. Testing the tick can also help isolate the harmful bacteria so your doctor can create a more effective antibiotic regimen.

- **Keep a Tidy Household:** They're called "deer ticks," but the ticks that can transmit *B. burgdorferi* are most commonly found on mice and rats. If you have cats, then the ticks can jump from the rats to the cats…and then to you.

- **Inspect Your Kids and Pets:** Remember that ticks prefer warm, dark places to feed, so if you think a tick might have attached itself to any of your family members—be they four-legged or two-legged—look in the best hiding places, including behind their ears, under their arms, in their hair, behind their knees, in their navels, even around their groins. It's recommended that you check for ticks once a day for three days after going anywhere that you might have been exposed.

- **Use More Than Your Eyes:** Tiny ticks can be tough to spot visually, but if run your fingertip over one, it might feel like a small scab. Any bumps should be inspected thoroughly.

- **Vaccinate Your Dog:** There is currently no vaccine available for people, but some dogs can be vaccinated against Lyme. Ask your veterinarian for more details.

- **Know the Symptoms:** Even though Lyme disease can mimic other conditions as it spreads throughout your body, the initial symptoms include "headaches, flu-like symptoms, joint pain, fatigue, and sometimes a rash." (Bay Area Lyme Foundation)

- **Look for the Rash:** But don't rely on it. If you think you have a bull's-eye-shaped rash (there are plenty of pictures of them online), go to a doctor right away.

- **Get Tested:** Depending on where you live, you may have to convince your skeptical doctor to test for Lyme. But if you have to, insist.

This is a thing? In 2012 Kyle Johnson set a world record
by holding 14 plastic Easter eggs in one hand.

BROADWAY BOMBS

*Not every musical can be a combination of catchy songs and a
compelling plot that allows it to run for years and years.*

Musical: *The Civil War* (1999)

Story: Perhaps it's because it was the bloodiest conflict in United States history. Or maybe it's because its political ramifications still resonate painfully today. But either way, the Civil War has never been a great subject for a Broadway musical. Among the failures: *My Darlin' Aida* (an adaptation of Verdi's *Aida* set in the 1860s South), an off-Broadway take on *Gone With the Wind,* and composer Frank Wildhorn's *The Civil War.* Rather than try to tell the story of the entire four-year war over a couple of hours, Wildhorn's show was a revue made up of songs about the war—songs that sounded like 1950s rock, country, and R&B, performed by Union troops, Confederate troops, and slaves.

Total Performances: 61

Musical: *Disaster!* (2012)

Story: It was a nostalgic romp through the 1970s, mashing up two pop-culture phenomena of the decade that didn't age well and which few people remember fondly: disaster movies and disco music. Created by comedy writer Seth Rudetsky and character actor Jack Plotnick, *Disaster!* takes place at the 1979 opening of a casino/discotheque floating in New York Harbor…and then, well, disaster strikes, just like in *Earthquake!* or *The Towering Inferno.* No original songs were written for the musical. Instead, characters sang familiar disco-era classics like Donna Summer's "Hot Stuff" and Gloria Gaynor's "I Will Survive." Unfortunately, *Disaster!* was not hot stuff…and it didn't survive.

Total Performances: 72

Musical: *Brooklyn* (2004)

Story: Not a musical about the history of the New York City borough, nor an adaptation of the 2015 Oscar-nominated movie. *Brooklyn* was a musical about a group of five garbage-covered, mentally ill homeless musicians—the self-proclaimed "City Weeds"—who live under the Brooklyn Bridge and decide to stage a musical right there on the street. (That musical is also called *Brooklyn* but, confusingly, it's centered on a woman named Brooklyn.) Tasteless? Yes. Offensive? Yes. David Cote of *Time Out* called it "an infantile urban fable…that deserves a loud Bronx cheer."

Total Performances: 284

There are more French speakers in Kinshasa, the capital of the
Democratic Republic of the Congo, than there are in Paris.

Musical: *Anyone Can Whistle* (1964)

Story: Composer and lyricist Stephen Sondheim is a Broadway legend, creator of many musically complex Broadway classics, such as *Into the Woods*, *Sweeney Todd*, and *A Funny Thing Happened on the Way to the Forum*. He got the biggest bomb of his career out of the way early, back in 1964. *Anyone Can Whistle*, which marked the Broadway debut of Angela Lansbury, is not your usual musical fare—it's about a town that concocts a fake miracle (a rock that spouts water) in order to attract tourists and their money. Then there's a breakout at the insane asylum. *New York Times* critic Howard Taubman said that Sondheim wrote "several pleasing songs, but not enough of them to give the musical wings."

Total Performances: 9

Musical: *Home Sweet Homer* (1976)

Story: A musical based on *The Odyssey*, Homer's epic about the warrior Odysseus's treacherous ten-year journey home to his wife, Penelope, after the Trojan War. It seemed like a good idea, but the production was seemingly cursed. It began with promise: the original book and lyrics were by screenwriter Erich Segal (*Yellow Submarine*, *Love Story*), and Yul Brynner, star of *The King and I*, signed on to star as Odysseus, setting himself up for a huge comeback. Before the show opened on Broadway, it toured the United States under the name *Odyssey*. Performances sold out as fans clamored to see Brynner, who frequently missed shows, claiming he was suffering from a difficult-to-beat bout of food poisoning incurred from a plate of short ribs at a New York restaurant. Despite the sellouts, critics savaged the musical—so much so that Segal took his name off the project. The scheduled Broadway run was canceled…until Brynner reminded producers that it was in his contract that the show play in New York at least once. So they gave him a single New York performance.

Total Performances: With its name changed to *Home Sweet Homer*, the musical opened at the Palace Theatre on Broadway as a matinee on January 4, 1976—its first and its *last* performance.

* * *

NAME THAT CANDY BAR

The candy bar known in the U.S. as Three Musketeers is sold in Europe under the name Milky Way. The American candy bar called Milky Way is called a Mars Bar in Europe. The American Mars Bar no longer exists—it was renamed Snickers with Almonds in the 1990s (and caramel was added).

Who inspired the tongue twister "she sells seashells by the seashore"?...

A LONG, STRANGE TRIP, PART II

Here's the last installment of our story about the odd couple who tried to circumnavigate the globe in an amphibious car. Fasten your seat belts—it's gonna be a bumpy ride! (Part I is on page 267.)

OUT OF THE FRYING PAN

The Carlins rested on Flores Island for about a week, then spent the next three months island-hopping eastward through the Azores, stopping to exhibit the *Half-Safe* whenever possible to raise money for the next leg of the trip. In late November they set off for Madeira, a Portuguese archipelago 600 miles to the east and about midway between the Azores and the west coast of Africa. The Carlins assumed that because the trip to Madeira was shorter than their trip to the Azores, it would also be easier. They were wrong—it was hurricane season. For days on end, the *Half-Safe* was battered by tropical storms with powerful winds and high waves that pounded the hull so violently, the Carlins feared it might be crushed in at any minute. "We go up, up, up & smack, down, down, down," Elinore Carlin wrote in her diary. "Used to think it was an exaggeration when people talked of seas 30, 40, and 50 feet high. I've now seen them."

> Average speed: 2 miles per hour. Reason: they were being cautious because they didn't have a spare tire. It had fallen overboard somewhere in the Atlantic.

The trip that was supposed to take ten days took them more than three weeks. That they made it at all astonished the authorities in Madeira, who, like the officials in the Azores, had given the couple up for dead. They didn't see how a ship could have ridden out the storm, let alone a couple of nuts in a jeep.

After resting up on Madeira for two months and making repairs to the *Half-Safe*, in February 1951 the Carlins set sail for the west coast of Africa by way of the Canary Islands. On February 23, they landed at Cape Juby, just south of Morocco, and entered the record books as the first—and still the only—people to drive across the Atlantic Ocean in an amphibious car.

BRITISH INVASION

The Carlins drove north from Cape Juby to Morocco. (Average speed: 2 miles per hour. Reason: they were being cautious because they didn't have a spare tire. It had

...One theory: an English seaside fossil shop owner named Marry Anning.

fallen overboard somewhere in the Atlantic.) In April 1951 they floated across the strait of Gibraltar into Europe, then embarked on a four-month driving tour of Europe. In August they crossed the English Channel and drove ashore at Kent, the same place where Julius Caesar landed during his invasion of the British Isles in 55 BC. (Caesar had to walk ashore.) In England, Ben Carlin was reunited with his old friend Mac Bunting, who was with him back in 1946 when they saw that first amphibious jeep and Carlin said he thought he could travel around the world in one. "By Jove, old boy," Bunting exclaimed, "you were right!"

SEEING, BUT NOT BELIEVING

One of the reasons the Carlins made their trip was for the fame and fortune that they thought it would bring them. Ben imagined himself writing books and articles and traveling the world giving paid lectures to a public eager to devour his every word. With book royalties and speaking fees rolling in, he would never have to work a real job again. But when Ben and Elinore arrived in England, they were surprised to see how little attention they received. After just a day or two the reporters stopped calling, and *Life* magazine, which had already done one article on the couple, backed out of doing a second.

The Carlins had also assumed that someone would sponsor a European exhibition tour of the *Half-Safe*, which would bring in the money they needed to repair the jeep and prepare the vehicle for the next leg of the trip. But there were no takers; the Carlins had to tour on their own. And when they did exhibit the *Half-Safe* to the public, they were astonished to discover that many people believed the whole thing was a hoax. People simply did not believe that anyone could, or would, cross the Atlantic in a jeep.

Instead of being showered with attention and cash, Ben and Elinore had to go back to work for two years to save up the money they needed to continue their journey. Ben found a job as an auto mechanic in Birmingham, and Elinore worked as a secretary in London. It was at this time that Ben wrote a book about the journey so far, titled *Half-Safe: Across the Atlantic by Jeep*. It sold more than 30,000 copies in five languages—an impressive figure to be sure, but far less than the Carlins expected.

HERE WE GO AGAIN

When he wasn't fixing other people's cars or writing his book, Ben Carlin worked on the *Half-Safe*, repairing damage, rebuilding the engine, and making various improvements. By April 1955, just shy of five years after leaving Halifax on what he thought would be a one-year trip, he and Elinore climbed back into the jeep, drove into the English Channel, and set off for France. From there they drove through Switzerland, Italy, Yugoslavia, Greece, and western Istanbul, then sailed across the

How do guinea pigs get back the nutrients they excrete?
The old-fashioned way: They eat their own poop.

Bosporus strait to Asia Minor, the part of Turkey that lies in Asia. Next they drove south and east through Syria, Jordan, Iraq, Iran, Pakistan, and then across India to Calcutta. They arrived there in the middle of summer, having driven more than 8,500 miles in just under three months—all of it at speeds of 25 mph or less.

In some ways, the trip from France to Calcutta was more grueling than their transatlantic crossing: The *Half-Safe* didn't have air-conditioning, and in the desert heat of the Middle East, temperatures inside the vehicle climbed as high as 180°F. Elinore, not a very big woman, lost 30 pounds during the trip due to chronic stomach problems. In India, Ben contracted dengue fever, also known as "breakbone fever" because of the terrible pain it causes to the joints, and was laid up in Calcutta for weeks.

> **Ben contracted dengue fever, also known as "breakbone fever" because of the terrible pain it causes to the joints, and was laid up in Calcutta for weeks.**
>
> **Perhaps worst of all, they were out of money. Again.**

Perhaps worst of all, they were out of money. Again.

DOWN UNDER

Luckily for the Carlins, they soon received an offer from Ben's publisher to go take the *Half-Safe* on a book tour of Australia. So they loaded the jeep onto a steamship and sailed for Australia, planning to return to Calcutta after the book tour and resume the trip where they'd left off. But the Australia trip, which had offered the promise of diversion from their difficult life in Calcutta, turned out to be a financial disaster. The books never arrived, so there was nothing for the Carlins to sell. By the time the tour was over, Elinore decided she'd had enough of both the trip and her marriage to Ben. Instead of accompanying him back to Calcutta, she returned home to the United States and filed for divorce. According to some accounts, she never saw Ben again.

MOVING ON

In December 1955, Carlin returned to Calcutta by steamship—alone. A few weeks later he climbed aboard the *Half-Safe* and set sail for Burma (Myanmar), across the Bay of Bengal. For the rest of the trip he covered some stretches by himself, and others with the assistance of hired crewmembers who'd signed on for parts of the trip.

From Burma, Carlin drove through Thailand, Laos, and Vietnam, then sailed across the South China Sea to Hong Kong. From there he sailed to Taiwan, then drove north across the island and sailed to Kyushu, the southernmost of the major islands of Japan, and then island-hopped northward across Japan. From Japan he sailed to the southernmost of Alaska's Aleutian Islands, and island-hopped all the way to Anchorage, where he arrived on September 2, 1957. He spent the next eight months driving all around the United States and Canada.

The Brazilian capital of Brasilia, founded in 1960, is designed to look like an airplane when seen from the air.

THANKS, BUT...

As Carlin traveled around North America, he was saddened to see that, just as in Europe, people weren't very excited about his trip. Some people still thought it was a hoax. He drove to Southern California and spent a few weeks in Hollywood trying to put together a movie deal, but no one was interested. When he drove through Michigan, he stopped at the Ford Motor Company's headquarters in Dearborn and tried to interest the publicity department in what he'd been able to accomplish with one of their amphibious jeeps. But Ford executives refused to meet with him, so he got back in the *Half-Safe* and drove away.

> He drove to Southern California and spent a few weeks in Hollywood trying to put together a movie deal, but no one was interested.

On May 13, 1958, just short of eight years after setting out across the Atlantic (and just shy of ten years after his first failed attempt to cross it), Carlin arrived back in Montreal, where he and Elinore had started their trip in July 1950. A few reporters were there to greet him, but there were no crowds. He'd been gone so long that most people had forgotten that he and Elinore had ever set off on such a trip. By his calculations, he'd traveled some 39,000 miles by land and another 11,000 by sea, and had spent roughly $35,000 doing it, the equivalent of nearly $300,000 today. But no one seemed to care.

END OF THE ROAD

Now that his journey was finished, Carlin handed over the *Half-Safe* to an American friend who owned a half-share in the vehicle, perhaps as collateral on a loan that Carlin had yet to repay. "I can't get rid of her fast enough. It's been a tortoise shell on my back for many years," Carlin told a reporter at the time. He wrote a second book, *The Other Half of Half-Safe*, but no one wanted to publish it, so he set the manuscript aside. It was not published in his lifetime.

Carlin lived out the rest of his life in obscurity, first in Canada and then in the United States. By the late 1970s, he was back in Western Australia. There he suffered a series of strokes that left him increasingly debilitated, until a final one killed him in 1981. Elinore Carlin died in 1996.

FORGET ME NOT

In his will, Ben Carlin bequeathed his entire estate—his meager life savings, his half-ownership stake in the *Half-Safe*, the unpublished manuscript of *The Other Half of Half-Safe*, and all of his photo albums, scrapbooks, correspondence, and other records of the trip—to the school he'd attended in Australia as a boy, Guildford Grammar School in Perth. It's because of this bequest that we know as much about the Carlins

What's a postprandial somnolence? *That's the technical name for a "food coma," getting sleepy after a big meal.*

and their strange adventure as we do, because the school took a lot more interest in their story than the rest of the world had.

In the early 1980s, the school tracked down the *Half-Safe*. It was still sitting abandoned in a barn in Ohio where Carlin and his partner dumped it not long after he'd finished the voyage. The school acquired the other half-interest in the vehicle from Carlin's partner, then had the jeep shipped back to the school. When it arrived in Australia, the school had it lovingly restored. Today it sits proudly on campus in a glass-walled building that was specially constructed to house it.

In 1989 the school published *The Other Half of Half-Safe*. It is still in print and can be purchased from the school directly. The rest of Ben Carlin's papers have been made a part of the Guildford Grammar School's archives, where they are available for researchers and scholars to study. In 2011 a journalist named James Nestor used the material to write *Half-Safe*, the first new book about the Carlins and their strange odyssey in more than 40 years.

INSPIRATION

The school has also named a classroom in Carlin's honor, and—in perhaps its greatest tribute to their oddly distinguished alumnus—it has incorporated his spirit of adventure and stubborn perseverance into the curriculum by creating the "Carlin Challenge," a contest that "encourages students in innovation, courage, research, and risk-taking."

If you ever find yourself in the city of Perth in Western Australia, be sure to take a trip out to Guildford Grammar School and have a look at the *Half-Safe*. It's in beautiful shape and looks like it's ready for another adventure. You might even be tempted to take it out into the Swan River, which runs through Perth, or even out into the Indian Ocean. But no matter how tempting it seems, resist the urge. If Ben or Elinore Carlin were still alive today, they'd probably tell you it's not such a good idea.

* * *

MORE GROANERS

- Lack of general knowledge is my Achilles' knee.

- I poured root beer in a square glass. Now I just have beer.

- Communism jokes aren't funny unless everyone gets them.

- I've been to the dentist a lot, so I know the drill.

The chocolate chip cookie was invented at the Toll House Inn in Whitman, MA, in 1930.

HISTORY'S WONDER WOMEN

After seeing the 2017 film, we decided to track down real-life Wonder Women—female warriors who defied their times to defend their people, without hot pants, bustiers, bulletproof bracelets, or a lasso of truth.

FU HAO: THE GENERAL

As consort of Shang dynasty king Wu Ding, Fu Hao could have faded into obscurity. That's what happened to Wu's other 59 wives. But Fu Hao climbed over the crowd to become the king's favorite, reportedly because of her skill as a tough military leader.

The Shang ruled China's Yellow River Valley from about 1556 to 1046 BC. They built huge walled cities, improved irrigation systems, mastered the use of bronze, and developed a writing system. Much of what is known about the Shang has been found on "oracle bones"—ox shoulder bones or turtle shells inscribed with questions related to important events of the day. Those included military events. Hundreds of oracle bones have been found with questions about the military exploits of Lady Fu Hao. For years, archaeologists (mostly male) pooh-poohed the existence of a Shang dynasty warrior queen. But in 1976, modern archaeologists found proof: Fu Hao's tomb. Unlike most Shang tombs, hers had remained undisturbed. Inside they found a bronze battle axe—proof of her military authority—130 weapons, 27 knives, dozens of bone arrowheads, and the skeletons of six dogs and 16 human slaves.

Fu Hao reportedly began her military career when one of the dynasty's fiercest rivals—the Tu-Fang—threatened attack the Shang while two of Wu Ding's top commanders were fighting elsewhere. Fu Hao stepped forward to offer her services. She'd had military training, knew the country's geography, and understood the subtleties of the art of war. Wu Ding granted her a bronze *jue*, a ritual bronze wine vessel, and empowered her as a military commander. Though the Tu-Fang had been gnawing at the kingdom's borders for generations, Fu Hao defeated them so decisively that they never challenged the Shang again.

Fu Hao quickly became Wu Ding's most powerful military leader and was China's first female general. A force of more than 13,000 soldiers followed her command. Other powerful generals fought beneath her standard as she led successful campaigns against neighboring kingdoms. Wu Ding granted his gifted general a fiefdom from territories she conquered. From that stronghold, she

Black gold: Printer ink costs $4,000 per gallon.

defended the kingdom's borders and launched attacks against other tribes. After her death (around 1200 BC), the Shang's military dominance weakened, despite Wu Ding's many prayers to her spirit for aid.

LOZEN: THE SHIELD

Historians call Victorio, chief of the Chihenne Apache, the "greatest Indian general who had ever appeared on the American continent." Apparently, the guerrilla warrior got a lot of help...from his younger sister, Lozen. At the age of 12, Lozen journeyed into the craggy mountains of southwestern New Mexico on a vision quest. There, oral tradition says, she was gifted with a supernatural power: the ability to locate her tribe's enemies.

Born around 1840, Lozen grew up during a time of relentless warfare. Squeezed between two powerhouses determined to wipe them out—Mexico and the United States—the Apache nation was harried to near-extermination. Lozen chose the warrior's path early, vowing neither to marry nor have children, but instead to give her life to the survival of her people. She dressed, fought, and trained with male warriors; and her acceptance into the Apache warrior society gave her the right to sit at council. Her eerie ability to sneak past enemy lines and quietly steal their horses earned her the name Lozen, which means "dexterous horse thief."

During the so-called Indian Wars of U.S. westward expansion, the favored government strategy to rid itself of natives was to have the military corral them in reservations. In 1877 Victorio's band was due to be forcibly taken to the San Carlos reservation in Arizona Territory, a place so desolate that it was called "Hell's 40 Acres." The Apache chief decided he would rather die fighting than watch his people die of disease or starvation, so he took the Chihenne to war.

To confuse their enemy, the tribe fanned out in different directions with Lozen leading the women and children toward the Rio Grande. They found the river a torrent of churning water. Her followers froze at the river's edge, as fearful of drowning as of capture by the cavalry. Lozen raised her rifle over her head, slammed a heel into her horse's shoulder, and drove him into the river. As he kicked into a swim, the frozen women and children surged forward, buoyed by their leader's courage. Once her people were safe on the other side, Lozen plunged back into the roaring water, determined to rejoin the warriors.

She soon peeled off from the warrior band to escort a pregnant woman across the Chihuahuan Desert to reunite her with her family. Along the way she delivered the baby, killed a longhorn with nothing but a knife, and butchered it for food. Next, she stole two horses and a soldier's saddle, ammo, canteen, blanket, and shirt. As Lozen trekked across the desert, delivering mother and baby safely home, Victorio and his remaining warriors were trapped and slaughtered by Mexican soldiers. Would that have happened if his "right hand" had been there? Many Apache said it would not.

Ouch! After a male bee mates, its testicles explode, and then it dies.

Strong as any man and braver than most, Lozen was, according to her brother, "a shield of her people."

MILUNKA SAVIĆ: THE FEARLESS

What's a poor Serbian farm girl to do when her brother is called up to fight the Bulgarians? Shave off her hair, dress like a man, and take his place in the army, of course. At least, that's what 21-year-old Milunka Savić did. In 1913, within weeks of enlisting, Savić was boots-deep in the biggest battle in the Second Balkan War. Rifle in hand, Savić charged into wave after wave of assaults with the kind of courage every commander wants to see in a grunt. Savić's commander was so impressed, he awarded her a medal and promoted her to corporal. But he didn't know that she was a woman.

On a subsequent charge into battle, a Bulgarian grenade blasted Savić's position. Medics tossed her onto a stretcher and carried her to the field hospital, where a doctor opened her shirt to remove shrapnel from her chest and...the jig was up. When her commanding officer found out he'd pinned a medal on the chest of a woman, he didn't know what to do. She'd proven herself not only capable but heroic. Could he punish a soldier of her caliber? Apparently not. But he did suggest a transfer to the nursing corps. Savić respectfully refused and told her commander that she would take no position in the army that would sideline her without a weapon with which to fight for her beloved Serbia. Her commander told her he'd think about it. Standing at attention, the wounded soldier replied, "I'll wait." Savić stood there for a full hour before her commander agreed to keep her in the infantry, and promoted her to junior sergeant.

Savić survived the Balkan Wars, but a peaceful life back home on the farm was not to be. A Serbian dissident assassinated Austria's Archduke Ferdinand and before long World War I was in full swing. Back on the front lines, Savić quickly earned her country's highest award, the Order of Karađorđe's Star (don't worry—we can't pronounce it either).

In the 2017 movie *Wonder Woman*, there's a scene in which Wonder Woman charges across a barbed wire–studded "no-man's-land," dives into an enemy trench, and dispenses a super-heroic smackdown. That could only happen in Hollywood, right? Not really. Savić reportedly did it in real life, capturing 23 Bulgarian soldiers and earning herself another Star.

Unfortunately, the Serbian army wasn't doing as well as Sergeant Savić and it retreated to join up with the French. How did the French general in charge react to Savić's presence? He bet her a case of 1880 cognac that she couldn't hit a bottle from 40 meters (131 feet). When she did, he welcomed her into the ranks. (It probably didn't hurt that she shared the cognac.)

By the end of the war, Savić had won the French Legion of Honor (twice), been awarded the Russian Cross of St. George, and received the British Medal of the Order of St. Michael, all for her kick-butt courage in battle. She was the only woman in

World War I to be given the French Croix de Guerre, the highest award for bravery the country bestows. Her heroism was so legendary that when she was sent to a concentration camp during World War II, the German officer who was supposed to execute her recognized her name...and ordered her release.

BOUDICCA: THE QUEEN

By 60 AD Rome had ruled Britannia for more than a century. But Emperor Nero was about to make a mistake that would (nearly) drive the Romans off the isle. He miscalculated the cost of enraging a tawny-haired Celtic queen named Boudicca.

Like many British kings, Boudicca's husband, Prasutagus, had allied his tribe—the Iceni—with the Roman invaders. That allowed him to keep partial control of his kingdom in eastern England (modern-day Norfolk). When he died, Prasutagus willed the kingdom to his two daughters and to the emperor. But Nero had no intention of sharing land, wealth, or power with women, and wasted no time in sending centurions to do what Romans did in those days: plunder the Iceni's wealth, flog the king's widow, and rape the daughters. The end? Nope. The beginning. Spear in hand, the tall, muscular queen called on the Iceni and neighboring tribes to unite and drive the Romans out of their lands, once and for all. And having seen their lands pillaged, they were inclined to follow her.

The mob marched first to the town of Camulodunum (now Colchester). The Romans had a good laugh over the idea of a ragtag bunch of malcontents led by a woman, and sent 200 troops to quell the rebellion. Bad plan. When the Romans arrived, they discovered that 120,000 men had answered Boudicca's call. The mob quickly slaughtered the Roman troops and then killed everyone in the city and burned it to the ground.

Boudicca wasn't done. As her rebel army grew—some accounts say to 230,000 fighters—she charged into Londinium (now London), slaughtered an entire Roman legion, and then burned *that* city to the ground. Before the legions finally stopped her, the Celtic queen and her minions had killed around 80,000 Romans. And, to the deep chagrin of the centurions, most of them accomplished their gory work using agricultural tools.

Ultimately, the Romans regrouped and ended the rebellion, but they were so humiliated by the near-rout that they almost withdrew from Britain. As for the Brits, they turned Boudicca into a national hero, finally erecting a bronze statue to honor her in 1902, nearly 2,000 years later. *Boudicca and Her Daughters* stands on the west side of Westminster Bridge. The warrior queen rides her chariot into battle with her daughters at her side. The inscription reads:

> "Queen of the Iceni who died AD 61 after leading her people
> against the Roman invader."

GO AHEAD–HAVE SOME MORE CHIPS

On page 100 we told you the stories of some of the people responsible for bringing potato chips to the world. Like the chips themselves, chip trivia is a hard habit to break once you've gotten started. (Have you heard about the chip that was "born in a Disneyland trash can"?)

HERMAN W. LAY

In the depths of the Great Depression in 1932, Lay got a job selling peanut butter sandwiches made by Barrett Foods, an Atlanta snack food concern. After the company's owner died in 1937, Lay bought the business and expanded into popcorn. In 1938 he added potato chips to his product line. Then in the early 1940s, rationing of sugar and chocolate during World War II made candy bars and other sweets hard to come by. Many people reached for potato chips as a substitute, and sales of Lay's Potato Chips soared. They were the first snack food advertised on television, which helped build Lay's into the first potato chip brand sold nationwide.

GUSTAVO OLGUIN & CHARLES ELMER DOOLIN

At about the same time that Herman Lay got his job selling peanut butter sandwiches in Atlanta, a man named Elmer Doolin was making pies and cakes in his family's struggling bakery in San Antonio, Texas. He'd thought about putting complimentary bowls of tortilla chips on the sales counter for his customers, but they went stale too quickly. Then in July 1932, he read a classified ad in the *San Antonio Express* placed by a man named Gustavo Olguin, a native of Mexico. He and his business partner, whose name has been lost to history, had a small business making *fritas*, or fried corn chips, using the same cornmeal dough, or *masa*, that is used to make tortillas. But he was homesick and wanted to return to Mexico, so the business was for sale. Price: $100, a lot of money during the Depression.

Doolin started making the fritas—he anglicized the word into "Fritos"— in the family kitchen.

Doolin went to Olguin's store for a demonstration of how he squeezed the *masa* dough through a handheld device called a potato ricer to give the corn chips their shape, then cut strips of the extruded dough into a pot of boiling oil. Doolin tasted the finished product and was impressed. He wanted to buy the business, but he didn't have $100. So he talked to his mother, Daisy Dean Doolin, and she agreed to pawn her wedding ring. When that brought just $80, Olguin's business partner lent Doolin the remaining $20.

The tires on NASCAR vehicles are filled with nitrogen. Why?
Nitrogen is safer because it doesn't expand as much when the tires heat up.

With help from his brother and his parents, Doolin started making the fritas—he anglicized the word into "Fritos"—in the family kitchen. They averaged 10 pounds of chips a day. These sold so well that in 1933 he expanded production to factories in Dallas and Houston. In 1945, Doolin licensed Herman Lay to manufacture and sell Fritos Corn Chips in the southeastern United States, where Lay was based. They went nationwide four years later. By the time Doolin died in 1959 at the age of 56, the Frito Company was selling $60 million worth of Fritos and other snacks a year. Two years later it merged with the H. W. Lay & Company to become Frito-Lay. Today Frito-Lay, a division of PepsiCo, is the largest distributor of snack foods in the world. (C. E. Doolin's other claim to fame: inventing Crunchy Cheetos in 1948. Cheetos Puffs weren't introduced until 1971.)

RICHARD MONTAÑEZ

In 1976 Montañez was a janitor working at the Frito-Lay plant in Rancho Cucamonga, California. It was there that a machine on the Cheetos assembly line broke one day and some of the Cheetos were not dusted with the orange cheese powder that gives the snack food their flavor. Rather than toss the cheeseless Cheetos in the trash, Montañez took them home. He remembered back to his childhood days in Mexico, where *elote,* corn on the cob sprinkled with chili powder, was a popular street food. "I see the corn man adding butter, cheese, and chili to the corn and thought, what if I add chili to a Cheeto?" He sprinkled some chili powder on the Cheetos and was surprised by how good they tasted.

Montañez's wife, friends and co-workers also thought the spicy Cheetos were delicious. That inspired him to call the president of Frito-Lay and tell him about his product idea. The president asked Montañez to make a presentation at a meeting of company executives in two weeks' time. Montañez and his wife spent those two weeks practicing his presentation, which they developed with help from a business book they borrowed from the public library. Montañez also bought a necktie—his first ever—for $3, and asked a neighbor to teach him how to tie it. He made his presentation to the executives, and they agreed to introduce the chili-flavored Cheetos under the name Flamin' Hot Cheetos. Today Flamin' Hot Cheetos outsell regular Cheetos by a wide margin, and Montañez spends a lot more time in the executive suite than he used to: He's PepsiCo's executive vice president of multicultural sales and community activation. "There's no such thing as 'just a janitor,' if you act like an owner," he says.

AN UNKNOWN SALESMAN AND ARCH WEST

C. E. Doolin was also an early investor in Disneyland, which opened in Anaheim in 1955. The Frito Company, and later Frito-Lay, operated the "Casa de Fritos" Mexican restaurant in the park for many years. Free with every meal: Fritos corn chips. The restaurant had no use for actual *tortilla chips*, since the Frito-Lay Company didn't make those. Then one day

When the Empire State Building opened in 1931, less than 25% of its offices were occupied. It was nicknamed the "Empty State Building."

West gave them a name similar to *doraditos*, the Spanish word for "little gold things"—Doritos.

in the mid-1960s, a salesperson for Alex Foods, the Los Angeles company that supplied the tortillas that were used to make the restaurant's enchiladas and other dishes, noticed that some unused tortillas had been tossed in the trash. Why let good food go to waste? The salesperson told the kitchen staff that if they cut the tortillas into triangles, fried them in oil, and added spicy seasoning, they would make delicious chips.

Casa De Fritos added the chips to the menu, apparently without telling the top brass at the Fritos Company, and they were a hit with diners. When Arch West, a vice president with Frito-Lay, paid a visit to Disneyland and saw the restaurant full of people enjoying the unfamiliar chips, he arranged for Alex Foods, and later Frito-Lay itself, to begin producing them. West gave them a name similar to *doraditos*, the Spanish word for "little gold things"—Doritos.

Even after West retired from the Frito-Lay executive suite, he continued on as a Doritos taste tester until shortly before his death in 2011 at the age of 97. One of the last experimental flavors he tasted: cheeseburger Doritos (they were so disgusting that he spat them out). At his funeral, West's family honored his request that they toss Doritos chips into his grave. "It will just be plain Doritos," West's daughter Jana Hacker told reporters. "Otherwise people will say, 'Thanks Jana, I've got nacho all over my hand.'"

(DIS)HONORABLE MENTION: TOM COLELLA

Colella, an electrician who lives in Perth, Australia, didn't invent a snack chip, but he did figure out a way to use them to play hooky from work: His employer issued him a personal data assistant that used GPS technology to track his location and report the information back to his employer. But as an electrician, Colella knew that if he placed the PDA in an empty bag of Twisties cheese curls, a snack food similar to Cheetos, the foil lining of the bag would act as a "Faraday cage" and block the PDA from sending or receiving signals. Thus blocked, Colella's location would not be revealed to his employer, and he could go wherever he wanted. It's estimated that Colella snuck off to play golf on the clock 140 times between 2014 and 2016. His fun ended when an anonymous tipster sent a letter to his employer, who promptly fired him. At last report, he was working as an Uber driver.

* * *

OOPS: In 1915 the *Washington Post* reported that President Woodrow Wilson had attended a play with his fiancée and soon-to-be First Lady, Edith Galt, saying, "Rather than paying attention to the play, the President spent the evening entering Mrs. Galt." (They meant to say "entertaining.")

The Greek philosopher Aristotle (384–322 BC) believed that the heart, not the brain, was the...

THE *PRINCESS* LETTERS

Did you grow up watching The Princess Bride *on VHS or cable TV? Or did your kids?*
Then you know all about this wonderful story full of romance, adventure, and Mandy
Patinkin as the vengeance-seeking Inigo Montoya ("You killed my father!
Prepare to die!"). Or do you? It turns out that there's another
chapter to the story—one you've probably never heard of.

PAGE TO SCREEN

Director Rob Reiner's film *The Princess Bride* hit movie theaters in 1987. It's a fairy tale
adventure about the noble Westley's (Cary Elwes) quest to reunite with his one true
love, Princess Buttercup (Robin Wright), and save her from the clutches of the evil
Prince Humperdinck (Chris Sarandon). Along the way, he becomes a pirate, acquires
three sidekicks—the revenge-obsessed Inigo Montoya (Mandy Patinkin), the crafty
Vizzini (Wallace Shawn), and the humongous Fezzik (Andre the Giant)—and even
dies, only to be revived by Miracle Max the medicine man (Billy Crystal).

Reiner presents the story as a book (*"The Princess Bride,* by S. Morgenstern")
being read by a grandfather (Peter Falk) to his grandson (Fred Savage). That framing
device is the major difference between book and movie. William Goldman wrote the
screenplay, and he also wrote the 1973 novel on which it's based—*The Princess Bride:
S. Morgenstern's Classic Tale of True Love and High Adventure.* The novel doesn't have
a story-within-a-story structure, so it has no grandpas and grandsons. Instead, it has a
50-page preamble in which Goldman explains that the book is actually an adaptation
of a much longer, long-out-of-print book by "S. Morgenstern," a legendary author
from the nation of Florin. Morgenstern, Goldman says, wrote *The Princess Bride,* and
he—Goldman—edited it down to just "the good parts."

FAKE NEWS

Goldman's introduction includes the story of how he discovered Morgenstern's book:
He needed a gift for his son, and so he sent his lawyer out to a bookstore in the middle
of a snowstorm, and *The Princess Bride* was procured.

However, absolutely *none* of that is true. No author named "S. Morgenstern" ever
existed. The existence of an uncut version of *The Princess Bride* is fiction. Florin isn't
a real country. (Even the part about Goldman's son is fictional—he doesn't *have* a
son.) Goldman wrote the entire book himself—the story and the "backstory." He's said
his inspiration came one night when his two daughters were young and asked for a
bedtime story; one wanted a story about a princess, and the other wanted a story about
a bride. So he wrote a combination.

...source of human consciousness, and that the brain's only function was to cool the blood.

REUNITED, AND IT FEELS SO GOOD

As the story of Westley and Buttercup unfolds in the book, Goldman frequently interrupts, informing the reader about the sections of Morgenstern's original text that he has supposedly excised or edited—mostly boring, overly long exposition. Just once does Goldman admit to writing any part of *The Princess Bride*. Goldman can't believe that although Buttercup and Westley reunite, Morgenstern doesn't do it in a big, emotionally powerful, audience-pleasing scene. So, Goldman tells the reader, he took it upon himself to write one…but the publisher wouldn't let him include it. He explains that Harcourt Brace Jovanovich felt it was sacrilege to try to improve on the work of "the great S. Morgenstern." However, he goes on, they reached a compromise: Readers could write to the publisher to request the scene, and it would be sent to them.

Over the years, thousands of people wrote to HBJ in search of the scene. But they never got it, because while Goldman had actually written the entirety of *The Princess Bride* and claimed that he hadn't, he never actually did write the one part he said he had. Readers who wrote in got an envelope in the mail from Harcourt Brace Jovanovich, expecting the long-lost Westley-Buttercup exchange, but instead got a long letter explaining *why* they couldn't read the scene they'd asked for.

After the greeting, Goldman immediately lets the reader know that they won't be reading what they wrote in to receive: It's all because of a lawyer (or "roadblock," as Goldman calls him) with the improbable (and definitely made-up) name of Kermit Shog. Goldman says that as soon as *The Princess Bride* was bound and ready to be shipped to bookstores, he received a call from his lawyer, a guy named Charley. (That's also a throwback to the *Princess Bride* prologue; Charley figured in Goldman's so-called procurement of the S. Morgenstern transcript—he's the guy that Goldman asked to head out into a blizzard and buy a book for him.)

Goldman writes that he knows something is amiss when Charley skips his customary "Talmudic humor" in favor of getting right down to business, urging Goldman to head down to his office "right away." Goldman indeed rushes down to Charley's office, speculating that someone close to him died, or he failed his IRS audit. Instead, when he arrives, he's ushered in by Charley's secretary, and he's introduced to Kermit Shog, who Goldman says looks like classic Hollywood actor Peter Lorre, only more "oily."

> "Mr. Shog is a lawyer," Charley goes on. And this next was said underlined:
> "*He represents the Morgenstern estate.*"
> Who knew? Who could have dreamed such a thing existed, an estate of a man dead at least a million years that no one ever heard of over here anyway?

A fence designed to keep dingoes out of sheep-grazing land in Australia
is longer than the distance from Seattle to Miami.

After claiming that Shog performed an impression of Peter Lorre in *The Maltese Falcon* ("Perhaps you will give me the Falcon now!") before backtracking and admitting it isn't true, Shog gives Charley and Goldman a moment to commiserate, and then he leaves. Goldman and Charley subsequently panic, and wonder how their publisher, Harcourt Brace Jovanovich, didn't even think to check to see if Morgenstern still even had an estate, and if they might be litigious. And then, Goldman writes, Charley emitted a low, sustained grunt, the kind lawyers make when they realize they've just lost a case before it's even started.

> "What does he want?" I said. "A meeting with Mr. Jovanovich," Charley answered.
> Now, William Jovanovich is a pretty busy fella, but it's amazing when you're confronted with a potential multibillion-dollar lawsuit how fast you can wedge in a meeting. We trooped over.

Kermit Shog gets his meeting with Jovanovich, who *somehow* found the time. Goldman notes that all the Harcourt bigwigs are in attendance, as are their lawyers, as is he—and Charley, of course.

> Harcourt's lawyer started things: "We're terribly terribly sorry, Mr. Shog. It's an unforgivable oversight, and please accept our sincerest apologies." Mr. Shog said, "That's a beginning, since all you did was defame and ridicule the greatest modern master of Florinese prose who also happened to be for many years a friend of my family." Then the business head of Harcourt said, "All right, how much do you want?"

Shog explains that his case is about more than money—it's about history, literature, legacy, and Florin itself. The attorney then explains that he doesn't want some cash to keep quiet and to make the case go away. No, he wants Harcourt Brace Jovanovich to publish the original, unabridged version of *The Princess Bride* in its entirety—no William Goldman and his "defilement" of the original manuscript. That's about the time, Goldman writes, when he was ready to wash his hands of the project and walk away, content to never let the reunion scene reach readers.

> But Mr. Shog wasn't done with me: "You, who *dared* to *defame* a *master's* characters are now going to put *your* words in their mouths? Nossir. No, I say." "It's just a little thing," I tried; "a couple pages only."
> Then Mr. Jovanovich started talking softly. "Bill, I think we might skip sending out the reunion scene just now, don't you think?" I made a nod. Then he turned to Mr. Shog. "We'll print the unabridged. You're a man who is interested in immortality

"Amphibian" comes from the Greek *amphibios*, which means "living a double life."

for his client, and there aren't as many of you around in publishing as there used to be. You're a gentleman, sir." "Thank you," from Mr. Shog; "I like to think I am, at least on occasion." For the first time, he smiled. We all smiled. Very buddy-buddy now. Then, an addendum from Mr. Shog: "Oh, yes. Your first printing of the unabridged will be 100,000 copies."

Despite those crushing terms—in which Shog, on behalf of the S. Morgenstern estate, got everything he wanted—it didn't end the negotiations with Harcourt Brace Jovanovich, or even William Goldman's involvmenet in the project. He claims that his version of *The Princess Bride* generated no less than 13 lawsuits, although he was only personally involved in 11. But after all those are settled, and the copyright on the Morgenstern version runs out in 1978, *then*, Goldman promises, readers might begin to receive that reunion scene.

All of you who wrote in are having your names put alphabetically on computer, so whichever happens first, the settlement or the year, you'll get your copy.

But wait, there's more: Goldman breaks the news that Kermit Shog was willing to negotiate on some of those terms, provided that Harcourt Brace Jovanovich published *another* Morgenstern book.

The last I was told, Kermit Shog was willing to come down on his first printing provided Harcourt agreed to publish the sequel to *The Princess Bride*, which hasn't been translated into English yet, much less published here. The title of the sequel is: *Buttercup's Baby: S. Morgenstern's Glorious Examination of Courage Matched Against the Death of the Heart.*

Goldman isn't too excited about it, but the prospect of an entire sequel to *The Princess Bride* could definitely make some readers forget that they'd written in for a measly scene.

A FEW MORE WORDS

In 1978—the year in which Goldman said the reunion scene could finally be published—Goldman added a postscript to the letter. Once again, he plays with the reader's perceptions of reality via a shaggy dog story, instead of just including the reunion scene. First off, Goldman tells the reader to disregard pretty much everything he'd said in the initial letter. He had some bad news, and guess what it entailed? Yep, an excuse as to why he couldn't include the scene. It would seem that Kermit Shog,

Web site: Spiderwebs are a Christmas tree decoration in Poland.

being native to Florin, didn't understand the American numeric system, and as such accidentally led Goldman, the publisher, and their attorneys to believe that *The Princess Bride* copyright ran out in 1978…it actually ended in 1987. Also, according to Goldman, the whole matter got even more complicated somehow.

> Worse, he died. Mr. Shog I mean. (Don't ask how could you tell. It was easy. One morning he just stopped sweating, so there it was.) What makes it worse is that the whole affair is now in the hands of his kid, named—wait for it—Mandrake Shog. Mandrake moves with all the verve and speed of a lizard flaked out on a riverbank.

The bright side to this, and yes, it's another diversion: the translation of *Buttercup's Baby* is complete. Goldman is looking forward to reading it, and the grad students at Columbia University who translated it say it's even funnier and more satirical than *The Princess Bride*.

JUST A FEW WORDS MORE

After the film version of *The Princess Bride* was released, igniting new interest in the original book, Goldman added some more to the letter. Also, the film just so happened to hit theaters in 1987, which is when Goldman's previous postscript claimed might be the year the reunion scene could be released, per the end of the copyright on Morgenstern's original manuscript.

Of course, Goldman explains that the reunion scene cannot be sent out anytime soon. His reasons this time are incredibly absurd: factors include a precious element, a trade war, and NASA.

> This is getting humiliating. Have you been reading in the papers about the trade problems America is having with Japan? Well, maddening as this may be, since it reflects on the reunion scene, we're also having trade problems with Florin which, it turns out, is our leading supplier of Cadminium which, it also turns out, NASA is panting for.
>
> What this means is that the reunion scene, for now, is caught between our need for Cadminium and diplomatic relations between the two countries.

Goldman closes the letter by remarking how happy he is that it was finally made—Mandrake Shog even saw it and improbably smiled "once or twice."

In 2003 Goldman updated the book for its 30th anniversary edition. He added a footnote referring readers to a website where they could enter an email address and receive the reunion scene. But what did they receive? The same letters that Goldman and his publisher had been mailing out for 30 years (only this time by email).

Monopoly's inspiration: The Landlord's Game, invented in 1903 by Elizabeth Magie. (She made $500.)

HISTORIC HORSES

Hi-yo, Bucephalus—away! (Hm. Doesn't have the same ring to it.)

HORSTORIES

You've heard of Mr. Ed and Silver (okay, lots of you younger people might not have heard of those famous TV horses), but most of you are probably familiar with famous racehorses like Secretariat, Seabiscuit, Phar Lap, and American Pharoah, and with famous fictional horses like Black Beauty (from the 1877 novel of the same name by Anna Sewell); Rocinante (Don Quixote's horse in the novel by Miguel de Cervantes), and Shadowfax (the stallion of the wizard Gandalf from J. R. R. Tolkien's *Lord of the Rings*). Well, let's see how many of you are familiar with these famous horses from history. (Bonus: You can use this to quiz your friends on their historic horse knowledge!)

BUCEPHALUS

The huge black stallion and "warhorse" of ancient Greek conqueror Alexander the Great (356–323 BC). Alexander was 13 years old when he acquired Bucephalus and rode him for the next 18 years, into numerous battles and over thousands of miles during his campaigns from present-day Greece to central Asia, until the horse's death, reportedly at the age of 30.

TRAVELLER

The gray American Saddlebred was ridden by General Robert E. Lee, commander of Confederate forces during the American Civil War. Traveller died in 1871, just a few months after Lee himself. (You can actually see what the horse looked like, because there are several photos of Lee and Traveller from the early days of photography.) Bonus fact: When Lee bought the horse in 1862, its name was Jeff Davis, named after Mississippi senator Jefferson Davis before he became president of the Confederacy. Lee renamed him Traveller.

BABIECA

Babieca belonged to Rodrigo Díaz de Vivar (c. 1043–1099), the popular Spanish folk hero better known as El Cid. According to legend, as a coming-of-age gift, El Cid's godfather gave the young man the pick of a herd of Andalusian colts. (Andalusians are a very old breed of horses, known for their stocky, muscular bodies, and thick manes and tails.) When El Cid picked what his godfather thought was a weak horse, the godfather yelled, "Babieca!", meaning "stupid." El Cid stubbornly stood by his pick,

The word "mascot" comes from the French *mascotte*, which means "lucky charm."

and named the horse Babieca in honor of the moment. (You can see Babieca's tomb in the cemetery of the San Pedro de Cardeña Monastery, near the city of Burgos, in north-central Spain.)

INCITATUS

The favorite horse of Roman emperor Caligula (12–41 AD). Legends involving the horse abound, including that he lived in a stable made of marble, had a manger of ivory, was fed oats mixed with flakes of gold, was made a consul in the Roman government, and that he was made a priest. (According to historians, most of the legends are untrue.)

MARENGO

The gray Arabian horse belonging to French emperor Napoleon Bonaparte. Napoleon rode the horse in many famous battles, including his last, the Battle of Waterloo, after which Marengo was captured by the British and shipped to England, where he died at the ripe old age of 38. Want to see him? His skeleton still stands at the National Army Museum in London. (Minus his hooves, one of which was made into a snuff box, which resides in the Household Cavalry Museum, also in London.)

SAMPSON

The largest and heaviest horse on record. The Shire breed horse, foaled in 1846 in Toddington Mills, England, stood 21.25 hands high at the withers (the top of a horse's shoulders). How tall is that? It's 7 feet, 2½ inches—more than an inch taller than Shaquille O'Neal. (And that's just at the shoulders. He was more than 9 feet tall measured to the top of his head.) Sampson's weight was estimated at 3,360 pounds.

BURMESE

The black mare was a favorite horse of Queen Elizabeth II. She was foaled in 1962 at a Royal Canadian Mounted Police ranch in Fort Walsh, Saskatchewan, and was presented to the queen in 1969, when the RCMP took part in the Royal Windsor Horse Show. The queen rode Burmese in 18 consecutive "Trooping the Colour" ceremonies (a military ceremony performed by members of Commonwealth armies since the 17th century), from 1969 until 1986. Burmese was put out to pasture on the grounds of Windsor Castle, and died there in 1990. (In the famous photo of Queen Elizabeth and President Reagan chatting while on horseback, that's Burmese that Her Majesty is riding.)

SERGEANT RECKLESS

A chestnut mare of the Mongolian breed, Sergeant Reckless really was a sergeant: she was given the official rank—a promotion from corporal—by the U.S. Marine Corps in 1954, after serving for nine months during the Korean War. The horse was purchased from a young Korean man in 1952, and became the packhorse for a Marine

The Pentagon has five sides because it was going to be built on a five-sided piece of land. The site changed, but the building didn't.

Recoilless Rifle Platoon. She carried ammunition and other vital supplies—often from supply sites to front lines *by herself*—during several combat operations. She was also used to carry wounded soldiers away from enemy fire and to safety. Sergeant Reckless was shipped to the United States in 1954, and was retired from service in 1960. Some of the medals she received for her Korean War service: two Purple Hearts, a Good Conduct Medal, a Presidential Unit Citation, a Korean Service Medal, and a United Nations Service Medal.

COMANCHE

The U.S. Army 7th Cavalry horse ridden by Captain Myles Keogh in General George Custer's disastrous Battle of the Little Bighorn against Native American tribes, in 1876. Like Custer and most of his men, Keogh was killed in the battle, but Comanche, despite being shot several times, survived. The horse, who got his name from Captain Keogh after being wounded in an earlier battle with Comanche Indians, lived out the rest of his years at Fort Riley in Kansas, and died there in 1891, at the age of 29. Then…he was taxidermied. His stuffed remains are on display in a glass case at the University of Kansas's Natural History Museum.

PROMETEA

And finally, one very recent historic horse: Prometea, a Haflinger horse (a small, chestnut-colored breed developed in northern Italy and Austria in the 18th century), who was born on May 28, 2003, in Cremona, Italy. What's so special about her? She was the first cloned horse in history, having been "born" at the Laboratory of Reproductive Technology. She was carried by and birthed from the horse she was cloned from, meaning she was born from her identical twin. Five years later, Prometea made equine history again, when she gave birth to a healthy foal, making her the first cloned horse to give birth.

* * *

HORSE SENSE

"A man on a horse is spiritually, as well as physically, bigger than a man on foot."
—John Steinbeck
"No hour of life is lost that is spent in the saddle."
—Winston Churchill
"It's hard to lead a cavalry charge if you think you look funny on a horse."
—Adlai E. Stevenson II
"Horse sense is the thing a horse has which keeps it from betting on people."
—W.C. Fields

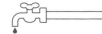

Before vacuums, people placed cloths called *druggets,*
or crumb catchers, over carpets to keep them clean.

PRESIDENTIAL ALSO-RANS

We all remember the candidates in the 2016 presidential election: Donald Trump and Hillary Clinton, right? But did you know that there were actually more than 400 other candidates in the race? Turns out anyone can fill out FEC Form 2, the one-page statement of candidacy, and file it with the Federal Election Commission, free of charge. You don't even have to use your real name. Here are some of the stranger entrants in the 2016 race.

Brink Sanity (Republican), The Brink of Sanity for President in 2016 Committee

Frosty Chicken (Independent), Frosty Chicken 4 Prez! Committee

Rarest Pepe (Unknown), Committee to Make Pepe Rare

Jean-Luc Picard (No Party Affiliation), United Federation of Planets

Ultra-MC Harry The MLG Wizard Potter UMC HP (Commandments Party), Gryffindor MLG C0DSW4G XXXDDDDDDD Committee

Mister Han James Solo (TRA), The Rebel Alliance Committee, Forest Moon of Endor

Reverend Pamela M. Pinkney Butts (Multipartisan), Pinkney Butts 2016 Committee

President Emperor Caesar (Democratic), President Emperor Caesar Committee

Mary Jane (Libertarian), Marijuana for President Committee

Some Lice (Republican), Committee of Lice

Why So Many Trolls (Independent), Trolls For President Committee

Ponzi Schemes Suck (Prohibition), Ashley Samuelson Committee

Anus The Goat (Democratic), Anus for President Committee

HipHop For President (Democratic), HipHop For President Committee

Paul Y. Potato (Write-In), People for Mr. Potato Committee

Devon "Deez" Nutz Padgett (Republican), Committee to Elect Deez Nutz

Mr. Grump (Independent), I'm Grump, And I'm Not So Grump, And We're The Game Grump—Arin and Danny Grump Committee

Coffee and Donuts (Non Partisan), Everybody Loves Coffee and Donuts Committee

Mr. Porcupines R. Spikey Jr. (American Independent), Spikey for President Committee

Zibble the Puppet (No Party Affiliation), Puppet Freedom Force Committee

Sister city of Boring, Oregon: Dull, Scotland.

Dank Ass Weed (Independent), Dank Ass Weed for President Committee

Lady Sparkle Kawaii (Independent), Lolitas on Liberty Committee

President Princess Khadijah M. Jacob-Fambro (Revolutionary Party), From One Alien to Another Alien "Lil Wayne" Dwayne Michael Carter Jr. "President Carter" Will You Marry Me? I Am God!!! President Princess Khadijah M. Jacob-Fambro Committee

Max Cat McCoy (Republican), Smugcat Committee

Buffy Anne Summers (Socialist), The Scoobies Committee

Michael Andrew, Duke of Leppert (Other), Big Booty Bitches Inc. Committee

HRM Caesar Saint Augustine de Buonaparte Emperor of the United States of Turtle Island (Absolute Dictator Party), Sovereign Citizens Committees HRM Caesar Saint Augustine de Buonaparte

Commandant Dog Eating Maniacal Fish Brained Ugly Moose Lookalike Fool That Will Be Elected (Republican), Oh No I Just Married My Sister OJ Simpson Oh No!!!!!!!!!! !!! Committee.

Moose the Dog (Jewish/Christian National Party), Your Mom Committee

Foot Cheese (None), Foot Cheese For President 2016 Committee

Osama Bin Liftin (UN Party), Bin Liftin For President Committee

Zorro the Cockroach (Communist), Osama bin Laden Committee

Kermit Frog (Boiling Frog), Kermit the Frog for President Committee

Mr. Jesus Iron Man Chris D Rockman Jr. (Independent), Jesus Iron Man Chris Rockman for President Committee

The Crawling Chaos Nyarlathotep (Communist), Church of Starry Wisdom Committee

The Ghost of Christmas Present MMXV (One Earth Party), Past Present Future Committee

Sydney's Voluptuous Buttocks (Independent), The Syd Buttocks Committee

@lolmynameisjon (Peace and Freedom), Lolmynameisjon for President 2k16 Committee

Disco Daddy (Other), LGBT Nationalist Party Committee

Fredrickson Asshat Kazoo (Other), Kazoos for the People Committee

This Is Fake (Republican), Fake For President Committee

Lucille Hamster (OE), Lucille Hamster for President Committee

Ms Bunny H. Carr?t (Unknown), Bunny for President Committee

Benjamin Dover (Independent), Ben Dover for America Committee

Q: Why did James McNeill Whistler's mother pose for the famous painting? A: Because...

ATTENTION EARTHLINGS! WARNING!

The atomic age of the 1950s spawned a whole new genre of science fiction movies that featured radioactivity, UFOs, paranoia about invasion, and scary warnings from outer space. Here are a few of our favorites. Watch them now, puny Earthlings!

The Angry Red Planet
MARTIANS GET MAD! THEN GET EVEN!

Year: 1959

Plot: It's Earth's first manned mission to Mars…and it's a disaster. The crew is attacked by a man-eating plant, then by a giant bat-spider monster, and then an amoeba creature with a spinning eye. Only two survivors make it back to Earth, and when they do, they find that their ship is carrying a message on its data recorder.

Message from the Martians: "Men of Earth, we of the planet Mars give you this warning. Listen carefully and remember: We have known your planet Earth since the first creature crawled out of the primeval slime of your seas to become man. For millennia, we have followed your progress. For centuries, we have watched you, listened to your radio signals and learned your speech and your culture, and now you have invaded our home. Technological adults, but spiritual and emotional infants, we kept you here, deciding your fate. Had the lower forms of life on our planet destroyed you, we would not have interfered, but you survived. Your civilization has not progressed beyond destruction, war and violence against yourselves and others. Do as you will to your own and to your planet, but remember this warning—do not return to Mars. You will be permitted to leave for this sole purpose. Carry the warning to Earth—"Do not come here." We can and will destroy you—*all* life on your planet—if you do not heed us. You have seen us, been permitted to glimpse our world. Go now. Warn mankind not to return unbidden."

The Thing from Another World
IT CREEPS…IT CRAWLS…IT STRIKES WITHOUT WARNING!

Year: 1951

Plot: At an arctic research outpost, scientists locate a crashed spaceship and its alien pilot frozen in the ice nearby. When they take the frozen body to the

…the model who was supposed to pose didn't show up that day.

base, it accidentally thaws. It turns out to be a plant-based life-form that feeds on blood. When it goes on a murderous rampage, the scientists make a last-stand attempt to stop it.

Warning from a radio reporter: "Every one of you listening to my voice. Tell the world. Tell this to everybody, wherever they are. Watch the skies. Everywhere. Keep looking. Keep watching the skies!"

The Day the Earth Stood Still
FROM OUT OF SPACE...A WARNING
AND AN ULTIMATUM!

Year: 1951

Plot: When humanoid alien Klaatu and his 8-foot-tall robot, Gort, land their spaceship in the heart of Washington, DC, the U.S. military goes all-out to destroy them, but that doesn't stop the aliens from bringing their powerful message to all of the people of Earth.

Message from the alien Klaatu: "I am leaving soon, and you will forgive me if I speak bluntly. The universe grows smaller every day, and the threat of aggression by any group, anywhere, can no longer be tolerated. There must be security for all, or no one is secure. Now, this does not mean giving up any freedom, except the freedom to act irresponsibly. Your ancestors knew this when they made laws to govern themselves and hired policemen to enforce them. We, of the other planets, have long accepted this principle. We have an organization for the mutual protection of all planets and for the complete elimination of aggression. The test of any such higher authority is, of course, the police force that supports it. For our policemen, we created a race of robots. Their function is to patrol the planets in spaceships like this one and preserve the peace. In matters of aggression, we have given them absolute power over us. This power cannot be revoked. At the first sign of violence, they act automatically against the aggressor. The penalty for provoking their action is too terrible to risk. The result is, we live in peace, without arms or armies, secure in the knowledge that we are free from aggression and war. Free to pursue more...profitable enterprises. Now, we do not pretend to have achieved perfection, but we do have a system, and it works. I came here to give you these facts. It is no concern of ours how you run your own planet, but if you threaten to extend your violence, this Earth of yours will be reduced to a burned-out cinder. Your choice is simple: join us and live in peace, or pursue your present course and face obliteration. We shall be waiting for your answer. The decision rests with you."

Wood you believe? Pound for pound, the most flatulent creature on Earth is the termite.

Earth vs. the Flying Saucers
WARNING! TAKE COVER!

Year: 1956

Plot: Flying saucers filled with aliens from a dying planet attack Washington, DC, and the U.S. military fights back. The saucer creatures meet with one of Earth's top scientists and tell him that they had come in peace, but it's a trick—they're really invading Earth. It turns out that the aliens, who wear suits made of solid electricity and have the power to extract information directly from the human brain, can be killed with handguns. The scientist invents an antimagnetic ray and successfully destroys the saucers before the saucers can destroy humanity.

Message from the aliens: "Attention! People of Earth, attention! This is a voice speaking to you from thousands of miles beyond your planet. Look to your sun for a warning!"

It Came from Outer Space
REACHING FROM THE SCREEN TO SEIZE YOU IN ITS GRASP!

Year: 1953

Plot: An astronomer named John Putnam and his girlfriend watch as a fiery meteorite crashes in the desert. But it's not a meteorite—it's a spaceship. Putnam reports the crash to the sheriff. The sheriff doesn't believe him. Meanwhile, several townspeople have started behaving like zombies. Putnam returns to the crash site, where the head alien tells him the crash was an accident and the aliens just want to repair their ship and leave. Putnam discovers that the aliens, who are one-eyed and slimy, have been abducting people and assuming their shapes so that they can go into town to gather the materials they need for their repairs. As a good-faith gesture, the aliens release the abductees. In return, Putnam helps hold off the hostile sheriff and his posse while the friendly aliens make their escape from Earth.

Warning from John Putnam when asked if the aliens are gone for good:
"No, just for now. It wasn't the right time for us to meet. But there will be other nights, other stars for us to watch. They'll be back."

* * *

"If you're too open-minded, your brains will fall out." **—Lawrence Ferlinghetti**

First state to make Christmas a holiday: Alabama (1836).

PLANET 9 FROM OUTER SPACE

If you're still smarting over the "demotion" of Pluto to dwarf planet status in 2006, take heart! The same astronomer who played a big part in Pluto's reclassification says there's credible evidence that a ninth planet—a real one this time—is lurking somewhere far beyond Neptune in the outer reaches of the solar system.

LOOKING UP

In 2012 two astronomers named Chad Trujillo and Scott Sheppard discovered what may be another dwarf planet in the *Kuiper belt*, a band of a billion or more of objects orbiting the Sun, in a Saturn-like ring, beyond Neptune. Pluto was the first object discovered in the Kuiper belt, and that was in 1930. Since then, more than 1,300 Kuiper belt objects, or KBOs, have been observed. Most are too small to be considered dwarf planets, but a handful of the KBOs discovered are similar to Pluto in size.

The object discovered by Trujillo and Sheppard in 2012 is likely to be a dwarf planet. When they reported their find to the International Astronomical Union, the organization responsible for naming planets and celestial bodies, the IAU gave it the designation 2012 VP113. But who wants to call it that? Trujillo and Sheppard referred to it simply as "VP" at first, and then nicknamed it "Biden," after then-U.S. vice president Joe Biden.

Trujillo and Sheppard were studying other distant objects in the Kuiper belt as well, and they noticed that 13 of the most distant—Biden included—had odd orbits that suggested they were being pulled by the gravitational force of an unknown planet in the solar system.

POINTERS

Trujillo and Sheppard's work prompted two Caltech astronomers, Mike Brown and Konstantin Batygin, to study the same 13 Kuiper belt objects. If the name Mike Brown sounds familiar, that could be because he was the guy who discovered Eris, a Kuiper belt object that has a greater mass than Pluto (but is slightly smaller in size). The discovery of Eris is what prompted the IAU to reclassify both Pluto and Eris, and other objects like them, as dwarf planets in 2006.

Brown and Batygin observed that the six most distant of the 13 Kuiper belt objects had orbits that all pointed in the same direction in space. They estimated that the odds of this happening purely by chance were 1 in 100. In other words, there was a 99

percent chance that the gravitational force of some unknown object had *caused* the orbits to point in the same direction.

In addition, the orbits of the six outermost objects were tilted roughly 30 degrees downward in relation to the orbits of Earth and the other planets in the solar system. Brown and Batygin calculated that the odds of that happening at random were even lower: less than one one-hundredth of 1 percent. That meant that there was a 99.99 percent chance that the gravitational pull of an unknown object (or objects) had caused the 30-degree tilt.

PULLERS

Like Trujillo and Sheppard, Brown and Batygin suspected that an unknown planet might be responsible for these odd orbits. But they had to consider all the possibilities, so they began running computer simulations of many different scenarios—one planet, more than one planet, lots of smaller objects, etc.—to find a scenario that would explain the orbits they had observed. One possibility they examined was whether a cluster of undiscovered Kuiper belt objects might be the culprit. But none of the cluster simulations they ran produced the orbits that had been observed.

Another possibility they simulated in their computer was a planet that orbited the Sun beyond the orbits of the six Kuiper belt objects. But no matter what size planet they used, or where they placed it in space, none of the simulations worked.

Next, they tried a planet in an "anti-aligned orbit," which meant that for part of its orbit, it was farther from the Sun than the other six objects, and for part of its orbit it was closer. And the planet's *perihelion*, or closest approach to the Sun, was 180 degrees on the opposite side of the Sun than the perihelions of the other six objects. When Brown and Batygin ran this simulation, it worked.

And there was a bonus: the simulation also provided an explanation for the unusual orbit of another Kuiper belt object called Sedna, which Brown, Trujillo, and a third astronomer, David Rabinowitz, discovered in 2003 and had puzzled over ever since. Unlike many other large bodies in the Kuiper belt, Sedna never gets close enough to Neptune to be strongly influenced by that planet's gravitational pull. Brown and Batygin theorized that the undiscovered planet, if it existed, might have pulled Sedna away from Neptune, and in the process reduced Neptune's influence on it.

> **Brown and Batygin suspected that an unknown planet might be responsible for these odd orbits.**

TRIFECTA

Another thing the computer model predicted—and which surprised Brown and

...blue beehive, something that would not be revealed until the very last episode of the show.

Batygin—was that some other Kuiper belt objects would orbit the Sun on a plane that was perpendicular to the plane of the planets as they orbit the Sun. If the planets were on horizontal plane (think east to west), these Kuiper belt objects would be orbiting on a vertical plane (north to south). And as Brown and Batygin quickly realized, five such objects had already been found, though their unusual orbits had not been explained.

Until now.

"When the simulation aligned the distant Kuiper belt objects and created objects like Sedna, we thought this is kind of awesome—you kill two birds with one stone," Batygin recounted in 2016. "But with the existence of the planet also explaining these perpendicular orbits, not only do you kill two birds, you also take down a bird that you didn't realize was sitting in a nearby tree."

FAR OUT

According to the computer model, "Planet 9," as it has become known, has ten times the mass of Earth and two to four times its diameter. The plane of its orbit is inclined about 30 degrees from the orbital plane of the other eight planets in the solar system.

> The only way to prove for certain that an undiscovered planet exists is to actually *discover* it.

And unlike the other planets, its orbit is highly elliptical, rather than circular. At its closest approach to the Sun, it is 200 *astronomical units* from the Sun. (One AU is the average distance between the Sun and Earth, or about 93 million miles.) At its most distant point, Planet 9 is 1,200 AU from the Sun. With this orbit, it would take somewhere between 10,000 and 20,000 years to complete one trip around the Sun.

Planet 9 may not always have been so far out. It may once have been much closer in, but may have traveled too close to Jupiter or Saturn and been flung by their gravitational field out into the far reaches of the solar system. Another possibility is that it is an *exoplanet,* or planet from another solar system, that floated near our solar system some 4.5 billion years ago, and was captured by the gravitational pull of the Sun or the planets and has been hanging around ever since.

SLINGSHOT

It's still possible that some other explanation exists; the only way to prove for certain that an undiscovered planet exists is to actually *discover* it. Brown, Batygin, and doubtless other astronomers are searching the skies along the proposed orbit of Planet 9, looking for visual evidence that it really is there. If the planet is at a point in its orbit where it's close to the Sun, any number of astronomical observatories around the world may be able to spot it. Even better, if it is nearby, it may already have been

Even the ancient Romans had wedding cakes...of sorts: They were barley cakes, and the groom broke one over the bride's head for good luck.

photographed in previous surveys of the sky, and all that needs to be done is to search the old images for an object that matches Planet 9's description, and that is traveling in the same orbital path.

But if Planet 9 is at a more distant point along its orbit, only the largest, most sophisticated telescopes will be able to see it. More bad news: as a planet moves farther away from the Sun, it slows down. This means that it spends more time in the part of its orbit that is far from the Sun, so it's more likely to be far away than it is to be nearby. Finding it, if it really exists, may prove to be quite a challenge.

PROOF IS IN THE PUDDING

Mike Brown's discovery of the dwarf planet Eris in 2005 led to the reclassification of Pluto as a dwarf planet, and many fans of the former planet still haven't gotten over it. The discovery of Planet 9 may help ease their pain. "All those people who are mad that Pluto is no longer a planet can be thrilled to know that there is a real planet out there still to be found. Now," he says, "we can go and find this planet and make the solar system have nine planets once again."

* * *

OOPS!

- Three Tennessee Air National Guard members got into big trouble following a 2018 swearing-in ceremony. Master Sergeant Robin Brown took her oath while holding up a dinosaur hand puppet mouthing the words: "I do solemnly swear that I will support and defend the Constitution of the United States against all enemies, foreign and domestic." Brown was promptly removed from her post, and the colonel who administered the oath received an official reprimand. So did the unit sergeant who filmed the ceremony…which went viral.

- The American men's curling team shocked the world at the 2018 Winter Olympics by coming from behind to win gold. Even the award presenters must have been shocked, because they awarded the men gold medals that read "Women's Curling."

- Beverly Harrison, 62, was living in an Alabama motel room in February 2018 when some family members brought her a ham. Harrison hates ham. She hates it so much that she threw it in the garbage and lit it on fire. Then she took her dog for a walk. While she was out, the fire heated up a nearby can of butane, which exploded, sending shrapnel and ham chunks flying and blowing out the room's door and window. When Harrison returned from her walk, she was arrested and charged with arson.

According to NASA researchers, the perfect length for a nap is 26 minutes.

JUST SAY NO TO CHICKEN POWDER

In 2017 the U.S. Drug Enforcement Agency declassified a report that listed all known nicknames, street terms, and strain names for various illegal drugs. Some of them refer to the color or shape of the product and others refer to…well, we don't really know. Regardless, please remember: Drugs are no laughing matter—even if some of these names for them are.

MARIJUANA
Blue Cheese
Gorilla Glue
Barbara Jean
Love Nuggets
Mother
Platinum Jack
Acapulco Gold
Big Pillows
Animal Cookies
Christmas Tree
Burritos Verdes
Gummy Bears
Hairy Ones

METHAMPHETAMINE
Colorado Rockies
Hawaiian Salt
Chicken Powder
Accordion
Pantalones
Bud Light
Peanut Butter Crank
Witches' Teeth
Pointy Ones

PCP
Water
Butt Naked
Dummy Dust
Horse Tracks
Alien Sex Fiend (when
    mixed with heroin)
Black Whack
Amoeba
Detroit Pink
Love Boat
Gorilla Biscuits
Embalming Fluid
Leaky Leak
T-Buzz

PRESCRIPTION PAINKILLERS
Rims
Wheels
Bananas
Blueberries
Hillbilly Heroin
Hulk
School Bus

OPIUM
Chocolate
Dream Gum
Gondola
Aunt Emma
Joy Plant
Chinese Molasses
Zero
Cruz
Midnight Oil
Toys

MDMA (ECSTASY)
Kleenex
Baby Slits
Scooby Snacks
Skittle
Doctor
Disco Biscuits

MUSHROOMS
Hongos
Alice
Boomers
Silly Putty

Anna Strong, a Revolutionary War spy, sent coded messages by
hanging petticoats and handkerchiefs on her clothesline.

RUSSIAN SPY WARS

The Cold War ended in 1991, but we appear to be entering Cold War 2.0. To help you understand Russian espionage, here is a glossary of its not-so-secret terms.

Active measures. The steps the Kremlin takes to influence the affairs of nations around the globe. The modern "active measures" arsenal includes propaganda, disinformation, deception, forgery, funding of extremist and opposition groups, election tampering, spreading conspiracy theories and rumor, cyberattacks, espionage, and....assassination.

Chekist. The KGB term for intelligence officers, used in honor of the *Cheka*, Vladimir Lenin's vicious and brutal secret police. In modern Russia, all current intelligence officers continue to commemorate their lineage by calling themselves *Chekists*, because as Russian president—and KGB veteran—Vladimir Putin says, "There are no former *Chekists*."

Honeypots. It's not specifically a Russian term, but refers to a trap of desire, designed to seduce an unsuspecting target. Once ensnared, the target is ripe for blackmail. The seducer may be a "swallow" (woman) or a "raven" (man). The honeypot itself can be sex, money, information, power—whatever is desirable and most valuable to the target.

Wet work (also wet affairs or liquid affairs). A euphemism for murder or assassination. The Russian term can be traced to 19th-century criminal slang used to describe any robbery that involved murder or the spilling of blood.

Department S. The most secret department of the KGB and where men and women were trained and deployed to live as deep-cover agents, known as "illegals" in the West. While the KGB no longer exists, Russia is still seeding deep-cover spies throughout the world. In 2010 the FBI conducted an operation called Ghost Stories, arresting ten illegals, some of whom had been installed in the United States before the fall of the Soviet Union.

Wet boys. The assassins who do wet work.

Kamera. The "Chamber"—a laboratory established by Lenin in 1921 to study and develop poisons into weapons. While it has been called many names over the years—the Special Room, Laboratory No. 1, and Lab X—its informal name has always been the Kamera. This is the place where the R&D focuses on killing people without leaving a trace.

Air-conditioning was invented by Willis Carrier in 1902—to lower humidity in a printing plant.

Deza (short for *dezinformatsiya*— "disinformation" or fake news). An old-school Soviet tactic—weaponizing lies to make the public doubt something that is true and demonstrable. From its very beginning, *deza* was meant to deceive. Stalin deliberately created the French-sounding term and then falsely declared it was of Western origin. In the hands of Russian espionage, *deza* is designed to embarrass, destabilize, and shift public opinion. While it's an old-school tool, the internet—along with social media, bots, and trolls—makes it much easier and faster to distribute.

Illegals. Deep-cover spies who live and work in their target country as ordinary citizens, keeping their real identities hidden from everyone, including their children. They may spend decades developing their "legend," or cover story, while working covertly for the Kremlin.

Spetsbureau 13 ("Department of Wet Affairs"). The top-secret department of the KGB/FSB whose agents have the license to kill.

Kompromat. A combination of two words—"compromising" and "material." In the hands of the Kremlin, *kompromat* is a collection of documented evidence that, if released, could destroy the reputation of an individual or business entity. Sex, pornography, financial crimes, and corruption are all dark material that the target would rather not have see the light of day. The fear of *kompromat* is almost as potent as the *kompromat* itself. The beauty of *kompromat* is that it doesn't matter if the evidence is real, just as long as it creates enough doubt so that it can be used for blackmail.

Glavy protivnik. That's Russian for "main adversary"—the Soviet Union's term for the United States during the Cold War. Given that the current tensions between Russia and America appear to be returning to Cold War levels, it should be no surprise to learn that, according to some sources, Putin has revived calling the United States its "main adversary."

* * *

ZPELLBOUND

Ever notice that prescription drug names seem to include Xs and Zs more often than regular words? (For example, Celebrex and Xeljanz.) That's because drug manufacturers have to come up with unique names in order to differentiate their products from all the other medications on the market. Result: "Z" appears in drug names 18 times more often than it does in regular English, and X appears 16 times more often.

In the video game *Walden,* players write in a journal, visit with Ralph Waldo Emerson, and walk in a forest.

THOU SHALT READ!

It's been said that what you read as a child stays with you in a way that no other book ever will…and it's true. Not only can children's books affect their readers, they're meant to do that very thing. They teach, indoctrinate, influence, and—at their best—they inspire. Here's a look at important milestones in the nearly 400-year history of children's literature and children's publishing.

1658 The world's first known picture book is published: *Orbis Sensualium Pictus (The World of Things Obvious to the Senses Drawn in Pictures)* by John Amos Comenius. This compendium of knowledge included pictures of everyday activities such as baking bread, brewing beer, and butchering animals. Each activity was described in detail. The barber, for example, cut more than just hair:

> Sometimes he cutteth a *Vein*
> with a *Pen-knife,*
> where the Blood
> spirteth out....

Within the *Orbis Pictus*, kids could find a little bit about "all things that can be shewed."

- To teach them their ABC's, it had a picture to illustrate each letter, along with a descriptive caption such as "the **G**oose gagleth," "the **C**hicken peepeth," and "the **F**rog croaketh."

- Kids could learn about shipwrecks ("Dead Folks" are carried out of the sea upon the shores), magnifying glasses ("a Flea appeareth…like a little Hog"), and marriage ("they are joined together," and "when she is dead he becometh Widower").

- There was even a section about "Monstrous and Deformed People," including the *crump-footed*, the *blubber-lipped*, the *great-nosed*, and the *bald-pated*.

The *Orbis Pictus* became the world's first international children's book sensation. At least for some children. Actually, just boys. "Come boy," the book begins, "and learn to be wise." (Girls do get a mention in a section called "The Seven Ages of Man." They're "the *other* sex.")

The daisy gets its name from the Old English *dæges ēage,* or "day's eye," because the blossom opens in the morning and closes at night.

1693   British philosopher John Locke wrote about politics and human consciousness, but he also had a lot to say about raising children, and wrote an influential book titled *Some Thoughts Concerning Education*. Learning to read, he insisted, should be fun. If children enjoy reading instead of dreading it, "there will be but very rarely an occasion for blows or force" in their education. Instead of being about learning to read, he said, children's books should share stories.

1765   Another John—John Newbery—took Locke's words to heart, publishing what has been described as the first children's novel: *The History of Little Goody Two Shoes*. The book was ostensibly written for the benefit of those

> *Who from a State of Rags and Care*
> *And having Shoes but half a Pair;*
> *Their Fortune and their Fame would fix,*
> *And gallop in a Coach and Six.*

If the story sounds familiar…it should. It's a rustic version of Cinderella. Farmer Meanwell and his wife hit hard times and lose their farm. Then the father and mother fall ill and die, leaving their children, Margery and Tommy, orphans. Life for Margery is tough. On top of being alone in the world: "Tommy had two shoes but *Margery* went barefoot." But a rich gentleman comes along and offers to take Tommy with him to London. And then a tearful Margery learns that the gentleman has ordered her a pair of shoes. "Two shoes!" she rejoices. She says it so often that she gets the nickname Goody Two-Shoes. ("Goody" is an archaic version of "Mrs." or "Miss.") Margery lives happily ever after—she learns to read, becomes a teacher, and marries a local landowner. No balls. No gowns. No fairy godmother. Just two shoes and a man of means.

1865   *Alice's Adventures in Wonderland* by Lewis Carroll (real name: Charles Dodgson) took children's books down a rabbit hole into what some believed must have been a drug-induced fantasy. The story had mushrooms that make you smaller or taller, a hookah-smoking caterpillar, and a Mad Hatter singing "Twinkle, twinkle little bat…how I wonder where you're at?" In response to those who see drug usage in his books, experts insist that while such modern interpretations may make for interesting scholarly theses, they do not reflect the author's actual habits or inclinations.

Temperature inside of a NASCAR car mid-race: 120°F.

In fact, Wonderland began in a rowboat on the Thames with Dodgson—a young Oxford mathematician—trying to amuse the dean's three children by making up a story. The book's main character was named for one of those children, 10-year-old Alice Liddell. In the story, Alice follows a white rabbit, falls down a deep hole, and lands in a room with a table and a bottle labeled "Drink me." After checking to make sure it's not poison, Alice does drink it, noting that it tastes of "cherry-tart, custard, pineapple, roast turkey, toffee, and hot buttered toast." Thus begins a tale destined to change children's books forever because it had one purpose: to entertain readers. That's what makes *Alice's Adventures in Wonderland* a milestone. Instead of trying to teach children, the author simply wanted to give them a smile (like the Cheshire cat's).

1960s

Short simple sentences. Three-letter rhyming words. Theodore Seuss Geisel (a.k.a. Dr. Seuss) brought back books that teach kids to read, but his snarky sense of humor, his playful way with words, and his whimsical illustrations also brought something new to the staid world of children's book: silliness.

He wrote his first in 1936. It was an ABC book featuring imaginary creatures. At the time, the "long-necked whizzleworp" and the "green-striped cholmondelet" did nothing for New York publishers. His work was so weird that 27 editors turned it down. In fact, if one of his old college friends hadn't become a children's book editor, he might never have found a publisher for his first published effort, *And to Think That I Saw It on Mulberry Street*. The long title itself might have done him in. But fortunately for the future of kids' books, he bumped into his friend on Madison Avenue, showed him the manuscript, and the rest is publishing history. "If I had been going down the other side of Madison Avenue," Seuss later said, "I'd be in the dry-cleaning business today."

That would have been a huge loss for generations of children who grew up with *The Cat in the Hat*, *Green Eggs and Ham*, and *Horton Hears a Who*...and an even bigger loss for his publishers. By 1960 three million Seuss books were in the hands of eager readers. By 2015 the number had climbed to more than 750 million. More than half a century after their original publication dates, Dr. Seuss's children's books continue to top best-seller lists.

Remember the creature in the *Alien* movies? The goblin shark grabs its prey by "shooting" its jaw almost entirely outside of its body.

1962

For generations, when it came to children's books, every book that rolled off the American and British presses reflected the dominant (white) culture. When people with dark skin showed up, they were never the heroes. Ezra Jack Keats changed that. Keats came from an immigrant family of Polish Jews who lived in Brooklyn. After years of illustrating books for other writers, he got the chance to write and illustrate his own book, and for his hero, he chose a spunky kid whose picture he'd clipped from a copy of *Life* magazine. The book, *The Snowy Day*, was about a little boy putzing around his neighborhood on a snow day. What's so groundbreaking about that? The kid—who Keats named Peter—was black.

Keats wasn't black, but he understood discrimination at a gut level: after all, he'd served in World War II and changed his name from Katz to Keats in a response to the violent anti-Semitism of his era. If the book had faded into obscurity, the door to diversity in children's books might have slammed shut. It didn't. *The Snowy Day* won the Caldecott Medal in 1963, given for the most outstanding illustrated book of the year. It also became a best-seller. For kids of color, it turned the mirror around so they could see themselves as heroes. "For the first time," one teacher wrote to Keats, "the kids in my class are using brown crayons to draw themselves."

1970s

Through the centuries, children's books changed to reflect changes in the culture around them. Those changes once oozed out slower than ketchup from a glass bottle. The youth-led culture shift of the 1970s was kind of like sticking a butter knife up the neck of that bottle. Stories that were different, dark, or debatable flowed into publishers' offices and a new generation of editors fought to give them a place on bookshelves.

Today's young readers may not know it, but they can thank their grandparents' generation for the fact that, these days, anything goes when it comes to children's books. They gave us books about boys playing with dolls (*William's Doll*, Charlotte Zolotow, 1972), books protesting the mutually destructive nature of war (*The Butter Battle Book*, Dr. Seuss, 1984), and books about protecting the planet (*50 Simple Things Kids Can Do to Save the Earth* by our own Uncle John, 1990).

They also gave us a children's book that would probably have shocked the socks off John Locke. In 1992 Chronicle Books, a San Francisco publisher founded during 1967's "Summer of Love,"

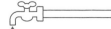

High flyers: A pilot flying over the Himalayas once spotted a flock of bar-headed geese at 29,000 feet.

published *The House That Crack Built*—a book about crack cocaine and the tragic results of the drug wars that plague America. Writing with a hip-hop beat, author Clark Taylor delivered lines such as "This is the Street of a town in pain/This is the Girl who's killing her brain." And *that* pretty much sums up how much children's books have changed since the days of Goody Two-Shoes.

1998

How many children's books have theme parks around the world? That would be one: Harry Potter. The Wizarding World of Harry Potter opened in Orlando, Florida, in 2010, and more attractions followed in California and Japan, Australia, and England. Before the parks, there were Potter-themed movies, toys, and a long list of spin-off books and merchandise. But before *that* came the real children's literature milestone: a book about a young wizard named Harry written by an unknown author, J. K. Rowling.

Anyone who hasn't heard J. K. Rowling's rags-to-riches story must have spent the last 20 years stuck inside a vanishing cabinet. Rowling went from a struggling single mom to one of the wealthiest people on the planet. The book that started it all—*Harry Potter and the Sorcerer's Stone*—saw its first UK edition published in 1997, and its first U.S. release in 1998. The book grabbed young readers like no other book in the history of children's literature. Reviewers from the *Glasgow Herald* declared they had "yet to find a child who can put it down." The seven books in the Harry Potter series have now sold 400 million copies.

As for the effect Rowling's writing had on children's publishing, there are two main time periods: before Harry and after Harry. Before Harry, children's literature was the often-ignored younger sibling of "real" publishing (meaning books for adults). "The publishing of children's books," wrote one industry expert, "tended to be in a ghetto." After Harry, the sky above the ghetto started raining money and children's books became big business. Rowling, now the world's richest author, is reportedly worth more than $1 billion; the value of the Harry Potter franchise has topped $25 billion. With that much money at stake, children's publishing became a whole new animal… with a hunger for more of the same. *Twilight*, *The Hunger Games*, and *Percy Jackson and the Olympians* are just a few of the fantasy series feeding the beast…and you can bet your Quidditch stick that we'll see more changes.

The largest-ever bag of potato chips (made by UK chipmaker Corkers in 2013) was 18 feet tall and contained 2,515 chips.

Here are a few more groundbreaking kids' books:

1958: *The Rabbits' Wedding* by Garth Williams
(interracial marriage, bunny style)

1962: *A Wrinkle in Time* by Madeleine L'Engle
(girls can be sci-fi heroes)

1970: *Are You There, God? It's Me, Margaret* by Judy Blume
(girls have periods)

1970: *In the Night Kitchen* by Maurice Sendak
(full-frontal nudity!)

1971: *The Lorax* by Dr. Seuss
(cutting down trees stinks)

1977: *Everyone Poops* by Taro Gomi
(everyone...well, you know)

1997: *The Adventures of Captain Underpants* by Dav Pilkey
(now we can say underwear!)

2005: *And Tango Makes Three* by Justin Richardson and Peter Parnell
(same-sex penguins can be loving parents)

2015: *Last Stop on Market Street* by Matt de la Peña
(even poverty has its upsides)

For a list of the most questionable kids' books to ever go to press, see page 466.

For a list of the most questionable kids' books to ever go to press, see page 466.

*   *   *

BOOING IS BORN

In ancient Greece, the playwriting competition at the annual Festival of Dionysia in Athens was considered the entertainment event of the year. Playwrights from all over the Greek world presented their latest tragedies, and at the end, one would be proclaimed the best. When a democratic-minded emperor named Cleisthenes took power in the sixth century BC, he let the audience be the judge: the crowd applauded the plays they liked and whistled at the ones they didn't. Those practices continued on to ancient Rome and its peculiar form of entertainment—gladiator battles—with crowds adding hissing to the whistling. (Hissing is basically whistling, but it's easier to do because it's done with the tongue and not the lips.) By the 13th century, the English had a word to describe the ominous sound of a displeased crowd whistling and hooting in unison: "hoot." Before long, people were just saying the word "hoot" instead of hissing or whistling, and by the 1800s "hoot" had evolved into "boo."

Live free or die: In Longyearbyen, Norway, dying is illegal.

NOT MY BEST WORK

The artist and the art. Sometimes they don't get along.

Frank Zappa: "Valley Girl"

Zappa hated the fact that his 1982 hit charted higher than any other song he released in a career that spanned more than 30 years. He'd intended it as a satire of teenage girls of California's San Fernando Valley and their distinctive speech ("like, totally" and "gag me with a spoon"). To his dismay, the song—featuring his 14-year-old daughter Moon Unit on vocals—gave national exposure to what had only been a Southern California fad, and soon Valley girls were everywhere. "It just goes to show," lamented Zappa, "that the American public loves to celebrate the infantile. I mean, I don't want people to act like that. I think Valley girls are disgusting!"

Beastie Boys: "(You Gotta) Fight for Your Right (to Party!)"

The same thing happened with the Beastie Boys' 1986 hit song. "There were tons of guys singing along...who were oblivious to the fact it was a total goof on them," said Beastie Boy Mike D. The band watched in amazement as "Fight for Your Right" reached #7 in the charts and was named one of the Rock and Roll Hall of Fame's "500 Songs that Shaped Rock and Roll." When the band reluctantly included it on a greatest hits album, they admitted in the liner notes that "it sucks."

Miles Teller: *Divergent*

Teller took the part as villainous Peter in the 2014 film for "business reasons"—it was his first role in an international movie, so he was hoping for a career boost, which he got. But he agreed with most of the critics who called the film a "disappointingly predictable" knockoff of *The Hunger Games*. "I was feeling dead inside," he said of his time on set. "I called my agent and said, 'This sucks.'" (Teller reprised his role in both sequels.)

Sir Anthony Hopkins: *Transformers: The Last Knight*

Hopkins played Sir Edmund Burton in the fifth installment of the Transformers movie franchise. Burton, a British astronomer, tells Mark Wahlberg's character the history of the Transformers on Earth. For the most part, the purpose of Hopkins's character

It takes up to 50 gallons of sap to create one gallon of maple syrup.

was to explain the plot—which wasn't easy because Hopkins didn't really get it himself. "Please don't ask me to explain it," he pleaded to an interviewer. "It's so very complicated, and there's the whole mythology of four previous films that come into play. I have to admit, I don't quite get all of it."

A. A. Milne: *Winnie-the-Pooh*

Milne considered himself a serious author. He wrote well-received grown-up fare like *The Red House Mystery* (1922), which Alexander Woollcott praised as "one of the three best mystery stories of all time." Milne also wrote 35 plays, four screenplays, and was a regular contributor to *Punch* magazine, which featured satire by the most revered British writers. By the mid-1920s, Milne had a reputation as one of the literary elite. But that all changed after he started writing stories about a teddy bear who lived in the woods. The Winnie-the-Pooh books became instantly popular and within a few years had overshadowed everything else Milne ever did. While he enjoyed the sudden fame, Pooh destroyed his literary credibility.

Worse yet, the Pooh books drove a wedge between Milne and his son, Christopher Robin Milne, who was the inspiration for the lead character. As the books' popularity grew, so too did the fame of the "real Christopher Robin." Capitalizing on this, Milne made his son answer all of Christopher Robin's fan mail, read excerpts at publicity appearances, and sing songs on a Winnie-the-Pooh novelty record. Later, when Christopher was at boarding school, the other kids played the record all the time just to taunt him. It wasn't long before he wanted nothing more to do with the books… or his parents. "My father got to where he was by climbing upon my infant shoulders," wrote a bitter Christopher later in life. The rift in their relationship never mended.

Arthur Conan Doyle: Sherlock Holmes

Holmes was more famous than Doyle, and Doyle really hated that. He was also annoyed that his detective stories, which he himself dismissed as an "elementary form of fiction," outsold his historical novels like *The White Company* (1891), about the Hundred Years' War. Doyle called that book his "greatest achievement." And what did he say about Holmes? "He takes my mind from better things." In fact, in 1893, Doyle grew so sick of the detective that he killed him off in a *Strand* magazine short story, "The Final Problem." Fans were so upset that many canceled their subscriptions. A few years later, Doyle brought Sherlock Holmes back to life, but, as he told his mother, "I weary of his name."

Tyrannosaurus rex couldn't run—it would've broken its legs if it tried.

Sylvester Stallone: *Stop! Or My Mom Will Shoot!*

One of the oddest movies ever made was this Sylvester Stallone film, an action comedy about a cop with a mom who's a mobster, or something like that. It doesn't matter. What does matter is how Stallone got the part: Arnold Schwarzenegger tricked him into it. At the time, the action stars were locked in a bitter rivalry over who had the bigger box office. On a few occasions, they even tried to steal each other's roles. Knowing this, Schwarzenegger got an idea when he read the "so very bad" script: he told his agent to leak it to the press that he has "tremendous interest" in the role, but he would only do it for an exorbitant sum. "Then they'd say," Schwarzenegger recalled in 2017, "'Let's go give it to Sly (Stallone). Maybe we can get him for cheaper.' So they told Sly, 'Schwarzenegger's interested. Here's the press clippings. He's talked about that. If you want to grab that one away from him, that is available.' And he went for it!" Schwarzenegger's instincts were spot on: *Stop! Or My Mom Will Shoot!* was universally panned, and Stallone has been apologizing for it ever since: "If you ever want someone to confess to murder, just make him or her sit through that film. They will confess to anything after 15 minutes."

* * *

WHO WAS ALICE?

Go Ask Alice, written by "Anonymous," was one of the biggest best-sellers of the 1970s. It purports to be the diary of a troubled teenager who made her first entry in 1969, at the age of 14. (The girl's name is never revealed in the diary; "Alice" is a reference to a line in the Jefferson Airplane song "White Rabbit.") The entries chronicle how the girl experiments with drugs, becomes an addict, and runs away from home. She turns to prostitution to support her drug habit, spends time in a mental hospital, and eventually kicks the habit. She reunites with her family, but—spoiler alert!—at the end of the book we are told that the girl died from an overdose, possibly accidental, three weeks after making the last entry in her diary.

The diary—if that's really what it is—was prepared for publication by Beatrice Sparks, a therapist and youth counselor who claimed she received it from a real teenage girl. But Sparks has never produced the actual diary, and after *Go Ask Alice* became a best-seller, she followed it up with similar "real diaries" of teenagers struggling with unwed motherhood, AIDS, gang violence, eating disorders, foster care, Satanism, and other timely issues. The U.S. Copyright Office lists her as the sole author of *Go Ask Alice* and all but two of these other works. *Alice* is still in print and has sold more than 5 million copies to date; modern editions include a disclaimer acknowledging that it's a work of fiction.

How revered were beans in ancient Rome? Four great families named themselves after them: Lentulus (lentil), Piso (peas), Cicero (chickpea), and Fabius (fava).

ACTORS WHO DIRECT

It's the classic "actor-becomes-filmmaker-and-blabs-about-it" story.

"I like acting better than anything else, but, you know, directing's good."

—Tommy Wiseau

"I don't like just showing up. I've never been good at, 'Hope it all goes well.' I want to be a part of why it goes well."

—Drew Barrymore

"Once you've directed a movie, it makes you understand that a lot of things that actors do are obnoxious."

—Seth Rogen

"The whole chameleon thing about acting; that's why I'm moving towards directing—it's a much more healthy occupation."

—Andy Serkis

"Directing is too hard, it takes too much time, and it doesn't pay very well."

—Harrison Ford

"Producing is hell, writing is frustrating, acting is really satisfying, directing is heaven."

—Salma Hayek

"When I direct and have to look at filmed scenes of myself, I suck."

—William Shatner

"You get money out of acting. You get gray hair out of directing."

—Tim Robbins

"Directing is really exciting. In the end, it's more fun to be the painter than the paint."

—George Clooney

"If I had to choose between a great acting job and a good directing job, I'd choose the directing job."

—Ron Howard

THE ART OF THE PHARM-MANTEAU

Drug naming companies have mastered creating a portmanteau, which is what happens when you combine two words to make another word.

BRAND NAME: Ambien
What it is: *Zolpidem*, a sedative that helps people sleep.
How it got its name: AM stands for morning. And *bien* means "good" in Spanish and French. If you take Ambien, you'll sleep soundly and have a "good morning."

BRAND NAME: Fosamax
What it is: *Alendronate sodium*, the chemical name for a drug that slows bone loss and increases bone mass in people with osteoporosis.
How it got its name: Os is Latin for bone, and "max" means great, so Fosamax means "for great bones."

BRAND NAME: Lasix
What it is: *Furosemide*, a diuretic, used to eliminate water and salt from the body. (It makes the user have to run to the bathroom.)
How it got its name: The name refers to how long the drug works. Lasix is short for "lasts six hours."

BRAND NAME: Latisse
What it is: An opthalmic prostaglandin that's also used to make eyelashes grow.
How it got its name: The Brand Institute considers this name their biggest success because they appealed directly to their consumers by combining "lash" with the name of the French painter and sculptor Matisse.

BRAND NAME: Lopressor
What it is: *Metoprolol tartrate*, a beta blocker that lowers high blood pressure and helps prevent strokes, heart attacks, and kidney problems.
How it got its name: "Lopressor" describes exactly what the drug does—"lowers (blood) pressure."

BRAND NAME: Macrobid
What it is: *Macrodantin/nitrofurantoin*, an antibiotic used specifically to fight urinary tract infections.
How it got its name: "Macro" is short for *macrodantin*, and "b-i-d" is short for *bis in die*, the Latin term doctors use for "twice a day."

BRAND NAME: Vicodin
What it is: A combination of the opioid pain medication *hydrocodone* and the painkiller *acetaminophen*.
How it got its name: Hydrocodone is approximately six times as potent as codeine, so the manufacturer combined VI ("six" in Roman numerals) with "codin," a sound-alike word for codeine.

BRAND NAME: Flomax
What it is: *Tamsulosin*, an alpha-blocker that relaxes the muscles in the prostate and the neck of the bladder, making it easier to urinate.
How it got its name: The drug "maximizes" urine "flow."

Near Reno, Nevada, there is a recycling plant that turns household garbage into jet fuel.

FOUND IN TRANSLATION

What do you do when you want to describe a specific feeling, but there's no single word in the English language that accurately describes it? You look to other languages. They seem to have a word for everything.

Let's Say... You stuffed yourself at dinner and all you want to do is fall into a coma.
There's a Word for That: In Italian that feeling is called *abbiocco*.

Let's Say... You have the *abbiocco*. Might as well loosen your belt to let your food digest.
There's a Word for That: The Dutch call that *uitbuiken*, which literally means "stomach out."

Let's Say... You want to describe a friendship so comfortable that the two of you can sit in silence together.
There's a Word for That: *Ah-un*, a wordless understanding between friends (Japanese, from the "Om" chant).

Let's Say... You met someone special and are feeling a dizzy euphoria.
There Are Words for That: *Bazodee* is what they call it in Creole. The word is derived from the French *pas solide*, meaning "unstable." If the infatuation makes you feel like there are butterflies in your stomach, that's *kilig* in Tagalog.

Let's Say... You place shiny stones in a stream to dazzle salmon long enough to catch one. (It could happen.)
There's a Word for That: *Éit* in Gaelic.

Let's Say... A few months after that first burst of *bazodee*, you and your partner settle into a trusting, comfortable understanding of each other.
There's a Word for That: *S'apprivoiser* (literally "being tamed" in French).

Let's Say... You yearn for the serenity of not caring about what can't be changed.
There Are Words for That: The Inuit (indigenous people of the Arctic region) call that mental state *ayurnamat*. If you start to feel so serene you "stare blankly into space without thinking of anything in particular," that's the state of *boketto* in Japanese.

Let's Say... A prankster jumps out and yells "Boo!" You're so scared that you jumped to your feet in fear and surprise.
There's a Word for That: You've just experienced what Filipinos call *balikwas* (Tagalog).

Let's Say... Someone tells a bad joke—either just a terrible joke or a funny joke that was told badly. In fact, it's *so* unfunny that you can't help but laugh.
There's a Word for That: In Indonesia, that kind of joke is called a *jayus*. (Here it's commonly known as a dad joke.)

Average speed of a fart as it leaves your body: 6.5 mph.

Let's Say... You feel really bad for the person who just bombed with that terrible joke.

There Are Words for That: Finns call the sensation of feeling bad for someone who publicly embarrassed themselves *myötähäpeä*. Germans call it *fremdschämen*.

Let's Say... Something makes you smile, a private joke you might share with another or maybe just yourself.

There's a Word for That: The Dutch call that *binnenpretje* (literally "inside fun").

Let's Say... You're at a party and you just want to go home.

There Are Words for That: You are *engentado* (Spanish), meaning you are over-peopled and need solitude. *Sturmfrei* (literally "storm-free") is German for finding your quiet place, like having the house all to yourself. The Japanese *datsuzoku* means a break from the routine and conventional. Even more extreme, *stushevatsya* is Russian for completely dropping out of worldly concerns.

Let's Say... It's been raining for what feels like years, but then the sun comes out, and everyone wants to go outside and play.

There's a Word for That: When Iceland's weather turns unexpectedly pleasant, some employers tell their workers to go out and enjoy a *sólarfrí*, literally a "sun holiday."

Let's Say... Someone hurt you once, and you gave them another chance. They hurt you again, and you gave them yet another chance. Then they hurt you *again!* And all you want to say is "Third strike, you're out!" But you want to say it in one word.

There's a Word for That: *Ilunga* is a word in Tshiluba—spoken by the Bantu people in the Congo—that essentially means "third strike, you're out."

Let's Say... You made a mistake (you put a fork in the microwave), and you learned from your mistake (don't put forks in the microwave).

There's a Word for That: Norwegians call it *etterpåklokskap* ("afterward wisdom").

Let's Say... You're in a group waiting for something momentous to happen.

There's a Word for That: *Qarrtsiluni* in Inuktitut, the language of the Inuit.

Let's Say... You just know that your friend is up to something mischievous. You don't know what, but they have "that look."

There's a Word for That: In Dutch, that look is described as *pretoogjes* ("fun eyes").

Let's Say... There's a proverbial elephant in the room—a topic everyone is thinking about but no one dares bring up.

There's a Word for That: They don't have elephants in Papua, New Guinea, so they use the word *mokita*.

The Sullivan Ordinance (NYC, 1908) banned women from smoking in public. It was vetoed two weeks later.

Let's Say... How come this page has two columns? What font is this? When is this article going to end?

There's a Word for That: Don't ask so many questions, you *pochemuchka* (Russian for "someone who asks a lot of questions").

Let's Say... You want a word to describe someone who is at once flashy, vulgar, and tasteless.

There's a Word for That: *Poshlost*. Russian-American novelist Vladimir Nabokov defined *poshlost* as "valuing not only the obviously trashy but also the falsely important, the falsely beautiful, the falsely clever, the falsely attractive."

Let's Say... You say that you love someone, but you really don't.

There's a Word for That: *Onsay* means "pretending to be in love" in Tibet's Bodo language.

Let's Say... Something hurts so good, like a deep-tissue massage that is excruciating on one level but so soothing on another.

There's a Word for That: Germans call it *wohlweh* ("good pain").

Let's Say... You want to squeeze someone because they're SO DARNED CUTE. (Please don't.)

There's a Word for That: Indonesians call this annoying temptation *gemas*.

Let's Say... When a loved one returns from a trip, you're elated to see them.

There's a Word for That: *Gjensynsglede* is how Norwegians describe the joy in seeing someone after a long absence (literally "goodbye happiness").

Let's Say... You want to describe a bittersweet mix of joy and sadness.

There's a Word for That: *Charmolypi* in Greek.

Let's Say... You tell yourself you're going to study up on all these foreign words and use them to impress people, but you know deep down that you won't.

There's a Word for That: Germans use *lebenslüge* ("life lies") to describe those falsehoods we tell ourselves just so we can stand to keep living with ourselves.

Let's Say... Someone from the Netherlands calls you a "party pig."

There's a Word for That: Don't worry. It's not an insult—just the literal translation of *feestvarken*, a Dutch event's guest of honor.

Let's Say... You have to perform a difficult task in front of a bunch of people, and you want to make it look easy.

There's a Word for That: *Sprezzatura* is Italian for the studied nonchalance you sometimes see in jugglers while making something difficult (like juggling chainsaws) look simple.

GOLDEN SLUMBERS

This gruesome bit of history comes to us from our European correspondent, Walter Closet. It's got everything a Dark Ages tale should have: barbarians, bones, popes, virgins, and gold. But is it just a legend…or did it really happen?

VIEW FROM ABROAD

From the outside, the Basilica of St. Ursula in Cologne, Germany, seems pretty ordinary by 16th-century standards. Its stone walls and bell tower are unremarkable, especially in comparison to the grandiose Cologne Cathedral that greets travelers as they exit Köln Hauptbahnhof, the city's main train station, a few minutes away. Though you can find the cathedral on dozens of different postcards in Cologne's gift shops, you'd be hard-pressed to find one featuring St. Ursula's. But there's something special about St. Ursula's—something that makes it one of the most unique houses of worship in Europe. Within one of its chapels (called the Golden Chamber), there's an ornate display that has been attracting the faithful and the merely curious for centuries. Its history begins with the legend of a British princess who lived a very long time ago.

THE LEGEND

In the fourth century, the kingdom of Dumnonia—a large chunk of southwestern Britain—was ruled by King Dionotus. He had a daughter named Ursula. When Ursula came of age, Dionotus arranged for her to marry Conan Meriadoc, the powerful governor of Armorica, a kingdom in what is now northern France. After a delay of several years, Ursula finally set out across the English Channel to Armorica, accompanied by ten women, each of whom, like Ursula, was accompanied by 1,000 virginal handmaidens. That means Ursula was traveling with 11,000 virgins.

As outrageous as that sounds, it gets worse: Armorica at the time was running low on fertile women. Conan had informed Dionotus about his kingdom's predicament, and the king had sent him thousands of women…but many of the ships were lost at sea and the remainder, once they reached mainland Europe, were hijacked by barbarians. Ursula's virginal entourage was to serve as a sort of dowry and, in exchange, Conan—a pagan—agreed to convert to Christianity.

The princess successfully reached Armorica but had an abrupt change of heart once she sailed into port. She insisted upon being allowed to go on a pilgrimage to Rome (with all 11,000 of her virgins) before she would marry Conan.

Most produced arcade game ever: Pac-Man. 400,000 Pac-Man cabinets were manufactured in the early 1980s; they sucked up 14 billion quarters from players.

ROAD TRIP

If you had to read *The Canterbury Tales* back in high school, you'll know that such pilgrimages were common in Europe for centuries. In Ursula's day, the Roman Empire had begun its decline, but Rome itself was still the largest, most exciting city on the continent. And it was the center of the Christian world.

According to the legend, when Ursula and her virgin troupe arrived in Rome, they caught the eye of Pope Cyriacus, who became infatuated with them. When it came time for the princess to leave, he and a few other higher-ups within the Vatican decided to hang up their robes and tag along with them while they continued their pilgrimage to visit holy sites around Europe before they returned to Armorica, where Conan was waiting for them. But during this era, central Europe was a dangerous place. The Huns were besieging the Roman Empire, which still controlled large segments of what is now Germany. Ursula made the unfortunate mistake of stopping in Cologne on the eve of an assault by a large group of Huns. In the ensuing massacre, all 11,000 virgins were beheaded; the princess was executed by bow and arrow.

TRUE, FALSE, OR SOMEWHERE IN BETWEEN?

If you find this story hard to swallow, you're not alone. Scholars have been bickering about the veracity of this tale for centuries. According to one theory, Ursula was traveling with a much more realistic *eleven* virgins, or possibly even as few as two. The discrepancy might have been caused by a monk or a cleric who made the numerical error while transcribing historical records during the Dark Ages.

There are also questions about the fate of Pope Cyriacus and his colleagues once the Huns entered Cologne. Perhaps they slipped away or maybe they too were killed. Records of Cyriacus's time as pope are almost entirely nonexistent, possibly destroyed by church leaders who were furious that he abdicated in order to travel with Ursula. They might have considered him such an embarrassment that they wanted to excise his name from official pontifical records.

GET REAL

The real story of Ursula's trek—if it ever even happened—is lost to the ages, and the lack of historical evidence led to Ursula and the virgins being removed from the Catholic Church's official list of martyrs, the Roman Martyrology, when it was revised in 1969. Nevertheless, the story of Ursula and her 11,000 virgins became a popular legend, especially in Cologne.

In the 12th century, a mass grave was discovered near the Basilica of St. Ursula, a church that had been built in her honor after her martyrdom led to sainthood. It was quickly determined that the bones within it *must* have belonged to Ursula and her

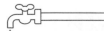

When you gotta go: Shortly after he became the second man to set foot on the Moon...

entourage. That's when church leaders decided to expand the building to house the remains. The bones were exhumed and many of the skulls were dipped in silver or adorned with gold, velvet, or other decorations. They're still there today, lining the walls of the Golden Chamber, an ornate chapel constructed in 1643 with funds donated by Johann Krane, a wealthy member of the imperial court of the Holy Roman Empire. Some of the bones have even been put into the shapes of Latin words that spell out phrases like "Holy Ursula, pray for us."

A BONE TO PICK

While it might sound macabre, chapels and catacombs filled with bones are fairly commonplace in Europe. Some of them, like the Catacombs of Paris, are even major tourist attractions that draw thousands of visitors every year. The Golden Chamber isn't quite that popular, but the odd tales surrounding it have guaranteed it a perpetual spot in tourism guides.

That's not to say that scholars and others haven't attempted to debunk the legends over the years. A local surgeon made the mistake of taking too close of a look at several of the bones on display in 1835. He determined that many of them belonged to men, children, and even one or two mastiffs. The citizens of Cologne were outraged and, reportedly, he had to hightail it out of town. As the old saying goes, when the legend becomes fact, print the legend.

> **DID YOU KNOW?**
>
> One of the most popular Catholic saints is St. Christopher, patron saint of travelers. Only problem: In 1970 the Church removed St. Christopher's feast day from the official Catholic calendar because it couldn't prove that he ever actually existed.

* * *

DÉJÀ VIEW: *PEOPLE* MAGAZINE'S MOST BEAUTIFUL WOMEN IN THE WORLD

1990: Michelle Pfeiffer

1991: Julia Roberts

1999: Michelle Pfeiffer (again)

2000: Julia Roberts (again)

2004: Jennifer Aniston

2005: Julia Roberts (once more)

2010: Julia Roberts (for a fourth time)

2016: Jennifer Aniston (again)

2017: Julia Roberts (the fifth time)

...Buzz Aldrin became the first man to pee on the Moon.
(He relieved himself into a special bag in his space suit.)

BY THE NUMBERS QUIZ

We took a bunch of famous lists and groups…and left out one of the things.
Can you remember what's missing? Answers are on page 501.

1 The first five American presidents are considered the nation's "Founding Fathers" for their role in creating it. Who'd we leave off the list?
James Monroe, George Washington, James Madison, Thomas Jefferson

2 These are the "seven deadly sins"—things you must never do. Okay, six deadly sins. Which one did we forget?
Pride, wrath, gluttony, lust, greed, envy

3 Up until 1967, the National Hockey League consisted of just six teams. Which of the "Original Six" isn't listed here?
Boston Bruins, Chicago Black Hawks, Detroit Red Wings, Montreal Canadiens, Toronto Maple Leafs

4 The English language is made up of eight "parts of speech." Which one isn't here?
Interjection, preposition, conjunction, adjective, adverb, verb, noun

5 There are four major entertainment awards in the United States. Which one got left out?
Oscar, Emmy, Tony

6 Living things on Earth are categorized into seven increasingly specific kinds of taxonomic classifications. Can you remember which one's not listed here?
Kingdom, Class, Order, Family, Genus, Species

7 Five nations have permanent seats on the United Nations Security Council. Who's not named?
China, Russia, the United States, the United Kingdom

8 *The Magnificent Seven* is a classic Western released in 1960. It starred seven top action heroes of the era. Which cast member did we forget to mention?
Yul Brynner, Charles Bronson, Robert Vaughn, Brad Dexter, James Coburn, Horst Buchholz

9 When old books and sailors referred to "the Seven Seas," they meant these six oceans…and what other one?
Arctic Ocean, Indian Ocean, North Pacific Ocean, South Pacific Ocean, North Atlantic Ocean, South Atlantic Ocean

10 Which book of the Pentateuch, or first five books of the Bible, did we leave off the list?
Exodus, Leviticus, Deuteronomy, Genesis

11 Exactly seven months have 31 days. Which one isn't here?
October, January, May, December, March, July

12 There are five freshwater Great Lakes in the upper Midwestern U.S. and Canada. Which isn't represented below?
Lake Michigan, Lake Ontario, Lake Superior, Lake Erie

13 In the 1990s, "the Three Tenors" thrilled audiences with their powerful operatic voices. We only named two here. Who's the third?
Luciano Pavarotti, Placido Domingo

14 There are 10 full-fledged provinces in Canada. Can you name the one we didn't?
Ontario, Newfoundland and Labrador, Quebec, Alberta, Prince Edward Island, Manitoba, British Columbia, Nova Scotia, New Brunswick

Centenarians are more likely to have been born in the fall. Why? One theory: Their mothers had…

IT'S ABOUT LYME: CELEBRITY EDITION

We told you about Lyme disease on page 389. Hundreds of thousands of people suffer from it, yet it gets a fraction of the press that other diseases do. That may be changing thanks to a slew of sick celebrities who are telling their stories about life in the "Lyme light."

George W. Bush: The former U.S. president contracted Lyme while he was in office, but fortunately he noticed the rash and was treated for the disease right away.

Richard Gere: Another star that got over Lyme disease quickly because he caught it early, Gere missed only a month of filming a movie in 2000—*Autumn in New York*—to recover from an antibiotic regimen. But the experience, he says, will affect him for the rest of his life: "This is one scary disease. I felt as though every ounce of strength had gone from my body."

Avril Lavigne: In 2015 the singer-songwriter told *People* magazine that she had been sidelined by Lyme. "I felt like I couldn't breathe, I couldn't talk, and I couldn't move. I thought I was dying." Despite her fame and fortune, Lavigne encountered many of the same obstacles as other sufferers: the doctors didn't believe her symptoms were related to Lyme disease. "I had doctors tell me I was crazy and they didn't want to test me. I had to learn about Lyme completely on my own."

Alli Hilfiger: The actor—daughter of fashion icon Tommy Hilfiger—was bitten by a tick in 1992 when she was seven years old. Her parents had the tick tested, but the results were inconclusive, so they forgot about it. After that, Hilfiger's teenage years were mired by a mysterious illness—at first her doctors thought it was multiple sclerosis, then fibromyalgia, and then rheumatoid arthritis, but none of the treatments were working. She was in nearly constant pain, her memory was failing, and she couldn't read. It got so bad that she was admitted to a psychiatric hospital. "I was convinced that bugs were crawling up my body," she recalls, "eating at my organs and brain." Finally, when Hilfiger was 19 years old, it was her psychiatrist who told her that the only thing that could explain all of her symptoms was Lyme disease. She tested for it again...and was formally diagnosed. In 2016

...plenty to eat the previous spring and summer, resulting in healthier children.

Hilfiger wrote a book about her struggles called *Bite Me;* she is still dealing with Lyme today.

Alec Baldwin: Baldwin's first tick bite was around the year 2000, and then he received more bites a few years later and has been battling chronic Lyme ever since. He kept it secret until 2017, when he finally opened up about his experiences: "I got the classic Lyme disease symptoms for…five years, every August, like this black lung, flu-like symptoms, sweating to death in my bed…The first time was the worst of all…I was lying in bed saying, 'I'm going to die of Lyme disease in my bed' and 'I hope someone finds me and I'm not here for too long.'"

Daryl Hall: Hall's symptoms began in 2006 as uncontrollable tremors. He tested negative for Parkinson's disease, which was a relief at first, but the symptoms kept getting worse: debilitating joint pain and stiffness. It got so bad that Hall had to cancel part of a tour. He told his ex-wife about his illness, and she told him to get tested for Lyme (she'd had the disease herself). "Lyme is many things," Hall explains. "One day you can feel like you have arthritis in your leg, and the next day it feels fine, and the next day you have brain fog. If you have any one of those symptoms and they are moving around your body, that is a big clue that you could have Lyme disease." In 2016 Hall announced he was mostly symptom-free, except for occasional flare-ups.

Marla Maples: The former wife of Donald Trump says she's been battling chronic Lyme for more than three decades, summing up the one thing that everyone who's dealt with Lyme can agree on: "It's a tragic disease."

* * *

BACK FROM THE DEAD

The coelacanth (pronounced "SEE-luh-canth") is a prehistoric creature that lived in the oceans off what's now Africa. These dinosaur-like fish grew to a six and a half feet long, and stalked undersea prey with their razor-sharp teeth as far as 2,300 feet below the surface. Like dinosaurs, they were thought to have died out 66 million years ago. But they didn't go anywhere—for millions of years, they quietly hung around in the super-deep parts of the ocean. A coelacanth was discovered in 1938 when one was inadvertently captured by a South African trawling boat.

How did the "English sweat" plague of 1485 get its name? Victims sweated to death in 24 hours.

A LETTER TO THE EDITOR

How much of an impact can a one-paragraph letter have on the world?

JUST WONDERING

Dr. Hershel Jick was a professor of medicine at the Boston University School of Medicine in the late 1970s. One of his interests was tracking both the positive and negative side effects of pharmaceutical drugs. To that end, he'd set up a database containing records of the more than 300,000 patients who'd been treated at the school's teaching hospital in recent years.

In the fall of 1979, Dr. Jick had a question about painkillers that he wanted answered: How many patients who'd been prescribed powerful opioid-based drugs while in the hospital became addicted to them? Opiates, also known as opioids, get their name because they are derived from, or are synthetic forms of, substances found in the opium poppy. Morphine and the street drug heroin are both opiates.

Dr. Jick asked a graduate student, Jane Porter, to search the database for the answer. She did the research and Jick summarized her findings in a 101-word letter to the editor of the *New England Journal of Medicine,* one of the country's most prestigious peer-reviewed medical journals.

"Although there were 11,882 patients who received at least one [opiate] preparation," Jick wrote, "there were only four cases of reasonably well documented addiction in patients who had no history of addiction. The addiction was considered major in only one instance...We conclude that despite widespread use of narcotic drugs in hospitals, the development of addiction is rare in medical patients with no history of addiction." As was customary with such letters, Jane Porter signed it first—because she did the research—and then Dr. Jick signed it. In time it would come to be known by the nickname "Porter and Jick."

The *New England Journal of Medicine* published the letter in its January 1980 issue under the headline "Addiction Rare in Patients Treated with Narcotics."

For more than a decade, the letter was ignored.

A LITTLE DAB WILL (HAVE TO) DO YA

In those days, opiates were administered only in hospital settings, and under the close supervision of a physician. This was because opiates are terribly addictive. It was drummed into doctors, from medical school onward, that opiates were dangerous for the patient. Prescribing them was done only as a last resort, and usually only for terminal cancer patients or people recovering from surgery. That was it. Even these patients

In 1827 France blockaded the port of Algiers for three years,
after its ruler swatted the French consul with a fly whisk.

were prescribed opiates for short periods of time and at low doses, often in a form that combined them with less addictive drugs, so that less of the opiate was needed. Percodan is a combination of aspirin and the opioid oxycodone, for example, and Percocet is oxycodone combined with acetaminophen, the active ingredient in Tylenol.

In a hospital setting, the patient could be closely monitored for signs of addiction and overdose. If necessary, the dosage of opiates could be reduced or eliminated entirely, and milder, less-effective drugs substituted in their place. Increased pain might be the result, but that was the trade-off that had to be made to spare the patient from becoming addicted to painkillers. Patients were *never* prescribed opiates that they could take at home after leaving the hospital. The risk that they would abuse the drugs and become addicted, or even die from an overdose, was thought to be far too great.

ON SECOND THOUGHT

In the mid-1980s, however, attitudes in the medical community began to change. Pain researchers—some of whom were already beginning to cite Porter and Jick as evidence to support their claims—came to believe that opiates could be safely prescribed to patients who had no prior history of drug addiction. The thinking was that some people had addictive tendencies, but most people did not. By questioning a patient carefully, a physician could determine whether a patient had tendency toward addiction. If they didn't, the physician could prescribe opiates with little risk of the patient abusing the drugs or developing an addiction.

> "At the core of this culture was the idea that these painkillers were virtually nonaddictive when used to treat pain."

Another idea that became popular was the belief that a patient's pain blocked the euphoria effect that makes opiates so addictive in the first place. People in pain could take the drug without fear of becoming addicted, because their pain would cancel out the euphoria and prevent addiction from taking hold.

Where pain had once been seen as an unfortunate but necessary trade-off to prevent patients from becoming drug addicts, now many in the medical community were beginning to see pain as an easily treatable symptom that in too many cases was going untreated. "All of this happened in about a decade," Sam Quinones writes in *Dreamland: The True Tale of America's Opiate Epidemic.* "At the core of this culture was the idea that these painkillers were virtually nonaddictive when used to treat pain."

TO BE CONTIN-UED

That's what the pain specialists had come to believe, but many ordinary physicians were still reluctant to go against a lifetime of training and prescribe opiates to their patients. Then in 1995, a drug company called Purdue Pharma won FDA approval for

Thanks! Spiders eat as many as 800 million tons of insects each year.

OxyContin, a time-release form of the synthetic opiate oxycodone, which is roughly 1.5 times more powerful than morphine.

Each OxyContin pill contained a massive dose of oxycodone, but because the pills were formulated to slowly release the drug into the body over twelve hours (the "contin" in OxyContin stands for "continuous release"), Purdue argued that they were a safer form of opiate, which the pain specialists already believed were fairly safe.

SALES PITCH

To win over skeptical physicians, Purdue launched a marketing campaign to convince them that OxyContin's time-release feature made it safe not just for cancer patients and people recovering from surgery, but for people suffering from other forms of pain as well. One piece of evidence cited over and over was Porter and Jick's letter to the *New England Journal of Medicine*, now 15 years old. Even though the *New England Journal of Medicine* is a medical journal that publishes peer-reviewed scientific papers, letters to the editor, including the one from Porter and Jick, do not receive the same rigorous, skeptical scrutiny when being considered for publication. Indeed, it's not clear that the Porter and Jick letter received *any* scrutiny before it was published. It was just a letter to the editor, after all. When Purdue Pharma and others cited Porter and Jick, it usually included just the headline ("Addiction Rare in Patients Treated with Narcotics"), the fact that it had been published in the *New England Journal of Medicine*, and—remarkably—the claim that Porter and Jick had supposedly found that "less than 1 percent of patients" to whom opiates are prescribed become addicted to them.

The letter from Porter and Jick wasn't a peer-reviewed scientific paper, and it *did not* make the claim that "less than 1 percent of patients" to whom opiates are prescribed become addicted to them. The only patients who had been studied were ones who were in a *hospital*, where they were carefully monitored by a *physician* for any sign of addiction.

Anyone who went to the trouble of looking up the letter and reading it for themselves would have discovered this right away. But doing so took some work. In 1995 the *New England Journal of Medicine*'s online archives went back just a few years; the only way to obtain information published as far back as January 1980 was to go to a medical library that had back issues on their shelves and retrieve the magazine by hand.

SEEING IS BELIEVING

Not many people did. When physicians read the headline "Addiction Rare in Patients Treated with Narcotics" and saw that Porter and Jick had been published in the *New England Journal of Medicine*, they naturally—and tragically—assumed that it was a peer-reviewed scientific paper. They accepted on faith that the claim that "less than 1

The name for the disease *malaria*—"bad air"—dates back to the days when people had no idea how it was spread. (You get it from mosquito bites.)

percent of patients" ever became addicted to opiates. And they assumed that there was strong scientific evidence to support it.

"That single paragraph, buried in the back pages of the *New England Journal of Medicine*," Sam Quinones writes in *Dreamland*, "was mentioned, lectured on, and cited until it emerged transformed into, in the words of one textbook, 'a landmark report' that 'did much to counteract' fears of addiction in pain patients treated with opiates. It did nothing of the kind."

AND AWAY WE GO

Purdue Pharma's sneaky marketing campaign paid off: physicians became much more comfortable prescribing OxyContin and other powerful opiates to their patients than they were before. And their patients, having been persuaded by the "experts" that the drugs were safe, eagerly took them, not just to control severe pain from surgery and terminal cancer, but also for sports injuries, broken bones, arthritis, and lower-back pain. They even took them for toothaches, headaches, and sore knees. The opiates weren't just administered in the hospital under medical supervision, either; patients were routinely sent home with bottles filled with pills more powerful than heroin, and were trusted to administer the drugs themselves, with no medical supervision at all. After all, if the pills were as safe as everyone said they were, what was the risk?

Some 76 million prescriptions for opiate-based painkillers were written in the United States in 1991, and the number climbed year after year. By 2012 it had more than tripled, to 282 million prescriptions. Purdue Pharma sold more than $3.1 billion worth of OxyContin that year; that one drug represented more than 90 percent of the company's total sales.

CHEW ON THIS

But as drug users already knew—and many patients prescribed OxyContin soon discovered—the time-release property that made the pills so "safe" only worked if the pills were swallowed whole, as directed. If the patient chewed the pills before swallowing them, they received the entire 12-hour dose of the drug at once. Crushing the pill and snorting it also worked, and so did dissolving the pill in water and injecting it with a hypodermic needle. The powerful high that resulted—more powerful than heroin—was very addictive.

As the number of prescriptions soared, so did the number of addicts. Studies have since shown that as many as 29 percent of patients prescribed opiates misused them, and as many as 12 percent became addicted, far more than the "less than 1 percent" that had been predicted. An estimated 6 percent of patients who abused OxyContin and other prescription opiates transitioned to heroin when their prescriptions ran out.

Jacques Cousteau's first dive was in Lake Harvey, VT. He visited there in 1920 as a kid.

And as the number of addicts soared, so did the number of deaths from overdoses. In 1999, 4,000 people in the United States died from drug overdoses. By 2016 the number had risen to 64,000 deaths, with opiates being responsible for two-thirds of overdose deaths that year. (By comparison, 58,000 Americans died in the Vietnam War, which lasted from 1964 to 1975.)

WHO, ME?

For a decade, Dr. Jick remained blissfully unaware of the role his letter was playing in the growing opiate epidemic. He barely even remembered writing it. It wasn't until 2005, when he was contacted by federal prosecutors building a criminal case against Purdue Pharma, that their subpoena jogged his memory. "I'm essentially mortified that the letter to the editor was used as an excuse to do what these drug companies did," he told the Associated Press in 2017.

> "We believe that this citation pattern contributed to the North American opioid crisis by helping to shape a narrative that allayed prescribers' concerns about the risk of addiction associated with long-term opioid therapy," they wrote.

Rather than go to trial, Purdue Pharma cut a deal in 2007 and pled guilty to misleading regulators, physicians, and the public about the addictive risks of OxyContin. They paid $600 million in fines. Three top executives pled guilty to misdemeanor charges of "misbranding" the drug; each of the three was sentenced to three years' probation and 400 hours of community service, to be served, ironically, in drug-treatment programs. They also had to pay $34.5 million in fines out of their own pockets.

In 2010 Purdue Pharma reformulated OxyContin pills to make them more difficult to crush into powder or dissolve in water. But the opiate epidemic continues, and the more than two million patients who are already hooked will struggle with addiction for the rest of their lives. They'll probably have company: In 2016, 236 million prescriptions for opiates were written in the United States; that year, an average of 90 people died from opiate overdoses each day.

PAPER TRAIL

In 2017 some University of Toronto researchers conducted a statistical analysis of all the times the Porter and Jick letter had been cited over the years. They identified a total of 608 citations from 1980 to 2017. Of these, 72 percent used it as evidence that addiction was rare in patients treated with opiates, and more than 80 percent neglected to mention that the patients studied by Porter and Jick were treated with opiates in a supervised hospital setting.

The researchers summed up their findings in a letter to the editor of the *New England Journal of Medicine*. "We believe that this citation pattern contributed to

Georgia Southern University (Statesboro, Georgia) is home to the
U.S. National Tick Collection, the "largest curated tick collection" in the world.

the North American opioid crisis by helping to shape a narrative that allayed prescribers' concerns about the risk of addiction associated with long-term opioid therapy," they wrote.

CAVEAT EMPTOR

That letter was published in the June 2017 issue of the *New England Journal of Medicine*. The journal also took the rare step of giving the original Porter and Jick letter, which is still in the journal's online archives, something that also appears on bottles of OxyContin: a *warning label*. Today an editor's note that appears above the article reads: "For reasons of public health, readers should be aware that this letter has been 'heavily and uncritically cited' as evidence that addiction is rare with opioid therapy."

"It's difficult to overstate the role of this letter," lead researcher Dr. David Juurlink told CBS News in 2017. "It was the key bit of literature that helped the opiate manufacturers convince front-line doctors that addiction is not a concern."

* * *

WINNERS OF THE DIAGRAM PRIZE FOR ODDEST BOOK TITLE

1978: *Proceedings of the Second International Workshop on Nude Mice*

1983: *Unsolved Problems of Modern Theory of Lengthwise Rolling*

1984: *The Book of Marmalade: Its Antecedents, Its History, and Its Role in the World Today*

1986: *Oral Sadism and the Vegetarian Personality*

1993: *American Bottom Archaeology*

1994: *Highlights in the History of Concrete*

1998: *Developments in Dairy Cow Breeding: New Opportunities to Widen the Use of Straw*

1999: *Weeds in a Changing World: British Crop Protection Council Symposium Proceedings No. 64*

2000: *Designing High Performance Stiffened Structures*

2001: *Butterworths Corporate Manslaughter Service*

2002: *Living with Crazy Buttocks*

2008: *The 2009–2014 World Outlook for 60-milligram Containers of Fromage Frais*

2009: *Crocheting Adventures with Hyperbolic Planes*

2010: *Managing a Dental Practice: The Genghis Khan Way*

2012: *Goblinproofing One's Chicken Coop*

2014: *Strangers Have the Best Candy*

2015: *Too Naked for the Nazis*

2016: *The Commuter Pig Keeper: A Comprehensive Guide to Keeping Pigs when Time Is Your Most Precious Commodity*

The Fugio Cent, the first copper penny minted in the United States (1787), bore the motto "MIND YOUR BUSINESS."

TAKE ME OUT TO THE BA' GAME

For almost 200 years, the Uppies and the Doonies have
met in Scotland annually to do battle in the Ba'.

AN UNTRADITIONAL TRADITION

Located at latitude 58° on the North Sea, Kirkwall is the capital of Scotland's Orkney Islands. Orcadians, who number about 20,000 on the archipelago of 70 islands, are more Viking than Scots. Every year since around 1800, they've taken time off from farming and fishing to compete (or cheer for their side) in one of the islands' most sacred traditions—the Game of Ba'. The game is sort of like rugby except that there are no uniforms, no referees, and no rules—just two teams, two goals, and a handmade leather ball stuffed with cork dust, weighing about three pounds.

The two teams are called the Uppies and the Doonies. The Uppies are the Orcadians born "above the gate," or north of St. Magnus Cathedral in Kirkwall. Their goal is to get the ba' (the ball) to touch the wall at the south end of town. The Doonies are born "below the gate," or south of the cathedral. Their goal is to get the ba' north to the sea and into the water. You are born an Uppie or a Doonie, and that is your team for life. Moving to a different part of town makes no difference; you cannot change sides. Each team is made of about 150 men over the age of 16—no females allowed. (There was a women's ba' in 1945 and 1946, but that was abandoned because the women played as rough as the men, and it wasn't deemed "ladylike.") Many team members have been playing for more than 20 years.

ON YOUR MARK, GET SET...

Shortly before 1:00 p.m. on Christmas Day and again on New Year's Day, everyone from grannies in wheelchairs and couples with babies in strollers gathers at the Kirk Green in front of St. Magnus Cathedral, where the game will begin. They cheer as the two teams march from above and below the green to meet at the Mercat Cross. Players are dressed in sweaters, torn jerseys and jeans duct-taped tightly around the ankles of their work boots. They press together in a massive circle waiting for a Kirkwall VIP to do "the throw up." As the cathedral bell chimes one, that person kisses the ba', tosses it into the air, and the scrum begins.

In 1989 a new league began: the Senior Professional Baseball Association. It struck out in 1990.

ANYTHING GOES

Three hundred men, all with their hands waving in the air, surge toward the player who has caught the ba'. They can stay pressed in this tight mob for as long as an hour, wrestling the ba' back and forth. When a ba' carrier finally breaks away, the scrum follows—up alleys, down streets, and through the crowd of spectators. To prevent glass windows from being obliterated by the crush of 300 men pushing full strength in one direction or another, every storefront is boarded up with thick wooden railings. This includes gas pumps at filling stations. As the mob surges in one direction, spectators leap onto railings, duck into doorways, and even take shelter in the red phone booths to avoid being crushed in the melee. Once the mob passes, the crowd follows, shouting to stragglers behind them, "They're heading doon Castle Street!" or "They're at the fire station!"

INTO THE NIGHT

Much of the game is spent with the teams in one giant pack, a thick column of steam rising from the spot with the ba'. Inside the scrum, a lot is going on—kicking, elbowing, shoving, even punching. Orkadians say a lot of old scores get settled during the Ba', as ribs are broken and eyes blackened. Team strategies include "smuggling" the ba' under a jersey from one player to another, and "the dummy run," which is one player breaking from the pack surrounded by a team of defenders. For a while, nobody knows who has the ba', so the mob gets divided, with one part heading in the wrong direction, following the fake-out. Hand signals and vocal cues are used to communicate with teammates. It's not uncommon for the game to last five hours or longer. At this time of year in the Orkneys, the sun sets before 4:00 p.m., so the players battle much of the game in darkness.

THE BA' MUST GO ON

The Ba' can take place in a blizzard or torrential rain—but it is never canceled. On Christmas Day 2017, play was stopped for 20 minutes while medics resuscitated a Doonie who had almost been crushed to death by a pile-on of players. Because the game can last for hours, it is part of the ritual for spectators to duck under a railing and into a pub for a "wee dram" of whisky and a warm-up before going back out to watch the game. Radio coverage provides blow-by-blow reports of the ba' so nothing is missed. Some Orkadians aren't fond of the ba' because it can be violent—many

DID YOU KNOW?

In the late 1800s and early 1900s, industrialist Andrew Carnegie donated millions to build more than 2,500 libraries around the world, 29 of which were built in his native Scotland. The one in Kirkwall, built in 1909, is the northernmost Carnegie Library in the world. (The books are now housed elsewhere, but the building remains.)

The Starbucks at the CIA's headquarters in Washington, DC, is like a normal Starbucks, except that...

players emerge with black eyes or broken arms, ribs, and noses. Others, mostly wives, complain that their husbands are gone on both winter holidays, spending more of their time in the pubs and at the Ba' than with family.

AND THE WINNER IS

As the game comes to its conclusion—the Uppies reach the wall, or the Doonies plunge the ball into the freezing cold waters of Kirkwall Bay—one more scrimmage occurs, usually between two or three players on the winning team. Why? Because the Ba' has two winners—the team and a single star player. This individual must be more than just the MVP of the current game: he must also have demonstrated his skill and dedication over a lifetime of playing. This honor has Olympic gold medal status on the island and gives even distant family members and in-laws bragging rights about his winning the Ba'. The finalists for this honor are pretty clear, but the single winner isn't decided until those last 15 or 20 minutes, when the players negotiate to determine who deserves the crown. Finally, one player is lifted up by the others, holding the ba' triumphantly over his head, and the winner is declared.

PARTY ON!

After the team has enjoyed a celebratory drink, it's traditional for the winner to invite all the players from both sides to his house for food and drink. If a Doonie has won, this signifies good fishing for the next year. If an Uppie wins—abundant harvests lie ahead. The celebration can go on for a week, with the prized leather trophy never leaving the winner's side.

* * *

AUTHOR: ANONYMOUS

When the novel *Sense and Sensibility* was first published in England in 1811, the author, a woman, was identified only as "A Lady." The practice of publishing anonymously was common for female authors at the time. Seeking a career as a writer was socially taboo—women were expected to obtain fulfillment only in their roles as wives and mothers. Remaining anonymous was a way of demonstrating that literary pursuits did not interfere with their more important duties. When *Sense and Sensibility* found success, the author published five more novels; in each she was identified only as "the Author of *Sense and Sensibility*." It wasn't until after her death in 1817 at the age of 41 that she was finally identified by her name: Jane Austen.

...the baristas aren't allowed to write customers' names on cups...
and they can't tell anyone where they work.

THE MATILDA EFFECT

Quick: Name five famous woman scientists. Let's see—there's Marie Curie, Jane Goodall, Rachel Carson, and…uhh…There's a reason it's tough to think of more names, and it's called the "Matilda effect."

BACKGROUND

The Matilda effect comes from the world of science, but it applies to the arts, business, and politics as well. It refers to a systemic bias against women, whose contributions are often credited to men. A recent *National Geographic* article described it like this: "Over the centuries, female researchers have had to work as 'volunteer' faculty members, seen credit for significant discoveries they've made assigned to male colleagues, and been written out of textbooks."

The term was coined in 1993 by science historian Margaret W. Rossiter, who was inspired by Matilda Joslyn Gage—a suffragist and political activist who worked alongside Susan B. Anthony to gain the right to vote for women. But she also strongly advocated for women to receive proper credit for their advances in science. Here's an excerpt from Gage's 1883 essay "Woman as Inventor":

> No assertion in reference to woman is more common than that she possesses no inventive or mechanical genius…But, while such statements are carelessly or ignorantly made, tradition, history, and experience alike prove her possession of these faculties in the highest degree. Although woman's scientific education has been grossly neglected, yet some of the most important inventions of the world are due to her.

On the next few pages you'll find the stories of just a few of the countless pioneering women who were met head-on by the Matilda effect.

TROTA of SALERNO (mid-1100s)

Accomplishments: The "Renaissance of the 12th Century" was a period of enlightenment in southern Italy. Women were actually allowed to be educated and have careers. One such woman was Trota di Ruggiero, a doctor and teacher at medieval Europe's first true medical school. Far ahead of her time, she was responsible for several crucial advances, including:

- First doctor known to call for a separate field of medicine dedicated to women's reproductive health, and the first to suggest that women would be better at treating women.

Mistletoe gets its name from the Old English *mistil tan,* "dung twig," because people thought it grew in places where bird droppings landed in trees.

- Among the first doctors to recommend a balanced diet and regular exercise for better health.

- Argued that pain during childbirth should be limited—a notion that went directly against the contemporary Christian belief that women should suffer during childbirth. And she administered opiates during childbirth to dull the pain.

- Among the first doctors to turn a fetus into the proper position while still in utero.

- Developed revolutionary Cesarean surgical techniques that led to lower postpartum death rates from infection.

Trota's legacy lives on thanks to her three seminal books: *Book on the Conditions of Women*, *On Treatments for Women*, and *On Women's Cosmetics* (which offered "treatments for frizzy hair, freckle removal, bad breath, and chapped lips"). Collectively, the books became known as a single work called *The Trotula*, which remained the definitive text on women's health for the next 400 years.

Matilda Effect: In the years following Trota's death, Italy's first renaissance came to an end, and women were once again denied educations. As such, later scholars falsely assumed that Trota had been a man—or even several men—all writing under the same pseudonym. (Some of the men given authorship weren't even doctors.) Eventually, it became scandalous to even suggest that *The Trotula*, a book dedicated to women's health, could have been written by anyone other than a man. It would take until the 16th century for that notion to finally be proven wrong. Today, Trota of Salerno is recognized as the world's first modern gynecologist.

CECILIA PAYNE (1900–79)

Accomplishment: Today, it's common knowledge that the Sun is made mostly of hydrogen and helium. But as recently as the 1920s, it was a widely accepted "fact" that the Sun was made of the same materials as Earth, and to suggest otherwise was scientific heresy. Cecilia Payne suggested otherwise. The British-born astronomer made the groundbreaking discovery about the true composition of stars in 1925 while working on her Ph.D. at Radcliffe College (now part of Harvard). When she presented her thesis to her professor, Henry Norris Russell, he told her it was the best thesis he'd ever read. (And it holds up today: Neil deGrasse Tyson called Payne's "Stellar Atmospheres" the "most brilliant Ph.D. thesis ever written in astronomy.")

Matilda Effect: Even so, Russell urged Payne not to publish her "clearly impossible" conclusion because it went against scientific consensus. So Payne reluctantly shelved her work. Four years later, Russell reached the same conclusion in his own research and published the results himself. Although he did acknowledge Payne's contributions

---

Air conditioners were first installed in Disneyland in 1963, eight years after the park opened.
Reason: The animatronic figures were overheating.

within the paper, he put his own name on the cover, and she had to stand idly by as a man was given sole credit for her discovery. Payne finally set the record straight in her book *The Stars of High Luminosity*. In 1956 she became Harvard's first female astronomy professor and the first woman to become department chair.

> "The giants—Copernicus, Newton, and Einstein—each in his turn, brought a new view of the universe. Payne's discovery of the cosmic abundance of the elements did no less."
>
> **—The American Physical Society**

ANNA ARNOLD HEDGEMAN (1899–1990)

Accomplishments: In her six decades as a civil rights activist, Hedgeman served as executive director of the YWCA, executive director of the Fair Employment Practices Commission, and Assistant Dean of Women at Howard University. She also served as director of Harry Truman's 1948 presidential campaign, and became the first African American woman to serve in the cabinet of a New York City mayor. But perhaps her greatest achievement came in 1963 when she helped organize Martin Luther King Jr.'s historic March on Washington for Jobs and Freedom, where he gave his "I Have a Dream" speech. Without Hedgeman's involvement, the march might not have ever happened.

That year, there were two civil rights marches planned on Washington, DC, one to be led by King in July, and the other by labor leader A. Philip Randolph in October. Concerned that the two marches might cancel each other out, it was Hedgeman who came up with the idea of combining the two into one. She arranged for the two civil rights leaders to meet and then helped them hammer out the details. Not only that, Hedgeman singlehandedly recruited more than 40,000 Protestants to attend, arranged transportation for more than 100,000 people, and made sure that everyone there got fed. Thanks in large part to her, the event was a huge success.

Matilda Effect: The core team that organized the March on Washington became known as "the Big Six," consisting of Martin Luther King Jr., James Farmer, John Lewis, A. Philip Randolph, Roy Wilkins, and Whitney Young. Notice someone missing? Anna Hedgeman. She was, as she later described it, "kept out of sight." You read that right: the men who fought for civil rights denied a woman a place at the table.

But what really got Hedgeman angry was the announcement—a week before the march—that no women would be allowed to deliver speeches. "Instead," wrote Hedgeman, "it was proposed that Mr. Randolph, as chairman, would ask several Negro women to stand while he reviewed the historic role of Negro women, and that the women would merely take a bow at the end of his presentation." Hedgeman drafted a passionate letter urging them to reconsider, which she read aloud at a meeting:

Per her request, Elizabeth Taylor's funeral began 15 minutes later than scheduled. (She wanted to be late to her own funeral.)

In light of the role of the Negro women in the struggle for freedom and especially in light of the extra burden they have carried because of the castration of the Negro man in this culture, it is incredible that no woman should appear as a speaker at the historic March on Washington Meeting at the Lincoln Memorial.

Because of Hedgeman's vigilance, one woman did get to stand at the podium and give "brief remarks"—Daisy Bates, a publisher and civic leader who had helped the "Little Rock Nine" black students attend an all-white school in Arkansas in 1957. The remarks weren't much, but it was another small step forward. Three years later, Hedgeman and 48 other women cofounded the National Organization for Women.

MARGARET KNIGHT (1838–1914)

Accomplishments: We take it for granted that paper grocery bags have flat bottoms. Before that advancement, paper bags were pretty much useless: they didn't stand up, and were so poorly made that they often broke. Margaret Knight changed all that. She'd been a successful inventor since her teens, when she invented an automatic shutoff for malfunctioning factory machines. Because women weren't supposed to apply for patents, Knight didn't, and she never made a dime from the invention, even as her design was being used in factories around the world and would go on to save countless lives.

In 1868 Knight was working at the Columbia Paper Bag Company in Springfield, Massachusetts, when she invented a wooden hand-cranked machine that could cut, fold, and glue a flat-bottomed bag. The result was a stronger and more stable paper bag than any that had come before it. This time, Knight wanted due credit, so she went against social norms and decided to apply for a patent. But first she needed an iron prototype, so she went to a machine shop in Boston to have one built.

Matilda Effect: When Knight applied for the patent, she was dismayed to learn that one had recently been granted to a rival inventor named Charles Annan for the exact same machine. Though Knight had seen Annan tinkering around at the machine shop, little did she know that he was spying on her and stealing her work. Despite her insistence that *she* invented the paper bag, no one at the patent office believed her, leaving her no other choice but to sue.

At the trial, Annan's lawyer argued that no uneducated woman could come up with such a contraption. But Knight had the facts on her side—and she had a lot of evidence. She produced all of her notes, explained her invention in detail, and called three witnesses who testified that she was indeed the inventor…and she won the suit. Result: In 1871 Knight became one of the first women ever to be granted a patent. And her flat-bottomed paper bag made an immediate impact on society (much in the

"Popsicle" is a registered trademark. Each Popsicle
is made from a patented formula that's kept secret.

way sliced bread would in 1928). England's Queen Victoria even presented Knight with the Decoration of the Royal Legion of Honour. Knight received at least 27 more patents in her life, including a numbering machine and improvements to the rotary engine. But the "Lady Edison," as some called her, had wanted to do much more: "I'm only sorry I couldn't have had as good a chance as a boy."

JOCELYN BELL (1943–)

Accomplishment: In the late 1960s, Bell was a postgraduate student at the University of Cambridge working on her Ph.D. in astrophysics when she detected and identified the first radio pulsars. The discovery proved for the first time that when a massive star went supernova, it didn't just blow up into nothing, but became a much smaller rotating neutron star. That breakthrough gave astronomers a much clearer picture of how the universe works.

Matilda Effect: Bell was working on the research project with two men—her thesis adviser, Antony Hewish, and the astronomer Martin Ryle. Bell's contribution was so important that, on the paper announcing the discovery, her name was listed second, right under Hewish, the professor. In 1974 the research team was awarded the Nobel Prize for Physics—well, not *all* of the team. The prize went to Hewish and Ryle only. Many scientists were upset by the snub. One of them was renowned astronomer Iosif Shklovsky, who told Bell, "You have made the greatest astronomical discovery of the 20th century."

It's not uncommon for the Nobel Prize Committee to favor men; only 16 women scientists have received the prize in the last 100 years. For her part, Bell was diplomatic: "I believe it would demean the Nobel Prizes if they were awarded to research students, except in very exceptional cases, and I do not believe this is one of them." But most disagreed, arguing that it was her discovery, and she should have been a Nobel laureate. Bell didn't let the slight slow her down: she's since served as president of the Royal Astronomical Society, and in 2015 was awarded the Women of the Year Prudential Lifetime Achievement award. But still no Nobel Prize.

NETTIE STEVENS (1861–1912)

Accomplishment: In 1536 King Henry VIII had his wife, Anne Boleyn, executed after she failed to bear him a son. That's a real example, albeit extreme, of the way women throughout history have been punished and scorned for not producing male children. In the early 1900s, geneticist Nettie Stevens discovered the tragic irony: it's the male's contribution—not the female's—that determines the gender of the child.

Stevens was one of many scientists who were trying to solve the gender determination mystery. Her breakthrough came while studying mealworms at Bryn

Olympic swimmers never drown. Even so, there were lifeguards at the 2016 Rio Olympics swimming events. (Brazilian law required it.)

Mawr College in Pennsylvania. She discovered that sperm carries both the X and the Y chromosome, while eggs only carry the Y chromosome. Therefore, she concluded, it's the male sperm that determines the offspring's sex.

Columbia University professor Edmund Beecher Wilson was conducting similar research, and he published his findings first—in 1900. But here's the thing: he came to the wrong conclusion. After studying only male mealworms, he concluded that environment was the major factor in determining gender. Stevens had studied both male *and* female worms, and it was she who correctly concluded—in 1905—that the male XY chromosomes are responsible.

Matilda Effect: Stevens's findings were mostly ignored. Not only was she a woman, but she was a woman stating that men had been wrong to blame women. One man who didn't ignore Stevens's findings was Wilson. After she published, he reassessed his work and came to the same conclusion she had. When he published a correction paper, he thanked Stevens for her contribution. Not that it made any difference. As science historian Stephen Brush writes: "Because of Wilson's more substantial contributions in other areas, he tends to be given most of the credit for this discovery." Sadly, Stevens's life and career were cut short when she died of breast cancer at age 50.

CAMILLE CLAUDEL (1864–1943)

Accomplishment: Claudel was one of the most talented sculptors of her day, on a par with her mentor, Auguste Rodin, of *The Thinker* fame. In 1884 the 19-year-old Claudel started her art career as one of the 42-year-old Rodin's assistants. From the beginning, he recognized her immense talent, and she quickly became an artist in her own right—at least to those who knew her.

Matilda Effect: Rodin took credit for a lot of work that was actually produced by Claudel, including *The Slave* and *Laughing Man* (she sculpted the heads). This wasn't necessarily because Rodin was a spotlight hog—it was also because of the times. In those days women weren't accepted as artists, and obtaining funding for expensive bronze sculptures was difficult. It was *especially* difficult for Claudel, whose themes were often overtly sexual. Rodin funded many of her pieces...and then signed his name to them to give them a wider audience. But he was the one who was celebrated for the work, not her.

It got even worse when they had a falling-out in the 1890s. The two had an intimate relationship. When Claudel demanded that Rodin leave his childhood sweetheart and marry her, he refused. Knowing that she could never have Rodin exclusively, or escape his shadow, she left him to make it on her own.

Rodin continued to fund Claudel's work for a few more years...until she created *The Age of Maturity*, a bronze sculpture of a man walking away from a pleading woman.

First U.S. theater that showed only movies: L.A.'s Electric Theater, housed in a circus tent (1902).

When Rodin saw the sculpture, he recognized the depiction of their relationship and was furious. He broke off all contact, and Claudel ended up begging for food in the streets. A few years later, her brother and mother had her committed to a mental institution, where she was diagnosed with schizophrenia. She stopped making art, destroyed most of her sculptures (only 90 remain), and blamed Rodin for stealing all the credit and destroying her life, once saying, "I am in no mood to be deceived any longer by the crafty devil and false character whose greatest pleasure is to take advantage of everyone."

Claudel died in obscurity, at age 78. In 2017, on the 100th anniversary of Rodin's death, the Camille Claudel Museum was opened in France, finally giving the artist the credit she deserved.

MILICENT PATRICK (1915–1998)

Accomplishments: Milicent Patrick was the Hollywood makeup artist who designed Gill-Man, the fishlike creature in 1954's *The Creature from the Black Lagoon*. Prior to that, she'd designed the makeup for Mr. Hyde in *Abbott and Costello Meet Jekyll and Hyde*. She was also a model, an actor who appeared in more than 20 movies, a concert pianist, and the first female animator to work for Walt Disney. To promote the film, Universal executives—no doubt wanting to capitalize on Patrick's good looks—sent her and Gill-Man on a nationwide public relations tour called "The Beauty Who Created the Beast."

Matilda Effect: Bud Westmore, the head of makeup at Universal, was miffed that anyone other than he would get credit for creating Gill-Man—especially a woman. And Westmore had clout. Accounts vary, but most insiders agree that it was Patrick who was primarily responsible for designing Gill-Man's look. Nevertheless, Westmore sent a string of angry memos demanding that her name be removed from the film's credits. He also made the studio change the tour name to "The Beauty Who *Lives with* the Beast." Patrick was afraid she'd lose her job if she stood up for herself, so she made sure to always say that creating Gill-Man was a team effort, and Bud Westmore was the head of that team. The gesture did little to placate Westmore, and he fired Patrick when she got back to Hollywood.

Who knows what other contributions Millicent Patrick would have made to movie monsters had she remained at Universal? After she was fired, her career never really rebounded. She acted in a few more movies, but not much was heard from her after 1970. Today, there's a building at Universal named after Bud Westmore, but not a single monument to the woman responsible for one of Hollywood's most enduring and iconic monsters.

William Herschel, the discoverer of Uranus, wanted to name it Georgium Sidus— "George's Star." It took 69 years for people to finally agree to call it Uranus.

THE CENSORED 11

The classic Warner Bros. Looney Tunes and Merrie Melodies cartoons have been a part of TV forever. But there are a handful out of that collection that never aired on TV.

THAT'S ALL FOLKS

In the 1950s and early 1960s, individual TV stations that bought the rights to air old Warner Bros. cartoons had the right to decide which ones they would—and would not—air. Originally, the cartoons had been produced for adult audiences and were run before feature films—which is a lot different from airing them on television for kids. Some themes that were acceptable in the 1930s and 1940s simply would not fly in the era of the civil rights movement. Result: A lot of those old cartoons were edited to remove racially "sensitive" material, which usually meant removing blackface jokes. Other cartoons had so much objectionable material that many stations chose not to air them at all.

In 1968 United Artists secured the rights to the Warner Bros. cartoon catalog. UA created a new syndication deal with TV stations that wanted those old cartoons. But by this time, social values and cultural awareness had changed so much that United Artists didn't give the stations a choice. The company decided that 11 cartoons from the 1930s and 1940s contained so much racist material—primarily *main* characters with a blackface appearance or stereotyped, exaggerated African American features—that to edit them would be to reduce them to nothing. Those 11 cartoons were excluded from the syndication package and essentially banned from distribution in the United States. Cartoon aficionados call these missing shorts "the Censored 11." They haven't aired on American television since 1968, and they're available only as low-quality bootlegs.

"Uncle Tom's Bungalow" (1937). Harriet Beecher Stowe's 1852 novel *Uncle Tom's Cabin* helped jumpstart the slavery abolition movement with its depiction of the difficult, unfair lives of slaves. As much good as it did, it's also so simplistic that its characters informed African American stereotypes for years, particularly Uncle Tom, a kind old slave who doesn't want to cause any trouble with his white masters. This cartoon exploits that stereotype and others. A slave trader sells Uncle Tom to a white woman, but Uncle Tom escapes and gets rich playing craps (an old stereotype of black behavior).

"All This and Rabbit Stew" (1941). This one follows the typical formula of an Elmer Fudd vs. Bugs Bunny cartoon, except in this one Bugs is being hunted by a black character—or rather a black *caricature*, complete with exaggerated lips and

Nazi Germany created children's board games with titles like "Jews Out!" and "Bombers Over England."

mumble-mouth speech impediment. This cartoon also ends with a game of craps (Bugs, of course, wins).

"Hittin' the Trail for Hallelujah Land" (1931). A Mickey Mouse lookalike named Piggy has to get his girlfriend, Fluffy, and a character named Uncle Tom out of various dangerous situations. Several blackface characters sing the cartoon's title song, which is an old African American spiritual.

"Sunday Go to Meetin' Time" (1936). A blackface character named Nicodemus plays craps, gets knocked on the head, and dreams he goes to his final judgment. He's found to be wicked, and sent to Hades, where a group of blackface demons bring him to the devil.

"Clean Pastures" (1937). In this religion-themed cartoon, God sends a slow-talking, slow-walking angel to Harlem to try to get people to renounce their wicked ways and come to heaven (called Pair-o-Dice). When that doesn't work, God sends black jazz-musician angels instead.

"Jungle Jitters" (1938). A traveling salesman tries to sell housewares to a tribe of cannibals in the African jungle. The homely queen of the village falls in love with him, and to escape her advances, the traveling salesman throws himself into a cooking pot, implying he'd rather get eaten than marry her. Oddly, the African cannibal queen was drawn as a Caucasian woman because the Hays Code (the morality guidelines for the motion picture industry at the time) forbade depiction of interracial relationships.

"Coal Black and de Sebben Dwarfs" (1943). After legendary cartoon director Bob Clampett was asked by the cast of an African American musical—Duke Ellington's *Jump for Joy*—why there were no black Warner Bros. characters, Clampett came up with this jazz parody of *Snow White and the Seven Dwarfs* where all the characters are in blackface.

"The Isle of Pingo Pongo" (1938). A travelogue about the inhabitants of a remote jungle island. It has all the usual black stereotypes: natives with bones in their hair, rings in their noses, and plates in their lips, carrying spears—along with jitterbug dancers and a jazz orchestra.

"Angel Puss" (1944). An African American boy named Sambo gets paid "four bits" (50¢) to drown his cat, but the cat outsmarts him and escapes, then paints himself white and pretends to be a ghost cat. The frightened boy eventually wises up, finds a shotgun, and kills the cat.

Food for thought: Massachusetts and Illinois both have towns called Sandwich.

"Tin Pan Alley Cats" (1943). Another Bob Clampett jazz cartoon in which a cat who looks and sings like jazz legend Fats Waller is so entranced by a jazz band in a nightclub that he drifts off to a surreal fantasy land where he encounters World War II villains Adolf Hitler, Joseph Stalin, and Hideki Tojo. When he comes back to reality, he's so freaked out by what he saw in his dream world that he gives up the jazz nightlife and joins the religious band playing outside the club.

"Goldilocks and the Jivin' Bears" (1944). A retelling of the "Goldilocks and the Three Bears" story, except the bears are blackface jazz musicians…and also Goldilocks (reimagined as a leggy young black woman in high heels) is nearly devoured by the Big Bad Wolf from "Little Red Riding Hood." The jazz trio saves her by playing a song so hot the Big Bad Wolf jitterbugs himself to exhaustion.

* * *

FACTIEST FACTS

- Country with the longest name (one word only): Liechtenstein (13 letters).
- City with the longest average round-trip home-to-work commute time: Washington, DC (60.42 minutes).
- Deepest subway station in the world: Arsenalna Station, on the Kiev Metro line in Kiev, Ukraine (it's 346 feet below street level; it takes a full five minutes for escalators to reach the surface).
- World's busiest shipping lane: the Dover Strait, between the UK and France (500–600 ships pass through the strait every day).
- Skinniest tower in the world: British Airways i360 Tower in Brighton, England (it's 531 feet tall—and just 12.7 feet in diameter, giving it a 40:1 height-to-diameter ratio).
- Deepest river in the world: the Congo River in central Africa (scientists have not been able to determine the Congo's exact depth; the deepest they have been able to measure is 720 feet).
- Largest irrigation system in the world: the Sukkur Barrage on the Indus River, near the city of Sukkur in northern Pakistan (a barrage is a type of dam with controllable gateways used to divert water; the Sukkur Barrage is more than a mile long, has more than 60 gates, and irrigates 7.63 million acres of land).
- World's widest human tongue: 3.37 inches (Byron Schlenker, Syracuse, New York).
- World's widest human tongue (female): 2.89 inches (Emily Schlenker—Byron's daughter).

Mini, but mighty: Caterpillars have seven times as many muscles as humans do.

STOP THE PRESSES!

If you saw a children's book with a title like one of these, would you be so intrigued that you'd pick it up? Probably…which could be why the authors gave them these titles. And, yes, these were all actually published.

My Parents Open Carry, by Brian Jeffs and Nathan Nephew

See Dick Bite Jane, by Elise Mac Adam

I Wish Daddy Didn't Drink So Much, by Judith Vigna

The House That Crack Built, by Clark Taylor

The Night Dad Went to Jail, by Melissa Higgins

I Love You Better than Boogers: A Silly Bedtime Book, by Paullina Schiavenato

Who Cares About Disabled People?, by Pam Adams

Good Touch, Bad Touch, by Robert Kahn

The Long Journey of Mister Poop, by Angèle Delaunois

Where Willy Went: The BIG Story of a Little Sperm!, by Nicholas Allan

All My Friends Are Dead, by Avery Monsen and Jory John

Pooh Gets Stuck, by Isabel Gaines

My Monster Farts, by Kate Clary

Hair in Funny Places, by Babette Cole

Gross Gus and the Time Out Chair, by Kally Mayer

The Loneliest Ho in the World, by Travis Heaten and Gary Andrews (a Christmas tale)

Scouts in Bondage, by Geoffrey Prout

Titanic Turds of the Animal Kingdom, by Anthony Sievers

It's You and Me Against the Pee…and the Poop, Too, by Julia Cook and Laura Jana, MD

Melanie's Marvelous Measles, by Stephanie Messenger

I Found a Dead Bird, by Jan Thornhill

First words said on Skype (2003): "Tere, kas sa kuuled mind?"
("Hello, can you hear me?" in Estonian.)

STRANGE CRIME

Featuring an ugly sweater, poisonous cheesecake, twin peaks, and a crook who scans the obits. (Shameless plug: For more bizarre crime stories like these, check out Portable Press's Strange Crime.)

THE ZEN BURGLAR

February 9, 2018, was a strange Friday night for Siosifa Lolohea. It's unclear how the Utah man started the evening, but it ended with him throwing two empty vodka bottles through the doors of the Orem Public Safety Building, breaking in, and then lying down on the floor "to meditate." Several police officers were in that very building typing up the day's reports, so they responded quickly. "He was a little upset that we were messing up his meditation period," said the arresting officer, "disturbing him while he was just trying to get some inner peace." The officer also pointed out that Lolohea didn't have to break the glass—if he had simply rung the bell, they would have been happy to let him in.

THE CHEESECAKE MURDERESS

A 42-year-old Brooklyn, New York, woman named Viktoria Nasyrova met a 35-year-old woman who happened to look a lot like her. The two women, both being from Russia, struck up a friendship. But Nasyrova had ulterior motives. In August 2016, she baked her doppelganger a cheesecake laced with a strong tranquilizer called phenazepam. After the unsuspecting woman had a few bites, she said she didn't feel well and went to lie down. While she was unconscious, Nasyrova carefully arranged the empty bottle and remaining pills to make it look like a suicide. Then she stole her friend's cash, jewelry, passport, and employment authorization card. Nasyrova's scheme might have worked...except the victim didn't die. She was found unconscious a day later and taken to the hospital, where she later told doctors the last thing she remembered was Nasyrova watching her eat the cheesecake. The attempted murderer faces up to 25 years in prison.

THE OBIT BANDIT

Bad: Losing a loved one. Worse: Having your home burglarized while you're at the funeral. In the 2010s, several grieving families in southern Massachusetts were faced with that predicament until police finally apprehended Randy Brunelle, 35, whom the press dubbed the "Obit Bandit." His first known funeral burglary was in 2012, when he robbed the home of a police officer who was attending his mother's wake. Brunelle

NFL quarterback Tom Brady didn't taste his first strawberry until 2018, when he was 40 years old.

spent 18 months in prison for that crime, but soon after he was released, more people's homes started getting ransacked while they were attending funerals. Suspecting that Brunelle was scanning the obituaries in order to find potential victims, detectives set up a sting operation. On a Saturday in February 2018, they patrolled the homes of people whose funerals were announced in the paper, and lo and behold, there was Brunelle's Honda Civic parked outside one of the houses. Caught red-handed, the Obit Bandit is again behind bars.

THE VALLEY OF DEATH

Washington's Snoqualmie Valley has seen a lot of odd, grisly crimes over the years. For example, in 1999 a dog ran up to a house on Southeast Reinig Road carrying a human hand that was later linked to a homicide. That's not uncommon—because the remote, wooded area is only about 30 miles from Seattle, it's become a notorious dumping ground for dead bodies. Then there's the tragic account of a Snoqualmie man who murdered his wife and two stepdaughters. According to the *Guardian*, "He kept a third stepdaughter captive in his bedroom for hours, dragging her out occasionally so he could refill his wine glass." (She later escaped.) It seems that every few years, another odd, grisly crime shakes Snoqualmie Valley residents, especially along Southeast Reinig Road. That happens to be the road where they filmed the opening of the cult TV show *Twin Peaks*, which centers around odd, grisly crimes.

THE THUMB THIEF

On January 8, 2018, a museum staffer at the Franklin Institute in Philadelphia made an alarming discovery: a terra-cotta warrior was missing his left thumb! The 2,000 year-old-statue, known as "the Cavalryman," was one of ten on loan from China, and is valued at $4.5 million (the thumb alone is worth five grand). News of the crime sparked outrage in China; the FBI took over the case. Agents reviewed several weeks' worth of CCTV footage until they found a suspect. On the night of December 21, 2017, a man wearing an ugly sweater entered the exhibit and then left a few minutes later. Thus began the manhunt. It turned out that, on the night in question, there'd been an "ugly sweater" themed party at the museum, which didn't help narrow it down. But FBI agents were finally able to track down 24-year-old Michael Rohana, who lived in Delaware. That night, he had left the party, broken into the exhibit, put his arm around the life-size clay soldier, taken a selfie, snapped off the warrior's thumb, and exited the room. (The next day, he posted a pic of the thumb on Snapchat.) A month later, Rohana received a visit from the FBI, who asked if he had anything he wanted to turn over to them. He sheepishly retrieved the artifact from his desk drawer. Rohana was arrested, and the Cavalryman got his thumb back.

Over your lifetime, your mouth will make enough saliva to fill two swimming pools.

THE END

No matter how we start, it all comes out in the end.

IN THE BEGINNING. What do you think is the very first human body part to form at conception? The brain? The heart? The spinal column? Nope—it's farther down. The moment the father's sperm pierces the mother's egg, a single cell forms, containing all the genetic information needed to make a baby. That cell quickly divides, and keeps dividing until it forms a hollow ball of cells called a *blastula,* which is so small that it can fit on the head of a pin. The blastula then folds in on itself and forms an opening called a *blastopore.* This tiny opening becomes the baby's first body part: the anus. Then the embryonic butthole turns itself inside out to form the second organ—the mouth, which explains why human beings belong to the subclassification of animals known as *deuterostomes,* or "second mouth."

BOTTOMS UP. It used to be the custom for royal women to give birth in front of witnesses. Reason: they needed to guarantee that the true royal offspring hadn't been switched with an impostor. In December 1778, more than 200 people of the court gathered at Versailles to await the delivery of Marie Antoinette's baby. After eight hours of labor, the queen's doctor announced, "The queen is about to give birth!" A stampede of courtiers quickly entered the royal bedchamber, shimmying up the curtains, jumping on the couch, and climbing onto the windowsills to get a good view of the queen's royal rear. The mob pressed so closely they nearly suffocated the queen. And as little Princess Marie Theresa made her first appearance in court, the queen passed out. The experience was so traumatic that King Louis XVI banned all future public viewings of royal births, limiting witnesses to a dozen or so close family members.

END RUN. Soon after Germany occupied Norway during World War II, the Nazis announced they were confiscating all of the sardines from the Norwegians' factories to feed their troops in the field and on U-boats. The Norwegians got angry…and the Norwegian resistance got even. They sent a message to their British contacts asking them to send a laxative that could be added to vegetable oil without detection. The Brits sent as much as they could get their hands on. The Norwegians then sneaked into sardine-canning factories at night and filled the sardine cans with croton oil, which is a very powerful laxative. When the Nazis shipped the tins of sardines to the U-boat bases across the continent, the sailors were in for a big surprise. Painful diarrhea can be horrible for anyone, but imagine being packed into a tiny submarine where every single member of the crew is suffering from "Norway's Revenge."

If bees were paid the minimum wage, a jar of honey would cost $182,000.

VIDEO GAME LAWSUITS

*What's more exciting than a video game? The legal battles that
ensue when video game companies sue each other.*

THE PLAINTIFF
Rock band No Doubt

THE DEFENDANT
Activision

THE LAWSUIT
Before she was a pop star and a judge on *The Voice*, Gwen Stefani was the lead singer
of the successful band No Doubt, with hits like "Just a Girl," "Don't Speak," and
"Ex-Girlfriend." The band's music was a logical choice to include in *Band Hero*,
Activision's 2009 entry in its best-selling *Guitar Hero* interactive video game franchise.
The members of No Doubt licensed their music and their likenesses to Activision,
but claimed they were unaware that the video game characters could be used to play
non–No Doubt songs. For example, a player could use a "Gwen Stefani" avatar to sing
and play a Taylor Swift song, or one by the cheesy 1980s hair metal band Poison. The
day after *Band Hero* was released, No Doubt sued Activision for using their images in
what the filing called "a virtual karaoke circus act."

THE VERDICT
The case never made it to court. After their lawyers negotiated for three years, the
band and the video game company reached a (sealed) settlement that didn't require
the game to be pulled from store shelves.

THE PLAINTIFF
Magnavox

THE DEFENDANT
Atari

THE LAWSUIT
Pong (1972) was the first famous video game, but it wasn't the first electronic game
played on a TV screen with a joystick. Nor was it the first video game in which play
was a simplified presentation of table tennis—two lines representing paddles, and a
white dot for a ball. Magnavox gave public demonstrations of a table tennis game
for its home video game system Odyssey, at department stores in early 1972. Nolan
Bushnell had just started a software company called Atari. (He and engineer Allan
Alcorn had been contracted by a casino chain to develop a driving simulator.) After

he played Magnavox's table tennis game at a demo in a Burlingame, California, department store, Bushnell asked Alcorn to develop a coin-operated electronic table tennis game as a test of his programming abilities. But Alcorn did such a good job, Bushnell released it commercially. When *Pong* became a sensation, Ralph Baer, inventor of the Magnavox Odyssey, sued Atari, alleging that the company had stolen his creation.

THE VERDICT

Bushnell's attorney advised him to take the case to trial, but Atari settled out of court in 1976 because Bushnell estimated that his legal costs were going to be more than all the money Atari had on hand at the time. As part of the settlement, Atari continued to produce *Pong* for arcades and home video game consoles, but Magnavox received licensing fees and a royalty for every game sold.

THE PLAINTIFF

Former college athletes Sam Keller and Ed O'Bannon

THE DEFENDANT

Electronic Arts and the Collegiate Licensing Company

THE LAWSUIT

Despite massive TV and merchandising deals that generate billions of dollars for companies and universities, the athletes who actually play college football, basketball, and other sports don't get paid a cent (other than scholarships)—they're amateurs. In 2009 former college basketball player Ed O'Bannon and former college football player Sam Keller sued EA, maker of the popular *NCAA Basketball* and *NCAA Football* video game franchises, and Collegiate Licensing, the firm that sets up all those college sports deals.

REASON

They didn't believe that their amateur athlete status applied to exploitation of their images that made other people rich. On behalf of all former athletes, they wanted royalties for allowing their likenesses to be used in those successful games.

THE VERDICT

After a long legal battle, Keller and O'Bannon settled out of court for an undisclosed amount. However, their lawsuit changed the way the video game industry operated *and* how the business of college sports work. After the suit was settled in 2013, EA permanently discontinued all NCAA-branded games. Not only that, but the company started writing checks. In early 2016, athletes whose faces were used in certain EA Sports collegiate titles started getting checks in the mail in the range of $1,200–$7,200.

First U.S. territory to grant women the vote: Wyoming, in 1869.
First U.S. state to elect a female governor: Wyoming (Nellie Tayloe Ross, in 1924).

THE PLAINTIFF

Atari

THE DEFENDANT

Philips

THE LAWSUIT

Developed in Japan by Namco and released to the rest of the world by Bally/Midway, *Pac-Man* was a global sensation in the early 1980s. Within 18 months of its release, the game about a yellow pie that eats white dots and avoids ghosts earned $1 billion in revenues. And that's just at arcades—in 1981 Namco and Bally/Midway were in the process of adapting or "porting" *Pac-Man* to home video game consoles, particularly the Atari 2600. But before *Pac-Man* could hit homes, Philips Electronics came out with a game called *K.C. Munchkin* for its Odyssey 2 console. It wasn't an *exact* clone of *Pac-Man*, but it looked like developers tried to make it just different enough from *Pac-Man* to avoid a lawsuit—the maze walls move around the screen, and the villains are monsters, not ghosts. But it was also a game about a circle that ate dots. Atari, which owned the home gaming rights to *Pac-Man*, sued Philips for copyright infringement.

THE VERDICT

Atari lost its initial case—it wanted an injunction to stop the sale of *K.C. Munchkin*—but the company appealed, and in 1982 an appellate court ruled that Philips *had* ripped off *Pac-Man*. Later that year, Atari released its home version of *Pac-Man*...and sold seven million copies.

*   *   *

...AND NOW A FEW WORDS ABOUT PIE

"Pie makes everybody happy."

—Laurie Halse Anderson

"Good apple pies are a considerable part of our domestic happiness."

—Jane Austen

"Stress cannot exist in the presence of a pie."

—David Mamet

"Pie fills the cracks of the heart."

—Kevin James (as Paul Blart, Mall Cop)

"Promises and pie crusts are made to be broken."

—Jonathan Swift

Black Sabbath, one of the first heavy metal bands, was from Birmingham, England, a city known for...

STALL OF FAME: THE "SHADY LADY"

Tombstone, Arizona, is famous for the 1881 "gunfight at the O.K. Corral,"
where Wyatt Earp and his brothers shot it out with the Ike Clanton gang.
But it's another town resident that has made it into the Stall of Fame.

TRANSPLANTS

In 1885 two Scottish newlyweds named Henry and Mary Gee arrived in the
burgeoning town of Tombstone, Arizona, where Henry found work as an engineer with
the Vizina Mining Company. The company ran a boardinghouse, and the Gees stayed
there until they finished building their own house in town.

While they were living in the boardinghouse, Mary Gee struck up a friendship
with Amelia Adamson, the woman who ran it. The two women remained friends
even after the Gees moved into their new home. And when a box from Mary's family
arrived all the way from Scotland, filled with seeds, bulbs, and cuttings collected from
the family garden, Mary gave one of the cuttings from a white Lady Banksia rosebush
to Adamson. She planted it behind the boardinghouse.

DOWN UNDER

The climate of the Arizona desert has little in common with that of Scotland,
which is as far north as Juneau, Alaska, and surrounded by the sea on three sides.
It's not clear how many of the seeds and bulbs that Mary Gee planted in her garden
survived. But the Banksia rosebush that Adamson planted in the sandy soil behind
the boardinghouse thrived. That it survived at all is not due to what was *in* the soil,
but rather what was *under* it. And what was under it had a lot to do with Tombstone's
history as a mining boomtown.

When the town was founded in 1879, following what turned out to be the richest
silver strike in the history of the Arizona Territory, only about 100 people lived in
Tombstone, mostly in tents and shacks built around the opening of the Tough Nut
Mine. But word of the discovery spread, and over the next several years Tombstone's
population exploded to nearly 15,000 people. By the time the Gees arrived in 1885,
the town was home to more than a hundred saloons and casinos, three newspapers,
four churches, an opera house, a bowling alley, and French, Italian, Mexican, and
Chinese restaurants. About the only thing it lacked was a sewer system. Not that it
really needed one: the warren of mine shafts that had been dug beneath the town

...its metal fabrication factories. (Sabbath guitarist Tony Iommi lost
the tips of two fingers working in a sheet metal factory.)

proved to be more than adequate to the task of "disposing" of Tombstone's sewage, so the townspeople never bothered to install a better system.

EUREKA

It apparently didn't take long for the roots of Amelia Adamson's rosebush to find their way down to a spot where some of this natural human "fertilizer" had collected. As soon as it did, the plant began to grow rapidly…and it never stopped. As the decades passed, the silver mines played out and most of the townspeople moved on. By 1910 fewer than 700 people lived in Tombstone. But the rosebush kept growing: by the 1920s, its creeping vines had taken over so much of the yard that the owners of the boardinghouse, which now operated as a hotel, built trellises to place the vines overhead, so that people wouldn't trip or trample them underfoot.

Soon the rosebush provided a large shady area on the patio in back of the hotel, and became a popular resting spot for people who wanted to get out of the desert sun. It became so popular, in fact, that in 1935 the hotel changed its name from Cochise House to the Rose Tree Inn. And the rosebush acquired a nickname as well: the Shady Lady.

STILL GROWING

In 1937 Robert Ripley of *Ripley's Believe It or Not!* fame visited Tombstone and saw the Shady Lady; by then it was nine feet tall, its canopy of miniature white tea roses covered an area of 2,750 square feet, and it was still growing. Ripley wrote it up in his newspaper column as the "World's Largest Rosebush."

More than 80 years have passed since Ripley passed through town. The Shady Lady has more than tripled in size since then…and it's still growing. Today the central "trunk" is 12 feet in diameter and the canopy covers more than 9,000 square feet. Guinness World Records has confirmed its status as the world's largest rosebush. The plant owes nearly all of its 130 years of prodigious growth to the mother lode of human "fertilizer" that it found in the mine shafts beneath Tombstone. The owners of the inn, which is now a museum, didn't need to fertilize the plant until 2015.

The Shady Lady will probably never be as famous as the gunfight at the O.K. Corral, but it is the center of attention during Tombstone's annual Rose Festival, held every year during March and April when the plant is in bloom. The museum's owners sell transplanted cuttings of the rosebush, so if you want a piece of the Shady Lady in your own garden, you can have it. (Where you get your fertilizer is your problem.)

Why do seagulls stand on one leg? Tucking one leg into its feathers keeps it warm, helping retain body heat on cold days.

SURVIVING '17

Between August and November 2017, planet Earth was battered by one natural disaster after another. Floods, fires, earthquakes, and hurricanes killed several thousand people, and displaced millions more. Yet out of the anguish and devastation came inspiring stories of survival and heroism. Here are six of them.

SIERRA LEONE MUDSLIDES

Details: When three times the seasonal average of rainfall soaked the western African nation of Sierra Leone in the summer of 2017, mudslides were inevitable. The capital city, Freetown (with a population of nearly one million) was directly in harm's way. Situated at the foot of a steep mountain chain, Freetown has an aging, clogged drainage system, and there were few escape routes for the city's residents due to crowded conditions and poor infrastructure. Early on a Monday morning in mid-August, following three days of relentless rain, it happened: a torrent of thick, red mud poured out of the mountains and demolished much of Freetown. More than 500 people were killed, with hundreds more remaining missing.

Survival Story: Unlike many who perished, Kelvin Kamara was awake when the mudslide came. He barely made it to high ground before the mud and debris overtook his street. But he didn't stay there; instead, he jumped into action. In the crucial moments that followed, Kamara frantically began searching for people who were trapped and in danger of being buried by the still-rising mud. By his own count, he helped save more than 40 people that morning.

HURRICANE HARVEY

Details: Harvey was the first of four major hurricanes to make landfall in the Americas in 2017. When the category 4 hurricane hit Texas on Thursday, August 24, it weakened and stalled for two days. But by the time it finally moved on, it had dropped more than 40 inches of rain in Houston and set an all-time U.S. record for the most rainfall in a 24-hour span. More than 30,000 people were displaced; just under 100 died. And one person was born.

Survival Story: Andrea Smith went into labor just as Harvey made landfall. She and her husband Greg had been watching the storm's approach for several days. They'd planned on going to the hospital on Sunday, but the water rose much faster than anyone had expected, and they found themselves trapped in their first-floor apartment. Although the young married couple are both doctors, neither had any experience delivering a baby, nor did they have any medical equipment. They tried calling 9-1-1,

Dodged: The International Olympic Committee has
rejected proposals to make dodgeball an Olympic event.

but no one answered. So they called the U.S. Coast Guard and were told that no one could rescue them until the rain stopped. With no way out, the Smiths enlisted help from Greg's mother and some neighbors and prepared to have the baby at home. But water was coming in under the door and rising fast. Reluctantly, Andrea and Greg made their way to an apartment on the second floor.

As Andrea was preparing to have her first child in a stranger's bed, a dump truck rolled up and parked out front. Greg ran outside in the torrential rain and yelled for help. The driver yelled back, "We're here for you!" Unbeknownst to the Smiths, one of their neighbors had managed to contact nearby firefighters, who procured the dump truck. Then, in pouring rain and waist-high water, friends and strangers formed a human chain to get Andrea and Greg safely from the building to the truck, where firefighters took care of Andrea as she was driven to the hospital.

A few hours later, little Adrielle was born. There were complications, though, and the baby girl was put straight into intensive care. She's okay now, but who knows what would have happened if Andrea hadn't made it to the hospital to give birth. "Moments like these," said Molly Akers, who filmed the human-chain rescue, "remind me of all the good in the world." That was one of 17,000 documented rescues during Hurricane Harvey.

CENTRAL MEXICO EARTHQUAKE

Details: September 19, 2017, marked the 32nd anniversary of a Mexico City earthquake that killed more than 10,000 people. To commemorate the tragedy, at 11:00 a.m. the country held its annual earthquake preparedness drill. Two hours later, a magnitude 7.1 quake struck central Mexico. During the 20 seconds of violent shaking, hundreds of buildings fell in Mexico City, and over 200 people were killed. (Despite the drill that had just taken place, no warning sirens preceded the earthquake, which caught the populace off guard.)

Survival Story: "I don't even know how I saved myself," said 12-year-old Luis Carlos Tomé through tears to a *Telemundo News* reporter. A few hours earlier, Luis was in his English class when the floor started to vibrate. He yelled for everyone to get out, and they all ran to the door. Unsure which direction to go, he went with his friends to the right. They were about to run down a staircase when the ceiling started falling in front of them, so they turned around and made their way—arms linked—to another staircase…which was shaking so violently that Luis had to jump over it as the air started filling with dust and rubble. He lost sight of his friends as he somehow made his way outside. When he turned around, what had been his school was now just a pile of rubble. Although 21 students, three teachers, and a janitor died at the school, Luis was beyond relieved that his little brother Jose had also made it out unscathed. "We cried," said Luis. "He was my biggest worry."

The number of human egg cells necessary to produce the next generation of the human race would fit inside in a single hen's egg.

SOUTH ASIA FLOODS

Details: Monsoon season hits Asia hard every year, but the summer of 2017 brought the worst flooding in decades. Rising waters killed nearly 1,300 people across Bangladesh, Nepal, India, and Pakistan. In Karwar, a city on the west coast of India, onlookers watched helplessly as six people were washed away in a flash flood. A search was begun immediately, but there was little hope that they would recover anyone alive. That grim forecast seemed more and more likely as four bodies were recovered. Two people were still missing, though. One of them was never found; the other was Yashwant Raikar.

Survival Story: The young man and his wife had been preparing for a family picnic at the base of a popular waterfall. They were making chicken kabobs when the torrent of water came gushing over the falls. People started making their way to higher ground, but then, "a young boy who was running to escape the flood fell down," Raikar later told the *Times of India*. "I pulled him to safety, but I fell down and was washed away." A tourist filmed Raikar and the five others get taken by the river. The footage was shown on the local news, which pronounced all six people dead.

But Raikar was in a fight for his life. "I was slammed against boulders and tree branches," he recalled, for more than a mile. "I caught hold of a tree branch and held on to it. After some time, the water level receded and I came out of the stream and fell unconscious." The next thing Raikar knew, he was in the hospital. His family was overjoyed that he was alive, as another of their relatives didn't make it. "I never thought the picnic would cost us so dearly," he said.

NORTHERN CALIFORNIA FIRESTORM

Details: With all the wildfires that roar through heavily populated Southern California, one wouldn't expect that the most destructive fire in the state's history would happen in the heart of Wine Country. "The Northern California Firestorm" was actually a series of more than 250 separate wildfires. The worst was the Tubbs Fire, which broke out on October 8 near the town of Calistoga. The cause: a tree branch that took down a power line in high winds. Those same high winds—some gusts reached 60 mph—quickly turned the fire into an inferno. There was no stopping it as it spread southwest through dry pine forests straight toward the city of Santa Rosa.

Survival Story: Jan and John Pascoe, 65 and 70 respectively, lived in the mountains just outside of Santa Rosa in a home they'd built 35 years earlier. As they were getting ready for bed on that calm Sunday night, the Tubbs Fire started about 11 miles away. At around 10:00 p.m., their daughter called and told them that several fires were burning in surrounding areas, and they needed to leave. Jan checked an app on her phone, which told her the closest flames were still several miles away. And they hadn't received a wildfire evacuation alert yet, so they thought they had some time. They started *preparing* to evacuate. Several crucial minutes later, a blast of wind hit the

It takes 872 gallons of water to produce just one gallon of wine.

house and Jan looked out the window and saw red. They threw what they could in their pickup truck and started racing down the driveway, but they were too late. A wall of flames blocked their way to the main road, forcing them back to the house. And then their worst nightmare came true: their home was surrounded by fire.

Then they remembered that their neighbor had a pool; it was about a third of a mile away. It wasn't very large, and only four feet deep, but it was their only hope. Jan called 9-1-1 to say they'd be in the pool if anyone came. (No one did.) Then they ran outside in their pajamas and traversed the burning mountainside all the way to the pool…only to discover that the water was freezing. They huddled next to it for as long as they could. Then a large pine tree burst into flames, followed by wooden railroad ties lining the steps to the pool. They had no choice. They got in.

Just then, the neighbor's house caught fire, and the air became hot enough to burn their skin on contact. Meanwhile, it was so cold under the water that they nearly got frostbite on their toes. Jan and John huddled together for warmth and used their shirts to shield their heads when they came up for air. "Just how long," John kept asking, "does it take for a house to burn down?" This one took six hours.

By the time the flames finally subsided, the sun had risen, and the Pascoes were still alive. Tired and shivering, they climbed out of the pool and surveyed the damage. Everything they owned was gone. "After being here for 35 years," John told the *Los Angeles Times*, "it's a bit hard to get my head around." More than 5,000 structures were lost in Santa Rosa that night. Even worse, the Tubbs Fire took 43 lives. It would have likely been two more if not for the Pascoes' quick thinking and their will to live.

IRAN–IRAQ EARTHQUAKE

Details: On November 12, 2017, a 7.3 magnitude quake struck rural Iran just inside the Iraqi border, and the damage was quick and severe. The already crumbling infrastructure proved no match for the violent tremors, and more than 70,000 people suddenly became homeless. The 630 confirmed fatalities made it the deadliest earthquake of 2017 (and it had competition). Worst hit was the town of Sarpol-e-Zahab. Most of its 35,000 people lived in apartment buildings, many of which tumbled to the ground.

Survival Story: Rescue efforts there were slow, and after two days and two nights that saw temperatures fall below freezing, searchers were finding only dead bodies. But then, while looking through some rubble, they discovered a little baby…alive. Very few details were released in press reports, but a widely circulated photo of the smiling infant shows that, other than a cut on the bridge of his nose, he appears to be fine. No one knows how the baby survived on his own for more than 60 hours in freezing temperatures without food—or even how he survived the earthquake in the first place. The rescue was called a "miracle" by the beleaguered survivors…who at that point really needed a miracle.

Research shows that red and yellow are the colors that most make people want to eat…

LIFE IMITATES
THE SIMPSONS

When a TV show has been on as long as The Simpsons *has, it's bound to intersect with the real world every once in a while—especially because the show contains so many references to cultural moments and current events. Still, when things happen on* The Simpsons *first and then they happen in real life, it's kind of eerie.*

On *The Simpsons:* At the end of "When You Dish Upon a Star," a 1998 episode guest-starring Alec Baldwin and Kim Basinger, director Ron Howard pitches a movie idea to his business partner, Brian Grazer. He does it on the lot of 20th Century Fox (parent company of *The Simpsons*), which a sign indicates is "A Division of Walt Disney Co."

In Real Life: Nearly 20 years after the episode aired, Disney announced plans to buy most of 20th Century Fox.

On *The Simpsons:* In the 2010 episode "Boy Meets Curl," Marge and Homer go on a date to an ice-skating rink but discover that the place has been taken over by a curling team. The two realize they're really good at the bizarre sport that involves sliding a stone across an ice rink toward a target, assisted by sweeping—Homer can bowl and Marge can sweep. They wind up on the U.S. Olympic team and win a gold medal over Sweden.

In Real Life: At the 2018 Winter Olympics, the U.S. men's curling team won its first-ever gold medal…over Sweden.

On *The Simpsons:* The depths to which the Springfield Elementary School cafeteria, and Lunchlady Doris, will sink to save a buck on food is a long-running, disgusting joke on *The Simpsons*. In the 1995 episode "The PTA Disbands," Doris makes a meal out of shredded newspaper and old gym mats.

In Real Life: In 2014 a health watchdog organization called the Environmental Working Group released a report revealing that a compound called *azodicarbonamide* had been found in 500 different processed foods, mostly bread products like Wonder Bread, Pillsbury rolls, and the bread used at the Subway sandwich chain. What's *azodicarbonamide*? It's a chemical ingredient that is added to bread—and yoga mats—to make them soft and pliable.

…which is why most fast-food companies use one or both of those colors in their logos.

On *The Simpsons:* The show aired a "flash forward" episode set in the distant future called "Bart to the Future." It begins with Lisa being inaugurated as the "first straight female president" of the United States. In a budget meeting with advisors, she laments that she "inherited quite a budget crunch from President Trump."

In Real Life: That episode aired in 2000, when the idea of Donald Trump becoming president was absurd.

On *The Simpsons:* In the 1992 episode "New Kid on the Block" (written by Conan O'Brien), Homer goes to an all-you-can-eat seafood restaurant called the Frying Dutchman. Of course, he eats until the place closes down for the night and the staff kicks him out. Claiming to still be hungry—despite having eaten hundreds of helpings of fried shrimp—Homer and his sleazy attorney Lionel Hutz sue the restaurant for false advertising.

In Real Life: In 2012 a man named Bill Wisth attended the weekly Friday night all-you-can-eat fish fry at Chuck's Place in Mequon, Wisconsin. After a few trips to the buffet, the restaurant ran out of fish. Claiming to still be hungry, Wisth refused to pay for his meal and summoned the media. "If the people who run the restaurant put up signs that say all-you-can-eat, but then selectively not want to fill that promise, that's false advertising," he told reporters. Wisth threatened to sue, but backed down when the owner of Chuck's Place claimed that Wisth had eaten more than 20 pieces of fish and had also violated the buffet's strict "no sharing" rule.

On *The Simpsons:* In "Elementary School Musical," from 2010, Lisa, Millhouse, Martin, and other nerdy kids (with gambling help from Homer) put together a pool to place their bets on who will win Nobel Prizes in various categories. Millhouse thinks Bengt Holmström is a lock for Economics, but he loses to Jagdish Bhagwati.

In Real Life: Bengt Homström isn't a made-up name—he's a real economist. And in 2016 Millhouse's prediction came true when Homström won the Nobel Prize for Economics.

* * *

A LUCKY FIND

In 2016 a "bargain hunter" (unnamed in press reports) bought an old, cracked teapot for $20 from an antiques store. The shopper had it appraised, only to discover it was made in South Carolina in the 1760s. The teapot was later sold at auction for $806,000.

The line went dead: In 2007 a Chicago man faked his death to try to get out of his cell phone contract. (It didn't work.)

HAMBURGER FACTS

This page would go great with a page of french fry facts, and maybe some milkshake trivia.

First patent for a mechanical beef cutter: E. Wade in 1829. In 1845 G. A. Coffman of Virginia improved on Wade's invention, and received a patent for a meat grinder, which made grinding meat fast—and cutting no longer had to be done with a knife or chisel.

Ancestor: the 18th-century Hamburg steak. German immigrants in New York City bought this cheap lunch-counter or restaurant item that was similar to a Salisbury steak. The beef was hand-minced, salted, smoked, served with onions and breadcrumbs on a plate, and eaten with a knife and fork.

Who came up with the idea to put cheese on it? In 1935 Louis Ballast of the Humpty Dumpty Drive-In in Denver got a trademark for the word "cheeseburger," but he never defended it, so the word and concept spread. (Actually, burgers with cheese had been available since the 1920s.)

Louis' Lunch, a lunch counter in New Haven, Connecticut, is regarded by many as the birthplace of the hamburger. In 1900 it started offering ground beef patties between bread slices for a quick lunch on the go. Louis' Lunch is still open today.

Another claim to the burger's invention: Fletcher Davis, who put ground beef on bread in Athens, Texas, in the 1880s. Then he took them to the St. Louis World's Fair in 1904, where the food was widely popularized.

Another claimant to the "inventor of the hamburger" title: Oscar Weber Bilby. On the Fourth of July, 1891, he had a party on his farm near Tulsa, Oklahoma, and served ground beef on his wife's homemade rolls—not bread. That's the birth of the hamburger on a hamburger bun.

In 2000 North Korea's "glorious leader," Kim Jong Il, told his people that he invented the hamburger.

McDonald's sells 75 hamburgers every second.

At the 1885 Erie County Fair—coincidentally in Hamburg, New York—Frank and Charles Menches ran a food stand selling pork sausages. When they ran out, they started serving ground beef sandwiches on rolls. That same year, Charlie Nagreen in Seymour, Wisconsin, sold the same thing at the Outagamie County Fair. The hamburger was born.

About 71 percent of all beef served in restaurants in the United States is in the form of hamburgers (or cheeseburgers).

Each week, the average American eats three hamburgers. Altogether, that's about 50 billion burgers a year.

60 percent of all sandwiches sold around the world are hamburgers.

First fast-food hamburger chain: White Castle, which opened in 1921 in Wichita, Kansas, selling burgers for five cents each.

Cardinals get their name because their bright red color reminded people of the red vestments worn by cardinals of the Roman Catholic Church.

THE HUNT FOR "PLANET X"

*Here's the unlikely tale of how a 23-year-old farm boy
was enlisted to search for a new and unknown planet
at the far edges of the solar system...and found it.*

EYES ON THE SKIES

Clyde Tombaugh grew up on a Kansas farm in the 1910s and 1920s. He was a bright kid: his hobby was building telescopes from scratch, using materials he found around the farm. About the only part he had to send away for was the thick ship's porthole glass that he needed to make the lenses, which he ground into shape by hand. It was a painstaking process that required skill, patience, and tremendous attention to detail. In 1928 he cobbled together a telescope using a crankshaft from a 1910 Buick and parts from a cream separator, and with it he spent hundreds of hours studying the night sky. The telescope worked so well that he was able to make meticulous drawings of the visible features on the surface of Mars and Jupiter.

Tombaugh's dream was to become a college professor or an astronomer at an observatory one day, and to do either he would need a college degree. But times were tough in Kansas. The Great Depression, which would sweep the country in late 1929, was already wreaking havoc in farm country. There was little chance of him or his family ever being able to raise the money he'd need to go to college. So Tombaugh set his dream aside and worked on his parents' farm, and he hired out to his neighbors' farms as well. He thought about starting his own telescope business one day, or maybe getting an apprentice job on the railroad, where he might one day work his way up to being an engineer.

TAKE A LOOK

In his spare time, Tombaugh continued to study the night sky through his telescopes and making drawings of the planets. When he read in an old copy of *Popular Astronomy* magazine that the Lowell Observatory in Flagstaff, Arizona, was also studying the planets (most observatories studied celestial objects that were more distant than the planets), he mailed some of his best drawings to the director of the observatory, Vesto Slipher, and asked Slipher for his professional opinion of the work.

Slipher "responded almost immediately with a letter, asking a series of questions, which I promptly answered," Tombaugh recalled in his memoir, *Out of Darkness*. "Then came another letter with more questions, one of them being, 'Are you in good physical health?' which again was promptly answered. I realized that there was more

The "Dont Walk" sign is misspelled. (It's missing the apostrophe.)

than just polite interest." In a third letter, Slipher explained that the observatory had ordered a new telescope that they were going to use to photograph the night sky, and they needed someone to operate it. The job would involve lots of overnight work in an unheated observatory, high atop a mesa that received as much as 15 feet of snow each winter. That's why Slipher asked about Tombaugh's health. "Would you be interested in coming to Flagstaff on a few months trial basis?" he wrote.

"Then came anoth[er] letter with more questions, one of th[em] being, 'Are you in goo[d] physical health?'"

By now Tombaugh had had his fill of farming. He wrote back to Slipher and accepted the job, and a few weeks later boarded the train to Flagstaff. (Muron Tombaugh's parting words to his son: "Clyde, make yourself useful, and beware of easy women.")

THE AMATEUR

That the Lowell Observatory was even willing to offer a job to a young man with no college degree and no professional experience was due in no small part to the institution's status as a pariah in the world of astronomy. It had its deceased founder, Percival Lowell—a wealthy former diplomat, amateur astronomer, and popular author—to thank for that.

For many years Lowell had been obsessed with the idea that the surface of Mars was crisscrossed with canals built by an intelligent race of Martians. That idea dated back to 1877, when an Italian astronomer named Giovanni Schiaparelli observed Mars through a telescope and saw what he described as *canali*, an Italian word that can mean either "channels" or "canals." Schiaparelli meant "channels," which are naturally occurring, like rivers or streams. But when his writings were translated into English, *canali* was mistranslated as "canal," and that led many people to jump to the more exciting conclusion that the lines were artificial structures made by Martians.

OUT OF LINE

Percival Lowell was one such person. He was so enthralled by the idea of intelligent life on Mars that he left the diplomatic service and used much of the wealth he'd inherited to build the Lowell Observatory on a 7,250-foot mesa, which he named Mars Hill. He outfitted it with a state-of-the-art, 24-inch telescope that cost $20,000, the equivalent of more than $500,000 today, and used the telescope to study the Martian surface.

And just as he'd hoped, when Lowell looked through his telescope he saw plenty of lines that he believed were canals. He shared his enthusiasm for the subject in countless newspaper and magazine articles, and in three books: *Mars* (1895), *Mars and*

In England's Great Frost of 1709, loaves of bread froze so hard that they had to be cut with axes.

ts Canals (1906), and *Mars As the Abode of Life* (1908). "These lines run for thousands of miles in an unswerving direction, as far relatively as from London to Bombay, and as far actually as from Boston to San Francisco," he wrote in *Mars and Its Canals*.

Lowell's books and articles were light on substance but they captured the public's imagination. They made him, in at least a superficial sense, the Carl Sagan or Neil deGrasse Tyson of his age—someone who took the arcane subject of astronomy and made it into something that ordinary people found thrilling. His influence is still felt today. When you think of aliens, do you think of Martians more than Venusians, Uranians, and Saturnians? You have Percival Lowell to thank for it.

RED AWAKENING

Lowell's books may have been popular with the general reader, but they gave professional astronomers fits. Many had made their own observations of Mars, and they had not seen any canals. Even Schiaparelli thought Lowell was imagining things.

> When you think of aliens, do you think of Martians more than Venusians, Uranians, and Saturnians? You have Percival Lowell to thank for it.

Lowell's critics were soon proven correct. In 1908 the Pic du Midi Observatory, set atop a mountain in the French Pyrenees, opened its doors. It had a better telescope than the one at the Lowell Observatory, and when Mars passed close to Earth in 1909, astronomers there took some of the highest-resolution photographs of the Red Planet that had yet been taken…and they showed no canals. There weren't any naturally occurring *channels* on Mars, either, at least none that could be detected by telescopes in 1909. Lowell, Schiaparelli, and others who'd thought they'd seen lines on Mars were actually looking at optical illusions. The lines may have been caused by flaws that were common in telescopes of the day; it's also possible that Lowell and the others were looking at the veins inside their own eyeballs.

DAMAGE CONTROL

Lowell had spent 15 years of his life and a good chunk of his fortune trying to prove his Martian canal theory. Being proven wrong was humiliating: "The Lowell Observatory became virtually an outcast in professional astronomical circles," Tombaugh recalled. But by then Lowell was already working on another project to redeem himself.

For several years, when he wasn't observing Mars, Lowell had been studying the orbits of Uranus and Neptune, the two outermost planets in the solar system. Neptune had been discovered less than a hundred years earlier, when discrepancies in the orbit of Uranus suggested that another large planet farther out was pulling on it. In 1846 one group of astronomers in England and another group in France both calculated

Actor Cuba Gooding Jr. carries a good-luck charm at all times.
He won't say what it is—he believes that if he does, it will stop working.

mathematically where in the solar system that planet was likely to be. Later that year, when a third group of astronomers at an observatory in Berlin used the calculations to look for the planet, they found Neptune in less than an hour.

But while Neptune explained some of the irregularity of the orbit of Uranus, it did not explain all of it, at least not according to the observations of Uranus that had been made up until then. And Neptune appeared to have some discrepancies in its orbit as well. That led many astronomers, Lowell included, to suspect that a *ninth* planet, even farther out than Neptune, remained to be discovered. Lowell saw in the search for "Planet X," as he called it, a chance to restore his and his observatory's reputation.

PASSING THE BUCK

Lowell began his search for Planet X in 1905. He was still looking in November 1916 when he suffered a stroke while working at the observatory and died at the age of 61. In his will, Lowell had set aside $1 million to keep his observatory funded after his death, but his widow, Constance Lowell, contested the will. It wasn't until the late 1920s that the estate was finally settled and the search for Planet X could be resumed.

Then a new problem arose: *Who* was going to search for Planet X? The astronomers who worked at Lowell were busy with their own serious research, and didn't want to be bothered with Percival Lowell's silly quest. The observatory couldn't afford to hire another professional astronomer, even if it could find one willing to risk their professional reputation by working for the Lowell Observatory.

But the terms of Lowell's will required that the observatory continue the search. Somebody had to look for Planet X, but who?

HOW SOON CAN YOU START?

It was at about this time that Clyde Tombaugh, the 23-year-old Kansas farm boy with a high school diploma and a love of building telescopes, sent his drawings of Mars and Jupiter to Vesto Slipher, the director of the Lowell Observatory.

Here was the perfect candidate for the task: Tombaugh loved astronomy, and he was smart enough to build sophisticated telescopes from scratch. He was also young enough and naive enough to accept any job assigned to him, no matter how menial or tedious—and the search for Planet X promised to be *very* tedious—freeing the other astronomers to continue with their own work. And with no college diploma and no professional experience, he could be hired on the cheap.

Tombaugh arrived at the observatory in January 1929 and began his photographic work the following April. That consisted of using the Planet X telescope to photograph a particular area of the night sky, then photographing the identical spot several nights later. He'd develop the two images himself and view them through a

Daylight Saving Time was adopted during WWI to save fuel. After the war, it was repealed.

device called a "blink comparator," which allowed him to quickly flip or "blink" from the first image to the second, which is how the device got its name. When he finished photographing one area of the night sky he'd move on to another area, and so on, until he'd taken pictures of every place a planet might be hiding.

The blink comparator made it easier to spot celestial objects that had changed position from one night to the next against the background of stars, which were so far away that they appeared not to move at all. Closer objects, such as asteroids or comets, and undiscovered planets, would "jump" from their spot on the first image to their new position on the image taken several nights later.

If an object moved a great distance, it was moving quickly and therefore was likely an asteroid or a comet. If an object moved more slowly, it might well be the planet that Tombaugh was looking for.

NEEDLE IN A SPACE-STACK

Each section of sky that Tombaugh studied in the blink comparator contained anywhere from 150,000 to nearly a million stars. It took him as long as a week to complete the "grim task," as he put it, of carefully studying a pair of images for several hours each day until he was satisfied that Planet X was nowhere to be seen. Only then could he move on to the next pair of images in his pile, and start the process all over again.

After ten interminable months of this mind-numbing, laborious searching, on February 18, 1930, Tombaugh was studying a pair of images of the constellation Gemini taken on January 23 and January 29, when he saw an object move from its position on the first image to the next. It was, Tombaugh observed, too slow to be an asteroid or comet.

> **He saw an object move from its position on the first image to the next. It was too slow to be an asteroid or comet.**

The object also exhibited what is known as "apparent retrograde motion." All of the planets in our system orbit the Sun from west to east, but when viewed from Earth, they occasionally *appear* to move from east to west. The phenomenon is similar to two cars driving down a highway side by side, with one car traveling 60 mph and the other traveling 55 mph. From the point of view of people in the faster car, the slower car appears to be moving backward.

In the case of astronomy, the "cars" are planets moving in circular orbits around the sun. No celestial objects besides planets demonstrate apparent retrograde motion, so Tombaugh knew that if he observed the phenomenon, he was looking at a planet. He had been careful to point his camera in directions where a planet, if it was present, would exhibit apparent retrograde motion. And just as he'd hoped, the object he was looking at appeared to move from east to west. And he could tell that the object was orbiting the sun at a distance far beyond Neptune.

NASA astronauts personally award Silver Snoopy lapel pins to NASA employees for...

"A terrific thrill came over me," Tombaugh remembered. "I switched the shutter back and forth, studying the images. This would be a historic discovery." He spent about 45 minutes looking at the images over and over again, then he got up and walked down the hall to Vesto Slipher's office and told him, "Dr. Slipher, I have found your Planet X."

BY ANY OTHER NAME

The observatory photographed Planet X for three more weeks, carefully studying its orbit. All the evidence pointed to it being a planet (as the term was then understood) orbiting the

> **"Dr. Slipher, I have found your Planet X."**

Sun. Then on March 13, 1930, the 75th anniversary of Percival Lowell's birth, the discovery of Planet X was announced. Clyde Tombaugh became a celebrity overnight, appearing in motion picture newsreels and countless newspaper and magazine articles around the world.

The first order of business following the announcement, besides continuing to study Planet X, was to name it. Suggestions included Zeus and Lowell (suggested by Percival Lowell's widow Constance, who had nearly bankrupted the Lowell Observatory when she contested her husband's will). Other names considered were Splendor, PAX, Utopia, Atlas, Burdett (after Tombaugh's hometown of Burdett, Kansas), Eagle, and Usofa ("U.S. of A.").

Because the Lowell Observatory discovered Planet X, they were the ones that got to pick a name and submit it to the American Astronomical Society for approval. After the list of suggestions was whittled down to three, members of the observatory got to vote on the finalists: Minerva, Cronus, and a name first suggested by Venetia Burney, an 11-year-old schoolgirl living in Oxford, England: *Pluto*, after the Greek god of the underworld. Her suggestion won unanimously, and she received an award of £5, the equivalent of about $500 today.

...AND NOW THE FINE PRINT

Remember, the reason Percival Lowell went looking for Pluto in the first place was because astronomers believed the orbits of both Uranus and Neptune were being affected by the gravitational pull of an undiscovered planet. Uranus has about 14.5 times as much mass as Earth, and Neptune has 17 times as much. An object would have to be quite massive in its own right to alter the orbits of these giants. When Pluto was first discovered, it was thought to possibly be even larger than Jupiter, which at 318 times the mass of Earth is larger than all of the other planets in the solar system combined.

But as the years passed and more was learned about Pluto, the estimates of its size and mass were revised ever downward. As early as 1931, its mass was calculated to be oughly that of Earth. In 1948 it was revised to 0.1 times the mass of Earth; then to 0.01 in 1976, then to less than 0.002 in 2006.

Adding insult to injury, beginning in 1992, other objects similar in size to Pluto were discovered in the same region of space, called the Kuiper belt. Enough of them had been found by 2006, including one, Eris, that had a 27 percent greater mass than Pluto, that the word "planet" was redefined in a way that excluded Pluto, Eris, and other large objects in the Kuiper belt. They were given the new classification "dwarf planet." Technically speaking, not only did Tombaugh not find Planet X, he didn't find a planet at all. (But he did confirm the existence of the Kuiper belt.)

INTO THIN AIR

So is Planet X still out there, close enough to Uranus and Neptune and massive enough to alter their orbits? Not likely: The way the orbit of a planet is calculated is by estimating the mass of the planet, and then using the mass of the Sun and the laws of physics to determine its orbit around the Sun.

Estimating the mass of Neptune is no easy task, considering that Neptune is 30 times as far from the Sun as Earth is. It was even more difficult in the 1890s, when Percival Lowell began his search for Planet X. Even the best estimates made in the 20th century turned out to be off, something that the *Voyager 2* spacecraft confirmed when it flew past Neptune in 1989 and determined that the planet was a bit smaller than expected. When Neptune's mass was corrected, the discrepancies in both its orbit and the orbit of Uranus—and thus the need for a Planet X to explain them—disappeared entirely.

CONSOLATION PRIZE(S)

Clyde Tombaugh, it turns out, had spent 10 long months doing unbearably tedious work that no one else at the Lowell Observatory was willing to do, slowly poring over millions of stars on hundreds of photographic plates, looking for a planet that *wasn't even there*. And still he managed to find Pluto. The discovery earned him worldwide fame, and he got to fulfill his dream of going to college when he was awarded a four-year scholarship to the University of Kansas. There he earned his bachelor's and master's degrees in astronomy. (When he tried to sign up for his first course, Introduction to Astronomy, the professor threw him out of the class. "For a planet discoverer to enroll in a course of introductory astronomy is unthinkable," the professor told him.)

> **"For a planet discoverer to enroll in a course of introductory astronomy is unthinkable."**

In 1898 the U.S. Congress refused to seat newly elected B. H. Roberts of Utah. (Reason: He had three wives.)

STILL SEARCHING

Tombaugh continued the search for undiscovered planets even after discovering Pluto. His worst fear was that Pluto might actually be a moon orbiting a much larger, undiscovered planet. And once the Lowell Observatory had publicized Pluto's location to the world, there was a very real chance that if he stopped searching, someone else might find the planet that Pluto was orbiting (if such a planet existed) and steal the credit for discovering it from right under his nose. "The thought of the possibility of this makes me shudder yet, after 50 years," he admitted in 1980. "I was determined that if there were more planets to be found, they would be found at the Lowell Observatory."

So he kept searching, working full time until he started college in the fall of 1932, then during school breaks until he completed his education. Afterward he returned to the search, and kept at it until 1943. By then the United States had entered World War II, and he was drafted into the military and assigned to teach navigation at a U.S. Navy training school in Flagstaff.

In all, Tombaugh spent 14 years looking for undiscovered planets. He never did find one, though he estimated that the areas he searched contained more than 44 million stars. As he searched through them all looking for planets, he also discovered 775 asteroids, and numerous other astronomical bodies as well. "Few astronomers have seen so much of the Universe to such minute detail," he wrote in 1980.

TO INFINITY

After World War II Tombaugh worked at the White Sands Missile Range, then in 1955 he achieved another of his life's dreams when he became a professor of astronomy at New Mexico State University. He worked there until he retired in 1973.

In 1997 Tombaugh passed away at the age of 90. Nine years later a portion of his cremated remains were placed aboard the *New Horizons* spacecraft, which blasted off on a mission to Pluto, the first spacecraft ever to visit the dwarf planet. On July 14, 2015, it passed within 7,800 miles of Pluto's surface before continuing onward.

Tombaugh's next and, presumably, last claim to fame will come sometime after 2038, when his ashes aboard *New Horizons* become the first human remains ever to leave the solar system.

* * *

Random Fact: All the American flags that were left on the moon have been bleached completely white by the sun.

Earlier in the day he was shot, John Lennon signed his autograph
for the man who killed him, Mark David Chapman.

ACCORDING TO THE LATEST RESEARCH

It seems like every day there's a report on some scientific study with dramatic new info on what we should eat, or how we should act, or who we really are. Did you know, for example, that science says…

JOKES CAN BE "TOO SOON"

Researchers: A joint study by the University of Colorado and Texas A&M University.

What They Learned: Jokes about a recent tragedy are the least funny 15 days after the event, and the most funny 36 days after, which the research scientists dubbed the "comedic sweet spot."

Methodology: The scientists asked 1,064 online participants to rate the humor of tweets pertaining to Hurricane Sandy—which caused severe damage to the Caribbean and eastern United States in October 2012. They chose to conduct the study during a hurricane because a hurricane doesn't show up unannounced like other disasters. This way, they could test the humor potential before, during, and after the event. They started a Twitter account a few days prior to landfall called @HurricaneSandy, and then posted humorous tweets about it, including this one:

"JUS BLEW DA ROOF OFF A OLIVE GARDEN FREE BREADSTICKS 4 EVERYONE"

Before the storm hit, when no one knew how catastrophic it would be, the participants rated the tweet as pretty funny. As the days passed, however, and stories of human turmoil and images of destroyed landmarks dominated the news, the tweets were considered less funny. They bottomed out about two weeks after the storm, when it was still "too soon."

Then, as people came to terms with the disaster, the humor served as a coping mechanism, and tweets were deemed funniest around a month after the storm. "A tragic event is difficult to joke about at first, but the passage of time initially increases humor as the event becomes less threatening," the researchers concluded. "Eventually, however, distance decreases humor by making the event seem completely benign." (They also noted that jokes about less devastating disasters require significantly less than two weeks to be funny.)

Bananas, which are tropical, can be grown in Iceland, using the warmth of volcanic steam vents.

YOU'RE LEAST LIKELY TO BE PUNCHED IN FEBRUARY

Researchers: Cardiff University's Violence Research Group

What They Learned: Violent attacks are mainly a summertime activity. That's due to longer daylight hours and warmer nights, when more people are out and about.

Methodology: The researchers studied several years' worth of medical reports from 151 "Emergency Departments, Minor Injury Units, and Walk-in Centres" in England and Wales. The fuel of these violent attacks: alcohol. The study's co-author, Jonathan Shepherd, noted: "Given that violence peaks in the summer months of May and July, a time when all-day drinking is more common, it would make sense for the government to step up alcohol campaigns and violence prevention efforts at this time." There was some good news: the researchers reported that violent crime numbers have gone down in recent years, especially in February.

SELFIES SPREAD LICE

Researcher: Marcy McQuillan, who offers lice-removal services in California's Bay Area

What She Learned: The act of two or more teenagers putting their heads together when taking a selfie is transmitting lice to an age group that has never had to deal with it before.

Methodology: In a 2014 interview with the website SFist, McQuillan said, "Every teen I've treated, I ask about selfies, and they admit that they are taking them every day." The result, she said, was a "huge increase of lice in teens this year." The interview went viral, and within a few days, rival news outlets ran the story with alarmist headlines, such as this one from England's *Daily Mail:* "Selfies are causing a rise in MUTANT head lice!" Referring to McQuillan as a "lice expert," the article stated that "the social media trend is causing an infestation of head lice among older children." The reasoning: because lice can't jump, they only spread when two people's heads touch, a common occurrence when posing for selfies. Worse yet, reported the *Mail,* the parasitic insects are becoming resistant to insecticides (hence the phrase "MUTANT lice").

What Real Scientists Say: Several critics pointed out a flaw in McQuillan's research: there wasn't any. But even though her conclusion wasn't based on any previous study, most media outlets reported it as if it were. According to an actual expert, Shirley Gordon, director of the Head Lice Treatment and Prevention Project at Florida Atlantic University, selfies do not spread lice. While it's theoretically possible, there's no data that shows an increase in head lice cases. Besides, she says, the insects aren't that agile; they need several seconds of close contact in order to spread, more than the time it takes to take a selfie.

Chitty Chitty Bang Bang was based on real 1920s English racing cars called Chitty Bang Bangs.

"It's a marketing ploy, pure and simple," Harvard University lice expert Richard J. Pollack told NBC News. "Wherever these 'louse salons' open a new branch, there always seems to be an epidemic. It's good for business."

YOU MAKE THREE KINDS OF MISTAKES

Researchers: Psychologists from Eotvos Lorand University in Budapest, Hungary (who conducted a study about stupidity because the subject is "surprisingly unexplored")

What They Learned: Any given mistake can be categorized into one of three broad groups, and its level of "offensiveness" depends on which one it lands in.

Methodology: The researchers collected 180 news articles about blunders big and small, and then had 150 volunteers fill out questionnaires to rate the blunders' severity. (Sample question: "On a scale of 1 to 10, how stupid was it?") One interesting takeaway: 90 percent of the respondents were in agreement as to which acts were stupid and which were merely strokes of bad luck. Then the researchers divided the acts of stupidity into three categories:

1. *Confident Ignorance:* When you falsely believe your abilities are greater than they are. For example, someone jumping off the roof of a building, falsely believing he will land safely because he saw someone do it on TV. This type of blunder ranked as the "stupidest" of the three categories, averaging 8.5 on the stupid scale. "What that tells us," said lead researcher Balazs Aczel, "is that you don't have to have a low IQ, in people's eyes, to act stupidly. You just have to misperceive your abilities."

2. *Lack of Control:* It's when you find yourself doing something really stupid because you think, at the time, the means will justify the end. Often the result of "obsessive, compulsive, or addictive behavior," this is the category that most political scandals fall under, such as the time South Carolina governor Mark Sanford went missing for several days while having a tryst with his mistress, and later claimed he was "hiking the Appalachian Trail," despite a mountain of evidence that showed otherwise.

3. *Absentmindedness—Lack of Practicality:* You might call this a "brain fart." It's what happens when you're walking down the sidewalk while texting and veer off into traffic. This is the category that the respondents found the least offensive in terms of stupidity.

Good news: being aware of these stupid categories can help you avoid committing them. Or, as the researchers put it, "These stupidity categories can potentially predict what environmental or inner states increase the likelihood that one would behave in a way that others could call stupid." (Duh.)

17th-century Canadian contraceptive: a potion made from crushed beaver testicles. (No word on how well it actually worked.)

LEANING TO THE LEFT MAKES THE EIFFEL TOWER SEEM SMALLER

Researchers: Psychologists from Erasmus University in Rotterdam, the Netherlands

What They Learned: "Body posture influences our estimations of quantity."

Methodology: The researchers devised a sneaky tactic to come to this conclusion. They asked 91 college students "39 questions that involved making estimations of a wide variety of quantities." When they asked the questions—which ranged from "How much coffee is in that cup?" to "How tall is the Eiffel Tower?"—the test subjects had to stand on a Wii Balance Board and use a crosshair on a screen to continually adjust their balance in order to remain upright. But the scientists manipulated the Wii, so the students were unknowingly leaning to the right or to the left. Interestingly, the left-leaners estimated the Eiffel Tower to be an average of 12 meters *shorter* than the right-leaners did. And not just the iconic Paris landmark. Nearly all quantitative estimates were lower when the subjects were leaning to the left. By contrast, there was little difference in the estimates of those who were standing straight up or leaning to the right.

The reason, the researchers posited, is that most of the participants were right-handed, so they were "slightly biased" toward their dominant side. While this might seem like a silly experiment, it helps prove the "embodied cognition hypothesis" that says "the content of the mind is partly determined by the form of the body." So the next time you're trying to gauge the size of something, stand up straight to get the most accurate estimate.

MCDONALD'S FRENCH FRIES CAN CURE BALDNESS

Researchers: Hair scientists at Yokohama National University in Japan

What They Learned: "Oxygen-permeable dimethylpolysiloxane (PDMS)" (more commonly known as silicone) can help "grow thousands of hair follicles suitable for transplantation."

Methodology: The researchers came to this conclusion after studying hair growth on mice. They released their findings in a scientific journal in February 2018…and then the story went off the rails. A writer at England's *Daily Mail* had read a recent report that McDonald's used PDMS as an antifoaming agent in its cooking oil, so after reading the results of this study, he made the "McDonald's cures baldness" connection himself. One problem: the Japanese scientists mentioned nothing about curing baldness—or McDonald's, for that matter.

Following the *Daily Mail* article, bogus reports of baldness-curing French fries spread like hotcakes. Australia's Channel 9 News reported: "Japanese scientists say eating McDonald's fries could cure baldness!" They claimed the scientists "have mass

Ed Sullivan missed Elvis's first appearance on *The Ed Sullivan Show*.
(He was recovering from a car accident.)

produced 'hair follicle germs' which fuel hair development."

What Real Scientists Say: The record was finally set straight by science writer and LifeHacker.com's health editor, Beth Skwarecki:

> Let's be clear: the scientists used silicone to build their hair cell growing chip. And McDonald's uses silicone in their frying oil. That is literally the only connection. The silicone is not an "ingredient" in a baldness "cure." And it certainly doesn't "come from" frying oil, as if frying oil were a natural resource to be mined.

When one of the researchers, Junji Fukuda, was asked by *Japan Times* to clarify the fast-food claim, he was befuddled: "I have seen online comments asking, 'How many fries would I have to eat to grow my hair?' I'd feel bad if people think eating something would do that!"

RUDE BEHAVIOR SPREADS LIKE A DISEASE

Researchers: Trevor Foulk, Andrew Woolum, and Amir Erez from the University of Florida

What They Learned: When a person in a position of authority is rude to a subordinate, other subordinates are more likely to think rude thoughts as well.

Methodology: Two groups of volunteers took a survey asking what they felt about various words—some positive (like "happy") and some negative (like "savage"). What the test subjects didn't know: the researchers arranged for an actress to show up late to each session and ask to be included. In one group, the tester politely told the woman that she would have to leave, which she politely did. In the other group, the tester humiliated the woman for her tardiness and rudely told her to get out, which she rudely did.

Both groups responded similarly to the positive words, but when they got to the negative words, "the people who watched a rude interaction had concepts about rudeness active in their mind, and thus were faster to respond to those concepts." In other words, once the rudeness is activated in your mind—whether it was directed at you, or you simply witnessed it—you're subconsciously more likely to respond in kind. It's not your fault, though—the rude response is automatic. Our advice: Just take a breath and go to your happy place.

* * *

"To be able to ask a question clearly is two-thirds of the way to getting it answered."

—**John Ruskin**

Fair? In ancient Rome, the birthdays of all adult males were celebrated.
Women's and children's birthdays were not.

SUNK BY THE *TITANIC*

If you're not from Chicago (and even if you are), there's a good chance that you've never heard of the SS Eastland disaster. It's one of the deadliest and least-remembered maritime tragedies in American history.

CAN'T HELP BUT WONDER

One of the first questions to arise from the sinking of the *Titanic* in 1912 was why there weren't enough lifeboats for everyone on board. The answer was simple, and naive: The thinking back then was that it made more sense to turn the ship itself into a giant lifeboat, by loading it up with safety features. For example, the *Titanic*'s hull was divided into 16 watertight compartments, and each one had electric watertight doors that could be closed remotely via a control panel on the bridge. As many as four of the compartments at the front of the ship could be breached and flooded with seawater, and the *Titanic* would still remain afloat.

The only reason large ships like the *Titanic* carried lifeboats at all was in case they developed mechanical problems and were dead in the water. The lifeboats would then be used to ferry passengers to another ship. But this could be done in turns; there was no need to have enough lifeboats to ferry everyone over in a single large group. At the turn of the 20th century, the idea that modern ships might actually sink seemed preposterous. In 1907 an English sea captain named Edward Smith remarked that he could not think of "any condition which would cause a ship to founder. Modern shipbuilding has gone beyond that."

THINK AGAIN

Five years later, on April 14, 1912, Smith was the captain of the *Titanic* when it struck an iceberg and ruptured not four but five of its forward watertight compartments, enough to send it to the bottom of the Atlantic. Some 1,500 people were killed the disaster, in large part because there weren't enough lifeboats on board for everyone.

After the *Titanic* disaster, it was clear that no ship was unsinkable. And that meant that ships needed to carry more lifeboats. The Seamen's Act of 1915, signed into law by President Woodrow Wilson in March of that year, was a step in the right direction; it required American-flagged ships to carry enough lifeboats for 75 percent of the passengers and crew. (The *Titanic* was built to carry 3,300 people but had lifeboats for only 1,100.)

> The idea that modern ships might actually sink seemed preposterous.

First American guide dog school: The Seeing Eye, Inc., established in Tennessee in 1929.

The Seaman's Act applied to all ships, not just new ones, and that meant that older ships had to be retrofitted with more lifeboats and other safety equipment. One such ship was the SS *Eastland*, a 275-foot-long "excursion steamer" based in Chicago.

ODD DUCK

The *Eastland* was an unusual ship. It was built in 1903 in a shipyard that had never built a passenger ship before, and would never build one again. Because it was designed to operate in the Chicago River and other shallow waters, it didn't have a bulky keel at the bottom of its hull. Keels typically contain a lot of weight, and since they're at the very bottom of the ship well below the waterline, that weight helps to keep the ship stable by preventing it from listing, or rolling too far to one side or the other. That's what the keel is for.

> The *Eastland* was an unusual ship. It was built in 1903 in a shipyard that had never built a passenger ship before, and would never build one again.

The *Eastland* had a system of ballast tanks at the bottom of the ship that served the same purpose as a keel. If the ship listed too far to the port (left) side, water could be pumped into the starboard (right) ballast tanks to add weight to that side, leveling the ship. If the *Eastland* listed too far to starboard, water could be pumped into the port tanks. Such a system might have worked with cargo that didn't move once it was loaded—the ballast tanks could be adjusted once to level the ship, then left alone. But passengers were another story: they moved around unpredictably, and if a ship was fully loaded, the ballast tanks had to be watched very carefully and adjusted regularly.

ON TOP

Another problem with the *Eastland*—and one that made its unusual ballast system much more problematic—was the fact that it was top-heavy. This was apparent from the moment it was launched in 1903, when it listed a full 45 degrees, or halfway over onto its side. That should have been a warning sign, but when the *Eastland* promptly righted itself, the builders concluded that the design was good and the ship was stable. When it listed again later that same year, this time with hundreds of passengers on board, "improvements" were made. But that didn't solve the problem. The *Eastland* continued to list dangerously, especially when it was overloaded, which was often. Several times it nearly capsized.

In the years that followed, more modifications were made to the *Eastland*, but not for safety. Quite the opposite, in fact. The ship was reengineered to travel faster, and to carry more people. A lot more people. By 1915, when the Seaman's Act went into effect, the ship that had been designed to carry 500 people now carried more than

Only U.S. president to have registered a patent: Abraham Lincoln, for a mechanism that lifted riverboats over obstructions (1849).

2,500. Most people tended to congregate on the upper decks, well above the waterline, which made the *Eastland* even more top-heavy.

Now that the Seaman's Act had gone into effect, all of those extra people were going to need lifeboats. Where the *Eastland* had once carried only six lifeboats, it now carried 11, along with 37 smaller life rafts and more than 2,500 life jackets, enough for everyone on the ship. Nearly everything was stored on the upper decks; the combined weight of all of this equipment was more than 40 tons, adding to the *Eastland*'s instability.

THE PICNIC

On July 24, 1915, three weeks after the last of the new lifeboats and other equipment were installed—and without any safety trials being conducted—the *Eastland* was scheduled for an excursion that had the ship filled to capacity: a day trip to Washington Park in Michigan City, Indiana, 38 miles southeast of Chicago on the Lake Michigan shoreline. The trip had been booked by the Western Electric Company to provide recreation for employees of the company's Hawthorne Works factory in Cicero, Illinois. The *Eastland* was one of five ships chartered to bring the factory's 7,000 workers to a picnic in the park.

The ship began loading at 6:30 a.m., and by 7:10 some 2,500 people were aboard. Because the weather was cold and drizzly, many mothers with small children moved inside to the main cabin. The ship loaded on the starboard (right) side, and because people congregated there after boarding, the *Eastland* initially listed to starboard. A short time later, it listed to port. The water in the ballast tanks was repeatedly adjusted in an attempt to level the ship, but the *Eastland* remained unsteady as people moved around.

OVER

When the *Eastland* began to pull away from the wharf, a crowd of passengers on the top deck suddenly moved from the starboard side of the ship to the port side, where the view was better. The ship was already listing to port, and when the passengers moved to the port side, the list became more pronounced, reaching nearly 30 degrees—so far over that water began flooding into the ship through the port side gangway. Terrified stokers and oilers belowdecks in the engine room abandoned their posts and fled in terror as water poured into their compartment.

On the upper decks, the danger was not as apparent, at least not to the passengers. Many of them, especially the children, thought the steep list was exciting. But the crew knew better and they instructed the passengers on the port side to move to the starboard side of the ship, quickly. By now, however, the angle

Most produced motor vehicle in history: the Honda Super Cub motorcycle.
More than 100 million have been made since 1958.

of the ship was so steep, and the deck so slippery from the wet weather, that the passengers were slow to move—too slow...and too late. The list increased to more than 45 degrees, then the ship rolled over onto its side, coming to rest in 20 feet of water just 20 feet from the wharf.

NO ESCAPE

Technically speaking, the *Eastland* didn't sink: the ship was nearly 40 feet wide, so when it rolled over in water 20 feet deep, half of the hull remained above the surface. But to the hundreds of people trapped inside the main cabin or belowdecks, that made little difference. They were tossed into great heaps when the ship rolled over, and in the mad scramble to escape as water flooded in, hundreds of them died either from drowning, or by being crushed or smothered beneath people, furniture, and other debris.

> **Many hundreds more passengers who had been standing on the upper deck were tossed into the river "like so many ants being brushed from a table."**

Many hundreds more passengers who had been standing on the upper deck were tossed into the river "like so many ants being brushed from a table," one witness remembered, and were now fighting for their lives. Many did not know how to swim, and were weighed down by their clothes. Helen Repa, a Western Electric nurse who was one of the first medical professionals to arrive, described the scene:

I shall never be able to forget what I saw. People were struggling in the water, clustered so thickly that they literally covered the surface of the river. A few were swimming; the rest were floundering about, some clinging to a little raft that had floated free, others clutching at anything they could reach—at bits of wood, at each other, grabbing each other, pulling each other down, and screaming! The screaming was the most horrible of all.

CLOSE TO SHORE

The tragedy might have been even worse if the *Eastland* had not rolled on its side so close to the wharf. Many people were able to swim to it and pull themselves from the water, and a few bystanders jumped into the water to try and save whomever they could. There were also plenty of boats around, and many rushed to render assistance. A tugboat called the *Kenosha* positioned itself between the Eastland and the wharf so that people standing on the overturned hull could walk to safety.

And yet for all that, the death toll was shockingly high: by the time the last bodies were pulled from the ship ("all the bodies that came up seemed to be women and children," Repa remembered), 844 people were dead. Among them were George

Yachts get their name from *jaghtschip,* a Dutch word meaning "hunt ship" or "chase ship." The Dutch used them hunt pirates.

Sindelar, a Western Electric foreman, his wife Josephine, and all five of their children aged 3 to 15. The Sindelars were but one of 21 families where both parents and all of their children were killed.

AFTERMATH

An investigation into the deadliest shipwreck ever on the Great Lakes blamed "conditions of instability," among which the ship's bad design, mismanagement of the ballast system, and overloading of passengers were cited. Four officers of the St. Joseph-Chicago Steamship Company were indicted on federal charges for manslaughter, and the ship's captain and engineer were charged with "criminal carelessness," but the charges were later dropped when a judge ruled that since the *Eastland* had operated for so many years without loss of life, the accused had little reason to suspect that the ship was unsafe. As for being compensated for their losses, the families of the deceased had to get in line behind the companies that salvaged the *Eastland*. By the time they were paid, there was little money left for anyone else.

After the *Eastland* was salvaged, the U.S. Navy bought it and turned it into a gunboat named the *Wilmette*. The ship remained in service through World War II, and for many years was a training ship on the Great Lakes. After the war, it was decommissioned and offered for sale to the public. When no one offered to buy it, the navy sold it for scrap in 1946.

* * *

ACTUAL & FACTUAL RANDOM FACTS

- Items that have been left behind in Uber cars: a 1.3-carat diamond, a mask made of rhinestones, tax returns, divorce proceedings, a skateboard, a slice of pizza, a marriage certificate, a cat carrier (with no cat in it), a Nintendo 64, a cardboard box full of hair extensions, a flute, a flat-screen television, a single Birkenstock sandal, two French bulldog statues, a jetpack, a wagon, a bulletproof vest, a leaf blower, a full laundry hamper, a tuxedo, a butcher knife, an air mattress, a bridal veil, a pool cue, a college diploma, and a superhero cape.

- "Moon River" lyricist Johnny Mercer split the profits from his song "I Wanna Be Around to Pick Up the Pieces When Somebody Breaks Your Heart" with a Youngstown, Ohio, grandmother named Sadie Vimmerstedt, who sent him the suggested title in the mail. "She did the title and I did everything else," Mercer said. "But I figure that's fifty-fifty, because, as far as I'm concerned, that's a hit title."

Hard to bee-lieve: You're 33 times more likely to be killed
by bees than you are to win the lottery jackpot.

ANSWERS

Edison Quiz (*Answers for page 11*)

1. Spain, Andorra, Monaco, Italy, Switzerland, Germany, Luxembourg, and Belgium.

3. In Russia.

9. This was a trick question: Australia is more than three times as large as Greenland, but on world maps that use what is known as the Mercator projection, geographical features near the North and South Poles are exaggerated in size. On these maps, Greenland appears much larger than Australia.

10. In Denmark.

12. Papua New Guinea.

14. He was a British engineer who invented a process for making steel by blowing air through molten pig iron, which made steel much cheaper to produce.

17. The Minute Man who rode on horseback from Boston to Lexington, Massachusetts, warning that the British were marching to Concord.

20. The Carthaginian (North African) general who conquered much of Italy in the third century B.C.

32. The city of Ajaccio, on the Mediterranean island of Corsica.

34. John Napier, a Scottish mathematician (1550–1617).

35. Montezuma II, who ruled the Aztec empire from 1502 to 1520.

37. An oval-shaped region of the North Atlantic known for slow currents and large quantities of seaweed floating on the surface.

42. Delaware, then Connecticut.

46. Montana.

59. The gravitational pull of the moon.

70. In Wisconsin.

71. It depends on the medium that sound is traveling through. At sea level and a temperature of 59° Fahrenheit (15° Celsius), it travels at 1,116 feet (340 meters) per second.

72. In empty space: about 186,282 miles (299,792 kilometers) per second.

73. A queen of ancient Egypt and lover of both Julius Caesar and Mark Antony. She committed suicide by causing a poisonous snake called an asp to bite her.

75. Sir Isaac Newton.

76. The average distance is 92,960,000 miles, or 149,600,000 kilometers.

79. A cloth made from wool or other animal-hair fibers matted together by pressure, moisture, and heat.

85. Marie Curie, in Paris in 1898.

86. Wilhelm Roentgen, in 1895.

92. Giuseppe Verdi, in 1853.

93. At sea level with an air temperature of 59° Fahrenheit: 0.0765 pounds per cubic feet x 6,000 cubic feet = 459 pounds.

98. Charles Goodyear.

101. Eli Whitney.

105. Silica sand (silicon dioxide), soda ash (sodium carbonate), and limestone (calcium carbonate).

110. A unit of energy equal to the amount required to raise a one-pound weight a distance of one foot.

121. The English composer John Stafford Smith wrote the music, originally for a drinking song called "To Anacreon in Heaven," in about 1780. Francis Scott Key wrote the words for the song in 1814.

125. Miguel de Cervantes, in 1615.

126. Victor Hugo, in 1862.

129. Auguste Rodin, in 1880.

130. It is named after Daniel Gabriel Fahrenheit, the Polish-Dutch physicist who invented it in 1724.

133. Mosquitoes (more specifically, female mosquitoes of the genus *Anopheles*).

134. The Spanish explorer Vasco Núñez de Balboa, who first spotted the Pacific from

It's estimated that $1.5 trillion worth of bribes are paid worldwide each year.

a mountaintop in what is now Panama, on September | 25, 1513. On September 29, he waded into the surf and | claimed the Pacific and a~ adjoining lands for Spain.

Television by the Numbers Quiz (*Answers for page 254*)

1. Susan
2. Matt
3. Jan
4. Theo
5. Jim-Bob
6. Jerry
7. Brian
8. Mushmouth
9. Jughead
10. Stephanie
11. Al (short for Alicia)
12. Jill
13. Ricky
14. Manny
15. Jack Paar

Occupational Name Quiz (*Answers for page 273*)

1. Bradley Cooper. A cooper is a traditional name for a barrel maker.
2. Karen Carpenter
3. Mike Judge
4. Margaret Thatcher. A thatcher is an old word for "roof builder"—specifically someone who builds roofs out of reeds or straw, also called "thatch."
5. Danny Glover. Yes, a person who makes gloves is a glover.
6. Dennis Miller. A person who grinds grain in a mill is called a miller.
7. Tim Cook
8. Tiki Barber
9. Cybill Shepherd
10. George Washington Carver
11. "Rowdy" Roddy Piper. (But Piper was Canadian, not Scottish, and his real last name was Toombs, a derivative of "Thomas.")
12. Elizabeth Taylor
13. Usher
14. Holly Hunter
15. Kyle Chandler. A chandler is the medieval English word for a candle maker.
16. Joey Bishop

"Princess Takes a Ballet Class" Quiz (*Answers for page 297*)

1. "What'd I Say"
2. "Yesterday"
3. "Don't Go Breaking My Heart"
4. "Let's Stay Together"
5. "Jailhouse Rock"
6. "Papa's Got a Brand New Bag"
7. "I Can See For Miles"
8. "Purple Rain"
9. "Call Me"
10. "The End"
11. "It's Too Late"
12. "I Wanna Be Sedated"
13. "Life on Mars?"
14. "Summertime Blues"
15. "Dancing Queen"
16. "Movin' Out"
17. "Surrender"
18. "Landslide"
19. "We Are the Champions"
20. "Do It Again"
21. "New Year's Day"
22. "Holiday"
23. "November Rain"
24. "Paint It Black"
25. "Burning Down the House"
26. "Free Fallin'"

Contronyms Quiz (*Answers for page 378*)

1. g; 2. l; 3. a; 4. x; 5. i; 6. e; 7. c; 8. y; 9. t; 10. z; 11. n; 12. q; 13. j; 14. p; 15. b; 16. d; 17. k; 18. v; 19. s; 20. w; 21. h; 22. f; 23. o; 24. m; 25. u; 26. r.

By the Numbers Quiz (*Answers for page 444*)

1. John Adams
2. Sloth
3. New York Rangers
4. Pronoun
5. Grammy
6. Phylum
7. France
8. Steve McQueen
9. Southern (or Antarctic) Ocean
10. Numbers
11. August
12. Lake Huron
13. José Carreras
14. Saskatchewan

Before the fruit orange was discovered, the English word for the color orange was *geoluhread*.

We are pleased to offer over 125 e-book versions of Portable Press
titles—some currently available only in digital format!
Visit *www.portablepress.com* to collect them all!

- ❏ Bathroom Science
- ❏ Best Movies of the 80s
- ❏ The Best of the Best of Uncle John's Bathroom Reader
- ❏ The Best of Uncle John's Bathroom Reader
- ❏ Dad Jokes
- ❏ Do Geese Get Goose Bumps?
- ❏ The Funniest & Grossest Joke Book Ever!
- ❏ The Funniest Joke Book Ever!
- ❏ The Funniest Knock-Knock Jokes Ever!
- ❏ The Grossest Joke Book Ever!
- ❏ How to Fight a Bear...and Win
- ❏ Instant Genius
- ❏ Instant Genius: Smart Mouths
- ❏ See Ya Later Calculator
- ❏ Strange Crime
- ❏ Strange History
- ❏ Strange Science
- ❏ Uncle John's Absolutely Absorbing Bathroom Reader
- ❏ Uncle John's Actual and Factual Bathroom Reader
- ❏ Uncle John's Ahh-Inspiring Bathroom Reader
- ❏ Uncle John's All-Purpose Extra Strength Bathroom Reader
- ❏ Uncle John's Bathroom Reader Attack of the Factoids
- ❏ Uncle John's Bathroom Reader Book of Love
- ❏ Uncle John's Bathroom Reader Cat Lover's Companion
- ❏ Uncle John's Bathroom Reader Christmas Collection

- ❏ Uncle John's Bathroom Reader Dog Lover's Companion
- ❏ Uncle John's Bathroom Reader Extraordinary Book of Facts
- ❏ Uncle John's Bathroom Reader Fake Facts
- ❏ Uncle John's Bathroom Reader Flush Fiction
- ❏ Uncle John's Bathroom Reader For Girls Only!
- ❏ Uncle John's Bathroom Reader For Kids Only!
- ❏ Uncle John's Bathroom Reader For Kids Only! Collectible Edition
- ❏ Uncle John's Bathroom Reader Germophobia
- ❏ Uncle John's Bathroom Reader Golden Plunger Awards
- ❏ Uncle John's Bathroom Reader History's Lists
- ❏ Uncle John's Bathroom Reader Horse Lover's Companion
- ❏ Uncle John's Bathroom Reader Impossible Questions
- ❏ Uncle John's Bathroom Reader Jingle Bell Christmas
- ❏ Uncle John's Bathroom Reader Nature Calls
- ❏ Uncle John's Bathroom Reader Plunges into California
- ❏ Uncle John's Bathroom Reader Plunges into Canada, eh
- ❏ Uncle John's Bathroom Reader Plunges into Great Lives
- ❏ Uncle John's Bathroom Reader Plunges into History
- ❏ Uncle John's Bathroom Reader Plunges into History Again

- ❏ Uncle John's Bathroom Reader Plunges into Hollywood
- ❏ Uncle John's Bathroom Reader Plunges into Michigan
- ❏ Uncle John's Bathroom Reader Plunges into Minnesota
- ❏ Uncle John's Bathroom Reader Plunges into Music
- ❏ Uncle John's Bathroom Reader Plunges into National Parks
- ❏ Uncle John's Bathroom Reader Plunges into New Jersey
- ❏ Uncle John's Bathroom Reader Plunges into New York
- ❏ Uncle John's Bathroom Reader Plunges into Ohio
- ❏ Uncle John's Bathroom Reader Plunges into Pennsylvania
- ❏ Uncle John's Bathroom Reader Plunges into Texas
- ❏ Uncle John's Bathroom Reader Plunges into Texas Expanded Edition
- ❏ Uncle John's Bathroom Reader Plunges into the Presidency
- ❏ Uncle John's Bathroom Reader Plunges into the Universe
- ❏ Uncle John's Bathroom Reader Quintessential Collection of Notable Quotables
- ❏ Uncle John's Bathroom Reader Salutes the Armed Forces
- ❏ Uncle John's Bathroom Reader Shoots and Scores
- ❏ Uncle John's Bathroom Reader Sports Spectacular
- ❏ Uncle John's Bathroom Reader Takes a Swing at Baseball
- ❏ Uncle John's Bathroom Reader Tales to Inspire

Ridley Scott directed *Blade Runner,* an adaptation of Philip K. Dick's novel...

- Uncle John's Bathroom Reader Tees Off On Golf
- Uncle John's Bathroom Reader The World's Gone Crazy
- Uncle John's Bathroom Reader Tunes into TV
- Uncle John's Bathroom Reader Vroom!
- Uncle John's Bathroom Reader Weird Canada
- Uncle John's Bathroom Reader Weird Inventions
- Uncle John's Bathroom Reader WISE UP!
- Uncle John's Bathroom Reader Wonderful World of Odd
- Uncle John's Bathroom Reader Zipper Accidents
- Uncle John's Book of Fun
- Uncle John's Canoramic Bathroom Reader
- Uncle John's Certified Organic Bathroom Reader
- Uncle John's Colossal Collection of Quotable Quotes
- Uncle John's Creature Feature Bathroom Reader For Kids Only!
- Uncle John's Curiously Compelling Bathroom Reader
- Uncle John's Did You Know…? Bathroom Reader For Kids Only!
- Uncle John's Do-It-Yourself Diary for Infomaniacs Only
- Uncle John's Do-It-Yourself Journal for Infomaniacs Only
- Uncle John's Electrifying Bathroom Reader For Kids Only!
- Uncle John's Electrifying Bathroom Reader For Kids Only! Collectible Edition
- Uncle John's Endlessly Engrossing Bathroom Reader

- Uncle John's Factastic Bathroom Reader
- Uncle John's Facts to Annoy Your Teacher Bathroom Reader For Kids Only!
- Uncle John's Fast-Acting Long-Lasting Bathroom Reader
- Uncle John's Fully Loaded 25th Anniversary Bathroom Reader
- Uncle John's Giant 10th Anniversary Bathroom Reader
- Uncle John's Gigantic Bathroom Reader
- Uncle John's Great Big Bathroom Reader
- Uncle John's Haunted Outhouse Bathroom Reader For Kids Only!
- Uncle John's Heavy Duty Bathroom Reader
- Uncle John's How to Toilet Train Your Cat
- Uncle John's InfoMania Bathroom Reader For Kids Only!
- Uncle John's Legendary Lost Bathroom Reader
- Uncle John's Lists That Make You Go Hmmm…
- Uncle John's New & Improved Briefs
- Uncle John's New & Improved Funniest Ever
- Uncle John's Old Faithful 30th Anniversary Bathroom Reader
- Uncle John's Perpetually Pleasing Bathroom Reader
- Uncle John's Political Briefs
- Uncle John's Presents: Book of the Dumb
- Uncle John's Presents: Book of the Dumb 2
- Uncle John's Presents: Mom's Bathtub Reader

- Uncle John's Presents the Ultimate Challenge Trivia Quiz
- Uncle John's Robotica Bathroom Reader
- Uncle John's Slightly Irregular Bathroom Reader
- Uncle John's Smell-O-Scopic Bathroom Reader For Kids Only!
- Uncle John's Supremely Satisfying Bathroom Reader
- Uncle John's The Enchanted Toilet Bathroom Reader For Kids Only!
- Uncle John's Top Secret Bathroom Reader For Kids Only!
- Uncle John's Top Secret Bathroom Reader For Kids Only! Collectible Edition
- Uncle John's Totally Quacked Bathroom Reader For Kids Only!
- Uncle John's Triumphant 20th Anniversary Bathroom Reader
- Uncle John's True Crime
- Uncle John's 24-Karat Gold Bathroom Reader
- Uncle John's Ultimate Bathroom Reader
- Uncle John's Uncanny Bathroom Reader
- Uncle John's Unsinkable Bathroom Reader
- Uncle John's Unstoppable Bathroom Reader
- Uncle John's Weird Weird World
- Uncle John's Weird Weird World: Epic
- The Wackiest Joke Book Ever!
- The Wackiest Joke Book That'll Knock-Knock You Over!
- Who Knew?

…Do Androids Dream of Electric Sheep? without finishing the book. (It was too boring.)

THE LAST PAGE

FELLOW BATHROOM READERS:

The fight for good bathroom reading should never be taken loosely—we must do our duty and sit firmly for what we believe in, even while the rest of the world is taking potshots at us.

We'll be brief. Now that we've proven we're not simply a flush-in-the-pan, we invite you to take the plunge: Sit Down and Be Counted! To find out what the BRI is up to, visit us at *www.portablepress.com* and take a peek!

GET CONNECTED

Find us online to sign up for our email list, enter exciting giveaways, hear about new releases, and more!

Websites: www.portablepress.com
www.bathroomreader.com

Facebook: www.facebook.com/portablepress

Instagram: instagram.com/portablepress

Pinterest: www.pinterest.com/portablepress

Twitter: @Portablepress

Well, we're out of space, and when you've gotta go, you've gotta go. Tanks for all your support. Hope to hear from you soon.

Meanwhile, remember…

Keep on flushin'!

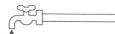